ECHOES OF DISTANT THUNDER

Books by Edward Robb Ellis

A DIARY OF THE CENTURY:
Tales from America's Greatest Diarist (1995)

ECHOES OF DISTANT THUNDER:
Life in the United States, 1914–1918 (1975)

A NATION IN TORMENT:
The Great American Depression, 1929–1939 (1970)

THE EPIC OF NEW YORK CITY:
A Narrative History (1966)

THE TRAITOR WITHIN:
Our Suicide Problem
(with George N. Allen, 1961)

ECHOES OF DISTANT THUNDER

Life In The United States, 1914–1918

EDWARD ROBB ELLIS

With a New Preface by the Author

KODANSHA INTERNATIONAL
New York • Tokyo • London

To the Memory of My Beloved Wife RUTH KRAUS ELLIS

Kodansha America, Inc.
114 Fifth Avenue, New York, New York 10011, U.S.A.

Kodansha International Ltd.
17-14 Otowa 1-chome, Bunkyo-ku, Tokyo 112, Japan

Published in 1996 by Kodansha America, Inc.
by arrangement with the author.

Originally published in 1975 by Coward, McCann & Geoghegan, Inc., New York.

This is a Kodansha Globe book.

Library of Congress Cataloging-in-Publication Data
Ellis, Edward Robb.
Echoes of distant thunder : life in the United States, 1914–1918 / Edward Robb Ellis.
p. cm.
Originally published: New York : Coward, McCann & Geoghegan, [1975].
Includes bibliographical references and index.
ISBN 1-56836-149-1
1. United States—History—1913–1921. 2. World War, 1914–1918—United States. I. Title.
E780.E55 1996
973.91'3—dc20 96-7143

Printed in the United States of America

96 97 98 99 00 BER/B 10 9 8 7 6 5 4 3 2 1

For permission to quote from copyrighted material, the author gratefully acknowledges the following: The Bobbs-Merrill Company, Inc., for excerpts from *My Memoir* by Edith Bolling Wilson, copyright 1938, 1939, by Edith Bolling Wilson, reprinted by permission of the publisher, The Bobbs-Merrill Company, Inc.; Curtis Brown, Ltd., for excerpts from *Movers and Shakers* by Mabel Dodge Luhan, copyright © 1935, 1936, by Mable Dodge Luhan, reprinted by permission of Curtis Brown, Ltd.; Mr. Raymond Ginger for excerpts from his book *The Bending Cross*, copyright 1949, by the Trustees Rutgers College in New Jersey, reprinted by permission of the Author; Holt, Rinehart and Winston, Inc., for an excerpt from *Baruch: The Public Years* by Bernard M. Baruch. Copyright © 1960 by Bernard M. Baruch. Reprinted by permission of Holt, Rinehart and Winston, Inc.; David McKay Company, Inc., for excerpts from *Triumph and Turmoil* by Edgar Mowrer, published originally by Weybright and Talley, Inc., reprinted by permission of David McKay Company, Inc.; *The New Republic*, Inc., for excerpts from *Early Writings of Walter Lippmann* by Walter Lippmann, reprinted by permission of *The New Republic*, copyright © 1914, 1915, 1916, 1917, 1918, 1919, 1920, *The New Republic*, Inc.; Charles Scribner's Sons, Inc., for excerpts from the following books: *Theodore Roosevelt and His Time*, Volume II, by Joseph Bucklin Bishop; *The World Crisis* by Winston Churchill; *Look Homeward, Angel* by Thomas Wolfe, reprinted by permission of the publisher, Charles Scribner's Sons, Inc.; Simon & Schuster, Inc., for excerpts from the following books: *The Movies* by Richard Griffith and Arthur Mayer, copyright © 1957, 1970 by Arthur Mayer and the Est. of Richard Griffith, reprinted by permission of Simon & Schuster; *Starling at the White House* by Colonel Edmund W. Starling as told to Thomas Sugrue, copyright © 1946 by Simon & Schuster, reprinted by permission of the publisher.

Contents

There is nothing new in the world except the history you do not know.

—HARRY S. TRUMAN

People move forward into the future out of the way they comprehend the past.

—NORMAN MAILER

Preface to the 1996 Edition

It is difficult to tell the truth. If you question this statement, hurrah for you! Nothing should be taken for granted. Everything should be questioned. Why? Because this is how to find the truth; because curiosity is the sign of a good mind. Education should teach questions, not answers.

If you doubt that it is hard to tell the truth, think about philosophers and theologians, diplomats and politicians, lawyers and jurors, Supreme Court justices—or even historians. As for salesmen and television commercials, forget it.

Philosophically, is there just one huge truth? Or does this truth consist of countless tiny truths? Just for the fun of it, pretend you are looking at Mt. Everest from a distance. It appears to be, in your imagination, one solid block of ice. Then let your imagination zoom in closer, like the lens of a camera, and you discover that this seemingly solid block of ice is composed of trillions of ice cubes.

Is truth an element or a compound? History is a compound, that we know for sure. It is a story told by a lot of different people, some dead and some living, all leaving different records, most of them saying different things.

Once there was a college class in which a minor crime supposedly was committed as students watched. It lasted only seconds. Then the students were asked what they saw, and each saw something different.

What does this have to do with history? It alerts us to the necessity of being skeptical about all we read. Each person judges others and sees events through the prism of his or her personality. Are you a man or a woman? Are you black or white? Are you twenty years old or eighty? Were you born in Texas or Massachusetts? These factors determine the way you look at life. When you feel secure enough to admit your ignorance, as wise men do, then you shed your prejudices.

But even then it is hard to identify the truth. The historian reads manuscripts and monographs, peruses books and newspapers, interviews old folks, visits ancient sites. But can we trust these sources, original and secondary? Some monographs are written to please a professor; once a mistake has been made, it often is repeated in newspapers; some books plead special interests; some old folks have faulty memories and time erodes sacred sites.

And, most important, let us understand that there is no such thing as total objectivity.

When I was a reporter with the United Press in Chicago, I covered a spectacular fire in an office building. So did other reporters. The next day

I read what was said about the fire by the two other wire services in town and by all the Chicago newspapers. They sounded as though each of us had covered a different event. No story was exactly like mine and none matched any of the others. Why? The journalists and wire services and papers had nothing to gain or lose by the way they reported the blaze. People often see what they expect to see, not necessarily what actually happens.

Consciously or unconsciously, people lie. You tell a sick woman in a hospital bed that she looks better. Sometimes you say that you feel well when actually you feel rotten, indulging in the so-called power of positive thinking. The wise man knows he is ignorant. The fool thinks he is wise. But, as Shakespeare wrote: "Lord, what fools these mortals be!"

When I was a student at the University of Missouri several centuries ago, as it seems, my major was journalism and my minor was history. When I graduated, I thought I knew a thing or two about American history, and I was right. All I knew about it was a thing or two.

As I began researching this book you hold in your hands, I did not know that there had been a Reign of Terror on the American home front during World War I. Plunging more deeply into my subject, I got a hint of violence here and there. Uncovering more and more puzzling data, I knew I needed guidance, so I went to the home of Roger Baldwin in Manhattan. When I met him, he was eighty-seven years old and his memory was sharp. He was a conscientious objector during the First World War and spent a year in a penitentiary because of it. Later he helped found the American Civil Liberties Union. Before he died in 1981 at the age of ninety-seven, he received the nation's highest civilian honor, the Medal of Freedom, from President Jimmy Carter.

I asked Mr. Baldwin which was worse—the suppression of civil liberties during the war or during the McCarthy era of the 1950's. To my astonishment, he declared that the hysteria was much worse in the war. Thus enlightened, I dug deeper and found data proving he was correct.

For example, the Espionage Act of May 16, 1918. It suppressed all freedom of speech and the press. It threatened anyone who dared to "utter, print, write, or publish any disloyal, profane, scurrilous, or abusive language about the form of government of the United States."

Who decided whether you were guilty under this act? The People. In a democracy "the People" is a cherished concept, but one often misused. Did your neighbor have the right to define this act in terms of his own heritage and prejudices? Did he report you to the government? That is exactly what many neighbors did.

People were beaten and killed because they said something or did something that other people considered harmful to the nation. Millions of naturalized immigrants had come here from Germany and central Europe and had relatives still living there. They were attacked because their behavior was not precisely what was desired by spread-eagle patriots. Samuel Johnson said that patriotism was "the last refuge of a scoundrel." He might have added "*mindless* patriotism."

When individuals coalesce into a mob, the group's collective intelligence equals the I.Q. of its most ignorant member. The individuals, acting as parts of a whole, do horrible deeds they would not do by themselves. They feel less responsibility. If there are a hundred men in the mob, then each individual feels only about 1 percent responsible for a crime. Conscience becomes as slippery as quicksilver.

But to go back, why was I at first unaware of the Reign of Terror? Partly because of the way textbooks are chosen. Educated idiots on some school boards in some parts of the country try to perpetuate the myth that the American past was perfect. Let us grit our teeth and admit that nothing is perfect. Some of my own white ancestors inflicted a holocaust upon red people and black people in this land. Let us be realists. Let us confess to the shame as well as the glory of the United States.

Schoolkids, for the most part, are bored by history. They are forced to read sanitized textbooks conforming to the bias of a given region. There is no such thing as boring history. There are only boring historians. Actually, history is exciting.

I write narrative history that is as truthful as I can make it, and I hope I do not bore you. I just tell what heppened. I try to do this with a smile.

New York City
December 1995

Preface

This is a story about what happened to men, women and children in the United States during World War I. I cannot call it *the* story, for historians see history differently, but it is a narrative, and it is concerned with people.

For centuries philosophers have debated the nature of ultimate reality, and certainly I am not wise enough to resolve this problem. However, I tend to believe that the most basic reality is the human soul—not institutions such as states, governments, churches or corporations, since they are abstractions and have no souls.

I agree with Sir Arthur Keith, the British anthropologist, who said, "The course of human history is determined . . . by what takes place in the hearts of men." Much the same thing was said by Dr. Carl G. Jung, the Swiss psychiatrist: "What is the fate of great nations but a summation of the psychic changes in individuals?"

I try to write history—*accurate* history—as though it were a novel, recounting the behavior of people and describing their emotions. Nonetheless, I am aware of the difficulty of combining truth-telling with storytelling. Never do I sacrifice truth for dramatic effect. Whenever I say a person *thought* or *felt* or *believed* this or that, I have evidence to document my remark.

To research and write a narrative history is like functioning as a detective who solves a crime or finds a missing person by collecting evidence and then studying the details until they coalesce into a meaningful pattern. Since I never wholly understand any era until I have written about it, I begin by confessing my ignorance to myself, collecting the facts, letting them astonish me and then following wherever they lead. I appreciate what Sherlock Holmes told Dr. Watson: "It is a capital mistake to theorize before one has his data. Insensibly one begins to twist facts to suit theories, instead of theories to suit facts."

In researching this book I did not work from original documents, since they exist by the *ton,* and had I gone to the archives I would not have lived long enough to complete this volume. I am painfully aware of all the episodes—many significant—which I had to omit because of the limitations of space. I understand what Tacitus meant when he wrote, "My purpose is not to relate at length every motion, but only such as were conspicuous for excellence or notorious for infamy."

And, sad to relate, some episodes in American history *are* infamous. Time and again, while researching this book, I was shocked to learn what horrible things were done by a few Americans. I felt heavyhearted as I wrote about these cruel events, but I included them because they are true and only the truth can set us free.

Life contains at least two constants: (1) the conflict between good and evil, and (2) endless change. Since human nature is partly good and partly evil, since we imperfect mortals are always changing and since history is a record of these changes, history is therefore a story of the endless conflict between good and evil. I believe we should learn as much as possible about the truth of this epic story because ignorance is the root of all evil.

I could not have written this book without the help of kind friends and strangers. To my friend and editor, Patricia Brehaut Soliman, I offer my appreciation for her sensitive editing, her enthusiasm and her confidence in me. I thank my agent, John Cushman, who suggested this book. For assistance beyond measure I am indebted to Selma Seskin Pezaro. I thank June Roma Dashiell Morgan for helping me formulate the title of this book. I owe especial gratitude to my daughter, Sandra Gail Ellis Emelio; to my sister, Kathryn Ellis Burton; to my brother-in-law, Robert C. Burton.

I furthermore thank Will Durant, Conrad Aiken, Roger Baldwin, Scott Nearing, John Tebbel, Boyd Lewis, Lucy Wind, Janet Steinberg, Patrick T. Finnegan, Henry Senber, Charles M. Schwarz, Jack and Barbara Waugh, Harry and Betty Gordon, Martin H. Linskey, Victor I. Kaspar, Warren Marr II, Carol Jennings, Judy Wildman, Lil and Ben Sherer and James F. McShea.

EDWARD ROBB ELLIS

New York, New York
October, 1974

PART I

Forecast: Sunny and Pleasant

Chapter 1

WOODROW WILSON IS INAUGURATED

Woodrow Wilson walked out of his Tudor home in Princeton, New Jersey, at noon on Monday, March 3, 1913, to leave for Washington to be sworn in as President of the United States.

As he came into the sunshine and wind, he covered his head with a tall black silk hat and nodded at secret service agents. They wore derbies and fell in behind him and his wife and their three daughters. All the girls were in their twenties. Mrs. Wilson walked on the left side of her tall husband, her bonnet only as high as his shoulder, a smile on her lips, carrying a fur muff, and the wind teased her fur stole from her neck. Wilson ignored the autos waiting to drive them to the railway station and began walking the short distance.

Old friends advanced with smiling faces and outstretched hands and he stopped and they shook and he thanked them for their congratulations. One was a Presbyterian minister, and Wilson listened and then said, "I appreciate your good wishes, but had you better not pray for me?" Eleanor Wilson was twenty-four and so excited she thought just about everyone in Princeton had come to see them off, and it furthermore seemed to her that half the population was about to accompany them to the national capital.

Students and alumni of Princeton University had asked to come along and bring a band and Wilson, who had rejected a military escort, was delighted to accept their request. He had served as president of the university and governor of the state before being elected President of the United States. Surrounded by students and graduates singing "Old Nassau" at the tops of their lungs, he reached the depot and boarded the private car at the end of the nine-car special train, while the celebrants scrambled into the other cars. As the train pulled away from the station, the Wilsons stood on the rear platform and watched the pull of perspective diminish the university's Gothic spires, which coalesced into a dot and then vanished.

At every railroad station between Princeton and Washington the platforms were packed with people who waved flags and yelled and craned their necks as the train streaked past, its whistle screaming. When the special eased into Union Station in Washington, the terminal was a sea of faces, and the agents guarding Wilson convoyed him through a door reserved for Presidents and saw him safely into a limousine. A woman bobbed and weaved through the throng, shrilling, "Which is Margaret? Which is Jessie? Tell me—which is Eleanor?" She was more eager for a glimpse of Wilson's daughters than for a peek at their father, who would become President the next day. Elsewhere in the city a suffrage parade was in progress; but the Wilsons were driven to their hotel by a route that kept them from the crowds, and Eleanor mistakenly assumed that the "cave dwellers"—the permanent residents of Washington—were so accustomed to the arrival and departure of dignitaries that they had become blasé. The limousine stopped in front of the Shoreham hotel at H and Fifteenth streets and Wilson and his family got out and walked inside and were escorted to their suite.

The outgoing President, William Howard Taft, had invited Wilson and his wife to the White House for tea at 6 P.M. Eleanor helped her mother dress. Wilson had bought his wife a diamond pendant, so there were jokes about the "crown jewel." Mrs. Wilson did not join in the fun but remained silent as Eleanor arranged her hair and adjusted her hat. This perplexed Eleanor. Then the girl kissed her mother and said she looked perfectly lovely, and suddenly Mrs. Wilson's cheeks crimsoned and she clapped her hands over her face and burst into tears. Eleanor was so astonished she could think of nothing to say or do at first, but she recovered and ran for a bottle of spirits of ammonia and told her mother to take a drink. After a swallow Mrs. Wilson declared she was all right; she had felt confused, but Eleanor must not worry, and above all, she must not tell anyone what had happened. But the girl saw a shadow in her mother's eyes.

Again she smoothed her mother's hair, and then the two of them went to find Wilson and Eleanor watched as her parents walked out of the suite. The moment they left she rushed into her own room and locked the door and paced the floor and sobbed. Becoming afraid that someone would hear her, she crawled under the bed and beat the rug with her fists and screamed to herself, "It will kill them both! It will kill them both!"

When Wilson entered the White House, he looked about curiously, for this was the first time he had been inside the executive mansion. He and his wife were graciously received by the fat and genial Taft, a Republican whom Wilson had defeated in the November election, along with Theodore Roosevelt. After a spot of tea and a bit of talk the Wilsons left and returned to the Shoreham, and then, all participants acting out the last letter of protocol, Taft and his wife drove to the hotel to return the call.

Taft had been busy this final day of his Presidency. Holding his last press conference, he talked to reporters about the triumphs and failures of his administration, declaring that most of all he was proud of having appointed six of the nine justices of the Supreme Court. With a chuckle, Taft added, "And I have said to them—damn you, if any of you die, I'll disown you!" The correspondents laughed. All that evening and late into the night Taft sat at his desk signing his name over and over again for autograph collectors, and when he finally went to bed, he still had so many people to satisfy that after tossing awhile, he arose at two twenty in the morning to write for another hour and a half.

That night in the Shoreham hotel the Wilson daughters tucked their mother into bed and questioned her about her visit with the Tafts. Eleanor was twenty-four, Jessie was twenty-six, and Margaret was twenty-seven. Mrs. Wilson told her girls that Mrs. Taft had given her so many helpful hints about running the executive mansion that she thought she would be able to manage it all right. Before Wilson left his home on Cleveland Lane in Princeton, he received a letter from Taft in which the President explained what his expenses were likely to be and how he might go about economizing. But for the first time in his life Wilson had felt obliged to borrow a large sum of money—$5,000. He felt uneasy about taking a loan but thought it necessary to have such a sum to set up housekeeping in the White House.

That same evening of March 3 politicians milled about in the New Willard hotel at Pennsylvania Avenue and Fourteenth Street, a historic place where Julia Ward Howe had written the words to "The Battle Hymn of the Republic" in a burst of inspiration one morning in 1861. One of the men was Josephus Daniels, a Southerner and small-town editor, who the previous month had received a handwritten letter from Wilson asking him to become secretary of the navy.

In the lobby Daniels happened to run into Franklin D. Roosevelt, a young state senator from New York who had come to Washington to attend the inauguration. Both Democrats, Daniels and Roosevelt had met for the first time the previous June in Baltimore at the Democratic convention that nominated Wilson for President. At that June encounter Daniels had considered Roosevelt "as handsome a figure of an attractive young man as I had ever seen," and the day he got Wilson's letter asking him to join the Cabinet he had told his wife he planned to ask Wilson to make Roosevelt the assistant secretary of the navy. Now the editor offered the senator this second-rank post in the new administration—subject, of course, to approval by Wilson and confirmation by the Senate. FDR accepted enthusiastically.

Inauguration day, Tuesday, March 4, 1913, the day was gray at first; but the clouds drifted away, and by midmorning the weather was warm. At eight o'clock Wilson arose in his suite in the Shoreham, and an hour later he was discussing Cabinet selections with William F. McCombs, chairman of the Democratic national committee, a man Wilson considered slightly vulgar. He also received William Jennings Bryan, who had helped him win the election and now was about to be rewarded with the office of secretary of state, a selection Wilson considered necessary although not wholly desirable.

When the two men left, Wilson telephoned his closest adviser, Colonel Edward M. House, to ask him and his wife to join the Wilsons at their hotel and then accompany them to the Capitol for the inaugural ceremony. The Colonel, who loathed ceremonies and crowds, also felt he could cement his hold on Wilson by remaining as invisible as possible, so he drove Mrs. House to the Shoreham and then continued alone to the Metropolitan club to loaf around with Hugh C. Wallace, who six years later was named American ambassador to France.

Mrs. Wilson and the girls were busy dressing for the great occasion. Eleanor had sent to New York for a bright-blue broadcloth suit, but it arrived in an unfinished condition, so there was much frenzied pinning and sewing to be done. Margaret also wore blue, Jessie had chosen a green outfit, and their mother dressed in brown, pinning on her "crown jewel."

Shortly after ten o'clock the Wilsons emerged from their hotel and stepped into a White House limousine provided by President Taft; Eleanor was impressed with its liveried chauffeur and footman. Some Princeton students fell in behind and followed the car along the streets and into the White House grounds and burst into a college song as Wilson got out at the front door. Military aides in full-dress uniform stood at intervals from the front door to the door of the Blue Room, and Wilson walked past them and was about to enter the room when he thought better of it and retraced his steps to the porch, where he removed his hat and waited until the students finished singing. His thin face showed that he was touched.

Waiting in the Blue Room was Thomas R. Marshall, soon to be sworn in as the Vice President, a Congressional committee waiting attendance upon him and members of Taft's Cabinet. Taft waited in his second-floor study until his personal aide informed him that now the President-elect was in the Blue Room, and then Taft came downstairs and joined the others. Walking over to Wilson, he gave him a cordial handshake and made a comment about the weather. Then he said he understood they were supposed to have their pictures taken together.

Taft took Wilson's arm and led him out of the Blue Room and out onto the south portico, where a score of photographers had set up their cameras. Noticing that Wilson still wore his overcoat, the President paused long enough to don his own overcoat and hat. With face powder supplied by a woman photographer a line had been drawn on the floor of the porch, and now the two men were asked to toe it for the benefit of the cameramen. Taft remarked that just four years ago he and Theodore Roosevelt had had their pictures taken in the identical spot. Wilson said dryly, "Is that so?" In the three-cornered election the previous November Wilson had beaten both Taft and Roosevelt for the Presidency.

After the last flash powder exploded and the last camera clicked, Taft escorted Wilson back through the White House and out the front door, both of them wearing tall silk toppers, Taft wearing black gloves, Wilson pulling on gray ones. Black servants held themselves stiffly, and smartly uniformed officers saluted as the President and President-elect stepped into a vehicle, this time a landau drawn by four horses. Since it had no top they were readily seen by the people thronging Pennsylvania Avenue, and as the horses clop-clopped toward Capitol Hill there were cheers for both of them. Wilson smiled and peered through his nose glasses. Taft positively beamed. Someone yelled to Taft, "You're a darn good loser!" and Taft waved his hand and laughed.

When they reached the Capitol, they entered the Senate chamber, Taft walking ponderously to his seat in front of the secretary's desk. Wilson, his face serious and somewhat perplexed, moved more quickly as he sat down; then he glanced at the ornate uniforms worn by foreign ambassadors, at the black robes of the Supreme Court justices, at the assemblage of Senators and Representatives. Mrs. Wilson and her daughters already sat in the gallery waiting to see Marshall take the oath of office as Vice President.

Before the start of this ceremony, however, Senator Miles Poindexter, a Republican from the state of Washington, launched into a long speech about the woman's suffrage parade held the previous day. Twelve noon was the time set for Wilson's inauguration on the east portico of the Capitol, but Poindexter droned on and on and on, doubtless aware that his oratory held captive as influential an audience as he was ever to address in his life. Up in the gallery Eleanor Wilson squirmed, then flushed with anger. No one was listening to him, tens of thousands of people were waiting outside the building to watch Wilson be sworn in, and Poindexter was upsetting the inaugural schedule; but he seemed oblivious. When the minute hand of the Senate clock clicked within a few seconds of twelve, a man leaned down from the front row center of the gallery and turned it back. Three times he turned it back. Someone sitting near Eleanor muttered, "He's a Republican! He's doing it on purpose!"

At last Poindexter shut up and sat down. Thomas R. Marshall now was escorted into the chamber to be sworn in. Marshall was a liberal Democrat, a seasoned politician and a witty and compassionate man. In time to come, as he presided over Senate sessions, he was to hear another Senator drone on about the needs of the country, whereupon Marshall turned to a man and spoke the line for which he is best remembered: "What this country needs is a really good five-cent cigar!" Now, after officially taking office, Marshall kept his speech mercifully brief.

Members of the inaugural committee then escorted Wilson and Taft out of the Senate, through the open ten-ton bronze doors, and out onto the steps on the east side of the Capitol. They were followed by the men Wilson had decided to name to his Cabinet, by leaders of both houses of Congress, by Mrs. Wilson and her party. From a waiting crowd of perhaps 100,000 people there ripped a roar.

Part of the American people had gathered at the Capitol to watch the transition of power from the Republicans to the Democrats. This was the first Democratic inauguration in twenty years—ever since Grover Cleveland took office a second time. Since then the nation had had only Republican Presidents—McKinley, Roosevelt, Taft. But Wilson was about to become a minority President, for in the election of November, 1912, Roosevelt and Taft had won more votes collectively than Wilson. If the Republicans had not been divided between the progressives for Roosevelt and the regulars for Taft, Wilson would have lost.

Mrs. Wilson left her seat on the steps of the Capitol and slipped down onto the ground, her secret service agents watching nervously, to take up a position directly beneath the large Presidential seal on the balustrade, to stare up at her husband with a look of rapture.

Wilson had removed his silk hat and stood bareheaded in the March weather facing Chief Justice Edward D. White, who wore a black robe and was about to swear Wilson in as the twenty-eighth President of the United States. Eleanor Wilson thought her father looked slender and distinguished and very grave. Wilson had asked that he swear his oath on his wife's Bible, and now he placed his left hand on an open page and held up his right hand and repeated the words spoken by the chief justice. After he pledged his honor, he kissed the Bible, and at that moment a shaft of light pierced a cloud and illuminated the new President.

As Wilson stood enshrined by the sun, he had the eerie feeling that he was not himself but a stranger, not the central figure in a solemn ceremony but only a spectator, and even the next day he wrote a friend, "Everything is persistently *impersonal*—I am administering a great office—no doubt the greatest in the world—but I do not seem to be identified with it; it is not me, and I am not it." After his election but before his inauguration he had told someone, "God ordained that I should be the next President of the United States." Now that he *was* the President of the United States, the administrator of the greatest office in the world, sure to be remembered by history, perhaps he recoiled in terror from the sin of pride, for Wilson was a Calvinist with a cold conscience.

As his wife stood and adored her husband with her eyes, unaware she was to die before the end of his term, as Eleanor had feared, the woman who was to become the second Mrs. Wilson sat in her home in Washington at 1308 Twentieth Street. She was Edith Bolling Galt, the handsome widow of a man who had owned one of the best jewelry stores in the city. Her sister-in-law, Mrs. Annie Bolling, had come to stay with her during inauguration week, and from the moment of her arrival she had talked of nothing but Wilson, Wilson, Wilson. This very morning Annie was up early to get ready to go to the Capitol to watch the ceremony, and she could not believe her ears when Mrs. Galt said she intended to stay home. When Annie expressed indignation, Edith told her she had seen the McKinley and Roosevelt inaugurations—and inaugurations were all alike. Annie snapped, "All alike? This is a Democrat and a great man! I'd go even if I had to stand on the sidewalk in the crowd. The idea—when you have that wonderful balcony of your own at Galt's—not to go!"

So the woman who was to become the First Lady of the land sat at home alone and did not know that just as Wilson was about to begin speaking some people pushed through police barriers to try to get closer to him. When the cops tried to force them back, the new President looked down and said, "Let the people come forward." Smiling up gratefully at him, they pressed closer to the white balustrade draped in white bunting. Then Wilson looked down at his manuscript with hooded blue-gray eyes and in his mellow tenor voice began reading his inaugural speech—only 1,500 words in length and one of the shortest in American history. The next day a newspaper said that "not since Lincoln has there been a

President so wonderfully gifted in the art of expression," and decades later historian Henry Steele Commager called Wilson's first inaugural speech "one of the most notable statements of democratic faith in our political literature, and for eloquence [it] compares favorably with Jefferson's first inaugural and Lincoln's second inaugural."

Wilson began:

> There has been a change of government. It began two years ago, when the House of Representatives became Democratic by a decisive majority. It has now been completed. The Senate about to assemble will also be Democratic. The offices of President and Vice President have been put into the hands of Democrats. What does the change mean? That is the question that is uppermost in our minds today. . . .

He was speaking naturally, with no oratorical flourishes.

> . . . . We have squandered a great part of what we might have used, and have not stopped to conserve the exceeding bounty of nature, without which our genius for enterprise would have been worthless and impotent, scorning to be careful, shamefully prodigal as well as admirably efficient. We have been proud of our industrial achievements, but we have not hitherto stopped thoughtfully enough to count the human cost, the cost of lives snuffed out, of energies overtaxed and broken, the fearful physical and spiritual cost to the men and women and children upon whom the dead weight and burden of it all has fallen pitilessly the years through.
>
> The groans and agony of it all had not yet reached our ears, the solemn, moving undertone of our life, coming up out of the mines and factories and out of every home where the struggle had its intimate and familiar seat. With the great Government went many deep secret things which we too long delayed to look into and scrutinize with candid, fearless eyes. The great Government we loved has too often been made use of for private and selfish purposes, and those who used it had forgotten the people. . . .

When Wilson finished and while the cheers thundered, Taft heaved his bulk out of his chair to the left of the new President and held out his hand and said, "I wish you a successful administration and the carrying out of your aims. We will all be behind you." They left the Capitol steps and were ushered again into the stately carriage, which wheeled back down Pennsylvania Avenue, followed by a cavalcade of cars. William Jennings Bryan rode in one automobile with his wife, and the acclaim along the avenue fell into a pattern—eruptions of applause for the new President, followed by outbursts for Bryan. Thrice defeated for the Presidency, Bryan now beamed and cried to his wife, "It is worth sixteen years of hard work to have devotion like this, isn't it?"

During the ceremony at the Capitol the White House had been silent and its staff apprehensive about their new master's personality. At 11:30

A.M. Mrs. Taft had put on her hat and furs to leave, so nervous that she dropped some magazines as she handed a couple of letters to Irwin "Ike" Hoover, the head usher. Cooks and butlers were busy preparing a buffet luncheon to be served when the Presidential party returned from the Hill. At twelve noon the old flag was replaced by a new one run up the staff over the executive mansion. As luncheon guests began arriving, the doorkeepers became slightly confused, for they were accustomed to Taft's colleagues and friends, not the new faces now appearing.

As these strangers assembled in the East Room, the carriage containing Wilson and Taft drove up under the porte cochere, and they got out and walked through the main doorway and into the vestibule and stopped at a spot on the floor decorated by the Presidential seal. The chief usher thought both men looked slightly embarrassed, now that they were relatively alone together, neither seeming to know what to do next. Then an usher approached and informed Wilson he was expected in the dining room.

Meantime, to avoid the crowd gathered in front of the White House, Mrs. Wilson and her daughters had entered the grounds by the south gate and walked into the basement. The first thing Eleanor saw was an enormous circular seat covered with vivid red velvet. The women were led through a series of rooms full of china, glass, paintings and antique furniture. They stepped into a small elevator lined with mirrors and rose to the first floor, got out and were ushered into the Red Room. There they primped and powdered until Taft joined them and graciously offered to show them their upstairs bedrooms. Then he took them down to the state dining room. Wilson warmly greeted his family. Eleanor whispered to her father that she thought his speech had been splendid, but she felt a chill of panic when she found herself surrounded by important-looking strangers.

Wilson had invited Mr. and Mrs. Taft to attend the luncheon, and Taft had accepted while his wife, busy with details of their imminent departure for the South, had declined. In the book Ike Hoover wrote about his forty-two years in the White House he said Taft had remained for lunch, looking sad and lonely, but the fact of the matter is that Taft changed his mind and left before eating. As he said good-bye to Wilson, he remarked, "Mr. President, I hope you'll be happy here." Wilson, still slightly shocked at finding himself President, looked blank and muttered, "Happy?" Taft's smile faded as he said, "Yes . . . I know. I'm glad to be going. This is the loneliest place in the world." Taft then left for Union Station to join his wife and board a train that departed at 3:10 P.M. to take them to Augusta, Georgia.

Wilson ate sparingly of the buffet, for he was eager to get to the reviewing stand erected outside to watch the inaugural parade. General Leonard Wood, the chief of staff, a career officer with no great love for the new President, assured Wilson a couple of times that there was no need for haste, but at last Wilson became irritated and ordered the general to leave, even if he had not finished eating, to start the parade. Once again clouds veiled the sky as Wilson took his place on the stand and stood the rest of the afternoon to review the river of bright uniforms flowing past. Almost himself again, he laughed and smiled and waved his hand.

When the last soldier had tramped away, he walked back inside and went to the Oval Room to attend a tea for his cousins, aunts and uncles and close friends. The room hummed with soft Southern accents, for most of his relatives were from the South. Eleanor Wilson gazed around the room, finished in rose color and magnificently proportioned, but thought the furniture was stiffly arranged. The furnishings used by the Tafts had been removed, while the Wilsons had not yet had time to settle in with their own belongings.

Next to the President, the hit of the party was a cousin, Florence Hoyt. Cousin Florence, as all called her, was a high-spirited cripple. Her train had pulled into the station while the inaugural ceremony was in progress, and through some oversight no one was there to greet her. She could find no cab. Hobbling back and forth on the sidewalk, she tried to hail passing cars but was ignored. She was seen by an old black man who sold frankfurters from a wagon pulled by a skinny horse, and he stopped and asked if he could help her.

Cousin Florence allowed that that was right nice of him, so he handed her into his rickety wagon and asked where to. She said to the White House. She told her relatives that the ancient black man had rolled his eyes in terror and argued with her as though she were a foolish child, but she sang out, "That's where I want to go, Uncle!" The reins trembling in his hands, he drove her to the grounds of the White House and wanted to let her off at a rear entrance, but she insisted instead that she would enter by the front door, so the gaunt horse plodded up the main driveway and under the porte cochere and was met by two liveried doormen who stared in amazement. They helped her down from the rattletrap, and as it creaked away, the bewildered driver shaking his head from side to side, she waved and thanked him and shouted that she was Mrs. Wilson's cousin from Baltimore.

Everyone laughed. Then the party took a new turn, for someone rushed into the room to cry that Aunt Annie had fallen on the stairs and twisted her back. This was Mrs. Annie Wilson Howe, the President's fifty-nine-year-old sister. Besides hurting her back, she had gashed her forehead on the marble stairway. A servant sent to find a doctor returned with Navy Lieutenant Cary Travers Grayson, a charming man with an aristocratic face. Taft had made Grayson the White House physician, and the previous day while entertaining the Wilsons at the White House, Taft had presented him to Wilson, saying, "Mr. Wilson, here is an excellent fellow that I hope you will get to know. I regret to say that he is a Democrat and a Virginian, but that's a matter that can't be helped." Now, as Dr. Grayson took charge of Aunt Annie, Eleanor Wilson listened to him speaking "educated nigger," as she put it, and chuckling with a voice that sounded like the tearing of silk. Wilson liked Grayson so much he kept him on as his official doctor, and the two men became close friends.

With the President's sister resting comfortably in bed, the rest of the family and friends strolled into the big dining room for the Wilson's first sit-down meal in the White House. The huge table was massed in roses that faded in and out of focus in the flicker of candles, while from overhead a great candelabrum shed soft radiance on the guests and the fatigue ironed into the face of the new President.

After the meal he was driven to the New Willard hotel, where the

Princeton Class of '79 was holding a smoker. It was in 1879 that Wilson had been graduated from the College of New Jersey, later renamed Princeton University, and this inaugural night 800 alumni had gathered in friendship. Some had arrived in Washington on Wilson's special train, and of course they hoped the new President would join them, although they thought he would be too tired to appear. But just as they were being served dessert, Wilson appeared in the banquet room, and they jumped up and cheered and gave him the seat of honor. When they called on him for a speech, it was to his Princeton friends that he confessed that he had felt all day long as though he were only a spectator watching someone else getting all the attention. After a happy hour and a half Wilson left and rode back to the White House.

He had broken tradition by canceling the usual inaugural ball. Both he and his wife felt such an affair would be too ostentatious for their simple tastes. When Eleanor heard the news, she shed secret tears, for her mother had bought her a pin set with small diamonds and Eleanor had hoped to wear it while being whirled about a dance floor by admiring young men. Elsewhere in the land there were inaugural balls that night, but Wilson contented himself by standing at a White House window to watch a fireworks display at the Washington monument.

Toward midnight some people left while houseguests went to their rooms and Wilson reached his bedroom and rang several bells, not knowing which one meant what. His confused calls were answered by a doorkeeper, and Wilson explained that his nightclothes were in his trunk and he wanted to know where it was. Servants began searching, and at last the trunk was found at the railway station. A car was sent to pick it up; but the car did not return to the White House until one o'clock in the morning, and by that time the President was asleep. In the Lincoln bed. Sleeping soundly in his underwear.

In his inaugural address he had dwelled on domestic events and devoted only a few lines to foreign affairs. Had he known of the storm soon to lash the earth he might not have slept so well.

Chapter 2

THE LONG PEACE

"We send this New Year Greeting January 1, 1914," wrote Andrew Carnegie in his own curious spelling, "strong in the faith that International Peace is soon to prevail, thru several of the great powers agreeing to settle their disputes by arbitration under International Law, the pen thus proving mitier than the sword. . . . Be of good cheer, kind friend.

> It's comin' yet for a' that!
> When man to man the world o'er
> Shall brothers be and a' that.

Carnegie's friends were not surprised to receive the aging capitalist's message of hope on that first day of the new year, for pacifism and optimism prevailed throughout most of the world. They knew that the previous June he had gone to Berlin to represent the American Peace Society at a fete celebrating Kaiser Wilhelm's quarter century as the emperor of Germany and the king of Prussia. The Kaiser had swaggered up to Carnegie and boasted, "I have given my people twenty-five years of peace." An ardent pacifist, Carnegie beamed and responded, "Your Majesty is our best ally." And after the Scottish-born Carnegie returned to his adopted country, he became chairman of a national committee formed to celebrate the fact that the United States and Great Britain had been at peace for a century. On December 24, 1814, the signing of the treaty of Ghent had ended the War of 1812 between the two powers.

The idea for the celebration was brought up for the first time at the 1909 commencement at Harvard by W. L. King, the Canadian minister of labor, who urged that a memorial be erected at Niagara on the American-Canadian border. The matter was taken up again at the Mohonk peace conference in May, 1910, and then at a June 10 meeting, when it was decided to form a temporary committee on organization, which later became a permanent organization. Several people put forward proposals about memorials that might be erected. One called for construction of a monument in the form of a water gate to be built between Detroit, Michigan, and Windsor, Ontario, on the American and Canadian sides of the Detroit river. Another plan was to place an arch on the Canadian frontier over the New York-Montreal highway, then under construction. Or perhaps in New York City there could be erected a structure dedicated to the cause of peaceful progress. Elihu Root, former American secretary of state, hoped that on February 15, 1915, the anniversary of the ratification by the American and British governments of the treaty signed at Ghent, all 150,000,000 English-speaking people throughout the world might "engage in silent prayer and contemplation." But as it turned out, on that date Germany was sending the United States a note agreeing to modify its savage submarine policy if Britain would let neutral nations ship food to Germany for consumption by civilians.

On the eve of the first worldwide war in history, most people believed that peace was permanent and progress inevitable. In 1910 Sir Norman Angell, a British economist and pacifist, wrote a book called *The Great Illusion* in which he "proved" that peace would endure because big nations could not war against one another for more than three months without going bankrupt; the book was published in twenty-five foreign editions. Henry Cabot Lodge, the historian, biographer and Republican Senator from Massachusetts, published a sketch of American-British relations under the significant title *One Hundred Years of Peace.* President Wilson spoke in his inaugural of "a growing cordiality and sense of community of interest among the nations, foreshadowing an age of settled peace and good will." In Berlin the Germans were constructing a huge stadium for the 1916 Olympic games, while in New York City the German-American Economic Association was cultivating stronger business ties between both countries.

In the first fifteen years of the twentieth century sixty-three peace societies were organized in this country alone. Dr. David Starr Jordan, the director of one of them, the World Peace Foundation, wrote in *War and Waste,* "What shall we say of the Great War of Europe, ever threatening, ever impending, and which never comes? We shall say that it will never come. Humanly speaking, it is impossible." *The Review of Reviews* said in its January, 1914, issue, "The world is moving away from military ideals; and a period of peace, industry and world-wide friendship is dawning."

On January 1, 1914, the London *Daily Chronicle* published an article by British Prime Minister Herbert H. Asquith in which he declared that the world was blessed with permanent peace. That same day the New York *Times* printed an interview with David Lloyd George, the British chancellor of the exchequer, who said people were sick of armaments and announced the time had come for reducing British naval expenditures. In the first 1914 issue of *Collier's Weekly* its editor predicted: "Fifty years from now the future historian will say that the ten years ending about January 1, 1914, was the period of the greatest ethical advances made by this nation in any decade."

All these gentlemen were forgetting the lessons of history and human nature. Since the beginning of that fragile vessel called civilization more than 5,000 years earlier, war had been a bloody commonplace in the annals of mankind. Ancient Greeks and Romans had fought, fought, fought—almost continuously. During the Middle Ages all Europe was fragmented into hostile social units that battled one another most of the time. In the seventeenth century the great European states were formally at war about 75 percent of the time, in the eighteenth century about 50 percent, and in the nineteenth century about 25 percent of the time. It should be noted that this 25 percent refers only to official wars and ignores irregular expeditions and the like.

No massive and official war between one European coalition and another had been fought on the continent since 1815, when the British under Wellington defeated Napoleon at Waterloo. But since then, of course, there had been the Spanish-American War of 1898, the Filipino War of 1899, the Boer War of 1899, the Boxer Rebellion of 1899–1900, the Russo-Japanese War of 1904–05, the Turko-Italian War of 1911 and the Balkan Wars of 1912 and 1913. But these wars, however savage and brutal, were only local in scope and did not convulse nations.

Americans, like most other peoples, tended to regard themselves as peaceful and nonmilitaristic—but this was not wholly true. In the first 150 years of its history the United States fought 110 wars or armed conflicts that involved some 8,600 battles or military engagements of one kind or another. In fact, throughout this century and a half there were only about 20 years in which American soldiers or sailors or marines were *not* fighting somewhere on some day or other. Between 1775 and 1921—which of course includes World War I—79 percent of the nation's total expenditures went for national defense—and *defense* is a tricky word.

At the beginning of 1914 no realist would dare argue that the human heart had been purged of hate and fear and envy and anger and greed and selfishness—but these basic human emotions, it seemed, now could be kept under control. Statesmen and storekeepers told one another that now there were practical means for keeping the peace, since a balance of power had been attained in Europe. And while the United States was a teen-ager among the nations of the earth, immature and crude and often empty-headed, Europe was the very shrine of modern civilization—by tradition, by education, by finance, by religion and by military and naval and political and diplomatic influence.

European sovereignty was vested in six great powers—Great Britain, France, Germany, Russia, Italy and Austria-Hungary—and in fourteen smaller states. Except for Sweden and Switzerland, all these states were also empires possessing colonies or in some degree dominating and exploiting other races and their resources. In the latter part of the nineteenth century Europe divided itself into two equally balanced camps held together by alliances and ententes. The Triple Alliance consisted of Germany, Italy and Austria-Hungary. The Triple Entente was composed of Britain, France and Russia. Each of these two great coalitions was as strong as the other—hence, the balance of power. Nonetheless, within this framework there was a ferment of economic rivalry, imperialistic aspirations, armament races, passionate nationalism, social immorality or amorality and a dangerous lack of effective international law. The Balkan Wars of 1912 and 1913 had resulted in a direct confrontation between Russia and Austria-Hungary, which for years had vied for mastery of middle Europe. Prior to these wars these two great powers had moved against each other indirectly, through the intermediation of various other nations in the Balkans. But now the diplomatic chessboard had been cleared of pawns; now the prime movers plotted their next plays.

Sir Winston Churchill once wrote:

The world on the verge of its catastrophe was very brilliant. Nations and Empires crowned with princes and potentates rose majestically on every side, lapped in the accumulated treasures of the long peace. All were fitted and fastened—it seemed securely—into an immense cantilever. The two mighty European systems faced each other glittering and clanking in their panoply, but with a tranquil gaze. A polite, discreet, pacific, and on the whole sincere diplomacy spread its web of connections over both. A sentence in a dispatch, an observation by an ambassador, a cryptic phrase in a Parliament seemed sufficient to adjust from day to day the balance of the prodigious structure. Words counted, and even whispers. A nod could be made to tell. Were we after all to achieve world security and universal peace by a marvellous system of combinations in equipoise and of armaments in equation, of checks and counter-checks on violent action ever more complex and delicate? Would Europe thus marshalled, thus grouped, thus related, unite into one universal and glorious organism capable of receiving and enjoying in undreamed of abundance the bounty which nature and science stood hand in hand to give? The old world in its sunset was fair to see. . . .

Chapter 3

WILSON: THE MAN AND THE PRESIDENT

Thomas Woodrow Wilson was born on December 28, 1856, four years before Lincoln was elected President for the first time, five years before the outbreak of the Civil War. That fratricidal bloodbath left a deep impression on him; as a boy he grew up on horror stories about what General Sherman had done to his beloved South, and once he saw Jefferson Davis marched along a street, a prisoner of Union soldiers.

Wilson's birth took place in his father's home at 24 North Coalter Street in Staunton, Virginia. The town lay within the Shenandoah valley, and its steep streets followed old Indian trails and provided long views of fertile fields and acres of orchards dripping blossoms in spring. In later years Wilson mused, "A boy never gets over his boyhood, and can never change those subtle influences which have become a part of him, that were bred into him when he was a boy."

His father, Joseph Ruggles Wilson, had been born in Ohio of Scotch-Irish ancestry. His mother, Janet (known as Jessie) Woodrow, had been born in Carlisle, England, near the Scottish border, into a learned and religious Scottish family distinguished through many generations for its scholars and Presbyterian ministers. Wilson's father was also a Presbyterian pastor, whose calling led him to move the family from Virginia to Georgia to South Carolina to North Carolina, giving the boy intimate knowledge of Southern geography and traditions. Wilson was one of four children—the third child and first son.

The Reverend Mr. Wilson was handsome and impressive, pious and learned, fond of romping with Woodrow but also given to teasing the boy frequently and sometimes mercilessly. The minister's wife was a plain-faced woman, serious and reserved, wholly devoted to her family. Woodrow, who clung to her, later said that "love of the best of womanhood came to me and entered my heart through those apron strings." When he turned six, he was not sent to public school but was tutored at home by his father—a perfectionist. Perhaps because of paternal pressure, Woodrow did not master the alphabet until he was nine, and although he enrolled in school at the age of ten, he did not learn to read easily for another year.

After Woodrow was able to write, he gave his compositions to his father for review. The Reverend Mr. Wilson would read what he had written, point to a sentence and ask, "What did you mean by this?" The boy would explain, usually in more simple terms, and his father would counter, "Well, you did not say it, so suppose you try again and see if you can say what you mean this time." While his father's insistence on simplicity shaped Woodrow's clarity of writing and precision of speech, this repeated experience traumatized him. He was afraid of his father. But even more fearful of expressing resentment and hostility toward such an authoritative figure, the boy remained obedient and respectful.

All his life Woodrow addressed his father in such extravagant terms—"my precious father," "my incomparable father"—that one is justified in posing certain questions: Did he actually hate his father? Was he afraid he might be destroyed if he let himself realize his true feelings? Did he shrink from trying to excel his father? After he became President, he said he regarded his father as a greater man than himself, rationalizing that his father had won less fame because he had lived out his life on a smaller stage. Was his repressed ambivalence toward his father the flaw that almost tore him apart?

After growing out of boyhood, Woodrow dropped his first name of Thomas. In 1873 he spent a year in Davidson College in North Carolina, then enrolled in the College of New Jersey at Princeton—which became Princeton University. A skinny, intense student, he studied public speaking, became a star debater, managed the college baseball team, pored over biographies of British statesmen, decided to become a lawyer as the first step in a public career. In 1879 he entered the law school at the University of Virginia, where he paid less attention to required legal reading than he did to the study of British and American political history.

Nonetheless, he passed his bar examination and in 1882 became a partner in an Atlanta law firm that failed to prosper. He moved to Baltimore to enter the graduate school at Johns Hopkins University, began writing and produced a book called *Congressional Government*, a clear and beautifully written analysis of American legislative practices. Submitted as his thesis, it won him a doctorate in philosophy from Johns Hopkins in 1886. He also was elected to Phi Beta Kappa.

A year earlier he had married Ellen Louise Axson, a young woman willing to endure the privations of life with the struggling teacher he was to become. They were ideally suited to each other, and their marriage was almost perfect. After teaching history at Bryn Mawr, he was called to Wesleyan University as a professor of history and political economy. In 1890—not yet thirty-four and only eleven years out of college—he returned to his alma mater of Princeton as professor of jurisprudence and political economy. A magnetic teacher, illustrating his points with jokes and dramatizations, he was so popular with students that when class ended they often applauded and stamped their feet appreciatively. Some felt he was the best teacher they ever had.

In 1902 Wilson became president of Princeton. Dissatisfied with outworn educational concepts, maintaining that "the object of a university is simply and entirely intellectual," irked by outside pressures and the privileges enjoyed by the sons of rich men, Wilson tried to revolutionize the academic life at Princeton. Wealthy students belonged to exclusive eating clubs serving as fraternal aristocracies. Wilson wanted to abolish the clubs and substitute something that came to be known as his quad plan. Modeled after the structure of British universities, his plan would have divided Princeton into separate colleges with students living in resident quadrangles, each with its own dining hall, study and social rooms.

But Wilson underestimated the power of his opposition. His plan was opposed by students belonging to the clubs, by some older members of the faculty, by a majority of the university trustees, by Princeton graduates constituting part of the Establishment along the eastern seaboard. As Wilson bitterly remarked, the power of the exclusive clubs proved greater than the interest of the university itself. He suffered the first big defeat of his career.

Nonetheless, his fight against academic and economic interests won him a reputation as a champion of the masses against the classes—and at a time when public feeling in New Jersey was running high against conservative Republicans called standpatters. So when the Democrats sought a liberal to run for governor, they turned to Wilson, who was well read in history and political economy but wholly inexperienced in practical politics.

As a matter of fact, Wilson was not the liberal some people thought he was. Years earlier he had made the puzzling statement that the automobile was sure to spread Socialism, he had expressed hostility to the very principle of labor unions, he had written books and articles advocating a conservative political philosophy, and once he even spoke disparagingly of popular democracy. But he began to change his mind after his defeat at Princeton by the rich and rigid, after he became sensitive to the dangers of monopolies and trusts. He developed into what might be called a conservative progressive—somewhat to the political right of both Progressives and Socialists.

Accepting the Democratic nomination for the governorship of New Jersey, Wilson campaigned through the state, and after one speech he was approached by a farmer who clapped him on the back and cried, "Doc, you're all right!" Telling this story, Wilson would add, "I knew then that I had arrived as a politician." The state's Democratic political bosses thought that in the high-minded university president they had found a man they could manipulate, only to learn they were wrong. Wilson told his audiences, "If you give me your votes, I will be under bonds to you—not to the gentlemen who were generous enough to nominate me." Tammany boss Richard Croker, watching Wilson's intransigence from the east of the Hudson river, rumbled, "An ingrate is no good in politics!"

On November 8, 1910, Wilson won the election, eighteen days later two Wilson for President clubs were organized in Virginia, and the following January 17 he was sworn in as governor of New Jersey. Before long he "licked the gang to a frazzle," in the words of a political reporter. Defying party hacks loyal only to the party, he instituted a series of important reforms: a primary election law, a public utilities act with a cutting edge, a corrupt practices act, an employers' liability act. Ten months after he took office in Trenton his state was being studied across the land as a shining example of the possibilities of reform, and for the first time Woodrow Wilson began to win national attention. He was succeeding because he was in tune with the times. "No reform," he observed, "may succeed, for which the major thought of the nation is not prepared."

Prepared, and waiting in the wings, was Edward M. House of Texas, a manipulator of politicians, a Machiavelli in search of a prince. Having served as the chief adviser to four governors of Texas, he had been rewarded with the honorary title of "Colonel." With an income big enough to provide the leisure he needed to play the game of politics, which fascinated him, Colonel House wanted power more than prestige and now felt himself ready to expand into the national political scene. In the fall of 1911 he and Wilson met for the first time and instantly fell into friendship, for they thought alike and shared the same principles, with House's realism balancing Wilson's idealism.

Shy, self-effacing and meek-looking, Colonel House had a balding head, huge ears, a mustache, almost no chin and narrow, sloping shoulders. His voice was a whisper and he never laughed out loud although sometimes he would smile a thin smile or perhaps let himself go in a half chuckle. His catlike eyes peered in cool calculation over high Mongolian cheekbones, and one of his enemies compared him to a tiger sneaking over dry leaves without making a sound. Wilson fondly compared the Colonel to a fox. In addition to being a superb political technician, Colonel House was a close student of human nature. He would listen carefully to everything Wilson said, quickly agree with him and only later try to slip across his own ideas, succeeding so well that Wilson came to regard House as his alter ego. The Colonel became convinced that this eloquent Eastern reformer was the man who should and could become the next President of the United States.

The Democratic national convention, held in Baltimore in the summer of 1912, was ferocious and protracted, but with the help of Colonel House and others, Wilson won the Presidential nomination on the forty-sixth ballot. The Republicans, split between regulars and progressives, were even more divided. The regulars picked incumbent President William Howard Taft as a candidate to succeed himself, while former President Theodore Roosevelt became the candidate of the progressive wing of the Republican party. In the ensuing campaign the main issue was the control of monopolies. As Wilson stumped the country, he shaped a creed called the New Freedom, arguing that monopolies were evils inimical to the existence of free enterprise.

In the election of November, 1912, Wilson won over both his rivals, getting 435 electoral votes to Roosevelt's 88 and Taft's 8. However, the popular vote proved that Wilson was to become a minority President. Roosevelt took 4,126,020 popular votes and Taft 3,483,922 for a combined total of 7,610,012 popular votes, while Wilson polled only 6,286,215 popular votes. Still, Wilson was to have a Democratic majority in both the Senate and House during both his first and second terms in office—which, of course, included World War I.

Elevated to the highest office in the nation only three years after he entered politics, Wilson felt both humble and proud. The month after his election he went back to Staunton, Virginia, to celebrate his fifty-sixth birthday, and one afternoon he visited an old aunt he had not seen since he was a child. She was senile and so deaf she used a long black ear trumpet. After an exchange of greetings, she asked, "Well, Tommy, what are you doing now?"

"I've been elected President, Aunt Janie."

"*What?*"

"President!"

"Well, well! . . . President of what?"

Grabbing her trumpet, Wilson roared into it, *"President of the United States!"*

She stared at him with weak eyes, smiled a skeptical smile, waved her hand and dismissed him.

Woodrow Wilson weighed 179 pounds and was five feet eleven inches tall, although he seemed taller than his actual height because he held himself erect and had broad shoulders that slanted down his lean body to a slim waist. Some people thought his head looked disproportionately large for his figure. He had a high-domed forehead and parted his thinning graying hair on the left side. His ears were long and pointed. His face was long and thin and angular, a series of triangles and rectangles, and he had a sharp nose. Clamped onto the bridge of his nose were rimless glasses that enhanced his prim and chiseled look. He had hooded blue-gray eyes, high cheekbones and a mouth that was small and taut and betrayed a hint of femininity within this obviously masculine man. Perhaps his most arresting feature was his elongated jutting jaw.

When he and his family moved into the White House on March 4, 1913, he brought along much of his old Princeton furniture to enable them to feel at home in this strange environment. There was his flat desk with drawers on either side, a plain wooden chair with a high back, a brown leather seat and arms whose black paint had worn off where his elbows had rubbed them. He also brought along his collection of canes, hundreds of canes.

In prewar days Wilson did not work hard as President. A creature of habits, he arose daily at 8 A.M. and a half hour later breakfasted on two raw eggs in orange juice, along with oatmeal and coffee. His physician had prescribed the raw eggs, but Wilson abhorred them, snorting, "I feel as if I were swallowing a newborn baby!"

By 9 A.M. he was in his office reading his mail and dictating replies to his stenographer. For personal correspondence, speeches and state papers, Wilson tapped his green bell-shaped portable Hammond typewriter, one that could be adapted to either English or Greek—although he knew no Greek. Whenever he traveled anywhere, he took his typewriter, for it seemed to have become a part of him. Forever prompt himself, and always expecting everyone else to be prompt, at exactly 10 A.M. he began receiving visitors, limiting them to only ten or fifteen minutes. Should any dare linger longer, the President would fix cold eyes on a spot on a wall above the man's head until the visitor got the message and departed.

At 1 P.M. Wilson lunched—always with his family. To the dismay of politicians and intellectuals, it was noted that the President was so much the family man that he did not socialize with Cabinet members or bureaucratic officials, Senators or Representatives, philosophers or professors, writers or painters—men whose wisdom and experience might have broadened his mind and augmented his statesmanship. Wilson doted on the company of women—his adoring wife and worshipful daughters and uncritical female friends. His closest male friend, Colonel House, had markedly feminine traits, although he was a contented husband, a good father to his two daughters and a fast man with a gun because of his Texas background.

By 2 P.M. Wilson was back in his office keeping more appointments. At 4 P.M. he quit work for the day, donning a Scots cap to take an auto ride along the same unvarying routes, changing into a cheap golf suit to play an indifferent game of golf or boarding the Presidential yacht, the *Mayflower*, to relax while gliding up or down the Potomac river. In the golden days of 1913 and the early part of 1914 life was simple, the world seemed safe, and Presidential problems were less numerous and pressing than they were to become from that time forward. After war broke out, Wilson was at his desk by 6 A.M. and often remained there until midnight.

At 7 P.M. he dined with his wife and daughters and then spent the evening with them, never really getting into the capital's social swing. For a man seemingly so austere in public, he was delightfully relaxed when in the bosom of his family. He liked to stretch out on a rug in front of the hearth to recite poetry from memory or to read aloud from the works of Keats, Wordsworth, Browning, Swinburne, Shelley and Tennyson. He could be playful and impish, gay and entertaining, putting a record on the Victrola and dancing a jig. A talented mimic, he convulsed his daughters with his repertoire of impersonations.

As the Grande Dame, he draped a feather boa over his shoulders, trailed a velvet curtain and uttered banalities in a falsetto voice. As the Drunk he staggered about, always on the verge of falling down, talking nonsense with a thick tongue. As the Englishman—and a good thing the British ambassador never saw this performance—Wilson wore an invisible monocle, behaved with fatuous pomposity, haw-hawed absurdities and pretended to react to everything with amusing slow-wittedness. Caricaturing the Villain he clumped around like the deformed King Richard III, dragging one foot behind him, clawing the air with stiff fingers and scowling a Barrymore scowl. Mocking Theodore Roosevelt, whom he disliked, he waved his fists and shrilled, "We stand at Armageddon and battle for the Lord!"

One or two nights a week he would attend the theater. Although he had no taste for serious drama, he was fond of everything else connected with the stage—comedy routines, variety acts, tap dancing, vaudeville—and he sometimes tapped his feet while a singer belted out a song. His favorite comedian was Will Rogers, the gum-chewing, rope-twirling cowboy who liked to hone his wit on politicians. One night Wilson went to Baltimore to see Rogers in the *Follies*. Aware that the President sat in the audience, the Oklahoma satirist poked gentle fun at him. Wilson beamed. Taking heart, Rogers then spoke directly to the President, using his name, and Wilson enjoyed it. Rogers said, "I see by the papers that them German submarines cain't operate in the warm Gulf Stream. If we can only heat the ocean, then we got 'em licked!" Wilson laughed. "Of course," Rogers added, "that's only a rough idea. I ain't got the thing worked out yet." The President howled.

Most people who met Wilson considered him an icicle. While he had a firm handshake and could put men at their ease whenever he wished, he never clapped them on the back, never called them by their first names, never behaved in that easygoing way glad-handers call "good fellowship." On display at a White House reception he could shake thousands of hands while keeping his face a mask except for the obligatory half-smiles he called "smirks." Later, alone in his bedroom, he would grimace to ease the facial strain, telling his wife his face needed resting as much as his other muscles needed exercise. His facial muscles were so flexible and his control over them so absolute that he could elongate or broaden his face and wiggle his ears. Shy and sensitive, Wilson was reserved even with people he liked, and in the company of pompous men he closed himself in like a castle with the drawbridge up.

Once he told his secretary, Joseph Tumulty, "I *am* cold, in a certain sense. Were I a judge and my own son should be convicted of murder, and I was the only judge privileged to pass judgment upon the case, I would do my duty even to the point of sentencing him to death. It would be a hard thing to do—but it would be my solemn duty as a judge to do it and I would do it, because the state cannot be maintained and its sovereignty vindicated or its integrity preserved unless the law is strictly enforced and without favor."

Had Wilson transformed himself into his own stern and moralistic father? Perhaps in part. However, after the United States got into the war, he pardoned several American soldiers convicted of sleeping while on guard duty.

Until he was more than forty, he was afraid he might be a coward, but he changed his mind after being aboard a ship that hit an iceberg and seemed in danger of sinking. Later, as President, he insisted on reviewing a parade from an exposed grandstand although the secret service knew of a plot to assassinate him. Like all of us, Wilson was a bundle of contradictions. His second secretary of war, Lindley M. Garrison, told another Cabinet member, "I was never able to understand Mr. Wilson and—with due deference—I doubt if you or anybody else could. He was the most extraordinary and complex character I ever encountered."

It would be impossible to understand Wilson without understanding his religious life. The descendant of a long line of Presbyterian ministers, the son of a Presbyterian pastor, himself a Presbyterian and a ruling elder of the church, having somehow missed that period of doubt which disturbs many young men, Wilson was utterly pious. He said grace before every meal, read the Bible every day, prayed on a daily basis, attended church regularly, was a connoisseur of sermons. As a Presbyterian he was, of course, a Calvinist—and the dour dogma of Calvinism declares that man is innately depraved, a corrupt sinner deserving eternal punishment, a creature whose only hope of salvation lies in election by God to a state of grace and eternal life.

Once he told his secretary, "You know, Tumulty, there are two natures combined in me that every day fight for supremacy and control. On the one side there is the Irish in me—quick, generous, impulsive, passionate, anxious always to help and sympathize with those in distress. And like the Irishman at the Donnybrook Fair, always willin' to raise me shillalah and to hit any head which stands against me. Then, on the other side, there is the Scotch—canny, tenacious, cold and perhaps a little exclusive. I tell you, my dear friend, that when these two fellows get to quarreling among themselves, it is hard to act as umpire between them!"

Regrettably, this was about as far as Wilson could go in explaining himself to himself. He was compulsive and tense, with nerves coiled like springs, and his energy was mostly nervous energy which he quickly burned up, leaving him without any reserve strength. Frail and sickly as a child, never having enjoyed robust health, Wilson entered the White House almost a sick man. His wife constantly worried about his health. According to the White House physician, Dr. Cary T. Grayson, when Wilson was professor and then president of Princeton, "he was frequently under the care of physicians for a stubborn stomach ailment, and three times he broke down." Besides his stomach trouble, for years he had been afflicted with respiratory upsets, blinding headaches, hemorrhoids, neuritis and phlebitis—"flea-bitten," he joked.

His migraines were so massive and prolonged they could be cured by no medicine; all he could do was sleep as long as possible. For his frequent digestive disorders he treated himself with a stomach pump and medicinal powders. Dr. Grayson took away his pump and powders and told him to drink orange juice and the raw eggs he hated. Deprived of his private remedies, Wilson laughingly accused his doctor of being a "therapeutic nihilist." Despite the President's afflictions, he retained his wit. Once when Grayson was tapping his chest, he grinned and said, "Why knock? I am at home." One of his favorite quotations was this definition of golf: "An ineffectual attempt to put an elusive ball into an obscure hole with implements ill-adapted to the purpose." Fond of limericks, Wilson especially liked this one:

For beauty I am not a star,
There are others more handsome by far,
But my face, I don't mind it,
For I am behind it—
It's the fellow in front that I jar.

Woodrow Wilson was the second Democratic President since the Civil War, the eighth born in Virginia, the eleventh elected from a state other than his native state, the first who had majored in history and government while in college, the first who had been the head of a major university. He entered the White House with supreme confidence in his own judgment. If an intellectual is one who enjoys thinking, then Wilson certainly was an intellectual. While thinking through an issue, he was fairly open-minded, but after making up his mind about a subject, he often grew stubborn. He regarded himself as an idealist, and believed that he was always on the side of righteousness—which marked him as slightly fanatical.

Like some great leaders, he was perhaps more sensitive to mankind as a whole than to individual men and women. He had keen powers of observation, his comprehension was swift and sometimes intuitive, and he was more interested in concepts than anything else. His doctor observed, "He thinks while he's exercising, while he's dressing or bathing." His secretary said, "He was always ahead of us in his thinking." Wilson's mind pounced on ideas, absorbed them, assimilated them, synthesized them. He cut through verbiage and went to the core of every concept. Nonetheless, he seldom was profound, and he had difficulty making those compromises so necessary in political life.

He could digest data speedily, dictate to his stenographer rapidly, and no one ever had trouble understanding what he meant. He often began a speech with the stilted phrase "May I not," which became as much a national joke as Theodore Roosevelt's 'Deee-*lighted!*" Before Wilson became President he wrote several books, among them a five-volume work called *A History of the American People*. Later he told his daughters, "I have never been proud of that history. I wrote it only to teach myself something about our country."

There had been a time when he wrote short stories, but instead of collecting money, he collected rejection slips. Surprisingly, in 1916 Wilson told a reporter that in the previous fourteen years he had not read a single serious book through to its end. To win his PhD, he learned German but soon forgot most of it and spoke no other foreign language. "To know English properly," he said, "has kept me so busy all my life I haven't had time for anything else." Sir Winston Churchill confessed that only because he was kept in the same class three times longer than anyone else did he "get into my bones the essential structure of the ordinary British sentence—which is a noble thing." Wilson was not widely traveled, was wholly indifferent to the scientific developments changing his world, had huge gaps in his knowledge of literature, knew next to nothing about classical art or music.

If someone told Wilson something he had read or heard, he might snap, "I know that!" Dissatisfied with his achievements, never wholly respecting himself, he had the unfortunate habit of denigrating others and trying to dominate them. After some encounters with Wilson, former President Grover Cleveland called him "intellectually dishonest." Supreme Court Justice Oliver Wendell Holmes wrote a friend about Wilson, "I can not admire either his intellect or the moral nature of one who writes as he does." Senator Henry Cabot Lodge said, "I think he is a man of ability, but he has no intellectual integrity at all." Lodge, an avowed enemy of Wilson, may have been thinking of the President's insistence that "the thing to do is to keep your mind open until you are bound to act. Then you have freedom of action to change your mind without being charged with bad faith."

Wilson was a genius at molding public opinion. As President he regarded himself as the "trustee of the people" and the "clearing house of the government"—although Washington correspondents complained he told them little about what was happening in the government. Nonetheless, he startled them with the candor of his remarks the evening of March 20, 1914, at the dedication of the new National Press Club at 15th and G streets:

> I have never read an article about myself in which I have recognized myself, and I have come to the conclusion that I must be some kind of fraud, because I think a great many of these articles are written in absolute good faith. . . .
>
> I tremble to think of the variety and falseness in the impressions I make—and it is being borne in on me that it may change my very disposition—that I am a cold and removed person who has a thinking machine inside which he adjusts to the circumstances, which he does not allow to be moved by any winds of affection or emotion of any kind, that turns like a cold searchlight on everything that is presented to his attention and makes it work.
>
> I am not aware of having any detachable apparatus inside of me. On the contrary, I would say that my constant embarrassment is to restrain the emotions that are inside of me. You may not believe it, but I sometimes feel like a fire from a far from extinct volcano, and if the lava does not seem to spill over, it is because you are not high enough to see the caldron boil. . . .
>
> I can hardly refrain every now and then from tipping the public with a wink, as much as to say, "It is only *me* that is inside this thing. . . . I know perfectly well that I will have to get out presently. I know that then I will look just like my proper size, and that for the time being the proportions are somewhat refracted and misrepresented to the eye by the large thing I am inside, from which I am tipping you this wink. . . ."
>
> There are blessed intervals when I forget by one means or another that I am the President of the United States. One means by which I forget is to get a rattling good detective story, get after some imaginary offender and chase him all over—preferably any continent but this one, because the various parts of this continent are becoming painfully suggestive to me. Some day after I am through with this office I am going to come back to Washington and see it. I am in the same category as the National Museum, the [Washington] Monument, the Smithsonian Institution, or the Congressional Library. . . .
>
> It would be a great pleasure if, unobserved and unattended, I could be knocking around as I have been accustomed to being knocked around all my life, if I could resort to any delightful quarter, to any place in Washington that I chose. I have sometimes thought of going to some costumer's—some theatrical costumer's—and buying an assortment of beards, rouge and coloring and all the known means of disguising myself, if it were not against the law. . . . If I could disguise myself and not get caught, I would go out, be a free American citizen once more and have a jolly time.

Wilson is probably the only American President who ever indulged in such a public psychological striptease. Since he usually was reserved, his behavior that night might be inexplicable were it not for his longing to be loved.

On another occasion he said, "There surely never lived a man with whom love was a more critical matter than it is with me!" This remark may explain his fondness for flattery, which he equated with loyalty, and helps us understand why he formed a Cabinet consisting mainly of second-raters. Seven of its ten members were suggested to him by Colonel House, and most were Southerners like himself. Seldom did he consult with Senators and Representatives; if he had something he wanted to tell them, he would send for them and then treat them like the teacher he was at heart. In 1913, talking about the acceptance of his leadership in Congress, "even by men of whom I did not expect it," he added in arch tones, "I hope that this is in part because they perceive that I am pursuing no private and selfish purposes of my own."

Except for military matters, Wilson failed to delegate much authority and tried to do too much himself. He did not enjoy the company of generals or admirals, cared little about strategy, and when the battles began, he left everything to the professional soldiers—unlike Franklin D. Roosevelt in World War II. Wilson refused to see patronage hunters, such as those who wore out Abraham Lincoln in the first few weeks of Lincoln's first administration.

Anyone wishing to see Wilson had to pass approval by Tumulty, his devoted secretary, a genial Irishman who tried to touch everything with a lighter touch than his boss. Tumulty swore that the President welcomed suggestions and criticisms, but this was denied by others. Shunning personal contacts for the most part, Wilson preferred to do business in writing, and on papers handed to him he would scrawl in a margin, "No, W.W.," or "Okeh, W.W." Asked why he did not write it "O.K." he replied, "Because it is wrong," and suggested that the inquirer look it up in the dictionary, where he would discover that "Okeh" was an Indian word meaning "It is so."

Woodrow Wilson was totally honest. Never mingling in Washington society, scorning nepotism, letting no friendship influence him, he refused all expensive gifts and would not permit Harper & Brothers to sell movie rights to one of his books after he became President. He set a high moral tone that permeated his entire administration—with one wretched exception. As a Southerner with paternalistic regard for blacks, he was insensitive to their rights and feelings. Otherwise, because of his rigid moralistic stance, he inspired awe and admiration from millions of Americans—but rarely the affection he wanted. Convinced that God had chosen him to lead the nation, a superb orator, a wooer of the masses, if not of individual men, this strange and straitlaced man had the gift of inspiring people with his noble vision, and this was all to the good—considering the oncoming troubles.

Chapter 4

THE IRON HEEL

In 1914 the United States of America consisted of forty-eight states, New Mexico and then Arizona having entered the Union only two years previously. The nation covered 3,026,789 square miles and had a population of 98,646,491, which averaged out to 33.17 persons per square mile.

Nearly one-third of the population was foreign-born, and of this third 15,000,000 were *European*-born immigrants, including 3,000,000 adults unable to speak English and 9,000,000 who read foreign-language newspapers exclusively. New York City alone had 500,000 non-English-speaking inhabitants. Immigration into this country had been running especially heavy since 1905, and between then and the peak year of immigration in 1914, nearly 10,500,000 foreigners had come here in hope of realizing their dreams. Between 1905 and 1914 three-quarters of these immigrants came from Slavic and southern regions of Europe, while less than 15 percent came from western and northern Europe. Next to Prague, Chicago had the largest concentration of Czechoslovaks in all the world. In Cleveland 34.9 percent of the city's residents consisted of aliens. Of the foreign-born whites living in this land 12.7 percent were illiterate; for the total population the figure was 7.7 percent. Twenty-nine percent of all the people in Louisiana over the age of ten were unable to read or write. Iowa's illiteracy rate of 1.7 percent was the lowest of any state in the union.

Chauncey M. Depew, the socialite president of the New York Central Railroad, suspected immigrants of wishing "to destroy our government, cut our throats, and divide our property." Depew failed to mention that his father was of French Huguenot descent. Men of Angle-Saxon ancestry dominated the nation's political and economic power structure, filling Cabinet posts and high governmental positions, running the Ivy League universities, controlling the rich and powerful railroads, making most of the big decisions about cultural life and the slant of the communications media. Many of them were the sons or grandsons of the old robber barons—white Anglo-Saxon Protestants for the most part. But New York City, now the largest city on earth, was becoming ever more Jewish and some of these Jews, especially the German Jews, were rising to positions of enormous influence. These German Jews tended to scorn the Jews lately arrived from Russia and Poland, men and women of lesser means and therefore of a supposedly inferior culture.

Shortly after getting here, the immigrants learned with a sense of shock that America was not the wholly democratic, classless and open-ended society they had thought it was, but rather a rigidly structured system that granted privileges to the rich while disadvantaging the poor. Yet it was a fact that the middle class was growing in size—although this is a relative statement and does not mean that the middle class was the largest segment of society, for it was not. Concentration of wealth was an evil so obvious and ominous that liberals of many persuasions had fought on many fronts over the previous decade or so to institute reforms—an end to child labor, fair wages, decent working hours and conditions, free education for all, equitable taxes, equal rights for blacks, the abolition of social and political corruption. Edward A. Ross, a professor of sociology at the University of Nebraska, had formulated what he called the concept of "social sin"—the idea that men sometimes harm others not only by open violence or overt threats, but also by indirect and distant means, in ways subtle and silent and sinister. Sarah N. Cleghorn, a Quaker poet, wrote this famous quatrain:

> The golf links lie so near the mill
> That nearly every day
> The laboring children can look out
> And see the men at play.

This was hardly the viewpoint of Dr. John James Stevenson, an educator, a famous geologist, a Presbyterian, a PhD and a member of Phi Beta Kappa. The 1914 spring issue of *Popular Science Monthly* published an essay by Dr. Stevenson called "Capital and Labor" in which he said in part:

> . . . a wife and child cannot be considered in connection with the relations of wage earner to wage payer. The only question concerns the worth of a man's services. Introduction of other matters would so increase the uncertainty of business affairs as to make them little better than a lottery. If a man's services are not worth enough to secure wages which would support a family, he should not marry. He may not complain because the community is unwilling to have him gratify his desires at its expense. . . .
>
> One is told that in each year 200,000 women in our land are compelled to sell their bodies to procure the necessities of life, and that each year sees 700,000 children perish because their parents had insufficient nourishment . . . if it be true . . . one must conclude that their deaths are a blessing to themselves and to the community. Such children should not have been born. . . . Unskilled labor is merely animated machinery for rough work and adds very little value to the final product. One E. H. Harriman is of more lasting service to a nation than would be 100,000 of unskilled laborers. Without a Harriman they would be a menace.

This tender expression of capitalism was praised by John D.

Rockefeller, Jr., as "one of the soundest, clearest, most forcible pronouncements" he had ever read.

After the Civil War, and especially after the depression of 1873–79 when large-scale production began, there was a trend toward the consolidation of economic power in this nation. As business and industry grew in size and complexity, brilliant and cunning men created one device after another to kill competition and grab control of all the means of production and thus the profits.

The first such device was the pool—a secret agreement between two or more firms to act together in fixing prices, limiting output, dividing up territory and sharing profits. The first pool in American history was the Michigan Salt Association, formed in 1868. The pooling of resources, from which the phrase gets its name, became a commonplace in the United States in the 1870's and 1880's, but in 1890 Congress passed the Interstate Commerce Act, which prohibited railways from banding together in this way to crush rivals.

The second device was the trust. John D. Rockefeller's Standard Oil Company, secretly organized in 1879 but amended and publicized in 1882, was the first trust. In its simplest form, a trust is property of any sort held by one party for the benefit of another. Similar to the pool, but an improvement upon it, the trust is a business combination in which holders of stock in previously competing firms surrender their shares to a new board of trustees in return for trust certificates. The trustees hold all the power, for only they can vote and only they can decide the size of the dividends to be paid. In the case of Standard Oil, holders of stock in many refining, pipeline and other companies signed over their holdings to a board of nine trustees at a stipulated price and then received trust certificates. Between 1879 and 1882 Standard Oil controlled 90 percent of the nation's refining capacity.

Other industries soon formed their own trusts. The American Cotton Oil Trust was set up in 1884; the National Linseed Oil Trust in 1885; the Distillers and Cattle Feeders Trust, known as the Whiskey Trust, in 1887; the American Tobacco Trust in 1901. These gigantic combines alarmed the public—expecially small businessmen, who were being squeezed out of industry after industry, and farmers, who felt they were being gouged by industrial monopolies. In response to their clamor, in 1890 Congress passed the Sherman Antitrust Law, which declared that every contract, combination or conspiracy in restraint of trade or commerce among the several states was illegal. But the Sherman Act was so loosely phrased and poorly enforced that by 1904, in defiance of this legislation, there were 318 industrial monopolies with a total capitalization of more than $7 billion and consolidating more than 5,300 plants or factories. When Theodore Roosevelt was President between 1901 and 1909, he was called a trustbuster, but rather than seek to destroy monster corporations, he sought instead to regulate them. During his term of office forty-four antitrust suits were started. Taft, his successor, who held office between 1909 and 1913, initiated ninety proceedings against monopolies.

The third device was the holding company. It came into vogue in the late 1890's as a successor to the still-powerful but discredited trust. A holding company is a corporation holding enough shares of other companies to control or influence their policies. Because stock in a holding company is scattered among many small holders, anyone owning as little as 10 to 20 percent of the stock can control the industry. A pure holding company has no assets other than the securities of its subsidiaries; a parent holding company engages in productive operations as well. For many years the United States Steel Corporation was the largest holding company in the nation. Until 1888 most states forbade a corporation to own securities in another firm except when granted permission by special legislation, and few such privileged charters were issued. However, in 1889 the New Jersey general corporation law was amended to let firms chartered under it acquire the right to own shares in other firms.

This was a fundamental and dangerous change in American corporate law. The New Jersey type of corporation was not required to have any operating duties whatsoever, other than to hold the shares of other concerns, elect officers, receive dividends from subsidiaries and turn them over to their stock- or bondholders. When the Standard Oil Trust was outlawed, it simply reincorporated as the Standard Oil Company of New Jersey. When J. Pierpont Morgan consolidated 60 percent of the steel industry in 1901, he established a holding company, the United States Steel Corporation, under New Jersey law.

Woodrow Wilson raised the issue of trusts and holding companies when he ran for the governorship of New Jersey in 1910. Ignorant of economics and corporate law, when he took office, he turned to the head of the chancery court of New Jersey and also a retired justice of the state supreme court, asking them to draft reform bills. They prepared seven laws, known as the Seven Sisters, which were passed by the New Jersey legislature. The Seven Sisters laws outlawed all attempts to create monopoly or suppress competition, made corporation officers personally liable for their acts, sought to prevent the watering of stocks and banned the creation of new holding companies. As a result, corporations moved to states with lax corporation laws, states such as Delaware, Maine, West Virginia and North Dakota.

By the turn of the century the United States was the richest nation on earth in terms of real gross national product per person. Obviously, however, this did not mean that wealth was shared equally by all Americans. In 1916 the United States Commission on Industrial Relations quoted a conservative statistician as saying that 2 percent of the people owned 60 percent of the wealth. In 1914 the world's five richest nations were: (1) the United States, with $150 billion; (2) Great Britain and Ireland, $85 billion; (3) Germany, $80 billion; (4) France, $50 billion; and (5) Russia, $40 billion.

Also by 1900 the United States had become the greatest manufacturing nation on earth, owned the most railway mileage and produced the largest amount of agricultural items. In 1914 artisans were dying out and industrialism was growing faster than agriculture. Besides exceeding other nations in productivity, the United States was the world's biggest consumer. In 1900 per capita consumption of manufactures in this country was 50 percent higher than in Great Britain and twice as great as that in Germany and France. Allan Nevins has said, "Americans either shared or had taken undisputed leadership in railroad construction; in structural engineering; in factory, business, and modern home architecture; in the quantity manufacture of motor vehicles; in the development of sanitary water systems; and in the new art of highway construction adapted to automobiles."

Just before the outbreak of war our five best foreign customers were—in this sequence—Great Britain, Germany, Canada, France and the Netherlands. Increased productivity in factories and on farms resulted in surplus capital which Americans invested in foreign enterprises. This was a new and vital factor in the history of the world. Ever since the discovery and settlement of the New World by Europeans, capital had flowed from Europe into America. Now the tide was changing. In 1914, although foreign investments in this country stood at a whopping $4 billion, American investments abroad had reached about $3.5 billion.

One of the great themes in American history is the maldistribution of wealth. Whether the majority of our citizens can retain their political freedom and social institutions when the privileged few control most of the wealth—this is an ageless and endless and disturbing question. In 1915 the Commission on Industrial Relations said in its final report:

> The control of manufacturing, mining, and transportation industries is to an increasing degree passing into the hands of great corporations through stock ownership, and control of credit is centralized in a comparatively small number of enormously powerful financial institutions. These financial institutions are in turn dominated by a very small number of powerful financiers.
>
> The final control of American industry rests, therefore, in the hands of a small number of wealthy and powerful financiers.
>
> The concentration of ownership and control is greatest in the basic industries upon which the welfare of the country must finally rest.
>
> With few exceptions each of the great basic industries is dominated by a single large corporation, and where this is not true the control of the industry through stock ownership in supposedly independent corporations and through credit is almost, if not quite, as potent.
>
> In such corporations, in spite of the large number of stockholders, the control through actual stock ownership rests with a very small number of persons. For example, in the United States Steel Corporation, which had in 1911 approximately 100,000 share holders, 1.5 percent of the stockholders held 57 percent of the stock, while the final control rested with a single private banking house. . . .

This private bank was the so-called House of Morgan, mostly owned and wholly dominated by J. P. Morgan. He was the only son of J. Pierpont Morgan, who had died in Rome in 1913. The elder Morgan certainly had been the foremost leader of American finance, and some newspapers called him the greatest financier who ever lived. After his death the New York *Tribune* devoted its first seven pages one day to the story of his life. Now the son had his own office in his own building at 23 Wall Street, a gray five-story structure, massive and forbidding in appearance, completed in 1914. The House of Morgan stood just across the street from the New York Stock Exchange building whose portico was decorated with eleven white marble figures, the central statue symbolizing Integrity.

Louis D. Brandeis, a Boston lawyer commonly called "the people's counsel" and a man who later became a justice of the United States Supreme Court, said in 1904 that "neither our intelligence nor our characters can long stand the strain of unrestricted power." He gave this example of how money and power were held in a few hands:

"J. P. Morgan (or a partner), a director of the New York, New Haven & Hartford Railroad, causes that company to sell J. P. Morgan & Co. an issue of bonds; J. P. Morgan & Co. borrow the money with which to pay for the bonds from the Guaranty Trust Company, of which Mr. Morgan (or a partner) is a director. J. P. Morgan & Co. sell the bonds to the Penn Mutual Life Insurance Company, of which Mr. Morgan (or a partner) is a director. The New Haven spends the proceeds of the bonds in purchasing steel rails from the United States Steel Corporation, of which Mr. Morgan (or a partner) is a director. The United States Steel Corporation spends the proceeds of the rails in purchasing electrical supplies from the General Electric Company of which Mr. Morgan (or a partner) is a director. . . . " And so on *ad infinitum.*

Brandeis said the control of capital is to business what the control of the water supply is to life, adding, "When property is used to interfere with that fundamental freedom of life for which property is *only a means*, then property must be controlled."

Partial and temporary control flowed from hearings by the famous Pujo Committee, whose counsel was Samuel Untermyer. Born in Virginia of German immigrants, Untermyer developed into an eminent attorney who earned $5,000,000 by the time he reached his early thirties, mainly by helping to organize several great industrial combines. The wealthier he grew, the more independent he felt until at last he became a traitor to his class—as rich men viewed such matters. Max Eastman, a radical, expressed it this way: "Having put away millions as attorney for the 'robber barons,' he had taken up public-spiritedness, somewhat as one takes up golf in advancing years, and made himself both feared and hated by those barons." On December 27, 1911, speaking before the Finance Forum of New York City, Untermyer shocked its members by declaring that eighteen financial institutions in New York, Boston and Chicago constituted a "money trust" that controlled the nation's economy through interlocking directorships. In February, 1912, the House of Representatives passed a resolution directing its committee on banking and currency to determine whether such a money trust did in fact exist. Democratic Congressman Arsène Pujo of Louisiana, the committee chairman, was named chairman of a subcommittee to investigate the matter, and he appointed Untermyer its counsel.

Hearings began on April 27, 1912. One after another of the nation's leading financiers and businessmen testified, many reluctantly, the star witness being J. Pierpont Morgan. Untermyer, who served the Pujo Committee without pay, had such intimate knowledge of high finance that he pried damaging admissions from some of the witnesses. All the committee's work was skillfully done and carefully evaluated. On February 28, 1913, five days before Woodrow Wilson was inaugurated as President, the Pujo Committee released its majority report.

A money trust *did* exist. The committee said so in this clumsy sentence:

> If by a "money trust" is meant an established and well defined indentity and community of interest between a few leaders of finance which has been created and is held together through stock holdings, inter-locking directories, and other forms of domination over banks, trust companies, railroads, public service, and industrial corporations, and which has resulted in a vast and growing concentration of control of money and credit in the hands of a comparatively few men—your committee has no hesitation in asserting as a result of its investigation that this condition, largely developed within the past five years, exists in this country today.

Newspapers gave massive coverage to the Pujo Committee hearings and its report. Farmers and factory workers, small businessmen and liberals were shocked by this proof that the United States was not a democracy but a plutocracy—government by rich men. Up went cries for reform. Forced at long last to pay some attention to public opinion, Morgan and other capitalists resigned their multiple directorships in most of the many corporations they controlled. When President Wilson delivered his first annual message to the Congress on December 2, 1913, he called for the prevention of private monopoly by the passage of more antitrust legislation. At the same time he declared that antagonism between government and business was at an end—but this was not exactly true.

In that same speech Wilson also called for the extension of citizenship to Puerto Rico, a further degree of self-government in Hawaii and ultimate independence for the Philippines. The United States had begun to develop into a colonial and world power in the 1880's, when it secured a dominant position in Hawaii and Samoa. In 1898, after defeating Spain in the Spanish-American War, after annexing the Philippine Islands, after clinching American power in the Caribbean and even projecting it into the northern part of South America, after starting construction of the Panama Canal through Central America, this nation developed into a great power in the fullest sense of the phrase. Its influence now extended far beyond its continental shoreline and land borders. Now other great powers had to consider the attitude of the United States in the settlement of major diplomatic problems.

To ram home this point, President Roosevelt sent an American fleet around the world in 1907–09. "In my own judgment," he later wrote, "the most important service that I rendered to peace was the voyage of the battle fleet round the world. I had become convinced that for many reasons it was essential that we should have it clearly understood by our own people especially, but also by other peoples, that the Pacific was as much our home waters as the Atlantic, and that our fleet could and would at will pass from one to the other of the two great oceans."

On December 16, 1907, sixteen battleships, six torpedo boats and four auxiliaries, with a total complement of 15,000 men, left Hampton Roads, Virginia, for San Francisco and then the horizon beyond, traveled 13,772 miles, sailed over every navigable ocean, crossed the equator four times, visited every continent on the globe and exchanged greetings with the warships of fourteen different nations.

After Wilson was sworn in as President, he became swept up in the expansionist fever, and diplomatically and militarily he interfered in the internal affairs of other nations on a more massive scale than ever before in the annals of the United States. When tyrants fell in countries such as Nicaragua, the Dominican Republic and Haiti, he sent marines to restore order for the sake of order, not for the sake of democracy. He also sent soldiers into Mexico.

Mass production, which was to change the world, was developed by the Ford Motor Company in Michigan between 1908 and 1914.

Henry Ford was not the father of mass production, as many people believe, but rather its midwife. Seldom is a theory, invention or technique the unique product of a single mind, since each genius learns from every genius of the past. Interchangeable parts had been used in the fifteenth century by Johann Gutenberg, the German printer. Standardized parts had been introduced in the eighteenth century by Eli Whitney in making guns. A completely mechanized grain mill had been built in 1784 on Red Clay creek in Pennsylvania by Oliver Evans. Conveyor systems were in use in American packinghouses by the latter part of the nineteenth century.

Ford began making automobiles in 1899, introduced his Model T in 1908, announced the following year his firm would build only the Model T chassis and that "any customer can have a car painted any colour he wants, so long as it is black." By 1913 Ford was the most successful auto manufacturer in the world, although he was not mentioned in *Who's Who* and that year the New York *Times* did not print a single article about him. At the end of 1913 Ford had 100,000 unfilled orders.

This backlog of orders met one condition necessary for mass production—a national market. Among the other necessities are sufficient working capital, standardized and interchangeable parts and a high state of technological development in manufacture, automatic control and transportation. Ford said that mass production embraces seven principles—power, accuracy, economy, continuity, system, speed and repetition. He put them together in expert combination.

The concept of the moving assembly line was formulated by Charles E. Sorensen, Ford's production chief. In his autobiography Sorensen wrote,

"The idea occurred to me that assembly would be easier, simpler, and faster if we moved the chassis along, beginning at one end of the plant with a frame and adding the axles and the wheels; then moving it past the stockroom, instead of moving the stockroom to the chassis." Although Ford was skeptical, he told Sorensen to go ahead and experiment with his plan.

Ford made his cars in a three-story brick building on Piquette Avenue in Detroit; stretching along one side of this factory was a long sign that said in white letters: THE HOME OF THE CELEBRATED FORD AUTOMOBILE. It was there, in July, 1908, that an assembly line was tested for the first time—not with the Model T but with the Model N. One Sunday morning that month Sorensen and some helpers put together the first car ever produced on a moving line. Developments and refinements were added over the next few years. The assembly line had to move at just the right speed, on just the right level, through just the right sequence of activities. By 1913 a Model T could be put together in twelve hours and twenty-eight minutes. By 1914 final assembly took only ninety-three minutes. In 1916 twelve "Speed Mechanics" dazzled New York audiences in the famous Palace theater by assembling a Ford on stage in two minutes flat. Mass production had been born.

Historian Lloyd Morris has written that mechanized mass industry changed American society more profoundly than any other single influence in the twentieth century. Mass production multiplied the productivity of the world's manufacturing industries. Since a keynote of mass production is simplicity in the operations performed by each worker, it decreased the need for mechanical skill by factory workers, while increasing the demand for skill in management, planning, designing and the marketing of products. It dehumanized labor and left workmen discontented.

But, on the other hand, many employers claimed they were working harder than any of their employees. This was easily explained, according to Louis D. Brandeis: In assuming responsibility for their work, the employers derived much satisfaction from it. Brandeis felt that the workers' dissatisfaction stemmed from the suppression of their individuality. In the February 14, 1915, issue of the Boston *Post* he said, "There are few things so interesting in life as work, under the proper conditions; and the way that employers generally work establishes the truth of this. They complain because their employees do not work similarly, do not feel the responsibility of the business. Let them give the employees a chance to bear responsibility, and the response will come."

Industrialization evolved so fast that in its wake it left a host of evils: slums, sweatshops, child labor, limited suffrage, unequal distribution of wealth, corrupt political machines, venal public officials, labor strife, discrimination against blacks, unfair tax laws, agrarian discontent, wasteful consumption of natural resources. Since the start of the twentieth century real wages either stood still or declined. The trouble was that in the transition from handicraft to machine production, labor did not get its fair share of the profits. Employees had no opportunity to help make policy decisions concerning those businesses or industries for which they worked. The men who owned the plants and railroads paid little attention to the welfare of those who helped them get rich. One businessman drawled that he would take up the labor question when he got around to it.

These cruel conditions came under attack by young reformers who wrote in magazines and novels that something should be done about abuses in the nation's economic, political and social life. These muckrakers, as Theodore Roosevelt called them, started their exposés in 1903, at a time when 10,000,000 Americans lived in poverty. Upton Sinclair attacked the meat-packing industry in a novel called *The Jungle*, Lincoln Steffens wrote *The Shame of the Cities*, Ida M. Tarbell turned out a critical *History of the Standard Oil Company*. Other journalists exposed the railroads, high finance, chicanery in the Senate, food adulteration, traffic in women and children, fraudulent advertising of patent medicines and the like. The muckrakers became so influential that Congress was forced to respond by passing remedial legislation.

Then the reforms advocated by the muckrakers were taken up by progressives—private individuals, enlightened politicians and others, who demanded an end to all abuses and mounted such pressure that a whole new body of laws was enacted at the federal, state and municipal levels. Unfortunately, though, many judges and lawyers had failed to keep in touch with social and industrial developments in America, and some of the new and necessary laws were voided in the courts. For example, in 1914 Arizona passed an old-age pension act, only to have it declared unconstitutional.

Woodrow Wilson was a conservative when he entered public life. He was against labor unions. He declared, "Government supervision . . . will in the long run enslave us and demoralize us." He urged the formation of a society of intellectuals to guide the nation's destiny and suggested that its chairman be J. Pierpont Morgan. However, as has been said, Wilson was able to change his mind. By 1907 he was agreeing that the muckrakers and progressives were on the right track. Soon thereafter he declared that the trouble with American society was that economic power and ownership of property had been concentrated in a few men, that they exercised political power out of all proportion to their numbers. By 1908 Wilson was saying, "Half our present difficulties arise from the fact that privileged interests have threatened to become too strong for the general interest, and that therefore the government has had to step in to restrain those who would enjoy the very privilege which it itself had granted." He denounced trusts. He said the only single possessor of rights and privileges should be the individual, not the corporation.

In the early years of this century perhaps the most popular American author was Jack London. The illegitimate son of a man who made a meager living practicing astrology, London was born in 1876 in the slums of San Francisco, so poor that he had to leave school after the eighth grade. He was self-taught for the most part, reading widely and finally evolving a philosophy drawn from the works of Herbert Spencer, Friedrich Nietzsche, Karl Marx and Rudyard Kipling. Before London killed himself in 1916 at forty, he had written an equal number of books. He called himself a Socialist, but in reality he was an individualist and romantic, enthralled by violence, anticipating Ernest Hemingway in his obsession with death and the courage of men close to death.

In 1907 he produced one of the most scathing indictments of capitalism ever conceived, a novel called *The Iron Heel.* Irving Stone has called this book "one of the world's great classics of revolution." Supposedly written in 1932, the novel describes alleged events in the United States between 1912 and 1918, when all the nation's capitalistic monopolies banded together into an organization called the Iron Heel and seized control of the country. The framework for the book is the papers supposedly left by the protagonist, Ernest Everhard, a Californian who was both a kind of superman and a Socialist. Fear of the Socialist party was the reason why the leaders of the Iron Heel launched a right-wing revolution. They stamped out all democratic forms and free institutions, liquidated the middle class, broke the power of labor, created a caste system with a plutocratic aristocracy at the top, maintained a secret police and a military junta.

Ernest Everhard and other Socialists rose in rebellion against this tyranny, used force to meet force, and averted war with Germany by means of a general strike in collaboration with German Socialist unions. In one chapter the hero faces the Philomath Club, whose members formed the richest oligarchy on the Pacific coast, defiantly pointing out the waste and evils of the profit system, predicting that industry will be taken over by the workers. The leader of the oligarchs answers him, shouting:

> "When you reach out your vaunted strong hands for our palaces and purple ease, we will show you what strength is! In the roar of shell and shrapnel and the whine of machine-guns will our answer be couched. We will grind your revolutionists down under our heel, and we shall walk upon your faces. The world is ours, we are its lords, and ours it shall remain. As for labor, it has been in the dirt since history began, and in the dirt it shall remain so long as I and mine have power!"

At the climax of the novel the slum classes, for whom Everhard and his fellow Socialists feel nothing but contempt, pillage a great city. For twenty years the revolutionaries wage underground war against the Iron Heel, but in the end they are defeated, and Everhard is executed. At this point the so-called Everhard manuscript breaks off, but then come footnotes written by an alleged twenty-seventh-century editor who said that the Iron Heel held power for 300 years, was overthrown at long last and then was succeeded by the Brotherhood of Man.

Anatole France wrote an introduction to the novel, saying, "Jack London has that particular genius which perceives what is hidden from the common herd, and possesses a special knowledge enabling him to anticipate the future." In 1907, the year the book was published, the word "Fascism" had not yet entered the language, but it was American Fascism that London was predicting. Not surprisingly, few newspapers even mentioned the book, while those that did urged that "the hand of the law should descend heavily" on Jack London. *The Iron Heel* sold only a few copies. But some who read it may have shifted uneasily in their chairs and wondered about the concentration of wealth in America and about the trusts, which continued to flourish. Socialists, for their part, accused Jack London of betraying their evolutionary cause by advocating revolution. *The History of Violence in America*, edited by Hugh Davis Graham and Ted Robert Gurr, published in 1969, had this to say: "The apocalyptic fury with which *The Iron Heel* concludes may well have been the sign of London's sanity as a social prophet. . . ."

Chapter 5

THE NEEDY AND THE GREEDY

A recession had begun in 1913. One business analyst called it "a year of doubt and uncertainty, occasioned largely by numerous federal and state investigations and the uncertain results of the new tariff law and other legislation. The year represented a selling movement in which investors and speculators liquidated heavily. During the entire year business men marked time while awaiting developments and showed a disinclination to take the initiative in making purchases for the future or otherwise extending their business operations."

By 1914 the recession had deepened into a depression, with business worse than at any time since the panic of 1907. Foreign trade declined, commodity prices weakened, an increasing amount of gold was shipped to Europe, coal and steel production fell, and unemployment rose. There was even a drop in vaudeville receipts, cabaret owners found almost no one willing to pay $7 for a quart of champagne, and Broadway producers could hardly remember when show business had been so bad.

Businessmen blamed everything on the Democratic administration's lowering of tariffs and filing of antitrust suits—but actually the depression was worldwide. After the end of the two Balkan Wars of 1912 and 1913 the former combatant nations stopped buying arms and other goods abroad. Treasury Secretary William G. McAdoo, who found the United States full of "a propaganda of pessimism which apparently had its source nowhere and in nothing," suspected a conspiracy among "the interests"—by which he meant the Republicans.

Republican Senator Henry Cabot Lodge of Massachusetts faulted the Democrats and wrote to Theodore Roosevelt, en route home from Brazil: "I feel greatly alarmed about the outlook, for I fear we are on the edge of a condition which will cause great suffering in all directions. It is not the fault of business." President Wilson was about to appoint officers to the new Federal Reserve Board, and McAdoo begged him to name men who would help break Wall Street's control over the nation's credit. "Please don't think me unduly fearful of the 'Money Trust,'" McAdoo wrote Wilson. "I am not. I simply know, after a year's experience in the Treasury, that it is not a fiction, but a real thing and I want to keep the upper hand for the people while we have it." Disregarding his secretary's advice, the President nominated conservative bankers and businessmen to represent the people on the board.

James Madison once said that governments destitute of energy will produce anarchy, and in 1914 the government under Wilson gave little energy to the problem of unemployment. Wilson said the depression was merely psychological, an opinion endorsed by businessmen but scorned by the unemployed. Speaking to a delegation of Virginia editors in the White House on June 25, the President predicted a gigantic business boom; he said this three days before the assassination at Sarajevo that sparked World War I, before he could have known that the European struggle would start the wheels turning again in American factories.

Earlier, on January 28, 1914, Jacob S. Coxey said the depression was so severe and unemployment so widespread that he intended to gather an army of 500,000 workless men and march them to Washington to protest. Newspaper editors snapped to attention. Coxey—"General Coxey" he called himself—was an American folk hero. A reformer, sportsman, farmer and rich businessman, he owned a profitable sandstone quarry at Massillon, Ohio. Colorful and unorthodox, Coxey also was a Populist and convert to Theosophy.

Back in 1894, amid the economic unrest resulting from the Panic of 1893, he had formed a "living petition" of unemployed who marched as the Army of the Commonweal of Christ from his hometown to the national capital. On May Day, 1894, he led 500 followers up Pennsylvania Avenue to Capitol Hill and spoke from the steps of the Capitol, urging the passage of legislation to create public works and build roads and thus give work to the workless—an idea adopted decades later by the New Deal. Coxey was arrested for trespassing, spent twenty days in jail, later got a hearing before a House subcommittee. In 1914 he was almost sixty years old but still vigorous.

On February 10 he announced he was a candidate for the governorship of Ohio on the Socialist ticket, then turned around and endorsed the Industrial Workers of the World—with whom Socialists would have nothing to do. He rounded up musicians and organized a band, and soon some of his instrumentalists were arrested for drunkenness. His self-confidence undimmed, Coxey pushed eastward from Ohio to Washington and on May 21 spoke again from the steps of the Capitol about the plight of poor people. But instead of the army of 500,000 unemployed of which he had talked, he was flanked by only a handful of followers. This was the end of Coxey's mild threat to the administration, although it was not the end of the nation's economic problems.

The situation was especially bad in California because jobless men had gone there in the hope of finding work in connection with the San Diego Panama-California Exposition, scheduled for the entire year of 1915. The result was too many hands for too few jobs. The California Building Trades Council blamed the presence of this excess labor pool on advertisements soliciting workers for the exposition. In San Francisco the city fathers put their unemployed to work on reservations.

Then Charles T. Kelly began making noises like Coxey. He also called himself a general—"General Charlie" Kelly. In 1894 he too had left for Washington with his own army of unemployed, but never made it. Kelly now announced in California that he would lead another crusade of poor people. Oakland cops broke up his tiny army, but its members regrouped and were fed by compassionate citizens. Kelly and the others then pushed on toward the state capital at Sacramento. The militia was summoned, Kelly and his adjutants were arrested, and the rest were driven from the city by policemen and firemen. For the next few days the scattered men loafed and fished in the countryside. People began to eye them suspiciously after hearing a rumor that they planned to push east into Illinois and capture the army arsenal at Rock Island. This did not happen. Some of Kelly's followers got as far east as West Virginia but drifted quietly apart.

Midwestern states were in trouble because their state employment agencies had more job applicants than jobs, while private charitable organizations were overwhelmed with demands for work or food. Conditions were equally grim in the Eastern states. In Boston a group of idle men angrily invaded the Chamber of Commerce building; they were ejected, and eighty were jailed as vagrants.

Early in 1914 Calvin Coolidge was elected president of the Massachusetts senate. Despite the troubled temper of the times, he chose in his inaugural speech to take a strong stand in favor of the vested interests. A Republican and a vice-president of a small savings bank, Coolidge said:

> Ultimately, property rights and personal rights are the same thing. . . . History reveals no civilized people among whom there were not a highly educated class, and a large aggregation of wealth, represented usually by the clergy and the nobility. Inspiration has always come from above. . . . As the little red schoolhouse is builded in the college, it may be that the fostering and protection of large aggregations of wealth are the only foundation on which to build the prosperity of the whole people.

Coolidge's elitist argument, reprinted far and wide, evoked bitter comments from the unemployed, from Progressives and Socialists and anarchists.

The first call for a constructive large-scale attack on joblessness came not from the federal government but from the American Association for Labor Legislation in affiliation with the American Sector of the International Association on Unemployment. These related groups held the first National Conference on Unemployment in New York City on February 27 and 28, 1914. The sessions were attended by nearly 300 delegates from twenty-five states and fifty-nine cities—economists, statisticians, employers, union leaders, social workers and officials from the federal department of labor. They decided it was necessary to solve not only the acute and current situation, but also the seemingly chronic joblessness inherent in an industrial society. This decision marked a new attitude in American history toward the unemployment problem.

New York City seems to have suffered most in the 1914 depression. An official of a conservative relief society estimated that the city had 325,000 unemployed—a statement that was challenged but not disproved. A police survey revealed that 26,000 homeless New Yorkers were sleeping in free lodging houses, in employment offices, in saloons, under bridges, in streets and parks. It was obviously impossible to care for all of them in the Municipal Lodging House at 432 East Twenty-fifth Street. Various labor and radical organizations banded together into a Conference of the Unemployed, and every night hundreds of idle restless men gathered in lower Manhattan to listen to inflammatory speeches and discuss what they might do to try to save themselves. Members of the Industrial Workers of the World conferred in their headquarters on West Street while local anarchists seethed in their office at 313 Grand Street.

The specter of anarchism terrified the royal and the rich. Anarchism began to take shape in Europe about the time of the revolutionary year of 1848 and was elevated into a political doctrine by a French journalist, Pierre Joseph Proudhon. He believed all government to be evil. Karl Marx expelled all anarchists from his Socialist movement but did not repudiate the anarchist ideal as an ultimate goal of Communist society—after the "withering-away of the state."

In the decade prior to 1914 anarchists had assassinated six heads of state—President Sadi Carnot of France in 1894, Premier Antonio Cánovas of Spain in 1897, Empress Elizabeth of Austria in 1898, King Humbert of Italy in 1900, President McKinley of the United States in 1901, and another Spanish premier, José Canalejas, in 1912. If Americans paid little attention to the assassination of anyone except their own President, they had learned about anarchists in the Haymarket Riot of 1886. On May 4 of that year anarchists and police clashed in Haymarket Square in Chicago. The anarchists had gathered for an open-air discussion of labor problems, the cops tried to break the meeting up because of radical remarks, a fight broke out, a bomb was thrown, and seven policemen were killed and sixty wounded. As a result, four anarchists were hanged, one escaped the gallows by killing himself in jail, two were sentenced to life imprisonment, and one was jailed for fifteen years.

That was bad enough, but another shudder ran through the nation in 1901, when an anarchist named Leon Czolgosz shot President William McKinley, who died of his wounds eight days later. The assassin said he had heard Emma Goldman, called the "Queen of Anarchists," declare "that all rulers should be exterminated. . . . [It] set me to thinking so that my head nearly split with pain." Theodore Roosevelt, who succeeded to the Presidency, told Congress that "anarchism is a crime against the whole human race, and all mankind should band against the anarchists." In 1903 Congress amended the Immigration Act to exclude all persons "teaching disbelief in or opposition to all organized government."

In the early part of this century anarchist newspapers were being published in Chicago and New York, there was a nest of anarchists at Paterson, New Jersey, and New York City had the Ferrer School at 63 West 107th Street. Founded in 1910 and named after the Spanish revolutionary Francisco Ferrer Guardia, who had died a year earlier, the Ferrer School was the first American institution "devoted to the constructive side of anarchism," according to its president, Leonard D. Abbott. One of the "Ferrer School boys" was a young Austrian immigrant named Frank Tannenbaum, who had worked as a busboy until he lost his job. Long after the trouble into which he was about to plunge,

Tannenbaum earned a degree as a doctor of philosophy, joined the history department of Columbia University, wrote books about prison reform and Latin American economic problems.

Abbott, Tannenbaum and a few others decided that one way to dramatize the plight of the unemployed in 1914 would be to invade New York churches to ask for work, shelter, food or money. After all, Abbott had declared that the Ferrer School was "a laboratory in which new social theories are tested." Tannenbaum met Emma Goldman, who took him to visit Mabel Dodge's elegant home, since Mabel always felt herself drawn to the underprivileged despite her wealth. Mabel liked young Tannenbaum and praised his "finely modeled features." Soon afterward he spoke at a meeting in St. Mark's Parish House, and reporters wrote that he advocated the use of force to get something done for jobless men and women.

The evening of March 5, 1914, with a blizzard raking Manhattan, the ardent young Austrian and 189 followers—many just boys—went to the old Bible House, where they received a handout, then to the Labor Temple, where they got nothing, and to the First Presbyterian Church, where they were given $25. Their next target was the Roman Catholic Church of St. Alphonsus on fashionable Fifth Avenue. Leaving his shivering followers outside, Tannenbaum entered the rectory next door to the church to ask the priest for permission to sleep in the church that bitter night, promising to do no damage and to clean up after themselves before they left the following morning.

"A Catholic church is no place to sleep," the priest said. "The Blessed Sacrament is there."

Tannenbaum then asked for food. The priest refused. Some money? Again the priest refused.

Tannenbaum said, "So this is your Christian Gospel?"

"Never mind about that!" the priest snapped. "I will not allow you to talk to me in that way!"

Tannenbaum left to tell his men they could not use the church and then returned to bid farewell to the priest, saying, "All right. . . . No harm done." He offered to shake hands, but the priest refused the gesture. By the time Tannenbaum emerged from the rectory a second time his wind-chilled followers had taken shelter inside. He went in after them with the intention of marching them out, but a detective materialized and tapped his shoulder and said, "Please wait. We are waiting for orders from Police Commissioner McKay." Then a uniformed cop blocked the church door and said none would be allowed to leave just then. Moments later Tannenbaum and his group were arrested and led to a police station where he was charged with unlawful assembly and inciting to violence; his followers were charged with disorderly conduct.

Newspapers blared:

> FRANK TANNENBAUM LEADS MEN INTO CHURCH. . . . YOUNG RADICAL ATTEMPTS TO SEIZE CHURCH FOR UNEMPLOYED MEN. . . . TANNENBAUM UNDER ARREST FOR ILLEGAL ASSAULT UPON FIFTH AVENUE CHURCH.

On March 23, 1914, the New York *Globe* said in an editorial that the community held two lawless elements reactionaries who incited the police to lawless violence and radicals who indulged in lawless attacks upon property. The paper quoted with admiration some words of the late Mayor William J. Gaynor, who had ordered his police officials not to interfere with the rights of those who held unorthodox opinions of the government or economic or social order.

When Tannenbaum and his fellow defendants went on trial, Mabel Dodge sat in court every day. New Yorkers were tense because dynamite had been found in the yard of St. Mark's Church. When a reporter asked why a society woman such as herself should be interested in the Tannenbaum case, Mabel Dodge replied, "Of course, I don't believe in dynamite and that kind of thing," then added that she was a student of current events and wanted to help organize labor. "If some of the unemployed have qualities that are not altogether desirable," she said, "I think the blame should be placed on their environment rather than on the men."

Former President Taft attacked the IWW, the governor of New York suggested that the city's unemployed be put on farms at state expense, police kept a crowd from invading All Saints Episcopal Church, a hundred homeless men were sheltered in the Memorial Building of St. George's Episcopal Church, and Tannenbaum and his followers were found guilty as charged.

When the judge asked Tannenbaum whether he cared to say anything, the young man rose and said, "There was once a person who said that society would forgive murder or arson, but that the one thing it would not forgive was the preaching of a new gospel. That is my crime. There is no instance in the world's history where the efforts of the slave class to free themselves has been considered legal. I belong to the slave class. I am accused of participating in an unlawful assembly. I don't know of any assembly on the part of the working class that would be lawful. Why is there all this nonsense about bloodshed? The capitalistic class sheds more blood in one year than the workers do in five . . ."

Tannenbaum made these remarks on March 29, 1914. Three weeks later blood was shed at Ludlow, Colorado.

Tannenbaum was given a year in jail and fined $500. Unable to pay this sum, he would have been forced to serve an additional 500 days behind bars if the IWW had not raised the money. His arrest and conviction that spring of 1914 touched off a series of demonstrations in New York City. After one rally in Union Square a throng of unemployed people marched up Fifth Avenue brandishing the black flag of anarchy, shaking their fists at churches and private clubs and blocking traffic. No arrests were made, but the demonstration was so frightening that individuals and organizations began to realize they had better create jobs lest all workers become radicalized.

With more New Yorkers out of work than ever before in the city's history, well-to-do people collected food from door to door for the starving poor and breadlines formed at big hotels. There was a general outcry that the city administration should help. The city chamberlain held, however, that the city could not afford the necessary money, while the city comptroller argued that it had no responsibility in the matter. Their attitude did not go down well with the New York *World*, which declared, "The unemployment problem in its present form cannot be considered only from a bookkeeper's point of view." Workshops were opened to provide jobs at 15 cents an hour. Mayor John Purroy Mitchel created a Mayor's Committee on Unemployment and named Elbert Gary to head it.

This was not the reform mayor's most brilliant appointment. Gary was board chairman of the United States Steel Corporation, the largest industrial corporation in the world, a firm that worked its men twelve hours a day seven days a week. It was common knowledge that Gary hated unions. Except for business matters, he fearlessly faced the past, belonging to the Society of Colonial Wars and the Sons of the American Revolution. It has been said, of course, that a conservative is one who worships a dead radical. A regular churchgoer, Gary said he believed in *all* the Bible, "not a little piece here and a little piece there, not some garbled kind of new book that somebody had created for these modern times." A couple of years earlier Gary had given his wife a $500,000 pearl necklace for Christmas, causing Louis D. Brandeis to comment, "Is it not just the same sort of thing which brought on the French Revolution? . . . Social unrest is largely caused by industrial oppression on one side and ostentatious extravagance on the other." Living in opulence at 856 Fifth Avenue, working in the rarefied atmosphere of boardrooms, Gary knew nothing about poor people. After his appointment he got off to a bad start by making a speech in which he said that the United States had been hurt by agitation, investigation and attacks inspired by dishonest motives. He was denounced by the American Federation of Labor, and his name was hissed at an unemployment meeting in Cooper Union. In the end, according to Norman Thomas, Gary "gave jobless workers a little food, practically no money, and occasional work rolling bandages."

Some of the unemployed were invited to a Manhattan town house to tell a group of social reformers and city officials what they thought should be done. Among those present was a *New Republic* writer, Walter E. Weyl, who was struck by something: "The unemployed were addressed as 'you fellows,' 'friends,' 'boys,' but the title 'gentlemen,' which is in vogue in almost every sector, was not used." Walter Lippmann, also of the *New Republic*, devoted another article to the contrast between the rich and poor, the dehumanization of the lives of poor people, saying:

> . . . even the so-called democracies are far from a decent sense of the value of life. Here in America life is extraordinarily cheap. There is almost no task so dull, so degrading or so useless but you can find plenty of human beings to do it. You can hire a man to walk up and down the avenue carrying a sign which advertises a quack dentist. You can hire rows of men for the back line of the chorus, just standing them there to fill up space. You can hire a man to sit next to the chauffeur; he is called a footman

> and his purpose is to make the owner of the car a bit more comfortable and a great deal more magnificent.

The New York City police commissioner reported a rise in thefts owing to bad business conditions. The City Club of Philadelphia began studying the unemployment problem, and so did the National Association of Manufacturers. Cincinnati gave jobs to the idle by instituting waterworks and sewage improvements. Boston was giving relief funds to one-fifth of its citizens. Cleveland's mayor asked every resident with a job to donate one day's pay to unemployment relief. Chicago police broke up a march of hungry men, shots were fired, and a detective was injured. Theodore Roosevelt gave $10,000 to people out of work. The Catholic Protective Association gave free legal aid to people arrested for begging. Hoboken, New Jersey, was suffering because the decline in shipping had left 8,000 German sailors idle on the docks. Churches organized labor bureaus. Members of the American White Cross visited the homes of rich New Yorkers to solicit funds for the jobless. Mrs. O. H. P. Belmont, a rich society woman, opened a soup kitchen for women. A hundred desperate men exchanged their blood for money at the Beth Israel Hospital in New York.

Most newspapers were owned by rich men, and many of them now became impatient and almost angry with the unemployed. The *Wall Street Journal* said the nation needed a revival of religion, since only religion "brings employer and employed together on the common platform of love and fear of God." Agreement came from the Reverend Billy Sunday, the most popular evangelist of the era, the darling of millionaires such as John Wanamaker and John D. Rockefeller, Sr. Far from feeling compassion for the underprivileged, Billy Sunday declared, "The man that stands around with his hands in his pockets will soon be trying to get them into somebody else's. . . . An idle brain is the devil's workshop." When it was pointed out to him that the idle wanted work but could find no jobs, the evangelist urged them to "go back to the farm and study expert dairying and help save the lives of 200,000 babies that die every year from impure milk that is sold. . . . Go out west and study to be a horticulturalist." White farmhands lucky enough to have work were paid only $1.17 a day with board, while many black farmworkers earned 75 cents a day or less.

In January, 1915, Billy Sunday went to Philadelphia to preach the Gospel and point souls toward Christ. Instead of emphasizing faith and hope, he might have dwelled more on charity, for in the City of Brotherly Love half the wage earners were without wages. His exhortations pleased the Reverend W. C. Poole, who felt that the evangelist had helped business because "business was taught that religion is profitable." Bile rose in the throat of Scott Nearing, an economics instructor at the University of Pennsylvania. Nearing wrote Sunday, saying in part:

> . . . The well-fed people, whose ease and luxury are built upon this poverty, child labor and exploitation, sit in your congregation, contribute to your campaign funds, entertain you

> socially, and invite you to hold prayer meetings in their homes. . . . The employers of labor have always welcomed anyone who could divert men's minds from worldly injustice to heavenly bliss. Turn your oratorical brilliance for a moment against low wages, overwork, unemployment, monopoly, special privilege and the other forces which grind the faces of the poor.

Billy Sunday's theme song might have been "Heaven Will Protect the Working Girl," a popular ballad of the day, but in the slums of Hell's Kitchen on the middle west side of Manhattan a social worker learned that an eleven-year-old Irish girl let down her skirt and put up her hair to make herself look older, then got a job wrapping packages in a chewing-gum factory. She was paid 85 cents a week. Whenever a city inspector visited her tenement, she hid under a table, for her mother was so poor that 85 cents meant a lot to the family. Elbert Gary said Billy Sunday was doing much good among working people.

It was not just liberals such as Walter Lippmann, Louis D. Brandeis and Scott Nearing who were concerned about the gap between wealth and poverty. Their views were shared by the Vice President of the United States, Thomas R. Marshall. He was a fun-loving philosopher who made great good sense, a native of Indiana, well educated and a Phi Beta Kappa, forever fair and politically fearless. In 1913 Marshall denounced inherited wealth so baldly that conservatives struck back. What hurt them was his statement that American laborers were paid only one-fifth of what they produced. This comment bred a flurry of letters in the New York *Times* challenging the Vice President's judgment and asserting that labor was very well paid.

Was it? In 1915 Dr. Howard Woolston, director of investigation for the New York State Factory Commission, said this: "More than half the people employed in the factories and stores investigated in New York City get less than $8.00 a week." Lippmann quoted Woolston and then went on to remark, "It is all very well to say of a woman that 'she is working for her living,' but suppose she is working and not making her living." In an article called "The Campaign Against Sweating," Lippmann further said:

> . . . But when a mercantile establishment pays its labor less than labor can live on, it is combining the evils of the mismanaged railroad and the get-rich-quick concern. It is showing a profit it has not honorably earned, it is paying a dividend out of its vital assets, that is, out of the lives, the health, and the happiness of its employees. A business that exists on labor paid less than a living wage is not a business at all, for it is not paying its fixed charges. They are being paid either by the family of the woman worker, or by her friends, or by private charities, or by the girl herself in slow starvation. . . . You cannot ruin a country by conserving its life. You can ruin a country only by stupidity, waste, and greed.

This was hardly the attitude taken by J. P. Morgan when he testified on

February 1, 1915, before the United States Commission on Industrial Relations. Heavyset, very well dressed, looking remarkably like his late father except that his eyes were less fierce, the private banker took the stand and first was asked about his business connections. Morgan told Commission Chairman Francis P. Walsh that he was a director of the United States Steel Corporation, the Northern Pacific Railway, the International Mercantile Marine and the Pullman Company, that—well, the other corporations in which his banking house was financially interested would be "a very long list" and he could not name all of them without consulting his books.

Walsh said that longshoremen were paid only $10 to $12 a week and then asked, "Do you think ten dollars a week is enough for a longshoreman to earn?"

"I do not know, sir," Morgan replied. "If that is all he can get and he takes it, I should think it was enough."

Under further examination Morgan said he had given no thought to the age limit or length of workday for children in industry. In fact, he said bluntly, he had no opinion regarding child labor, wages of laborers or working hours.

Callous indifference to the plight of wage earners also was characteristic of Thomas Edison, the great inventor. He owned and operated a storage-battery plant at Silver Lake, New Jersey, and when his son Charles went to work for him in 1914, the young man was appalled by conditions in his father's factory. After working a twelve-hour day, the men were left sodden with fatigue. Across the street from the Edison plant there stood a long line of cheap gin mills, where the work-numbed Edison employees drank themselves into forgetfulness. Although young Edison almost worshiped his famous father, he had the courage to argue with him about Edison's labor policy.

When war broke out in Europe in August, 1914, the initial reaction in the United States was a worsening of business conditions. The immediate effect was a decline in foreign trade, throwing longshoremen and sailors out of jobs, snatching work away from clerks and stenographers in import houses and in offices in the financial district of New York. With the halt of new construction, unemployment then spread further among workers in the steel, cement and lumber industries.

But when the embattled nations across the Atlantic turned to America for supplies of every kind, joblessness in this nation began to fall in certain lines of work. By February, 1915, the combatants had placed with American business war orders worth more than $59,000,000. This gave employment to machinists and others in heavy industry without at first helping clerical and mercantile employees. American businessmen, who had marked time and acted cautiously over the preceding two years, now began purchasing for the future and otherwise expanding their business operations. The 1915 agricultural harvest was bountiful, bank clearings rose, foreign exports became abnormally large, and the leading iron and steel plants—which had been operating at only about 40 to 45 percent of capacity—now ran at full capacity. America was becoming the bread-basket and arsenal of the Allies.

Chapter 6

THE LUDLOW MASSACRE

On Monday morning, April 20, 1914, the sun rose over Manhattan at five thirteen o'clock, and moments later John D. Rockefeller, Jr., was up and dressed and saying his prayers.

The only son of the richest man on earth, he was forty, short and slight, his head too large for his body, square-faced, gray-eyed and very pale. As a student at Brown University in Providence, Rhode Island, his favorite subjects had been economics and sociology, and he called himself "a conscientious student, plodding, hard working, but not brilliant." Despite his modesty, he was elected to Phi Beta Kappa. He was correct when he said he lacked an analytical or philosophical mind, and he was not widely read. Living within the shadow of his world-famous father, he had a fragile ego, once writing the elder Rockefeller: "Of my ability, I have always had a very poor opinion." But he worshiped his father, calling him "a perfect saint" and declaring "there never was another father so kind, so loving and so generous as you are." Down into middle age the younger Rockefeller was glad to black his father's shoes. The elder Rockefeller, for his part, was extremely fond of his son and namesake and heir apparent, whom he smilingly addressed as "Mr. John."

Mr. John believed in hard work, high morals and no nonsense. He neither smoked nor drank, although he did enjoy good music and the theater, riding and skating and squash. In 1910 a judge had appointed him foreman of a New York City grand jury investigating white slavery, and Mr. John said that "it was such a grim, depressing subject, and they couldn't have picked anybody who knew less about it." Unable to express his feelings easily, stern with himself, he was formal and aloof with others. Whenever he signed a letter, he wrote his name slowly and carefully, his handwriting was always precise, and he had the habit of carrying in his hip pocket a four-foot folding rule.

Although in later years he widened the focus of his religious interests, in 1914 he was an old-fashioned Baptist and taught the Men's Bible Class at the Fifth Avenue Baptist Church. In one of his Sunday-morning talks he developed an analogy between business consolidations and the cultivation of an American Beauty rose. He also said, "The growth of a large business is merely survival of the fittest. It does the greatest good to the greatest number, although perhaps at the expense of the few. . . . [It is] merely the working out of a law of God and nature." In 1914 God and nature and the Rockefellers was a hard combination to beat.

John D. Rockefeller, Sr., lived in an ivy-clad town house at 4 West Fifty-fourth Street, the present site of the outdoor garden of the Museum of Modern Art. His son lived a couple of doors away at Number 10 in a mansion with several drawing rooms and family suites, walls hung with Gobelin tapestries, floors covered with Persian rugs woven with gold and silk threads. This luxurious home had its own infirmary, library, music room, squash court and private playground. Mr. John was a stern but loving father to his one daughter and four sons. The most mischievous of the boys was five-year-old Nelson A. Rockefeller. Nelson liked to amuse his sister and brothers by clowning around, his pranks sometimes getting him sent from the table for a spanking. Thin-lipped Mr. John tolerated no horseplay as he addressed himself to God. If this Monday morning was like other mornings in his routine life, no doubt he said grace before they ate, murmured amen, opened his eyes and smiled at his family.

When breakfast was finished, he left his mid-Manhattan home to drive south to 26 Broadway near the Battery and walked into the Standard Oil Building, erected by his father and soon to be enlarged. This dignified limestone structure curves in conformity with Broadway as it bends to meet Beaver Street. Mr. John's fourteenth-floor office was rather depressing—a few overstuffed chairs in need of repair and rolltop desks set on mustard-colored carpets and starkly outlined against bare walls. Since his father's retirement, Mr. John had been taking over more and more of the Rockefeller business interests and philanthropies. As he entered his office, he was greeted by his secretary, Charles Heydt, and may have been handed some papers by his attorney, Starr J. Murphy. They were keeping him in touch with events, so Mr. John thought, in faraway Colorado, where coal miners had walked out of Rockefeller mines and off property owned by other companies. But on this April morning nothing critical seemed to be happening on the slopes of the Rocky Mountains. It was too early in the day.

At Ludlow, Colorado, 2,000 miles west of New York and 6,000 feet higher, the sun rose at 5:19 A.M., two hours later than in Manhattan. Ludlow showed on no map, since it was not even a village but a temporary tent colony for some of the striking miners and their wives and children, a flat area on the eastern slope of the Rockies. The state capital of Denver lay some 200 miles north. The nearest coal mine—idle because of the strike—was a mile or so up a twisting canyon. In the dim light of the new day babies wailed, dogs yapped, chickens squawked and men stood and yawned and stretched and looked with sleepy eyes at a setting of black-scarred hillsides dotted with the low-growing pines called piñons, at a ranch pasture here and there, at a railway track and in the pale distance the humps of Colorado's Black Hills. Washing flapped on lines strung between poles, and grouse scurried for cover.

The mines of northern Colorado were relatively unimportant, but this southern part of the state near the New Mexico line was heavy with bituminous coal, vein after vein of black gold that could make a man rich. In 1914 coal barons in that area were so numerous that Colorado Springs residents boasted that their town was the richest per capita in the United

States. One of its landmarks was El Pomar, an elegant estate owned by a mine operator named Spencer Penrose, renowned for his parties that sometimes lasted an entire week. The hamlet of Redstone was graced by a million-dollar mansion built by John C. Osgood, retired president of the Colorado Fuel and Iron Company. Osgood said that miners living in their own flimsy shacks were probably healthier—because of the fresh air blowing through the cracks—than fellow workers who lived in company-built houses. Senator George S. McGovern has called such men "industrial barons who were anarchists for profit."

Of the many coal companies in the state the largest was the Colorado Fuel and Iron Company, mostly owned and wholly managed by the Rockefellers and their deputies. Although his father had held a controlling interest in the firm a dozen years, Mr. John had not visited there within the previous decade. In the early part of this century one of the nation's worst evils was absentee ownership, and in the case of the Rockefeller mines absenteeism was at its worst. It is ironic that Mr. John complained that the mine strike was caused by outside agitators when he was controlling the business, or thought he was, 2,000 miles to the east.

The twenty-four Rockefeller mines employed 15,000 miners, brawny men recruited by company agents in middle and southern Europe—Greeks, Montenegrans, Bulgarians, Serbians, Italians, Tyroleans, Croatians, Austrians, Savoyards—men of thirty-two nationalities who spoke twenty-seven different languages. Many were unable to read or write or even speak English. With take-home pay of $1.68 per day, they lived "under a despotism so absolute," according to one magazine writer, "that the radical press is not far wrong in calling them slaves." As early as 1903 the *Rocky Mountain News* of Denver wrote that "as the Colorado Fuel and Iron Company goes, so goes the [Republican] party. It has always been the dominating influence in party affairs, for it controls enough votes in the various counties in which it operates to hold the balance of power."

The plight of the striking miners was summed up by Ethelbert Stewart, chief clerk of the federal bureau of labor statistics, in these words:

> Theoretically, perhaps, the case of having nothing to do in this world but work, ought to have made these men of many tongues as happy and contented as the managers claim. . . . To have a house assigned you to live in, at a rental determined for you, to have a store furnished you by your employer where you are to buy of him such foodstuffs as he has, at a price he fixes; to have a physician provided by your employer, and have his fees deducted from your pay, whether you are sick or not, or whether you want this particular doctor or not; to have churches, furnished ready-made, supplied by hand-picked preachers whose salary is paid by your employer; with schools ditto, and public halls free for you to use for any purpose except to discuss politics, religion, trade-unionism or industrial conditions; in other words, to have everything handed down to you from the top; to be . . . prohibited from having any thought, voice or care in anything in life but work, and to be assisted in this by gunmen whose function it was,

> principally, to see that you did not talk labor conditions with another man who might accidentally know your language—this was the contented, happy, prosperous condition out of which this strike grew. . . . That men have rebelled grows out of the fact that they are men. . . .

Every mine or town on company property was a camp—either open or closed. The few open camps were incorporated towns whose mayors and council members were company employees, and a public highway led into them. But most were closed feudal enclaves lacking public roads, their gates guarded by company marshals, many deputized by the local sheriff and empowered to make arrests. Additionally, many closed camps had been gerrymandered into separate election districts. Miners had to pay poll taxes in company polling places run by company officials who tallied their ballots. There was no pretense of democracy. If a strong-willed miner became restless, he would be "kangarooed"—beaten up—or some pit boss or marshal would snarl, "Down the canyon with you!" This meant he was fired from his job, evicted from his company-owned house and the company property, driven down toward the flatlands with no money in his pockets.

Mining accidents were a bloody commonplace. This was admitted even by the mine operators' chief periodical, *Coal Age*. In 1913—a year when 434 men died in a catastrophic Welsh explosion—total British fatalities numbered 1,742. That same year 2,785 men died in American mines—and Colorado's record was the worst of any state. Between 1886 and 1913 the Colorado mining industry averaged 7.14 deaths per 1,000 workers—double the national figures in the industry and four times greater than in Illinois, Iowa and Missouri, where the mines were unionized. But if a Colorado miner tried to sue a company for a crippling accident, his suit was sure to be thrown out by company-dominated jurors. From 1890 to 1913 only six damage suits were brought against coal firms in Huerfano county, and in not a single one of them was a company forced to pay compensation. During this same period not a single damage suit was filed in Las Animas county against the Colorado Fuel and Iron Company.

Although a state law said it was illegal for any employer to prevent a worker from joining a union, the coal operators broke the law all the time. But while denying laboring men the right to organize, businessmen had formed themselves into protective groups. For example, there was a Colorado Mineowners Association and the Citizens' Alliance—organized with the help of the Denver Chamber of Commerce and sprouting branches all over the state.

The illegal and dehumanizing conditions in the coalfields angered the United Mine Workers of America. Organized in 1890, the union had a nationwide membership of about 450,000 in 1913 and enjoyed contractual relations with coal companies in seventeen states—but not in Colorado. In 1913 the UMW sent organizers into the southern mine fields to try to help the miners, but when they reached company towns, they were met at the gates by armed marshals who curtly forbade them to enter to talk to the men inside. Then the union's policy committee asked Colorado Governor Elias M. Ammons to ask the operators to agree to hold a conference. He approached the presidents of two of the twenty firms involved, but they refused to meet any union spokesmen. L. M. Bowers, board chairman of the Rockefeller firm, wrote Mr. John in New York that "the word *satisfaction* could have been put over the entrance of every one of our mines." This false and unfair opinion was taken at face value by Mr. John. Next, the union gave the governor a list of the miners' grievances, but when it reached Mr. John he did not even bother to read it.

The union's scale committee said:

> First—We demand recognition of the union.
>
> Second—We demand a ten per cent advance in wages on the tonnage rates.
>
> Third—We demand an eight hour workday for all classes of labor in or around the coal mines and at coke ovens.
>
> Fourth—We demand pay for all narrow work and dead work, which includes brushing, timbering, removing falls, handling impurities, etc.
>
> Fifth—We demand a check-weightman at all mines to be elected by the miners, without any interference by company officials in said election.
>
> Sixth—We demand the right to trade in any store we please, and the right to choose our own boarding place and our own doctor.
>
> Seventh—We demand the enforcement of the Colorado mining laws and the abolition of the notorious and criminal guard system which has prevailed in the mining camps of Colorado for many years.

The main issue was union recognition. Regarding the fifth point, operators often cheated workers by using rigged scales so the men often had to dig from 2,500 to 2,800 pounds of coal to get credit on the scales for 2,000 pounds. Although this seven-point program hardly constituted a revolutionary plot, the owners declared that the union wanted to infringe on the "liberty" of the miners and thwart the owners' rights to manage their own property.

In the summer of 1913, anticipating a strike, the Rockefeller firm and other coal companies began importing gunfighters hired by the Baldwin-Felts detective agency, a strikebreaking outfit in West Virginia, along with other thugs brought in from Texas, New Mexico and Mexico. Many had criminal records, but they were deputized by the sheriffs of southern Colorado without any inquiry into their backgrounds. Albert Felts, acting as a kind of ordnance officer for the mineowners, also began stockpiling handguns and rifles and at least eight machine guns brought from West Virginia. Felts also had a car shipped from Denver to Pueblo, and in a Rockefeller shop in that town he converted it into a crude armored car the miners came to call the Death Special. Its sides were walled with steel three-eighths of an inch thick, and it was outfitted with two machine guns.

Watching the operators beefing up their manpower and firepower, the workers decided they had better arm themselves for their own protection. They got encouragement from Socialist leader Eugene V. Debs, who wrote in the *International Socialist Review:*

> The time has come for the United Mine Workers and the Western Federation of Miners to levy a special monthly assessment to create a GUNMEN DEFENSE FUND. This fund should be sufficient to provide each member with the latest high power rifle, the same as used by the corporation gunmen, and 500 rounds of cartridges. In addition to this, every district should purchase and equip and man enough Gatling and machine guns to match the equipment of Rockefeller's private army of assassins. . . .

Hardware stores sold a record number of weapons and dynamite. A union official ordered 300 rifles from the East; but a spy tipped off the owners, and the lot was seized as it entered Colorado. At a later date the United States Commission on Industrial Rights said, "In all discussion and thought regarding violence in connection with the strike, the seeker after truth must remember that government existed in southern Colorado only as an instrument of tyranny and oppression in the hands of the operators; that, once having dared to oppose that tyranny in the strike, the miners' only protection for themselves and their families lay in the physical force which they could muster."

The company gunmen now began attacking miners, union organizers and officials. The union wrote to ask for a conference, but the owners failed to reply to a single letter. On September 15, 1913, the union held a meeting in its office on the third floor of the German-American Trust building in Denver, and two days later it issued this formal call: ". . . all mine workers are hereby notified that a strike of all the coal miners and coke oven workers in Colorado will begin on Tuesday, September 23, 1913. . . . We are striking for improved conditions, better wages, and union recognition. We are sure to win."

In preparation for the strike the union had leased tracts of land at more than a dozen spots outside company towns, had brought in canvas tents to put up tent colonies, had installed stoves and kitchens, had dug sanitary trenches and storage pits. The day the strike began the weather was horrible. Clouds smudged the tips of distant peaks, rain fell like shrapnel, the temperature sank, and then the rain changed into sleet and snow. More than 12,000 men and women and children began moving out of the coal camps. Don McGregor, a reporter for the Denver *Express*, described the scene:

> No one who did not see that exodus can imagine its pathos. The exodus from Egypt was a triumph, the going forth of a people set free. The exodus of the Boers from Cape Colony was the trek of a united people seeking freedom. But this, yesterday, that wound its bowed, weary way between the coal hills on the one side and the far-stretching prairie on the other, through the rain and mud, was an exodus of woe, of a people leaving known fears for new

> terrors, a hopeless people seeking new hope, a people born to suffering going forth to new suffering. And they struggled along the roads interminably. In an hour's drive between Trinidad and Ludlow, 57 wagons passed, and others seemed to be streaming down to the main road from every by-path. Every wagon was the same, with its high piled furniture, and its bewildered woebegone family perched atop. And the furniture! What a mockery to the state's boasted riches. Little piles of rickety chairs. Little piles of miserable looking straw bedding. Little piles of kitchen utensils. And so worn and badly used they would have been the scorn of any second-hand dealer. . . .

At strategic sites near canyon entrances and railway stations there had been erected tent towns—at Ludlow, at Suffield, at Sopris, Starkville, Walsenburg, Rugby, Monson, Aguilar, Forbes, El Moro, Pictou, Cokedale, Oak Creek and other places. The largest was the forty-acre plot called Ludlow in Las Animas county a few miles northwest of Trinidad on the north-south line of the Colorado Southern Railroad. This was a flatland area, its horizon broken by the Black Hills to the northeast, the Spanish Peaks to the west and Fishers Peak to the southeast. An earthen saucer holding tents with timbered floors, a big kitchen serving as a community kitchen, an even larger tent for use as a schoolroom, a wooden stage for public meetings, even a baseball diamond scratched out of the soil. And the people elected their leaders and settled down to a new kind of life.

Ludlow had 1,200 people living in 275 tents. The union, which had set up strike headquarters in rented rooms in Trinidad, paid a weekly strike benefit of $3 to each man, $1 for each wife, 50 cents for each child. Ludlow's leader was Louis Tikas, born in Greece and educated at the University of Athens, a man of cultivated manners who was well liked by all nationalities in the colony. Although he spoke English with an accent, he spoke it well. Of average height, his build slim, he held himself erect and had a dark skin and a shock of thick black hair. His charisma, his even temper and his courage enabled him to control some of the hot-tempered miners and endeared him to their anxious wives. They waited. They suffered. Winter came. After one storm the snow lay more than two feet thick on the ground, and J. F. Welborn, president of the Rockefeller firm, jeered, "This ought to make a good many of the strikers who are living in tents provided by the organization seek the comfortable houses and employment at the mines."

But the people stayed where they were. Company thugs and mine guards began harassing the tent colonies. The striking miners became furious when they saw strikebreakers heading into the canyons to do their work. Both sides became violent—buildings were dynamited, shots were exchanged, here and there a shack was blown up—and everyone realized that these isolated incidents could not long remain isolated. The coal kings demanded that the governor send the national guard into the region to quell the growing trouble, but they wanted the soldiers not so much to bring peace as to break the strike itself. L. M. Bowers, board chairman of the Rockefeller interests in Colorado, wrote Mr. John that pressure was being exerted on "our little cowboy governor" by the operators, bankers, Denver Chamber of Commerce, Denver realtors and Denver's ministerial alliance, while the editors of the fourteen largest newspapers in the state demanded that the militia be summoned.

Elias M. Ammons, the "little cowboy governor," was caught in the middle of an ugly situation. The eldest of six children in a poor family, he worked hard as a boy, came down with measles that weakened his eyesight, lost more of his sight during a hunting season when he was accidentally shot in the head. Ammons became associate editor of the Denver *Times*, bought some cattle and became a rancher, was elected president of the Colorado Cattle and Home Growers Association, acquired interests in Denver banks, in 1890 took office in the state assembly, and in the 1912 election that swept Woodrow Wilson into the White House, was elected the Democratic governor of Colorado. Most of the state's other top officials were also Democrats, as were a majority of the state senators and assemblymen.

Upton Sinclair, who later won a Pulitzer Prize for letters, declared that the state legislature was composed of "hand-picked machine politicians, and all its orders were given from the offices of the Colorado Fuel and Iron Company." This was basically true even though Rockefeller's overseers were Republicans. Sinclair's accusation was amplified by the New York *World*, which editorialized that "the State of Colorado had abdicated in favor of great corporations and their murderous hirelings." As events worsened, one state senator growled that all the state needed was "three hundred men who could shoot straight and quick."

On October 28, 1913, the harassed governor signed an executive order calling out the national guard. He did not proclaim martial law, which would have subjected all civilian government to military rule. Unfortunately, he assumed that martial law obtained automatically when the soldiers took to the field. This was to cause complications. At first the striking miners welcomed the militiamen in the mistaken belief that their uniforms would serve as shields between themselves and company gunmen. Some of the soldiers encamped near the Ludlow colony went to dances in the big tent, ate with the miners and their families, played baseball and hunted with them. But the miners became uneasy when they saw that some of the uniformed men were mine guards they knew all too well, when they learned more about the national guard officers.

The state troops were commanded by Adjutant General John Chase, an eye, ear, nose and throat doctor with a practice in Denver, past middle age, a stern antiunionist, a sanctimonious man and an ardent militarist. Taking advantage of the confusion about the existence or nonexistence of martial law, General Chase conducted himself like a warlord in an occupied territory. His deputies were like him. Major Patrick Hamrock was a Denver saloonkeeper who boasted that he was one of the best shots in Colorado. Major Edward J. Boughton, the militia's judge advocate, was an attorney for a mineowners' association in Cripple Creek. Lieutenant Karl E. Linderfelt, called Monte, was a swaggering and sadistic soldier of fortune with a blind hatred of the strikers whom he called "Wops," a former mercenary in the Mexican revolution and a veteran of the 1906 American massacre of Filipinos.

General Chase rode around in a car owned by the Rockefeller interests, was paid $400 a month and received a weekly expense account of $175. His field force was as ridiculous as a Central American revolutionary army, for its 695 men were commanded by 397 officers. Incidents multiplied. One day a little boy left a tent to get a drink of water and was shot and killed by soldiers. The guardsmen provoked the strikers into fighting, drunkenly insulted girls on the street, tried to sneak into homes in nearby towns to get at unprotected women, arrested scores of people without cause, ignored writs of habeas corpus, held their prisoners incommunicado in the Trinidad jail—whose eight ministers denounced the strikers and praised the militia. General Chase set up a so-called Military District of Colorado, placed himself at its head and announced that "military" prisoners would be tried by his picked men—although the civil courts still were functioning.

On December 29, 1913, Chase sent soldiers into Ludlow forcibly to vaccinate the colonists on the pretense that they were threatened by an epidemic. In charge of this detachment was Lieutenant Linderfelt. Prancing along on horseback, he suddenly accused a fifteen-year-old boy of stretching wire across a road to trip his cavalrymen. The boy denied it. The lieutenant smashed him over the head with a rifle butt. Louis Tikas saw this happen and angrily protested. Linderfelt leaned down from his horse, hit Tikas in the face with his fist and screamed, "I am Jesus Christ, and my men on horses are Jesus Christs—and we must be obeyed!"

Into the area came a legendary labor agitator, Mary Harris Jones, known across the country as Mother Jones. In 1914 she was eighty-four and so robust that she was to live to one hundred. She had been born in Dublin, schooled in Toronto, anguished by the death of her husband and children in a yellow fever epidemic in Memphis, worked as a dressmaker in Chicago until the big fire, became a militant labor leader and spellbinding orator, devoted her whole life to the class struggle. Introduced at a meeting as a great humanitarian, she yelled, "Get it right! I'm not a humanitarian. I'm a hell-raiser!" Replying to a Congressman who asked where she lived, Mother Jones snapped, "Wherever there's a fight!" She had been slandered and arrested and jailed and run out of various states—a little old lady with a shrill voice, her handsome Irish face framed by white hair under a black bonnet. After a firsthand look at the troubles in Colorado she suggested that the governor be hanged. The militia promptly arrested her, expelled her from the state and nabbed her again when she slipped back in.

On January 23, 1914, more than 1,000 miners' wives and sympathizers staged a demonstration in Trinidad demanding the release of Mother Jones. As they marched down a street they met a cordon of cavalrymen with drawn sabers, commanded by General Chase, who wheeled his horse back and forth past the front rank of women, shouting at them to halt. Seeing a sixteen-year-old girl watching with an open mouth, he bellowed at her to back away, and his spurred boot struck her in the breast. Union propagandists later charged that he gave the girl a vicious kick. Whatever the truth, the next moment the general's horse stumbled, floundered into a parked buggy, and Chase fell out of the saddle. The women screamed with laughter. The red-faced general stiffly remounted and yelled at his men, "Ride the women down!" His cavalry charged —three times. A foreign-born observer said it reminded him of Cossacks in action. Chase swung his pistol menacingly from side to side. The soldiers tore American flags from the hands of the women, some of whom struck back with signs and banners. Sabers flashed. One woman was slashed across the forehead; another nearly had an ear cut off; a third was cut on the backs of her hands as she tried to protect her face. A guardsman slammed his fist into the face of a ten-year-old boy.

The Denver *Express* published this headline:

GREAT CZAR FELL! AND IN FURY
TOLD TROOPS TO TRAMPLE WOMEN

Its story began: "A craven general tumbled from his nag in a street in Trinidad like Humpty Dumpty from the wall. In fifteen minutes . . . soldiers with swords were striking at fleeing women and children. . . . Then there was bloodshed. The French Revolution, its history written upon crimson pages, carries no more cowardly episode than the attack of the gutter gamin soldiery on the crowd of unarmed and unprotected women. . . ." Don McGregor of the *Express* became so enraged he quit his reportorial job, strapped on a revolver and joined the strikers.

Edward Keating, a former city editor of the *Rocky Mountain News* in Denver, now a Democratic Congressman in Washington, marched to the White House to call on President Wilson. He poured out his indignation, but when he finished, Wilson asked, "What can I do? After all, this is a state matter, and I am President of the United States."

"It won't be a state matter very long, Mr. President. I have seen two of these strikes. They are not pink tea affairs. This will probably be worse than either of the others."

"But what can I do?"

"Call John D. Rockefeller to the White House," Keating suggested. "Urge him to meet the authorized spokesmen of his employees."

Wilson hesitated. "I can't do that," he said, "but I will help you. I will write to Mr. Rockefeller and ask him to do what you have suggested."

Subsequently the President met with his labor secretary, the first in the nation's history, William B. Wilson. In the past the secretary had been an organizer and then secretary-treasurer of the United Mine Workers. He had spent time in jail for his union activities and still called miners "brothers." He told Ethelbert Stewart, chief clerk of the bureau of labor statistics, to go to New York to see John D. Rockefeller, Jr. Mr. John was vacationing in Maine. When he returned, he refused to see Stewart but told his attorney, Starr J. Murphy, to meet the man from Washington. Murphy told Stewart that labor policies in Colorado were set by the mine managers on the basis of their firsthand knowledge. "We here in the East," Murphy added, "know nothing about the conditions and would be unwilling to make any suggestions to the executive officers."

Stewart told Murphy to tell Rockefeller that the President wanted him to accept federal arbitration of the coal strike so that it would be unnecessary to send federal troops into Colorado. Mr. John rejected the President's request. He believed that nine-tenths of the strikers opposed the strike, which he felt had been fomented by outside agitators, and feared that if the union were recognized it then would demand the right to say which men might work, which would be an invasion of their liberty. It did not seem to matter to Mr. John that coal operators in seventeen other states recognized the union and had signed contracts with it.

He was reflecting the opinion of his father, who once said, "I have watched and studied the trade unions for years. Times change, but men change very little. It is hard to understand why men will organize to destroy the very firms or companies that are giving them the chance to live and thrive, but they do it, and soon the real object of their organizing shows itself—to do as little as possible for the greatest possible pay." There had been a time when Woodrow Wilson felt much the same way, saying he opposed the union movement because unions encouraged workers "to give as little as he may for his wages." Wilson was changing his mind but the Rockefellers were slower to learn.

On January 29, 1914, six days after Chase's cavalry charge on women and children, the United States House of Representatives voted to investigate the situation in Colorado. Members of the House subcommittee on mines and mining traveled to Denver, and on February 9 they opened hearings in the senate chamber of the Colorado statehouse. Representative Martin D. Foster of Illinois, a former physician, presided as chairman. The state's chief coal mine inspector testified that his office was too understaffed to function properly. The state labor commissioner testified that coal operators dominated the state politically and freely flouted state laws. A Rockefeller manager testified that Lieutenant Karl Linderfelt had been a mine guard before donning a guardsman's uniform.

Albert C. Felts of the Baldwin-Felts detective agency gave the committee a peek at the operations of strikebreaking detectives. He said he provided coal companies with mine guards without anyone bothering to inquire into their backgrounds. He said it was the custom for sheriffs to deputize private detectives entering a strike area because it was necessary for such agents to cooperate with local authorities; in all the states where his firm operated, he met only one sheriff who refused to commission his men. He admitted obtaining at least four machine guns and said they were paid for by the coal operators. He revealed that the Death Special had been rebuilt from an automobile provided by W. C. Babcock, vice-president of the Rocky Mountain Fuel Company.

John C. Osgood, retired board chairman of the Colorado Fuel and Iron Company, testified rigidly: The miners did not need a wage increase. The fuss about faulty scales was really due to the foreigners' distrust of one another. The eight-hour-day issue was a fraud. He would never dream of dealing with the United Mine Workers.

Subcommittee members left Colorado for Washington, and toward the end of March they invited Mr. John to testify before them in the national capital. He wrote his father: "I have replied that I would be in Washington on Monday next in answer to the invitation. Mr. Murphy will go with me. What possible value any knowledge which I may be able to impart may be to this inquiry I do not know. However, since the invitation has been extended I felt it wise to accept it without hesitation."

On April 6, 1914, John D. Rockefeller, Jr., appeared for the first time as a witness before a Congressional committee. He was composed during the four hours of questioning. Chairman Foster, who asked most of the questions, was polite, if firm. Mr. John could not remember the exact date the strike began. He did not know what wages were paid the miners. He did not know the condition of the company houses in which they lived. He was forced to admit that although he was a director of the Colorado Fuel and Iron Company, he had not attended a board meeting in the last ten years.

"Do you realize," the chairman asked, "that since last September this strike has been reported in the press of the country, that the governor of Colorado has called out the militia to police the disturbed district, and that the conditions prevailing in that district were shocking, according to such reports, and that the House of Representatives deemed it a duty to undertake this investigation?"

"I have been fully aware of all those facts."

"And yet neither you, personally, nor the board of directors, have looked into the matter."

"I cannot say as to whether the board of directors have looked into the matter or not, their meetings being held in the West."

"What action has been taken personally to find out about the trouble in Colorado?"

Gesturing toward some papers on the desk in front of him, Rockefeller replied, "This correspondence will give you the whole thing."

"Personally, what have you done—outside of this—as a director?"

"I have done nothing outside of this That is the way in which we conduct the business."

Foster glared, and his voice took on an edge: "What remedies have you personally suggested to end this industrial disturbance?"

"The conduct of the business," Rockefeller replied evenly, "is in the hands of the officers, and so long as they have our entire confidence we shall stand by them. We could not conduct the business in any other way."

Mr. John went on to say that as far as he knew, the miners had no real grievances. He had no idea whether his company had bought guns or hired detectives. No, he knew nothing about the Death Special. He said he had done all he could to reduce the liquor problem among the workers who, "being largely foreign," drank a lot. He said it was costing the company about $1,000,000 "to stand for the principle which we believe is to the ultimate interest of those men."

"And that is to fight the union?"

"That is to allow them to have the privilege of determining the conditions under which they shall work."

"And not that men shall get together and talk over their own interests?"

"They have every right to do that."

"Collective bargaining and sale of their labor—you want to fight that?"

"I did not say that. Not that outside men, who have no interest in them or in their employers, shall come in and impose upon them that organization."

"You are an outsider with respect to Colorado, are you not?"

"I do not live there. I am an outsider except in a representative capacity. . . . "

Later in the hearing Foster said, "But the killing of people and shooting of children—has not that been of enough importance to you for you to communicate with the other directors and see if something can be done to end that sort of thing?"

"We believe," Rockefeller replied, "the issue is not a local one in Colorado. It is a national issue—whether workers shall be allowed to work under such conditions as they may choose. As part owners of the property, our interest in the laboring men in this country is so immense, so deep, so profound, that we stand ready to lose every cent we put in that company rather than see the men we have employed thrown out of work and have imposed upon them conditions which are not of their seeking, and which neither they nor we can see are in our interest."

"You are willing to let these killings take place rather than go there and do something to settle conditions?"

"There is just one thing that can be done to settle this strike, and that is to unionize the camps—and our interest in labor is so profound, and we believe so sincerely that that interest demands that the camps shall be open camps, that we expect to stand by the officers at any cost. It is not an accident that this is our—"

"And you would do that if it costs all your property and kills all your employees?"

"It is," Mr. John intoned, "a great principle."

It was such a great principle that his father, delighted with his "splendid effort at Washington before the Committee," gave Mr. John 10,000 shares of the common stock of the Colorado Fuel and Iron Company.

On April 20, 1914, two weeks after Rockefeller testified in Washington, patches of snow quilted the earth at Ludlow. After the children finished breakfast in the mess hall, they ran outside to romp with their dogs, while their mothers began washing the dishes. Louis Tikas felt apprehensive. The day before he had received a telephone call from Major Hamrock, who said he wanted the strikers to release a boy being held in the camp against the boy's will. Tikas had asked the boy's name, then said no one by that name was in the colony. The major had snarled that he knew damned well the boy was there and that he better be handed over or his soldiers would come get him. In midmorning an uneasy Tikas summoned his camp police. These men, like all the strikers, wore red bandannas around their throats. Uneasily shifting their feet, they peered around the horizon, and when their eyes focused on Water Tank Hill to the south, they saw massed soldiers and a shiny object that looked like a machine gun. Then they heard an explosion. A second! A third! Three crude dynamite bombs made by Lieutenant Linderfelt had been set off. At this signal guardsmen began firing down into the colony with small arms and machine guns.

The time was 10:01 A.M.

The miners yelled to the women to grab the kids and take shelter. Then, clutching rifles in their hands, they spread out to draw the fire away from their families, sprinting to railway tracks and dry gullies and flopping into them to use them as breastworks as they shot back at the attackers. They raged. They cursed. They squeezed off round after round at their half-invisible enemies, up toward blazing muzzles along the rims of hills. The soldiers shot again and again at the miners and down into the camp. Bullets cut through tents, shredding the canvas, ricocheting off iron stoves, splintering furniture, shattering mirrors. Dogs barked. Chickens squawked. Here and there a miner bounded out and ran a few paces to hit the dirt again, take aim, fire.

A bullet pierced a tent and bored through the head of an eleven-year-old boy, the son of William Snyder. He died instantly. His father and mother stared in disbelief. She screamed at her husband, "For God's sake, save my children!" Soldiers ran up to the door of the tent and glared at Snyder. One yelled, "What in hell are you doing here?" He roared, "Trying to save my children!" A guardsman shouted, "You son-of-a-bitch! Get out of there, and get out damn' quick at that!" Mrs. Snyder ran outside. Her husband cried to the attackers, "Hold on! I had a boy killed in there!" A man bellowed, "Get out damn' quick!" Snyder picked up his son's body, lost his hold, staggered outdoors, put down his son's body to get a better grip. He begged, "Help me carry him to the depot!" A soldier snarled, "God damn you! Aren't you big enough?" Snyder was slipping into shock. "I can't do it," he moaned. But he stooped down, boosted the boy's body onto his shoulders and, straightening up, took the hand of one of his little girls and began staggering away. A soldier stopped him, screaming, "God damn you, you son-of-a-bitch! I gotta notion to kill you right now!" But Snyder lived to tell this tale to a coroner's jury.

Another miner named Ed Tonner had a French wife who was the mother of five children and within a day or two of giving birth to her sixth. During the daylong attack she shielded them with her body within a pit inside a tent, flinching at the gunfire, her eyes widening when she saw that her canvas tent walls had become "just like lace from the bullets." As darkness fell, she heard "something like paper was blowing around." The back of her tent was ablaze. About 7 P.M. Linderfelt and his troops had charged the colony and now were setting fire to it. Mrs. Tonner boosted her children out of the pit, pulled herself up and out, herded them outdoors and over to another tent occupied by Mexicans. Then she screamed, "My God! I forgot one! I forgot one!" She was about to run outside again when a woman called, "It's all right! They're all here!" Mrs. Tonner quieted down but could not stop shaking. She heard moans. The tent in which she had taken shelter had other children who were being wounded by bullets. Mrs. Charles Costa whimpered, "Santa Maria, have mercy! . . ."

William Snyder ran inside, his hands held out in despair. "Oh, my God, Miz Tonner, my boy's head's blown off! My God! If your children won't lay down, just knock 'em down—rather 'n see 'em die!" From outside the tent they heard voices: "We got orders to kill you, an' we're gonna do it! . . . We got plenty of ammunition, so turn her loose, boys!" Mrs. Tonner began to go into labor. Grabbing her children, she burst out of the tent with them and stumbled a mile to a spot far from the battlefield. Later she said, "You talk about the Virgin Mary! She had time to save her baby from all the trouble, and I thought to myself I was havin' a time, too. . . ."

She was lucky she left when she did. Inside the tent the miners had dug a pit eight feet deep and eight feet long; during the day's attack this hole had been crammed with frightened people. Some of them, like Mrs. Tonner, crawled out and ran to safety elsewhere, but when the soldiers set fire to the tent, the pit was jammed with eleven children and two women. All suffocated to death. The Denver Public Library has a photograph of this "Death Pit," as the miners came to call it.

The miners had fought back as best they could, but near the end of the day they began to run out of ammunition, so Louis Tikas ordered them to regroup in the Black Hills to the east, while he went back to the tent to do whatever he could to save the women and children. According to some miners, he had decided to surrender himself in exchange for a cease-fire and an end to the burning of the tents. But near the intersection of a railway track and a wagon road he was captured by militiamen, one of whom shouted, "We've got Louie the Greek!" The soldiers also grabbed the colony's paymaster, James Fyler, and a third man who was never positively identified. Exactly what happened to the three is known only from subsequent testimony from the military.

Apparently they were brought before Lieutenant Linderfelt shortly before 9 P.M. The lieutenant admitted cursing Tikas for not stopping the battle. Then Tikas "called me a name any man with red blood in his veins will not stand," and Linderfelt swung his rifle at Tikas' head. Tikas raised an arm to ward off a blow so powerful that the rifle stock broke. His arm and head spurted blood, but he did not fall. A soldier yelled, "Hang the damned red-neck!" A lynch rope was thrown over a telegraph pole. Linderfelt told his men to lay off and turned the three prisoners over to Sergeant Cullen. Then the lieutenant left to collect men at the depot for a final charge across the flat. His sergeant told a couple of guardsmen to watch the prisoners. Since all stood erect within the glare of the burning tents, they offered tempting targets to sniping miners. The soldiers took cover. The moment the prisoners were left alone they dashed in the direction of the tents and all were caught in a crossfire, according to the military, and killed. Tikas was shot in the back three times. The fact that two of the bullets passed clear through his body proved they were the steel-jacketed kind fired from the soldiers' Springfield rifles.

The Ludlow massacre of April 20, 1914, took the lives of forty-five men, women and children—including the two women and eleven children who died in the one pit. Three attackers were killed. When the battle ended, the miners went back to their camp and found a shambles of blackened tent poles, naked bedsprings, shards of glass, broken pottery, scorched floorboards, charred clothing, blood.

News of the massacre jolted the nation. The New York *Times*, which was fond of the Rockefellers, placed most of the blame for the tragedy on the strikers but deplored the militia's "horrible blunder" at Ludlow. It went on to say, "The Ludlow camp is a mass of charred debris and buried beneath is a story of horror unparalleled in the history of industrial warfare. In holes that had been dug for their protection against rifle fire, the women and children died like rats when the flames swept over them." William Randolph Hearst's New York *American* scolded the Rockefellers. The Chicago *Tribune* criticized the miners. The San Francisco *Chronicle* called the miners no better than Mexicans. This was at a time when Americans were debating whether to recognize General Victoriano Huerta's claim to the presidency of Mexico, and the New York *Evening Post* commented, "Victoriano Huerta might well prefer to sever relations with a Government under which it is possible for women and children to be mowed down by machine guns in a frenzy of civil war."

A New York magazine called *Survey* said:

> The employers who have disobeyed the laws, the state which has not enforced them; the employers who hired mine guards to assault and intimidate, the state which took those mine guards in company pay into its militia, made some of them officers and then turned them on the strikers; the employers who had machine guns shipped from West Virginia, the state which took those machine guns and turned them on the tented camps where dwelt the families of the strikers—what answer have they to the question of responsibility for war?

The Denver *Express* said, "Mothers and babies were crucified at Ludlow on the cross of human liberty. They tried to help their men folk rise in Rockefeller-ruled southern Colorado. Their crucifixion was effected by the operators' paid gunmen who have worn militia uniforms less than a week. The dead will go down in history as the hero victims of the burnt offering laid on the altar of the great god greed. . . ."

Except for the labor press, the most bitter outcry came from the *Rocky Mountain News* in an editorial called "The Massacre of the Innocents":

> The horror of the shambles at Ludlow is overwhelming. Not since the days when pitiless men wreaked vengeance upon intruding frontiersmen and upon their women and children has this western country been stained with so foul a deed.
>
> The details of the massacre are horrible. Mexico offers no barbarity so base as that of the murder of defenseless women and children by the mine guards in soldiers' clothing. Like whitened sepulchers we boast of American civilization with this infamous thing at our very doors. Huerta murdered Madero, but even Huerta did not shoot an innocent little boy seeking water for his mother who lay ill. [Pancho] Villa is a barbarian, but in his

> maddest excess Villa has not turned machine guns on imprisoned women and children. Where is the outlaw so far beyond the pale of humankind as to burn the tent over the heads of nursing mothers and helpless little babies?
>
> Out of this infamy one fact stands clear. Machine guns did the murder. The machine guns were in the hands of mine guards, most of whom were also members of the state militia. It was a private war, with the wealth of the richest man in the world behind the mine guards. . .

The Colorado Fuel and Iron Company filed a $500,000 libel suit against the *Rocky Mountain News* but did not press the case through the courts to a conclusion. Members of the Denver Chamber of Commerce voted to boycott the newspaper. Governor Ammons blamed everything on the press: "The greatest difficulty I had was the absolute misrepresentation of everything in the public press—as we were powerless either to correct it or to get the facts stated to the public." This was an interesting argument, since most of the state's big newspapers were for the operators and against the miners.

The first word that Mr. John received in his New York office of the event in Colorado came in a telegram composed by L. M. Bowers, board chairman of the Colorado Fuel and Iron Company. Much of this information was false. Bowers told Rockefeller that the strikers had launched an unprovoked attack on heavily outnumbered militiamen, causing casualties and a fire in the strikers' colony with explosions that proved the existence of dynamite in the tents. Bowers suggested that this information be given to "friendly papers." Many years later Mr. John said, "The Colorado strike was one of the most important things that ever happened to the Rockefeller family."

This was an understatement. "Rockefeller" became a curse word to millions of Americans. Mr. John began to understand that he had made a grave error in letting distant subordinates make policy decisions, in accepting their reports unquestioningly, in failing to take matters into his own hands as had been suggested by the Congressional subcommittee. He made no instant and total change in his business philosophy, but he was shaken by the realization that instead of a respected businessman, he now was regarded by many Americans as a murderer. There was scant consolation in an editorial in the reactionary New York *Sun*, which said, "Unfortunately, a generation of truckling to the violent striker has bred in labor ranks a belief that the harrying of rival workers and the spoiling of plants was the strikers' accorded right. The words meant as a warning were taken up by the labor leaders as a challenge. Rifles and ammunition were distributed among the workers. Inevitable bloodshed followed. The event in Colorado should lead to a re-awakening of consciousness of justice and individual rights."

During the first months of the strike Mr. John had received bad advice from a close associate, a Baptist clergyman named Frederick Taylor Gates. In 1893 the Reverend Mr. Gates had become associated with the elder Rockefeller, helping him manage his business interests and plan his philanthropies. When the old man retired and gave his son control of all his enterprises, the minister remained as a counselor to Mr. John. Gates was out of touch with changing industrial relations and social issues. After the Ludlow massacre the Baptist preacher trumpeted. "The officers of the Colorado Fuel and Iron Company are standing between the country and chaos, anarchy, proscription and confiscation, and in so doing are worthy of the support of every man who loves his country." Gates was neither the first nor the last capitalist to equate patriotism with profits.

His strident and fatuous argument did not go down well with novelist Upton Sinclair. Soon after the massacre Sinclair went to Manhattan's Carnegie Hall to listen to eyewitness reports of the tragedy; although the hall was crowded, the meeting got scant attention in New York papers. Sinclair decided to do all he could to avenge the innocent dead and bring the Rockefellers to heel. "At first," he wrote, "I thought I would go to young Mr. Rockefeller's office and watch for him in the hall, and give him a horse-whipping. But this would have been hard on me, because I am constitutionally opposed to violence, and I did not think Mr. Rockefeller worth such a sacrifice of my feelings." Nonetheless, Sinclair gave a public talk called "How to Kill J. D. Rockefeller, Jr."

Reporters and editors flocked to Colorado. The strikers, crazed by grief and rage, had gone on a rampage, attacking coal camps along a forty-mile front, burning and tearing down mining equipment, lurking by the hundreds in the hills ready to ambush a train said to be bringing more soldiers and guns and ammunition to the combat zone. Three mine guards were killed in one battle, while in another, nine company workers were slaughtered. Union trainmen working runs through the state refused to move reinforcements of militiamen. Some guardsmen became so frightened that they mutinied, shed their uniforms and deserted. Various unions throughout Colorado voted to buy rifles and bullets for the marauding miners. Armed and ugly men captured Trinidad near Ludlow and took over the city government. Governor Ammons quavered, "The whole state is in rebellion!"

One of the first journalists to arrive was Max Eastman, editor of the left-wing magazine *The Masses*. He called the massacre "the most depraved act of savagery committed against a labor union in my time." Then he wrote:

> After viewing the flattened ruins of the little colony of make-shift homes, the open death hole, the shattered bedsteads, the stove pipes still standing, the dishes and toilet trinkets broken and black—the larks singing so incongruously over them in the sun—it was a joy to travel up the canyons and feed one's eyes upon those gigantic tangled piles of machinery and ashes that had been the operating capital of the mines. It was no remedy—it solved nothing—it was not even adequate retribution—but it was good for the eyes.

The *Central Christian Advocate* blamed everything on revolutionary plotters: " . . . in Las Animas County . . . the commune has leaped to its feet." Max Eastman posed as a reporter for a proper Christian magazine, hired a room in a hotel in Trinidad and invited the proper ladies of the town to tea to tell him how they felt about recent events. Among the dozen who accepted was the governor's sister and the wife of the Presbyterian minister. For an hour and a half Eastman jotted down their comments. The minister's wife said, "They ought to have shot Tikas to start with." Other elegant ladies observed, "The miners are nothing but cattle, and the only way is to kill them off. . . . You know, there's a general belief around here that those women and children were put in that hold and sealed up on purpose because they were a drain on the union. . . . Yes, those low people—they'll stoop to anything. . . . They're brutal, you know. They simply don't regard human life. And they're ignorant. They can't even read or write. They don't know anything. They don't even know the Christmas story!"

The Law and Order League of Women, composed of Denver's so-called Sacred Thirty-Six, met to express sympathy for the governor and the militia "in their great ordeal" and denounced "vicious people and a prejudiced and inaccurate press corrupted either by money or by the influence of the labor vote."

John Reed, a *Masses* reporter who worked for Eastman, also prowled through Colorado in search of background information and leads to further developments. In Denver he listened as the anguished governor double-talked the press. By this time a militia captain had admitted that 90 percent of the men in his company were mine guards wearing national guard uniforms. Even so, the governor said, "The Colorado National Guard is composed almost exclusively of young professional and business men, some of them sons of the best families of this state." Lieutenant Governor Stephen R. Fitzgerald said that even if the strikers were correct in their claims about the behavior of the militia, this could not justify attacks on innocent mine guards and harmless scabs and the destruction of mine property. John Reed, a strikingly handsome young man, met a charming young Denver widow who was so impressed by his impassioned defense of the strikers that she sent East to buy two machine guns which she hid in her cellar, ready to smuggle them to the coalfields if the guardsmen returned.

J. C. Osgood was president of the Colorado Field and Iron Company and also board chairman of the Victor American Field Company. Osgood announced that the fire at Ludlow had been started "in some manner which has not yet been investigated or explained." And all the violence, Osgood added, was the fault of "ignorant foreigners" who had "practically been made anarchists by the labor organizers and agitators sent among them by the officers of the United Mine Workers." He did not mention that these "ignorant foreigners" had been recruited by the coal barons in Europe.

The Colorado war became more ferocious and widespread. Two more battles were fought at Ludlow. Strikers dynamited the town of Primrose. The miners of Colorado Springs quit their jobs to rush south to reinforce the rampaging strikers. An attack was launched on the post office in the town of Higgins. Men with red bandannas around their necks lay in ambush, ready to attack any train that might try to bring more troopers into the roiling region. The revolt spread to the state's northern coalfields, where assaults on three towns were made by bushwhackers now armed with their own machine guns. The governor wired the President begging him to send federal soldiers into the state, but Wilson hesitated. What with the Mexican situation and the strife in Colorado, the President was under severe strain.

Congressman Foster, the subcommittee chairman who had interrogated Mr. John in Washington, left for New York in the hope of conferring with the elder Rockefeller, but was ushered instead into Mr. John's office. Mr. John still refused to do anything to end the bloodshed, telling Foster to get in touch with officers of his company in Denver, since they were the only ones who could deal with the situation. Shaking his head in disbelief, the Congressman told reporters that Rockefeller's attitude was little short of defiance not only of government but of civilization itself.

Foster later got a statement from Denver in which company officials described the events at Ludlow and concluded:

> We cannot enter into negotiations of any character with the officers and agents of the United Mine Workers of America, who alone are responsible for the terrible reign of disorder and bloodshed which has disgraced this State. Instead of it being our duty to do so, we conceive it to be the duty of the officials of the U.M.W. of A., who called the strike, to now call it off. They can do so if they see fit, and by so doing they will, within an hour, in a great measure restore industrial peace and prosperity to this State.

With Mr. John and his deputies remaining so rigid, the nation's press erupted in a new rash of criticism. The Cleveland *Press* said, "Rockefeller holds the situation in the hollow of his hand. . . . The charred bodies of two dozen women and children show that *Rockefeller Knows How to Win.*" In West Virginia, the Parkersburg *Despatch* observed, "The work of Mr. Rockefeller in the slums of New York becomes sounding brass and tinkling cymbal."

Although Upton Sinclair had abandoned his idea of horsewhipping Mr. John, he had not given up. On April 29, 1914, he and four women began picketing the Standard Oil building at 26 Broadway. They wore black crepe armbands on their left sleeves and walked up and down in silence. This mute and melancholy protest drew a crowd, and finally the police cleared the street. Reporters closed in to question Sinclair, but he kept his vow of silence. A cop told him he had to stop picketing. Breaking his silence, the writer politely told the officer he had checked in advance and he was violating no law. As he started to resume his silent protest, he was arrested. His four women companions were also taken into custody.

All five were led to a police station whose sergeant surprised Sinclair by letting him describe the massacre for the benefit of reporters who had followed him to the precinct house. A couple of hours later when the first editions of afternoon papers hit the street, Sinclair was quoted in stories running three and four columns long. As he later wrote in his book *The*

Brass Check, Sinclair exulted, "Such a little thing, you see! You have to get yourself arrested, and instantly concrete walls turn into news-channels!"

Sinclair and the women then were taken to the Manhattan jail called the Tombs, a heavy pile of masonry with an Egyptian-like façade. From there they were herded into a courtroom. A city magistrate informed them they were being charged with "using threatening, abusive and insulting behavior." Behavior—not language—since they had picketed in silence. Surprisingly, the arresting officer admitted that Sinclair's conduct had been that "of a perfect gentleman," but even so all five were found guilty and fined $3 each. Refusing to pay, they were remanded to the Tombs—but not before the magistrate, like the police sergeant, let Sinclair speak his piece in full, so once again New York reporters and newspaper readers got an earful about the Ludlow Massacre. While the New York *World* sneered that Sinclair was seeking "pink tea martyrdom," it nonetheless sent a special correspondent to Colorado.

Back in his cell, Sinclair began a hunger strike. He also wrote a letter appealing for help from another crusader for civil liberties, the Reverend John Haynes Holmes of the venerable and exclusive Unitarian Church of the Messiah in Manhattan. In his reply, Holmes said of the massacre that "a more terrible and inexcusable horror has never been perpetrated, I believe, in the history of this nation." But the minister added, "I cannot for the life of me see that you are accomplishing anything by this funeral parade business."

Mrs. Sinclair now resumed the picketing with eight companions, one the California poet, George Sterling. A poet in her own right, Mary Sinclair was a stately woman who wore exquisite clothes and a military cape. Not a single cop tried to stop her. A reporter had told the police she was the daughter of "one of the wealthiest men in this section who controls large banking interests." Day after day this Free Silence demonstration, as papers began calling it, continued on Lower Broadway, and slowly it was joined by hundreds and finally thousands of people. Mr. John stayed away from his office. The New York *Times* said he had a cold that threatened to turn into pneumonia.

Conditions in Colorado were worsening, a guerrilla-style labor war now raging within a half-moon-shaped area about fifty miles long. Some mines were kept working by strikebreakers. The Colorado Federation of Labor asked all unions to arm and aid the strikers. The militia took and held the towns of Lynn and Aguilar, but the guerrillas still skulked through the hills and swooped down every now and then in devastating raids. The New York State Socialist party begged President Wilson to protect the workers. Once again Governor Ammons asked the President to send in federal troops. At a mass meeting on the lawn of the statehouse in Denver one of the principal speakers was George Creel, a Western newspaperman soon to become one of the best-known men in the nation. Creel characterized the governor and lieutenant governor as "traitors to the people and accessories to the murder of babes," called for their impeachment, urged that the state seize the mines, shouted that "every prayer Rockefeller utters is an insult to the Christ that died for suffering humanity!" Charles S. Thomas, a United States Senator from Colorado, tugged at Creel, pleading, "George! George! For God's sake—tone it down!" After a two-day battle the strikers captured the town of Chandler. Nurses began entering the area to tend the wounded and dying. The Church of the Social Revolution asked President Wilson to end the carnage.

Having appealed to the elder Rockefeller, only to be turned down, having sent a labor department expert to propose mediation, only to have him refused, having learned of Mr. John's refusal of Congressman Foster, knowing from his testimony before the subcommittee that Mr. John intended to do nothing, aware that the situation had gone beyond the control of the Colorado militia, having twice been asked for federal troops by Governor Ammons—President Wilson finally decided to act. He ordered regular army soldiers into the troubled region.

From Fort Russell, Wyoming, Fort Leavenworth, Kansas, and Fort Robinson, Nebraska, spur-jangling regulars began converging on the southern coalfields of Colorado, taking over the towns of Trinidad and Canyon City. Coal company officials and agents were eager to help them, but U.S. Major William A. Holbrook announced that the federal troops under his command would be absolutely neutral and make no distinction among the strikers, militia or mine guards. Even as President Wilson issued a proclamation ordering all citizens to retire peaceably to their homes, a fight raged at Walsenburg, the citizens of Boulder armed themselves to battle the strikers, and the Italian ambassador to the United States asked secretary of state Bryan to protect Italians from being killed in Colorado. Now the matter had taken on international significance.

Released from jail, Upton Sinclair gave up his hunger strike and went West to see conditions there firsthand. Arriving in Denver, he interviewed Governor Ammons and then wrote an article for the Denver *Express:*

> I went yesterday afternoon to see your Governor. I wish to be very careful what I say of him. He is apparently a kindly man; in intellectual caliber fitted for the duties of a Sunday-School superintendent in a small village. He is one of the most pathetic figures it ever has been my fate to encounter. He pleaded with me that he was a ranchman, a working man, that he was ignorant about such matters as mines. When I pointed out to him that, according to government figures, there were twelve times as many miners killed and injured by accidents in the southern Colorado fields as elsewhere, his only answer was that he had heard some vague statement to the effect that conditions were different in other places. He pleaded tearfully that he had brought upon himself the hatred of everyone, he admitted that he was utterly bewildered and had no idea what to do in this crisis. His every word made evident his utter ignorance of the economic forces which have produced this frightful situation. He cried out

> for some solution; yet, every time I sought to suggest a solution, and to pin him down to a "yes" or "no" upon a certain course of action, he lost control of himself and cried out that I was trying to make him "express an opinion." He, the Governor of the State, had no business to have an opinion about such a dispute!

Sinclair later said, "It is no accident, of course, that a man of this type comes to be Governor of a State like Colorado. The corporations deliberately select such men because they wish to be let alone, and they prefer men who are too weak to interfere with them."

It was on April 30, 1914, that the President sent troops into Colorado. Before the end of the first week of May they numbered 1,590 enlisted men and 61 officers. Wilson wanted to withdraw them as soon as possible, but first the state's governor had to restore order and take control. Ammons was so frightened and uncertain that he did little, other state officials did almost nothing, and with the situation still in violent flux the members of the state legislature indifferently prepared to adjourn on May 16. The President sent the governor a stern telegram saying that the governor's "constitutional obligations with regard to the maintenance of order in Colorado are not to be indefinitely continued by the inaction of the state legislature." Wilson added that he could not conceive that Colorado was "willing to forgo her sovereignty, or to throw herself entirely upon the government of the United States."

In Manhattan picketing continued in front of the Standard Oil building, although not all the marchers remained mute, as Sinclair had wished. Roars of anger broke out every now and then, while one demonstrator yelled that John D. Rockefeller, Jr., "should be shot down like a dog!" Other pickets began showing up near Mr. John's town house on West Fifty-fourth Street, then more of them appeared in the vicinity of his country estate where he was holed up with his "cold." One of his aides mailed a $2,500 check in preliminary payment for the installation of limestone carvings of children with baskets to adorn the east façade of the Rockefeller retreat at Pocantico Hills.

Pocantico Hills lies 30 miles north of New York City in Westchester county near Tarrytown. Straddling a high ridge separating the Sawmill from the Hudson river, it provides a magnificent view of the Hudson where it widens into the Tappan Zee. In 1893 John D. Rockefeller, Sr., had begun buying parcels of property near Tarrytown, and by 1914 the estate included more than 3,000 acres. A half century later these grew into 4,180 acres—a fief 6 miles square laced with 70 miles of private roads. After fire gutted the main house on Kijuit Hill, the elder Rockefeller built himself a fifty-room Georgian mansion with dormer windows—and this single building cost $2,000,000. Mr. John had his own house on the grounds, while a new house was constructed and given to each of his sons as they matured. The Rockefeller family preserve was a bower of orchards, groves of trees, a vegetable garden and four great flower gardens containing statuary, fountains and waterfalls.

To this lush and lovely enclave, or near it, flocked hordes of pickets, most of them from New York City, shouting, speechmaking men and women eager to have their bitterness heard by the man they held responsible for the Ludlow tragedy. The Rockefellers doubled their guards both inside and outside their miles of barbed-wire fences, high stone walls and iron gates. While the demonstrators knew they had scant chance of glimpsing either Rockefeller, let alone making a personal appeal to them, they hoped at least to make their presence felt.

They tried to hold a street meeting in Tarrytown, and some were arrested. Their spokesman then asked the town trustees whether they might tell the story of Ludlow in a local theater or hall, since they had been banned from the public streets. Go ahead, said the town fathers. But not a single owner of a theater or hall would rent them his place. At last a wealthy woman, Mrs. Charles J. Gould, offered the use of an open-air theater on her estate almost next door to the Rockefeller gardens. Her neighbors sniffed that this was in bad taste, and they especially resented the thought of letting Upton Sinclair—that Socialist!—speak anywhere near their homes. But speak he did. Held on the evening of June 22, 1914, the rally was attended by some 300 Tarrytown residents, mostly poor, a few rich, and in the crowd there were even some laborers from the Rockefeller estate. A United Mine Workers organizer named John W. Brown described the strike in faraway Colorado, sketched conditions in the Rockefeller mines, told how men and women and children had been gunned down by thugs hired by these same Rockefellers who lived next door, behind all those trees. And before the people adjourned, they adopted a resolution declaring the Rockefellers had treated their workmen so brutally that their property should be confiscated by the President of the United States.

Resentment against the Rockefellers was hardly a local phenomenon. Up and down and across the country people of various political complexions railed at the Rockefellers, while anarchists tried to use the Ludlow massacre as a lever to overthrow both capitalism and the state. One of the most flamboyant anarchist leaders, Lithuanian-born Emma Goldman, turned the power of her personality to this issue, lecturing on the meaning of the massacre, exhorting everyone to abolish all government by whatever means. "In the zeal of fanaticism," she wrote in her autobiography, "I had believed that the end justifies the means. It took years of experience and suffering to emancipate myself from the mad idea. Acts of violence committed as a protest against unbearable social wrongs—I still believed them inevitable."

The hot night of July 3–4, 1914, an explosion shattered a room in a tenement on Lexington Avenue in Manhattan and damaged several floors in the building. At first police thought the blast had been caused by a gas leak, but as they picked their way through the debris they learned that a bomb had gone off. The detonation killed Mrs. Marie Chevez, Arthur Caron, Charles Berg and Karl Hanson, and it injured several other persons. After questioning the survivors, the police concluded that the bomb had been made to assassinate John D. Rockefeller, Jr., but exploded accidentally and prematurely. With hotheads still lurking around Tarrytown, the Rockefellers beefed up their protection by hiring Burns' detectives.

When Emma Goldman heard the news she became agitated, for Caron, Berg and Hanson were fellow anarchists and had been among the

Tarrytown demonstrators. She also knew the woman who had rented the apartment where the bomb exploded, a Louise Berg. Upton Sinclair was also upset. He knew Caron as a French-Canadian youth whose wife and baby had starved to death during a textile strike in Lawrence, Massachusetts; after that Caron went to New York to take part in an unemployment demonstration, was arrested by the police who beat him in his cell, breaking his nose and rupturing an eardrum.

"It was interesting," Sinclair wrote, "to observe the conduct of the New York newspapers during this affair. It made, of course, a tremendous excitement. Bombs are news; they are heard all the way around the world. But the outrages which have caused the bombs are not news, and no one ever refers to them. No one makes clear that these outrages will continue to cause bombs, so long as the human soul remains what it is."

The bodies of the dead anarchists were cremated and their ashes placed on view in a yard in the rear of a residence occupied by Alexander Berkman, another anarchist leader and Emma Goldman's lover. He denied published reports that the dead were members of the Industrial Workers of the World. When he announced that a memorial service for them would be held in Union Square, the New York *Times* published an editorial protest. But the meeting was held, Berkman did speak, and the police arrested another speaker, Rebecca Edelson. Sentenced and taken to the workhouse on Blackwells Island, she threatened to smash the prison furniture, went on a hunger strike, was forcibly fed.

Upton Sinclair announced that he was opposed to the use of bombs, and all responsible Americans, however furious they felt with the Rockefellers, agreed with him. Now that Mr. John knew some anarchists had hoped to kill him, now that he could not pick up a newspaper or magazine without reading criticism of himself, he decided to take steps to protect himself. One of his advisers urged him to buy advertising space in newspapers to tell his side of the story. Another suggested that he buy an entire newspaper so he could explain himself on a daily basis. Mr. John asked for advice from Arthur Brisbane, a Hearst editor sometimes called the "master of the commonplace." Brisbane recommended that he hire Ivy L. Lee, an executive assistant of the Pennsylvania Railroad and a near genius as a press agent.

Mr. John asked Lee to visit him, described his problem and asked whether Lee had any suggestions. Lee proposed that he study public opinion and then be allowed to help shape the policies of the Rockefeller coal company so that it might win public approval. Mr. John hired Lee at $1,000 a month after persuading the railroad to release its publicity man to work for the Rockefellers. Although the elder Rockefeller was opposed to the employment of a press agent, he accepted his son's decision.

Lee went to Colorado to see conditions for himself and soon reported to Mr. John that he had not been receiving accurate information from his Western mine managers. These men put Lee in touch with the governor, who let the press agent draft a letter to President Wilson to go out over the governor's name. But for some reason the letter never was mailed. Lee then wrote and distributed a series of bulletins called "Facts Concerning the Struggle in Colorado for Industrial Freedom"—although George

Creel and Upton Sinclair called them lies rather than facts. Among other things, Lee falsified the salaries of union officials to make it appear they were paid more than they actually received. The press agent also published speeches that had been made about the strike by some of Colorado's Representatives in Washington, men Sinclair described as "the 'kept' Congressmen of the coal-operators." Union members soon were calling Lee "Poison Ivy Lee."

The Ludlow massacre was investigated by a half dozen groups—among them two Presidential commissions, the subcommittee of the House committee on mines and mining, the United States Commission on Industrial Relations. But despite their adverse findings, Mr. John continued to refuse to negotiate with the United Mine Workers, who began to run out of money. The strike that began on September 23, 1913, was called off on December 10, 1914. It was a defeat for the strikers and a victory for the Rockefellers. This Colorado coal war of 1913–14 had resulted in many deaths; the figure of seventy-four has been used, but to this day no one knows the exact toll.

The matter of the eleven children and two women who died in the "Death Pit" was investigated by a coroner's jury, which returned this verdict: "We find that [the victims named] came to their death by asphyxiation, or fire, or both, caused by the burning of the tents of the Ludlow Tent Colony, and that the fire on the tents was started by militia-men, under Major Hamrock and Lieutenant Linderfelt, or mine guards, or both."

A national guard military court was convened in the officers' quarters of the state rifle range at Golden, west of Denver. It was a farcical tribunal since all its officers were cronies of General Chase. A few militia officers, troubled by their consciences and afraid of a whitewash, pointedly avoided taking any part in the proceedings. They had heard a superior officer say, "We've got to take care of these men of ours. We've got to vaccinate them so no court in the land can touch them at some future date. A man's life can't be put in jeopardy twice in the courts, and we'll take care of these boys." Within a fortnight ten officers and a dozen men were tried. All were acquitted. And in time to come not a single militiaman or mine guard was put on trial in a civil court. At hearings of the military court Lieutenant Linderfelt was tried for the murder of Louis Tikas but was released with a light reprimand for striking a prisoner; he was also demoted in rank. That was all.

Unlike the coroner's jury, a grand jury sided with the operators, reporting, "The evidence produced before us clearly shows that the crimes were committed by armed mobs, acting in pursuance of well-defined, carefully matured plans, having for their object the destruction of property and human life. These mobs were composed of members of the United Mine Workers of America and their known sympathizers. . . . The organization through its officers in Colorado bought the guns and ammunition and directed criminal activities. . . ."

A total of 124 union officials and strikers were named in 163 indictments—most of them indictments for murder—handed down by a Las Animas county grand jury whose twelve members were handpicked by the sheriff from a list of 88 coal company partisans, rather than being drawn from a panel supplied by the county commissioners, as prescribed by law. And the governor appointed as judge a man who was an attorney for a coal company.

Among the defendants was John Lawson, a high official of the union, who was accused of murdering a mine guard named John Nimmo near Ludlow long before the massacre. The indictment did not allege that Lawson had done the actual killing or even been near the spot where Nimmo died. It simply declared that Nimmo had been shot by *some member* of the United Mine Workers, and since Lawson was a union official, he was responsible. The jury found Lawson guilty, and the judge sentenced him to prison for life. This was so flagrantly outrageous that even some Rockefeller supporters were shocked. Lawson appealed to the Colorado supreme court, and public opinion forced it to act. The coal company lawyer who had sat as a judge was branded as grossly biased, and he was prohibited from presiding at any subsequent trials. After long and complex legal action, Lawson and three others of the accused were acquitted, their verdicts resulting in dismissal of all other untried cases. Having spent $6,000,000 in strike benefits and legal fees, the union was close to bankruptcy.

But this was not quite the end of the matter. The United States Commission on Industrial Relations decided to hold further hearings. In 1912 Congress had created this commission to study "the general condition of labor in the principal industries of the United States" in order to find "the underlying causes of dissatisfaction in the industrial situation." As Walter Lippmann expressed it, the commission members had "before them the task of explaining why America, supposed to have become the land of promise, has become the land of disappointment and deep-seated discontent." President Wilson appointed its nine members, including its chairman, Francis P. Walsh. A native of St. Louis and an able attorney, Walsh was hated by corporations. The *Saturday Evening Post* described him as one who "is not happy when he is not fighting for something he thinks is right."

The commission began its hearing at 10 A.M. on January 25, 1915, under the crystal chandeliers of the former board of estimate room in city hall in New York City. Chairman Walsh boomed, "Will the house please be in order and will the audience maintain as perfect order as possible." Pause. "Mr. Rockefeller."

Among the reporters covering this hearing was Walter Lippmann, who wrote for *The New Republic.* In a subsequent article, Lippmann said:

> Mr. Rockefeller seemed terribly alone on Monday when he faced the Industrial Relations Commission. There was an atmosphere of no quarter. A large crowd watching intensely every expression of his face, about twenty cameras and a small regiment of newspaper men, a shorthand reporter at his elbow, and confronting him the Commissioners led by the no means reassuring Mr. Walsh—except for an indefatigably kindly police sergeant who gave him one glass of water after another, not much was done to pamper the witness. He met what he knew to be his accusers with the weary and dogged good humor of a child trying

> to do a sum it does not understand for a teacher who will not relent.
>
> From the first Mr. Rockefeller was on the defensive. He began by reading the long statement which was printed that evening in the newspapers. The statement was very carefully prepared; much thought and labor had evidently gone into it, but as a matter of style it did not sound in the least like anything that Mr. Rockefeller had to say on his direct oral examination. Perhaps we did him an injustice, but it never occurred to us to suppose that Mr. Rockefeller had written the document himself. Nevertheless, Mr. Rockefeller read the paper well. . . .

Lippmann doubted the sincerity of the witness when Mr. John read that "combinations of capital are sometimes conducted in an unworthy manner, contrary to law and in disregard of the interest of both labor and the public . . . such combinations cannot be too strongly condemned nor too vigorously dealt with." Lippmann, nonetheless, could not bring himself to believe that Rockefeller himself hired thugs or wanted them hired.

> His intellectual helplessness [Lippmann mused] was the amazing part of his testimony. Here was a man who represented an agglomeration of wealth probably without parallel in history, the successor to a father who has with justice been called the high priest of capitalism. Freedom of enterprise, untrammeled private property, the incentives of the profiteer, culminate in the achievements of his family. He is the supreme negation of all equality, and unquestionably a symbol of the most menacing fact in the life of the republic. . . . His tragedy is that of all hereditary power, for there is no magic in inheritance, and sooner or later the scion of a house is an incompetent. Yet the complicated system over which he presides keeps him in an uncomfortably exalted position, where all men can see its absurdity. . . .

The Commission on Industrial Relations published its findings in four reports. It blamed the coal strike on the operators. It confirmed most of the accusations made against company gunmen and state militiamen. It accused Mr. John of approving measures intended to coerce the Colorado state government and flout the President of the United States. It blamed Mr. John and his father for employing incompetent and reactionary men as executive officers of their corporations. It described the prosecution and conviction of John Lawson as "the crowning infamy of all the infamous record in Colorado of American institutions perverted and debauched by selfish private interests. It is anarchy stripped of every pretense of even that chimerical idealism that fires the unbalanced mind of the bomb thrower. It is anarchism for profits and revenge, and it menaces the security and integrity of American institutions. . . ."

In 1917 crowds flocked to Ludlow to dedicate a United Mine Workers' monument erected beside the "Death Pit." In front of a stone pillar there stands a statue of a miner, his thumb hooked in his belt, his sad eyes gazing into the distance. To his left is a figure of a woman crouching protectively over a child. Carved into the pillar are these words: "In memory of the men, women and children who lost their lives in freedom's cause at Ludlow, Colorado, April 20, 1914."

In 1960 John D. Rockefeller, Jr., died, and two years later a granite commemorative plaque was unveiled at the foot of the Channel Gardens at Rockefeller Center in mid-Manhattan, a site visited daily by an estimated 175,000 people. The upward-sloping surface of this plaque contains Mr. John's credo, which begins with these words: "I believe in the supreme worth of the individual and in his right to life, liberty, and the pursuit of happiness. . . ."

In 1969 a report submitted to the National Commission on the Causes and Prevention of Violence was published as a book entitled *The History of Violence in America: Historical and Comparative Perspectives.* This says, "The Ludlow conflict was in truth an actualization of the apocalyptic visions of class warfare of Jack London in *The Iron Heel.*"

Chapter 7

MORALS AND MANNERS

One day in 1912 a nude French girl waded out into the Lake of Annecy in eastern France and struck a pose for an artist sitting on the shore. The artist was Paul Emile Chabas, famous for his nude paintings and something of a celebrity in Paris. This particular day he had hired as his model a lovely, wondrously proportioned peasant girl. Since the weather was chilly, she tried to keep warm by hugging herself, and despite her goose pimples, she held this pose until Chabas finished painting her. Later he said, "I love that picture. They call it my masterpiece, and perhaps it is." He entitled it "September Morn."

He gave permission for his painting to be reproduced by Braun and Company, a New York firm that had an art shop at 13 West Forty-sixth Street. The manager, Philippe Ortiz, had 2,000 lithographs made of "September Morn" and offered them for sale at 10 cents apiece, but even at this low price they did not sell well.

Early in 1913 Harry Reichenbach walked into the store and asked for a job. Reichenbach was a press agent who later won fame as the so-called Father of Ballyhoo, but at this time life was hard for him. He had just moved to Manhattan to open a publicity office and had found a few clients, although not enough, so he had had to give up his hotel room and sleep on the desk in his office. When he saw the lithographs of "September Morn," he had an idea. He told Ortiz that for $45, the monthly rental for his office, he could guarantee the sale of all 2,000 prints. Although the manager was dubious, he told Reichenbach to go ahead and try.

The first thing the press agent did was to display several prints of the nude Frenchwoman in the window of the shop. Then he made an anonymous phone call to Anthony Comstock, head of the Society for the Suppression of Vice, pretending to be shocked by the very display he had created. Comstock, about to crack down on boys peddling pictures of tango dancers, paid no attention. Reichenbach called again and again without being able to stir the celebrated reformer into action. At last the press agent visited Comstock's office to protest in person, yelling, "This picture is an outrage! It's undermining the morals of our city's youth!" Actually, as he later confessed, "there was no more immorality or suggestiveness to it than sister's photograph as a baby in the family album."

Comstock caught fire. Charging out of his office, he hurried to the art store, where he found a group of boys in front of the window, ogling, giggling, pointing. Comstock was unaware that Reichenbach had hired the boys at 50 cents apiece to stage this show of mock horror. Stalking inside, Comstock told the clerk, "That is not a proper picture to be shown to boys and girls! There is nothing more sacred than the form of a woman, but it must not be denuded. I think everyone will agree with me that such pictures should not be displayed where school children passing through the streets can see them."

Aware of Comstock's reputation for ferocity, the clerk promised to dismantle the display, but when Ortiz returned, he insisted that every copy of "September Morn" remain in full view. On May 10, 1913, Comstock had Ortiz arrested on a charge of displaying an obscene drawing. When the news got around and when people saw for themselves the innocence of the painting, they ridiculed Comstock, and some wrote to newspapers to oppose the action he had taken. When the case came to trial, Ortiz was acquitted.

The publicity made "September Morn" the most famous nude painting in the world. Ortiz sold his 2,000 prints and ordered more, which he priced at $1 apiece. Other art dealers offered "September Morn" for sale, and some men went into the business of publishing prints for the sole purpose of reproducing and peddling it. Manufacturers turned out "September Morn" statues, dolls, calendars, umbrellas and cane handles. Drunks drew the French model with their fingers in the sawdust on the floors of saloons, and sailors had her image tattooed on their chests. More than 7,000,000 copies of the Chabas painting were sold.

The original was bought by M. Leon Matoncheff, a rich Russian, who took it to Moscow. Later it was acquired by C. S. Gulbenkian, a wealthy Armenian, who hung it in his posh Paris town house. And on September 1, 1957, New York's Metropolitan Museum of Art placed on public exhibition the painting Comstock had thought was corrupting the morals of Americans.

Dr. Sigmund Freud wrote a friend on July 8, 1915, "Sexual morality as defined by society, in its most extreme form that of America, strikes me as very contemptible. I stand for an infinitely freer sexual life, although I myself have made very little use of such freedom."

In the second decade of the twentieth century America's moral code, derived from the prudery of the Puritans and the hypocrisy of the Victorians, had begun to loosen a little. Men declared, and most women believed, that while it was all right for men to "sow their wild oats" before marriage, good women never did. Married farmers bedded servant girls in straw and rich businessmen kept mistresses in fine apartments —"birds in gilded cages," they were called—but these extramarital affairs were hushed up, mentioned only snickeringly by men to other men and mostly ignored by high-minded, if suspicious, wives.

Seduction was more difficult then than now because women wore corsets difficult to unlace and shed quickly. Men doted on large breasts, so women tried to accommodate them. In a magazine Mrs. Louise Ingram of Toledo, Ohio, placed an advertisement promising: BUST DEVELOPED ONE OUNCE A DAY. In 1914 the *World Almanac* printed this advertisement: "Thin women by the thousands have been amazed at the results of our generous Free Trial Treatment of Dr. Whitney's Nerve and Flesh Builder. . . . It has been astonishing how little additional flesh and bust development it has required to make many of our thin patrons attractive."

College students sang:

> Mrs. X had bosom trouble,
> She was flat across the bow;
> Then she took three bottles of Compound,
> Now they milk her like a cow!

The United States divorce rate was higher than in any other country supplying statistics—and it was rising. In 1861, when Nevada was a territory, a husband and wife could get divorced there if one of them resided in the territory for six months. But not until about 1906 did Easterners begin to take advantage of the Nevada divorce law. In 1914 Reno passed a law requiring a year's residence, but two years later the Nevada legislature restored the six-month law.

Between 1867 and 1906 the American divorce rate rose 30 percent every five years; population increased only about 10 percent during this period. Different states had different laws on divorce with a total of perhaps thirty-six various grounds for dissolving marriage. By 1914 one marriage in every ten was ending in divorce. Still, any wife who divorced an adulterous husband knew she courted criticism from other wives who clung painfully to relationships empty of meaning.

In this restrictive atmosphere there were few American women who practiced free love, but among this tiny minority was Isadora Duncan. Born in San Francisco in 1878, she became the greatest American dancer of her day and the first in modern times to elevate her profession to the level of a creative art. When her father left her mother for another woman and she saw her mother's unhappiness, Isadora decided at twelve that she would "live to fight against marriage and for the emancipation of women and the right of every woman to have a child or children as it pleased her."

Giving herself to her art and a succession of men, Isadora Duncan was impulsive and irresponsible. She had dark soft hair, an upturned nose and blue-gray eyes, stood an erect five feet six and weighed 125 pounds. And when she danced, she enchanted everyone, for she was so graceful and light she was like a breeze moving across water. After successful dance recitals in Europe she returned and settled awhile in Manhattan. In a business building she found a loft she converted into a studio, decorating it with curtains the color of robins' eggs. She called it the Ark. It had low couches piled with pale cushions, soft orange electric lights, and sometimes she lit candles set in candelabra on a big black piano. Within this sensual, seductive, bohemian environment she taught dancing to the

Russian children she had brought back with her, but felt she could help even more children if she were given permission to use one of the city's armories.

She turned for help to her friend Mabel Dodge, a rich bohemian with acquaintances in both the artistic and financial worlds. Mrs. Dodge asked assistance of Walter Lippmann, and he agreed to do all he could. The mayor of New York was persuaded to visit Isadora's studio to watch her pupils perform and then listen to her plea for use of an armory. Lippmann later said, with a touch of irony, "The idea was that he, as the head of the government, was to be struck mad by a vision of beauty and that we were all to dance on Fifth Avenue."

When John Purroy Mitchel took office on January 1, 1914, as the mayor of New York, he was only thirty-four and the youngest mayor in the city's history. Handsome and vigorous, a practical idealist and cultivated gentleman, Mitchel radiated Irish charm. He was also Catholic, married and the father of a daughter. Mabel Dodge wrote of Isadora that "the instincts of her blood could always report to her the degree of a man's virility."

One afternoon Mrs. Dodge arrived at Isadora's studio with Lippmann, his blue serge suit a harsh note amid its subtle colors. Isadora wore a flowing Greek gown. Soon the mayor was ushered in and introduced to Miss Duncan. An uncertain look on his face, he bowed, held his derby against his flat belly with one hand and tugged at his chin with the other. Her eyes widening, Isadora cried, "Why, I thought you would be an old, old man with a long white beard!" Seizing his free hand, she pressed a note into it. The mayor glanced down astonished, for Isadora had scrawled Plato's remark that the world would be better off if philosophers were kings and kings philosophers. Then she took his hand in both her soft hands and pressed it to her warm body, pulling him toward a couch covered with orange cushions. Sensing this beautiful woman was about to enthrone him on a divan, Mitchel broke away and dashed to a piano stool, grabbing at the piano to steady himself. Shrugging her magnificent shoulders, Isadora murmured she would not think of trying to *force* the mayor to recline on the couch with her. Slowly spilling herself on the cushions under an orange light, she laughed softly and let her gown fall loose to expose one breast.

The mayor coughed.

Now her pupils ran from the corners of the room to fall gracefully at her feet. With a grandiose sweep of her hand, Isadora cried, "*These* children have always had a *beautiful* life! *They* don't have to get up in the morning and go down to breakfast with their cross fathers and mothers! *They* don't have to go to school with horrid dirty books in satchels! *They* don't have to go to church on Sunday and listen to stuffy old men in ugly buildings!"

Then she went on to observe that if there were to be real freedom in New York, why, of course the family would have to be abolished.

The mayor said, "I had hoped we would see something of your work. . . ."

Isadora had wanted much from this man. She had wanted Mitchel's permission for room to teach a thousand poor children how to dance, how to appreciate the finer things of life; but she had seen him flinch at the sight of her bare breast, and she felt this revealed him as a Philistine. Coldly and self-destructively, she said, "Oh, I do not think the children feel like dancing this afternoon." And dismissed them.

With just a hint of courtesy, the mayor got up and left. Isadora laughed merrily, glanced at her thunderstruck friends and cried, "Come! Let us rest and drink wine and forget that young man. How could New York be other than it is with a ruler like that? Marguerite! Can you fetch us some white wine?"

Walter Lippmann stormed out in disgust. Later he wrote of Isadora Duncan, "Essentially she was doing what every archaic moralist does who tells men to be good, be true, be beautiful, and forgets to say how."

Prostitution had existed in the United States since colonial days. In the early part of this century it flourished in red-light districts in many cities, protected by police, patronized by men both respectful and notorious. Various vice commissions and civic groups had tried to stamp out prostitution but were unsuccessful, in the main, because as each new law was passed, it was ignored by the public and public officials alike. After all, sin was profitable.

When evangelist Billy Sunday trod his sawdust trail into Norfolk, Virginia, many of his backers were respectable church members, propertied men with income from the ownership of houses in which prostitution was practiced. Buster Clark was king of the red-light district in Terre Haute, Indiana, a man said to be as honest as any in the business, one who drove pimps out of town and would not let a girl work unless she had had previous experience. Chicago had more than 1,000 brothels with annual earnings of $16,000,000. The renowned red-light district of New Orleans consisted of twenty-eight city blocks and had not been disturbed in a half century. In the segregated area of El Paso, Texas, the whores were told to obey the "Rules of the Reservation," which said among other things that they might not "sit with legs crossed in a vulgar manner and must keep skirts down."

After it was revealed that rings of vicious men—and even some women—were seducing and ensnaring innocent girls for purposes of prostitution, Congress passed the Mann Act in 1910. This imposed a heavy fine and imprisonment on anyone transporting a female across state lines for an immoral purpose. In passing this law, Congress was not trying to ban prostitution, since it lacked the constitutional authority to do so; the act was based on the power of Congress to regulate interstate commerce. The Mann Act became known as the white slave act, and the thought of evil men garnering girls for wicked purposes titillated some repressed Americans, men and women alike, gave rise to the publication of covertly erotic books and articles and sermons and to the production of spuriously righteous movies. Sex entered the American cinema over the bodies of the so-called white slaves.

To cite one example, New York newspapers published advertisements announcing that on November 24, 1913, Joe Weber's theater would present "TRAFFIC IN SOULS—The sensational motion picture dramatization based on the Rockefeller White Slavery Report and on the investigation of the Vice Trust by District Attorney Whitman—A $200,000 spectacle in 700 scenes with 800 players, showing the traps cunningly laid for young girls by vice agents—Don't miss the most thrilling scene ever staged, the smashing of the Vice Trust."

In 1910 John D. Rockefeller, Jr., had served as chairman of a Manhattan special jury investigating white slavery and become so disturbed that after his duties ended he decided to try to find a way to combat the "social evil," as prostitution was called. He founded the Bureau of Social Hygiene and hired Abraham Flexner. The son of immigrants from Bohemia, Flexner was a noted educator and had made a survey that criticized the nation's medical schools. Rockefeller asked him to go to Europe to see how prostitution was handled there. As a result of his study abroad, Flexner wrote a book published in 1914 and still considered a classic in its field, called *Prostitution in Europe.*

Here were his conclusions:

> There are obviously two sides to prostitution. It is not only unjust but ineffectual to single out the woman for any special kind of treatment, whether by the police authorities or by the health authorities. In so far as the woman is concerned, prostitution is a constantly changing status, depending upon the causes which have led to the individual's demoralization. Some of the causes are permanent and to a considerable extent irremediable, as, for example, low mentality; others vary. Here a woman is driven to the streets by the consequences of seduction under the influence of alcohol; another by the breakup of home or the destruction of home life, resulting from the constant influx of detached young men and women from the country into the large towns; and loneliness, sheer loneliness, even among employed persons, is not infrequently a decisive factor. Economic conditions are of course important, but they are by no means the sole factors. . . .

Between 1912 and 1915, according to the International Reform Bureau, more than fifty American cities gave up their policy of tolerating or regulating brothels. Chicago formed a Morals Commission to study prostitution. In 1912 Americans learned that in Germany some people had organized the first nudist camp of modern times. Enrico Caruso, the great Italian tenor, was arrested in Manhattan's Central Park for pinching a woman. In Oak Park, Illinois, a boy named Ernest Hemingway read that the charge against Caruso was "mashing" and asked his father what this meant. Dr. Hemingway merely called it a "heinous crime," leaving the boy bewildered and fantasizing Caruso doing terrible things to a beautiful lady with a potato masher.

Anyone flouting the nation's moral laws was criticized, prosecuted and persecuted. Another sometime resident of Oak Park was the architect

Frank Lloyd Wright, who became so discontented with his marriage that he asked his wife for a divorce. She said that if he repeated his request a year later, she would agree. At the end of the year he asked again, but she told him she had changed her mind. Outraged, Wright declared that "only to the degree that marriage is mutual is it decent." One day he went for a ride with Mrs. Mamah Bouton Borthwick Cheney, the wife of a Chicago businessman, and never came back. Instead, he took his married mistress to Italy for two years and then settled with her and her children in Spring Green, Wisconsin. One night in August, 1914, while Wright was away on business, his butler went mad, ran amok and murdered seven people, including Mrs. Cheney and her two children. Moralists hailed this tragedy as "just retribution." Gutted by grief, the genius buried his beloved mistress with his own hands.

For decades Americans had been scandalized by the polygamy of the Mormons, but before the turn of the century Mormon men had ceased marrying more than one woman. During the first part of this century, however, the leader of a religious cult entered into multiple marriage with several young women. He was Benjamin Franklin Purnell, a broommaker from Kentucky who declared that education was less useful than dung, a man who left his first wife and entered into bigamous marriage with a second woman who became high priestess of his odd cult.

A striking figure, Purnell weighed 200 pounds, grew a full beard and long hair, wore a white hat and a white suit adorned with a heavy gold chain. In 1895 he had proclaimed himself the younger brother of Christ and announced that his mission was to assemble 144,000 men and 144,000 women—all of whom would live forever. In 1902, near Benton Harbor, Michigan, he established a commune he called the House of David. At its peak it had 500 members, many of whom regarded Purnell as God. All the men were bearded and long-haired. They organized a baseball team and astounded folks by playing the game bare-handed. Purnell told his disciples that sex was sinful, and he prohibited any of them, even married couples, from having intercourse. They seem to have believed and obeyed him, for only two children were born in the commune.

Nonetheless, between 1910 and 1923 the "King" of the House of David took one girl after another as his wife—nearly forty of them—but never appeared at any of his weddings. Some disciples became disenchanted, left the colony, were denounced by the faithful as "scorpions" and began spreading rumors. In 1910 fifty-four women of the commune signed an affidavit declaring they had *not* had sexual relations with Purnell. This launched a series of brushes with the law. On one occasion, according to a witness, Purnell fled to Chicago disguised as a woman. In 1923 the state of Michigan filed suit to dissolve the House of David, and in court two girls accused Purnell of indulging in immoral practices under the guise of religious ritual. He was found guilty of "immoral conduct with many girls of the colony." A court ordered the dissolution of the House of David, although this decision was later reversed. In 1927 Purnell died, a broken old man.

Public schools gave children no courses in sexual education. This was left to parents, most of whom were too shy or moral or ignorant of the subject to tell their sons and daughters anything helpful. Many youngsters became confused when their father or mother obliquely talked about the "facts of life" or "the birds and the bees." When members of the National Education Association met in Oakland, California, in August, 1914, they submitted many learned papers, but only two were concerned with sex hygiene. Various publishers issued bland sex manuals either used or ignored by parents too timid to tell their children about sex.

Aging men worried about their virility could turn to "Doc" John R. Brinkley for supposed assistance. Born in North Carolina, he wandered about the country, got a spurious diploma from something called the Eclectic Medical University of Kansas City, began practicing medicine in Milford, Kansas, a tiny livestock and grain center. In 1917 he became a goat-gland specialist. According to him, a farmer complained that for sixteen years he had been sexually dead. The farmer led the talk to the subject of goats, then to goat glands, finally suggesting that Brinkley get a pair and implant them in his body. After the operation the farmer's wife gave birth to a boy whom the grateful father named "Billy" in honor of the goat. Proclaiming that he had found the secret of sexual rejuvenation, Brinkley became rich and infamous. The Kansas medical society accused him of malpractice, and the Kansas state medical board revoked his license to practice medicine on the grounds that the transplantation of goat glands into humans was biologically worthless. Brinkley nonetheless became so wealthy that he wore several diamond rings on his fingers, owned four cars, several yachts and a private airplane and ran three times for governor of Kansas.

Sunday, June 28, 1914, the day the archduke of Austria was assassinated at Sarajevo, a newspaper in middle America published this headline: HOT DEBATE OVER CORSET. The subject of corsets had been argued by delegates to the Women's National Medical Association meeting in Indianapolis, Indiana. Dr. Louise Eastman advocated wearing corsets because she found that as she became heavier, a corset kept her from looking "bunchy," as she put it. Dr. Flora Smith, on the other hand, told her sister physicians she was unable to understand why "women thought it necessary to improve on nature."

Most American women wore corsets, corset covers, brassieres, bust confiners, long silk slips, cambric underskirts and dresses reaching to their ankles. One popular item was the hobble skirt, which evoked comment from Louis H. Chalif, founder of the Chalif School of Russian Dancing in New York. He thought the hobble skirt was related to a popular dance called the turkey trot, saying:

> If a lady's feet are so tied that she cannot dance, other parts of her body will dance, and they did—the shoulders and hips. The

> original turkey trot consisted of very short steps and very ample body movements. The steps but not the spirit came from the hobble skirt. For a while we had the curious phenomenon of women dressed like moderns and dancing like Hottentots. The spirit of this dance came from the music, which came from the Africans, who got it from nature. . . . The spirit of the dance could not be resisted.

Women's clothing was inexpensive. For $3.35 a young lady could buy a dress made of washable cotton rice cloth in a flowered pattern with collar, lapels, wide girdle and fancy turn-back cuffs of white pique. One style had elbow-length set-in sleeves and an underskirt with a flounce made of raised striped voile. The waist front and girdle were trimmed with mother-of-pearl buttons. Another popular fashion was the blouse and skirt. Some blouses were made of all-wool double-twisted warp serge, while tunics could be divided and loose-hanging, with a yoke effect in front and double box panel ending in open plaits to provide fullness. Women had their choice of high shoes with laces or shoes studded with as many as fourteen buttons. No lady would think of going outdoors without a hat—broad-brimmed, slanting low over the right eye and decorated with feathers or artificial flowers.

Women took pride in long hair. Some enhanced their own with genuine human hair in single puffs, biscuit coils, band switches, basket twists, outside front pompadours, coronet braids and long switches braided into their own hair. In their coiffures they wore decorative combs. Since shiny skin was considered improper, women dabbed their noses and cheeks with talcum powder. Daring females reddened their cheeks with rouge and smeared their lips with lipstick. Except for farmers' wives, most women carried vanity cases in their handbags.

Men's fashions, as well, cost little. For $10.50 a man could buy a pure wool twill navy blue serge suit. Collars were high, vests almost mandatory, and two-button jackets popular. Trousers were narrow and came down only to the tops of shoes, so there was no break in the sharp vertical line. Ten dollars could purchase a spring overcoat made in a loose-fitting baggy style with kimono sleeves finished in a heavy welt seam giving a split-sleeve effect. This overcoat had slash pockets, while the arm slings on the inside facing of the garment made it possible to wear the coat as a cape.

In summer a man could wear a $7 Palm Beach suit with a stripe formed by a green pinstripe almost invisible against a black background. There were three-button sack styles with patch pockets. Some men wore hats and some caps; like women, few would leave the house without putting on some kind of headgear.

Small children wore rompers costing 20 cents and playsuits priced at 35 cents. Older boys donned wool or cotton knickerbockers reaching to their knees and held in place there by elastic bands. The sum of $3.75 would buy a boy a dark-blue pencil-striped Palm Beach cloth suit with a single-breasted coat having three outside patch pockets, yoke effect, and plaits to the waist. For $6 a young man could get a suit of dark navy blue manipulated serge, one-half wool worsted and one-half cotton, the coat a two-button single-breasted sack, slit in back, half lined with English twill lining. The conservative peg-top pants had belt loops, side buckle straps, a watch pocket and cuff bottoms. The watch pocket, on the right side of the pants near the belt, might hold a nickel-plated watch with an engraved back that cost as little as 77 cents. Schoolgirls wore bloomers made of black sateen and blue chambray gingham, cut in full sizes and finished with elastic at the knees. These bloomers—almost a uniform for girls between the ages of eight and sixteen—were priced as low as 29 cents.

Almost every boy carried a pocketknife—not for use in gang rumbles, as happened later, but for cutting branches off trees, sharpening sticks, opening cans, slicing bait for fishing. One popular number was the Wilbert Dakota Cowboys' Knife with three blades, priced at 60 cents and guaranteed for a year. Boys delighted in knives thick with a variety of pull-out devices—double bolsters, corkscrews, awls, can openers, screwdrivers, tack pullers, spear blades, etc. Germany, noted for its cutlery industry, manufactured many of the knives owned by American boys.

In the days before television commercials, boys sprawled on their bellies to flip through thick mail-order catalogues displaying all kinds of treasures. They paid particular attention to bicycles costing $17.95, acetylene gas or carbide bicycle lamps at $1.95, bicycle tool bags for 25 cents and bicycle bells and horns costing only 38 cents. Shotguns and rifles, pistols and automatics enchanted boys and alarmed their mothers. It was possible to buy almost any kind of weapon through the mail. For $15.98 one could get a double-barreled shotgun, a leather leg o'mutton gun case, patent globe sights, Three-in-One oil to clean the gun, and twenty-five smokeless shells. A .22 caliber single shot rifle came for as little as $2.65. Then there was Colt's army special revolver at $15.50, Colt's automatic pistol at $12, and the self-cocking Smith & Wesson revolver at $14.50. Boys whose mothers forbade them to buy anything so lethal had to content themselves with air rifles shooting pellets and costing as little as $1.20.

Halloween and the Fourth of July were days of delight to boys and times of terror for adults. On Halloween nothing that could be moved was safe from skylarking boys, who hoisted buggies onto the roofs of stores and even the steeples of churches, plundered fields of pumpkins, shot out streetlights, daubed sidewalks and storefronts with red paint, rampaged through streets like Atilla and his Huns. One of their prime targets was outhouses, which they would tip over and then run away. In Illinois a youth fired his .22 rifle at a privy and accidentally killed a man inside; he felt such remorse that all the rest of his life he wore a flower in his buttonhole to remind himself of his youthful folly. On the Fourth of July young men were so careless in their use of firecrackers, skyrockets, spinwheels and the like that the holiday would end with long casualty lists of people who burned their hair and lost their eyes and sometimes even their lives.

It was the custom of most Americans to bathe only once a week and generally in a bathtub, since few homes had showers. The favored time was early Saturday night, after which one would go out on the town to hang around the post office, village square or neighborhood bar. In 1914 some stores displayed shower equipment that could be installed over the bathtub. One standard bathroom item was the bathtub seat, made of oak, finished in white enamel and hooked over the sides of the tub.

Except for Saturday night, Americans entertained themselves mostly at home. They would gather around the piano in the parlor to sing solos or harmonize, and so-called barbershop quartets were highly regarded. A conservatory piano could be bought for as little as $142. Mothers devoted to culture forced reluctant sons to take piano lessons or study the violin, the mothers dreaming of concert careers for their offspring, the boys dreaming of open fields and dogs and guns and fish.

More to the taste of some youths were banjos costing $1.95 or rosewood mandolins priced at $3.95 and up. Harmonicas were especially popular, for they were easy to play, easy to carry in a pocket, and talented people could make beautiful music with them. People lacking talent but fond of music turned to player pianos with perforated rolls of paper and operated by pumping two pedals. In 1914 Americans had their choice of hundreds of player-piano selections, songs such as "Onward, Christian Soldiers," "Moonlight Bay" and "Meet Me Tonight in Dreamland."

More and more cameras were sold. A consumer could buy a daylight loading roll film Kewpie Kamera for as little as $1.65. George Eastman of Rochester, New York, was the nation's "Kodak King" with a near monopoly of the camera market in the United States, earning an annual profit of 171 percent on all the products he sold in 1912; even so, Eastman was an enlightened industrialist and one of the country's five leading philanthropists. Except for the poor, almost every family owned a camera and filled albums with snapshots of Uncle Ed and Aunt Mabel and Cousin Harold.

Another source of home entertainment were stereopticon slides and postcard projectors. These "magic lanterns" were also educational, for they enabled children to see reproductions of Niagara Falls, the streetcars of San Francisco, the Woolworth building in New York, the national Capitol in Washington and the like. Some projectors were powered with electric bulbs, while others had gas burners with mantles.

Electric consumption was rising, although many Americans used gas and oil and kerosene for illumination and cooking and heating. On the market were new all-purpose lighting fixtures adaptable to either liquid fuel or electricity. A common household chore was cleaning glass lamp chimneys smudged by smoke from wicks that burned improperly or had been turned too high.

Most homes had front rooms kept spotlessly clean, although they seldom were used unless company came to call. To children the parlor was a formal stale place to be studiously avoided, since one had to mind his manners there. They associated the parlor with the parish priest or local minister, for it was here that the holy man was entertained with whiskey or tea, which he drank while peering over his spectacles at wayward youngsters. Still, some parlors were fascinating, for they had curio cabinets with perhaps a bottle of water from the Holy Land, curiously gnarled pieces of driftwood, pink seashells that could be held to the ear to hear the sound of waves.

In many ways it was an era of innocence, although it also had its dark side.

Chapter 8

CRIME AND THE DRUG PROBLEM

In 1914 Americans worried about the national crime rate.

New York and Chicago had more murders than England, Scotland and Wales combined, and eight times more burglaries than London. Even Detroit and Cleveland exceeded London in burglaries. Street robberies, too, were far more numerous in the United States than in European countries. In one American city after another the local police found themselves overwhelmed with the volume of crime, which continued to soar.

Raymond B. Fosdick, who investigated this problem for the Rockefeller Bureau of Social Hygiene, observed:

> In America the student of police travels from one political squabble to another, too often from one scandal to another. He finds a shifting leadership of mediocre calibre—varied now and then by flashes of real ability which are snuffed out when the political wheel turns. There is little conception of policing as a profession or as a science to be matured and developed. It is a *job*, held perhaps by the grace of some mysterious political influence, and conducted in an atmosphere sordid and unhealthy.
>
> Instead of confidence and trust, the attitude of the public toward the police is far more often than not one of cynicism and suspicion, expressing itself, occasionally, in violent attacks which are as unjust as they are ineffective. In the interim between these spasms of publicity the average police force sinks in its rut, while crime and violence flourish.

One example of foolish police work occurred in New York on February 24, 1914, when a murdered girl's eyes were photographed in the hope of finding an imprint of the murderer on her sightless eyeballs.

There was widespread agreement that less and less respect was being shown for the law. Why? Louis D. Brandeis thought he knew one answer: People did not respect the law because it did not express their will. "To secure respect for the law," he said, "we must make the law respectable."

Brandeis was talking about individuals, not organized gangsters. In the course of American history criminals had banded together in ethnic groups—Anglo-Saxon desperadoes in the West and Southwest, Irish and Chinese and Jewish gangsters in the big cities. Now some Italians were becoming a menace to society.

Like most immigrants, Italians had come to the new world in quest of freedom and a better standard of living. Most worked long hours at respectable jobs, but a few decided it would be easier to prey on fellow immigrants. New Orleans became the first American city in which Italian gangs rose to power; in 1890 its chief of police was assassinated in front of his house by members of the Mafia, to whom he had traced several crimes. In New York City predominantly Italian neighborhoods formed in the Williamsburg section of Brooklyn and on Manhattan's lower east side, and by the early part of this century hardworking people began receiving extortion threats signed by the Black Hand. This was the menacing symbol of two Italian secret societies, the Mafia of Sicily and the Camorra of Naples.

In 1906 New York was lucky enough to get a truly great police commissioner, Theodore A. Bingham. With a wave of Black Hand violence sweeping across the city, within the police department Bingham created a secret unit called the Italian Squad. It was headed by Detective Lieutenant Joseph Petrosino, who had been born near Naples and as a boy had been chilled by stories about the evil practices of the Camorra and Mafia. Petrosino began compiling dossiers on members of the Italian secret societies transplanted to New York. Then, eager to find evidence of ties between the Mafia of Sicily and New York, he sailed for the island off the tip of the Italian boot. He had taken pains to cover his trail, but one day in 1909 as Petrosino paused in the Piazza Marino in Palermo, two men came up behind him, unhurriedly drew revolvers from their jackets, fired four bullets into his back and head, killing him. Bingham angrily denounced his murder, but when he quit as police commissioner four months later, the department's special Italian Squad was dissolved.

The fifth New York police commissioner to follow Bingham was Arthur Woods, who took office in April, 1914, at an annual salary of $7,500, and one of the first problems to engage his attention was the Black Hand. The 1916 edition of *The American Yearbook* presents a much too optimistic evaluation of the war waged by the new top cop against the Mafia:

> . . . So successful has been the policy adopted of close surveillance and quick arrest of these malefactors on the commission of any crime, no matter how trivial, with the detention of witnesses and the skillful working up of evidence, that in two years the *omerta*, or conspiracy of silence, once the most effective factor in preventing convictions in Italian cases, has practically disappeared from the courts. Respectable Italians now carry complaints of the Black Hand to the police of their own accord. . . .

The yearbook went on to say that the Black Hand had just about been wiped out.

The editor who wrote this piece would have been surprised to learn that more than a half century later the Black Hand, or Mafia, was stronger than ever.

While city residents worried about organized criminals of foreign origin the folks in the West were beset by hard-riding outlaws, many of them native Americans. This latter problem came as a surprise to Bernard M. Baruch, a Wall Street speculator soon to become one of the most powerful men in the nation. In the summer of 1915 Baruch took some relatives and friends to San Francisco to attend the Panama-Pacific International Exposition. On their way back East they visited Yellowstone Park. They were riding in one of several sightseeing stagecoaches when the vehicle ahead of them bucked to an abrupt halt. Baruch leaned out and saw a man wearing a blue mask gesturing with a rifle as the passengers in the coaches ahead tossed their valuables onto the road. The financier was carrying a considerable sum of money, much of it in large denominations. Thinking fast, he threw most of the bills under the seat in front of him, and his wife stashed her pearls there, too. By this time the rifle-brandishing bandit was beneath the windows of their coach, shouting at them, "Chuck! Chuck!" Baruch tossed out a roll of about forty $1 bills. The masked bandit waved them on, but their coach had not gone far before a United States cavalry unit came galloping down the road to their rescue. The whole affair had been such authentic Western lore that in his memoirs the bemused Baruch said he felt he had been watching a Western movie.

Lynchings were so frequent that Brandeis said they showed that criminal law had broken down; he called the American lynching record "a monument of inefficiency." Between 1865 and 1955 more than 5,000 blacks were lynched by white mobs. In the twentieth century the worst year was 1901, when 130 persons were lynched—105 blacks and 25 whites. Most of the white victims were policemen trying to protect black prisoners from white citizens taking the law into their own hands.

In 1914, 45 lynchings resulted in 50 deaths. One of these outrages took place early in the year in Louisiana. K. McKnight, T. Lewis and M. Suden were accused of murdering a postmaster, were denied any kind of trial and were murdered out of hand. One of the three victims was an old black man with an excellent reputation in his neighborhood. There was absolutely no evidence against him. Grabbed by a crowd of enraged whites, he refused to confess to a crime of which he was innocent and was burned at the stake in full view of everyone.

In Texas the Houston *Post* editorialized:

> The conviction is irresistible that the old man who was burned to death had nothing whatever to do with the crime. If he had been guilty, the torture to which he was subjected would have forced a confession and the wonder is that he did not confess, anyhow, in the agony of his roasting flesh as many innocent

> victims have done in the hope of escaping torture. In all probability the guilty murderers of the village postmaster are at large, while the blood of innocents rests upon the hands of those who took it upon themselves to discharge the functions of the law.

The systematic brutalization of prisoners was a commonplace in some prisons across the land. For example, in Beaufort, North Carolina, in the early part of 1914, county authorities authorized the county prison superintendant to "keep in his possession a lash 18 inches long and more than two inches in diameter, and said lash may be split three times one-half way from the end. No convict may be whipped more than once during two consecutive days, and none shall receive more than 25 lashes at more than one whipping."

The plight of prisoners led to some prison reforms.

In January, 1914, Katharine Bement Davis, a sociologist, became the commissioner of corrections in New York City in the reform administration of Mayor Mitchel. She was the first woman in American history to serve in such a capacity. She had a gigantic job, for her jurisdiction embraced fifteen penal institutions handling 125,000 prisoners a year. Shocked by the conditions she found, Miss Davis instituted a series of reforms: abatement of the drug traffic, the segregation and classification of women prisoners, the improvement of prison diets, the expansion of medical facilities, the regrading of prison personnel. She also ordered that prisoners taken from New York City to Sing Sing should go by bus, so they would not have to suffer the shame of being stared at, as happened when they were sent upstate by train.

In December, 1914, Thomas Mott Osborne took office as warden of Sing Sing, and before the end of his career he did more than anyone in Western civilization to improve the treatment of criminals. From the start he began making wholesale changes in the grim penitentiary on the east bank of the Hudson river. He stopped guards from smuggling narcotics to prisoners. He let the convicts decorate their cells with pictures and knicknacks. He gave each man two suits of underwear so one could be washed while the other was being worn. He permitted the prisoners to write more letters than before. He encouraged them to organize their own orchestra and to play baseball. When state officials warned Osborne he was smashing too many rules, he said, "I like to smash rules."

A Harvard graduate, cultured and independently wealthy, a good family man with four sons, Osborne underestimated the cunning of politicians and contractors and others wishing to keep Sing Sing a nest of corruption. In 1915 a Westchester county grand jury accused him of mismanagement and immorality, but Osborne was innocent, there was no evidence, a judge dismissed the charges against him, and his case never came to trial. After resigning as warden of Sing Sing in 1916, he wrote two books, *Society and Prisons* and *Prisons and Common Sense*.

In his first book he described the prison system as "the organized lunacy of the people." One passage read:

> An aching, overwhelming sense of the hideous cruelty of the whole barbaric, brutal business sweeps over me; the feeling of moral, physical and mental outrage; the monumental imbecility of it all; the horrible darkness, the cruel iron walls at our backs; the nerve-wracking routine; the whirring dynamo through the other wall; the filth, the vermin, the bad air; the insufficient food, the denial of water and the overpowering, sickening sense of accumulated misery—of madness and suicide—haunting the place.

One icy afternoon in the spring of 1914 the hostess of a famous bohemian salon on lower Fifth Avenue near Greenwich Village discovered that one of her guests had peyote buttons in his pocket. She was delighted. The idea of almost any new experience appealed to thirty-five-year-old Mabel Dodge, for she felt one should "be alive like fire." Although she had inherited money from her parents and had a wealthy husband, she scorned materialism, considered America ugly, shunned the high society of the Vanderbilts and Astors, abhorred businessmen and surrounded herself with artists. Her salon was perhaps the only one in America that ever matched the intellectual salons of Paris.

Her peyote-carrying guest was Raymond Harrington, whom she was meeting for the first time; he was a cousin of one of her regular guests, Hutchins Hapgood. Harrington was an anthropologist just back from Oklahoma where he had lived with Indians. Looking at his tight face and sunken eyes, she said that while she had never met an Indian, she thought he looked like one, and the others agreed.

"Of course"—Mabel Dodge beamed—"we must all try your peyote. . . ."

Although she was a free spirit she never used drugs and knew nothing of the magnitude of the narcotics problem in this country. According to Edward M. Brecher and the editors of *Consumer Reports*, in a book called *Licit & Illicit Drugs*, "the United States during the nineteenth century could quite properly be described as a "dope fiend's paradise."

In 1900 a well-known pharmaceutical company advertised heroin as a sedative for coughs. In 1903 the *Medical Examiner and Practitioner* published an advertisement saying, "The problem of administering heroin in proper doses in such form as will give the therapeutic virtues of this drug full sway, and will suit the palate of the most exacting adult or the most capricious child, has been solved by the pharmaceutical compound known as Glyco-Heroin." In a Coca-Cola history called *The Big Drink* E. J. Kahn, Jr., wrote, "In its formative days, the drink did contain a minute quantity of cocaine, since this drug was not removed from the coca leaves that constituted a tiny fraction of its makeup, but even before the passage of the Pure Food and Drug Act, in 1906, the last trace of cocaine had gone."

In passing this act, Congress banned the sale of any drug whose label failed to state "the quantity or proportion of any alcohol, morphine, opium, heroin, alpha or beta eucaine, chloroform, cannabis indica, chloral hydrate or acetanilide, or any derivative or preparation of any such substance contained therein." In the decade 1860–69 a total of 21,176 pounds of smoking opium was legally imported into the United States; between 1900 and 1909 importations rose to 148,168 pounds. In 1909 the importation of smoking opium was prohibited. In 1910 William James died; during his lifetime the great American psychologist and philosopher had experimented with mescal.

The first international conference on narcotics met in Shanghai in 1908–09, and the presiding officer was an American, Bishop Charles Brent of the Protestant Episcopal church. He also was chairman of the American delegation to the International Opium Conference held at The Hague in 1911. Out of these sessions came the first international opium agreement.

Dr. Charles B. Towns, an American authority on opiates, wrote in 1912 that "opium smoking is vastly less vicious than morphine-taking." The next year surveys taken in Jacksonville, Florida, and throughout the state of Tennessee showed that white people used more opiates than black people; furthermore, more women than men consumed opiates because of the widespread medical custom of prescribing them for "female troubles."

In 1915 an article in the *Journal of the American Institute of Criminal Law and Criminology* spoke of society women who "indulge in opium to calm their shattered nerves." Despite the ban on the importation of smoking opium, between 1900 and 1914 the per capita consumption of opiates in the United States was eighteen times greater than in Germany.

The 1914 edition of the *World Almanac* published a quarter-page advertisement saying, "MORPHINE . . . If you are a sufferer from the drug habit, write us and we will convince you beyond a shadow of a doubt that you can be cured without suffering, inconvenience or loss of time. Absolute secrecy guaranteed. Thousands of successes and unquestionable testimonials. Address Carney Common Sense Treatment, 565 Lebanon St., Melrose, Mass."

In 1914 the American Public Health Association adopted a resolution declaring that "the use of habit-forming drugs such as opium, cocaine, chloral and similar drugs in this country is increasing with such appalling rapidity as to have assumed the proportions of a national evil." Movie theaters showed two-reel melodramas exposing "cocaine's deadly lure to youth." A sociologist estimated that 60 percent of the children in New York City had tried cocaine or opium. Mrs. William K. Vanderbilt, a Manhattan society leader, launched a campaign against the use of drugs. And in 1914 some American Indian tribes formally adopted the use of peyote as a sacrament in their religious rites.

Peyote, Raymond Harrington told Mabel Dodge and her guests, was nothing to play with. In a grave voice he said that if they tried it they must do so ritualistically, as the Indians did. Only in this way would they be able to transcend ordinary consciousness and perceive a new and higher kind of reality, for the drug had magical qualities. But before they began eating the peyote button, they had to improvise the tools and symbols employed in the Indian ceremony and convert the second-floor salon into a rude temple. Harrington went outdoors and came back carrying a branch of a tree to serve as an arrow. To simulate a campfire, he put a light bulb on the floor and covered it with a red Chinese shawl that Mabel Dodge owned. Then he made a Peyote Path by unrolling a long roll of white paper in a narrow strip along the floor. When all this was done, he suggested that the guests retire to their rooms to wait until it was dark to begin the ceremony.

Mabel Dodge could hardly wait. She was a strange woman, enchanting but not beautiful, inwardly tense but outwardly calm, able to sit still and listen to others. She read enormously and was one of the first Americans to be psychoanalyzed. "I have always been myself," she wrote, "and at the same time someone else; always able to be the other person, feel with him, think his thoughts, see from the angle in which he found himself. This has caused me many inward conflicts, and it has always drawn people to me in the same degree that I flowed out to them and identified myself with them, and it has always made people want to kiss me, to manifest an actual nearness and union, finding it comforting and consolatory. It is the only genius I have ever had but it is enough."

Hapgood had a master's degree from Harvard, had studied at German universities and then taught at Harvard and the University of Chicago. He was a journalist, novelist and essayist, a shambling bearlike man, gentle in manner, distinguished in appearance, with a voice that commanded attention because it was as deep as an organ. With him was his wife, the former Neith Boyce, lithe and beautiful, with pale skin and red hair and green eyes; formerly an editor, she now devoted herself to rearing their four children. Hapgood enjoyed talking endlessly about man's soul—a taste his wife did not share. He felt he should be free to enjoy love affairs with other women but so adored his lovely wife he found no other female physically attractive.

Another guest was Max Eastman. A many-sided man, he was a poet, critic, editor, revolutionary, pagan. A year earlier he had published his first book, a study of the psychology of literature called *The Enjoyment of Poetry*, and it became so popular it went into more than twenty editions. That previous year, as well, he had become editor of the radical magazine *The Masses*. Extremely handsome, Eastman was quick of mind but so slow-speaking and slow-moving that he was known as "the sleepy Adonis." He lived in Greenwich Village not far from Mabel Dodge's home with his wife, the former Ida Rauh, a beautiful woman with an air of perpetual sadness, an advocate of free love, the radical daughter of rich parents. She had converted her husband to Marxism. She was studying law, and later she was admitted to the bar. Ida had accompanied her husband to Mabel's place.

Another guest was Genevieve Onslow, who struck Eastman as being frog-eyed. Slender and brown and tense, she chatted incessantly about mysticism. She had left her rich father to travel alone around the world, and now she had just returned from China. Then there was Robert Edmond Jones, called Bobby, who was to become the most influential artist-designer in the modern American theater. A Harvard graduate *cum laude,* Jones described himself as "violent, passionate, sensual, sadistic, lifted, heated, frozen, transcendental, Poesque." Someone said that "with his red beard he had the look of Jesus starving in the desert."

Also present was a painter, Andrew Dasburg, huge-chested and handsome, with sulky lips and eyes Mabel considered as blue as cornflowers, limping and carrying a cane. Still another was identified by Mabel in her memoir only as Terry, an anarchist, poor and thin and always hungry, with blue Irish eyes and iron gray hair. Mabel regarded Terry as "a splendid talker, a dreamer, a poet, a man. Wonderful Terry!"

At 9 P.M. Mabel and her guests gathered again in her all-white salon. We know much about her peyote party because both she and Eastman wrote about it in detail in their memoirs.

At Harrington's request Mabel had turned off all the lights except for the bulb glowing under her red shawl. They all sat on the floor with the Peyote Path running eastward from their midst. Harrington, who was to enact the role of Indian chief, sat near the fake campfire, the improvised arrow in one hand, some eagle feathers in the other. In a little heap on the floor in front of him was the peyote—"small, dried-up buttons," Mabel thought, "with shrivelled edges, and it had a kind of fur on the upper side." Harrington told them that once they began eating the peyote they must begin to sing, keep on singing, and continue their ceremony until the morning star rose.

He sat cross-legged with his face so grave that suddenly Mabel laughed, but he ignored her and took a peyote button and popped it into his mouth. Chewing hard, he raised his chin and began howling like a dog. He kept his howl on one pitch and continued wailing, increasing the tempo, and as he howled, he gestured to the others to eat the peyote. One after another, they reached out and took a button and nervously put it into their mouth. The taste was so bitter they felt nauseated. As Mabel swallowed, she felt her mouth and limbs go numb and found her mind filled with laughter. Harrington handed the arrow to Hapgood and pantomimed to him to sing; he also signaled the others to take a second button. Hapgood held the arrow stiffly in front of himself and then began his own kind of howl—disjointed and without rhythm. Mabel was so shaken with "ghoulish laughter" that she held her second button in her hand and forgot to eat it. When her mind came together again and she remembered what she was supposed to, she decided she had had enough and slipped the button under her billowing skirt.

Everyone seemed to sit at a great distance from her, as though she were seeing them through the wrong end of a telescope, and all struck her as appearing ridiculous. Bobby Jones resembled a Persian miniature, Hapgood looked like a Lutheran monk, Genevieve's big eyes were enormous as she stared at a spot on the rug, and Terry was hypnotized by the glowing end of his cigarette and seemed to swell into enormous size. In the glow of the bulb under the red shawl everyone's face, Mabel felt, underwent strange changes like a kaleidoscope held to one eye and twirled. As the night wore on the mood became ever more peculiar, with everyone chanting or singing, sounding outlandish, and at last Mabel arose and nodded toward the bedrooms, and they understood her and the party broke up.

As Max and Ida Eastman left, he spat the bitter dose of peyote onto the snowy street, and then he and his wife walked the short distance to their home and went to bed. Later he rose to consciousness out of swirling dreams and realized he was hearing a pounding on his door and someone screaming, "Ida! Ida!" Opening the front door, he found Genevieve clad only in a nightgown and fur coat, so chilled she shook like a harp string, raving mad. The Eastmans welcomed her and put her to bed and piled blankets on her and tried to "call her gibbering mind back to reality," as Eastman phrased it. He was so worried he telephoned Herman Lorber, a physician who was a friend to many artists in Greenwich Village. The doctor told him to go to a drugstore and buy a certain sedative, give it to the girl and then take her back to Mabel's place in the morning.

When the Eastmans and Genevieve arrived in the salon, it looked to them like a den of wild animals. Hapgood was pacing back and forth, and as dawn crept through the windows, he stopped to speak to Mabel; she thought he looked shrunken and awe-stricken. Hapgood cried, "Mabel! I have learned something wonderful! I cannot put it into words exactly, but I have found the short-cut to the soul!"

"What is it?"

"The death of the flesh! I *saw* it! I saw the death of the flesh occur in my body and I saw the soul emerge from that death."

His wife smiled a strange and beautiful smile and said, "I saw no such thing. . . . As I sat there, I saw the walls of this house fall away and I was following a lovely river for miles and miles through the most wonderful virginal forest I have ever known—"

Dasburg interrupted, saying, "I saw what sex is—and it is a square crystal cube, transparent and colorless, and at the same time I saw that I was looking at my soul!"

Harrington sprang to his feet. In the dim light his face looked green and his eyes were filled with terror. "I can't breathe! . . . My heart! . . . Get me something! Some fruit—"

Mabel ran to the kitchen for an orange, and when she returned, she found Hapgood bending over Harrington, who had sunk to the floor and now sat with his hands covering his face, his body wracked with convulsions. "You don't know what you did to me," Harrington muttered to Dasburg—who had done nothing to him. Dasburg reacted as though he *had* done something to Harrington, mumbling over and over, "I *had* to do it!"

Mabel, who had felt a pang of fear when she learned that Genevieve had slipped out of her house, was grateful that the Eastmans had brought her back. But her relief tightened into anxiety as she watched the girl: "Genevieve was just gibbering. She was making curious rapid movements, her eyes rolled in her head, she ran with dreadful haste into her room, Neith and Ida and I after her." Holding two Chinese slippers to her breast, Genevieve babbled with white lips that she wanted to see her father, because she had something to tell him.

When Dr. Lorber arrived, he was led to Genevieve. Seemingly unaware of his presence, she held the slippers and stared at a corner. He walked back and into the salon and snorted, "Dope—hey?"

Hapgood confessed that all of them had eaten peyote. The doctor said he had never heard of it but wondered whether it was like mescal. He returned to Genevieve, gave her some medicine, told Mabel she was so sick she needed a nurse and warned Mabel not to let Genevieve out of her sight. The sick girl let herself be led back into the salon, sank down onto a chaise lounge, stared out a window and wept.

The doctor walked over to Terry, whom he knew, and spoke to him. For the first time since eating the peyote Terry smiled—a smile Mabel considered "illuminated." Terry blurted, "I have seen the universe and man! It is wonderful!" Then he put on his hat and coat and left, and that was the last Mabel ever saw of him.

A nurse came for Genevieve and took her away, and Mabel never saw her again, either, for the poor woman spent the next several years in a mental institution. In the slang of a generation yet unborn, Genevieve had freaked out on dope. But none of the others suffered any lasting effect,

Mabel was terrified. "What bothered me most was that I should be personally acquainted with a situation that was ambiguous enough to deserve, even at any angle, the name of a 'Dope Party.' Horrors! I had heard of such gatherings and they were the antithesis of all I wished to stand for. The level of my life, at least in my own eyes, was infinitely raised above such sordid sensationalism. The very word 'dope' annoyed me, and seemed to cling to me like pitch."

No reporter learned about her peyote party, but that spring of 1914 the New York *Times* published articles about men and women arrested for selling heroin and cocaine, about a dealer who sold drugs to children, about a cocaine peddler being shot and then arrested, about the apprehension of dope smugglers, about raids on homes containing cocaine, about the passage of a New York state law controlling narcotics.

One of the richest women in the world, Evalyn Walsh McLean, was at that time breaking herself of her morphine addiction. Her father had been enormously rich and she had married another wealthy man, Ned McLean, son of the owner of the Washington *Post* and *Cincinnati Enquirer.* He was so neurotic and alcoholic that the McLeans were forever fighting and making up. In the northwestern part of the District of Columbia they built a mansion costing $835,000 and named Friendship, where they entertained Cabinet members and Supreme Court justices, Senators and Representatives, lords and ladies, journalists and lobbyists.

Mrs. McLean paid $154,000 for the Hope Diamond reputed to bring ill luck—and of this she had plenty. An auto accident killed her younger brother and injured her so severely that she had to have an operation which left one of her legs shorter than before. Never comfortable with herself, deeply disturbed, loathing boredom, she was frenetic in her pursuit of pleasure and got hooked on morphine. In her autobiography she wrote in detail about obtaining morphine from drugstores, hiding it here and there in her home, taking the drug and then suffering terrifying hallucinations thick with the shapes of evil beasts.

Evalyn Walsh McLean managed to cure herself of her drug habit, but thousands of other Americans agonized over their addiction, frequenting an underground drug world which concerned scientists called a national evil.

Chapter 9

WILSON AND THE BLACKS

Black voters had had difficulty trying to decide which of the three candidates they preferred in the Presidential election of 1912: William Howard Taft, Theodore Roosevelt or Woodrow Wilson.

Taft, during his term in the White House, had refused to appoint blacks to federal offices in the South. Roosevelt had braved criticism by dining with black educator Booker T. Washington in the White House, but he had annoyed blacks by his summary dismissal of black soldiers after the 1906 riot in Brownsville, Texas, and now he was trying to lure Southern Democrats into his Progressive ranks by organizing a lily-white party apparatus in the South. Wilson, as most of the nation's 10,000,000 blacks very well knew, had been born in Virginia, his wife in Georgia, and when he was president of Princeton, that university had banned black students. Nonetheless, Wilson wooed the black vote during the 1912 campaign, telling J. Milton Waldron that he sought their support. Waldron was president of the Washington branch of the National Association for the Advancement of Colored People and also leader of a black Democratic club in the District of Columbia. Wilson told Waldron there was nothing to fear from a Democratic Congress because when he became President, he would veto hostile legislation, administer the laws impartially and would not exclude blacks from office on the basis of color.

American blacks had two outstanding leaders, Booker T. Washington and W. E. B. Du Bois, but they were often at odds. Washington, the president of Tuskegee Institute in Tuskegee, Alabama, advocated "dependence, and through compromise, an emergence into an economic, social and cultural stability never quite equal to the white man's." Du Bois, on the other hand, was a sociologist and writer who urged instead "a fight to obtain without compromise such rights and privileges as belonged to members of the civilization of which he was a part." Washington came out for the Democratic candidate, saying, "Mr. Wilson is in favor of the things which tend toward the uplift, improvement, and advancement of my people, and at his hands we have nothing to fear." Other black leaders and some white spokesmen for their cause worked hard for Wilson, helping him win the largest number of black votes ever obtained up to that time by any Democratic Presidential candidate. After Wilson's election and a month before his inauguration, a black leader in

Washington, D.C., wrote, "From the training, high character and Christian sentiment expressed by President-elect Wilson, before and since his election, I see an open door of hope for the negro."

But the blacks were doomed to quick disappointment. Soon the South Carolina governor, Coleman L. Blease, evoked wild applause when he shouted, "Whenever the Constitution comes between me and the virtue of the white women of the South, I say to hell with the Constitution!" At the first Congressional session after Wilson took office there was introduced a rash of bills designed to end the immigration of blacks from the West Indies, to prohibit blacks from holding commissions in the armed forces, to segregate blacks on civil service rolls and the like. Wilson, the first Southern-born President since the Civil War, was characteristically Southern in his attitude toward blacks—fond of them but paternalistic. Furthermore, his Cabinet was weighted with Southerners and Westerners who shared his view of race relations.

The two federal departments with the most black workers when Wilson took office were the post office and treasury departments. The post office was run by Postmaster General Albert S. Burleson, born in Texas the son of a major in the Confederate army, while the treasury was administered by Treasury Secretary William Gibbs McAdoo, who had been born in Georgia the son of a man who had been attorney general of Tennessee; a liberal white editor said sarcastically that McAdoo's only fear was that Wilson would become too friendly with "colored people." At a Cabinet meeting a month after Wilson became President, Burleson raised the question of segregation, complaining that friction occurred whenever white and black railway mail clerks worked in the same car. Announcing he had conferred with black leaders who agreed with him, Burleson declared that segregation was best for the black man and for the postal service itself. No Cabinet member objected to the fact that Burleson was about to rob some black Americans of part of their civil liberties. Wilson remarked that he had made the blacks no particular promises, except to do them justice, and hoped the matter could be taken care of in a way that would cause the least friction.

Neither the President nor any of his Cabinet members publicly announced they had adopted a policy of segregation, but segregation nonetheless soon became an established fact in the post office department's shops and rest rooms and lunchrooms; in the treasury offices, in the bureau of printing and engraving, and in the census bureau. According to the black press, Mrs. Wilson had become upset when she visited some departments and found white and black clerks lunching in the same room. Whether this was true or false, it was common knowledge that the President's wife worked tirelessly to alleviate living conditions among the district's 96,000 black residents—one-third of the population of the capital—and especially among those who existed in wretched back alleys. As for segregation in government offices, Wilson himself said there was a social line of cleavage which unfortunately corresponded with a racial line. Burleson and McAdoo discharged black political appointees in the South and let local postmasters and collectors of internal revenue demote or dismiss black civil service workers. Supposedly, these civil service employees were under the protection of the Civil Service

Commission. In Atlanta the new federal collector of internal revenue said, "A Negro's place is in the cornfield."

Blacks and white liberals reacted with surprise, disappointment and anger. Oswald Garrison Villard, a white editor and author, criticized McAdoo. The treasury secretary protested that he was without prejudice but revealed himself by adding, "I shall not be a party to the enforced and unwelcome juxtaposition of white and Negro employees when it is unnecessary and avoidable without injustice to anyone." The editor of the New York *Amsterdam News* wrote, "When the Wilson Administration came into power . . . it promised a 'new freedom' to all the people, avowing the spirit of Christian democracy. But on the contrary we are given a stone instead of a loaf of bread; we are given a hissing serpent rather than a fish." Booker T. Washington, totally disillusioned, wrote, "I have recently spent several days in Washington, and I have never seen the colored people so discouraged and bitter as they are at the present time."

These reactions surprised and disturbed Wilson. He told Villard segregation had been initiated at the suggestion of the heads of several departments and approved by influential blacks in the hope of reducing friction in federal agencies. He declared that this policy was not to be misconstrued as an attack upon blacks since he considered segregation beneficial to them.

On September 4, 1913, the Reverend Howard A. Bridgman wrote Wilson a letter complaining about the way the federal government was treating blacks. Bridgman was a Congregational minister, an educator, author and Republican. Four days after receiving this letter and fifty-one years after Lincoln's Emancipation Proclamation, Wilson wrote:

> In reply to your kind letter of September fourth, I would say that I do approve of the segregation that is being attempted in several of the departments. I have not always approved of the way in which the thing was done and have tried to change that in some instances for the better, but I think if you were here on the ground you would see, as I seem to see, that it is distinctly to the advantage of the colored people themselves that they should be organized, so far as possible and convenient, in distinct bureaux where they will center their work. Some of the most thoughtful colored men I have conversed with have themselves approved of this policy. I certainly myself would not have approved of it if I had not thought it to their advantage and likely to remove many of the difficulties which have surrounded the appointment and advancement of colored men and women. . . .

Villard, a grandson of abolitionist William Lloyd Garrison, was publisher of *The Nation* magazine and the New York *Evening Post*. His prestige, together with the fact that he had helped elect Wilson, enabled him to keep in touch with the President. Villard urged Wilson to name fifteen eminent whites and blacks to a privately financed National Race Commission to conduct "a non-partisan, scientific study of the status of the Negro in the life of the nation." The idea for the commission had come from a Southerner, R. H. Leavell, associate professor of economics at the Agricultural and Mechanical College in Texas. At first Wilson seemed to welcome Villard's suggestion, but with the passage of time he decided against it. Too embarrassed to tell Villard in person, the President wrote to say he was helpless because of the attitude of certain Senators, not only those from the South but also others from different parts of the country. While Wilson was not so helpless as he said he was, antiblack sentiment and legislation were not confined to the South. Dr. Charles W. Eliot, president-emeritus of Harvard, told Villard he believed in the social separateness of blacks because in a democracy "civilized white men" would not be comfortable living beside "barbarous black men."

If the President had cared enough to delve into the facts, he would have learned that the black population was growing at a much slower rate than the whites because many blacks lived in poverty, had a high rate of infant mortality, suffered from malnutrition, had a higher death rate than whites. Ever since 1877, when the North abandoned Reconstruction after the South promised to protect the constitutional rights of blacks, the blacks had been disadvantaged. Many could not vote because of the so-called grandfather clause in the constitutions of several Southern states. In general, these grandfather clauses waived certain voting requirements, provided that the citizen's grandfather had had the right to vote at the time of the Civil War; since almost no blacks had been allowed to vote in the South during that war, this trick disenfranchised many blacks.

State laws, backed by court decisions, restricted marriage between blacks and whites, prohibited the two races from attending the same schools, forbade them to ride in the same public vehicles or ordered the blacks to sit in restricted areas of these conveyances. These were called Jim Crow laws after a song of that name introduced in 1830 by Thomas Rice. In 1912 the Louisiana supreme court modified one such law by ruling that blacks might not be put off streetcars reserved for whites if there were no seats in the cars set aside for blacks. In 1915 in Washington the House approved a bill banning the marriage of white persons and persons with one-eighth or more of "Negro blood"; it was never considered by the Senate.

In 1915 the Alabama supreme court of appeals decided a strange case: A white sheriff was taking a black prisoner to jail on a train. This posed a problem, for if the sheriff kept his prisoner with him in a car reserved for whites, the law officer would get into trouble. On the other hand, if he took the black felon into the train's Jim Crow car, filled with other blacks, they might help the prisoner escape, and then the sheriff would be in another kind of trouble. He compromised by leading his handcuffed prisoner into a smoking compartment for whites, only to have the conductor eject them both. After the disgruntled sheriff finally got his prisoner safely inside jail, he sued the Mobile Railway Company. When the case was tried, the sheriff won. However, the railroad appealed. When the matter reached the highest court in Alabama, four of its seven judges held that the conductor had been within his rights in ejecting the sheriff and prisoner and that the white officer had not been denied the equal protection of the law. But the majority said nothing about granting the equal protection of the law to the black prisoner.

Conditions became so bad that in 1910 the National Association for the Advancement of Colored People was founded in New York, and by 1914 it had more than 6,000 members in its fifty branches. Booker T. Washington established the National Negro Business League; in 1914 there were 40,000 Negro business concerns in the nation. One of the most interesting of the black business leaders was Mrs. C. J. Walker. When she was a laundress in St. Louis in about 1905, she concocted a preparation that allegedly would straighten the hair of black women. The laundress blossomed into a cosmetician, moved to Indianapolis, where she established a factory and laboratories to produce cosmetics, opened a training school for her beauty culturists and agents. Eventually she settled in New York, where she publicized herself as "Madame C. J. Walker of New York and Paris," and when she died in 1919, she left an estate worth more than $1,000,000.

One of the nation's most popular blacks in the early part of this century was Bert Williams, a comedian and songwriter. Born in the Bahamas, with one white grandfather whose wife was an octoroon, Williams had skin so light that when he began working in a minstrel show in California, he had to blacken his face with burned cork. Then he teamed up with another black man named George Walker, the two appearing in vaudeville and finally reaching New York in 1896. After Walker's death Williams became a single and shot to stardom in the *Ziegfeld Follies*. He had a sad rich bass voice, and although in real life he was intelligent and industrious, onstage he pretended to be stupid, a melancholy victim of hard luck and a world too difficult to understand. He was the first black to star in a film, *Darktown Jubilee*, but despite his talent and fame, his image on the silver screen evoked hisses, catcalls, boos and boycotts. The movie even triggered a Brooklyn race riot that took the lives of two men. That was in 1914. Never again did Bert Williams appear in any motion picture.

A special hero to black people was John Arthur Johnson, better known as Jack Johnson, a prizefighter six feet one inch tall and weighing between 205 and 220 pounds in his prime. A native of Galveston, Texas, he went to Sydney, Australia, in 1908 to take on the world's heavyweight champion, a Canadian named Tommy Burns, pounding Burns so savagely that cops stopped the bout in the fourteenth round. John claimed this made him the world's champion. Fond of luxury and women, Johnson angered many whites by traveling with an entourage of flagrantly blond white women, and then by marrying three white women. In the ring he seemed so invincible that white supremicists yearned for a "Great White Hope" to put the black boxer in his place. But Jack Johnson won undisputed claim to the title by knocking out Jim Jeffries in Reno, Nevada, on July 4,1910, and when this news spread across the nation, when it became known that a black man had taken the symbol of physical supremacy from the white race, rejoicing blacks began a celebration that turned into disturbances that churned into riots across the country that resulted in the deaths of a couple of dozen people. Freewheeling life-loving Jack Johnson continued to offend white bigots until April 5, 1915, when white pugilist Jess Willard knocked him out in twenty-six rounds in Havana, Cuba.

Herbert Bayard Swope of the New York *World* went to Havana to cover this championship match and then wrote a 4,000-word story with racial overtones unthinkable in time to come. In part, Swope said:

> . . . John Brown was a friend of the negro. He came from Ossawatomie, Kansas, and operated about fifty-five years ago. Jess Willard comes from old John Brown's stamping ground, hailing from Pottowatomie, Kansas, but he certainly had no love for the colored brother in his heart, judging from the way he tore after Johnson this afternoon, and never in the history of the ring, which stretches back hundreds of years, was there such a wildly, hysterically, shriekingly, enthusiastic crowd as the fourteen thousand men and women who begged Willard to wipe out the stigma that they and hundreds of thousands of others, especially in the South, believe rested on the white race through a negro holding the championship.

The year Johnson lost was the year in which Booker T. Washington died. To black intellectuals, Washington's career as an educator was more important than Johnson's career as a fighter. Born on a Virginia plantation in 1856, Washington was so poor he never slept in a bed until after his family and other blacks were freed from slavery by the Emancipation Proclamation. Soon after that historic event the Washington family moved to Malden near Charleston, West Virginia, where not a single black could read or write. After laboring in a local salt furnace, young Booker spent three years in a school intended to overcome black illiteracy, paying his way by working as a janitor, waiter and brickmason. In 1881 some Southern white men opened a black normal school called Tuskegee Institute in Tuskegee, Alabama, and chose Washington to run it. Intelligent and ambitious, reading the Bible daily and speaking with something of the majesty of its style, he administered this institution for the next thirty-four years. He developed into the nation's preeminent black educator and the greatest black leader since Frederick Douglass. Harvard gave him an honorary degree, Teddy Roosevelt entertained him in the White House, and other honors rained down upon this man born of a slave. Sincere and natural, gentle and humorous, Washington once said, "No man, black or white, from North or South, shall drag me down so low as to make me hate him." With his death on November 14, 1915, American blacks were left without a spokesman respected by a majority of all Americans. W. E. B. Du Bois, who was never quite able to take his place, nonetheless criticized Washington, saying, "In stern justice we must lay to the soul of this man a heavy responsibility for the consummation of Negro disfranchisement, the decline of the Negro college and public school, and the firmer establishment of color caste in this land."

Washington had died with a heavy heart because of what was happening to his race in the District of Columbia under the Wilson administration. One Cabinet member who had failed to speak out against segregation was Navy Secretary Josephus Daniels, born in North Carolina and the son of a man who built ships for the Confederacy during the Civil War. His assistant, Franklin D. Roosevelt of New York, employed white servants in the house he used in Washington. One day while visiting the Roosevelt home Daniels rebuked Mrs. Roosevelt, saying, "Negroes are meant to be servants, and not white people." Eleanor Roosevelt had trouble restraining herself from making a sharp retort to her husband's boss.

Black discontent was expressed in protest rallies, speeches and petitions. One petition with 20,000 signatures was taken to the White House by leaders of the National Independence Equal Rights League, who protested against the discrimination practiced against blacks in the federal service. The group's spokesman was William Monroe Trotter, a black editor and intellectual who had feuded with the National Association for the Advancement of Colored People when some of its leaders had urged the election of Wilson. Now, face to face with the President, Trotter complained about the administration's treatment of blacks. Wilson replied that "segregation is not humiliating but a benefit, and ought to be so regarded by you gentlemen." Giving no ground, Trotter pointed out that during the preceding fifty years blacks and whites had worked side-by-side in federal jobs without friction. Wilson made a sharp reply. Trotter launched into a long speech criticizing the President and threatening to vote against him and all other Democrats. Wilson lost his temper. Cuttingly he accused Trotter of trying to blackmail him and threatened "if this organization is ever to have another hearing before me, it must have another spokesman. . . . Your manner offends me!" This confrontation ended with the President ordering the black leader out of the White House.

D. W. Griffith boarded a train in New York one February day in 1914 to head for Los Angeles, where he intended to produce the world's greatest motion picture. A film director for six years, now thirty-nine years old, Griffith considered himself a genius. This opinion was beginning to be shared by the actors and technicians who accompanied him to the West coast, for they marveled at his cinematic innovations and his sensitive handling of players. A tall, rangy Southerner who looked like a cowboy, Griffith had pale eyes and a hawklike nose, lordly features, a long chin and wide mouth, and he radiated charm and authority. While few mortals ever realize their dreams, he did exactly this when he finished directing and producing *The Birth of a Nation*.

In many ways it *was* the world's greatest motion picture. It was the first twelve-reel film to be produced. It revolutionized the art of filmmaking. It was the first that fully exploited the technique of editing. It left its mark on moviemakers in other countries. It was seen by more people than perhaps any other film in history. It was the first movie to be taken seriously by the intelligentsia. It challenged the supremacy of the stage. It was the first film to be premiered in Los Angeles. It raised the price of admissions to movie theaters. It set new styles in fashion. It was the first motion picture ever shown in the White House. It involved the President of the United States and the chief justice of the Supreme Court in a controversy. It caused the passage of new censorship laws. It triggered riots and arrests, lawsuits and intrigues. It made several millionaires. It launched Louis B. Mayer on his fabulous movie career. It was one of the most vicious pieces of antiblack propagands ever produced. It revived the Ku Klux Klan. It was still being shown sixty years after it was made. It was *The Birth of a Nation*, and it remains a subject of endless dispute.

David Wark Griffith was born on January 22, 1875, in La Grange, Kentucky. His father was Jacob Wark Griffith, a former colonel in the Confederate army and a two-term member of the Kentucky legislature, a hard-drinking, loud-talking romantic who paid little attention to his farm because he liked to spend his time in taverns recounting his battle experiences and extolling the glory of the South before the War Between the States. His alcoholic and blustering behavior won him the nickname of "Roaring Jake." The father died when the boy was only seven. D. W. Griffith, who idolized his father, apparently never questioned any of the stories he heard as a child. The widowed mother moved the family to Louisville, where she opened a boardinghouse which failed to prosper, so young Griffith had to drop out of high school to take one odd job after another. After appearing in an amateur show in a Baptist church he became stagestruck; his mother never took this seriously. He ushered in a theater, clerked in a bookstore until he was fired for reading on the job, was hired as an actor by a stock company performing *Faust* in Louisville. He left to tour with the company, endured the poverty and misadventures common to most young men in the theater, finally decided to become a dramatist.

He wrote a play called *A Fool and a Girl*, which opened September 30, 1907, in Washington, D.C., and closed in a week. Griffith then switched from the stage to movies, which were just becoming popular, trying to sell scripts to production companies. Later in 1907 he wrote a scenario based on *Tosca*, which he offered to Edwin S. Porter of the Edison Company. Porter rejected his scenario but hired the handsome young man to play the leading role in a film called *Rescued from an Eagle's Nest*. After that Griffith was able to sell scripts to the Biograph Company, which also employed him as an actor. In 1908 the Biograph director, Wallace "Old Man" McCutcheon, became sick and Griffith took his place. Never having thought about becoming a movie director, Griffith had qualms at first, telling his wife, "Now if I take this picture—directing over and fall down, then, you see, I'll be out of my acting job." At last he elected to risk it—and risked a great deal, for in directing his first film, *The Adventures of Dollie*, he broke most of the established cinematic rules and shot the entire picture in only two days.

In those pioneering days of the motion-picture industry, films were short, crude, and made solely for entertainment. The standard movie consisted of a single reel 1,000 feet long. In 1909 Griffith produced an average of three films a week for Biograph. But he rebelled at the speed, at the artistic limitations of short films, at the idea that a motion picture had to conform to stage standards. Other movie directors failed to understand that the cinema was a new art form calling for techniques unknown in the legitimate theater. Each scene in a movie was filmed like a scene in a play, the camera grinding from one fixed position as the actors walked onto the set, performed, then exited. Directors stuck to medium-length shots, obeying the dictum of Charles Pathé: "Will you gentlemen never learn that in the cinema an actor must be photographed so that his feet touch the bottom of the screen and his head at the top?"

Why? Griffith asked himself. He began improvising, moving the camera while the action was proceeding, taking close-ups to reveal subtle expressions on a player's face, coaching his actors to shun the heroic gestures common to stage actors, shooting extremely long shots of lovely landscapes, sustaining the suspense of the drama, experimenting with backlighting, photographing at night, inventing the fade-in and fade-out, the iris effect, watching the action from both high and low angles, making radical experiments in the cutting and editing of his films. Terry Ramsaye, the film historian, has said that although Griffith did not provide a whole new cinematic vocabulary, he gave the screen its syntax. Charlie Chaplin said, "The whole industry owes its existence to Mr. Griffith."

Having tested his wings and finding they bore him to new artistic heights, Griffith became increasingly annoyed with one-reel films, and whenever he began a new one, he snarled that he was "grinding out another sausage!" By 1911 he had persuaded reluctant Biograph officials to let him make two-reel movies, but even these had a playing time of only two minutes. Two years later he took a company of players to California because of its abundant sunshine and because it was far from the heavy hands of studio executives. Secretly, there on the West coast, he began the production of a film called *Judith of Bethulia*, which was to be four reels long and sexy. Anita Loos, a proper young lady just breaking into the movie industry as a scenario writer, visited Griffith on the lot and was shocked to see him filming dancing girls "wearing little more than beads, their faces dead white, with black smudged eyes and violent red lipstick."

While Griffith was working in California, he was dismayed to read in a trade paper that a director named Enrico Guazzoni had shot a nine-reel film in Italy called *Quo Vadis?* It had an arena scene costing $10,000 and showing 900 actors and extras. *Quo Vadis?* opened on April 21, 1913, in New York's Astor theater on Broadway at a top of $1.50. Among other things, this Italian film had a nude girl on the back of a bull, which helps explain why it played on Broadway for twenty-two weeks. While this nine-reel movie proved Griffith's contention that longer films could and should be made, he felt hurt at the thought of an Italian company's getting the jump on him. After he returned to New York, a Biograph executive told him, "The time has come for the production of big fifty thousand dollar pictures. You are the man to make them. But Biograph is not ready to go into that line of production. If you stay with Biograph, it will be to make the same kind of short pictures that you have in the past." Disgusted, Griffith quit.

Harry E. Aitken, a film distributor branching out into production, offered to form a new company called Mutual Film Corporation to give

Griffith his chance. Under this arrangement, Griffith would get a budget of $5,000 for each four- or five-reel picture he produced for Aitken, with the option of producing two independent films a year. Accepting, Griffith persuaded many actors and technicians to leave the Biograph studio and let him lead them into greener pastures. One was Frank Woods, called Daddy by his colleagues because of his mop of white hair; Woods was one of the industry's first scenario writers. Griffith made Woods the head of his new scenario department, and before long the story editor urged Griffith to make a movie of a novel written by Thomas Dixon, Jr., whose name Griffith already knew.

Dixon and Griffith had much in common: Both were born in the South; both romanticized it; both worshiped their fathers. Dixon was born in 1864 in Shelby, North Carolina, the son of a Baptist minister who had been one of the founders of the original Ku Klux Klan. Dixon's first story, written when he was in his teens and published in a college magazine, had to do with the Klan. Winning a law degree in 1885, Dixon was elected to the North Carolina legislature when he was only twenty—too young to vote. He served only briefly, resigned to practice law, then abandoned his legal career to become a Baptist preacher like his father. After serving two congregations in his native state, he took charge of a church in Boston and then accepted a call from the People's Temple in New York City. Magnetic and eloquent, Dixon attracted the largest congregation of any Protestant preacher in the country at that time; but he also tended to be sensational, and once he was indicted for slander. Seeking an even larger audience, he quit the ministry in 1899, lectured for four years, finally began writing novels.

A professional Southerner, savagely antiblack, eager to avenge the "Lost Cause" and defend the moribund Klan, Dixon lightly described himself as "a reactionary individualist." In 1902 he wrote a novel called *The Leopard's Spots* in which he tried to show what would happen if the black man were "lifted above his station"; it sold 100,000 copies during the first year of publication. The following year he produced *The One Woman: A Story of Modern Utopia*, which also became a best seller. It dealt with a crusading clergyman of philandering tendencies who becomes involved in a murder trial. (Griffith, during his brief career as an actor, had been hired and then fired as the leading man in the movie version of this Dixon novel.) In 1905, in the interest of "racial purity," Dixon published his third novel, *The Clansman: An Historical Romance of the Ku Klux Klan*. It depicted Klansmen as a band of dedicated knights rooting out an intolerable menace. A reviewer for the Boston *Literary World* said of Dixon, ". . . He loves to tell his story as he wishes it told, and his style, melodramatic, strained, uneven though it be, is yet strong and vital in parts." *The Clansman* sold well as a novel, became a stage play performed by stock companies, was filmed as a movie on a site near New Orleans. However, owing to legal snarls about the screen adaptation, the film version was never seen by the public. Dixon, who had followed Griffith's career from afar, now had produced another screen treatment of *The Clansman*, which Woods showed to the famous director.

Griffith caught fire. He felt the story was precisely the one he needed to film the greatest movie the world had ever seen. Epic in scope, it spanned the five years before the Civil War, the war itself, then Reconstruction. Teeming with action, it had battlefield scenes and ghostly night-riding Klansmen. It also appealed to Griffith because it concerned a Confederate colonel who came back from war to find his beloved South had been changed beyond recognition. When he was a child, this was the very thing he heard from the lips of his own father. Griffith asked Aitken to buy Dixon's scenario. The former minister wanted $10,000 for his script. Aitken did not have that much money. Aitken persuaded Dixon to accept a $2,500 check and a promise of a share in the movie's profits.

Billy Bitzer, a cameraman who had quit Biograph to work for Griffith, did not share the director's enthusiasm for *The Clansman*, saying, "I had read the book and figured that a Negro chasing a white girl was just another sausage, after all, and how would you show it in the South?" Lillian Gish, an unknown actress whom Griffith discovered and then cast as the heroine of his film, also had reservations; she feared that the story's racial episodes might cause trouble in the future. But Griffith could not be dissuaded. In their book called *The Movies*, Richard Griffith and Arthur Mayer quoted Miss Gish: "As the son of 'Roaring Jake' Griffith, he firmly believed that the truth of the Civil War and Reconstruction had never been told, and he was quite ready to tell, through this new medium of the silent screen, the story he believed in above all else in the world."

Seeking to outdo *Quo Vadis?*, Griffith decided to make a twelve-reel film with a playing time of two and three-quarter hours. Aitken set his budget at $40,000. Griffith chose other unknown actors for leading roles, held a few readings in New York, then entrained with his players and technicians for Los Angeles. There he conducted long rehearsals, hired hundreds of extras, collected equipment and props, oversaw construction of indoor sets in the Kinemacolor studio at 4500 Sunset Boulevard.

Assisted by Karl Brown, Bitzer shot the entire movie with just one camera, a hand-cranked Pathé, at speeds of twelve to eighteen frames per second. Griffith did not stick closely to Dixon's script; in fact, he regarded every script as only an outline, and worked from notes on his own ideas of how each scene should be played. Into *The Clansman* he wove episodes from Dixon's other novel, *The Leopard's Spots*. He could be accurate, as when he settled a dispute among his actors about the horse ridden by General Robert E. Lee, telling them it was an iron-gray charger named Traveller. But he also was inaccurate, overlooking the fact that the Klan had run its course before Southern blacks won power in state legislatures.

Shooting began on July 4, 1914. Interiors were filmed in the Sunset Boulevard studio, battle scenes at an outdoor site that later became the property of Universal, plantation scenes in the cotton fields of Calexico in southern California. The summer was so hot that Griffith shaved his head and wore a floppy straw hat with holes cut in it. A month after production began the war broke out in Europe, compounding Griffith's problems. Horses were so much in demand by the Allied armies that the best ones were sold abroad, leaving Griffith with nags, for the most part, except for the horse resembling Lee's famous Traveller. Cotton is used to make explosives, so Griffith had trouble getting all he needed to manufacture the white robes worn by marauding Klansmen in the picture. The director hired some blacks as extras, but since California had few experienced black actors, he had burned cork applied to the faces of white actors to make them look like blacks.

Billy Bitzer was a cameraman of great imagination and daring. Wishing to give the movie the tone and texture of Mathew Brady's historic photographs, he obtained a collection of Brady prints from a gullible librarian by giving her a box of chocolates. Griffith wanted close-ups of the flying hooves of the cavalry horses and the steeds ridden by the Klansmen, so Bitzer sprawled on the earth as the horsemen galloped up in clouds of dust, hoping he could roll out of the way in time if an iron shoe slashed down near his head. During one take Griffith saw that his cameraman was in danger and dashed into the center of the action, waving and yelling to divert the horses. Bitzer was not hurt that time, but later a horse kicked in the side of his wooden camera; soon it was repaired with tape and shooting resumed. Griffith had hired fireworks experts to shoot off smoke bombs for battle scenes, but most exploded outside and above camera range. "Lower!" he yelled. "Lower! Can't you shoot those damn bombs lower?" One fireworks technician yelled back, "We'll hit the cameraman if we do!" But he and the other experts began aiming the bombs closer until—*Bang!* One whizzed past Bitzer's ear. The next one slashed between his legs and peppered the skin of his hands with blue powder marks that remained the rest of his life.

These special effects, the salaries of hundreds of extras, the cost of buying the horses and feeding them, the cotton and uniforms and meals and everything else needed for the movie, soon took Griffith over his $40,000 budget. Aitken managed to raise another $20,000, but after that he could find no businessman willing to risk capital in a venture they were unable to understand. Production was halted from time to time to enable Griffith and Aitken to try to find other sources of investment money, which now came principally from small tradesmen and even from optimistic members of the cast. By the time the last scene had been filmed *The Clansman* had cost $110,000—an astronomical sum for a motion picture in those days.

Griffith spent the next three months cutting his film, editing it, arranging for subtitles and supervising its musical score. Having a special interest in music to be used as a background for the silent screen, he worked closely with composer Carl Breil. Although they supplied a couple of new tunes, most of the score consisted of black spirituals, along with passages from such classics as Wagner's *The Ride of the Valkyries* for scenes showing galloping Klansmen. The arrangement was scored for thirty-piece orchestras such as were to be found in big cities, although in small towns each movie house had but one lonely pianist thumping out the music.

By 1915 motion pictures had become so popular that there were 17,000 movie theaters in the nation, more than 900 of them in New York City alone. New theaters were being built and legitimate playhouses were installing screens to show films. Every day 5,000,000 people paid a total of $1,000,000 to see movies that ran much longer than the one-reelers they had enjoyed during the previous seven years or so. The beginning of the end of the nickelodeons came on April 11, 1914, with the opening of the Strand theater in Manhattan on the northwest corner of Broadway and Forty-second Street. Seating about 3,000 people, the Strand was by far the largest movie house in the United States. Costing more than $1,000,000, it also was the nation's most opulent cinema shrine, with a beautiful lobby and staircases, above the proscenium a mural representing "The Dreams of Life" and side walls with panels symbolizing "The Senses." Ordinary folks could forget their troubles by paying only 10 to 50 cents to enter this dreamland.

Griffith now faced the problem of distributing *The Clansman*. There were more than 200 producing and distributing companies in the nation, but few distributors cared to handle a film that ran to twelve reels. Furthermore, throughout the industry there raced the gossip that Griffith had made a dangerous film, "a dirty nigger picture." He solved his distribution problem by forming the Epoch Film Corporation, planning to skim off the cream of the profits by controlling all road showings of the picture in major cities. After that he would sell exhibition rights for small-town screenings under a system called a "state's rights" arrangement. Louis B. Mayer of Massachusetts controlled the largest chain of movie theaters in New England, and one of his scouts, unafraid of this "nigger picture," told Mayer that *The Clansman* was a surefire hit. Mayer wired Griffith a $25,000 offer for exclusive rights to New England showings of his film—the highest bid ever made for the exhibition of any movie. Griffith accepted. Mayer made a $1,000,000 profit on this deal and went on to become one of the most powerful movie moguls in Hollywood.

The Clansman was shown at a sneak preview in Riverside, California, in January 1915. The world premier was held the following February 8 in Los Angeles in the Clune Auditorium, which seated an audience of 2,600. Because of rumors that blacks might attack the movie house and disrupt the performance, police were there in numbers, but the threatened riot failed to materialize. Joseph Henabery, an actor who played the part of Abraham Lincoln in the movie, later said, "I'll never forget that first big showing. It was here in Los Angeles, and the picture was still called *The Clansman*. The audience was made up largely of professional people and it was our first big showing—the whole industry's first big showing. I had never heard at any exhibition—play, concert or anything—an audience react at the finish as they did at the end of *The Clansman*. They literally tore the place apart. Why were they so wildly enthusiastic? Because they felt in their inner souls that something had really grown and developed—and this was a kind of fulfillment." The picture played in Los Angeles for seven months, an unparalleled run for any film or even legitimate play.

Griffith took a print to New York for a special showing at the Rose Gardens, Broadway and Fifty-first Street. Thomas Dixon, who had kept in touch with Griffith during production of the movie, in which he held a 25 percent interest, was in the select group that saw it the night of February 20, 1915. It has been said that when the screening ended and the houselights came up, Dixon shouted to Griffith, "*Clansman* is too tame!

Let's call it *The Birth of a Nation!*" Although the director never denied this story of how the title was changed, it may not be true, for it seems that the name *Birth of a Nation* already had appeared in the trade press.

Dixon and Woodrow Wilson had known each other years earlier when both were studying law at Johns Hopkins University in Baltimore. Presuming on this friendship, the novelist persuaded the President to let him show *The Birth of a Nation* in the White House. Wilson, a constant theatergoer, agreed. This was the first time any movie ever was screened in the nation's executive mansion. Dixon later wrote a letter to Presidential Secretary Tumulty, saying recklessly, "Of course I didn't dare allow the President to know the real big purpose back of my film—which was to revolutionize Northern sentiments by a presentation of history that would transform every man in my audience into a good Democrat! And make no mistake about it—we are doing just that thing. . . . Every man who comes out of one of our theatres is a Southern partisan for life—except the members of Villard's Inter-Marriage Society, who go there to knock." This last comment was a slanderous sneer at Oswald Garrison Villard who, despite his concern for blacks, never organized any such society. Still later, Dixon boasted to Wilson's face that *The Birth of a Nation* "is transforming the entire population of the North and West into sympathetic voters. There will never be an issue of your segregation policy." Dixon was wrong, for segregation under the Wilson administration had already become a social issue. But the Southern-born President saw nothing wrong with the movie's rabid antiblack slant, failing to recognize it as brutal propaganda. After the White House screening Wilson was quoted as saying, "It is like writing history with lightning, and my one regret is that it is all so terribly true."

Dixon then won the aid of Navy Secretary Daniels of North Carolina in obtaining an appointment with Edward White, the chief justice of the United States Supreme Court. Born on his father's plantation in Louisiana in 1845, once a Confederate soldier captured by soldiers of the Union army, the chief justice now was seventy, fat and popular and renowned for getting right to the point of any conversation. Dixon was ushered into his bulky presence. Aware of the justice's reputation, Dixon said immediately that he wanted him and other members of the court to see a movie about the Ku Klux Klan which had won the praise of President Wilson. According to Dixon's report of this encounter, at the mention of the Klan the justice showed instant interest.

"You tell the true story of the Klan?"

"Yes," Dixon replied. "For the first time."

White removed his glasses and leaned back in his swivel chair, then brought his face close to that of the author and said reflectively, "I was a member of the Klan, sir. . . . through many a dark night I walked my sentinel's beat through the ugliest streets of New Orleans with a rifle on my shoulder. . . . You've told the true story of that uprising of outraged manhood?"

"In a way," Dixon purred, "I'm sure you'll approve."

"I'll be there!"

The fact that the President and chief justice saw *The Birth of a Nation* and approved of it helped pave the way for its New York opening. This occurred the evening of March 3, 1915, in the Liberty theater at 234 West Forty-second Street. The Liberty seated 1,200 people and charged from 50 cents to $2 for its stage plays. Now it charged $2 for the best seats in the house to see the Griffith production, which meant that movies had become as important as stage plays. At the end of the long film Griffith made a curtain speech, although no reporter seems to have preserved his remarks. Dixon also made an appearance, telling the Manhattan audience he would let none but the son of a Confederate soldier produce the film version of his story. The author may have remembered that during the Civil War New York City was strongly pro-Southern in sentiment.

The next morning the New York *Times* praised the movie as a movie:

> . . . an impressive new illustration of the scope of the motion picture camera . . . an historical pageant. . . . The civil war battle pictures, taken in panorama, represent an enormous success. One interesting scene stages a reproduction of the auditorium of Ford's Theatre in Washington, and shows on the screen the murder of Lincoln. In terms of purely pictorial value the best work is done in those stretches of the film that follow the night riding of the men of the Ku Klux Klan, who look like a company of avenging spectral crusaders sweeping along the moonlit roads. . . .

However, the *Times'* critic was aware of the movie's social implications, for he spoke of its "inflammatory material" and lamented "the sorry service rendered by its plucking at old wounds."

Censorship of movies was in its infancy. In 1909 some New Yorkers had organized the National Board of Censorship of Motion Pictures; by 1915 the name had been changed to the National Board of Review. Pennsylvania enacted the first state censorship law in 1911, and two years later similar laws were passed by the legislatures of Kansas and Ohio. As various states and cities tried to decide what might or might not be shown on the screen, there existed no overall guideline; the result was confusion and a series of court decisions. After the New York premiere of *The Birth of a Nation* a white reformer named Lillian Wald led 500 blacks and white liberals to city hall to attend a hearing on the film in the presence of Mayor Mitchel. They protested that the Griffith picture misrepresented blacks, was malicious propaganda and maligned an entire race. The mayor agreed and ordered several especially offensive scenes cut from the print being shown in the Liberty playhouse. Thereafter, the film settled down to a long run in the Liberty, and subsequently in other theaters, a total of more than 825,000 New Yorkers seeing it in 1915 alone.

Boston was something else. Boston was the home of the abolitionist movement, the stronghold of Villard's grandfather William Lloyd Garrison, perhaps the greatest of all abolitionists, and it still was regarded as a problack city. With *The Birth of a Nation* scheduled to open on April 9, 1915, the local branch of the National Association for the Advancement of Colored People mounted a campaign against it, using the slogan "The Assassination of a Race." Villard helped by refusing to advertise the film in the newspaper and magazine he owned, by writing that it was "a deliberate attempt to humiliate 10,000,000 American citizens and portray them as nothing but beasts." Miss Mary Ovington, a Unitarian, Socialist, descendant of an abolitionist and a social worker of independent means, wrote a pamphlet attacking the movie. Boston had been the birthplace of Massachusetts Senator Charles Sumner, perhaps second to Lincoln and Garrison in helping blacks win freedom. Sumner had been dead since 1874, but his secretary, Moorfield Storey, was still alive although along in years, and now he headed the Boston branch of the NAACP. Storey objected to the fact that *The Birth of a Nation* implied that Sumner's mulatto housekeeper was also his mistress.

In the two weeks before the film was due to open in Boston it was publicly denounced by black leaders, ministers, teachers and others. The NAACP's magazine, *The Crisis*, said the movie portrayed the black as "an ignorant fool, a vicious rapist, a venal and unscrupulous politician, or a faithful but doddering idiot." Few white Americans seemed to know or care that by 1915 a few American blacks had earned degrees as doctors of philosophy. Booker T. Washington, only seven months from death, lamented that "the managers of this play encourage and even skillfully initiate opposition on account of the advertising the play receives when attempts are made to stop it." *The New Republic* published a Francis Hackett article calling Dixon "a yellow clergyman." On the other hand, Dr. Charles W. Eliot, the former president of Harvard, made the curious charge that the picture tended to pervert white ideals.

But all these outcries did not prevent the movie from opening in Boston's Tremont theater on its scheduled date. As many had feared, a disturbance broke out in front and soon developed into a race riot. Boston police, unable to control the situation, called upon firemen for help. The next day news of the riot was spread from coast to coast by newspapers that only whetted the appetites of people in other cities to see this provocative film. In Boston, a few days after the riot, hundreds of blacks stormed the Tremont, demanding the right to buy tickets, and when they were refused, another melee erupted. This time 260 cops battled the angry demonstrators, and 6 blacks were arrested.

Now thoroughly aroused, 2,000 blacks from the greater Boston area, together with 250 white sympathizers, met in Faneuil Hall, which Daniel Webster had called the "cradle of American liberty." They demanded a stop be put to the showing of the movie. Their arguments were heard by Governor David I. Walsh and Mayor James M. Curley. The end result was passage of a municipal law creating a Boston motion-picture censorship board consisting of the mayor, police commissioner and chief justice of the municipal court. Actually, this was a board of appeal rather than a board of censorship, for it let any movie be shown and only later evaluated.

All this hubbub delighted Thomas Dixon, who said, "The silly legal opposition they are giving will make me a millionaire." After *The Birth of a Nation* broke theater records across the United States and then in various world capitals, Dixon did become a millionaire, and so did Griffith. The director, however, was bewildered and hurt by the protests against his artistic masterpiece, declaring he loved blacks, insisting it portrayed "bad white people as well as bad Negroes," adding the blacks were bad "only because the white people made them so." In Minneapolis the mayor's ban on the film was upheld by a court "in the interest of public welfare and the peace and good order of the city."

There are many valid questions about censorship and freedom—and no easy answers. Griffith thought he had the answer. He wrote a foreword that was spliced into the beginning of the film before the action commenced. In it he said, "We do not fear censorship, for we have no wish to offend with improprieties or obscenities, but we do demand, as a right, the liberty to show the dark side of wrong, that we may illuminate the bright side of virtue—the same liberty that is conceded to the art of the written word—that art to which we owe the Bible and the works of Shakespeare." Griffith then wrote a brochure called *The Rise and Fall of Free Speech in America;* its cover showed Liberty with her hands bound behind her by reels of celluloid film. He quoted Louis Sherwin, drama critic of the New York *Globe:* "This is absolutely against public policy, against the spirit of the Constitution, against the very life and essence of what should be true American and democratic ideas. The mere fact of the races constituting the population of the United States being shown in an unpleasant light is no argument whatsoever. If this factor is to be seriously considered, there is hardly any limit to which censorship may not go."

This argument was spurned by members of the NAACP. They decided to try to counteract *The Birth of a Nation* by producing their *own* movie, one favorable to blacks and presenting the truth about the Reconstruction period. Villard arranged to have a scenario prepared by a writer for the Universal Film Company. Universal agreed to produce a film twelve reels long, as long as the Griffith movie, provided the NAACP raised $10,000 of the estimated production cost of $60,000. The $10,000 could not be collected, however, so the picture was never made. Then the NAACP planned a more modest venture by backing a "race play" called *Rachel,* which was presented in New York and Washington, but only to black audiences. Independent film companies having nothing to do with the NAACP tried to capitalize on Griffith's success by turning out a couple of movies, one called *The Nigger* and the other *Free and Equal*, but neither amounted to much.

The leading man in *The Birth of a Nation* was Henry B. Walthall, born on an Alabama plantation, the grandnephew of a Confederate general. Small, slender and handsome, with dark curly hair and a mustache, he played the part of Colonel Ben Cameron, known in the picture as the Little Colonel. In one scene he was shown refusing to shake the hand of a male mulatto. With the movie being seen everywhere in the nation, young American men began imitating his haircut, the style of his collar, his suits and neckties. The role of his daughter Elsie was played by Lillian Gish, slim and fragile, her golden hair cascading below her waist. Plumpness, which had been fashionable among American women, went out of style as a result of *The Birth of a Nation.* They began dieting in the hope of looking as reedlike as Miss Gish, and they tried to imitate her mannerism—demure and controlled but suggesting latent passion.

Griffith's picture made screen history by remaining on Broadway forty-four weeks, although now and again blacks and some whites demonstrated in front of the Liberty. In the hinterland theatergoers paid the same top Broadway price for the best seats. In the St. Louis area white realtors lingered at theater doors to hand out copies of their trade paper urging passage of city laws segregating residential areas. In Atlantic City, New Jersey, the city fathers banned the film and then reversed themselves. A few governors suppressed it in their respective states. In Lafayette, Indiana, a white man shot and killed a fifteen-year-old black boy immediately after seeing *The Birth of a Nation*.

Despite Dixon's remark about opposition to the movie making him a millionaire, he tried to quash criticism by pointing out that the President and chief justice had seen and liked his picture. This worried Wilson's secretary, who urged the President to write "some sort of letter" showing that he did not approve *The Birth of a Nation*. Wilson said, "I would like to do this, if there were some way in which I could do it without seeming to be trying to meet the agitation . . . stirred up by that unspeakable fellow Tucker." The President meant William Monroe Trotter, the black leader he had ordered out of the White House. Wilson let Tumulty say he never had approved of the film and three years later when the nation was at war and black men wore uniforms, he said he disapproved of the showing of this "unfortunate production." Second thoughts were had, as well, by Chief Justice White; he threatened to denounce the movie in public unless Dixon stopped claiming he had endorsed it.

The picture won rave reviews in the South. One Southerner who took a special interest in it was William J. Simmons. He was born in Alabama in 1880, the son of a farmer who belonged to the original Ku Klux Klan, and as a boy he was fascinated by Klan lore. When he grew up, he became a Methodist minister, livened revivals with sermons such as "The Kinship of Kourtship and Kissing," was unable to live on his tiny ministerial salary, was turned out of the church for "inefficiency and moral impairment." Simmons became a salesman—and failed again. At last he learned he had a talent for organizing fraternal societies. Promoting one group after another, he began earning $15,000 a year as district manager of the Woodmen of the World. Simmons stood six feet tall, weighed 200 pounds, had gray eyes, light red hair, a prominent nose, square chin and a powerful speaking voice.

In the fall of 1915 he read that *The Birth of a Nation* was to be shown in a theater in Atlanta, Georgia. Simmons decided this was his golden opportunity, his chance to revive the Klan, which had died out in the 1870's. He convened a meeting of forty men from various fraternal orders, including two members of the original Klan and the current speaker of the Georgia legislature. Sharing his warped vision, they agreed to found a new Klan, so Simmons told them to meet him in front of the Piedmont hotel the evening of the day before Thanksgiving.

When they gathered, Simmons said he had hired a bus to carry them to Stone Mountain, a huge granite dome near Atlanta. That night in northern Georgia the weather was so cold that some men said they had no intention of going that far. However, thirty-four braved the elements and rode to the mountain and shivered and stumbled about with flashlights to gather stones, as he had ordered. Simmons used the stones to make a crude altar and also provide a base for a cross made of pine boards padded with excelsior. They soaked the cross in kerosene, Simmons touched a match to it, and as the flames scratched the sky, the ceremony began. Grandiloquently, Simmons proclaimed the birth of the Knights of the Ku Klux Klan and declared that he had assumed the title of the Founder and Emperor of the Invisible Empire.

A week later, when *The Birth of a Nation* opened in Atlanta, a local newspaper published an advertisement for the film and next to this was another advertisement heralding "The World's Greatest Secret, Social, Patriotic, Fraternal, Beneficiary Order." Subsequent Klan publicity characterized the organization as "A Classy Order of the Highest Class." On December 4, 1915, the state of Georgia granted a charter to the revived Klan. Its members were a mite less than "classy," since most of them came from Georgia's middle class—rural clergymen, planters, farmers. One of the early members was Robert Ramspeck, who later was elected to Congress from Georgia. Although national headquarters were opened in Atlanta, the Klan was *national* in name only at that time; until 1920 it never had more than 5,000 members, all natives of Georgia. But Simmons was doing well selling memberships, insurance, hoods and gowns.

The first Ku Klux Klan, organized at Pulaski, Tennessee, in December, 1865, consisted of former Confederate soldiers and other Southerners opposed to the Reconstruction policies of the radical Republican Congress and eager to maintain "white supremacy." Simmons' second Klan was also antiblack, but it went far beyond racism, for it also was anti-Catholic, anti-Jewish, anti-alien, anti-Darwin, antiliberal, and after the Russian revolution it became passionately anti-Red. Because of its broader, if negative, base, the new Klan came to have an appeal defying mere regionalism. In a long flamboyant statement about its aims, Simmons said it held "that our civilization cannot be safe in a democracy that is un-Christian, or that is half white and half of color." He always claimed that the Klan had the endorsement of D. W. Griffith, although there seems to be no evidence the famous director ever made any public statement to this effect. After the war began Georgia Klansmen proved their patriotism by hunting down draft dodgers.

Griffith, smarting from criticism and censorship of *The Birth of a Nation*, decided to produce an even more colossal film and call it *Intolerance*. Created on a scale so gigantic as to be awesome, *Intolerance* nonetheless lacked the cinematic artistry of *The Birth of a Nation*, which continued to play to vast audiences in the United States and abroad. *The Birth of a Nation* cost a total of $110,000, ultimately grossed something like $50,000,000 and became one of the most profitable pictures ever filmed. Nearly sixty years after it was made it still was being shown in art theaters and by film societies, while generations of blacks continued to resent it.

PART II

Revised Forecast

Chapter 10

THE ASSASSINATION AT SARAJEVO

On the last day of his life the archduke of Austria arrived by imperial train at Sarajevo in what today is central Yugoslavia.

Sunday morning, June 28, 1914. Sunshine glinting from swords and medals of dignitaries waiting at the railway station to greet Franz Ferdinand von Este and his wife. Sarajevo, the capital of Bosnia, lay in a valley with hills in the foreground and mountains beyond. Most inhabitants were Muslims, and the city had a semi-Oriental look. Mosques pointed slim minarets at the bright sky, hand-woven rugs were displayed in the Turkish bazaar, townspeople clattered down narrow cobblestoned streets to the center of town where a little river called the Miljachka was almost dry, now that summer heat had begun. The archduke, who had been afraid the heat would be oppressive, was pleased to feel his cheeks brushed by a breeze wafting from the dim mountain ranges.

Stepping off the train, he took salutes from officials wearing red fezzes, inspected troops at a nearby parade ground, then got into the second car of a six-car motorcade, maneuvering his sword so the scabbard would not become entangled in his legs. He sank down into a leather seat, and his wife sat down beside him. Peasants, enjoying the pageantry of royalty, gaped at the tall, fleshy man, for he was the nephew of Franz Josef I, the emperor of Austria and king of Hungary, and also heir presumptive to the Dual Monarchy. A vain man, the archduke had insisted upon being sewn into his green uniform, that of an Austrian field marshal. His neck bulged over the collar of his tunic. His decorations clinked. On his head he wore a visored shako, its high crown plumed with white feathers. He was firecely mustached like Kaiser Wilhelm of Germany, whom he admired. His consort, Sophie, wore a white dress, string of pearls, and a broad-brimmed hat slanting down the right side of her plump and lovely face.

The mayor and chief of police got into the first car of the royal motorcade. Marshal Oskar Potiorek, the despised military governor of Bosnia, took his place in the second automobile with the visiting couple, riding backward and facing them. The royal car had its top down and flew the gold and black fanion of the House of Hapsburg. The marshal waved his hand, and the procession began rolling along the Appel Quay, a broad avenue rimming the embankment. And along the scheduled route, from the railway station to city hall, there lurked six young terrorists armed with bombs and revolvers.

To understand what brought the Austrian archduke so close to a half dozen potential assassins, one must know something of the tangled history of the Balkans.

For more than four centuries the Ottoman empire of the Turks had dominated the easternmost peninsula of southern Europe. "Balkan" is a Turkish word for mountains, and in those rugged highlands east of Italy and across the Adriatic sea, the peaks and valleys and rivers kept the people physically isolated and psychologically fragmented. A surrealistic nightmare of clashing cultures, religions, languages and ethnic groups, the Balkans had become the despair of the great powers of Europe.

Russia beat Turkey in a war in 1878, and the ensuing treaty of Berlin forced Turkey to surrender its provinces of Bosnia and Herzegovina to Austria-Hungary. This Dual Monarchy was not granted outright title to the two provinces but was allowed to administer them. The capital of Bosnia was Sarajevo, while the capital of Herzegovina was Mostar. The peace treaty also compelled Turkey to relinquish Serbia, which became an independent kingdom in 1882. Lying to the east of Bosnia-Herzegovina, Serbia was landlocked and trade-starved, without access to any seaport, unable to market its products without the consent of its neighboring states. Austria-Hungary, which coveted Serbia, tried to dominate it economically and intimidate it politically, starting a tariff war in an attempt to prevent Serbia from extending its market for livestock and agricultural produce. But the end result was that Serbia diverted its trade into other and better channels.

In 1908 Austria-Hungary violated the treaty of Berlin by forthrightly annexing Bosnia and Herzegovina, converting them into dual territories within the Dual Monarchy, robbing them of many political rights, oppressing the people. This infuriated Serbia and angered all of the empire's South Slavs—Serbs, Croats and Slovenes. The annexation crisis raged from October, 1908, until March, 1909, and almost provoked the World War five years before it actually erupted. Serbia, regarding herself as the natural protector of all the Slavs, mobilized for war. So did Austria-Hungary. Serbia knew, though, it could not win a war with the powerful Hapsburg empire without the help of the Slavs of Russia—but Russia backed down under pressure from Germany. The annexation was accepted by Serbia. Sullenly.

Seeking to strengthen herself by alliances, Serbia formed the Balkan League, signing treaties with Bulgaria and Greece. The league was attacked by Turkey in the First Balkan War of 1912, but Turkey was whipped by Serbia, Bulgaria, Greece and Montenegro and lost almost all its remaining European territories. Then the victorious Balkan allies quarreled among themselves about the division of the land they had taken from Turkey, leading to the Second Balkan War of 1913. Encouraged by Austria-Hungary, Bulgaria attacked Serbia and Greece, with Turkey and Rumania coming in on the side of the Bulgarians. But Serbia won a second time. As a result of these two Balkan wars Serbia increased its area by 82 percent while its population rose from 3,000,000 to more than

4,500,000. Swollen with success, the hero of all the South Slavs, eager for access to the sea, Serbia began talking about taking Bosnia-Herzegovina away from Austria-Hungary as the first step in the creation of a Greater Serbia. This alarmed Austria-Hungary, whose general staff began to plan the liquidation of the upstart state.

Out of this welter of events—so confusing to Americans—came the so-called Balkan Question. This was the question of the relations of the Balkan states to one another, to Russia, to Turkey and to the nations of central Europe. The decline of the Ottoman empire, the subsequent disappearance of Turkish authority in Europe and the rise of a crazy quilt of small and poor and antagonistic states in the Balkans—all this created a power vacuum and made war inevitable. It was for this reason that statemen and journalists spoke of the Balkans as a powder keg. In 1897 Otto von Bismarck, the first chancellor of the German empire, prophesied that someday the great European war would come from "some damned foolish thing in the Balkans." In 1913 the British ambassador in Vienna, Sir Fairfax Cartwright, wrote a friend, "Serbia may some day set Europe by the ears and bring about a universal conflict on the Continent."

Franz Ferdinand had come to Sarajevo not from desire but out of a sense of duty. The two Austro-Hungarian army corps regularly stationed in Bosnia were scheduled to stage military maneuvers some thirty kilometers south of the capital, and the archduke felt he had to make an appearance since he was inspector in chief of the imperial army. But he hesitated. His health was not the best, he had heard that Sarajevo was a furnace in the summer, an Austrian flag had been burned only days before his departure from Vienna, and there even was a rumor that an attempt would be made on his life. Hoping to be urged to stay home, he had asked Emperor Franz Josef what to do:

"Do as you wish," the emperor grunted.

Uncle and nephew did not get along well and seldom saw each other, communicating mostly in writing. The fifty-year-old archduke hated his eighty-four-year-old uncle for clinging to the throne in the sixty-fourth year of his reign, thus cheating him out of full royal powers. The old emperor was reactionary, fixed in his ways and surrounded by decaying aides who tended to recall the past rather than anticipate the future. Insofar as any Hapsburg could be liberal, the archduke was more progressive than the emperor, although not so wise, and already had decided what changes he would make when the old man died and left him the empire. For one thing, he would weaken the authority of the Germans in Austria and the Magyars in Hungary by giving the smoldering Slavs in the southern part of the empire a greater sense of participation in the affairs of state. Nearly 2,000,000 Serbs lived in Bosnia-Herzegovina alone.

During the annexation crisis of 1908–1909 Franz Ferdinand opposed those Austrian jingoists who demanded war with Serbia. While he was much too ambitious and autocratic to let anything diminish the power he expected to inherit, nonetheless he had an occasional gleam of statemanship. He thought he could curb Serbia's militarism and satisfy Slavic discontent by instituting reforms and reconstituting the empire. It would be better, the archduke felt, if the Germans and Magyars shared some of their power with the Slavs. Perhaps this could be done by converting the Dual Monarchy into a Triple Monarchy—"trialism" this concept was called. If the Slavs got greater autonomy, they might abandon their hope of uniting with Serbia, becoming instead loyal subjects of the Hapsburg regime. But the archduke's very moderation antagonized the youths now lying in wait for him since they would settle for nothing less than reunion with "Mother Serbia."

Down through the years, as Franz Ferdinand waited for his uncle to die, he absented himself as much as possible from the court in Vienna. Sourly he commented that "the monarchy has fallen into the hands of Jews, Free Masons, Socialists and Hungarians and is ruled by them." The first part of this remark by the ardent Catholic archduke echoed the anti-Semitism tainting the otherwise sweet life of the capital. Perhaps Sigmund Freud, a Jewish doctor practicing something called psychoanalysis in Vienna, could have explained why Franz Ferdinand was a cynic. "I regard everyone I meet for the first time," said the archduke, "as a cheap fellow, and wait until he does something to justify a better opinion in my eyes."

His life had not been easy despite the royal trappings. Until his father died, it had been unthinkable that he ever would become next in line to succeed the emperor. When he came down with tuberculosis, he was deserted by many, especially those connected with the court, and he neither forgot nor forgave this betrayal. His peacemongering during the annexation crisis further alienated him from Vienna's ruling clique. Then there was the agony of his love affair and marriage.

He lost his heart and reason to the Countess Sophie Chotek, who came from a Czech family that was ancient and noble but not royal. When the emperor learned his nephew wanted to marry her, he muttered, "Love makes people lose all sense of dignity." For her part, Sophie declared, "Greatness is dearly bought." She was ambitious and clever, a rigid Catholic, a tattletale and ill-natured to almost everyone but Franz Ferdinand. He begged his uncle to let him take Sophie as his morganatic wife, meaning she never could become empress and none of her children by him could claim the throne or his property.

The emperor said no. The archduke threatened to kill himself. This chilled the emperor's heart, for his own son had taken his life in 1889 and his wife had been assassinated in 1898. Kaiser Wilhelm of Germany, Czar Nicholas of Russia and Pope Leo XIII interceded in behalf of the anguished archduke, and at last the old emperor relented.

On June 28, 1900—exactly fourteen years before his arrival in Sarajevo—Franz Ferdinand swore a solemn oath of renunciation which declared that his impending marriage was "not an eligible but a morganatic marriage." After this formality the marriage declaration was registered, and soon thereafter he married Sophie. Nine years later the emperor gave her the title of Duchess of Hohenburg and the privilege of being addressed as "Highness." Even so, members of the imperial family inflicted subtle but cruel humiliations on the archduke's consort. The Kaiser, on the other hand, went out of his way to pay attention to her whenever they met, endearing himself to the man who someday might become the emperor of Austria-Hungary. Franz Ferdinand and Sophie had an extremely happy marriage; she gave him three children whom he so adored that he would throw away all royal dignity to sit on the floor and play with them.

Otherwise, the archduke was a haughty man with no intimate friends. Like so many other royal personages of that era, he was an almost psychopathic butcher of wild game. While visiting Britain he was taken by King George V to a park to shoot ducks, and the prince of Wales later said, "There I watched the Archduke, who could match my father as a wing shot, pull two hundred and seventy-three birds down out of the air." Not long before the archduke arrived in Sarajevo he boasted he had just killed his three thousandth stag. He was given to fits of black depression and rages so violent his wife thought he was going mad. Restless, energetic and iron-willed, he had executive ability and took care of business matters rapidly and efficiently. After the death of his father left him next in line to the throne, he buckled down to the study of politics, and he also mastered the languages of all the nations he would someday rule.

Now, this summer day in Sarajevo as his limousine purred along the Appel Quay, he saw houses displaying his picture in their windows, saw Austrian flags and native rugs unfurled as decorations. While all this was heartening, every so often he also saw defiant Serbian flags. Loyal Sarajevo newspapers were welcoming the archduke to the city, but the town's leading Serbian paper had published only a brief announcement of the royal visit and then underlined the insult by printing a big picture of King Peter of Serbia. There were no soldiers holding back the crowds; except for the few at the parade ground, they were being kept in the field for further military maneuvers. Security, in fact, was dangerously scant; only gaudily dressed gendarmes lined the curbs—too few of them, at that. Some spectators cheered, while others remained ominously silent. The military governor of Bosnia was pointing out the girls' high school and the Austro-Hungarian Bank on the left side of the river. The time was 10 A.M.

Waiting near the bridge was a teen-ager named Nedjelko Chabrinovitch. A native of Herzegovina and a communicant of the Serb Orthodox faith, he had quit school because of poor grades, quarreled with his father and left home, tried one trade after another, became a printer, wrangled with his employers, left Sarajevo for Belgrade, the capital of Serbia. There he got a job in an anarchist printing shop. A flaming Serb nationalist and fanatical Pan Slav, he joined a secret Serbian revolutionary society named Union or Death, but more commonly known as the Black Hand. This society had no ties with the Black Hand so troublesome to the New York City police of 1914.

Union or Death had been organized in 1911 by an archconspirator, Colonel Dragutin Dimitrijević, chief of the intelligence department of the Serbian general staff. To this day historians are not sure whether Serbian Cabinet members knew about all of the colonel's intrigues. Controlled by a central committee of eleven, this secret society had rules and bylaws. Article I declared that its aim was "the realization of the national ideal: the union of all Serbs." Article II stated that the organization preferred "terrorist action to intellectual propaganda, and for this reason must be kept absolutely secret from non-members." Still another article said, "Every member on entering the organization must realize that by this act he forfeits his own personality and that he can expect within it neither glory nor personal profit." Any of its terrorists who attacked a public official was supposed to take his own life immediately. During the initiation ceremony the novitiate was led into a room lit by a single candle on a table covered with black cloth and displaying a cross, a dagger and a revolver. The fanatics who joined the Black Hand swore never to betray it, which explains why Chabrinovitch and the others involved in the attack on the archduke said at their trial they had no connection with it. Instead, they claimed to belong to a Serbian group called National Defense, ostensibly a cultural society but actually an agency for espionage and subversion throughout southern Austria.

Chabrinovitch had left the anarchist printing shop in Belgrade, gone to Trieste to work on a newspaper, then returned to the Serbian capital, where he got another job in the government printing house. At Eastertime in 1914 a friend in Sarajevo clipped an article about the archduke's impending visit, pasted it on a card with no comment other than "Greetings," mailed it to the Green Garland coffee house in Belgrade where Chabrinovitch picked up his mail. As early as October, 1913, he had told another friend he intended to kill Franz Ferdinand. In February, 1914, Chabrinovitch had been joined in Belgrade by Gavrilo Princip.

Princip was a frail, slim young man of nineteen with burning blue eyes. Born in western Bosnia amid the wild mountains near the Dalmation border, he also belonged to the Serb Orthodox faith. His father was a postman who gave him no financial support, and after many fights, the boy left home. He went to Sarajevo and enrolled in the local high school, finding living quarters in a roominghouse run by the mother of Danilo Ilitch. Ilitch had fallen under the influence of Vladimir Gatchinovitch, who was subsidized by the Black Hand to organize secret cells in Bosnia. Princip was an avid reader and at first a diligent student, but he missed many classes because of an illness that may have been tuberculosis. This June, 1914, he had not yet passed his final high school examinations, but this did not bother him because he had begun to devour revolutionary propaganda and now considered himself a professional terrorist. He was poor and sick and hopeless.

At the urging of Ilitch he left Sarajevo for Belgrade, where he was intitiated into the Black Hand. He met Chabrinovitch, and the two recruited a third conspirator, named Trifko Grabezh. All three were trained in pistol shooting and the use of bombs by agents of the Black Hand. Night after night Princip dreamed he was a political murderer struggling with policemen and soldiers. These pawns of the scheming Serbian colonel, these teen-agers, were dead serious in their intention of assassinating Franz Ferdinand, but they also suffered from adolescent romanticism. They regarded themselves as giant killers, as national heroes. Princip often visited the grave of an earlier political assassin and swore to do his own bloody deed. Chabrinovitch, an hour or so before his attack on the archduke, had his photograph taken.

Three weeks before the archduke was due in Sarajevo the three left Belgrade and slipped out of Serbia carrying six bombs, four Browning revolvers, a map of Bosnia, 150 dinars in cash and phials of potassium cyanide with which to take their lives afterward. They were able to enter Bosnia without being searched and their weapons found because the border guards belonged to the Black Hand. After arriving in Sarajevo, the trio recruited three local youths to help them carry out their deadly plan. Princip went back to Ilitch's house to live quietly until the moment presented itself.

Ten A.M., Sunday, June 28, with Chabrinovitch lurking near the Cumurja bridge. He was armed with a bomb. When the royal motorcade came abreast of him, he pulled out the bomb, knocked off its cap against a post, stepped forward and hurled it at the archduke's car. The chauffeur saw him and hit the accelerator. The bomb landed on the folded top of the archduke's car, bounced off and exploded beneath the third automobile. The blast injured an aide-de-camp riding in the third car and slightly injured several spectators. Sophie felt something graze her neck and put up her hand to touch her skin. The archduke's face was scratched, probably by the flying cap of the bomb.

Chabrinovitch pulled out his poison and swallowed it. Then he leaped over the embankment and down into the shallow riverbed. Policemen jumped in after him, knocked him down, collared him, jerked him to his feet and beat him with the flats of their swords. Although he was throwing up almond-smelling vomit, Chabrinovitch managed to scream, "I am a Serb! A hero!" In the royal car the military governor of Bosnia cried that a bomb had gone off. The archduke snapped that he had been expecting something of this sort. The governor, Potiorek, then reported that an officer in the third car had been hurt. Courageously but foolishly, the archduke ordered his own car stopped so that they might look after the wounded man. On making sure that everything possible was being done for the aide-de-camp and the bleeding spectators, the archduke shouted, "Come on! The fellow is insane. Gentlemen, let us proceed with our program." Potiorek ordered the chauffeur to drive fast and not stop again until they reached city hall.

After they reached the Rathaus, the mayor began his welcoming speech but had read only a few words when Franz Ferdinand roughly interrupted, "Enough of that! Herr Burgermeister, I come here on a visit and I get bombs thrown at me. It is outrageous!" There was an embarrassed pause. Then the mayor resumed reading his prepared address: "All the citizens of the capital city of Sarajevo find their souls are filled with happiness, and they most enthusiastically greet Your Highness' most illustrious visit with the most cordial of welcomes. . . ." This time the royal visitor let him finish. While this brittle ceremony was proceeding in city hall, Chabrinovitch was being questioned at a police station. The gendarmes, believing the prisoner was involved in a plot and had information that might save the royal couple when they left city hall, were none too gentle. But he refused to talk—just then, at least—buying enough time to let one or another of his five co-conspirators finish the job he had bungled.

At the close of the reception a member of the archduke's retinue asked whether a military guard could be provided. Potiorek barked, "Do you think Sarajevo is filled with assassins?" At last it was decided that when

Franz Ferdinand left the Rathaus, he would not follow his scheduled itinerary, calling for him to drive through narrow Franz Josef Street in the crowded part of the city. Instead, he would ride at a fast clip back along the Appel Quay and from there to the hospital; the archduke insisted on going to the hospital to see the injured aide-de-camp. After that he would visit the museum. While no military guard was given him, as requested, an officer did take up a protective position on the running board on the left side of the archduke's car.

But no one thought to tell the archduke's chauffeur of the change in plans. After driving back along the quay, he slowed to make a right turn into the block-long Rudolph Street leading into Franz Josef Street. Potiorek roared at the driver, "Not that way you fool! Keep straight on!" The confused chauffeur stopped the car opposite the Latin bridge so that he might shift into reverse. Princip happened to be standing near the bridge. The time was 10:45 A.M.

Earlier in the day, while the motorcade was en route to city hall, Princip had taken up a position three blocks away from Chabrinovitch, and when he heard the bomb explode and saw the archduke's car leap forward with the archduke unharmed, he realized Chabrinovitch had failed. Princip felt the world collapse. Having run toward the spot, having seen his friend dragged away by angry policemen, Princip thought for a fleeting moment of shooting Chabrinovitch and then taking his own life. Princip carried a loaded Browning revolver. Who knew what tortures would be inflicted on Chabrinovitch? Surely he would talk, name names, reveal everything. But the moment faded before he could act, so Princip wandered away in shock. He did not know that at the sound of the explosion the other four terrorists had panicked and run, one racing to his uncle's house to hide his bomb in a toilet. Princip, his head aswirl and his knees rubbery, stumbled into a coffeehouse to sip shakily from a cup and try to think things through.

When he emerged, he stepped into the doorway of a barbershop at the intersection of Appel Quay and Rudolph Street across the quay from the embankment. To his astonishment he saw the archduke in a car with the chauffeur shifting into reverse—less than ten feet from him. Fate, so it seemed, had given Princip his own chance. The officer on the running board stood on the left side of the car opposite Princip. He had a clear shot at the archduke, since Sophie was leaning back against the seat. Princip jerked out his automatic and fired. The bullet pierced the archduke's neck. Princip now aimed at Potiorek and fired a second time, but his hand may have trembled or Sophie may have tried to shield her husband's body with her own, for he accidentally shot her in the abdomen.

Then the assassin turned his gun toward his own head with the intention of killing himself, but passersby grabbed his hand. After firing the two shots into the car, he thought he had missed because for the next couple of seconds the archduke sat as erect as ever. Sophie screamed, fainted, collapsed against her husband. He remained upright, but blood gushed from his mouth and crimsoned his green tunic. Potiorek bellowed at the driver to get the hell to the governor's palace. The car leaped forward and picked up such high speed that the wounded archduke tried to brace himself against his wife's fallen figure. His dulling eyes on his wife's blood-spattered white dress, the archduke murmured, "Sophie! Sophie! . . . Don't die! . . . Live for our children!" Asked if he were in pain, he replied, "It is nothing. Six more times he said, "It is nothing." But each time his voice was weaker. He died about 11:30 A.M. Doctors had lost time cutting him out of his uniform.

The next morning the New York *Times* published a four-column headline:

HEIR TO AUSTRIA'S THRONE IS SLAIN
WITH HIS WIFE BY A BOSNIAN YOUTH
TO AVENGE SEIZURE OF HIS COUNTRY

Summer lay like a pageant across the land, both on the continent and in the United States, each day ripe with a high-hanging sun, and people held faces and hands toward the heavens as they smiled and declared they could not remember a time when the weather was lovelier. Americans were far more concerned with swimming and boating and motoring and such pleasures than with the news from—where? Sarajevo? Never heard of it. Bosnia? What's that? Oh, in the Balkans! Well, that's just a lot of comic-opera countries fighting with one another, so what's it got to do with us? It was not just the average citizen who was unfamiliar with the site of the double assassination. Brand Whitlock, the United States minister to Belgium, was in his summer home outside Brussels writing a new novel of rural life in Ohio, and when he heard the news from Sarajevo, he confessed, "I had not the least idea where it was in this world, if it was in this world." In 1914 few American newspapers maintained European staffs of their own and published very little foreign news. Americans could not be faulted for their ignorance of what was going on in the Balkans. On June 29 the Atlanta *Journal* did not consider the murder of the archduke and his wife sufficiently newsworthy to be published on its front page. That same day the New York *Sun* editorialized, "It is difficult to discuss the tragedy at Sarajevo yesterday without laying oneself open to the reproach of heartlessness. For while it is only natural that one should be stricken with horror at the brutal and shocking assassination of Archduke Francis Ferdinand, it is impossible to deny the fact that his disappearance from the scene is calculated to diminish the tenseness of the situation and to make for peace both within and without the dual empire."

When Emperor Franz Josef was told that his nephew had been killed, he moaned, "Horrible! I am spared nothing! The Almighty does not allow Himself to be challenged with impunity. . . ." The day of the assassinations Sigmund Freud sat down in his study in Vienna and wrote a letter to a friend: "I am writing while still under the impact of the astonishing murder in Sarajevo, the consequences of which cannot be foreseen." Kaiser Wilhelm of Germany told an intimate, "I cannot imagine the old gentleman in Schönbrunn [Franz Josef] will go to war, and certainly not if it is a war over Archduke Franz Ferdinand." The Kaiser's former chancellor, Prince von Bülow, said of the tragedy, "It can be an embarrassment or a disembarrassment." In Paris, General

Zurlinden, the respected military commentator for *Figaro*, wrote, "There is nothing to cause anxiety."

In those days news traveled only as fast as words could be tapped out on a telegraph key. At 12:30 P.M., June 28, the British vice-consul at Sarajevo sent a wire to the British foreign office in London reporting the news; it arrived at 4 P.M. London time. Lloyd George, the British chancellor of the exchequer, was just about to stop work long enough to take tea when his secretary handed him the red dispatch box. He unlocked it and took out the telegram. "This means war," said Lloyd George—but he meant just another Balkan war, not a world war. The British government was so engrossed in other matters that Cabinet members did not even bother to discuss this fresh trouble in southeastern Europe. When the British king, George V, heard the news, he wrote in his diary, "Terrible shock for the dear old emperor."

Frederic C. Penfield, the American ambassador in Vienna, wired news of the assassinations to the state department in Washington. It was departmental officials, no doubt, who prepared the first draft of a personal telegram to be sent by President Wilson to the old emperor; this left Washington on June 29. The next day State Secretary Bryan had a note of regret hand-delivered to the Austrian ambassador in Washington. David Franklin Houston, the secretary of agriculture, later scribbled a memorandum saying, "I had noted with passing interest the news of the assassinations of the Austrian Archduke and his wife at Sarajevo on June 28th . . . but as . . . there was no clear indication that the developments would be brought very near home to us, I decided to take a short vacation. There had been so much fighting and turmoil in the Balkans that I had become accustomed to them." Herbert Hoover was a private businessman in 1914. After he became President and after he left the White House, he wrote in his memoirs, "On June 28, 1914, when news came of the assassination of the Archduke at Sarajevo, the world took it as just another of those habitual Balkan lapses into barbarism—and we went about our accustomed business with little more thought than that. Other incidents had happened before in the Balkan states and, after a week or so of threats and rumors of war, things had always quieted down."

That summer of 1914 Joseph C. Grew was home on leave from his post as secretary of the American embassy in Berlin; later he became the American ambassador to Japan during the administration of Franklin D. Roosevelt. In his memoirs Grew says:

> . . . Fate is supposed to announce her dreadful purposes with a knell, or series of knells. The first knell struck for me on the golf course at Manchester-by-the-Sea in America. I met an old Austrian friend whom I had not seen for years and asked him to dinner. "I'm sorry," he said, "I can't come; we've just had bad news," and then as an afterthought he added: "Our Archduke Francis Ferdinand has been murdered in Bosnia." I expressed my condolences and we parted, but the news did not then convey to me its full significance. I wonder to how many it did.

Brigadier General John J. Pershing, commanding the 8th infantry brigade along the Mexican border, was on leave and vacationing with his family in Cheyenne, Wyoming. In his memoirs he wrote:

> My wife and I had been in France in 1908 and witnessed the excitement of the French people during the crisis that followed the seizure by Austria of the provinces of Bosnia and Herzegovina. It was suspected even then that Austria had similar designs against Serbia, and the animosity that had grown up between them, added to the fears and ambitions of the nations likely to be aligned on either side, furnished plenty of inflammable material to start a war. But the thought of a world war, impending, perhaps imminent, actually stunned one's senses.

Vladimir Ilich Lenin was an exile from Russia living in a village of Austrian Galicia in what today is part of Poland. From time to time he had joked that the czar of Russia and the Kaiser of Germany might bring about a war which would result in a Socialist victory—but then he would grin and shrug his shoulders as though to dismiss such revolutionary wish-thinking. In 1913 Lenin had written Maxim Gorky, "War between Austria and Russia would be very useful to the cause of the revolution in western Europe. But is is hard to believe that Franz Josef and Nicholas will grant us this pleasure." On June 28, while returning from a Sunday stroll with some Russian émigré friends, Lenin heard of the murder of the Austrian archduke. It took him by surprise.

Adolf Hitler, who had failed as a student of architecture in Vienna, left the capital and moved to Munich, where he floundered as he tried to find himself. After hearing the news from Sarajevo, he wrote, "I was filled with muffled dread at this vengeance of an inscrutable destiny. The greatest friend of the Slavs had fallen under the bullets of Slav fanatics."

Chapter 11

THE WAR BEGINS

In the opening days of August, 1914, Mrs. Woodrow Wilson died and Western civilization began its long day's journey into night.

The tragedy at Sarajevo climaxed the hostility between Austria-Hungary and Serbia. Most members of the Austrian crown council urged war against Serbia, but Hungarian premier, Count Stefan Tisza, argued instead for diplomatic action to avoid larger European complications. He was defied by the Austrian foreign minister, Count Leopold von Berchtold, who saw the murders as an excuse to finish Serbia forever, declaring that a *fait accompli* would halt Russia or any other great power that tried to intervene. A diplomat left Vienna for Sarajevo to investigate the crimes; while he proved the part played in it by the Black Hand, he could find no conclusive evidence of Serbian complicity.

Berchtold sent another envoy to Berlin to solicit Germany's help. The Kaiser promised to support any action taken by the Dual Monarchy against Serbia, and the German chancellor repeated this pledge. They behaved rashly, since neither knew the scope of Berchtold's plans. Germany's "blank check," as it came to be called, is hard to explain. Some historians consider it proof of Germany's wish for war; others regard it as diplomatic folly. In any event, Berchtold overcame internal opposition to his pugnacious policy and drew up an ultimatum which Austria-Hungary presented to Serbia on July 23, 1914.

The ultimatum demanded reparation and suppression of the Pan-Serbian movement in a form that meant Austrian intervention in Serbia's domestic affairs. Serbia conceded almost everything—but this made no difference to the hawks in Vienna. Rejecting Serbia's reply, they declared war against it on July 28. That same day Myron T. Herrick, the American ambassador to France, cabled from Paris to Washington: "Situation in Europe is regarded here as the gravest in history. It is apprehended that civilization is threatened by demoralization which would follow a general conflagration. . . ."

European statesmen anxiously sought compromise or delay, but now began the mobilizations that were to end with 64,129,000 men under arms. Now the web of treaties, some of them secret treaties, entangled every European nation except the Scandinavian countries, Holland, Spain and Switzerland. Now came the culmination of decades of armament races, balance-of-power politics, economic rivalry, imperialistic clashes, fervent nationalism and the chaos resulting from the absence of adequate international law. Austria, Germany, Bulgaria and Turkey drew together into the Central Powers. Russia, France, England, Belgium, Serbia, Montenegro, Portugal, Rumania and Greece linked arms as the Allies. Now came one declaration of war after another.

Saturday, August 1—Germany declares war on Russia. . . . The German people remind one another that the previous evening the Kaiser had declared that the "sword has been forced into our hand." . . . In New York City a German-American paper called the *New Yorker Herold* publishes this headline: ALL GERMAN HEARTS BEAT HIGHER TODAY. . . . President Wilson, stunned by the news, paces the lonely corridors of the White House. . . . Colonel Edward M. House, in Europe to promote disarmament, writes Wilson about Secretary of State Bryan, "Please let me suggest that you do not let Mr. Bryan make any overtures to any of the Powers involved. They look upon him as purely visionary and it would lessen the weight of your influence if you desire to use it yourself later." . . . Theodore Roosevelt tells a friend, "As I am writing, the whole question of peace and war trembles in the balance; and at the very moment . . . our own special prize idiot, Mr. Bryan, and his ridiculous and insincere chief, Mr. Wilson, are prattling about the steps they are taking to procure universal peace." . . . Secretary of Agriculture David Franklin Houston feels the end of things has come and stops in his tracks, dazed and horror-stricken. . . . Franklin D. Roosevelt, the assistant secretary of the navy, hears the news while en route to Reading, Pennsylvania, and on the train he writes his wife, "A complete smash up is inevitable. It will be the greatest war in the world's history."

Sunday, August 2—German troops enter Luxembourg and invade Belgium to attack France. . . . The New York *Times* views the war as a crusade for "the crushing out of the imperial idea, the end, once for all times, in those three empires of absolute rule and the substitution for all-powerful sovereigns and their titled advisors of an executive with power to carry out only the will of the people." . . . The Chicago *Tribune* says, ". . . This is the twilight of the kings. Western Europe of the people may be caught in this debacle, but never again. Eastern Europe of the kings will be remade and in the name of God shall not give grace to a hundred square miles of broken bodies." . . . Walter Hines Page, the American ambassador to Great Britain, sits down in his country house in Surrey and writes, "The Grand Smash is come. . . . I walked out in the night a while ago. The stars are bright, the night is silent, the country quiet—as quiet as peace itself. Millions of men are in camp and on warships. Will they have to fight and many of them die—to untangle this network of treaties and alliances and to blow off huge debts with gunpowder so that the world may start again?"

Monday, August 3—Germany declares war on France, and Belgium asks Britain for aid. . . . Colonel House writes President Wilson, "Our people are deeply shocked at the enormity of this general European war, and I see here and there regret that you did not use your good offices in behalf of peace." . . . An ocean liner sails through the Panama Canal for the first time. . . . Franklin Roosevelt returns to Washington and goes straight to the navy department where "as I expected, I found everything asleep and apparently oblivious to the fact that the most terrible drama in history was about to be enacted." . . . Ellen Slayden, the wife of Congressman James L. Slayden, rides a train from Little Rock to St. Louis and writes in her diary, "The Little Rock *Gazette* is made thrilling with news of Europe's madness. Germany invading Luxembourg. . . . The paper has a cartoon, 'As it was in the beginning,' two hairy apelike men attack each other with stone hammers." . . . Joseph C. Grew, secretary to the American embassy in Berlin, scribbles, "We issued 418 passports today. . . . All very tired tonight—I have lost over four pounds in three days. . . . All foreigners forbidden to leave Germany today until after the mobilization. . . . Some people cannot speak without crying." . . . In London an American mining engineer named Herbert Hoover goes to his office, hears on the phone that Germany has declared war on France, sadly reflects that the blows come swiftly, gazes out a window at British troops passing in the streets below. . . . An aging educator and diplomat, Andrew D. White, arrives at Yale, goes for a drive in the beautiful countryside with Professor William Lyon Phelps, tells Phelps, "You will live to see the end of this war, but I shall not."

Tuesday, August 4—Germany declares war on Belgium, and Britain declares war on Germany. . . . President Wilson issues a proclamation declaring the neutrality of the United States. . . . Wilson also writes to ask whether Colonel House thinks he should offer to negotiate between the warring powers. . . . Grew writes in Berlin, "Telegrams come in every minute from Americans in different parts of Germany asking for help, some of them hysterical." . . . Winston Churchill, the first lord of the admiralty, stands in the admiralty office in London, its windows open to the warm night air, waiting with admirals and captains and clerks for the expiration of the British ultimatum to Germany, and "as the first stroke of the hour boomed out, a rustle of movement swept across the room."

Wednesday, August 5—Austria declares war on Russia, and Belgium declares war on Germany. . . . The New York *Times* publishes a dispatch from London: "The crowds last evening and this morning began to betray growing excitement. A procession of young men marched along by Whitehall and up the Strand, cheering. It was headed by a squad carrying the Union Jack of England and the tri-color of France. As it passed Trafalgar Square there was some booing, but the cheering outweighed it. Fleet Street last evening was jammed by crowds watching the bulletins. Occasionally they sang 'The Marseillaise' and 'God Save the King.' "

God save the people. God save the souls of the millions upon millions of soldiers and noncombatants about to perish. In one Protestant country after another frightened men and women opened the Bible and read in Revelation:

> . . . and, lo, there was a great earthquake; and the sun became black as sackcloth of hair, and the moon became as blood;

> And the stars of heaven fell unto the earth, even as a fig tree casteth her untimely figs, when she is shaken of a mighty wind.
> And the heaven departed as a scroll when it is rolled together; and every mountain and island were moved out of their places.
> And the kings of the earth, and the great men, and the rich men, and the chief captains, and the mighty men, and every bondman, and every free man, hid themselves in the dens and in the rocks of the mountains;
> And said to the mountains and rocks, Fall on us, and hide us from the face of him that sitteth on the throne, and from the wrath of the Lamb;
> For the great day of his wrath is come; and who shall be able to stand?

Neither Woodrow Wilson nor his wife was well when they moved into the White House, and they brought along a traveling medicine kit which he himself always packed. Mrs. Wilson had a fall on March 1, 1914, and when their daughter Eleanor visited them, she thought her mother looked pale and ill, bearing out her earlier apprehensions on inauguration day. The President said to Eleanor, "She gave us a scare. She fell in her room a few days ago and she won't stay in bed and rest.' Mrs. Wilson smiled at their daughter and then said teasingly of her husband, "This goose keeps worrying about me for no reason at all."

On April 1, 1914, Wilson wrote a friend, "I am sorry to say that Ellen does not make as rapid progress in the recovery of her strength as we had hoped. She is entirely out of the woods, so far as the effect of her fall are concerned [sic], but it has left her very weak indeed and she only sits up for a little while every day and has not yet got back appetite enough to build her up." At Easter, when the Wilsons vacationed at White Sulphur Springs, Virginia, they took along a nurse. After they returned, Mrs. Wilson mustered enough energy to be driven to the Capitol to hear her husband speak to Congress, and she managed to receive guests on May 7, when Eleanor was married, but near the end of May she gave up and remained in her second-floor bedroom with its flowered chintz and gay cushions and lamps.

Wilson and his wife deeply loved each other. He had met her in April, 1883, when legal business took him to Rome, Georgia, where she was born, and they were engaged by the following September. She was small and gentle, golden-haired and rosy-cheeked, quick in movements and slow in speech, with a Southern drawl. Ellen Louise Axson—Woodrow called her Nell some of the time—was born in 1860, which meant she was three years his junior. Her father was a Presbyterian minister, and so was his. After reading Hegel and Kant and the major English and Scottish philosophers, she had gone through a period of religious doubt, something that never happened to Woodrow, but in the end she remained true to her religious heritage. She enjoyed reading aloud; her favorite authors were Shakespeare, Wordsworth and Browning. After she became engaged to Woodrow, but before marrying him, she lived awhile in New York City, where she studied painting at the Art Students' League, for she wanted to become a painter. They were married in Savannah, Georgia, in 1885. He later wrote, "A man who lives only for himself has not yet begun to live—has yet to learn his use, and his real pleasure, too, in the world. It is not necessary that he should marry to find himself out, but it is necessary he should love."

Ellen idolized her husband. In fact, she considered him the greatest man of his time. Nonetheless, she was an independent thinker, constructively critical, always listening to him intensely, forever ready to comfort and reassure him. He regarded her as his best literary critic; carefully she went over his prepared speeches and he discussed with her his every important move. While they never quarreled, she had a couple of habits that annoyed him. He declared it took her longer to say anything than anyone else in the world, and he disliked her habit of folding her arms as she listened to him. He would cry, "Don't do that, Nell! It pushes out your upper arm." She would unfold her arms, only to fold them again unconsciously moments later.

Like a proper Southern belle, she disliked boisterousness, and whenever he playfully chased their daughters around tables, she would ask, "Woodrow, what *is* the matter with you?" He would laugh at her and call her a Proper Member of the Family, then tickle their mischievous daughter Nellie, whom he classified with himself as the Vulgar Members. But despite her air of propriety, Mrs. Wilson could become excited by an intellectual discussion, her artistic temperament showing. In the White House she found an attic room with a skylight and converted it into a studio. There she painted pictures of such merit that a gallery sold them anonymously, and she donated the money she earned to crippled children and to an educational fund for Southern mountain people. During the Hayes administration the great English painter George Frederic Watts had presented the President with his famous picture called "Love and Life," but Mrs. Hayes had banished it from the White House because she was shocked by its two lovely nudes. Mrs. Wilson, the daughter of a Presbyterian preacher, was not shocked; she found the Watts masterpiece in the Corcoran gallery and had it returned to the White House.

After giving birth to three daughters, her figure thickened, and when the bloom faded from her cheeks, she crushed red rose petals and rubbed them on her face with a rabbit's foot. Before Woodrow became President, she seldom had much money and owned no jewelry, no furs, but this did not bother her because she took little interest in the way she dressed. Eleanor said of her mother, "She had excellent taste but no chic." Titters ran through Washington drawing rooms when the President's wife announced she would never spend more than $1,000 a year on her wardrobe. For a woman familiar with the works of great philosophers, though, she had small regard for the capital's social life, while at the same time she necessarily and graciously presided over receptions and musicals at the White House, gave two or three tea parties a week and received callers almost every afternoon. One Congressman's wife sneered, "She never seemed to enjoy the greatness her husband had achieved; her manner was almost apologetic, her hands limp and cold."

This critic was quite wrong, for Mrs. Wilson was thrilled by Woodrow's accomplishments.

Whenever she found time, she went to the Library of Congress to read rare books and gaze at art treasures, but mostly she concentrated on humanitarian work. She toured government offices, getting rest rooms installed for women workers. A member of the Board of Associated Charities, she often met with social workers and listened patiently as they described the misfortunes of needy families. But the cause that lay closest to her sensitive heart was the brutal living conditions of the capital's 96,000 blacks. Only three weeks after moving into the White House she discovered that behind the city's fine façade there were miserable black slums, filthy, diseased and overcrowded. Laden with food and clothing, she would leave the elegance of the executive mansion to descend into the slum quarters, and while the blacks knew by her drawl that she was a Southerner, they also knew she was sincere in her concern. Breaking her self-imposed rule of never asking her husband to do anything for her in his capacity as President, she begged him to appoint a commission to survey conditons in the back alleys. He did. Soon she was leading Congressmen along back streets lined with squalid shacks and heaped high with garbage. Ellen Wilson was the Eleanor Roosevelt of her day. Congress would later approve an act creating a corporation called the Ellen Wilson Memorial Homes. It was intended to provide sanitary housing for the working class in the District of Columbia; but later it was declared unconstitutional, and all her good work came to nothing. This pending legislation was on her mind as she lay dying.

On June 7, 1914, the President said in a letter:

> I am very, very blue and out of heart today. My dear one absolutely wore herself out last winter and this spring and has not even started to come up the hill again. She can eat and retain almost nothing, and grows weaker and weaker, with a pathetic patience and sweetness all the while which makes it all the more nearly heart-breaking for those of us who love her. There is nothing at all the matter with her organically: It is altogether functional; and the doctors assure us that all with care will come out right. But a nervous break down [*sic*] is no light matter and my heart is very heavy.

Mrs. Wilson was not having a nervous breakdown. She was suffering from Bright's disease—inflammation of the kidneys—complicated by tuberculosis of both kidneys. Woodrow became so alarmed about her failure to eat that he would take a tray of food to her bedside, sink onto his knees beside her and plead, "You'll soon get well, darling, if you'll try hard to eat something. Now, please take a bit, dear." But her condition worsened, and she slept badly, and he fell into the habit of rising at 3 A.M. to slip into her bedroom to see how she was resting. Later, alone at his desk and trying to choke down his own breakfast, he would turn to Dr. Cary T. Grayson, medical adviser to the White House, and ask, "How is she, Doctor?"

Grayson did not wish to give Wilson false hope, so most of the time he would reply, "I am sorry to say, Mr. President, that I cannot report any improvement." Eleanor Wilson thought her mother looked very small and white. One day Eleanor found her at her desk writing indignant letters to Senators who were attacking her husband.

Eleanor paid no attention to the assassinations at Sarajevo because of her mother's conditon, and now she began worrying about her father, too, for his step had lost its spring, his face was gaunt and gray and lined. On July 28 when Austria-Hungary declared war on Serbia, Eleanor lunched at the White House, and the President told her the news in a low voice, adding, "It's incredible! Incredible! But don't tell your mother anything about it." Eleanor asked whether he thought the whole world would become involved. Wilson stared at her in a daze, suddenly clapped his hands over his eyes and moaned, "I can think of nothing—nothing, when my dear one is suffering!"

On August 4, when Britain declared war on Germany, the President sat beside his sleeping wife, fighting back his mounting terror and struggling to write a message to the warring nations that tendered his "good offices in the interest of European peace." Dr. Grayson had called in two other physicians for consultation. The three agreed that Mrs. Wilson's condition was hopeless, so at last Wilson learned the bitter truth. He was too shocked to say a word, but for the first time Eleanor saw him weep. Grayson now became as alarmed about Wilson as he was about his wife.

Ellen told her husband she knew she was dying. She said that after she was gone, she wanted him to marry again. Time after time she asked about the progress of her bill to give the poor good housing; legislative leaders acted quickly, and Wilson was able to tell her that her measure had passed. For the last time she smiled her radiant smile. She never did learn that war had broken out in Europe. Austria declared war on Russia on August 6, and Wilson was told his wife could not last more than a few hours. He and their three daughters gathered at her bedside. His two sons-in-law waited in another room with Presidential Secretary Tumulty, who loved Mrs. Wilson as though she were his own mother. In attendance were two nurses, ready to do whatever they could, but nothing could be done. Dr. Grayson was by her bed. Ellen roused herself from a semistupor, took his hand in her feeble hand, drew his face near her lips and spoke her last words: "Please take good care of Woodrow, Doctor." At the moment of her death her husband was holding her hand while their daughters knelt at the bedside, and Ellen Louise Axson Wilson gave up her soul as twilight softened the city. Wilson's face was hard as marble. Looking across the bed at Grayson, he asked, "Is it all over?" The doctor nodded. The President straightened up and folded her arms across her breast. He walked to a window and stared south across the gardens his wife had had planted in the Ellipse, stared past the Washington monument toward the Potomac river beyond and began sobbing.

"Oh, my God! What am I going to do? What am I going to do?"

Over in Europe young men had been torn from their families and friends, uprooted from homes and desks and workbenches, thrust into uniforms of various colors, armed with guns and revolvers and bayonets, told that it was their duty to kill other young men, and then they were sent marching down roads and over fields and across marshes, millions upon millions of soldiers whose heavy boots thudded the earth and set up vibrations that quickened the continents and oceans and came to be felt around the entire globe, while one of the most powerful men in the world, the President of the United States, was paralyzed with grief.

"I sometimes feel," Wilson mourned, "that the Presidency had to be paid for with Ellen's life, that she would be living today if we had continued in the old simple life at Princeton." Friends and associates saw his gray, grim face and tensed with concern. Franklin D. Roosevelt took one look and thought Wilson was about to have a nervous breakdown. Some who did not know the President speculated that he might marry again, while a few crass gamblers even took bets on it. Colonel House, Wilson's closest adviser, wondered whether he would be able to hang onto his sanity. House's anxiety turned to terror when the grieving President muttered that he wished someone would kill him.

One day Wilson left impulsively for New York to visit Colonel House in the Colonel's apartment at 145 East Thirty-fifth Street, and late that evening he said he wanted to go out for a walk. And, the President snapped, he did not want any secret service agents or policemen following him. Colonel House argued, pointing out that it was much too dangerous for him to walk the streets of Manhattan at that hour without any protection. Wilson insisted. Colonel House, born in Texas and a good shot with a pistol, slipped a revolver into his pocket and led Wilson out a service entrance. Neither the nervous Texan nor the rash President was aware that two New York detectives fell in behind them, careful to stay out of sight while still remaining close enough to the President to protect him. Colonel House's anxiety grew when Wilson said he wanted to stroll the main streets of mid-Manhattan. The colonel later said:

> I remember we went up Fifth Avenue and through Forty-second Street and Times Square. The theater crowds were out. We had people jostling all around us, but not a soul recognized him. It was an extraordinary experience. I wouldn't have believed it could happen, particularly when you consider how striking was his face, and that he was the most widely photographed man in the country at the time. If anyone had attacked him, I don't know what I could have done. People were so thick around us that it would have been difficult for me to shoot, although I seldom had my hand off my gun. I thought at that time, and on several occasions afterward, that the President wanted to die.

Chapter 12

AMERICANS TRAPPED IN EUROPE

Herbert Hoover had been sent to Europe by his adopted state of California for the purpose of inviting the various governments to participate in the Panama-Pacific Exposition to be held in San Diego in 1915. At the age of forty he was a successful businessman, and rich; but his name was unknown to the public, and none could have predicted that he would become the thirty-first President of the United States. He worked out of London, where he maintained both an office and a home. Going from country to country on the continent, he persuaded many foreign nations to enter exhibits in the forthcoming exposition. While engaged in this civic work, he also took care of his own business, he and his associates having quantities of ore on ships bound for Belgian, French, German and American ports. Then came war.

It was the height of the tourist season and 120,000 Americans were traveling on the continent and in Great Britain. More than 10,000 were in Germany, 3,000 in Berlin itself. As nation after nation sprang to arms, borders were sealed, passenger ships were taken off the transatlantic run, banks and hotels refused to accept American currency, a bank holiday was in effect in Britain, and the bewildered Americans suddenly found themselves entrapped and immobilized in a world becoming a nightmare. Besides the vacationers, there were American employees of companies with offices abroad, and they too suffered. Also stranded in Europe were 150 American vaudeville acts—80 in Germany and Austria, 20 in France, 15 in Russia and the rest scattered elsewhere. American acts playing in London were paid in paper money difficult to convert into dollars. Here in the United States it began to appear that school openings would be delayed because 30,000 American teachers were unable to get back home.

The fate of American tourists was the responsibility of the state department, which was ill equipped to cope with an emergency so unexpected and massive. Secretary of State Bryan rolled up his shirt sleeves and worked long hours trying to make the necessary arrangements. Swift authorization was given to American embassies and consulates in London and other capitals to combat the crisis. They needed help. In London the embassy and consulate were overwhelmed by frantic people demanding that their checks be cashed, that they be given lodgings and that they be put aboard ships to sail home. Walter H. Page, the American ambassador to Great Britain, became the target of panic-stricken Americans. "Those two first days there was, of course, great confusion," he wrote. "Crazy men and weeping women were imploring and cursing and demanding—God knows it was bedlam turned loose. I have been called a man of the greatest genius for an emergency by some, by others a damned fool, every epithet between these two extremes. Men shook English banknotes in my face and demanded United States money and swore our Government and its agents ought to be shot. Women expected me to hand them steamship tickets home. . . . Yesterday one poor American woman yielded to the excitement and cut her throat." Page was kept so busy that he went three days without a bath and almost no sleep. Joseph C. Grew in the American embassy in Berlin wrote in his diary, "The State Department keeps cabling instructions to pay so and so $1000 which has been deposited in Washington, but where on earth the *cash* is to come from they do not seem to consider."

William Howard Taft, the former President, was horror-stricken, writing, "Nothing like it has occurred since the great Napoleonic Wars . . . nothing has occurred like it since the world began. It is a cataclysm. It is a retrograde step in Christian civilization." On August 2 Woodrow Wilson was still so stunned he spoke of "this incredible European catastrophe."

Late that Monday afternoon, August 3, the day Germany declared war on France, Herbert Hoover got a phone call from an old friend, Robert P. Skinner, the American consul general in London. Skinner said 1,000 American tourists were milling around the consulate and on the street outside, all penniless because they were unable to exchange their own currency and letters of credit for British money. Could Hoover think of anything to do? He knew of course that it was a British bank holiday and all banks had closed for four days. Hoover walked the one block from his office to the consulate and saw at a glance that Skinner had not exaggerated. Beefy-faced American men were pounding the counter and demanding to know whether the American government was going to protect its citizens. The consul general had better goddamn well straighten out the British about the rights of Americans! He ought to tell the American banks in London to open up at once! It was a disgrace! Then, anger turning to fear, they wondered whether London was about to be bombed by German planes or zeppelins.

Hoover asked to use Skinner's telephone. He called his own office and asked two of his staff engineers to bring to the consulate the few hundred pounds in gold and British currency he had had the foresight to withdraw from banks the previous Friday to pay staff salaries. Hoover then told Skinner he was willing to exchange British money for dollars at the usual rate—or he would lend anyone ten shillings each to tide him over the night if he was totally without any kind of cash. Skinner begged the people to calm themselves, explaining what was about to be done. Obeying Skinner's orders, they formed five lines and filed in orderly fashion past a few tables where Hoover and the others sat with the currency at hand. Did Miss Jones have no American currency whatsoever? Word of honor?

Okay, Miss Jones. Sign this IOU for ten shillings with your name and London address. Here is the English money. Come back again tomorrow.

When the last of the troubled Americans had received this temporary help, Skinner called Ambassador Page to report how Hoover had assisted him. Page said he too was being besieged and was completely without money. Would Skinner please send Hoover from the consulate to the embassy? The ambassador and the engineer knew each other slightly, having dined together on a few formal occasions. When Hoover got to the embassy, he found things there far worse than they had been at the consulate. Now tens of thousands of Americans were pouring into London from the continent. All British sailings to the United States had been canceled. Three American businessmen had scheduled an evening meeting to discuss what should be done, and Page asked Hoover to attend. Such was the beginning of Herbert Hoover's public career.

The meeting was held in the fashionable Savoy hotel, its glass-covered terrace overlooking the Thames. The management gave the Americans free use of its grand ballroom and the entire floor on which it was located. Nearly 2,000 arrived and milled anxiously around awhile, finally electing a committee that consisted for the most part of rich men. Hoover listened to speech after agitated speech. Then he suggested that since most of the committee members would go home as soon as possible, he would form another organization composed of Americans who were permanent residents of London, and they would try to restore order. Selflessly, Hoover did not mention the fact that for some time he had had reservations to return to America aboard the *Lusitania*; aware that his help was needed, he chose to remain awhile. Agreement came from members of the newly elected committee, who collected thousands of dollars from their fellow travelers, gave it to Hoover and then disbanded. He telephoned some American engineers and asked them to meet him in the Savoy the next morning. Before leaving the hotel about midnight, he reached the ambassador and consul general by phone to tell them that as of nine o'clock the following day he and his helpers would be ready "to take on all comers." The excitement and confusion, he confessed, left him "stunned and unstrung."

But not too stunned and unstrung to take on a relief job of gigantic proportions, one demonstrating for the first time Hoover's remarkable ability to organize. Himself an engineer, he surrounded himself with other engineers—hardheaded realists. From among them and the tourists themselves he organized a voluntary staff of 500 who soon sat at scores of tables listening to stories and appeals for help. Many Americans, sure the end of the world was near, wanted to talk to a countryman. Others sought financial aid. All wanted transportation back to security. They came to the Savoy in droves from the embassy and consulate, which were unable to service them.

Somerset Maugham said that in a crisis unselfish people become noble while selfish people become monstrous. A United States Senator wired Ambassador Page: SEND MY WIFE AND DAUGHTER HOME ON THE FIRST SHIP. Well, as Page wrathfully wrote in his memoirs, "his wife and daughter are found three days later sitting in a swell hotel waiting for me to bring them stateroom tickets on a silver tray!" Some American tourists threshing about in London bombarded Senators and Representatives, Cabinet members and state governors, with cables insisting on immediate relief. An embassy aide rushed into Page's office to say that a man from Boston carried letters of introduction from Senators and governors and demanded, since he would have time before sailing, that he be provided with a secretary to escort him to London picture galleries. The young assistant asked, "What shall I do?" The ambassador snarled, "Put his proposal to a vote of the two hundred Americans in that room and watch them draw and quarter him!" An American woman wrote Page a four-page letter ending with the request that he drop everything and come to her hotel five miles away to tell her about the sailing of steamships. Six solemn and nervous American preachers arrived with a resolution urging the ambassador to telegraph "our beloved, peace-loving President to stop this awful war." The harassed, embarrassed and exhausted ambassador—not a businessman like Hoover, but a man of letters—sighed to himself: "Lord save us! What a world!"

The Hoover committee functioned with extraordinary smoothness. A half dozen young American men, bright and familiar with finances, sized up the applicants as they entered relief headquarters, then divided them into three groups: white cards for those of seemingly substantial means; red for doubtful ones; blue for those who were absolutely destitute. Hoover and nine other businessmen had opened an account in a London bank that was guaranteed up to $1,000,000. Drawing on this, they and their assistants handed out cash to moneyless Americans. By the time the emergency ended they had disbursed more than $1,500,000 and were cheated out of less than $300. Some tourists got money as a charitable donation which they were not expected to repay. Hoover said in admiration, "It was a monument either to the shrewd judgment of our youngsters or to the honesty of the American school teacher and traveller."

But one woman went on a hunger strike because the Hoover committee would not send her home at its expense in quarters better than steerage; a staff member gave her an easy chair in the lunchroom, and the display of food broke her will within a few hours. Thousands of American girls were in continental boarding schools; their parents cabled them to come home, but their teachers were afraid to let them travel through war-torn countries. Hoover sent older women into Germany, France and Switzerland to collect the girls and bring them safely across the channel to London. After he had arranged passage home for one old woman, she refused to sail until he gave her a written guarantee that she would not be torpedoed on the Atlantic. He thought a moment and then wrote out the statement she wanted. Later he chuckled: "I knew that there wasn't one chance in ten thousand that her ship would be harmed. If she came through all right, she'd say I kept my word. If she was sunk, she'd never have time to blame me."

The sudden explosion of war jarred people out of their customary habits of thought and evoked many strange reactions. The very balance of nature seemed upset. In one area in Britain all the bees died—all except those owned by one woman who had lots of honey to sell. Her neighbors were curious to know why she alone had succeeded with her bees. Her face brightening, the woman said, "Ah! As soon as the war broke out I went and told my bees all about it." In ancient Rome a flight of bees was considered a bad omen; Appian said that a swarm of bees lit on the altar and foretold the fatal issue of the battle of Pharsalia.

And strange things were happening to the Hoover committee in the Savoy hotel. Into this posh and proper place there came a dozen American Indians, clad in feathers and beads and buckskin, and also ten cowboys, wearing chaps, leather vests and sombreros. They belonged to a small Wild West show that had been performing in Poland when the war started. The Polish government had commandeered their horses and cow ponies, their money ran out, and they had to feed their orangutan to their starving tiger and lion. Unable to pay for their lodgings, they had slipped out in the dark of night, leaving the innkeeper their tent and elephant and other wild beasts. After the Polish border opened a crack, they were allowed to leave the country to travel to Hamburg, Germany, which had been their port of entry from America. To escape the innkeeper, they had been forced to leave their luggage behind, so they wore their gaudy costumes which were more valuable than their street clothes.

In Hamburg the Indians and cowboys met a twelve-year-old American boy who had been sent from home to visit his grandparents in Croatia. His ship had just docked in Hamburg, the boy had descended to the pier, and the first thing he'd seen was a band of "redskins" wearing war bonnets. Dumbfounded, he stopped in his tracks. Black Feather, the Indian leader, approached the boy and came straight to the point. "Kid, you got any money?" Yes, the boy did have money, which he now shared with the Indians and cowboys, enough money to take all of them from Hamburg to London.

Now this spectacular group stood before Herbert Hoover in the Savoy. After listening to their story, Hoover said he had enough money in his loan fund to arrange steerage passage for them, but Black Feather seemed to have something else on his mind.

"What else can I do for you?" Hoover asked.

"Well," Black Feather replied, "you see, we took the kid's money. I'd like to be sure he gets it back. Can't you advance it to him? I own two hundred acres of apple orchard in Montana and I'll make good as soon as I get home."

That evening Hoover told this story at a dinner party. Among the guests was a rich American woman who had reserved a suite on the SS *Baltic.* She said she had a spare cabin the boy was welcome to use. The next day Hoover relayed the offer to the boy, who shook his head and said, "Thank the lady, but I'd rather go in steerage with my friend Black Feather."

In Berlin when war began was another Wild West show. Its Indians were Onondaga, members of one of the Five Nations composing the Iroquois League in colonial New York, men with fierce pride in their ancestry. Berlin authorities interned them "for their own protection," beat them, insulted them. The United States government managed to obtain their release after the unreeling of yards of red tape. Subsequently, the Onondaga issued a formal declaration of war against Germany. Furthermore, all the 540 braves living on a reservation near Syracuse in central New York were urged to enlist on the Allied side.

Herbert Hoover had his wife and two small sons with him in London. Five times he booked homeward passage for them and five times had the reservations canceled. At last, on October 3, he saw them off at the pier and sighed in relief. After Mrs. Hoover landed safely in New York, she cabled her husband to say that all was well, adding that Herbert, Jr., their eleven-year-old, had eaten seven cream puffs in one day during the voyage. The point was that the boy had triumphed over his fear of seasickness, but by this time British censorship was in full swing and British officials misinterpreted the cream puff remark as some kind of sinister message in code. Hoover was asked to explain, which he did, but the British agent who questioned him appeared dissatisfied and warned him of the dire fate awaiting spies.

Dr. Nicholas Murray Butler, the president of Columbia University, was in Paris with his wife and friends on June 28, when newsboys raced along boulevards hawking extras telling of the assassination at Sarajevo. Soon, he wrote, "Austria was openly threatening Serbia and that there was restlessness in Russia and Germany was quite obvious. Nevertheless, a general European war, to say nothing of a world war, seemed so grotesque an outcome of even the tragic happenings in the Danubian country that it did not occur to any of us as at all possible."

He and Mrs. Butler continued their vacation, going to Venice, but after their arrival he became alarmed for the first time on July 31. On that day Germany proclaimed a "state of threatening war" and sent Russia an ultimatum demanding an end to all warlike preparations. The Butlers and three friends left Venice to drive by car across northern Italy toward Milan. On Sunday morning, August 2 they departed from Milan in the hope of reaching Lausanne, Switzerland, before nightfall, but to their surprise they found the road blocked by masses of cavalry and artillery moving north. They turned around and drove back to Milan, where they abandoned their automobile and boarded a train bound for Paris. Just when they thought all was going well, they were told by a conductor that the French border had been closed; the train would not continue to Paris, after all, but if they wished, they could get off at Lausanne. At one o'clock in the morning they left the express at Lausanne and found themselves alone in the railway station except for the handful of other passengers who got off with them. The portly and dignified university president unloaded their trunks from the baggage car with his own hands, as he later wrote in astonishment. They went to the Hotel Cecil, but it was so crowded that the five members of the Butler party had to sleep the rest of the night on sofas and in bathtubs. Early the next day Butler returned to the station, where he found an old German-Swiss employed by the railroad, and the educator never forgot what he said: "Sir, this is not a peoples' war. This is a kings' war."

Butler questioned him. Yes, the French border was closed. No, there was no chance of getting to Paris. Butler said, well, then, there was nothing for him and his friends to do but to go back to Milan. Impossible, said the old man. When the train left for Milan it would carry only Italians who had been summoned home. Frustrated, Butler glanced idly about him and saw a railway car marked "Reserved." What was that? Well, that was a car used by public officials. And who was using it now? No one. In his best commencement day voice, Dr. Butler intoned, "Very well. Let's loosen the brake and bring it down the track." The old man wanted to know why. Butler said, "I'll show you." The university president and the puzzled railway worker pushed the car down the track to a convenient place, halted it, loaded Butler's luggage inside. Butler returned to the hotel, brought his party back to the station, and when the southbound train pulled in at 8:15 A.M. he stepped up to its conductor, saluted, and said in pompous French, "This is the special reserved car that you had instructions to take back with you to Milan." The bluff worked. The conductor politely tipped his hat, had the train backed up to the car Butler had commandeered, and five minutes later the Butler party was rolling back to Milan.

George B. McClellan, Jr., was having his own troubles. McClellan was the son and namesake of the controversial Civil War general, a leader of Tammany Hall, a Congressman from New York, a two-term mayor of New York City, an extremely well-educated and cultured man who had written four books. On August 3, the day Germany invaded Belgium, he was in southern Austria with his friend John C. Van Dyke, a professor of the history of art at Rutgers University. When they got back to their hotel, they found a young woman, apparently a caretaker, sitting on a stool with her head in her hands, sobbing. McClellan put his hand on her shoulder and asked, "Fraülein, what's the matter?" She wailed, "Ach! Herr Gott! They have taken my man from me and they are going to kill him!" Mobilization had been ordered in Austria. That morning when McClellan and Van Dyke left the hotel it had been full of guests, but now it was empty. Every hotel employee under sixty had been pressed into service. The government had commandeered every cow and goat in the neighborhood. The two American men put their heads together, decided that most tourists in Austria would head through Switzerland for France, so maybe they could avoid this crush by descending instead into Italy. "It was a very bright idea and would have been successful," McClellan wrote, "if some twenty-five thousand other Americans had not had exactly the same thought."

After a series of misadventures they reached Milan. The American consulate there was sheer bedlam—men cursing, women weeping, the consul demoralized. Amid this babble McClellan ran into Dr. Butler and Frederick W. Vanderbilt, grandson of Cornelius Vanderbilt, the founder of the fabulous Vanderbilt fortune. Butler had exactly 27 cents in Italian money in his pocket, and this was all he was to have for the next three weeks. One member of his party was able to draw $10 a day on his letter of credit, and this enabled all of them to pay for incidentals. At the Cavour hotel the manager not only let them stay free of charge, but also gave them money to ride a train from Milan to Genoa. The American consulate in Genoa presented the same mad scene they had witnessed in Milan: Hundreds of frantic Americans were laying siege to the consul, demanding money and help in getting home. The consul, beside himself with worry and excitement, told Butler he had cabled for help to the state department in Washington, but had not even received a reply.

Butler, Vanderbilt, McClellan and other influential Americans stranded in Milan decided that the best way to get home would be to charter their own ship, and to this end they organized a mutual help committee. But, rich though they were, they had almost no cash, and at first no one seemed willing to honor their various kinds of credit. Some of the men got a boat and rowed out into the harbor to look at anchored ships, seeing one called the *Principe di Udine*, an 8,000-ton vessel owned by the Lloyd Sabaudo Line. Her regular run was to and from Buenos Aires, but now she was about to be laid up a few weeks for overhauling and cleaning. The Americans conferred with shipping line officials, who said they would charter the liner for 400,000 lire—a price soon raised to 500,000 lire. Butler said in his memoirs they "would have signed the contract just the same if 4,000,000 lire had been asked."

After red-tape snarls and setbacks, the Americans convinced the shipping officers that they had enough credit to pay for the ship. It could accommodate 400 closely packed people. Now came the question of which of the many hundreds of Americans in Milan should be picked to sail. At last it was decided to give preference to those who were alone or old or for this or that other reason were entitled to special consideration. The committee set rates for passage at $250 for first-class cabin, $150 for second-class cabin, and $75 between decks. The men were berthed on the starboard side, the women on the port side, and even in first class as many as three persons were jammed into one room. The panic-stricken and grateful passengers could pay for the trip in a variety of ways—letters of credit, American Express notes, personal checks, and in one case a simple IOU. Exactly 399 lucky Americans were chosen; only about 25 were known personally to committee members; the passengers came from thirty-seven states. They sailed from Milan on August 12, the day German artillery was making rubble of forts in Belgium. A British destroyer guided the refugee ship through the heavily mined Strait of Gibraltar. After the *Principe di Udine* emerged into the open Atlantic, a strange ship closed in on her, and it was feared that they were about to be captured by a German naval vessel; but it turned out to be another British vessel, and after much apprehension this strange voyage ended at the port of New York on August 24. Dr. Nicholas Murray Butler still had only 27 cents.

Here in the United States hundreds of thousands of Americans worried about relatives and friends caught behind the battle lines in Europe. The machinery of foreign exchange had collapsed; the warring nations had severed communications with one another; steamship sailings had been canceled; German submarines were prowling the waters between the continents. President Wilson urged Congress to appropriate money to bring our penniless refugee citizens home, and on August 3 the Senate and House authorized the expenditure of $250,000. This was not enough, so the next day the Congress came up with $2,500,000 more. On August 6 the private banking house of J. P. Morgan & Company became the official American financial representative of France, and within hours $6,000,000 was transferred from the Bank of France to Morgan, Harjes & Company, which then made this sum available in credit to Americans helpless in Paris.

By this time the American ambassador to Great Britain had compiled a card catalogue with the names of all Americans stranded all over Europe. As yet, however, no one had solved the problem of how to bring them home. President Wilson and Secretary of State Bryan suddenly realized that the United States had almost no merchant marine. While there were about 5,500,000 tons of shipping under American registry, most operated along the coasts or in inland waterways. Only fifteen American-owned oceangoing ships flew the Stars and Stripes, and of these all but six were passenger liners with little cargo capacity. American exports were carried in foreign bottoms for the most part. Congress began considering bills to enlarge the merchant marine.

The American ambassador to Germany, James W. Gerard, was under heavy pressure in Berlin. Signing 1,000 passports a day gave him writer's cramp, so his embassy assistants had a stamp made of his signature to lighten his load. Nonetheless, the pleas and demands of Americans stranded in Berlin were so fatiguing that he began fumbling decisions, finally broke down, mumbled over and over again he felt he was dying.

The U.S. government decided to send two cruisers to Europe with gold to be distributed among the hapless Americans. Since this nation was not at war, our ships were neutral and therefore not legitimate prey for any belligerent warship, although there was a chance they might hit a floating mine and be sunk. The *Tennessee* sailed on August 6 and the *North Carolina* two days later. They carried $8,000,000 in gold. The man in charge of this treasure was Henry S. Breckinridge, assistant secretary of war; he was accompanied by army officers and officials of the treasury and state departments. When the cruisers got to the continent and Great Britain, they put in at one port after another so that Breckinridge and his staff might speed the gold to the various capitals.

Among those benefiting from the arrival of the *Tennessee* was Gertrude Stein, an expatriate American writer, and her companion, Alice B. Toklas. They had a home in Paris, but the outbreak of war had trapped them in Britain with almost no cash. Miss Stein wired a cousin in Baltimore to ask for money while Miss Toklas made the same request of her father. One day they were told to report to a certain office in London to claim the funds sent them aboard the *Tennessee*. To the surprise of the two women the American officials measured their heights, weighed them on a scale and then gave them their money. Miss Stein had not seen her cousin in ten years, while Miss Toklas had not seen her father in six. How in the world did each relative know their height and weight? After the war Miss Stein's cousin visited them in Paris, and when they put this question to him, he said that as best he could remember he had asked Washington for copies of their passports, from which he got this data.

Although the gold shipment had relieved the financial distress of the Americans abroad, there remained the problem of getting them home. The Germans offered the use of their ships anchored in American and

Italian ports when war began, so Bryan began making arrangements. Would the British let refugee-laden ships travel without molestation? Yes—provided they were operated by American crews, flew the American flag and returned to neutral ports when their relief task was ended. And the French? Well, at first the French refused to guarantee safe passage. To Europe Bryan sent seven army transports and a commercial vessel. American consuls on the continent hired other ships, and at last transatlantic trips were resumed by British, French and Italian lines. A committee was organized in New York City to help New Yorkers entrapped in Europe. It was headed by former Mayor Seth Low, money was collected, help was given 2,000 families overseas, and committee members met 135 ships carrying 103,276 refugees, who told reporters horror stories about what was happening abroad.

The repatriation crisis was over by the middle of September, 1914.

Chapter 13

LIES AND SPIES AND SABOTEURS

One evening in the spring of 1915 when his wife was out of town, Franklin D. Roosevelt dined in the exclusive Metropolitan Club in Washington, D.C. He later wrote Eleanor about the German ambassador, "Von Bernstorff was at the next table trying to hear what we were talking about." To the young assistant secretary of the navy this incident was merely an annoyance, but later he learned his name was high on a list of American officials marked for assassination by secret German agents. Our own secret service gave him a revolver and shoulder holster, but he went armed for only three days because, as he said to his wife, he "would normally be dead with the assassin half a mile away."

Count Johann Heinrich von Bernstorff had been the imperial German ambassador to the United States since 1908, and down through the years he had ingratiated himself with some influential Americans, with other diplomats in the capital and with Washington correspondents. Born in London in 1862 while his father was the Prussian minister to the Court of St. James's, Bernstorff was a Prussian Junker and a count, extremely well educated, a brilliant man and an envoy of wide experience. He had married an American woman, Jeanne Luckemeyer. Although he was a nobleman and looked it, although this was an era in which few diplomats condescended to talk to newspaper reporters, Bernstorff made himself available to the Washington press corps.

The German embassy was a big red brick building dominating the block-long Massachusetts Avenue terrace in the northwest section of the city. The Bernstorffs refurbished it soon after their arrival and gave lavish dinners and musicales. The ambassador often entertained correspondents, freely granting interviews, sometimes agreeing to write articles for magazines, never letting reporters leave without a gift of a bottle of wine, a box of cigars or some German delicacy. Bernstorff frequently visited publisher William Randolph Hearst's apartment on Riverside Drive in Manhattan, and he had hoodwinked the President's closest adviser, Colonel House, into believing he was a sincere friend of the United States.

Actually, Bernstorff was an unscrupulous master of intrigue. Broad-shouldered and slim-hipped, he held himself erect like the German army officer he once had been. His blond hair began high on his broad forehead, his blond mustache was upturned and tipped like the Kaiser's, and his alert face narrowed to a pointed chin. Some Americans who at first were charmed by him decided later there was something unpleasant about the way his full lips writhed when he smiled.

The news of the assassinations at Sarajevo had reached Bernstorff the evening of June 28, 1914, while he was dining with the Spanish ambassador in the Metropolitan Club. On July 7 he left for Berlin to be briefed by the German foreign office and by Colonel Walther Nicolai, head of Section III-B, the military intelligence department of the German general staff. Then in the early days of August, with his country now at war with the Allies, Bernstorff sailed back to the United States.

In his cabin he kept $150,000,000 in German marks intended for use in trying to subvert the neutral United States, influence public opinion and thwart the flow of American-made munitions to Britain, France and Russia. There was danger his liner might be stopped at sea by a British warship, boarded by a searching party and his money found. Rather than let this happen, Bernstorff was prepared to throw the cash overboard—all $150,000,000 of it. However, he arrived safely in New York on August 23 and was whisked through customs without his luggage being searched since, of course, he had diplomatic immunity. Even if American customs agents *had* found his millions, they would have been able to do nothing about them, because this nation was neutral and because none knew Bernstorff's plans. Before returning to his post in Washington, he deposited the money in the Chase National Bank in Manhattan in a joint account with Dr. Heinrich Albert, Germany's paymaster in this land; Albert had made the return trip with Bernstorff. The $150,000,000 was only the first of the many millions that flowed through their hands.

That bloody August, 1914, Bernstorff's first problem was to find a way to return to Germany all the German army reservists living in North and South America. Under the German army system every young German male served full time for two or three years, depending on his branch of the service, followed by four or five years in the regular reserves. The fact that a man had emigrated to the United States did not exempt him from service in the German army if called to the colors. At the start of the war in Europe the state department was flooded with inquiries from foreign-born men now residing in the United States. Many did not wish to return to their homelands to don uniforms, so they asked what penalties they might suffer if they remained here. The state department referred the questioners to officials of their own countries.

But some of the German reservists living here erupted in a frenzy of patriotism. Long in existence in New York City was a German Veterans' League, and now the city was overrun with blond, blue-eyed Teutons marching through the streets, wearing straw hats and derbies, keeping step to bands, carrying German flags and cheering. These parades infuriated other New Yorkers who sympathized with the Allies, tempers flared, skirmishes broke out, and at last the mayor issued a proclamation barring all but American flags on the streets and prohibited martial parades by any nationalistic groups.

In Berlin a brittle interview took place between the German foreign secretary, Gottlieb von Jagow, and our ambassador to Germany, James W. Gerard. The German official said ominously, "If there is a war between Germany and the United States, you will find there are 500,000 German reservists in your country ready to take up arms for their mother country, and the United States will be engaged in a civil war." Gerard coldly replied, "I do not know whether there are 500,000 German reservists in the United States, but I do know there are 500,000 lamp-posts in my country and that every German residing in the United States who undertakes to take up arms against America will swing from one of those 500,000 lamp-posts."

While the government never did learn the exact number of German reservists here, there were not the 500,000 Jagow had boasted about, but somewhere between 150,000 and 200,000. Most were middle-aged or older. Nonetheless, the total included perhaps 15,000 to 18,000 young reservists in the prime of life. As for German *officers*, there may have been 800 to 1,000 scattered throughout North and South America. In 1916 in Belgium, Herbert Hoover met a German colonel who had lived in the United States and been an important official in a large American manufacturing firm.

Although Berlin had ordered Bernstorff to send the reservists home, this was easier said than done. American officials, still officially neutral, could understand the desire of German soldiers to return to the fatherland, and they did not blame German envoys for trying to make this possible. But with the British controlling the seas, reservists could not travel on German, Austrian, Bulgarian or Turkish passports, since the ships on which they sailed were subject to search by the British fleet. The ambassador passed his problem along to his military attachés, Captain Franz von Papen and Captain Carl Boy-Ed.

They set up a secret organization to procure or forge American passports, for the British would have to honor any passport issued by the neutral United States. The man picked to head this underground apparatus was Hans von Wedell, a German reserve officer who had become an American citizen and had spent six years in New York as a lawyer and newspaper editor. He opened an innocent-looking office in Manhattan at 11 Bridge Street. From German consulates all over the United States a stream of German reservists was directed to New York, where, they were told, they would be given proper papers and be put aboard ship.

Wedell gave them money and sent them to various areas—to the Bowery, to the Yorkville section of Manhattan, to waterfronts in New York and New Jersey. Bums and drifters and money-hungry seamen of other neutral nations accepted from $10 to $25 for their passports. These were altered, the names and pictures of German reservists substituted for those of the rightful owners, and then the Germans would sail away from American ports to other neutral ports in Scandinavia, Holland and Italy.

The American government soon got wind of this passport ring and put some of its own undercover agents to work. Albert G. Adams, an operative for the justice department, disguised himself as a Bowery bum who shot off his mouth about his love for Germany. He was approached by a German who wanted to buy his passport. After haggling over the price, Adams and the German agreed on $20 for every passport Adams could get from native-born Americans and $30 each for passports of naturalized citizens. Adams promised to obtain four perfect passports and did—since they were made and issued by the state department, at the request of the treasury department, for this very purpose. President Wilson was told about the passport ring, and although he characterized the evidence as "sensational," he insisted that no word of it be leaked to the press. Apparently he hoped that if the government caught and prosecuted a few of the ring's small fry, he then might persuade Bernstorff to end his illegal activity. This would preserve the sanctity of American passports and our neutrality as well.

The four perfect passports given the German by Adams were doctored by the Germans and then issued to four reservists, whose real names were Sachse, Meyer, Wegener and Muller, under the false names of Wright, Hansen, Martin and Wilson. On January 2, 1915, in the port of New York, justice department agents boarded the SS *Bergensfjord*, a Norwegian liner bound for Bergen, Norway, ordered all male passengers to line up on deck, picked out the reservists and arrested them. Subsequently these Germans pleaded that they had accepted the passports because of their patriotism; they were fined $200 each. This raid and other arrests and a change in the form of the American passport put an end to the German passport fraud—but not until after hundreds or maybe thousands of German reservists managed to sneak back to the fatherland.

The spreading of propaganda was another of Bernstorff's missions in neutral America. Wartime propaganda is at least as old as Herodotus, who described a propaganda plot thought up by Themistocles during the Persian War. But although propaganda was an ancient art, World War I was the first so-called press agents' war in all history, for never was so much money spent and never had so many writers and artists been hired to try to brainwash whole segments of humanity. This, it should be understood, was done by all the major powers on both sides in this global conflict. And truth, as always, was the first casualty. In the words of R. W. Rowan, "The worst characteristic of propaganda after 1914 was its *volume*, and its worst ingredient a sickening pap of optimistic exaggeration which, in supplanting bitter truths about blunders, defeats and tragic failures, actually prolonged the war and protected the tenure of viciously incompetent leaders. It not only prolonged the war but made its mark upon the terms of peace. . . ."

In August, 1914, the German Information Service was established in New York City. This was a propaganda agency financed and directed by the German foreign office in Berlin. Besides paying the salaries of a permanent staff, besides subsidizing individuals and periodicals, it received help from people such as Professor Hugo Münsterberg of Harvard. Born in Germany, Münsterberg had been invited here in 1892 by Harvard, where he became a professor of psychology. On August 6, 1914, even before Bernstorff's return to the States, the New York *Globe* published an article by Münsterberg in which he made an all-out appeal for fair play for the Kaiser and Germany. That same day the Brooklyn *Eagle* aired the opinions of Charles Vezin, a merchant and artist who had been born in Philadelphia and educated in Germany. Outlining the German viewpoint of the war, Vezin declared that the Kaiser wanted peace and that Germany was fighting in behalf of all civilization. The German Information Service organized a new press agency called the International Press Exchange, bought control of the *New York International Monthly*, tried to purchase some of the fifty-five German-language newspapers in the United States, and helped George Sylvester Viereck.

Viereck was a talented and tempestuous man, passionately pro-German in both world wars. Born in Munich of a German father and an American mother, he was brought here to live when he was eleven, and his abilities quickly blossomed. In 1907, at twenty-three, the poet, novelist and editor was featured two successive times on the first page of the Sunday New York *Times* literary supplement. Among other things, Viereck became literary editor of his father's German-language magazine *Der Deutsche Vorkämpfer*. He must have entered into a secret agreement with Bernstorff before the ambassador left to visit Germany, for it was August 23 when the diplomat returned, while it was on August 10 that Viereck issued the first issue of his new weekly paper *The Fatherland*, hailing the Kaiser in glowing terms. *The Fatherland* appealed to so many German-Americans that soon it had a circulation of 100,000 copies. The Canadian post office banned it because of its overt German propaganda. After the United States went to war with Germany, Viereck was expelled from the Poetry Society of America and the Authors League and became so detested he nearly was lynched.

Germany's chief propaganda agent in the United States and the head of the German Information Service was Dr. Bernhard Dernburg, a former colonial minister who came here as the representative of the German Red Cross. As a propaganda adviser he hired an American named William Bayard Hale. Born in Indiana and claiming descent from Nathan Hale, Hale had studied at Harvard, become an Episcopalian priest and then quit religion for journalism. Long before the war he wrote a series of articles about President Theodore Roosevelt that won him an assignment from the New York *Times:* in 1908 he was sent to Germany to interview Kaiser Wilhelm. For two hours, in growing astonishment, Hale listened as the emperor spoke with reckless candor, railing against Great Britain and its "ninny" rulers, declaring flatly that he expected to go to war against Britain. The Kaiser's frankness and hostility so alarmed the *Times* that its editors sent Hale to the White House to confer with Roosevelt, who said he felt the story should not be published. While the piece never appeared in the *Times*, Hale wrote an emasculated version of the interview that was accepted by *The Century* magazine. German officials became alarmed when they heard of this development, bought out the entire edition, sent a cruiser here to get the copies and even the type and burned them in the ship's boilers out in the Atlantic.

In 1912 Hale wrote a campaign tract for Woodrow Wilson and consequently regarded himself as Wilson's biographer. Dr. Dernburg wrongly believed that Hale had a key to the back door of the White

House; actually, by the time the Germans hired Hale relations between him and Wilson had cooled and then frozen into enmity. After Dernburg made a speech trying to justify the sinking of the *Lusitania*, it was charged that Hale had been its author, but he insisted he merely edited the speech. Hale ground out German propaganda, criticized British activities on the seas, headed a movement to halt the export of American arms to the Allies. Dernburg paid him $15,000 a year. Hale also received $15,600 a year for journalistic work he did for Hearst, who was unaware of Hale's German connection. In a message to the German foreign office, Bernstorff called Hale "a confidential agent of the Embassy."

Living in Paris when war began was Willard Huntington Wright, a serious writer best remembered for the detective stories he wrote under the pseudonym of S. S. Van Dine. He rushed to the western front in the hope of writing news dispatches about the fighting but was put off by the censors. Wright returned to Paris, packed his belongings, moved to London and wrote a book about Nietzsche, the German philosopher. One night he visited a Swiss citizen who had lived in London for several years and shared Wright's enthusiasm for Nietzsche. As he was about to leave, his host handed him a letter and asked him to mail it, saying, "You see it is perfectly harmless." This remark aroused Wright's suspicions, which escalated when his host's wife took the unsealed letter out of the room and then returned with it in a sealed envelope. When the American writer declined to mail the letter, he was ordered out of the house. Wright went back to his London hotel room and found that it had been searched during his absence. The next few days he was shadowed by detectives wherever he went. With a little digging, Wright discovered that his host was a German spy.

Returning to the United States, Wright became the literary editor of the New York *Evening Mail*. This influential paper was owned by Henry L. Stoddard and financed by George Perkins, a Morgan partner and the manager of Theodore Roosevelt's Progressive campaign of 1912. After the defeat of Roosevelt and the decline of the Progressive party, no more money came from Perkins, so Stoddard decided to sell his newspaper. A syndicate of rich German-Americans, backed by the German government, tendered Stoddard a discreet offer to buy the *Evening Mail*, but he turned them down.

Wright got his job on the paper partly with the help of H. L. Mencken, the Baltimore journalist and gadfly. From 1912 to 1914 Wright had edited a magazine called *The Smart Set*, which then had been taken over by Mencken and George Jean Nathan. Both of Mencken's grandfathers and his maternal grandmother had been born in Germany, and he was so ruthlessly pro-German that some people called him a "literary Uhlan." But, prejudiced though he was, Mencken also was ferociously independent. In 1914 he was approached by a man named Revere, whom Mencken considered a stock speculator, but who in fact was an agent for the Germans. Revere made Mencken an either/or proposition: Either he would buy *The Smart Set* from Mencken, or he would hire him as the editor of a pro-German review. Looking a gift horse in the mouth, Mencken said that if he became the editor of a periodical, he wanted $1,000 a month and absolute control. The agent vanished, and that was that. Pro-German and seemingly anti-American, Mencken told his friend Theodore Dreiser that when he died his last words would be: "I regret that I have but one rectum to leave to my country."

Wright also felt sympathetic toward Germany despite his brush with the German spy in London. In his *Evening Mail* office he had a secretary who complained that his book reviews were unpatriotic, stole his letters and even refused to jot down the titles of German books he was discussing. He set a trap for her. One day he began dictating a letter to the *Evening Mail*'s correspondent in Washington, a letter that was deliberately suspicious, full of alarming and imaginary details and references to conversations he said he had had with the German ambassador. The moment the girl finished typing the letter she tore it from her typewriter, ran out of the office and down into the street and handed it to the first cop she saw. In the end the police accepted his explanation of the matter, but Wright received bad publicity and became so notorious that he was fired from his job and later lost his health. While he was recuperating from a nervous breakdown, he made a fortune writing detective stories about a mythical private eye named Philo Vance.

The Germans persisted in their efforts to get control of the New York *Evening Mail,* and at last they won it through a series of complex undercover tricks. First, the German government gave several hundred thousand dollars to Herman Sielcken. Born in Germany, Sielcken came to the United States, made a fortune in coffee, returned to his native land, invested heavily in German government bonds; he was German in thought, deed and hope. The second link in this secret chain was paymaster Dr. Heinrich Albert. The third was Edward A. Rumely, an American who had taken a medical degree at a German university and helped manage the family business, manufacturing farm equipment. The fourth was the New York law firm of Hays, Kaufman & Lindheim; the senior partner, Arthur Garfield Hays, was of German descent, pro-British in sentiment, but did legal work for the German embassy in Washington. The fifth link was S. S. McClure, born in Ireland, an emigrant to the United States, a man who became one of the best editors in the history of American journalism as the owner of a muckraking magazine named *McClure's Magazine.* After a long illness he sold his periodical but nonetheless yearned to edit a first-rate newspaper.

Rumely knew McClure and asked him to negotiate with Henry L. Stoddard, the owner of the *Evening Mail.* McClure asked Rumely where he expected to find enough money to buy the paper. Rumely, who knew he was about to be financed by the German government, lied to McClure, saying he had the backing of a syndicate of wealthy Americans. Rumely went on to say he had a contract to sell $1,000,000 worth of diesel tractors to Germany but could not make delivery because of the British blockade. Rumely declared that the British had no right to interfere with American trade, wondered why the U.S. government tolerated Britain's high-handed activities, asked why no New York paper ever discussed such matters. He said he wanted the *Evening Mail* to convert it into a neutral paper. He promised to create an S. S. McClure Newspaper Corporation as a holding company to buy the paper. Rumely would become the company president and publisher of the paper, while McClure would take title as editor-in-chief. McClure believed he could make the paper the best in the land, so he signed a two-year agreement with Rumely. "I love Great Britain as a son loves his mother," said Irish-born McClure in all sincerity—and let himself be duped by Rumely. On May 30, 1915, sale of the *Evening Mail* was consummated. Now Germany had another powerful propaganda organ in the United States. The naïve McClure soon found himself feuding with Rumely about the contents and tone of the paper. Rumely had the last word because he was publisher and held the purse strings, so the *Evening Mail* began veering toward the German point of view.

Much later there was revealed another curious newspaper connection, this one concerning Arthur Brisbane. Born here of Scottish descent, Brisbane was a leading editor and columnist for the Hearst chain at a salary of $104,000 a year. Despite his own ample income and rich real estate holdings, Brisbane accepted a "loan" of $375,000 from thirteen wealthy German-American brewers to buy the Washington *Times* in the nation's capital. The leading intermediary in this deal was C. W. Feigenspan, a New Jersey brewer. Interestingly, Brisbane gave no collateral, no lien, to Feigenspan and his colleagues. This strange arrangement came to the attention of some United States Senators, who ordered Brisbane to testify before a Senate subcommittee. Brisbane, who had been called pro-German because of his savage attacks on President Wilson, nervously told his inquisitors that the brewers' generosity was not due to any pro-German sentiments in his writings but rather, he believed, due to their fear of the advent of Prohibition and, like them, he favored beer and light wines. Brisbane was not penalized; when he died in 1936, he left a fortune of $8,000,000.

German armies, which had won spectacular successes on the western front since the beginning of the war, went on the defensive in November, 1914. One problem worrying the German high command was the increasing flow of American-made munitions to Britain, France and Russia. With the European war settling into stalemate, the Germans decided on a campaign of sabotage. On November 18, 1914, German naval headquarters sent secret coded instructions "to all destroying agents in ports where vessels carrying war materials are located in England, France, Canada, the United States and Russia." It mattered not to the Germans that the United States was neutral. German operatives were "to organize explosions on ships sailing to enemy countries." This sabotage work was to be done by personnel having "no relations with the official representatives of Germany."

German sabotage in the United States began on January 3, 1915, with a mysterious explosion aboard the SS *Orton* in Erie basin, a busy waterfront section of South Brooklyn. Fifteen days later an incendiary fire did $1,500,000 worth of damage to the John A. Roebling's Sons Company plant at Trenton, New Jersey; the factory was making steel rope for the Allies. On January 26 Bernstorff received a coded cable from the German foreign office that had been prepared by the German secret service. It gave him the names and addresses of three Irish-Americans willing to do Germany's dirty work in America, and it said in part, ". . . In the U.S. sabotage can be carried out in every kind of factory for supplying munitions of war. . . . Embassy must in no circumstances be compromised. . . ."

Although Germany had planted spies in England and France before the war, at the beginning of hostilities it had only one spy in the United States. This was Dr. Walter T. Scheele. As a young man Scheele had served in a German artillery regiment, then came to this country to engage in chemical research. From the start he was told to place himself at the disposal of the German military attaché in Washington, to make regular reports about explosives and new chemical discoveries relating to warfare. Paid only $1,500 a year for his undercover work, he provided reports so valuable to the German government that he was never called back to active duty but was elevated to a major in the reserves. As a cover Scheele called himself president of the New Jersey Agricultural Chemical Company. His contact at the German embassy was Captain Franz von Papen, the military attaché, a wily and durable character with a face like a fox who later became the German chancellor, connived with Hitler, quarreled with Hitler, was nearly killed by Hitler's elite guard. The German naval attaché, Captain Carl Boy-Ed, received his non-Teutonic name from his Turkish father. Bernstorff entrusted Papen and Boy-Ed with the task of creating a sabotage apparatus in the United States.

Papen recruited a German reservist named Werner Horn, gave him a small German flag, paid him $700, ordered him to blow up the Canadian Pacific railroad bridge spanning the St. Croix river between Vanceboro, Maine, and Canada. On February 2, 1915, Horn got off a train near the bridge, walked up to it carrying a suitcase full of dynamite, planted the charge, lit the fuse, pinned the black-white-red flag on the sleeve of his overcoat, walked away. His homemade bomb failed to explode. A few hours later he was found and arrested. Having been told by Papen that the German flag on his sleeve made him a German soldier, Horn demanded that he be treated as a prisoner of war—but American authorities did not see it that way. Canadian officials wanted to extradite him to try him in one of their courts, but he was prosecuted in the United States and found guilty—not of sabotage, though, since there was not yet any federal statute covering sabotage—but rather for transporting dynamite on an interstate passenger train.

In February, 1915, a bomb was found in a cargo hold of the SS *Hennington Court,* and the SS *Carlton* mysteriously took fire. In March there was an explosion in a Du Pont plant at Haskell, New Jersey. In April a blast wrecked a powder plant at Alton, Illinois, and then some caps for shells detonated in a New Jersey depot. But these early acts of sabotage did not satisfy the Germans, who were becoming ever more alarmed about the help that American manufacturers were giving the Allies. Franz von Rintelen, who was to become a German spymaster, said after the war:

> It was accepted in all quarters in Berlin that something of a more forceful nature must be done than hitherto. Indeed conferences took place in the war ministry, the foreign office,

> and the finance ministry, in each of which I outlined my plans, insofar as I could gauge the situation from my post in Berlin. The impression of energy and determination which I contrived to make gave considerable satisfaction. Men of action, particularly men like Helfferich and Zimmermann, could not help smiling when I concluded one speech with: "I'll buy up what I can, and blow up what I can't." One and all they resolutely agreed with me that sabotage was the only alternative.

Naval Commander von Rintelen was a dashing officer on the staff of the German naval intelligence service. At perhaps the highest political level in Germany it was decided that he should go to the United States as a director of sabotage—independent of the German embassy, operating under the direct authority of the German war minister. Given $500,000 in letters of credit, taking the name of Emile V. Gaché, pretending to be a Swiss citizen, handed a Swiss passport faked in Germany, he traveled to Christiania (Oslo), Norway, where he boldly visited the American and British consulates and obtained visas. Then he sailed for the United States aboard the SS *Kristianiafjord* and landed in New York on April 3, 1915.

Rintelen was as daring and resourceful a saboteur as ever set foot on this soil. He spoke English fluently and before the war had moved in high Anglo-German-American social circles. While living in New York, he had worked for a Wall Street investment house and become the only German not of royal blood to win membership in the exclusive New York Yacht Club. Brilliant and fearless, charming and forceful, he came from an aristocratic family, his easy carriage and fine features reflecting his breeding. Curiously, he looked more Italian than German.

On March 31, 1915, four days before his arrival, Connecticut granted a charter of incorporation to the Bridgeport Projectile Company. The legal work of creating this firm was done by the New York firm of Hays, Kaufman & Lindheim, who knew they were working for the Germans. The money came from Dr. Albert. Connecticut was becoming a booming war center as the Allies placed ever more orders for war matériel, munitions factories springing up and other plants being constructed to make accessories such as springs for shells, bases for machine guns and the like. Under the distant and invisible direction of Albert a congeries of factories and workshops was built at Bridgeport by the Bridgeport Projectile Company.

The Germans hoped to: (1) place such huge orders for lathes, milling machines and other scarce tools that they would slow down plant expansion elsewhere in the United States; (2) divert munitions intended for the Allies by accepting contracts for arms they had no intention of making; (3) pay very high wages and thus stir up discontent among workers; and (4) actually make armaments in the hope of getting them to Germany or some other part of the world for use against the enemies of the fatherland. At first this audacious scheme worked so well that men high in American financial circles mistakenly believed that the British were the secret financiers of the Bridgeport Projectile Company. Its officers drew up sly contracts with cancellation clauses devoid of penalties for failure to deliver the goods as promised. Arms contracts were signed with unsuspecting agents of the British and Russian government, together with innocent American manufacturers.

Shortly after Rintelen got to New York, he tried to do much the same thing by organizing a fake corporation called E. V. Gibbons, Inc., with offices on Cedar Street in lower Manhattan. The German foreign office gave him unlimited money with which to buy great quantities of ammunition in the hope of cornering the market or at least diminishing the help the Allies were getting from American manufacturers. By the spring of 1915, however, the daily production of munitions in this country was so enormous that the spymaster began to realize he could not achieve his first goal of buying up everything. Later he confessed, "If I had bought up the market on Tuesday, there still would have been an enormous fresh supply on Wednesday." So he switched from economic sabotage to physical sabotage and propaganda.

Rintelen got in touch with David Lamar, an unscrupulous and shadowy financier known as the Wolf of Wall Street, a schemer who had sucked John D. Rockefeller, Jr., into an empty deal in which Rockefeller lost about $1,000,000. After Mr. John met Lamar for the first time, he said, "One look at him was enough. I knew I had been sold out." Lamar was now out on bail after being indicted for trying to defraud J. P. Morgan & Company as well. For an enormous sum of money, perhaps hundreds of thousands of dollars, Lamar agreed to organize a front called Labor's National Peace Council. Its announced aim was to embargo arms shipments to the Allies. Among those who joined the council were labor leaders and public officials sincerely wishing to maintain the neutrality for which President Wilson had called, together with isolationist Congressmen, lame-duck politicians and German and Irish laborers.

In his memoirs Rintelen recalls:

> The first thing I did was to hire a large hall and organize a meeting, at which well-known men thundered against the export of arms. Messrs. Buchanan and Fowler, members of Congress; Mr. Hannis Taylor, the former American Ambassador in Madrid . . . together with a number of University professors, theologians and Labour leaders appeared and raised their voices. I sat unobtrusively in a corner and watched my plans fructifying. None of the speakers had the faintest suspicion that he was in the "service" of a German officer sitting among the audience.

Soon the council claimed to represent 4,500,000 peace-loving workers and farmers. William Jennings Bryan, wholly ignorant of the origin of the council, was one of those who spoke at its meetings. Subtle attempts were made to win over Samuel Gompers, president of the American Federation of Labor, who had been born in England and favored the export of arms to the Allies, but he knew the council was a German-front organization. Gompers declared, "The American labor movement as a body is loyal to America. . . . It has nothing to do with those anti-American, pro-Kaiserist activities of which the Peoples' Council [*sic*] is the promoter, and is, in fact, exactly in opposition to them."

The port of New York, which includes the New Jersey waterfront, was the principal harbor from which arms were shipped to Europe. Vessels were loaded by 23,000 stevedores paid $14 a week. Beginning in May, 1915, German agents tried to trigger a longshoremen's strike and halt the flow of arms to the Allies. This was at a time when Britain and France were on the defensive along the western front, when Britain was low on ammunition and switching to a coalition government, when Irish-Americans were angry about the British mistreatment of the Irish. Many stevedores were of Irish descent. Among them was seventeen-year-old Gene Tunney, a checker on the docks in the Chelsea area of Manhattan, a man who later became the heavyweight boxing champion of the world.

The Germans chose a rich Boston grocery dealer, Matthew F. Cummings, to make an approach to the Irish-American officers of the New York district council of the International Longshoremen's Association. The council president, T. V. O'Connor, happened to be visiting in Canada at the time, so Cummings first spoke to Richard Butler, secretary of a longshoremen's local. Cummings said he represented a group of wealthy Irish-American merchants in Boston and declared that what he was about to propose had the endorsement of Professor von Mach of Harvard University. If union officers would pull a five-week strike that would cripple the port of New York and end the export of arms and food to Britain and France, they would be given $1,035,000 to split among them. Furthermore, every dockworker, however lowly, would be paid a strike benefit of $10 a week.

Butler stalled until O'Connor could return from Vancouver. The German and Irish-American Bostonians may have thought they had an easy mark in another stevedore boss, Paul Kelly, for Kelly was not only an Irish-American but once had been a gang leader. However, every single longshoreman official rejected an offer that would have made him rich, and one of them leaked the story to the New York *World*. Shippers using the port of New York were relieved to learn that their dockworkers—badly underpaid dockworkers—were loyal. Richard Butler felt, though, that in the future the union would be unable to strike for more pay or better working conditions without being suspected of having been bribed by the Germans; he wished the story had not been leaked to the *World*.

The *World* saluted the patriotism of the dock wallopers in an editorial: "Most members of this organization are poor and all are hardworking. If they could have been hired to strike and riot, the foreign commerce of the United States might have been paralyzed, atrocious crimes might have been committed and charged against unionism, and public sentiment in this country relative to war might have been very emphatically influenced. . . ."

But if American stevedores refused to play into German hands, there were other ways to cripple commerce. Papen put Rintelen in touch with Dr. Scheele. Rintelen asked him to invent some incendiary device which could be dropped into the holds of ships carrying munitions. After a few experiments Scheele fabricated a bomb from a lead pipe full of acids that would ignite at a given time. His laboratory was at 1133 Clinton Street, Hoboken, New Jersey, but Rintelen wanted a safer place in which to mass-produce these cigar-shaped explosives. Since the outbreak of war British warships had bottled up some ninety German vessels in the port of New York; one of them was the *Friedrich der Grosse*. Under international law she was considered German soil, so Rintelen ordered Scheele to establish his secret factory aboard her. The ship's crew happily went to work, aware they could not be disturbed by American officials, and soon this floating factory was producing fifty cigar-bombs a day.

By one means or another German agents then dropped or planted the bombs in the holds of munitions ships or in their bunkers—their coalbins. After a vessel left the Atlantic seaboard for Europe, the hidden explosive would ignite and start a fire. At first ship's masters could not understand why so many ships caught fire at sea, one of them saying, "There was a maddening certainty about it that suggested that every ship that left port must have nothing in her hold except hungry rats, parlor matches, oil waste and free kerosene." To save his crew and cargo from being blown up, a captain would order the burning hold or bunker flooded with sea water. This damaged the ammunition, but after it was unloaded in a British or French port, the shells would be dried out and sent to the front. Many of these salvaged shells failed to explode, and after handling thousands of these duds, Allied artillerymen angrily blamed American manufacturers for defective workmanship.

Fear of strange bombs caused a tragicomic incident in New York City. Mabel Hite of the vaudeville team of Donlin & Hite died in 1915 and was cremated. The funeral parlor made a mistake and sent an urn containing her ashes to Murray's Roman Gardens, a restaurant at 228 West Forty-second Street near Broadway. When the restaurant manager received this curious delivery, he became alarmed and called the police. An inspector of the police department's bureau of combustibles picked up the package and soaked it in water. The dead woman's husband and partner, Mike Donlin, a great baseball player turned vaudevillian, promptly filed a suit against the funeral home for damaging his wife's ashes.

Dr. Scheele's cigar-bomb was only one of a number of incendiary devices used by the Germans. Some were made to look like tins of food or children's toys or ordinary lumps of coal. One of the most ingenious inventions came from Robert Fay. After the war broke out, Fay became a German lieutenant, saw severe fighting and was impressed by the quality of the captured American shells. This was before the brine-soaked duds began arriving at Allied lines. Fay told his commanding officer he had a scheme for preventing the delivery of American munitions to Europe. He was bucked up the chain of command and found himself talking to ranking members of German military intelligence. Impressed with his plan, they gave him a neutral passport and $4,000 in American currency and sent him to the United States aboard the SS *Rotterdam*. Wearing civilian clothes, as befits a spy, Fay landed in New York on April 23, 1915.

He was an engineer and spoke English with ease. He had been ordered to report not to Rintelen but to Papen. The spy and the German military attaché met for the first time in New York at the Deutscher Verein, or German Club, housed in a five-story building at 112 Central Park West. They discussed Fay's sabotage mission and from then on communicated through an intermediary, for Papen did not want Fay to be seen at the office he had taken in Manhattan.

Fay moved into a boardinghouse in Weehawken, New Jersey, across the Hudson river directly west of Manhattan's Forty-second Street. His plan was to blow the rudders off ships aiding the Allies and thus halt the flow of arms to the Allies. Renting a garage, he began by constructing a mock-up of the stern of a ship and attaching a genuine rudder to it. Then he invented a time bomb which American experts later described as mechanically perfect. To the rudder he attached the bomb containing a detonator with a needle-shaped pin at its lower end. This pin connected with the shaft of the rudder, turned when the rudder turned, bored into the detonator, finally pierced the fulminate and set off a blast that would blow off the rudder and cripple the ship

During his experiments Fay hurt himself, but not badly enough to cause him to abandon his project. Hiring a motorboat and docking it at Weehawken, Fay finally was ready. One night he started out in his boat, chugged down the river and into the upper bay, pretended to have engine trouble as he neared a munitions ship, edged up to its rudder without being seen, attached his bomb and shoved off. Soon he used this trick to plant another explosive on the rudder of a second big ship. Both put out to sea and had their rudders blown off. One of the helpless vessels signaled for help and was towed to safety, but the crew of the other ship had to abandon it and let it drift by itself along the Atlantic seaboard.

Identical explosions on one ship after another aroused suspicion, of course, so Fay dared not continue to skulk about the port of New York in a motorboat. Instead, he made a small cork float, put another bomb on it and swam out into the water, pushing his odd craft ahead of himself in the darkness of night. This was no small feat. Silently easing up to the stern of still another arms-carrying ship, Fay attached his explosive to its rudder and again slipped away undetected. For weeks thereafter the German saboteur carried on his dangerous work, not only in New York, but also in Baltimore and other ports along the coast. The Allies and Americans were unable to explain why munitions ships suddenly lost their rudders at sea.

Then one day the French military attaché stationed in New York got a telephone call from Carl Wettig, managing director of the Whitehall Trading Company. Wettig said that Paul Siebs, a man who rented desk space from him, had asked him to buy some TNT and deliver it to a garage in Weehawken. The Frenchman informed the New York City police department, which relayed this tip to William J. Flynn, chief of the secret service division of the treasury department. A trap was laid for the man who had ordered the TNT. Wettig and two police agents took twenty-five pounds of the explosive to Fay's garage, but Fay was not there. However, they were directed to Fay's boardinghouse at 28 Fifth Street, learned he was not home either, persuaded his landlady to let them examine his room. There they found a chart of the harbor and papers showing Fay had rented a motorboat. Now they knew he was their man.

The next several days nothing happened, but then the municipal and federal investigators heard from Wettig that Fay wanted him to witness a new test of his bomb. The test was to be held in some woods near Grantwood, New Jersey. Since New York City cops lacked authority in New Jersey, Flynn sent secret service men to the site. From a hiding place they watched as Fay touched off a couple of blasts, then closed in and arrested him. Returning to Fay's garage, they found bomb parts.

It was October 24, 1915, when Fay was nabbed. Examined by federal agents in the New York police headquarters, he surprised them by confessing everything. He said he had been detached from military duty on the front and sent here by the German secret service, revealed that his mission was known to the military and naval attachés at the German embassy, admitted he had made bombs in his Weehawken garage and attached them to the sterns of munitions ships. He also said he had been told not to make any trouble if caught. Who gave him this order? Fay replied, "Von Papen." His confession implicated three accomplices, who were arrested and charged, along with him, of conspiracy to destroy vessels to the detriment of the owners of the ships and their cargoes. On May 8, 1916, Fay and two others were found guilty and sentenced to serve terms in the federal penitentiary at Atlanta, Georgia.

Despite Fay's confession, the New York *Deutsches Journal* fatuously theorized that he was not really a German but an English provocateur. On the other hand, the New York *Journal of Commerce* said, "Nothing has done the cause of Germany in this war more harm in the estimation of the people of this country than these schemes, vainly designed to help that cause by committing crimes in its behalf." Vainly? Fay and Rintelen and other German saboteurs destroyed or damaged millions of dollars' worth of cargo in thirty-six ships and also provoked friction between the Allies and American manufacturers about the quality of American-made munitions.

Rintelen was a careful man but had an Achilles' heel—vanity. Early in the summer of 1915 he vacationed at a fashionable hotel at Kennebunkport, Maine, where he met a charming young American woman named Anne L. Seward, whom he sought to impress. In an intimate mood he confided to her that he was a secret German agent and had planned the destruction of the *Lusitania*. Rintelen was such an accomplished spy he had no need to embellish his feats with this lie about the *Lusitania*, but his vanity drowned his caution. Miss Seward knew Secretary of State Robert Lansing, who had succeeded to this post after Bryan resigned. She wrote Lansing to say she had information so vital she dared not commit it to paper. He sent his assistant to Maine to see Miss Seward, who poured out her fantastic story. Federal officials took her seriously and put agents on Rintelen's trail, who soon learned he really was the master spy he claimed.

When this report reached President Wilson, he became so alarmed that he wrote, "I am sure that the country is honeycombed with German intrigue and infested with German spies." Wilson and Lansing carefully kept this news about Rintelen from other Cabinet members, from Colonel

House and especially from newspaper reporters. For a while the President half believed that German agents in America had, at this and that secret spot, laid concrete foundations for future use by German artillerymen. He ordered an investigation, specifying that it be discreet, for "if the rumor got abroad it would inflame our people." But rumors did fly, and neighbors became suspicious of German-born householders with concrete floors in their cellars and garages.

Although the federal government now knew about Rintelen's mission, it lacked the hard evidence to convict him in a court of law, so he continued to go about his business. He was joined by Erich von Steinmetz, a captain in the German navy, who entered this country disguised as a woman. Steinmetz brought along cultures of germs that could cause glanders, a contagious and fatal disease, when injected into horses and mules intended for shipment to the Allies. After he arrived, he tested his bacteria and found it seemed to have lost its potency. Boldly he took his cultures to the Rockefeller Institute in New York and asked that they be analyzed, saying he planned to use them in experimental work. The Rockefeller scientists, unaware that they were being used by a German agent, tested the cultures and pronounced them dead.

But this was not the end of Germany's germ warfare against the United States. Anton Dilger was sent here with more bacteria. A German-American graduate in medicine from Johns Hopkins University in Baltimore, Dilger was in Germany when the war began and promptly offered his services to the imperial government. Colonel Nicolai of the German army intelligence division gave him cultures of glanders—and also anthrax germs. Anthrax is an infectious and usually fatal disease of animals such as cattle and sheep and occasionally of man. Dilger set up a secret laboratory in Chevy Chase, Maryland, a fashionable suburb of Washington, where he began breeding the germs on a large scale.

In the fall of 1915 he was ready to try to kill livestock awaiting shipment to Britain and France. The fieldwork was done under the direction of J. Edward Felton, a black foreman of black stevedore gangs in Baltimore and a man already in the pay of the Germans. Felton organized a ring of a dozen black assistants. Going to a corral near Van Cortlandt park in New York City, to Norfolk and Newport News in Virginia and to other sites where livestock had been gathered, they set to work. Each carried Dilger's germs in small glass bottles plugged by corks penetrated by long needles extending into the liquid cultures. They strolled along fences enclosing the animals and jabbed them with the needles. They also contaminated fodder and water. As a result, thousands of horses and mules and cattle died, and so did some of the American men who tended them.

One of the most curious German intrigues concerned young men from India residing in the United States. There were only a few of them, and for the most part they were either students or common laborers. Like many of their relatives in India, these students wanted to oust the British from their land and establish their own rule. An Indian nationalistic organization was founded here in the United States, branches were established from coast to coast, and the prime focal point of Indian discontent was at the University of California at Berkeley. A postgraduate student named Har Dyal founded a newspaper called *Ghadr (Revolution),* which was published in Urdu and other Indian dialects. Calling for an uprising in India, it preached assassination and bombings. This savage doctrine displeased American authorities, who arrested Har Dyal and held him for deportation as an undesirable alien.

His case interested German representatives in the United States. A part of Germany's geopolitical strategy in the war was to foment an uprising in India to serve the double purpose of keeping native Indian regiments from joining the British expeditionary force in France and divert British troops to India. German agents approached Har Dyal after he was released by American officials, and persuaded him to go to Berlin. When he reached the German capital, he was taken in hand by the secretary in charge of the Indian section of the German foreign office. Together they formed the Indian Independence Committee.

In December, 1914, Ambassador von Bernstorff received a coded cable saying, "A confidential agent of the Berlin Committee, Heramba Lal Gupta, is shortly leaving for America in order to organize the importation of arms and the conveyance of Indians [plotters] now resident in the United States to India. . . ." Bernstorff was ordered to give this Indian 150,000 marks for his work. The following January ten carloads of freight containing 8,000 rifles and 4,000,000 cartridges were sent to the revolutionary Indians at San Diego, California. In May Papen went to Seattle, Washington, to try to induce Hindu laborers to dynamite railway bridges and tunnels in the Canadian northwest, but nothing came of this scheme. Heramba Lal Gupta arrived here to plot with Bernstorff and Papen, British intelligence agents found his trail, and by 1917 the entire Hindu-German apparatus in the United States was discovered and broken.

Meanwhile, the German ambassador was furthering his propaganda work among Irish-Americans and even members of Congress. On December 1, 1914, an impressive 16,000 German-Americans and Irish-Americans met in Chicago to found the German-Irish Central Legislative Committee for the Furtherance of American Neutrality. They hoped to persuade Congress to declare an embargo on the growing shipment of arms to the Allies. Bernstorff gave the committee $5,000. On January 30, 1915, leaders of the German-American community in Washington, D.C., formed another group, the National German-American League. They warned politicians they would "support only such candidates for public office, irrespective of party, who will place American interests above those of any other country, and who will aid in eliminating all undue foreign influences from official life." Ostensibly, this was in keeping with President Wilson's plea for neutrality by all Americans, but actually it meant that pro-German elements in this country were trying to prevent American-made arms from reaching Britain and France. Some Senators and Representatives, especially those from communities with large German-American populations, were influenced by this propaganda. This new National German-American League developed into a powerful lobby of some 3,000,000 members.

Besides having these two huge pressure groups working for him, Bernstorff actually tried to bribe members of Congress. He cabled Berlin, "I request authority to pay up to fifty thousand dollars in order, as on former occasions, to influence Congress through the organization you know of, which perhaps can prevent war. I am beginning in the meantime to act accordingly. In the above circumstance a public official German declaration in favor of Ireland is highly desirable in order to gain the support of Irish influence here." This secret message fell into the hands of Secretary of State Lansing, who made it public. Newspapers played it up in emotional headlines, and Americans responded angrily. Some Congressmen demanded an investigation, and one, Representative J. Thomas Heflin of Alabama, declared he could name thirteen or fourteen members of Congress who had "acted in a suspicious manner." Bernstorff's chagrin over publication of his cable probably was offset by his success in spreading suspicion within the very halls of Congress. Lansing said there was no need for a Congressional investigation, though, and declared emphatically that the Bernstorff message cast no reflection on any elected official. "If there is any misunderstanding," Lansing said, "I wish to say very emphatically I do not see how the Bernstorff message in any way reflects upon Congress or any member. Apparently, it was the purpose to employ agencies to influence them of which they would have no knowledge and in case they were influenced it would be entirely innocent. I do not know what the organization was. This exposé is apropos of German methods of peace propaganda, and there is no intention of casting suspicion on members of Congress."

Friday night, July 2, 1915, a bomb exploded in a reception room of the Senate wing of the Capitol building in Washington. The blast shattered a telephone and switchboard, hurled fragments of it through the walls of nearby phone booths, ripped plaster from walls and the ceiling, smashed open doors including the door to the office of the Vice President, gouged holes in the walls, splintered mirrors and crystal chandeliers and sent glass flying in every direction. Alarmed federal officials tightened security in and around government buildings and launched an investigation. Soon a letter signed "Brown" was received with a threat to blow up the Capitol.

The next morning J. P. Morgan was eating breakfast in his three-story fifty-six-room stone mansion near Glen Cove on the fashionable north shore of Long Island. He and his wife had as weekend guests Sir Cecil Spring-Rice, the British ambassador to the United States, and Lady Spring-Rice. The mustachioed forty-seven-year-old Morgan was the prime purchasing agent for all munitions and other supplies bought in this country by both Great Britian and France. The Morgans and Spring-Rices were discussing the bombing of the Capitol, which had been reported in the morning papers. The doorbell rang. Henry Physick, the butler, opened the front door.

There stood a tall, slender thin-faced man who held out a card and said he must see Mr. Morgan. The butler asked the nature of his business. The stranger said he could discuss it only with Mr. Morgan. The butler looked at the card which said "Summer Society Directory, Thomas C. Lester, Representing." When the butler hesitated, the man said reassuringly, "I am an old friend of Mr. Morgan. He will see me." If the man had been an old friend of Morgan, he would have been known to the butler, who again asked that he state his business. The stranger put both hands into the pockets of his jackets, and when he brought them out again, each held a gun. His face changing, he snarled, "Don't dare and try to stop me!"

With two guns aimed at his body the butler walked inside and calmly said, "You will find Mr. Morgan in the library." This was a ruse, for the library lay at the west end of the mansion while Morgan was dining in its east end. When the gunman reached the library door, the butler politely stepped aside. Now that the weapons were not at his back, he turned and ran toward the breakfast room, shouting, "Upstairs, Mr. Morgan! Upstairs!" Then the butler fled down the stairs to the basement. Morgan was surprised by his butler's outcry. He leaped out of his chair, dashed out of the breakfast room and ran up a rear staircase to the second floor, followed by his wife and their visitors.

They ran from room to room to try to find out what was happening, but saw nothing unusual. Then another servant shouted that a strange man was coming up the steps from a downstairs hall near the library. Morgan hurried to the head of the stairway and saw the intruder. The gunman yelled, "Now, Mr. Morgan! I have got you!" Mrs. Morgan tried to protect her husband by throwing herself at the man, but Morgan pushed her aside. When the gunman reached the landing, Morgan jumped him. The man fired twice. Then he pulled the triggers again and again, but both pistols misfired. The staircase smelled of burning cordite.

Morgan's 220 pounds bowled over the slender gunman. They wrestled. Morgan pinned the man's left hand to the floor of the landing. His wife and the servant wrenched the gun from the man's right hand. By this time the butler had left the basement and was bounding upstairs carrying a heavy lump of coal. He smashed it down on the man's head, stunning him. Morgan eased off the limp body. Other servants came and tied the gunman hand and foot. Morgan walked to a telephone and called a doctor. Until then none knew he had been wounded. He had been hit twice. The first bullet entered his groin and lodged near the base of his spine. The second also smashed into his groin near the right thigh, went clear through the flesh and emerged. Soon afterward Morgan had an emergency operation, and the bullet near the spine was extracted without complications.

Glen Cove police were soon on the scene. They found a stick of dynamite in the prisoner's pocket and two more which he'd accidentally dropped on the lawn of the Morgan estate. Taken to the Mineola jail, the culprit identified himself as Frank Holt and made this statement:

> I went to the Morgan home in order to force him to use his great influence to stop the shipment of explosives. That is why I took some explosives with me, in order to demonstrate to him, *ad oculos*, what the use of machines of murder means, but I did not wish to hurt anyone. I wanted him to be in the same danger, him and his family, that we are imposing on Europe. . . . I tried to

> shoot in the air, but some one grabbed my hand. . . . He was the very last one that I should have hurt. He was to go out and do the work I could not do.

What kind of killer would use a phrase such as *ad oculos* (before one's eyes)? He was not who he said he was but finally was identified as Erich Muenter, a PhD who had taught German at Cornell and then at Harvard. In 1906 he had vanished after being indicted for the murder of his wife, who had perished at Cambridge of arsenic poisoning. Now he was remarried, and his second wife was found in Texas. Muenter boasted that it was he who had planted the bomb in the Capitol the day before, declaring he wanted to blow up the building to show the American people the dangers of dynamite. He refused to eat, tried to slash his wrists and on July 6 managed to kill himself in the Mineola jail by throwing himself from an upper tier of cells to the concrete floor below. His second wife told police he had written her to say he had planted time bombs on several eastbound liners. A search was made of ships in the port of New York but nothing suspicious was found. A few days later, though, a blast wrecked the SS *Minnehaha* bound for Europe with a cargo of munitions.

There was general agreement that Muenter had been mad. Six American newspapers theorized he had been driven insane by the pro-German clamor for an arms embargo. The St. Louis *Star*, published in a city with a huge German population, said Muenter's diseased mind "was given its peculiar bent by an arms embargo harangue that has been indulged in by the pro-German press, the misnamed Neutrality Leagues and the so-called Independence Leagues, which have been too long tolerated in this country, as the crimes of the madman witness."

Sir Cecil Spring-Rice, unnerved by recent events, believed the attack on his friend Morgan was part of a vast plot. He wrote a letter to the British secretary of state for foreign affairs, Sir Edward Grey, saying that the Germans "expect any measures [by the United States] against Germany to be followed immediately by explosions on board United States ships and at all arsenals, by the crippling of means of communication, by the appearance of submarines and by armed demonstrations by large bodies of well-disciplined men. . . . Extraordinary measures of precaution have now become necessary in all arms factories, at the docks and on board vessels, even vessels of the United States Navy. It is probable that German agents are everywhere and excellently organized."

Since the middle of May 1915 American secret service agents had been shadowing Germans and German-Americans suspected of violating neutrality and disrupting production. They especially distrusted George Sylvester Viereck, editor of *The Fatherland*. Early in the afternoon of Saturday, July 24, 1915, a secret service man named W. H. Houghton trailed Viereck to the Hamburg-American Steamship Company building at 45 Broadway in lower Manhattan. While Viereck was inside, Houghton called the New York office of the secret service and spoke to another operative, Frank Burke, asking for assistance. It was a hot day, and Burke had looked forward to a leisurely afternoon; but he agreed to join Houghton in front of the Broadway building.

About 3 P.M. the two agents saw Viereck emerge with a man to whom he paid obvious deference. This was paymaster Dr. Heinrich F. Albert. Albert was fifty, six feet tall, weighed about 190 pounds, had fair hair and blue eyes and ruddy cheeks scarred with cuts from his student dueling days. He was mustached, hawk-nosed and very well dressed, and carried a bulging briefcase. He and Viereck walked to the Rector Street station of the Sixth Avenue elevated line and boarded a northbound train. Burke sat down directly behind the two men, while Houghton took a seat across the aisle. When Viereck got off at the Thirty-third Street station, Houghton also got off to follow him.

The weather was humid, the train soothing, and Albert fell asleep. When the elevated train jerked to a halt at the Fiftieth Street station, he awakened so suddenly that he dashed for a door—forgetting the briefcase on the seat beside him. Burke grabbed it and started for another door. The German saw him and tried to bull his way past passengers to get at Burke but was blocked by a fat old woman hanging onto a leather strap. Albert ran out a door, clattered down the steps of the elevated station and took up a position on the sidewalk where he could see everyone else descending. Suddenly he caught sight of Burke clutching his briefcase and sprang at him. Burke, who was more agile than the middle-aged German, jumped onto a streetcar and told the conductor that the man chasing it was crazy. When the conductor looked back and saw the expression on Albert's face, he believed the agent and called out to the motorman to pass the next corner without stopping. Burke stayed on the streetcar for five blocks, changed to another, got off and walked into a drugstore and telephoned his chief, William J. Flynn. Flynn told Burke to stay where he was, came for him in an automobile, drove him back to the Manhattan office of the secret service.

Since the United States and Germany were not at war, since this nation was a declared neutral, the American agent had no legal right to steal the German's briefcase. It was crammed with documents, most of them in the German language and marked *Streng Vertraulich* (Strictly Private). Flynn could not read German, but the more closely he examined the papers, the more he felt, in mingled delight and apprehension, that Burke had found something of such great value that he needed guidance from above. His highest superior was William G. McAdoo, secretary of the treasury, now vacationing in North Haven, Maine. Flynn telephoned McAdoo and told him guardedly of the find. McAdoo ordered Flynn to take the next train to Maine and bring the briefcase with him. At the northern vacation retreat McAdoo and Flynn carefully went through the documents, the secretary's eyes bulging in astonishment, for here was proof that Dr. Albert was playing a leading part in German propaganda, espionage and sabotage in the United States.

Just as Flynn had been reluctant to take sole responsibility for these stolen papers, so was McAdoo. He drove with them to Cornish, New Hampshire, where President Wilson was vacationing in a mansion owned by the American author Winston Churchill. After Wilson had looked at Dr. Albert's files, he told McAdoo to confer with Secretary of State Lansing and Colonel House. They finally decided to give the documents to Frank Cobb, editor of the New York *World*. The *World* was the semiofficial organ of the Wilson administration, and Cobb was so close to Wilson that the President had offered him a Cabinet position. Cobb was told he might publish the papers, provided he did not reveal how they came into his possession. Colonel House wrote Wilson, "It may, in my opinion, even lead us into war, but I think the publication should go ahead. It will strengthen your hands enormously. . . . The people will see things as those of us that know the true conditions have long seen them, and it will make it nearly impossible to continue the propaganda."

Beginning on August 15, 1915, the New York *World* broke the story, which the *Star* of London called "The greatest 'scoop' in the history of journalism. This was the first headline:

HOW GERMANY HAS WORKED IN THE U.S.
TO SHAPE OPINION, BLOCK THE ALLIES
AND GET MUNITIONS FOR HERSELF,
TOLD IN SECRET AGENT'S LETTERS

From August 15 through August 23 the *World* continued to publish the Albert papers. And each article in the series named names: Theobald T. F. A. von Bethmann-Hollweg, chancellor of the German empire, Count Johann von Bernstorff, Captain Franz von Papen, Dr. Heinrich F. Albert, down to minor conspirators. These German agents were scheming, said the *World*, to influence newspapers, publish books, infiltrate the Chautauqua lecture circuit, hire professional lecturers and writers, finance propaganda films, start strikes in munitions plants, corner the supply of liquid chlorine used to make poison gas, acquire the Wright Aeroplane Company and its patents, keep American cotton from reaching Britain, operate their own arms factory at Bridgeport, prevent the Allies from obtaining a supply of phenol from a firm owned by Thomas A. Edison, etc.

The *World* summed up: "And throughout the correspondence there was evidence of an extreme care in the outlay of money, showing that full value was wanted for every German mark spent on conspiracy in this country. It was estimated that the cost to Ambassador Bernstorff of the activities exposed could not have been less than $2,000,000 a week."

This sensational exposé, reprinted in other papers from coast to coast, triggered outbursts of rage against Germany. Twelve years later George Sylvester Viereck wrote, "Albert's portfolio was a veritable box of Pandora; it unloosed every half-hatched plan of the Germans; the inner workings of the propaganda machine were laid bare. . . . The loss of that portfolio was like the loss of the Marne." He referred to the first battle of the Marne in France when the German advance on Paris was called off by the Kaiser under circumstances that remain controversial.

Dr. Albert defended himself in an article he wrote for the *World*. He denied everything, protested he had not violated American hospitality, said all he had tried to do was to overcome Allied propaganda in this nation, admitted he had received letters about fomenting strikes but denied answering any of them. However, in a letter to his wife he characterized Uncle Sam as "a great, strong lout suffering from shrivelling of the brain, to whom you ought to talk in high language about fine principles and then deny everything, especially if you are in the wrong."

Bernstorff called the *World*'s articles "inspired and romantic tales," but went on to say it was his "right and duty . . . to place difficulties in the way of the export of war materials to the Allies, either by the purchase of factories or war material, in spite of the fact that for the present we are not able to make any use of these goods. If we possessed the means and opportunity we would buy up every munition factory in the United States."

Treasury Secretary McAdoo was ambivalent: On the one hand, he felt "the British were doing the same thing, but we had no documentary proof." On the other, he wanted Bernstorff denounced and all German "secret and commercial agents" in the United States sent home on the first ship. President Wilson told McAdoo things were not that simple. While the Albert papers certainly proved the existence of German propaganda and economic sabotage, they revealed nothing about physical sabotage—the blowing up of plants and ships. Wilson's views were reflected in a statement given the press by Attorney General Thomas W. Gregory, who said there was insufficient evidence for the federal government to take any legal action. Even so, the *World*'s revelations shook official confidence in the good faith of the German government at a time when the American government was trying to be neutral, frightened politicians who had been speaking at German-American meetings and provoked newspapers into publishing strong anti-German sentiments. The New York *Sun* declared that Germany's undercover plots in this land belonged "morally in the same classification with political assassination."

The United States swarmed with 3,000 German spies, according to the Providence *Journal.* This Rhode Island newspaper was edited by Australian-born John R. Rathom, who claimed to have his own secret agents planted everywhere, even inside the German embassy. He published one lurid story after another, some containing damning coded messages that Rathom claimed had been plucked from the airwaves by his own wireless operators. Many of these allegations were written by Dr. Joseph Goricar, who had spent fifteen years in the Austro-Hungarian consular service but claimed he had resigned from his post in San Francisco when he was ordered to function as a spy as well as a consular official. The *Journal* declared that American arms plants were being blown up by agents of Germany and Austria-Hungary—and this, at least, was true. Dr. Goricar was denounced by Dr. Konstantin Theodor Dumba, the Austro-Hungarian ambassador to the United States, who called him a paid agent of the Russian government. Despite the skepticism felt by some readers about the paper's shotgun accusations, the Brooklyn *Citizen* thought it unnecessary to credit Goricar's allegations "in order to reach the conclusion that a vast conspiracy exists in this country, having for its object the destruction of American factories filling war-orders for the Allies and setting fire to passenger- and cargo-ships plying between American ports and the ports of the Allies."

Some of the *Journal*'s exposés may have been planted in the paper by British agents. In fact, Interior Secretary Franklin K. Lane believed that its editor might be "running the spy system of the British Embassy." Later it was learned that Rathom was working closely with Captain Guy Gaunt, the British naval attaché in Washington, who had organized an espionage and counterespionage system in our national capital. All told, the British had three intelligence units active in this country. British secret service was headed by Sir William Wiseman, who had headquarters in New York City and cloaked his real mission by representing himself as the director of W. Wisdom Films, Inc. British military intelligence in this land was commanded by a Colonel Thwaites. All three services carefully watched Captains Papen and Boy-Ed and now were on the trail of Germany's master spy, the indiscreet Commander Franz von Rintelen.

It was the British naval intelligence arm that brought him to earth. Early in the war this unit broke all of Germany's codes, including its most secret code. Unaware of this, the Germans continued to use their violated codes, and the British deciphered all wireless messages to and from the German government and its agents in neutral countries. Not long after Rintelen boasted to the charming Anne Seward that he was a German spymaster, he received a coded order to report immediately to his superiors in Berlin. In disguise and carrying his fake Swiss passport, Rintelen left on the first Dutch ship for Europe, and when it touched at Dover on August 13, 1915, he was arrested by British security officers.

Taken to London and examined by Admiral Sir Reginald Hall, chief of British naval intelligence, Rintelen learned to his horror that the message calling him home had been composed and dispatched by the British. Hall told Rintelen that Papen had "wired and wirelessed your name so often to Berlin in good, honest, straightforward German that he just placed you in our hands. It seemed almost deliberate." Rintelen, whom our ambassador to England called the "one genius that the war has developed," was interned in Great Britain. After the United States entered the war, it demanded his extradition, the British released him into custody of the Americans, Rintelen was tried in a federal court for violation of the Sherman Antitrust Act (the Espionage Act not yet having been passed), and he was sentenced to four years in the federal penitentiary at Atlanta, Georgia. He complained about such crude treatment of a *von*, a naval officer and a gentleman, but he was lucky to get off so lightly.

The United States lacked a good counterintelligence apparatus. Frank Burke of the secret service had pulled off a brilliant, if illegal, coup by snatching the Albert papers, but the federal government was without any big efficient agency to keep track of spies and saboteurs. As has been indicated, the American-based British did all they could, and further help came from a private underground organization known as the Bohemian Union. It was created by Emanuel Voska, a native of that part of the Balkans now included in Czechoslovakia, an ardent Czech nationalist who had fled his homeland fifteen years before the war—with Austro-Hungarian police hot on his heels.

A stonecutter when he arrived here, he worked hard, bought several marble quarries, became rich and was elected president of the American Sokol, or Czech nationalistic athletic organization. Proud of his American citizenship and eager to avenge himself on the tyrants who had made life hard for him in his native land, Voska put together his own counterapparatus. Taking the undercover name of Victor and using his own money, he recruited 84 full-time agents from among the 320,000 members of the various Czech and Slovak societies in the United States. He sent couriers from America into Austria-Hungary, supplied volunteer guards for munitions dumps and wharves in this country, placed Bohemian waiters in hotels and cafés frequented by Germans and German-Americans. Justice department agents raided Victor's organization in the mistaken belief that it was pro-German, but he did not reveal his true name or tell the government what he was doing because, apparently, he hoped to maneuver the neutral United States into the war on the side of the Allies.

Early in 1915 one of Victor's operatives said he thought that James F. J. Archibald was a German agent. Archibald was an American reporter who had covered the Spanish-American War for the San Francisco *Post*, had witnessed the first landing of American troops in Cuba, had been the sole American casualty in that first engagement. In other journalistic adventures south of the border he picked up the title of "Captain" and posed as a man of mystery. After war broke out in Europe, he went to Germany, where he wrote pro-German articles and then became a courier for the Central Powers, carrying secret dispatches through the British naval blockade between Europe and America. The evening of August 19, 1915, Archibald dined in a Manhattan hotel with Bernstorff, Konstantin Dumba, the Austro-Hungarian ambassador, and Papen. This was six days after the British nabbed Rintelen and at a time when the New York *World* still was publishing the Albert papers. The four were foolish enough to joke about Archibald taking a sword cane back to Germany with him. They did not know their waiters were some of Victor's agents.

Victor, who had planted four of his men in the Austro-Hungarian consulate in New York, already had learned that key saboteurs were about to withdraw secret files from their safes. Now he heard from one of his waiters that Archibald planned to leave for Europe on August 21, so he presumed that the newspaper correspondent might carry these papers to Berlin and Vienna. In the consulate the documents were packed by one of Victor's own operatives, and then they were delivered to Archibald aboard the SS *Rotterdam*. Victor then tipped off Captain Guy Gaunt, who sent a coded message to London and Admiral Sir Reginald Hall.

Archibald sailed from New York, and when his ship put into Falmouth, England, British authorities grabbed him and searched his luggage. They found nothing. For two days the British detained the vessel while they continued looking, and when at last they broke into the ship captain's safe, they found what they sought—thirty-four incriminating documents. The sword cane was never found; it may have been just a topic of jest. The British arrested Archibald on a charge of committing an unneutral act, since he was an American traveling on an American passport, but soon they let him go. However, the papers were forwarded to London, and copies were made and given to the American ambassador, who cabled their highlights to President Wilson. British naval intelligence also made sure American newspapers received copies.

The President, already shaken and angered by the Albert papers, suffered another shock. Archibald had carried evidence that the Austro-Hungarian ambassador was scheming to foment strikes in arms and steel plants from Bethlehem, Pennsylvania, to Chicago. This plot had been suggested to Dr. Dumba by Martin Diennes, alias William Warm, a New York correspondent for a Hungarian-American paper in Cleveland called *Szabadsag (Freedom)*. Dumba's government had told him to warn all Austro-Hungarian subjects in the United States that if they worked in any factory that made arms for enemies of the fatherland, they would be guilty of treason and could be imprisoned or hanged. One of the thirty-four papers was a letter from Dumba to the foreign minister of his country in which Dumba urged adoption of the Diennes plot regardless of cost. In another report Dumba said American policy might be influenced by domestic political considerations, and referring to Wilson, he spoke of "the self-willed temperament of the President." Still another document was a letter from Papen to his wife that said, "They unluckily stole from the good Albert in the Elevated a whole thick portfolio. . . . Well! One must after all have things go like this. . . . How splendid on the Eastern Front! I always say to these idiotic Yankees that they shut their mouths and better still be full of admiration for all that heroism."

On September 5, 1915, reporters flocked to Dumba's summer residence at Lenox, Massachusetts. The stoop-shouldered, thick-lipped, walrus-mustached ambassador blandly admitted everything. And he said, "There are thousands of workingmen in the big steel industries, natives of Bohemia, Moravia, Carniola, Galicia, Dalmatia, Croatia, Slovania and other peoples of the races from Austria-Hungary, who are uneducated and who do not understand that they are engaged in a work against their own country. In order to bring this before them, I have subsidized many newspapers published in the languages and dialects of the divisions mentioned. . . . It is difficult to get at these workers en masse, and a peaceful walkout of these workingmen would be of the greatest advantage to my government."

Well! The diplomat's undiplomatic confession enraged Americans. Two days later Dumba left Lenox and returned to Washington to confer with Secretary Lansing, who scorned him as "a natural-born intriguer." By this time the President and Lansing had agreed that the United States should demand Austria-Hungary recall Dumba. Wilson was eager to dismiss Bernstorff as well but had no evidence on which to base any serious charge against him. It was decided that for the time being nothing would be done about Bernstorff, while the government would make all possible use of the Dumba affair.

To Colonel House, who had become something of a father confessor to the foreign diplomatic corps, Dumba wrote, "As to the unfortunate incident which is the cause of my departure, I was certainly wrong because I made the mistake of being found out." He made his intrigues sound as trivial as cheating on a college exam. The matter was seen differently by the New York *Times*, which editorialized: "In the whole history of our relations with foreign countries, there never has been another diplomatic representative at our national capital who has in such an open and unabashed way taken measures to make himself altogether unacceptable." So Dumba was sent packing. His departure did not, however, end the war of nerves, for German saboteurs continued to blow up ships and factories.

Time was running out, though, for the German military and naval attachés. Papen and Boy-Ed had been shadowed by federal agents since the early part of 1915, dossiers on their activities had been compiled, both had been implicated in the Albert and Archibald papers, Robert Fay had confessed to his connection with Papen, and now the names of both were being mentioned in court proceedings against those German spies and saboteurs who had been arrested and indicted. Secretary Lansing told Bernstorff that the United States demanded their recall because "of what this government considers improper activities in military and naval factors." Bernstorff thought this demand was "intended to serve as a safety-valve—lest Congress should break off diplomatic relations with us." He obtained an interview with Colonel House, who noticed that for the first time in the ambassador's long career in this country he was "visibly shaken." House said Bernstorff was afraid he would be the next one sent home.

On December 7, 1915, President Wilson delivered his annual message at the opening session of the sixty-fourth Congress and talked about German lies and spies and saboteurs:

> I am sorry to say that the gravest threats against our national peace and safety have been uttered within our own borders. There are citizens of the United States, I blush to admit, born under other flags, but welcomed under our generous naturalization laws to the full freedom and opportunity of America, who have poured the poison of disloyalty into the very arteries of our national life; who have sought to bring the authority and good name of our government into contempt, to destroy our industries wherever they thought it affective [*sic*] for their vindictive purposes to strike at them and to debase our politics to the uses of foregin intrigue.
>
> Their number is not great as compared with the whole of those sturdy hosts by which our nation has been enriched in recent generations out of virile foreign stocks; but it is great enough to have brought deep disgrace upon us and to have made it necessary that we should promptly make use of processes of law by which we may be purged of their corrupt distempers. . . .
>
> I urge you to enact such laws at the earliest possible moment. . . . Such creatures of passion, disloyalty and anarchy must be crushed out. They are not many, but they are infinitely malignant and the hand of our power should close over them at once. They have formed plots to destroy property, they have entered into conspiracies against the neutrality of the government, they have sought to pry into every confidential transaction of the government in order to serve interests alien to our own. It is possible to deal with these things very effectively. I need not suggest the terms in which they may be dealt with. . . .

Such was the genesis of the Espionage Act of 1917, which destroyed almost all freedom in this land. In 1915 President Wilson had good cause to worry about national security, what with German agents honeycombing the country, but in the days ahead the countermeasures would become repressive measures that penalized the innocent.

Late in December, 1915, Papen and Boy-Ed were sent home—Papen to keep his historic rendezvous with Hitler. But their departure failed to end sabotage. In fact, six months later the Germans brought off their greatest coup in their underground war against the United States—the Black Tom holocaust.

Black Tom Island was not an island but a man-made peninsula jutting out from the Jersey City waterfront into the upper bay of New York just behind the Statue of Liberty. In all America this was the most important site for the transfer of munitions from trains into ships. The Lehigh Valley Railroad Company, which owned Black Tom, had crammed the mile-long landfill with railway tracks and warehouses and piers. American-made arms consigned to the Allies moved through this complex. Freight cars were shunted onto the peninsula, munitions were taken from the cars and loaded onto barges tied to the piers, and then the barges were tug-towed to waiting Allied ships to be loaded aboard. But since Allied agents were unable to keep just the right number of ships present to receive the munitions, for days or even a week at a time the explosives would remain inside the railway cars. At the time of the tragedy there were thirty-four such carloads at Black Tom—seventeen cars of shells, eleven of high explosives, three of nitrocellulose, two of combination fuses and one of TNT—a total of 2,132,000 pounds of munitions.

At 2:08 A.M., Sunday, July 30, 1916, Greater New York was rocked by the most massive explosion in its history. Thirty-two minutes later a second blast ripped the night, and during the next six hours shells exploded like strings of cosmic firecrackers. Their thunder was heard 100 miles away in Connecticut and Maryland and Pennsylvania. Bridges, skyscrapers and apartment buildings trembled; people were jolted out of bed; metal zinged through the air and gouged holes in the Statue of Liberty; other hot fragments rained down on Ellis Island and terrorized immigrants who were brought to the relative safety of Manhattan; hospital patients slammed awake and quaked in dread; householders ran into the night screaming. In Jersey City almost every window was shattered, in the Customhouse near the Battery half the windowpanes were broken, the nearby Aquarium had its skylights splintered, not a window remained intact in the House of Morgan at 23 Wall Street, $1,000,000 worth of damage was done to windowpanes in the Wall Street area, and over in Brooklyn and in Manhattan as far north as Forty-second Street windows were reduced to shards of glass. Damages estimated at $45,000,000 were inflicted on buildings within a radius of 25 miles around Black Tom. From a distance all New York City seemed in flames. Later it was found that deep craters had been gouged in the bottom of the Hudson river. Black Tom was utterly destroyed, and seven persons were killed.

In a letter to the *Times* a man compared the roar of this blast with the bombardment of Antwerp by zeppelins, so New Yorkers and some people in New Jersey got a bit of the feeling of the war over in Europe. Residents of a town in Maryland reported that not only did they hear the explosions, but they also felt shock waves. Government men combed the ruins of Black Tom for clues to the disaster's origin, engineers inspected the pockmarked Statue of Liberty, and insurance agents picked their way through the debris in the belief that the detonations were of incendiary origin. The governor of New Jersey and the mayor of Jersey City issued alarmed statements about the dangers of letting such a heap of munitions build up near big cities. A newspaper article explained why the concussions caused windowpanes to burst outward rather than inward, powder cases drifted down the shore of New Jersey to the alarm of residents in that area, and President Wilson ordered the Interstate Commerce Commission to investigate.

Was the Black Tom tragedy the work of German saboteurs? This question was put to the German-American Mixed Claims Commission, which was created after the war. This commission also studied the January 11, 1917, explosion in the munitions plant of the Canadian Car and Foundry Company at Kingsland, New Jersey. Legal wrangling went on year after year after year. Among the witnesses who testified before the commission were Bernstorff, Papen and Boy-Ed. In 1930 the international body handed down a decision in favor of Germany, but an American commissioner contested it, the matter was reconsidered, and a final determination was made on October 30, 1939. A total of 153 damage suits were settled with the payment by Germany of a total of $49,991,242—but this, of course, was more than two decades after German agents crippled the shipment of arms to the Allies.

When the United States declared war on Germany on April 6, 1917, most German agents in this country fled to Mexico, and their sabotage and espionage came to an end. But in the absence of an effective internal security organization the Kaiser's marauders had been successful in launching a reign of terror which, in turn, spawned an overreaction, a homegrown reign of terror that almost tore this nation apart.

Chapter 14

THE SINKING OF THE LUSITANIA

Ethel Barrymore was alarmed. The dark-eyed actress had discovered that her close friend and favorite producer Charles Frohman planned to sail to England to visit playwright James M. Barrie. Frohman had booked passage on the *Lusitania*, a British ship operated by the Cunard line, and what frightened Miss Barrymore was a fact known to all Americans—German submarines were prowling the Atlantic in the hope of sinking any vessel flying the Union Jack. While this was ominous enough, there was more. Frohman, whose father had been born in Germany, knew Papen and Boy-Ed, and both had hinted that he would do well not to take the *Lusitania*. The ebullient producer told friends about their cryptic warnings—and laughed.

At fifty-five Frohman was regarded by the American press as "the Napoleon of the drama." Having taught himself more about the nation's theaters and audiences than anyone else, he had brought order into the disorderly booking business and become a charter member of a theatrical syndicate that controlled sixty playhouses. He owned six more theaters and managed twenty-eight stage stars, one of whom was Miss Barrymore. Despite the business depression of 1914 Frohman had booked more than 500 plays in the United States, France and Great Britain.

Frohman had a figure like a frog and a face like a cherub. His temperament was sunny, his companionship delightful. He was a bachelor, and a prudish one at that, but he freely gave his affection to talented authors and players, making money for them and building them into stars without ever demanding a contract. They knew his handshake was as reliable as the sun. Miss Barrymore's uncle John Drew, a popular actor, felt especially close to the producer. Drew shared his niece's anxiety and tried to dissuade Frohman from sailing on the *Lusitania*. Frohman waved aside his arguments. Drew sent him a telegram: IF YOU GET BLOWN UP BY A SUBMARINE I'LL NEVER FORGIVE YOU.

Frohman was not well. He had fallen and hurt his knee, and a bruise had developed into arthritis that affected all his joints. Now he used a cane he jokingly called "my wife." He had a suite of rooms in the Hotel Knickerbocker on the southeast corner of Broadway and Forty-second Street two blocks from the Empire theater, which he had built and still owned. From Boston, where she was appearing in *The Shadow*, Miss

Barrymore wrote Frohman to beg him to stay at home. The day before he was due to sail he limped around dictating to his male secretary his next season's program. A thought occurred to him. Wishing to jot it down in the red notebook he carried, he pulled the notebook from a pocket, looked at it, grunted in surprise: "Queer! There's no more room." Then he turned to his partner, Alf Hayman, to ask whether Hayman thought there really was any danger in crossing the Atlantic at this time. Hayman replied, "Of course I do." Frohman limped toward the door, saying, "Well, I must go anyway." Then he paused, grinned, jested: "Al, if you need to write to me, just address the letter care of German submarine U-4."

The next day was Saturday, May 1, 1915. A light rain sprinkled the city. In the morning Frohman appeared in the lobby of his hotel with a cigar in his mouth, wearing a black hat and double-breasted suit. He was followed by his valet carrying a bulging briefcase containing plays he wanted to read on the voyage. Helped into a taxi, Frohman turned around to make sure a second cab he had hired to carry his luggage was behind him, then settled back and was driven to Pier 54 on Manhattan's west side. Frohman struggled out and found himself almost beneath the *Lusitania*'s bow. Despite the fact that he was a seasoned traveler, he was impressed with her.

The *Lusitania* was built by John Brown and Company at Clydebank, Scotland, and launched on June 7, 1906. She and her sister ship, the *Mauretania*, were made for the Cunard Steamship Company under special agreement with, and subsidized by, the British government. The key condition was that the *Lusitania* should be "capable of maintaining a minimum average ocean speed of from 24 to 25 knots in moderate weather." This assured the British the supremacy of speed in the transatlantic service, the coveted blue ribbon which had passed to the Germans some years previously. Her maiden voyage from Liverpool to New York was made in September, 1907, and the following November the *Lusitania* set a record by racing from Fastnet to New York in four days, eighteen hours and forty minutes. Then she broke her own record by crossing the Atlantic in only four and a half days. This speed later was surpassed by the *Mauretania* under the guidance of the skipper who now was in charge of the *Lusitania*. During her nine years of service she had carried a quarter million passengers.

Now that the war was on and other vessels had been taken out of service, the *Lusitania* was the largest, fastest and most powerful steamer still on the Atlantic run. She had nine decks. Her bridge was as tall as a six-story building. She measured 216 feet from her keel to the tips of her twin masts. Her four red and black smokestacks, according to a Cunard advertisement, were gigantic enough "to drive a coach and horses through." Stretching 790 feet from stem to stern, she was 34 feet longer than the Capitol building in Washington. She took her name from a Latin word for an ancient country in what is now Spain and Portugal. She cost $9,000,000. Each month depreciation, maintenance and other charges came to $150,000. Each trip to and from New York cost another $150,000. That was before the war. Now, said Cunard officials, she was operated as a public service and without profit.

She could carry 7,000 tons of coal. She had 192 furnaces and 25 steam turbines that could push her to a top speed of 27 knots—even faster than the contract stipulated. But the war was such a drain on Britain's manpower that her captain was unable to sign on enough crew members; now she had only forty-one able-bodied seamen instead of the usual complement of seventy-seven, and she also carried fewer stokers than usual. Because of this shortage of muscle, only nineteen of her twenty-five boilers had been fired for this voyage from New York to Liverpool. While this meant her speed would be cut to about 21 knots, she nonetheless held a 6-knot margin over the fastest U-boat in service. Like the luckless *Titanic*, the *Lusitania* was considered unsinkable. Her hull was divided into 175 separate watertight compartments. Along the full length of this 32,000-ton ship the double bottom was five feet deep. One U.S. Senator so admired the *Lusitania* that he said she was "more beautiful than Solomon's Temple—and big enough to hold all his wives."

At 8 A.M. this sailing day her two masters-at-arms took their places at the head of the main gangway to welcome the passengers with traditional British courtesy. The passengers were slow in arriving, but reporters and photographers swarmed aboard the ship. There was something different about this departure. Morning editions of New York papers had published, next to a paid Cunard schedule, this strange notice:

NOTICE

TRAVELERS intending to embark on the Atlantic voyage are reminded that a state of war exists between Germany and her allies and Great Britain and her allies; that the zone of war includes the waters adjacent to the British Isles; that, in accordance with formal notice given by the Imperial German Government, vessels flying the flag of Great Britain, or any of her allies, are liable to destruction in those waters and that travelers sailing in the war zone on ships of Great Britain or her allies do so at their own risk.

IMPERIAL GERMAN EMBASSY

On February 4, 1915, Germany had proclaimed the waters around the British Isles a war zone and announced that beginning February 18, enemy merchant ships would be destroyed on sight in the forbidden area. Furthermore, no provision would be made for the safety of passengers and crew members. On February 22 an order from the Kaiser was issued: "His Majesty desires that the submarine commanders be expressly informed that, on account of political difficulties which have arisen with the United States and Italy, it is necessary that they act with the greatest circumspection in dealing with ships of these two countries, to avoid sinking one of them by mistake." Apart from this word of caution, Germany launched its ruthless *Handelskrieg mit U-Booten* in February, 1915. There is evidence suggesting that British leaders actually *welcomed* it, since undersea war was likely to embroil Germany in tensions with the United States and perhaps even edge her into war on the side of the Allies. On March 28 an American citizen perished in the sinking of the

British liner *Falaba* in the Irish Sea. On May 1 the American tanker *Gulflight* was hit by a torpedo launched by a German sub engaged in a fight with a British naval patrol off the Scilly Isles, and two Americans died.

More than a week before the *Lusitania* was to sail the New York German community decided to place an advertisement in fifty American papers warning passengers they ran a risk if they traveled on the British liner. One newspaper editor checked with the state department, whose duty officer said it would be dangerous to publish such an ad. His paper, and others across the country, declined to print the warning. George Sylvester Viereck, however, managed to get the German embassy's warning published in the morning editions of the New York *Times* and *Tribune*.

One of the reporters now aboard the *Lusitania* showed the embassy's advertisement to the ship's senior third officer, John Lewis, and asked to see the captain. Lewis refused. Instead, he had someone telephone Charles Sumner, the New York general manager of the Cunard line, asking him to come to the pier and speak to the press.

Some *Lusitania* passengers had read the notice and reacted in terms of their personalities—they winced or shuddered or laughed. William H. Brown of Buffalo, New York, did not laugh; the previous night he had dreamed the *Lusitania* was torpedoed and he was lost at sea. Another who saw nothing funny about the warning was Professor I. B. Stoughton Holbourn, the laird of a tiny island in the North Sea and an authority on classical literature; he had had several nightmares about going down with the *Lusitania*. As some passengers approached the dock, they were waylaid by strangers who warned them not to sail. Other passengers boarded ship and then received ominous telegrams signed John Smith and George Jones; a few of these chilling wires were signed *Morte* (Death). At the last minute the Reverend W. M. Warlow of Bennington, Vermont, became so frightened he canceled his reservation and booked himself instead on the *New York* of the American Line. Actress Ellen Terry also canceled her passage, while the Isadora Duncan dance troupe switched to another vessel. Newsreel photographers set up their cameras on the pier and shot hundreds of feet of film of ordinary passengers and celebrities, laughingly telling them, "We're going to call this 'The *Lusitania*'s Last Voyage'!"

Reporters insisted on seeing the ship's master, William T. Turner, to ask for comment on these ghoulish warnings. They found him in the company of thirty-eight-year-old Alfred Gwynne Vanderbilt, worth more than $42,000,000, a sportsman and horse lover now about to go to England to offer his services to the British Red Cross. One reporter asked Vanderbilt whether he was afraid of U-boats.

"Why should we be afraid of German submarines?" Vanderbilt asked in turn. "We can outdistance any submarine afloat."

Another reporter reminded Vanderbilt that he had canceled his passage on the *Titanic*, which later hit an iceberg and sank, asking whether he expected to be as lucky now as he had been three years previously. The handsome young man smiled a faint smile.

Captain Turner put his hand on Vanderbilt's shoulder and said to reporters, "Do you think all these people would be booking passage on the *Lusitania* if they thought she could be caught by a German submarine? Why, it's the best joke I've heard in many days—this talk of torpedoing." He and Vanderbilt laughed. "Germany," the captain continued, "can concentrate her entire fleet of submarines on our track and we would elude them. I have never heard of one that could make twenty-seven knots. We *can* do that, and we are willing to show them, when the opportunity arrives."

The captain did not mention the *Lusitania*'s reduced speed on this trip.

The Cunard representative, Charles Sumner, came aboard and made himself available to the press. When asked what he thought about the warning from the German embassy, he gestured at the passengers boarding the great liner and laughed. "You can see how it has affected the public." Had anyone canceled his reservation? No, Sumner replied, not a single one. This was untrue.

During the crossing Charles Frohman was to have two companions, playwright Charles Klein and actress Rita Jolivet; she had just finished playing the lead in *What It Means to Be a Woman*. Ethel Barrymore hastened down from Boston to New York to bid Frohman *bon voyage*, and when he saw her, his face lit up. He told Miss Barrymore that the next season he planned to produce *Our Mrs. McChesney*. "It's an ideal play for you," he said. "It has womanliness and wholesome humor." As they parted, Frohman surprised Miss Barrymore by kissing her cheek, and the last she saw of him he was leaning on his cane at the rail.

Shortly before noon Captain Turner walked down the gangway to pick up his sailing orders. None had been received, he was told, so he was to take the same course as the last time. Some ships from British cruiser squadron "E" would rendezvous with him 10 miles south and 40 miles west of the Fastnet rock on the extreme southwest tip of Ireland. The skipper went back aboard, and about 12:30 P.M. the *Lusitania* cast off. Her horn bawled three times, so loudly and in such a deep register that people clapped hands over their ears and saw in surprise that its vibrations fluttered their clothing. Huffing tugboats pulled at the liner and eased her out into the Hudson, where she slowly swung her bow to the south. Visitors left on the pier could see the full length of her port side, her dark hull and white superstructure and the name LUSITANIA in big gold letters. The bow was an almost vertical line silhouetted against the Jersey shore which seemed to be moving, rather than the ship herself. The four huge propellors began churning. Deckhands aboard ship released lines that flopped into the water, and then the thick ropes were drawn dripping onto the tugs, which now fanned out and away and behind, leaving the ship alone in her majesty. In the sky the knotted clouds loosened and lowered and changed to fog as the vessel glided through the lower bay and down to Sandy Hook to drop the pilot, then knifed through offshore swells and into open sea. The ship's orchestra was playing.

A tinny gramophone was playing aboard the U-20. The German submarine had left the homeland on April 30 and had been hunting in the

Irish Sea since May 5. One of the songs blaring from the gramophone was "Rose of Stamboul," a popular ballad with heavy Wagnerian overtones. *Unterseeboot-20* was a happy ship. She was skippered by Kapitänleutnant Walther Schwieger, who was thirty-two but looked younger because his face was as smooth and open as a schoolboy's. Rugged and blond, educated and urbane, he had a personality so charming he made life a little easier for the three other officers and thirty-five enlisted men inside their sweating 650-ton iron prison. He had let the men bring along their pet dogs, and one had just whelped a litter of pups.

The U-20 could make only 9 knots submerged, but when she rose to the surface to charge her wet-cell storage batteries, she had a top speed of 15 knots. Each of her cigar-shaped torpedoes was 21 feet 6 inches long, could bore through the water at 22 knots, had a 4-mile range and was loaded with 290 pounds of a new explosive called trotyl. The German submariners, with the gallows humor of men at war, had a pet name for each torpedo—Yellow Mary, Bertha, Shining Emma and the like. They knew what they had to do.

Early in the afternoon of Friday, May 7, 1915, the *Lusitania* was gliding along the southwest coast of Ireland about 10 miles off County Cork, so close to shore that voyagers on the port side could see low green hills. Some passengers were still lunching in the dining room, and one said, "It's been such a dull, dreary, stupid trip! I can't help hoping that we get some sort of thrill going up the channel." The sky was bright. The sea was calm. An officer on the bridge was taking a fix on the dim shape of the lighthouse on a spit of land called the Old Head of Kinsdale. To let him get a bearing the ship had to hold her course on a straight line, which was dangerous in those sub-infested waters. But the six lookouts saw nothing suspicious.

On April 16 the British admiralty had given ships' captains this memorandum:

> War experience has shown that fast steamers can considerably reduce the chance of successful surprise submarine attack by zigzagging, that is to say, altering the course at short and irregular intervals, say in ten minutes to half an hour. This course is almost invariably adopted by warships when cruising in an area known to be infested with submarines. The underwater speed of a submarine is very low, and it is exceedingly difficult for her to get into position to deliver an attack unless she can preserve and predict the course of the ship attacked.

Captain Turner misunderstood this memorandum. He thought zigzagging was to be used only after a sub had been sighted.

Out of sight below the surface and 700 yards off the *Lusitania*'s starboard bow the U-20 was idling along. A broadside view of the great liner lay in the center of the hairlines of the periscope manned by the submarine commander. On this sunny day the time was now 2:09 P.M.

Schwieger cried, "Fire!"

On the ship a lookout on the fo'csle head slams a megaphone to his mouth and yells, "Torpedo coming on the starboard side!" Like a bubbling arrow, the torpedo flashes toward the *Lusitania*. Captain Turner stands on the navigation bridge on the port side. He has binoculars at his eyes studying the Old Head of Kinsdale. At the cry he swivels his head to the right and sees the telltale wake just below the surface. The torpedo whomps into the starboard side behind the bridge. An explosion. It sounds like a heavy door slammed shut. Another blast. The decks rise and then settle back. A pillar of water and smoke and coal and wood and steel splinters soars high above the tall radio antenna. Then in slow motion the debris cascades down onto the upper deck. The ship shudders. Ten seconds later she lists fifteen degrees to starboard.

In the second-class dining room glass shatters, lights flicker out, women scream, everyone is knocked down. The chief radio operator runs out of the dining room, races through passageways, scrambles up a ladder, charges into the radio shack and takes over the key from an assistant. Agile fingers flicking the key, he rattles out an emergency signal: "Come at once, big list, 10 miles south Old Head Kinsdale." Electric power weakens. Operator anxiously eyes extra dynamo in corner of shack.

In the many-storied engine room a deafening concussion, blinding flash of light, darkness, the hiss of steam. Stokers crawl out onto an open deck. Their faces are smudged. Passengers bewildered. They pour onto various decks. The wooden lifeboats on starboard side swing further from the side. So far no panic. Captain Turner's first thought is to beach the ship. He orders lifeboats readied for lowering but issues no order to abandon ship. The ship has twenty-two wooden lifeboats suspended from davits, eleven boats on each side. But the seaman shortage means lowering crews available for only ten boats on each side. On the starboard side two sailors and two passengers begin lowering a boat with sixty persons in it. The captain gives a hand signal for everyone to stay aboard. There had been no lifeboat drills, passengers had not been assigned boat stations, most life belts are in cabins rather than distributed about decks. Officers shout there is no danger and ship will right herself. When the torpedo hit, the ship had been making 18 knots. She continues to lunge ahead, erratically, listing evermore to starboard and beginning to settle by the bow. The quartermaster is at the helm behind the compass watching the list indicator—a pendulum showing how far the ship sways off even keel. The indicator has been shivering on either side of the fifteen-degree list mark. Now it trembles higher. Twenty degrees. Danger of capsizing. An ominous creaking of the ship's beams and joints and plates. Bow deeper, stern higher. People fall down. They pull themselves erect, or nearly so. They drag uphill toward the looming stern and away from the sinking bow.

Panic. Here and there an oasis of calm. Passengers, white-faced, fight their way into lifeboats. Some of the strong push the weaker aside. A New York export broker waves a revolver at dumbfounded sailors and screams he'll shoot the first man who refuses to help launch boats. On E deck all portholes are underwater. Now those on D deck are submerged. Seventy-four open portholes on the two decks. Water cascades through them at the rate of almost four tons a minute. The smoking salon is crazy-angled. Upended chairs. A man from St. Louis reaches into a heap of splintered glass, gets a bottle of ale, opens it and drinks. On deck a boat swings out prematurely. Its occupants are dumped into the sea. A woman muses that people move about like "a swarm of bees who do not know where the queen has gone." People babble that the sub will machine-gun them after they get into the water. A reporter helps a six-year-old girl into a boat. A woman takes the girl in her lap. Women cling in terror to an iron pipe railing. They are afraid to let go and get into a boat. Two men peel off their clothes. They dive off the boat deck. Quickly they are swept astern. The ship keeps plowing ahead. On the boat deck a man tears off all his wife's clothing and fastens a life belt around her naked body.

The bow is awash. The lower the bow, the higher the stern. Panting people crawl up this slippery iron mountain. Those lucky enough to reach the stern see they are frightfully high above the sea. The sea is littered with debris. Deck chairs. Empty lifeboats. Menacing. A ship's fireman climbs onto a railing, poses, arches off into a graceful dive. A watching passenger considers this a meaningless *beau geste.* Passengers stare at a stoker. His face is a scarlet smear. His head is open like a "spongy bloody pudding." Three Irish girls sing "There Is a Green Hill Not Far Away." In the radio shack the operator is too busy tapping out his signal to loosen his sweaty collar. The ship groans. She heels further to starboard. Now her smokestacks threaten to crash down on people struggling in the water.

The submarine commander watches through his periscope and writes in his log: "3:25 P.M. [His clocks are an hour earlier than those on the *Lusitania.*] It seems as if the vessel will be afloat only a short time. Submerge to 24 meters and go to sea. I could not have fired a second torpedo into this throng of humanity attempting to save themselves. . . ."

On the *Lusitania* a Wisconsin auto manufacturer wraps an arm around a stanchion and loads and snaps his camera. A seaman begins lowering himself on a rope toward the water. Halfway down he sees he is over the revolving blades of a propeller. He pulls himself hand over hand back onto the slanting deck. Vanderbilt helps a teen-age girl into a lifeboat. It capsizes. She is a strong swimmer. She looks back and sees her father and mother beside Vanderbilt. She knows that never again will she see her parents. A woman slides down a rope. Her skirt balloons out, and she floats down on the ocean. On B deck a steward sees Vanderbilt helping an hysterical woman. The steward yells to get off before it's too late. He doesn't know Vanderbilt can't swim. Vanderbilt tells his valet, "Find all the kiddies you can, boy!" On B deck near Vanderbilt stands Charles Frohman. Cigar in mouth. Calm. He has linked arms with pretty Rita Jolivet, her brother-in-law George Vernon and an English soldier named Captain A. J. Scott. Frohman has no life belt. The Englishman removes his life belt and forces Frohman to put it on. Moments later Frohman takes it off and asks Scott to help him work it onto a terrified woman.

Frohman is most concerned with Miss Jolivet. His eyes are on her. He tells her to hang onto a rail and save her strength. She shivers with fear. She knows the arthritic producer cannot survive immersion in the ocean. The water churns closer to the four holding arms. Frohman smiles and says, "Why fear death? It is the most beautiful adventure in life." The actress knows this is a quotation from Barrie's *Peter Pan*. The water engulfs the four of them. They are tumbled about. Her shoes are torn off. That is the last she ever sees of Frohman.

The *Lusitania* sinks in eighteen minutes. She is eight miles south southwest of the Old Head of Kinsdale.

. . . sea . . . horizons . . . sky . . . sun . . . debris . . . screams . . . overloaded lifeboats . . . people treading water . . . others in life belts . . . here and there a body . . . islands of bodies . . . five men fight for fingerholds on a floating keg . . . an old man treading water with his head far above the surface . . . Royal Gwent Singers weakly harmonizing "Nearer My God to Thee" . . . lapping waves . . . the taste of salt in the mouth . . . nausea . . . a woman clinging to a board . . . an Italian chanting as he drifts by with arms locked around a tin tank . . . Captain Turner swimming . . . sea gulls swoop down on him . . . are they attacking or curious? . . . he beats off the birds with his arms . . . a man in a boat blubbers about his bonds and someone hits him on the head with an oar . . . the sound of somebody singing "Tipperary" . . . a professor tows a man to a boat and sees he is dead . . . columns of smoke on the horizon . . . rescue ships . . . far away . . . hope revived . . . terror as the water closes over one's head . . . the sun glints off a woman's diamond ring and she is located and saved . . . in a boat a minister rips off his pants and waves them at the end of an oar . . . a man in the water is insane with fear because he has no life belt . . . he grabs a woman floating by . . . she tries to fight him off . . . she blacks out . . . when she comes to, she is alone on her back staring into the sky . . . a dead woman bobs past a lifeboat . . . her face is green . . . another woman clutches her dead baby . . . the water rocks the corpse of a ten-year-old boy . . . a woman survives by floating on the body of a fat man . . . and all alone, as alone as it is possible to be alone in the universe, a woman lies on the water with her legs apart giving birth to a baby. . . .

Early in the afternoon of Friday, May 7, 1915, William Jennings Bryan sat over lunch in the Shoreham hotel in Washington gobbling food; the fat secretary of state hated booze and adored food. At the table with him were other Cabinet members and Presidential Secretary Tumulty. Bryan wiped his mouth, got up and left the dining room, and a reporter approached and handed him a press bulletin saying that the *Lusitania* had been sunk. The bulletin did not say how many lives had been lost. Bryan hastened toward his waiting car and was waylaid by other reporters asking for comment, but he told them he did not want to say anything just then. He was driven to the state department building, where he fidgeted in his office while awaiting confirmation of the news from Page, the

American ambassador to Great Britain. In London the ambassador was preparing to give a dinner in the embassy in honor of Colonel House and his wife when word reached him that at 4 P.M. Greenwich time the *Lusitania* had been torpedoed. This report mistakenly added that all passengers and crew members had been saved, so Page did not think it necessary to cancel the dinner. Before long, though, he got further word that lives had been lost, that in fact the affair was a tragedy of colossal proportions. By this time it was too late to put off the dinner, which became one of the most mournful in the social history of London.

President Wilson had finished lunch in the White House and was about to leave for a golf course when a clerk handed him a bulletin about the *Lusitania.* Abandoning all thought of golf, Wilson waited in his office for further news, and only late in the afternoon did he leave for a brief spin in an automobile. He did not check with Bryan, nervously waiting at the state department. With the arrival of more reports and further details of the holocaust, Tumulty tried to call Wilson's attention to them, but the President was in such a state of shock he said, "Tumulty, it would be much wiser for us not to dwell too much upon these matters." His eyes were sad. Rescue ships were bringing survivors to Queenstown, Ireland, and at 7:55 P.M. Wilson heard from the American consul at Queenstown that the loss of life would be heavy. Aware that Americans had been killed by Germans, conscious that this would imperil his neutrality policy, facing his most severe test since taking office, Wilson could hardly bear the news. In the evening he surprised his secret service guard by leaving the White House, walking out into the night and a light rainfall, striding for blocks with sightless eyes and ears heedless of the cries of newsboys racing up and down the streets of Washington. Back in his study he learned at 10 P.M. that perhaps 1,000 passengers had perished.

The *Lusitania* had sailed from New York with 1,957 on board—1,257 passengers and about 700 crew members. Among the passengers were 159 Americans. The death toll came to 1,198. Among these casualties were 124 Americans. One hundred and twenty-four American citizens—men and women and children—killed by the Germans. Few events in American history carried the impact of the sinking of the *Lusitania.* There had been the Boston Massacre, the taking of the Alamo, the sinking of the battleship *Maine*—and now this! Innocent Americans slaughtered by a government with which we were officially at peace.

The evening of the tragedy Senator Henry Cabot Lodge stood on the steps of his home on Massachusetts Avenue looking at the huge headline in a Washington paper when a couple of friends stopped on their way home from the British embassy. They asked Lodge whether he thought the disaster would force President Wilson to take drastic action. A bitter look swept across the face of the Senator. Scornfully, he cried, "Words! Words! Words!" At about the same moment and only a few blocks away Bryan mused aloud to his wife, "I wonder if that ship carried munitions of war? I will have Lansing investigate that! If she did carry them, it puts a different face on the whole matter! England has been using our citizens to protect her ammunition."

To report the holocaust, American newspapers broke out what editors jestingly called the Second Coming type—headline letters of enormous size. On May 8 the New York *Times* published a predawn extra surpassing anything of its kind in the nation; the entire front page was given to the disaster while the tone of the writing was objective, almost clinical. Then the *Times* commissioned Joyce Kilmer to write a commemorative poem which he entitled "The White Ships and the Red." Because of the news, H. L. Mencken withdrew a piece he had written about the German philosopher Nietzsche from the forthcoming issue of the *Atlantic* because "I do not want to appear a spokesman for Germany, for I am an American by birth and the son of native-born Americans." The normally fearless Mencken may have felt that his passionate pro-Germanism might backfire on him, now that American passions had been aroused. Many newspapers were violently emotional, even in their news columns. The largest crowds since the outbreak of war now gathered outside Manhattan newspaper buildings to read bulletins scrawled in black grease pencils on white newsprint and then posted in the windows. Many spectators yelled that the United States should declare war on Germany. Angry crowds rioted in Liverpool, England. In Washington the British, French and Dutch ambassadors called on Bryan to express sympathy for the loss of American lives. Switzerland protested to Germany about the three Swiss citizens who had been killed. Memorial services were held in Manhattan's Cathedral of St. John the Divine.

Germany issued a statement charging that the *Lusitania* was carrying war matériel and was also armed with guns. The statement said the loss of life was the responsibility of Cunard officials who chose to rely on the protection of the British fleet rather than heed Germany's repeated warnings. The German military attaché, the same Captain Franz von Papen, said, "It is deplorable, if true, that so many lives have been lost. . . . But it was absolutely criminal for the Cunard Company to carry—and for the British government to allow the line to carry—neutral passengers in a ship which was transporting explosives and munitions of war." Dr. Dernburg told Cleveland reporters that the German navy had the right to destroy without warning *all* ships carrying contraband; he said this was especially true because the *Lusitania* was a British auxiliary cruiser. In Germany the common people rejoiced at the news, and a medal was struck off to celebrate this "victory." Mary Heaton Vorse, an American journalist in Berlin to report the effect of the war on civilians, described the reactions of some Germans. "It serves them right!" they said of the drowned Americans. "Travelling on a munitions ship! Why should they travel on a munitions ship? People who travel on a munitions ships must expect to be blown up!"

In London some British officials had difficulty concealing their sly satisfaction at the turn of events. Winston Churchill later wrote, "At the summit true politics and strategy are one. The manoeuvre which brings an ally into the field is as serviceable as that which wins a great battle." Colonel House was in London, and on the morning of May 7, before the *Lusitania* was shot down, he strolled in Kew Gardens with Sir Edward Grey, the British foreign minister. Apropos of nothing, Sir Edward turned to Wilson's emissary and asked, "What will America do if the Germans sink an ocean liner with American passengers aboard?" House replied, "I believe that a flame of indignation would sweep the United States and that by itself would be sufficient to carry us into war."

Henry Watterson, the fiery editor of the Louisville *Courier-Journal*, exploded in print: "Must we as a people sit down like dogs and see our laws defied, our flag flouted and our protests whistled down the wind of this lordling's majestic disdain? Must we as a nation emulate at once the impotence and the docility of China. . . ?" Theodore Roosevelt wrote, "Of course I shall not be satisfied with any delay in asserting in a most emphatic way all our rights—our right to send ammunitions of war to France and England, the right of American vessels to travel freely on the high seas, and the right of American citizens to travel freely on belligerent merchant ships on the high seas. It is not enough to assert these rights. We should insist upon their strict observance." On May 9 Colonel House cabled Wilson from London, I BELIEVE AN IMMEDIATE DEMAND SHOULD BE MADE UPON GERMANY FOR ASSURANCE THAT THIS SHALL NOT HAPPEN AGAIN . . . AMERICA HAS COME TO THE PARTING OF THE WAYS. House also told Ambassador Page, "We shall be at war within a month."

Reporters polled dozens of Senators and Representatives; all agreed a horrible crime had been committed, but only three felt we should go to war because of it. The governor of Connecticut said that any controversy arising from the tragedy could be settled by arbitration. The governor of Nebraska said 90 percent of the citizens of his state favored "adjusting these differences by arbitration and by civilized and intelligent methods." The British ambassador to the United States reported to his government, "The general feeling here is that the United States government ought to keep out of it."

Frank Cobb, the editor of the New York *World* and a confidant of the President, visited him in the White House and then quoted Wilson:

> I do not know whether the German government intends to keep faith with the United States or not. It is my personal opinion that Germany has no such intentions, but I am less concerned about the ultimate intentions of Germany than about the attitude of the American people, who are divided into three groups: those who are strongly pro-German, those who are strongly pro-Ally, and the vast majority who expect me to find a way to keep the United States out of war. I do not want war, yet I do not know that I can keep the country out of war. That depends on Germany, and I have no control over Germany. But I intend to handle this situation in such a manner that every American citizen will know that the United States has done everything it could to prevent war. Then if war comes we shall have a united country . . . and there need be no fear about the result.

On May 9 Wilson and Bryan communicated for the first time since the sinking. Bryan sent the President a clipping from the Washington *Post* listing the contraband carried by the *Lusitania* and suggesting that ships carrying risky cargo should not be permitted to carry passengers. Wilson was at work typing a rough draft of a note to Germany.

The German foreign office in Berlin, at the suggestion of Ambassador von Bernstorff, composed a word of regret and explanation, which was received by the state department and newspapers on May 10. It said, "The German Government desires to express its deepest regrets at the loss of lives on board the *Lusitania*. The responsibility rests, however, with the British Government, which, through its plan of starving the civilian population of Germany, has forced Germany to resort to retaliatory measures."

Wilson saw his secretary eyeing him and said, "I suppose you think I am cold and indifferent and a little less than human, but, my dear fellow, you are mistaken, for I have spent many sleepless hours thinking about this tragedy. It has hung over me like a terrible nightmare. In God's name, how could any nation calling itself civilized purpose so horrible a thing?" Tumulty had never seen the President looking so careworn. The evening of May 10 Wilson made his first public comment on the matter in a speech to thousands of newly naturalized citizens in exposition hall in Philadelphia. Toward the end of his talk the President spoke a phrase that was to be remembered for decades: " . . . There is such a thing as a man being too proud to fight. There is such a thing as a nation being so right that it does not need to convince others by force that it is right."

The following morning a friend asked Wilson why he had said something so easily misinterpreted. The President replied, "That was just one of the foolish things a man does. I have the bad habit of thinking out loud. That thought occurred to me while I was speaking, and I let it out." That morning Tumulty showed Wilson some 300 telegrams received at the White House during the night; most expressed indignation at his statement. Bryan, a pacifist, liked its ring: "Too proud to fight." But Americans in London felt humiliated when they saw news vendors wearing posters suspended from their necks that said in big letters : TOO PROUD TO FIGHT! George W. Wickersham, former U.S. attorney general, criticized Wilson for "sexless diplomacy"—whatever that meant.

Wilson was grateful to get a letter from former President William Howard Taft saying, "It seems to me that it is the duty of every thoughtful, patriotic citizen to avoid embarrassing you in your judgment and not to yield to the impulse of deep indignation which the circumstances naturally arouse, and demand at once a resort to extreme measures which mean war. . . . War is a dreadful thing. It would involve such enormous cost of life and treasure for us that if it can now be avoided, in a manner consistent with the dignity and honor of our country, we should make every effort to this end." Irvin S. Cobb, an American war correspondent who had seen soldiers die, felt that Wilson's controversial phrase "should be nailed in letters of flame across the national firmament and kept burning there."

That morning of May 11 Wilson convened his Cabinet to weigh the tone of the note he was preparing to send to Germany over Bryan's signature, a note written mainly by Wilson with help from Bryan and from Robert Lansing, counselor to the state department. All the Cabinet members agreed that the American people did not wish to become involved in the war. Lansing wanted the government to demand that Germany disavow the attack on the *Lusitania*, apologize, pay an indemnity, guarantee the future safety of Americans traveling abroad. Should Germany decline to meet these conditions, Lansing added, he thought we should sever diplomatic relations with Germany. Wilson rejected Bryan's recommendation that the administration issue a statement warning Americans against traveling on ships such as the *Lusitania,* for the President considered this a "weak yielding to threat and danger."

In the end Wilson decided on language asserting the "indispensable" right of United States citizens to sail the high seas, demanding repudiation of the sinking of the *Lusitania,* calling for reparations for damages. Bryan had long been aware that Wilson acted as his own secretary of state and preferred advice about foreign affairs from Colonel House rather than from his official secretary of state. After the Cabinet meeting Bryan wrote Wilson, "Mr. President, I join in this document with a heavy heart." Bryan believed that, above all, this nation should retain its "role of peacemaker."

On May 12 Wilson sent the draft of his note to the state department, where Lansing rewrote it in more diplomatic style and sharpened the language a little. Although American officials were unaware of it at the time, in Germany's supreme headquarters there was much fright over "the monstrosity of the deed," according to German Admiral Karl von Müller. The sinking of the *Lusitania* and reports of German atrocities in Belgium had set up jagged vibrations: That same May 12 French composer Camille Saint-Saëns landed in New York, and among those meeting him at the pier was a Wagnerian singer, Madame Katscherra. The old musician backed away from her in horror crying, "No! No! Away! You are a German!"

The night of May 14 the first *Lusitania* note to Germany was telegraphed in code to the American embassy in Berlin—thirty-one pages of cipher that was decoded by embassy secretary Grew, other staff members and their wives. The next morning Ambassador Gerard took the note to the German foreign office, where he was received by Gottlieb von Jagow, the German foreign secretary. Gerard had been instructed to read the document aloud to the German minister, but Jagow asked to read it himself since he understood written English better than spoken English. Jagow interrupted his reading, looked up and laughed. "Right of travel on the high seas? Why not right of free travel on land in war territory?"

When the note was published in American papers, it won Wilson more approval than anything he had said or done since his appeal for neutrality in August, 1914. William Allen White, the Kansas editor and Republican bigwig, told a friend, "I hope that you agree with me that President Wilson is doing splendidly in the foreign situation. I find myself in the attitude of endorsing him against my will." The *New Republic* commented, "The note is quiet, dignified, and firm. It is a model of restraint and understatement. It offers no ultimatum. It utters no threat." The St. Louis *Times* and Milwaukee *Free Press,* published in cities with large German-American populations, were the only two English-language papers in the nation to side with the Germans on the *Lusitania* matter. In Baltimore 8,000 German-Americans pledged their loyalty to the President. And Eleanor Roosevelt wrote a former schoolmate, a German woman named Carola von Passavant:

> . . . As to the opinions we have formed of the Germans in the war, I can only speak for myself, for my husband as you know is a member of the government and not allowed to express any opinions, but I think among the people here there is great respect for the people of Germany and also for the wonderful efficiency and preparedness of her army. Sympathy is pretty well divided I think on both sides. . . . Just now you know the feeling is very tense but I cannot help hoping some understanding may be reached.

On May 16 the German foreign office heard Bernstorff warn that America would declare war on Germany if it sank another passenger ship carrying Americans. In another secret dispatch the German ambassador told German officials:

> . . . We might as well admit openly that our propaganda here has *collapsed completely* under the impact of the *Lusitania* incident. [Italics by Bernstorff.] For anyone who knows the character of the American people, this was to be expected. . . . In the American nature two personalities that are seemingly contradictory live side by side. The cool, calculating businessman cannot be recognized when his passions take over—here they are called "emotions." In such moments he can only be compared to a hysterical woman, and all talk is to no avail. . . . Our propaganda cannot begin again until this storm has abated.

The *Berliner Tageblatt* said, "When one of our submarines again succeeds in sinking a passenger ship, we will no doubt hear another wild outburst of rage. But that our submarines will continue to sink large steamers is to be expected as a matter of course."

On May 19 Theodore Roosevelt wrote his son Archie, "There is a chance of our going to war; but I don't think it is very much of a chance. Wilson and Bryan . . . are both of them abject creatures and they won't go to war unless they are kicked into it." In a letter to an English friend Roosevelt said that if he were President, he "would . . . have taken a stand which would have made the Germans either absolutely alter their conduct or else put them into war with us." Thomas Edison said publicly, "How can we help by going to war? We haven't any troops, we haven't any ammunition, we are an unorganized mob." The inventor was criticized for calling Americans "an unorganized mob."

On May 24 the liner *New York* docked in Manhattan with some *Lusitania* survivors and the bodies of some who had perished. Among the dead was Charles Frohman, whose corpse had been embalmed in Queenstown. Actress Billie Burke gasped with grief, while another star, Maude Adams, let it be known she had not been the producer's wife. Reporters crowded around Rita Jolivet to hear her describe Frohman's final moments aboard the doomed vessel. The producer's character was eulogized in resolutions passed by Actors' Equity Association and the

American Federation of Musicians. Richard Le Gallienne wrote a poem praising Frohman. On May 25 thousands of people lined Fifth Avenue in front of Temple Emanu-El, with its two minarets, to gape at the famous actors and authors and theater managers who walked inside to hear a funeral service preached by Rabbi Joseph Silverman. The casket bore a sprig of violets from Maude Adams.

On May 25 tension increased between the United States and Germany when the American steamer *Nebraskan* was torpedoed off Fastnet Rock near the southern shore of Ireland; hit near the bow, as had happened to the *Lusitania*, the ship was able to limp back to Liverpool. Wilson protested, and Germany apologized, saying the submarine commander had mistaken the *Nebraskan* for a British merchantman and and calling it "an unfortunate accident."

On May 28 Germany replied to Wilson's note about the *Lusitania*. After pointing out that the imperial government already had expressed regret over the loss of neutral lives, it went on to say that Germany could not "escape the impression that certain important facts having a direct bearing on the sinking of the *Lusitania* may have escaped the attention of the American Government." And what were these alleged facts? The *Lusitania* had been built as an auxiliary cruiser for the British navy. On her last voyage she carried Canadian soldiers. She had been armed with cannon concealed belowdecks. She carried a large cargo of munitions.

True? False? It was true that historically the British admiralty relied on Britain's passenger liners to double as auxiliary cruisers in wartime. It was true that the British government paid the entire cost of constructing the *Lusitania*. It was true that the government insisted she be capable of mounting twelve 6-inch guns. However, British officials said she had been rejected for war work, denied she carried Canadian troops, denied she was armed, denied she carried munitions. But Winston Churchill, the first lord of the admiralty from 1911 to 1915, later wrote in *The World Crisis* that the ship's cargo included "a small consignment of rifle ammunition and shrapnel shells weighing about 173 tons." *Small?*

The German charges were answered by the American government in these words:

> Of the facts alleged in your Excellency's note, if true, the Government of the United States would have been bound to take official cognizance in performing its recognized duty as a neutral Power and in enforcing its national laws. It was its duty to see to it that the *Lusitania* was not armed for offensive action, that she was not serving as a transport, that she did not carry cargo prohibited by the statutes of the United States, and that, if in fact she was a naval vessel of Great Britain, she should not receive clearance as a merchantman. . . .

Decades were to pass before all the facts became known. A British journalist, Colin Simpson, dug into documents and in 1973 published a book about the *Lusitania* in which he said the ship had been heavily armed, that her manifests had been falsified to hide a large cargo of munitions and other contraband. Simpson charged that the British admiralty was strangely negligent in protecting the *Lusitania* against attack and presented evidence showing that for some thirty years the United States government withheld vital information about the matter from the public.

On August 4, 1914, when Great Britain declared war on Germany, the *Lusitania* was moved into drydock for the installation of twelve 6-inch guns. The following September 17 she was listed in the admiralty fleet register as an armed auxiliary cruiser and was so entered in the Cunard ledgers. When Churchill armed the *Lusitania*, he robbed her of the right to be treated as an unarmed merchantman, and elsewhere in his history of the war he wrote: ". . . The first British countermove, made on my responsibility . . . was to deter the Germans from surface attack. The submerged U-boat had to rely increasingly on underwater attack and thus ran the greater risk of mistaking neutral for British ships and of drowning neutral crews and thus embroiling Germany with other Great Powers." Furthermore, the admiralty ordered British merchantmen to fly the flag of a neutral power when in British waters and on the copy sent to Cunard, according to Colin Simpson, there was written: "Pass the word around that the flag to use is the American."

The day the *Lusitania* had left New York the last time she had been inspected by Dudley Field Malone, collector of the port of New York, with the help of a so-called Neutrality Squad. Soon after the ship was sunk a *summary* of her manifest was published in several American newspapers, which said she carried contraband and munitions. Various Senators and Representatives commented on her cargo in newspaper interviews. Herman Winter, assistant manager of the Cunard line, was quoted as saying that for years the company had been "sending small-arms cartridges abroad in the *Lusitania.*"

About two and a half years after the tragedy Senator Robert La Follette of Wisconsin said in a speech, "Four days before the *Lusitania* sailed President Wilson was warned in person by Secretary of State Bryan that the *Lusitania* had six million rounds of ammunition on board, besides explosives." Bryan, then no longer the secretary of state, replied, "I read a statement which was purported to have been made by Senator La Follette in a speech in Minneapolis to the effect that four days before the sinking of the *Lusitania* I had notified the President that there was ammunition on board the vessel. When I passed through Washington last Wednesday I notified the state department and also Senator La Follette that the Senator had been misinformed, and that I had not known until long after the sinking of the *Lusitania* that it carried ammunition in its cargo."

Some Senators became so furious that they tried to expel La Follette from the Senate. Now on the defensive, he asked the treasury department for a true copy of Malone's report and was referred to the state department. The state department refused to give the Senator a copy on the ground that it had become a part of the government's secret archives—an early instance of self-imposed bureaucratic secrecy. As late as 1938 a writer asked the government for access to cargo manifests of ships sailing from New York in 1915, only to be told that by an act of

Congress on May 17, 1928, authorization had been given to destroy all cargo manifests for 1915–16.

Senator La Follette had not given up when he was refused by the state department. His law partner got in touch with Malone, who agreed to meet La Follette, and the two conferred at 158 Waverly Place in Manhattan. La Follette explained what had happened. Malone said he thought it outrageous to refuse a United States Senator access to an official document—one of his own making, in fact. Malone later gave La Follette a copy of his report. Malone also supplied the Senator with carbon copies of affidavits signed by members of the Neutrality Squad and other officials who had helped him inspect the *Lusitania*.

These documents showed that she carried 5,468 cases of ammunition. There were 4,200 cases of metallic cartridges shipped by the Remington Arms-Union Metallic Cartridge Company and consigned to the Remington Arms Company of London, with the ultimate consignee the British government. There also were 1,250 cases of shrapnel shipped by G. W. Sheldon & Company for the Bethlehem Steel Company and consigned to the deputy director of ammunition stores at Woolwich, England.

The Cunard line had indeed let noncombatants sail on a ship laden with ammunition. A court awarded Mrs. May Davies Hopkins a $40,000 life insurance settlement on a policy taken out by her late husband, A. L. Hopkins, president of the Newport News Shipbuilding and Drydock Company. Other litigants were not so lucky; Cunard won a lawsuit of about $6,000,000 in claims filed by people who had suffered losses. And in 1919 the admiralty branch of the United States District Court in New York absolved Cunard of all liability, declaring that the sinking and consequent loss of life and property had been "caused solely by the illegal act of the Imperial German Government, acting through its instrument, the submarine commander." This decision said the line was "not liable to any extent for any loss, damage, or injury, nor for any claim whatsoever in any way arising out of, or in consequence of, the unlawful attack by a German submarine."

Long before this in Queenstown, Ireland, a coroner's jury of Irishmen, who normally felt better disposed to Germany than England, had returned this verdict:

> The deceased died from prolonged immersion and exhaustion on the sea eight miles south south-west of the Old Head of Kinsdale on Friday, 7th May, 1915, owing to the sinking of HMS *Lusitania* by torpedoes fired without warning by a German submarine. We find that this appalling crime was contrary to international law and the conventions of all civilized nations and we therefore charge the officers of the said submarine and the Emperor and Government of Germany under whose orders they acted with the wilful and wholesale murder before the tribunal of the civilized world.

It had been on May 28 that Germany replied to Wilson's note. Most American newspapers denounced the German document. The New York *World* called it "the answer of an outlaw who assumes no obligation toward society." The *World* also published a Rollin Kirby cartoon showing the corpses of women and children with Uncle Sam standing at their feet and facing the Kaiser, who was shrugging off all responsibility for their deaths. Actually, the Kaiser was afraid the United States might enter the war on the side of the Allies. On June 1 the German fleet received this order:

> His Majesty the Emperor points once more to the necessity of sparing neutral ships in the conduct of submarine operations until further orders are given. Further attacks on neutral ships would permit the danger of serious political complications, and these have to be avoided at any cost in the present circumstances. His Majesty makes it the solemn duty of submarine commanders not to attack unless they have the well-founded conviction that the ship in question is an enemy ship. In cases of doubt it is better to let an enemy freighter escape than to sink a neutral ship. You will also attempt to convey this order to U-boats now at sea.

Wilson did not know of this order when he convened his Cabinet on June 1. He wanted advice about what to say next. Should he send another note to Germany? One Cabinet member asked whether a strong protest would also be sent to Great Britain. Bryan, sitting to the right of Wilson with his eyes closed, now opened them, leaned forward, and began speaking excitedly. He said he always had insisted on dispatching a note to Great Britain, since it was illegally preventing our exports from going wherever we had a right to send them, and, he added heatedly, the Cabinet seemed to him to be pro-Ally. "You people are not neutral!" Bryan snapped. "You are taking sides!" Wilson cut Bryan down with a voice like a cold sword: "Mr. Secretary, you have no right to make that statement. We are all trying to be neutral against heavy difficulties."

And there *were* difficulties. Theodore Roosevelt wrote a judge: ". . . President Wilson has failed, and has caused the American people to fail, in performing national and international duty in a world crisis. There was not the slightest occasion for diplomacy or mediation. . . . The time for thought or for words had passed." No diplomacy? No mediation? No thought? No words? Just headlong action plunging the United States into war? Seemingly this was what Roosevelt wanted. Small wonder Wilson felt his burden intolerable.

The President was receptive when Bernstorff requested an interview, and when the two met in the White House, Wilson betrayed none of the animosity he felt for the German ambassador. Both stressed their wish to find some peaceful solution to the crisis. Bernstorff later told the German foreign office, ". . . Wilson kept coming back to the point that to him only humanitarian considerations are important, and that an indemnity for all Americans who perished on the *Lusitania* is secondary to the humanitarian considerations. His efforts are directed at a total abolition of the submarine war. . . . If we would abandon the submarine war, he would press the British into abandoning the starvation policy."

A few hours after Germany and England went to war on August 4, 1914, some British commandos put to sea in trawlers, made their way to the German naval base at Emden and cut Germany's deep-sea cables. Bernstorff now told Wilson that one of the greatest obstacles to a peaceful settlement of the *Lusitania* case was his difficulty in communicating with the foreign office in Berlin. Would the President let him use the American state department wires if he promised to send no information compromising American neutrality? Wilson consented to this arrangement until the end of the *Lusitania* negotiations. This was decades before the installation of a hot line between the White House and the Kremlin.

Bernstorff wired Berlin:

> . . . neither the President nor the American people want war with Germany. Therefore, Mr. Wilson has the best chance to gain public approval for himself if he averts conflict with us honorably, by beginning a peace movement in a grand style. . . . The President and the government over here are much more neutral than one would generally assume. . . . It is a fact perhaps astonishing to us, but a fact none the less, that prominent Americans often come here from Boston, New York and Philadelphia—general centers of English support in this country—and complain of the pro-German attitude of the government.

The day after Wilson saw Bernstorff he began drafting a second *Lusitania* note, crouching over his typewriter all day and far into the night as he searched for just the right word to express his precise meaning, writing and rewriting and then rewriting again. Mark Twain once said: "The difference between the *right* word and the *almost* right word is the difference between lightning and the lightning bug." Wilson wore himself out and went to bed at 2 A.M. on June 4. A little after nine o'clock that day Bryan came to the White House to go over the draft with the President. At 10 A.M. Cabinet members and Counselor Lansing gathered to hear Wilson read his document. Still later in the day former President Taft said at Bryn Mawr College, "If we had a jingo in the White House, this country would now be at war with Germany. Instead, our chief executive is a man who appreciates his responsibility."

Wilson often suffered blinding headaches, but now they were worse. He was torn by the realization that on the one hand, Americans wanted to avoid war, while on the other, they expected him to take a firm and honorable position. How could he reconcile these two desires? Well, in his second *Lusitania* note he managed to strike a balanced position. He said Germany's submarine war posed a grave threat to freedom of the seas, and he declared the German government was misinformed, since the ship had been unarmed and carried no Canadian troops. "Whatever be the other facts," Wilson said in his climax, "the principal fact is that a great steamer, primarily and chiefly a conveyance for passengers, and carrying more than a thousand souls who had no part or lot in the conduct of war, was sent to the bottom without so much as a challenge or warning, and that men, women, and children were sent to their deaths in circumstances unparalleled in modern warfare."

As Wilson read aloud, Bryan listened glumly and silently. Like the

President, he had not slept much and felt exhausted. The following day Bryan wrote Wilson a letter reviewing the three points Bryan thought most vital—arbitration of the dispute, action to prevent U.S. citizens from traveling on ships carrying munitions and a protest to Great Britain. With a touch of bitterness Bryan pointed out that Wilson had consented to the first and third measures—and then changed his mind. With ever more emphasis creeping into his sentences, Bryan wrote, "I beg to renew the suggestions most urgently, believing as I do, that without them the note as you outlined it at the cabinet meeting would be likely to cause a rupture of diplomatic relations and this might rush us into war in spite of anything we could do. . . . This may be our last chance to speak for truth."

Bryan did not feel Wilson actually wanted war or even was being flagrantly provocative; he just thought the President was not doing all he could to avoid the dangers of war. At issue was a difference of opinion between two highly principled men. Aware he would be unable to change Wilson's mind, vexed because of the President's habit of writing diplomatic papers himself, chagrined because Wilson turned to Colonel House for advice on foreign affairs, Bryan decided to resign as secretary of state. He went to the home of Treasury Secretary McAdoo and nervously announced his decision. McAdoo rushed to the White House to tell Wilson. The President said he was not surprised but thought Bryan's resignation at this critical moment might lead the Germans to believe there was a wide difference of opinion inside the American government. Wilson sent McAdoo back to Bryan to beg him to stay. Bryan quavered, "I think this will destroy me, but whether it does or not, I must do my duty according to my conscience, and if I am destroyed it is, after all, merely the sacrifice that one must not hesitate to make to serve God and his country."

Accompanied by McAdoo, Bryan returned to the White House to spend an hour passionately arguing that Wilson's proposed note surely would lead to war. Wilson yielded no point to Bryan but tried to dissuade him from resigning. The longer they talked, the more agitated Bryan became. Wilson pressed a button, and when a servant came, he said, "Mr. Bryan wants a drink of water." Bryan's hand shook so much that as he raised the glass to his lips, he spilled some water. As he left the Presidential study, Bryan blurted, "Colonel House has been secretary of state, not I, and I have never had your full confidence!" That night Bryan sent Wilson his resignation. He said he was unable to concur in Wilson's note "without violating what I deem to be an obligation to my country."

The next day was June 8, and the Cabinet met without Bryan. The members were discussing Wilson's second note when he was interrupted. Turning back to them, Wilson said, "Gentlemen, Mr. Bryan has resigned as secretary of state to take effect when the German note is sent. He is on the telephone and wants to know whether it would be desirable or agreeable for him to attend the Cabinet meeting. Would be it embarrassing? What do you think?" The men agreed Bryan's presence would not upset them. Moments later Bryan walked in, and the other men stood up, their faces solemn. Bryan looked careworn. He took his seat and leaned back and closed his eyes. At the end of the meeting Bryan invited his colleagues to lunch with him at the University club. To those who accepted he said he could not "go along with" the President in this note because he thought it might lead to war. "I think I can help the President more on the outside. I can work to control popular opinion so that it will not exert pressure for extreme action which the President does not want. We both want the same thing—peace."

Wilson wrote Bryan to say he accepted his resignation "with a feeling of personal sorrow." Actually, as Wilson soon told Colonel House, he was "greatly relieved now that Mr. Bryan had gone," since Bryan had been a constant source of concern to him. Early in the afternoon of June 9 Bryan went to the White House to bid formal farewell to the President. Each congratulated the other on the purity of his motives. At the end of their talk they stood up and clasped hands, and both said simultaneously, "God bless you!"

Bryan sadly told friends, "I go out into the dark," and for a while he moved as through midnight. When news of his resignation was made public, there was much excitement—perhaps the greatest since Wilson took office, according to Agriculture Secretary Houston. Interior Secretary Lane told Bryan, "You are the most real Christian I know." This was hardly a general opinion. The New York *World* published another Kirby cartoon showing Bryan speaking in a theater where the Kaiser sat in the first row applauding him while Americans left the hall. The *World* called Bryan's resignation "unspeakable treachery not only to the President but to the nation." *Life* magazine published this doggerel: "*I want to be a neutral and with the neutrals stand. / A smile upon my ego, the German vote at hand.*" Page, the pro-British ambassador to England, wrote a letter about Bryan and snarled: ". . . Of course he's a traitor: he always had a yellow streak, the yellow streak of a sheer fool."

William Howard Taft said in a letter, "Bryan as usual is an ass, but he is an ass with a good deal of opportunity for mischief." German-Americans and the Hearst press tried—unsuccessfully—to lure Bryan into their camp. Some people considered Hearst pro-German because he owned a German-language newspaper in New York and was openly anti-British. Theodore Roosevelt wrote Senator Lodge, "It is possible that Wilson, who is the worst President by all odds we have had since Buchanan with the possible exception of Andrew Johnson, may find that his break with Bryan is of more permanent hurt to him than anyone else." Franklin D. Roosevelt wrote his wife, "What d'y' think of W. Jay B? It's all too long to write about, but I can only say I'm disgusted clear through." Eleanor Roosevelt commented, "I'm so glad Bryan is out, but I can't help admiring him sticking to his principles." She added that Bryan's pacifism appealed to her.

Bryan's resignation mystified some people. Chandler P. Anderson, a state department legal adviser, wrote in his diary, "The extraordinary part of the situation is that the note which Mr. Bryan refused to sign . . . in some ways is less rigid than the previous note." Senator Lodge said that "why Bryan should let his name go on the first note and then refuse to sign the mild performance that appears in this morning's papers is difficult to understand." In a signed editorial Hearst declared the United States had no right to demand that Germany stop its submarine warfare. "Marse Henry" Watterson, the Southern editor, roared in print, "Men have been shot and beheaded, even hanged, drawn and quartered, for treason less heinous. The recent Secretary of State commits not merely treason to the country at a critical moment, but treachery to his party and its official head. . . . With the mind of Barnum and the soul of a Tittlebat Titmouse he waited for the opportune moment, and when it arrived he struck, wantonly and shamelessly."

Robert Lansing, who had helped draft Wilson's notes to Germany, was elevated from state department counselor to secretary of state. During Bryan's frequent absences from the capital to lecture on the Chautauqua circuit, where he appeared on the same bill with jugglers and female impersonators, Lansing had served as acting secretary. In selecting Lansing, Wilson made a wise choice, for Lansing was one of the nation's best international lawyers, often had represented the United States before international tribunals and knew much more about foreign affairs than Bryan. Although the second *Lusitania* note was mainly Wilson's work, it was sent to Germany over Lansing's signature, according to protocol. This second note, like the first, won the approval of most Americans. Neither harsh nor provocative, it was instead statesmanlike and courteous, although it firmly reiterated the same principles and demands, and it rejected Germany's arguments.

Meanwhile, the German ambassador had given the state department four affidavits declaring that the *Lusitania* had been armed with guns despite denials by Cunard officials, the British government and Dudley Field Malone. A departmental investigation resulted in the arrest of one of the four men who had signed these affidavits. His name was Gustav Stahl, and he was a reservist in the German army. Taken before a grand jury, Stahl swore he had seen four masked cannon on the ship. He was charged with perjury, pleaded guilty, was sentenced to eighteen months in jail.

British Ambassador Cecil Spring-Rice sent Senator Lodge a poem expressing his contempt of the President. In this poem Wilson speaks to the Kaiser:

I told you not to do it: I said that it was wrong
I meant it and you knew it: my words were kind but strong . . .
you knew that I was frowning and sharpening my pens.
Yet you would persist in drowning my fellow citizens.
About a hundred were destroyed;
I was exceedingly annoyed . . .
excuse the observation,—I wouldn't hurt your feelings,—
But really, Kaiser, the excuse—
It simply was the very deuce.

T. S. Eliot of St. Louis had gone to England to study at Oxford, and a month after the *Lusitania* sank he married an Englishwoman named Vivienne Haigh-Wood. Eliot wanted to take his bride to America to meet his family, but she refused because she was afraid of German submarines. After all, following receipt of Wilson's second note in Berlin the *Tägliche Rundschau* declared, "The torpedoing will go on." German

Count Ernst von Reventlow wrote in his diary, "If President Wilson persists in his refusal to recognize the German declaration of a war zone, we are not able to conceive of an agreement or even a real understanding."

Gerard, the U.S. ambassador to Germany, detested German military leaders and disliked civilian officials as well, but nonetheless did all he could to avoid a rupture between the two powers. He wrote Colonel House, ". . . It seems rather ridiculous to enter this awful war to enforce a right which is of no practical use. Americans can just as well travel on American, Danish or Norwegian ships and keep us out of complications." Gerard kept the state department informed of the progress of discussions in Berlin but did not reveal that he had helped prepare the draft of the German reply. When this reply was received in Washington and published in newspapers, editors across the land denounced it as totally unresponsive and unacceptable. George Harvey of the *North American Review* editorialized, "Not one of our moderate demands is accorded even the courtesy of frank recognition; all are in effect denied; each and every one is either tacitly spurned or imprudently rejected." But despite the anger and regret expressed in the press, especially the metropolitan press along the Atlantic seaboard, most Americans did not want to go to war with Germany over the *Lusitania.* Bernstorff correctly sensed the national mood when he told the German chancellor that "one should not be fooled by the eastern press in the United States. These as well as other powerful spokesmen take up for England and would gladly welcome a war with Germany. But for Mr. Wilson and the overwhelming majority of the American people, this is *not* the case."

The President wrote his third and final *Lusitania* note to Germany. Delivered on July 21, 1915, it declared that such "illegal and inhuman acts" would, if repeated, "constitute an unpardonable offense against the sovereignty of the neutral nation affected." This time Wilson's tone was so firm the Germans decided to relent a little lest they find themselves embroiled in war with the United States. Bernstorff gave Secretary of State Lansing a letter saying, ". . . I beg to inform you that my instructions concerning our answer to your last *Lusitania* note contains the following passage: 'Liners will not be sunk by our submarines without warning and without safety to the lives of noncombatants, provided that the liners do not try to escape or offer resistance.' "

Wilson had won the diplomatic war—for the time being. He won it by patience and self-control and farsightedness. He won it in the interests of Americans and the peoples of all neutral nations. The editor of North Carolina's Charlotte *Observer* echoed the feelings of many citizens when he wrote, "*The Observer* is not given to irreverence, but . . . it is now strengthened in the conviction that has possessed it for some time that Wilson was a divinely appointed leader of the people."

Chapter 15

SUPERMAN VERSUS THE PROFESSOR

On May 7, 1915, the day the news of the *Lusitania* reached this country, Theodore Roosevelt was in a courtroom in Syracuse, New York. The former President was the defendant in a $50,000 libel suit filed against him by the notorious New York Republican boss, William Barnes, Jr.

Roosevelt was handed a telegram saying the *Lusitania* had been sunk by a submarine. No details. People watching him saw anxiety on his face. When court adjourned, he went to the home of Horace Wilkinson, where he was a houseguest, and paced up and down. About midnight Wilkinson went to Roosevelt's room to awaken him to say a reporter was phoning from New York City and wanted comment on the sinking. Teddy told his host, "All right! I'll speak to him. I always talk with the boys."

He listened as the reporter gave him details. Roosevelt exclaimed, "That's murder! . . . Will I make a statement? Yes! Yes! I'll make it now. Just take this—" Then he dictated: "This represents not merely piracy, but piracy on a vaster scale of murder than old-time pirates ever practiced. . . . It is warfare against innocent men, women and children, travelling on the ocean, and our own fellow countrymen and countrywomen, who are among the sufferers. It seems inconceivable that we can refrain from taking action in this matter, for we owe it not only to humanity but to our own national self-respect."

The next morning Roosevelt told his lawyers his statement probably alienated two German-Americans on the jury, but added, "I cannot help it. There is a principle at stake here which is more vital to the American people than my own personal welfare is to me." His fears were groundless. The jury found in his favor, believing his charges that a corrupt political ring composed of members of both major parties had controlled the New York state government from 1898 to 1910.

Theodore Roosevelt and Woodrow Wilson fought each other over the issue of taking the United States into the war on the side of the Allies or remaining neutral. It was a clash of giants. In 1962 seventy-five students of American history rated the performances of our Presidents, deciding that Wilson was our fourth greatest President while Roosevelt ranked seventh. Their differences became a duel between a professor and Superman, between Wilson's cool mind and Roosevelt's hot blood, and the nation's fate hinged on the outcome.

Roosevelt once said of himself, "I am only an average man but—by George!—I work harder at it than the average man." The truth is that Roosevelt was the antithesis of the average man. After he died his friend Dr. W. Sturgis Bigelow said, "I don't know what you would call him. A man? A creature? An entity, perhaps? Call him what you want, he was more than a man. If one could imagine the impulse and force of a divinity inhabiting a human body with the divinity's overpowering energy and only a human mind, one might begin to get his measure." Henry Adams, another friend, remarked, "Theodore is never sober—only he is drunk with himself, and not with rum." Adams also ascribed to Roosevelt "the quality that medieval theology assigned to God—he was pure act."

Roosevelt brimmed with self-confidence and at all times he was so spectacularly himself that he was one of the most colorful men who ever lived. On occasion after occasion he gambled his life so recklessly that he astonished and frightened his peers. He rode to the hounds on Long Island and often fell off his horse and bled copiously but paid almost no attention to his wounds. After a gunman shot him in the chest, he declared, "I did not care a rap for being shot"—and with a sense of astonishment one finds himself believing that Teddy really meant what he said. Although his wrath was as explosive as a bomb, he forgave the man who tried to assassinate him.

Roosevelt slaughtered seventeen lions on an African safari and engaged in pillow fights with his sons in the White House. He proclaimed that "no triumph of peace is quite so great as the supreme triumphs of war" but won the Nobel Peace Prize for helping settle the Russo-Japanese War. He hunted panthers in Colorado and considered a baby's hand the most beautiful sight in the world. He lectured at Oxford and the Sorbonne and wrangled steers in Dakota. He lost the sight in his left eye while boxing in the White House and continued to read mountains of books. He climbed the Matterhorn and quoted from the classics. He crowed in delight when he saw one of his sons playing with a tin sword, and debated with naturalist John Burroughs on whether the chippy sparrow's song went *twee, twee* or *twee, twee, twee.* He knocked down bullies, took on Japanese jujitsu wrestlers, chopped wood and wrote more than any other American President, dipping his pen into an inkwell hollowed from the foot of a rhinoceros. While he sometimes exhibited pity, he often denounced the "weak and craven" and branded Russian novelist Leo Tolstoy a "moral pervert." A British statesman called him a mixture of "St. Vitus and St. Paul . . . a great wonder of nature." A relative said with a sigh, "When Theodore attends a wedding he wants to be the bride, and when he attends a funeral he wants to be the corpse." William Allen White said, "If he was a freak, God and the times needed one."

Theodore Roosevelt was born on October 27, 1858, at 28 East Twentieth Street in Manhattan, a descendant of Claes Martenzen van Rosenvelt who came from Holland to New York in about 1644. In his veins flowed the blood of Dutch, Scotch, English and Huguenot ancestors, although during World War I he talked a lot about his

"German" blood. His father, who became friendly with Abraham Lincoln, was collector of the port of New York, a rich glass importer with substantial banking interests, a Republican and a Presbyterian, famous for his philanthropies. "My father," Theodore wrote, "was the best man I ever knew. He combined strength and courage with gentleness, tenderness, and great unselfishness. I never knew anyone who got more joy out of living than did my father, or anyone who more wholeheartedly performed every duty." His mother was beautiful and willowy and fragile, a woman of great charm but so delicate that her mind became vague, such a fanatic about cleanliness that she kept her furniture covered with sheets. Theodore was the second of four children; he had two sisters and one brother. His brother, Elliott, the father of Eleanor Roosevelt, who became Mrs. Franklin D. Roosevelt, became an alcoholic. Theodore hated the taste of beer and drank whiskey or brandy only when prescribed by a physician.

As a child Theodore was so nearsighted he had to wear thick glasses that gave him an owllike expression, sickly and frail, pallid and wispy and weak-armed and racked by asthma. He always remembered his father "carrying me in my distress, in my battles for breath, up and down a room all night. . . . I could breathe, I could sleep, when he had me in his arms." The weakling turned in on himself at first, learning to read when very young and devouring books the rest of his life, able to concentrate even in a room full of noise. He never went to school but was tutored at home. As a boy he began collecting birds and mice and snakes, converting his bedroom into a museum and vowing to grow up to become a naturalist. When he was thirteen, he was sent to Maine because of its pure air, and two local boys his age taunted the four-eyed weakling; Theodore flew into a rage, but his tormentors easily and humiliatingly kept him at arm's length. From that day forward he exercised strenuously to build up his body, especially his biceps, filling a room on the second floor of the family home with barbells and horizontal bars and a punching bag. Later in life he said, "There were all kinds of things of which I was afraid at first . . . but by acting as if I was not afraid I gradually ceased to be afraid."

By sheer willpower he turned himself into a rugged, deep-chested man of cyclonic energy, becoming so impressed by his accomplishment that afterward he scorned any kind of weakness in anyone. Asked how he felt, he always answered that he felt as strong as a bull moose. His favorite motto was a West African hunting proverb: "Speak softly and carry a big stick; you will go far." He had another favorite aphorism: "Don't hit at all if it is honorably possible to avoid hitting, but *never* hit soft!" During summer vacations his father would take the family to Europe and Africa, and young Theodore explored the Nile, rode a donkey on the Sahara, took a horseback tour of the Holy Land, was left in Germany one year to learn to speak German. Fifteen years old and residing in Dresden, he let his hair grow long in imitation of a German poet—"*a la* mop," Theodore called it. He came to admire German characteristics and continued to admire them until 1914.

A tutor prepared him for Harvard, which he entered in 1876. Living apart from his Victorian family, he took to dressing like a dude and grew reddish sideburns that reached to his chin. Weighing 135 pounds, he yearned to become Harvard's lightweight boxing champion—although without his glasses he hardly could see his opponent—and had himself photographed stripped to the waist, a proper pugilistic scowl on his square face. He failed to win the title. Having spent so much time in the company of his father's friends and being widely traveled, he was unawed by his professors, believed he knew more than they and often rose in class to dispute them. Nonetheless, he was a serious student and applied himself to his books. When he was a sophomore, his father died and left him $200,000; Theodore never had to earn a living.

His wealth and social rank enabled him to mingle with Boston's Brahmins, and in his junior year of college he met and fell in love with Alice Hathaway Lee, herself a proper Bostonian. She was lovely and high-spirited and had such a gay disposition that her friends called her Sunshine. Teddy's wooing was so headlong that at first she reacted with alarm; she became positively frightened when he bought a pair of Italian dueling pistols and threatened to challenge any rivals to a duel. Still, he did not neglect his studies. The life of a professional naturalist was not for him, he decided, since he loved the outdoors and hated to say inside smelly laboratories bent over a microscope. Turning his attention to history, he discovered in his senior year that no history had been written about American naval action in the War of 1812, so he began one—the first of his many books. It was published in 1882. Elected to Phi Beta Kappa, he was graduated in 1880—twenty-first in a class of 117.

Now for marriage. Thoroughly Victorian, he wrote in his diary: "Thank Heaven, I am at least perfectly pure." The male virgin married Alice on his twenty-second birthday, October 27, 1880, in Brookline, Massachusetts. The newlyweds took no immediate honeymoon but moved into an upper floor of the Roosevelt home in Manhattan, and Theodore enrolled in the Columbia Law School. A legal profession, as he soon discovered, was not to his taste because the law moves slowly and he wanted to gallop through life. In the absence of anything better to do, he continued awhile to read law, hiking three miles to attend class, joining the national guard, boxing daily and racing around Central Park on horseback. At last he and his bride left for a belated honeymoon, sailing to Europe and traveling to Switzerland, where he immediately announced he would scale the Matterhorn. It had been conquered for the first time only sixteen years previously, and Alice begged him not to risk his life; but—as she knew he would—he picked his way to its high and icy peak.

Back in Manhattan, the Roosevelts took an apartment of their own and had two maids to take care of them. Not really caring to enter law, his *Naval War of 1812* unfinished, Teddy Roosevelt did some hard thinking about the kind of career he should choose. Politics. This was the thing. When friends protested that politics was a dirty business and beneath him, he mused that this merely meant the people he knew did not belong to the governing class, "and I intended to be one of the governing class." In 1882 he joined New York City's Twenty-first District Republican Club, informally known as the Jake Hess Club in honor of its burly leader. Club headquarters were over a saloon on Fifth Avenue between Fifty-eighth and Fifty-ninth streets on a site later occupied by the Savoy-Plaza hotel.

Jake Hess did not know what to make of this ebullient and aristocratic young man in fashionable clothes and wearing nose glasses attached to a black silk ribbon, but Roosevelt announced he was ready to begin at the bottom as a precinct worker. A Hess lieutenant named Joe Murray saw a golden opportunity and persuaded Roosevelt to run for election to the state assembly in Albany. Roosevelt became a candidate, was hailed by the New York *Times* as "a public-spirited citizen, not an office seeker," and won. At twenty-three he was the youngest member of the legislature.

Nothing like Teddy Roosevelt had ever been seen in the state capital. He had a magnetic quality that made him the center of attention wherever he went. Side-whiskered, sandy-haired and sometimes overdressed, the volatile and brash young legislator amused some people and offended others—including upstate legislators whom he would charge, hand held out, braying, "You're from the country, aren't you?" But whenever he arose in the well of the assembly chamber and sought attention by shrilling "Mistuh Speak-ah!" when they heard the Harvard accent lacking an *r*, when they saw his face split into a grin showing big teeth and when they began to realize the incredible breadth of his learning, when they watched the chopping motion of his right fist pounding down into the palm of his left hand, when his energy smashed into them like a tidal wave—then they realized that here was a young man to be reckoned with.

The silk-stocking Republican soon allied himself with the reform minority, and before long he accused financier Jay Gould of trying to corrupt a state supreme court justice. Gould, he declared, was "part of that most dangerous of all dangerous classes, the wealthy criminal class." Roosevelt's reform tendencies worked on alternating current: While he voted to abolish sweatshops in New York City's cigar industry, and while he voted to limit the working hours of women and children employed in factories, he refused to support much needed prison reform. He was no radical but rather a conservative reformer—a rare bird. Irritating his seniors and fascinating political reporters, he made shrill attacks on rich men and rigid institutions and was scorned by reactionaries as "a Harvard goo-goo"—one committed to good government.

On February 12, 1884, his wife gave birth to a daughter who was named Alice Lee Roosevelt, and two days later the new mother died of Bright's disease. That February 14 was the most terrible day in Roosevelt's life, for on that same day he also lost his mother, who died of typhoid fever. He was so stunned he did not know what he said or did but moved as through a mist. Later he wrote of his dead wife, "And when my heart's dearest died, the light went out of my life forever." Never again did he speak her name, not even to their daughter. While it is impossible to measure another's grief, it is permissible to point out that even this double tragedy failed to mature Teddy Roosevelt. Emotionally, all the rest of his life, he remained an adolescent; Cecil Spring-Rice, his friend who became the British ambassador to the United States, once said, "You must remember that the President is about six."

Despite Roosevelt's declaration that he overcame fear by facing fear, it seems he never overcame that most basic of all fears—seeing himself as he really was. There is a sense of cosmic loneliness when one is not in intimate touch with his basic nature, and Roosevelt, who seldom was introspective, never understood who or what he was. It is possible that he tried to shield himself from himself by engaging in furious action and by surrounding himself with relatives and friends. In rare moments when alone and quiet he sank into a depression, tortured by fears and doubts. There is external evidence of this internal insecurity. Roosevelt spoke and wrote balanced sentences—the moment after he took a position he immediately qualified it. It is possible to explain this trait by saying that he was a politician who did not wish to offend anyone—except when he was hammering away at Woodrow Wilson during the war—but it is equally possible that deep within himself he felt a certain ambivalence. He could say, "There have been abuses connected with the accumulation of great fortunes, yet it remains true that such fortunes confer . . . immense incidental benefits upon others." Senator Henry Cabot Lodge, who had been a young history instructor at Harvard when Roosevelt was a student, once told him, "You see things too darkly." Roosevelt proved his confusion of emotion with motion when he mumbled, "Black care rarely sits behind the rider whose pace is fast enough."

Before the deaths of his wife and mother he had gone to the Bad Lands of the Dakotas and purchased two cattle ranches. Now he donned an authentic cowboy outfit—a sombrero, a kerchief at his thick neck, a Western shirt with fringed sleeves, a gun at his hip, chaps and boots and spurs. With an extra pair of glasses tucked in a pocket, he galloped across the plains, hunted antelope, rode herd at night, ate from a chuck wagon, faced down or knocked down toughs who sneered at the Eastern tenderfoot, and finally won the respect of wranglers and hunters. But none of them ever quite recovered from the shock of hearing Roosevelt, during a roundup, rally them with the cry "Hasten forward quickly!" The wide spaces and blue sky and clean air helped heal his soul.

And he continued to write—book after book about his experiences in the West, about famous men, about history. He wrote well, constructing sentences as straight and strong as a bridge. His vocabulary spanned the spectrum of most of the arts and sciences. In his political papers and speeches he was a master of invective, much of it cruel, and to our language he contributed telling phrases—"race suicide," "muckraker," "submerged majority," "waging peace." Because he was always in a big hurry, his historical and biographical research was too shallow to be scholarly. He never produced a masterpiece, but he did enjoy popularity as an author. His book *African Game Trails* sold more than 1,000,000 copies. History, to him, was largely the record of the lives of great men, although he never probed deeply enough into their hearts and minds to find their motives and uncover the sources of their psychic drives. Instead, he always felt offended by any behavior he considered abnormal and saw life as white or black, remaining forever a prisoner of his Victorian morality. He declared that Goya and El Greco painted morbid rubbish, scorned the spirit-probing novels of Flaubert, denounced the psychological insights of Jung and Adler as "dirty nonsense." Of a novel by Henry James he said, "I think it represents the last stage of degradation . . . the book is simply diseased." He became friendly with journalist Lincoln Steffens, who told him one day "my impression is that you don't think things out in your mind but . . . mull them over somewhere else in your nervous system and form your conclusion in, say, your hips." Surprised, Roosevelt blurted, "Do you know—that's true! I do think down there—down there somewhere." In his unconscious, of course.

Writing and ranching failed to satisfy his lust for power, so he returned to Manhattan and in 1886 became the Republican reform candidate for the mayoralty of New York City. He lost the election, placing third. One day he ran into Edith Kermit Carow, whom he had known since he was three and she an infant in her cradle, and to his astonishment he fell in love with her. She was a quiet, reserved woman who read even more books than he, the only female he had ever known who shared his enthusiasm for zoology and natural history. He was shocked at the realization that he, a grieving widower, could feel tenderness toward another woman. Pacing the floor, banging his fist into his palm, he muttered, "I have no constancy! I have no constancy!" Undecided about marrying Edith, he returned to Dakota. She went to London to live, he followed her there, and they were married in the British capital in 1886. The best man was Cecil Spring-Rice. Over the next several years the second Mrs. Theodore Roosevelt gave him four sons and one daughter. She called him "Theodore," not "Teddy," since she knew he disliked the nickname. She was neither awed nor overwhelmed by her dynamic spouse. Whenever he uttered some outlandish statement, she would say, "Now, Theodore, you know that is just one of those remarks that make it so difficult sometimes for your friends to defend you." With an air of injured innocence, he would protest, "Why, Edie, I was only—"

Senator Lodge, a kind of guardian angel to Roosevelt during much of his life, persuaded President Benjamin Harrison to appoint Roosevelt a civil service commissioner at $3,500 a year, so the ambitious young politician moved to Washington, where he soon began to attract national attention. He quashed corruption in the New York customhouse, fought campaign assessments of federal employees, removed thousands of federal jobs from political patronage and performed so well that he was reappointed after Grover Cleveland became President. These accomplishments might have been enough to satisfy an average man, but Roosevelt's temperament was so dynamic he considered civil service work much too routine for his talents. Besides, he wanted to return to his home state to enhance his image as a Republican reformer, and he thought he might get the chance to run the police department of the world's largest city. The department was being reorganized into a four-man board of commissioners, and Mayor William L. Strong remembered that when Roosevelt had been a state assemblyman, he had probed the city's police record. The mayor appointed him to the board, Teddy was elected its president, and soon he shunted the other commissioners into obscurity.

Roosevelt swept over the city like a hurricane. Eccentrically dressed in a pink shirt and a black silk cummerbund whose tasseled ends hung to his knees, he dived into the slums in the company of police reporters, swooped down on cops sleeping on their beat, put an end to the beating of prisoners and police graft, supported special agencies, placed police promotion on a merit system, infuriated his colleagues and delighted plain citizens. He feuded with Comptroller Ashbel P. Fitch and at a city hall hearing declared that Fitch was no fighter and would run away.

"I would never run away from you!" Fitch snapped.

"You would not fight!"

"What shall it be," Fitch challenged, "pistols or—"

Roosevelt snarled, "Pistols or anything you wish!"

The mayor interrupted. "Come! Come! If this does not stop I will put you both under arrest!"

Roosevelt made the mistake of enforcing all laws—good or bad. A state statute called the Raines Law permitted hotels to serve liquor on Sunday—and defined a hotel as any structure with ten bedrooms and facilities for serving meals. Besides insisting on the letter of every law, Roosevelt now broke the law himself by ordering his policemen to arrest anyone who sold booze on Sunday. This outraged workingmen who liked to slip into a place for a friendly glass and infuriated the newspapers and the mayor as well. After two years of strife and storm Roosevelt discovered something that ultimately dawns on all New York police commissioners—his was a thankless job. He resigned.

Once again he was helped by Senator Lodge. Roosevelt wanted to be named assistant secretary of state in the new administration of President William McKinley. Lodge conferred with the President, who would not give Teddy that position but did appoint him assistant secretary of the navy, largely because of Roosevelt's book about the American navy in the War of 1812.

In 1897 Roosevelt moved back to Washington. The secretary of the navy, and his superior, was John Davis Long, a former governor of Massachusetts. A somewhat timid man, always tactful, conservative in outlook and calm in judgment, Long was no match for his energetic and often insubordinate assistant. Roosevelt knew Admiral Alfred Thayer Mahan and subscribed to the admiral's theory of naval superiority as the key to international power. An ardent expansionist, Roosevelt trumpeted that "great masterful races have been fighting races." He hailed conquest and annexation as a mark of racial superiority over the "weak and craven," for he despised the powerless brown and yellow people of distant lands just as he despised anyone lacking muscle. As tension developed between the United States and Spain because of Spanish atrocities in Cuba, Roosevelt hoped President McKinley would take quick positive action, and when the President hesitated, Roosevelt sneered that he had the spine of a chocolate eclair. Young Roosevelt, who always felt he knew more than his superiors, insisted that an attack on the Spaniards in Cuba would result in "a bully war!"

Secretary Long, aware of Roosevelt's rash impulsiveness, was afraid to leave his office lest his deputy do something precipitous, but one day he was forced to leave Washington briefly. In his absence Teddy cabled Admiral George Dewey in the Pacific, ordering the American fleet to Hong Kong. "In the event of a declaration of war," Roosevelt told Dewey, "your duty will be to see that the Spanish squadron does not leave the Asiatic coast, and then offensive operations in Philippine Islands." This directive helped assure Dewey's subsequent victory in Manila Bay. Then the American battleship *Maine* blew up and sank in the harbor at Havana, and Roosevelt, eager for action, quit his job in the navy department.

In April, 1898, war was declared between the United States and Spain, and Congress soon authorized the formation of three cavalry regiments. With the help of his friend Leonard Wood, an army physician, Roosevelt recruited men for the 1st United States volunteer regiment, which reporters quickly dubbed the Rough Riders. They were an odd assortment of volunteers—former outlaws from the West, polo players from the East, jaunty Southwesterners, fuzzy-cheeked Ivy Leaguers and a variety of drifters. Although Roosevelt was two years older than Leonard Wood and far better known, Teddy deferred to him because Wood had had regular army experience and fought Indians in the West; he made Wood colonel of the regiment while he became lieutenant colonel. The Rough Riders' theme song was "There'll Be a Hot Time in the Old Town Tonight." Before dashing off to war, Roosevelt ordered an optician to make him a dozen extra pairs of steel-rimmed spectacles and telegraphed Brooks Brothers in New York to tailor him "a blue cravenette lieutenant colonel's uniform without yellow on the collar and with leggings."

On the supreme day of his entire life, and in an engagement that has passed into American folklore, Roosevelt led his horseless cavalrymen through waist-high brush in a charge up Kettle Hill near San Juan Hill at Santiago, Cuba. He exulted in the whine of bullets, one of which narrowly missed him, and he even took perverse satisfaction from the casualties suffered by his own men. War correspondents wrote reams of copy about the colorful lieutenant colonel, and at the end of the ten-week war Roosevelt found himself a national hero. In the ensuing debate over the disposition of part of Spain's former empire, he stood with the imperialists, declaring, "We have no choice as to whether or not we shall play a great part in the world. . . . All that we can decide is whether we shall play it well or not."

Only forty years old, Roosevelt was now the most popular man in the nation with the exception of Admiral Dewey. He knew he stood a good chance of winning some high office, and even as he began writing a book about his Rough Riders, he was approached by an emissary of Thomas Collier Platt, the tall, lean and solemn Republican boss who ruled New York state. Platt, who had watched Teddy's obstreperous performance as an assemblyman, disliked the upstart but wanted to use his popularity. Roosevelt was told he could have the Republican nomination for governor—provided he cleared appointments and decisions with Boss Platt. Roosevelt accepted these terms, to the dismay of reform Republicans. He won the nomination, campaigned up and down the state in the company of some of his Rough Riders, won by a small majority and was inaugurated in January, 1899.

The new governor tried to do the impossible by instituting reforms while keeping on good terms with Boss Platt. Roosevelt always insisted it was a principle of leadership with him never to undertake a reform that would put him so far ahead of other people as to leave him out of touch with them. He was far more pragmatic than idealistic. He scoffed at reformers "who bathed every day and didn't steal, but whose only good point was 'respectability.'" No longer did anyone call him a "goo-goo."

Both as governor of New York and President of the United States, according to one critic, Roosevelt "stood close to the center and bared his teeth at the conservatives of the right and the liberals of the extreme left." To Boss Platt's surprise and chagrin, the young man developed into a good governor, tightening laws regulating sweatshops, urging closer supervision of utilities and insurance firms, even overseeing passage of a state tax on corporation franchises. This was too much for Platt, who exploded in fury. "I want to get rid of the bastard!" he snarled. "I don't want him raising hell in my state any longer. I want to bury him!"

The place to bury him, Platt decided, was in the Vice Presidency of the United States. President McKinley, who was preparing to seek reelection in 1900, was cool to the idea of Roosevelt as his running mate, and Teddy himself opposed it, saying, "I will not accept under any circumstances, and that is all there is about that." Famous next-to-last words. Teddy knew Platt was promoting him for the Vice Presidency only "to get me out of the state." Mark Hanna, national chairman of the Republican national party and the politician who had masterminded McKinley's election four years previously, referred to Roosevelt as "the mad cowboy." Teddy ordered the New York state delegation to the convention in Philadelphia not to vote for him and sat in his hotel room reading *The History of Josephus* as his worshipers burst inside chanting, "We want Teddy!" but when he strode onto the convention floor, he was wearing his jaunty Rough Rider hat and the delegates went wild. This irked Hanna, who turned to Senator Lodge and growled, "Teddy ought to be spanked." Some biographers have said that Roosevelt wore the hat to cover a wound in his scalp, but if this were true, why did he wear his campaign hat since he knew what effect it would have? McKinley won renomination, Roosevelt was nominated for second place on the ticket, Teddy waged a vigorous campaign, the Republicans won, and he found himself the Vice President of the United States. Sinking into a depression, he grumbled, "I shall probably end my life as a professor in some small college." If Roosevelt was depressed, Hanna was alarmed, wailing to a friend, "Don't any of you realize there's only one life between this madman and the White House?"

On September 6, 1901, McKinley was shot by an anarchist in Buffalo, New York, and died of his wound eight days later. Roosevelt was sworn in as the twenty-sixth President, pledging himself "to continue absolutely unbroken the policy of President McKinley for the peace, prosperity, and the honor of our beloved country." Thunderstruck, Hanna gasped, "Now that damned cowboy is *in* the White House!"

At an early White House reception the new President's wife saw former President Cleveland and cried, "Oh, Mr. Cleveland, my husband is so young!" Only forty-two years and ten months of age when he attained this highest office, Roosevelt was the youngest American ever to become President. He was the first President to ride in an automobile, the first to fly in an airplane, the first who won the Nobel Peace Prize, the third born in New York and the fourth to marry a second time. He took to the Presidency like a lion devouring raw meat. A conservative with progressive leanings, a man who mirrored the feelings of a majority of Americans, saturated with the prejudices of his class and upholding its interests, asking advice of industrialists and bankers, Roosevelt often acted without consulting the Congress, stressed executive leadership and expanded the powers of the Presidency as never before in American history. Typically, at first he tried to do everything himself, but he slowly learned to delegate authority and eventually came to trust his subordinates. His prodigious energy sent a river of decisions flowing from the Oval Room.

Basing his ideas of reform more in terms of old-fashioned right and wrong than on economics and sociology and political science, distrusting any idea of progress contrary to his concept of morality, he battled the abuses of big business and became the first President ever to attack the trusts. Once he said, "The great bulk of my wealthy and educated friends regard me as a dangerous crank because I am trying to find a remedy for evils which, if left unremedied, will in the end do away not only with wealth and education, but with pretty much all of our civilization." Roosevelt declared that property should be the servant of the people, not their master. He had less intention of busting trusts than of making them behave; his successor, William Howard Taft, filed more antitrust suits than Roosevelt. Teddy promised a square deal all around and preached conservation with all the ardor of a forest ranger. Wanting an American canal dug through the narrow neck of Central America, and getting it, he chuckled, "I took the canal zone and let Congress debate, and while the debate goes on, the canal does also."

Chapter 16

GERMAN ATROCITIES?

On May 12, 1915, five days after the sinking of the *Lusitania*, the British government published a document called *Report of the Committee on the Alleged German Atrocities*.

Prime Minister Herbert H. Asquith had appointed a committee to investigate rumors that German soldiers were brutalizing innocent civilians and helpless soldiers in Belgium and northern France. The head of the committee was Viscount James Bryce, the famous British historian and diplomat. Brilliant and bearded, Bryce was well known in the United States, for he had written *The American Commonwealth*, renowned as a foreigner's view of American history and government, and between 1907 and 1913 he had served as the British ambassador to the United States. Woodrow Wilson had idolized Bryce for years, while to other educated Americans he was something of a literary god.

The Bryce Commission, as it came to be called, was staffed at the top by eminent British historians, barristers and editors, but the work of collecting the evidence was left to thirty anonymous barristers who failed to swear witnesses, made no effort to get on-the-spot proof of alleged atrocities, and neglected to check stories with neutral observers. Nonetheless, they said that in the first few months of the war they took depositions from 1,200 eyewitnesses to the behavior of German soldiers and consulted diaries kept by German fighting men who had been killed, captured or wounded.

Drunk on militarism, Germany indeed had launched a campaign of *Schrecklichkeit* (frightfulness). German Major General Disforth said, "Frankly, we are and must be barbarians, if by this we understand those who wage war relentlessly and to the uttermost degree. There is nothing for us to justify and nothing to explain away. Every act of whatever nature committed by our troops for the purpose of discouraging, defeating and destroying our enemies is a brave act and a good deed, and is fully justified." Patriotic Germans fervently recited or sang Dr. Ernst Lissauer's savage "Hymn of Hate." Just before German troops invaded Belgium in order to wheel left to attack France, German Chancellor Theobald von Bethmann-Hollweg contemptuously referred to his nation's neutrality treaty with Belgium as a "scrap of paper."

The Bryce report said:

> In the minds of Prussian officers war seems to have become a

> sort of sacred mission, one of the highest functions of the omnipotent State, which is itself as much an army as a State. Ordinary morality and the ordinary sentiment of pity vanish in its presence, superseded by a new standard which justifies to the soldier every means that can conduce to success, however shocking to a natural sense of justice and humanity, however revolting to his own feelings. The spirit of war is deified. Obedience to the State and its war-lords leaves no room for any other duty of feeling. Cruelty becomes legitimate when it promises victory.

While this German attitude was shocking, it was nothing new in history. During the Civil War a like opinion had been expressed by Union General Philip "Little Phil" Sheridan, who thought that "the proper strategy" required that "the people must be left nothing but their eyes to weep with."

In every war ever fought some soldiers have behaved barbarously, since war itself is barbarous. And, as Herbert Hoover has pointed out, "every army has a percentage of criminally minded, and the abolition of moral restraints in war is scarcely calculated to lift their souls into the realm of idealism." At issue in the Bryce investigation were the questions of whether the alleged atrocities were widespread and sanctioned officially. The conclusion was—both. The purpose of these excesses, according to the report, was "to strike terror into the civilian population and dishearten the Belgian troops, so as to crush down resistance and extinguish the very spirit of self-defense." Bryce and his colleagues charged that the Germans had disregarded the rules of war and violated the Hague Convention, that sadistic crimes had been committed by individual German soldiers on their own initiative and that other bestial acts were done by soldiers acting under orders from their officers.

It was charged that German soldiers hacked off the breasts of Belgian women. They cut off the hands of Belgian babies. They used iron spikes to gouge out the eyes of Belgian men. They cut off people's legs. They raped women. They crucified Canadian soldiers with bayonets thrust through their hands and feet. They fired on stretcher-bearers. They dropped poisoned candy from airplanes for French children to pick up and eat. They drove civilians inside their homes, set fire to the houses and roasted them alive. They executed men, women and children. They cut off ears. On and on and on went this list of deeds so degenerate that the mind faded and fainted to blank out disgusting reality—if it was reality.

The Bryce Commission report was published in American newspapers beginning on May 12, 1915. In those days there was no such thing as a scientific public opinion poll, so we lack exact knowledge of the effect of the report on Americans, but it seems that a majority believed the Germans guilty of the atrocities. Since it was a fact that mighty Germany had attacked puny Belgium without just cause and since Prussian generals boasted of their barbarism, it was easy to believe that German soldiers had behaved outrageously. And the American public had been conditioned to believe horror stories because of lies told by those yellow journalists, Hearst and Pulitzer, about Spanish atrocities in Cuba just before the outbreak of the Spanish-American War. It is true that some Spaniards had behaved wantonly; on the foundation of fact Hearst and Pulitzer had erected a superstructure of fantasy. Americans further felt that Viscount Bryce was such an eminent scholar and so respectable a man that he would not lend his name to a collection of lies. Herbert Hoover knew Bryce, and long after the war Hoover wrote, "There exists a vast literature upon German atrocities in Belgium and France. It is mostly the literature of propaganda. Even Lord Bryce was drawn into it—and greatly exaggerated it."

Many important American newspapers lent their prestige to the Bryce report. The New York *Evening Post* said Germany "stands now branded with a mark of infamy such as in our times has not been stamped upon the face of any people." The Louisville *Courier-Journal* said, "The last hope that German atrocities in Belgium might have been exaggerated is dissipated by Viscount Bryce's report." The Philadelphia *Public Ledger* said, "No denunciation could add to the force of this plain tale," and it added that the Bryce report would be "accepted by Americans as final."

The alleged atrocities were believed by Walter H. Page, the passionately pro-British American ambassador to the Court of St. James's; in a letter to President Wilson he said he was convinced the Germans had perpetrated some of the most barbarous deeds in history. They were believed by Elihu Root, who had served as both secretary of war and then secretary of state; he spoke of "barbarity unequaled since the conquests of Genghis Khan." They were believed by advocates of prohibition, whose lobbyists in Washington spread the word that the atrocities were committed by Boche soldiers while under the influence of alcohol.

But there were disbelievers, too. The Boston *Globe* reminded its readers that the Bryce report was "not a verdict" but "a partizan [*sic*] statement full of partizan, tho [*sic*] strong evidence." The New York *Staats-Zeitung* dismissed the report as "a rehash of stories long since twice-told and long ago disproved." The St. Louis *Republic* said, "There was abundant evidence that the German private and non-commissioned officer regarded this policy of 'frightfulness' exactly as American privates, corporals, and sergeants would have regarded it, and that only the cast-iron discipline of the German military machine forced them to become the unwilling instruments of it." Other papers declared that if the report was true, it was a damning indictment of German militarists but not of the German people.

George Bernard Shaw was a disbeliever. England had taken in homeless Belgian civilians and wounded Belgian soldiers, and the famous writer spoke scornfully of "the stories of atrocities which the refugees brought, and which they soon had to supplement liberally from their own imagination, so great was the demand for them." Near Shaw's home in Hertfordshire a young Belgian soldier convalescing from wounds gave a graphic description of "how a beautiful woman, with her hands chopped off at the wrists, had held up the bleeding stumps and said 'Avenge me, brother.'" Another disbeliever was Robert Graves, the British soldier-poet, who wrote, "Propaganda reports of atrocities were, we agreed, ridiculous. We no longer believed accounts of unjustified German atrocities in Belgium; knowing the Belgians now at first hand. . . . We did not believe that rape was any more common on the German side of the line than on the Allied side."

American war correspondents in Europe differed in their opinions about the veracity of the Bryce report. E. Alexander Powell of the New York *World* drove his car through Belgium while the fighting was raging and later he interviewed General von Boehm, commanding officer of the 9th imperial field army and the mouthpiece of the German General Staff. The general told the reporter there was no truth to reports that atrocities had been inflicted on civilians. Boldly the reporter told the general that in one case after another that had come under his "personal observation" he had found women and children who had been tortured. But after reporting this conversation, Powell made no comment other than that he would leave it to "readers of the *World* to decide for themselves just how convincing are the answers of the German General Staff to Belgian accusations."

Edgar Ansel Mowrer of the Chicago *Daily News* got into Belgium behind the German lines, and in his memoirs he wrote, "Every Belgian had an atrocity story to tell. True or false, they awakened a deep hatred for the Germans in all those Belgians who could not be terrorized. . . . By this time I had become convinced that the German Army had indeed done most, if not all, of the terrible things with which the Belgians and their Allies reproached them." Mowrer visited one village after another and talked to ragged and starving Belgians, but in his book he does not pinpoint a single case of a handless child or crucified soldier.

A group of other American correspondents—Irvin S. Cobb, Harry Hansen, Roger Lewis, John T. McCutcheon and James O'Donnell Bennett—found some Allied and neutral newspapers while they were in Europe and were dumbfounded to read the atrocity stories. To the New York headquarters of the Associated Press they sent this joint cable:

> IN SPIRIT FAIRNESS WE UNITE IN DECLARING GERMAN ATROCITIES GROUNDLESS AS FAR AS WE WERE ABLE TO OBSERVE. AFTER SPENDING TWO WEEKS WITH GERMAN ARMY ACCOMPANYING TROOPS UPWARD HUNDRED MILES WE UNABLE REPORT SINGLE INSTANCE UNPROVOKED REPRISAL. ALSO UNABLE CONFIRM RUMORS MISTREATMENT PRISONERS OR NONCOMBATANTS. . . . NUMEROUS INVESTIGATED RUMORS PROVED GROUNDLESS. . . . DISCIPLINE GERMAN SOLDIERS EXCELLENT AS OBSERVED. NO DRUNKENNESS. TO TRUTH THESE STATEMENTS WE PLEDGE PROFESSIONAL PERSONAL WORD.

But stories of German atrocities spread like a prairie fire across the country year after year of the war, including that period after we became involved in it. According to one rumor, five American soldiers had been captured by the Germans, had had their tongues cut out, were returned to America and now lay aboard a hospital ship anchored in the Potomac river off Washington. A somewhat different version was heard by Senator George W. Norris of Nebraska. He heard about only one doughboy whose tongue was amputated, after which he was sent back here and was being treated in the Walter Reed hospital in the national capital. Norris did not think it possible for a man to live after his tongue had been cut out. He also felt that such grisly stories caused unnecessary excitement among Americans and retarded our cause. The Senator, known as a fighting liberal, wrote to the surgeon general of the army, told what he had heard and asked for the facts. From the surgeon general there came a prompt reply declaring the story false, denying that any such patient was in the hospital and furthermore saying he knew of no such incident. Norris carried this denial to the man who had told him the atrocity tale. This rumormonger flared in anger and declared that the surgeon general knew nothing about the matter; only the hospital superintendent had the facts. Norris then wrote to the superintendent, who said flatly that there was no basis for such a story. Soon after this in the Senate cloakroom Norris recounted what he had done and the answers he had received, but to his amazement not a single Senator doubted the truth of the original rumor. While he argued with the others, into the cloakroom came Senator Joseph I. France of Maryland, a highly respectable physician. Norris told him the story and without a moment's hesitation the doctor said it would be impossible for a man to live with his tongue cut out at the root. But to the despair of the Senator from Nebraska, even this failed to convince his colleagues, who afterward shunned him.

Senator Burton K. Wheeler of Montana suffered similar shock over something that happened in his home state:

> Mickey McGlynn, an organizer of the radical Non-Partisan League, objected to a story circulated in Miles City that a trainload of Belgian children whose arms had been cut off by the Germans was to cross the state. McGlynn was charged with saying: "The Germans never done that; it was done in the factories in Chicago. They were sent through the country to create feeling against the German nation." A mob took McGlynn to the basement of the Elks Club, beat him up severely, and drove him out of town. Prominent businessmen and lawyers were involved in the beating.

On July 24, 1918, in a trial held in Detroit, William Powell was sentenced to twenty years in prison and fined $10,000; one of the charges against him was his statement that German barbarities were only fiction.

After the United States went to war and Americans were urged to buy Liberty Bonds, a bond salesman in Iowa made a speech in which he told a frightful story. He said he knew a husband and wife, unable to have children of their own, who sent to Belgium to adopt two Belgian children. When the tots arrived, they were without hands, for the Germans had maimed them. A Des Moines newspaper editor ordered one of his photographers to find and photograph these tiny victims of German brutality, regardless of how long it took. The photographer never found them for the simple reason that they did not exist. The ultrapatriotic orator finally confessed he had made up this story to whip up emotion to enhance the sale of bonds.

Clarence Darrow, the freethinking criminal attorney of Chicago, believed the Bryce report at first but later changed his mind after getting to Europe and visiting the western front. In France he rode on a train with several men wearing uniforms but without any battle experience. When the conversation turned to the alleged German atrocities, Darrow scoffed. The others berated him. Up rose a man who identified himself as a clergyman from Montreal, Canada. Since early in the war, said the pastor, he had worked with the YMCA and other groups near the front but never had he been able to verify a single claim of German brutality. Before leaving Montreal, he had heard what supposedly happened to some Canadian nurses in a field hospital captured by the Germans. According to this rumor, the Germans had chopped off the nurses' hands. The minister became so concerned, he told Darrow and the others, that he made a personal investigation, and in the end he discovered the story originated in a letter written by a nurse in France who said her hands were sore.

When Darrow got back to Chicago, he spoke in a Baptist church to an audience eager to hear of atrocities, but the lawyer disappointed them, saying, "I had gone over hating the German warriors because they were press-agented as the most horrible bloodthirsty soldiers, committing fiendish atrocities. But I found that the German soldiers are like all other young boys forced to go to war: round-faced, innocent, bewildered, not understanding what it was for—excepting to obey orders or be court-martialed—dreading and fearing, fighting against their will, hoping that the hideous thing would soon be over and they might return to normal life." Darrow ended by offering to pay $1,000 to anyone who could prove that a single French or Belgian child had had its hands cut off. No one ever collected this reward.

Darrow felt that the atrocity stories had been created out of whole cloth by British propagandists—and he was partly correct. One of the most shocking rumors concerned a German corpse factory. It was said that the Germans—efficient as always—salvaged bodies from battlefields, tied them into bales, shipped them back to Germany and processed them into soap, grease and fertilizer. Here in the United States the magazine *Life*—the predecessor of the magazine published by Henry Luce—published a sketch of a German factory with smoking chimneys, a grim fortresslike plant with signs in German and English identifying it as "Establishment for the Utilization of Corpses." Here is what really happened: A German paper published a picture of dead horses being shipped to a rendering plant. Brigadier General J. V. Charteris, chief of British army intelligence, cut the caption off this photograph and then attached the caption to another captured picture showing dead German soldiers being taken away for burial behind the front lines. When the Germans learned they were being accused of using human corpses to make soap, they explained that in the German language the word *kadaver* referred only to animal corpses, never human corpses, but their truthful rebuttal made no impression on the Allied press.

The Germans became so enraged by Allied atrocity stories that they countered with accusations that innocent German soldiers had been wantonly attacked by Belgian and French noncombatants. According to the German point of view, the Belgians were guilty of violating the rules of the Geneva Convention of 1906 by waging guerrilla warfare. Naturally, they failed to mention the cardinal point that Germany had invaded Belgium. In the propaganda battle the Germans were disadvantaged by the fact that at the start of the war the English had cut their transatlantic cable, the Americans had seized two German wireless stations in the United States, and this left British propagandists in control of most of the news flowing from Europe to America.

Taking a leaf from the British book of lies, the Germans fabricated their own tales of atrocities. They said that Allied soldiers gouged out the eyes of German prisoners, that the French put cholera germs in wells in areas controlled by the Germans, that a Belgian priest wore a chain of German finger rings around his neck. A war correspondent for the *Berliner Tageblatt* claimed that cigars and cigarettes had been filled with explosive powder and then sold or given to German soldiers.

Kaiser Wilhelm sent a hypocritical letter to President Wilson in which he said:

> The old town of Louvain [in Belgium] . . . had to be destroyed for the protection of my troops. My heart bleeds when I see such measures unavoidable and when I think of the misdeeds of the guilty. [By "the guilty" the Kaiser meant all those Belgians who had fought his soldiers.] The cruelties practiced in this cruel warfare, even by [Belgian] women and priests, toward wounded [German] soldiers and doctors and hospital nurses, were such that eventually my generals were compelled to adopt the strongest measures to punish the guilty and frighten the blood-thirsty population for continuing their shameful deeds.

It simply is not true, as people like to believe, that the truth will always come out. Voltaire said: "History is a pack of lies, agreed upon." Mark Sullivan, the American journalist and historian, wrote that about 90 percent of the atrocity stories were false, but millions of Americans who were adults during the First World War went to their graves believing them. And as recently as 1973 a New York man in his early sixties recalled that as a child in Manhattan he had suffered spasms of terror during that war because he felt that any day the Huns would come goose-stepping down his street and torture his family. But the immediate effect of this grisly propaganda was to inflame passions and intensify the conflict here in the United States between pacifists and the apostles of preparedness.

Chapter 17

NEUTRALITY, PACIFISM AND PREPAREDNESS

On August 4, 1914, as Europe went to war, President Wilson had sat beside his dying wife and written the first of ten proclamations declaring that the United States would remain neutral. During the next two and a half years he gave most of his time and energy and thought to the intertwined issues of neutrality, pacifism and preparedness. Wilson was not a pacifist, as some of his critics charged, but he did hate war and feared that if this nation were drawn into the European conflict, it would breed militarism at home and weaken our social and economic reforms. He also hoped that by remaining above the battle, we might be able to mediate peace among the warring nations.

His August 4 proclamation was long and legalistic. Citing the federal penal code of 1909, he forbade Americans to enlist in any of the contending armies or do anything else to help either side. Nonetheless, a couple of days later D. P. Dowd became the first American to sail from the United States to enlist on the Allied side, while some Americans living in Paris formed a volunteer regiment to fight with the French and marched in civilian clothes behind their flag down the boulevards and off to camp.

The day following his first proclamation the President prohibited all wireless stations from handling the messages of any embattled power. The next day Navy Secretary Josephus Daniels banned all wireless messages transmitted in cipher, and the federal weather bureau discontinued publication of its daily weather map of the northern hemisphere for lack of data usually sent here from Europe. Wilson appointed a neutrality board to advise all federal departments on the ways they might and should remain neutral. And on August 19 the President told Congress, "The effect of the war upon the United States will depend upon what American citizens say and do. . . . The United States must be neutral in fact as well as in name during these days that are to try men's souls. We must be impartial in thought as well as in action. . . ."

Impartial in *thought*? Even the anxious and idealistic Wilson knew this was impossible. The outbreak of war had surprised and confused Americans. Since the beginning of the century so many peace societies had been organized that many citizens had come to believe war obsolete and unthinkable. As they received very little foreign news in their periodicals, they knew almost nothing about the web of European treaties and alliances now ripping apart at the seams. They were unable to understand the connection between the assassination at Sarajevo and the subsequent ultimatums and declarations of war. In time to come even Wilson was to declare that the war had been caused by "nothing in particular." Thunder now crackled below the horizon, and its echoes began to disturb Americans. Senator John Sharp Williams of Mississippi expressed the feelings of most people when he said he was "mad all over, down to the very bottom of my shoes, and somewhat sick and irritable, too" at this "outbreak of senseless war, setting all Europe aflame."

Remain neutral? Some Americans did stay neutral without even trying because they simply had no interest in that faraway war; this was especially true in small and isolated rural communities. Other Americans, a little more sophisticated, seesawed between fear and hope, anger and caution. Public opinion about American participation in the war fractured along several fissures.

First there was the matter of racial descent. At the beginning of the war there were 15,000,000 European-born immigrants in the United States. Among them were 3,000,000 adults who spoke no English and 9,000,000 adults who read only foreign-language newspapers. New York City alone had 500,000 inhabitants unable to speak English. These foreign-born folks naturally continued to feel warmly toward their fatherlands. German-Americans and Austro-Americans and Hungarian-Americans believed in the righteousness of the cause of the Central Powers. The English-hating Irish-Americans longed to see Great Britain humbled. Many Russian-Americans had fled to America to escape the tyranny of the czar, but now they had relatives in the Russian army and therefore hoped for a Russian victory.

Along the Atlantic seaboard there was strong sentiment in favor of the Allies among college graduates and rich people—the bankers and businessmen and industrialists who constituted the Establishment—most of them of Anglo-Saxon heritage. But the cities teemed with foreign-born workers who were generally neutral and pacifist, although some, as has been said, still felt emotional ties with their native lands. In the South there were some Americans of French descent who favored the French cause, but the farther the distance from the eastern seaboard, in the Midwest and far West, the less the concern about that distant war.

Pacifists were against American involvement in the war for a variety of reasons. There were racial pacifists, such as the German-Americans, who did not want their adopted country to fight the fatherland. There were religious pacifists, who were opposed to war on principle, sects such as the Quakers and Mennonites and Dunkards and Molokans. Surprisingly there were few pacifists among Catholic or Episcopalian priests or among the ministers of the major Protestant denominations. Fewer than a hundred preachers identified themselves as pacifists. Anarchists and Socialists freely voiced opposition to the war on humanitarian grounds and because of the connection between war making and profit taking. Emma Goldman lectured against preparedness—the concept that the United States should immediately arm itself to the teeth. The Socialist party took this official stand: "The working class must recognize the cry of preparedness against foreign invasion as a mere cloak for the sinister purpose of imperialism abroad and industrial tyranny at home." Norman Thomas began editing a pacifist magazine called *The World Tomorrow*. George Bernard Shaw, an Irish-born Socialist, said in England that if soldiers had any brains, they would shoot their officers and go home to attend to their own affairs.

The issues of neutrality, pacifism and preparedness split the Democratic party, which controlled Congress. At first, with difficulty, Congress managed to remain neutral. In the Senate there sat many men, most of them Republicans, who always had been in favor of a large navy and who now redoubled their efforts to build one. In the autumn of 1914 a great debate about preparedness began in Congress, led in the Senate by Senator Henry Cabot Lodge, the ranking member of the Senate naval affairs committee, and in the House by Lodge's son-in-law, Congressman Augustus P. Gardner, also of Massachusetts. Both were Republicans. Franklin D. Roosevelt, who was a Democrat and an advocate of preparedness, helped Gardner by slipping facts and figures to him. Congressman Claude Kitchin of North Carolina, the Democratic majority leader in the House, was a rural progressive with dark suspicions of the war makers, and his attitude was shared by Congressman James Hay of Virginia, also a Democrat, who was chairman of the House military affairs committee.

The Cabinet was divided, too. Secretary of State William Jennings Bryan came as close as possible to that pure neutrality suggested by President Wilson. Navy Secretary Josephus Daniels was an out-and-out pacifist who also entertained suspicions of navy lobbyists; he was unaware that his assistant, FDR, was helping the other side. But all the other Cabinet members were pro-Allied from the start. Secretary of Agriculture David Franklin Houston said, "The Allies are in the right. . . . I have been on their side since the first day the Germans moved." War Secretary Lindley M. Garrison began demanding that the United States prepare at once for war. To Daniels and Garrison the President sent this note:

> I write to suggest that you request and advise all officers of the service, whether active or retired, to refrain from public comment of any kind upon the military or political situation on the other side of the water. I would be obliged if you would let them know the request had come from me. It seems to me highly unwise and improper that the officers of the Army and Navy of the United States should make any public utterance to which any color of politics or military criticism can be given when other nations are involved.

Wilson's neutrality echoed the attitude of most Americans. There were some who believed nothing could drag this nation into the European conflict, while there were others who considered neutrality tentative at best and a mere stopgap measure until such time as we might find ourselves involved. But the longer we waited, the better. The President said, "I do not know whether the German government intends to keep faith with the United States or not. It is my personal opinion that Germany has no such intentions, but I am less concerned about the ultimate intentions of Germany than about the attitude of the American people, who are divided into three groups: those who are strongly pro-German, those who are strongly pro-Ally, and the vast majority who expect me to find a way to keep the United States out of the war."

Theodore Roosevelt, who later became Wilson's most savage critic over the issue of neutrality, said at first, "I am certain that the majority are now following Wilson. Only a limited number of people could or ought to be expected to make up their minds for themselves in a crisis like this; and they tend, and ought to tend, to support the President in such a crisis. It would be worse than folly for me to clamor now about what ought to be done, when it would be mere clamor and nothing more." Roosevelt's benevolence to Wilson lasted only about two months; after that, he must have wished he could eat his own words.

Senator Robert F. La Follette of Wisconsin applauded Wilson, declaring that his "course in the present world crisis is high statesmanship and splendid patriotism." La Follette was afraid that if we got into the war, our struggle for democracy would be set back a generation. The like-minded Wilson told Daniels that "every reform we have won will be lost if we get into this war." Senator Lodge, who despised Wilson and admired Roosevelt, said in August, 1914, he hoped for "strict neutrality as between belligerents"—but, like Teddy, he soon changed his mind and came out for involvement. Before long former President William Howard Taft was to say of his fellow Republicans, "Lodge and Roosevelt would get us into the war if they could." Nonetheless, Taft himself came around to preparedness. Wilson, in an off-the-record interview with the New York *Times,* said, "it will be found before long that Germany is not alone responsible for the war." Taft disagreed, blaming Kaiser Wilhelm II for being "behind it all the time." Roosevelt, in turn, disagreed with Taft, declaring, "To paint the Kaiser as a devil, merely bent on satisfying a wicked thirst for blood, is an absurdity, and worse than an absurdity. I believe that history will declare the Kaiser acted in conformity with the feelings of the German people and as he sincerely believed the interests of the people demanded." But Dr. Charles W. Eliot, president emeritus of Harvard, urged Wilson to unite with the Allies "to rebuke and punish Austria-Hungary and Germany."

Neutrality is a concept of international law that dates back to the seventeenth century. It concerns the attitudes and actions of a nation at peace and trying to maintain friendship with nations at war. In 1793, when France and England went to war, George Washington issued a proclamation declaring the United States neutral. In 1904, when Russia and Japan were fighting, the then President, Theodore Roosevelt, put forth another proclamation saying we would take no part in the conflict. In previous centuries impartiality had been difficult, but now it had become ever more difficult with the shrinking of the world owing to the industrial revolution, improved communications and transportation, the growing complexity of international trade and the like.

In the early part of World War I Irvin S. Cobb returned from Europe, where he had worked as a war correspondent, to make a nationwide lecture tour. He wrote:

> To walk the tightrope of a strict neutrality was a sufficiently difficult task already, without the peril that some outsider might inadvertently deliver himself of a prejudiced prolog. If, for example, I admitted that punitive reprisals of a cruel sort had been perpetrated in invaded Belgium, that was an affront to every pro-Teuton in the audience, while on the other hand, did I deny that hideous atrocities against civilization and prisoners had taken place—or at least hadn't to my personal knowledge and to the best of my belief—any violent British partisan was likely to denounce me as a lying apologist in German pay.

Another war correspondent, Richard Harding Davis, fumed over Wilson's neutrality:

> Were the conflict in Europe a fair fight the duty of every American would be to keep on the sidelines and preserve an open mind. But it is not a fair fight. To devastate a country you have sworn to protect, to drop bombs upon unfortified cities, to lay sunken mines, to levy blackmail by threatening hostages with death, to destroy cathedrals is not to fight fair. . . . When a mad dog runs amuck in a village it is the duty of every farmer to get his gun and destroy it, not to lock himself indoors and toward the dog and the men who face him preserve a neutral mind.

The god of war, like nature, abhors a vacuum. There was not a civilized nation on earth that did not feel some vibrations from the clash of armies in Europe. The concept of neutrality was an ideal in a real and ugly world. Wilson himself was unable to practice what he preached. In that interview with the *Times* he had said he hoped neither side would win, but on August 30, 1914, he said that if Germany won, the course of civilization would be changed. The day the *Lusitania* sank he turned with tear-filled eyes to his secretary and said, "If I let myself listen to my own heart, I should see red." To Walter H. Page in London Colonel House wrote, "The President wished me to ask you to please be more careful not to express any unneutral feeling, either by word of mouth, or by letter and not even to the State Department." But when Brand Whitlock, the American minister to Belgium, told Wilson, "in my heart there is no such thing as neutrality—I am heart and soul for the Allies," the President confessed, "So am I. No decent man could be anything else."

One of Wilson's daughters expressed admiration for the French, then checked herself and cried, "Oh, dear! Was that unneutral?" Franklin D. Roosevelt wrote to his wife, "I just knew I shall do some awful unneutral thing before I get through!" Vice President Thomas R. Marshall told someone seated beside him at a Gridiron dinner in Washington that he read none of the official documents issued by the belligerents "because then I might have a conviction about it, and that wouldn't be neutral."

Wilson admitted in a speech in Chicago that he was "careful to refrain from reading the details in the newspapers" of what was happening in Europe, and in Kansas City he said he "would not draw a passionate breath" for fear of disturbing "the nice equipoise in America."

In the fall of 1914 the President summoned into his office Henry Breckinridge, acting secretary of war. Wilson was holding a copy of the Baltimore *Sun* and was "trembling and white with passion." Pointing to a two-line story on a back page, he said the item hinted that the general staff was preparing a plan to be used in the event of war with Germany. Was that true? Breckinridge said he did not know. Wilson ordered him to make an immediate investigation, and if this report were true, then he would relieve every officer on the general staff and instantly order him out of Washington. The agitated Breckinridge reported to General Tasker Howard Bliss, acting chief of staff. Bliss told him that the law creating the general staff required it "to prepare plans for national defense." Bliss then went on to say that if the President acted as he had threatened, it would create a great political row. Wilson calmed down and never again brought up the subject. After this incident, however, the War College camouflaged its work and made almost no further *official* studies.

William Allen White, editor of the Emporia (Kansas) *Gazette* and a power in the Republican party, wrote Wilson, "it seems to me in this time of world madness we should retain our sanity. Running amuck with the rest of the world will accomplish nothing for humanity's ultimate gain." Evangelist Billy Sunday sermonized, "A lot of fools over there are murdering each other to satisfy the damnable ambitions of a few mutts who sit on thrones." Herbert Hoover, a peace-loving Quaker, wrote in his memoirs, "I had been deeply opposed to America's entering the war on many grounds—among them were my familiarity with European power politics and my little faith in our ability to change those forces and, in consequence, to make a lasting peace."

Republican Senator Warren G. Harding of Ohio made a statement that was meaningless because, as always, he hedged his every comment so as to offend no one. Declaring that he "heartily favored" preparedness, Harding then added, "It is not wise to rush militarism and we will not do it." Wilson found it at first difficult and finally impossible to maintain neutrality while also insisting on the right of Americans to travel on ships owned by nations at war.

The President, a Presbyterian who prayed every day, set aside October 4, 1914, as "a day of prayer and supplication, and do request all God-fearing persons to repair on that day to their places of worship, there to unite their petitions to Almighty God that . . . He vouchsafe his children healing peace and restore once more concord among men and nations." That "Peace Sunday" the nation's churches were filled, but the New York *Tribune* had a subhead saying SOME PREACHERS SEE NEED OF WAR. American prayers meant little to the Belgians, who the following day removed their seat of government from Antwerp to Ostend. The apostles of preparedness went about asking rhetorically, "Do you want our women and children to share the fate of the Belgians?" They also sneered at pacifists as "milk-faced grubs."

One preparedness leader was Frederic Louis Huidekoper. A native of

Pennsylvania, a Harvard graduate *cum laude*, he was a lawyer who gave more time to his avocation of writing military history than to his profession. Since 1897 he had engaged in extensive research in the war offices of the major European capitals. When war broke out in 1914, he returned to Britain, France and Germany to observe conditions at first hand. After getting home he worked feverishly for five months writing a book called *The Military Unpreparedness of the United States*. Its 556 pages of text were followed by 162 pages of references studded with quotations from famous men down through history. His book had this theme: "Adequate preparation for war has never yet in history been made after the beginning of hostilities, without unnecessary slaughter, unjustifiable expense and national peril." The introduction was written by General Leonard Wood, violating the President's order to officers to make no comment on the pressing questions of the day.

Huidekoper became one of the founders of the National Security League. At a big meeting in New York City on December 1, 1914, he and some associates decided that the American public should be awakened to an understanding of our lack of preparedness for war. They insisted the league was nonpolitical, although in fact it was dominated by Republicans. League leaders said their new society was broad enough to embrace all branches of the military establishment; already in existence was an Army League and a Navy League. The Navy League was a "big navy" lobby whose officers included top executives of corporations that would earn huge profits if more warships were constructed. Most of the founders of the National Security League lived in the industrial Northeast and were industrialists and financiers, and they received eager support from most of the metropolitan press of this region. The league was incorporated under laws of New York state, and headquarters were established at 31 Pine Street in the financial district of Manhattan.

League members said they believed: (1) There was no assurance we would not become involved in the war; (2) a peaceful policy, even supported by treaties, was no iron-clad shield against war; (3) until a sound plan for a world alliance was evolved and agreed on by the major powers, this nation must arm to protect itself; (4) the United States was not strong enough to maintain its international policies; and (5) our defenselessness was due to the failure to adopt the plans of our military leaders.

One of the founders of the league was Henry L. Stimson, a rich lawyer who had been secretary of war under Taft. Stimson wrote, "In any discussion of the military needs of this country, the first thing to be avoided is the formulation of any ill-matured suggestions by civilians who have no special knowledge on the subject." In other words, let the generals and admirals decide everything. This elitist concept was challenged by Oswald Garrison Villard, the pacifist publisher of the New York *Evening Post*, who wrote, "The preparedness policy signifies an entire change in our attitude toward the military as to whom we inherited from our forefathers suspicion and distrust. A cardinal principle of our policy has always been the subordination of the military to the civil authority as a necessary safeguard for the republic." This was much the attitude of Navy Secretary Daniels, a Southern editor with liberal leanings except in racial matters. Daniels said, "It is folly to talk of or to advocate clothing a chief of staff or a chief of naval operations with authority independent of the head of the navy."

The National Security League recruited 100,000 members in all forty-eight states, organized them into nearly 200 branches, set up seventy-four committees whose members were appointed by mayors, created seventeen committees administered by governors. The league thus became a huge and powerful propaganda machine promoting preparedness by means of speeches, books, articles and drawings.

One day in November 1916 a group of writers met for lunch at 16 Gramercy Park South in a handsome town house owned by the Players Club; in the past it had been owned by actor Edwin Booth and was remodeled for him by architect Stanford White. The luncheon had been arranged by Hermann Hagedorn, an author born in New York City of parents of German descent, a Harvard graduate who spent a semester at the University of Berlin; after the war began he felt a little guilty about his German ancestry. His luncheon companions included S. Stanwood Menken, an attorney who was president of the National Security League, and Hamlin Garland and Cleveland Moffett, both members of the publicity committee of the American Defense Society, another preparedness group.

They decided to pull authors, artists, illustrators, publicists, editors and others into a group to fight with pen, brush and voice "for their country's honor and their country's life." They named themselves the Vigilantes. The birth of this new organization was announced in a pamphlet that said, "There has been a disposition to associate the Vigilantes with those beloved roughnecks of the early California days, who established order in the frontier towns and camps by methods distasteful to tender souls. We find no fault with this. In fact, we are rather proud of being linked up with the stern and vigorous pioneers who effectually squelched the anarchists and I.W.W. of their day." This declaration whitewashed the fact that vigilantes were men who cracked down on outlaws only by taking the law into their own hands.

The new Vigilantes said their purpose was to give wide publicity to "the best available type of patriotic publicity" through newspapers, news syndicates and magazines. They volunteered to "write articles, stories, or to draw cartoons, on demand, absolutely without charge" on any subject which their managing editor might pick. For managing editor they chose Charles J. Rosebault, formerly of the New York *Sun*, installing him in their new headquarters at 505 Fifth Avenue in New York City. Theodore Roosevelt gave them a generous contribution. The Vigilantes also asked several millionaires for help and instantly began receiving checks running into three and four figures. Denouncing pacifism and promoting preparedness, they put together syndicated propaganda which they mailed for free use to newspapers and magazines in every part of the country. One of their favorite targets was Senator La Follette, who continued to argue against American involvement in the European war.

One of their heroes was General Leonard Wood, who ranked with Roosevelt and Lodge as a beater of preparedness tomtoms. Hagedorn later wrote a two-volume worshipful biography of the political general.

Energetic and restless, a prima donna in all he did, simplistic in thought and intemperate in speech, Wood had "an apoplectic soul," in the words of Walter Lippmann. Openly defying the President's order that no military officer might comment publicly about the military or political situation, he was ferociously critical of his commander in chief, even going so far as to call Wilson a rabbit. In late 1914 the President wrote, ". . . I do think that General Wood is pursuing a questionable course hardly consistent with the right spirit of the service." Some urged Wilson to discipline his insubordinate officer. Hagedorn found excuses for Wood, saying "he was at heart a Saxon wielder of a two-hand sword; a diplomat on occasion, but no courtier at all. He could, like other strong, ambitious men, do things for which he was sorry afterward, but he could not dip the shoulder and incline the knee."

In December, 1916, Wood testified before a Senate subcommittee against federalizing the national guard and advocating universal military training. With the war stalemated and with Wilson writing notes to the combatants suggesting they state their peace terms, Wood became a guest speaker at a preparedness dinner sponsored by the Vigilantes. On the evening of December 18 the tall, burly general, his blue eyes scowling, his sandy mustache a grim line, marched into the banquet hall and was greeted with wild applause that failed to relax his stern features. When he rose, he said, "Gentlemen, I have just received word that the President has today dispatched another note to the German government. In this note he states that, so far as he can see, the aims of Germany and the Allies are the same." Jeers from the diners. Snorts of disgust. "Gentlemen," Wood cried, "we have no leadership in Washington!" This was such strong medicine that some Vigilantes felt Wood may have gone too far and would be criticized—as a matter of fact, he was rebuked by the secretary of war.

Among the authors who served the Vigilantes were Samuel Hopkins Adams, Gertrude Atherton, George Ade, Rex Beach, Booth Tarkington, Ellis Parker Butler, Charles Hanson Towne, Julian Street and Irvin S. Cobb. Their talents were an important influence in shaping public opinion. They helped the National Security League, the American Defense Society, the American Bankers Association, the League to Enforce Peace and the United States Chamber of Commerce. Irvin S. Cobb became a member of the executive committee of the Vigilantes, and after the war he regretted having succumbed "to the prevalent hysteria" and having written propaganda under "the spell of that madness which we mistook for patriotism." Hermann Hagedorn also became ashamed of the Vigilantes' "silly chants and little hymns of hate."

The protracted and nationwide debate about preparedness was clouded by the vagueness of the word "preparedness." "When *I* use a word," Humpty Dumpty told Alice in *Through the Looking-Glass*, "it means just what I choose it to mean—neither more nor less." And so it was with both those for and against preparedness.

One of the best definitions was written by Louis D. Brandeis, a Boston lawyer whom Wilson named to the United States Supreme Court. Brandeis said, "'Preparedness' implies far more than adequate military equipment and training. It implies conservation and development of all the resources of the nation, human and material. It implies that in industry and in agriculture there will be constant effort to improve the methods and means of production. It implies that men and women will be trained for the vocations they are to pursue, and that opportunity shall exist to make their labor effective. . . ."

In the *New Republic*, Walter Lippmann wrote:

> Preparedness is an easy word to use, but an infinitely difficult thing to achieve. It costs a price which a democracy like our own has not yet shown the slightest inclination to pay. I do not mean price measured in army and navy bills. I mean price measured in a willingness to create democratic organization at the sacrifice of sectional, private, class and personal interests. When I read the names of the men who dominate the Republican party and think of their almost unbroken record of resistance to the nationalization of industry, their record on the tariff, on patronage, on "pork," on the relation of business to government, of government to the farmer, of power to the labor union, I wonder whether the leopard can change his spots. . . .

Three months before the formation of the National Security League, the President had laughingly referred to the discussion about preparedness as "good mental exercise," adding that that kind of talk had been going on ever since he was a boy of ten. Seven days after the meeting that launched the league, he sent Congress a message:

> It is said in some quarters that we are not prepared for war. What is meant by being prepared? Is it meant that we are not ready upon brief notice to put a nation in the field, a nation of men trained to arms? Of course we are not ready to do that; and we shall never be in time of peace so long as we retain our present political principles and institutions.
>
> And what is it that it is suggested we should be prepared to do? To defend ourselves against attack? We have always found means to do that, and shall find them whenever it is necessary without calling our people away from their necessary tasks to render compulsory military service in times of peace. We are at peace with all the world. No one who speaks counsel based on facts or drawn from a just and candid interpretation of realities can say that there is reason to fear that from any quarters our independence or the integrity of our territory is threatened. . . .

No one? Realistically or not, Theodore Roosevelt said on September 5, 1914, that if Germany conquered Britain, the Germans then would invade the United States within five years. He also recalled that during the War of 1812 the British invaded our country and burned both the Capitol and the White House. General Wood, commander of the army's department of the east, put his staff to work surveying the Atlantic seaboard, noting every beach and harbor where hostile forces could be landed, selecting artillery and trench positions from which an invasion might be repulsed.

William Howard Taft said our coastal defenses were good, but men were needed to operate them. A war correspondent, Frederick Palmer, home from Europe to lecture on preparedness, considered it foolish to think of a German invasion "until the British and German navies should make common cause against us." A Congressional committee was sent to see whether our coastal defenses were adequate, decided they were not and stated it would cost millions of dollars to make them sufficiently strong. The Detroit *Free Press* snorted that of course such work would cost millions, but it wouldn't cost us 10 cents to mind our own business and stay out of the war.

Despite Wilson's wrath toward the general staff for preparing a plan to be used in the event of war, War College officers drew up another one, complete with maps and charts, for resisting hypothetical invasions of the United States. It called for 500,000 men, trained for at least a year, for the first line; 500,000 for the second; and 500,000 more to be raised immediately for replacement of casualties. These officers also felt it might be necessary to evacuate our North Atlantic ports if they were attacked by invaders with heavy guns.

According to Colonel House, who urged preparedness, Wilson said that "no matter how the great war ended there would be complete exhaustion, and, even if Germany won, she would not be in a condition seriously to menace our country for years to come." House argued the point with the President but lost. When Secretary of State Bryan announced there was not "the slightest danger" of a German invasion, House sneeringly characterized him as "innocent" as "my little grandchild, Jane Tucker." Congress became so alarmed that on January 28, 1915, it merged the United States revenue cutter service with the United States life saving service, thus creating the United States coast guard.

General Wood was adamant in his pursuit of preparedness. In the fall of 1914, with 90,000 regular soldiers in uniform, he said the army was "just about equal to the police forces of Boston, New York and Philadelphia." On December 24, 1914, Wood wrote a friend:

> The United States is today exactly in the position Harvard would be in if she had about one good football player weighing about 110 lbs., and another substitute perhaps turning the scales at 120 pounds, but rather poorly trained, the first representing the Army and the second the Militia. They know they have got a game ahead with a first class team trained to the hour and with at least five men for every position. No one knows when the game is coming off, but we know it is coming some day, and what is worse, we know we are not getting ready for it. . . .

The preparedness agitators decided to use terror tactics to frighten the American people into arming themselves. Frederick Palmer wrote, "I was told that throwing a scare into the masses was the only way to arouse them to the need of preparedness."

Irénée du Pont, vice-president of the Du Pont de Nemours Company, which was getting rich making explosives for the Allies, wrote a letter to Washington to warn that the firm's Carneys Point smokeless powder plant, located on the Delaware river opposite Wilmington, could be destroyed by German commerce raiders with quick-firing guns. At Lake Hopatcong, New Jersey, the Du Pont people had built an experimental laboratory for Hudson Maxim, the white-bearded inventor who had perfected smokeless gunpowder. He also invented an explosive he named Maximite, after himself. It was 50 percent more powerful than dynamite and could blast a shell through the heaviest armor plate; during one test with it Maxim had his left hand blown off. Now he wrote a book called *Defenseless America* in which he savagely denounced pacifists, called Germans "Huns" and argued that America could keep out of the war only by making itself a mighty military nation.

Defenseless America fell into the hands of J. Stuart Blackton, who read it in one night. Blackton was a British-born motion-picture pioneer who lived in this country and had worked with Thomas Edison. He decided to turn Maxim's book into a film preaching preparedness, and when he told Theodore Roosevelt his plan, Teddy heartily encouraged him. Blackton wrote a scenario, persuaded the Vitagraph Company to produce the picture and directed the shooting. Entitled *The Battle Cry of Peace*, it was a super spectacular—by both the standards of that day and the present one. It made a star of Norma Talmadge, who played the heroine. Blackton used 16,000 national guardsmen, 800 Civil War veterans, tons of black powder, seventeen airplanes, several seaplanes, dirigible balloons, submarines, dreadnaughts and torpedo boats.

The picture showed a defenseless America invaded by foreign soldiers wearing uniforms similar to those of real German soldiers. It depicted citizens being murdered while trying to protect their homes, the sinking of two battleships, a mother killing her two daughters to prevent them from falling into the clutches of bestial, lust-crazed soldiers. The climax of the movie showed the bombardment of New York City, its skyscrapers shattered by enemy gunfire and crashing down into streets boiling with panic-stricken people. On August 6, 1915, the melodrama was screened for officers in the Naval War College at Newport, Rhode Island, and the following month it premiered in the Vitagraph theater on Broadway with reserved seats costing $10. When a censor cut a whole scene in the film, the theater manager had the episode played in pantomime by actors on the stage in front of the screen. Far more disturbing than any of the censored newsreels of the actual fighting in Europe, *The Battle Cry of Peace* was shown the length and breadth of America, stimulating hatred for the Germans and an increased demand for armaments.

On December 1, 1915, airplanes flew over Detroit to drop leaflets advertising the picture. This enraged Henry Ford, who had declared he would burn down his auto factory rather than manufacture anything that could be used in battle. "I have prospered much," Ford said, "and I am ready to give much to end this constant, wasteful 'preparation.'" True to his word, the previous September he had donated $10,000,000 to be used to campaign against preparedness. Ford now placed full-page advertisements in newspapers from coast to coast in which he said, "For months the people of the United States have had fear pounded into their brains by magazines, newspapers and motion pictures. No enemy has been pointed out. All the wild cry for the spending of billions, the piling up of armaments and the saddling of the country with a military caste has been based on nothing but *fiction*. . . ." Ford went on to hint that *The Battle Cry of Peace* was basically a scheme to sell stock in Hudson Maxim's munitions corporation. Maxim and Blackton chafed, while Vitagraph—afraid people would stop seeing its film and box-office receipts would drop—filed a million-dollar suit against Ford. After the filing of a few legal motions the suit was dropped.

Another book hitting pacifism and hailing preparedness was written by Thomas Dixon, who had propagandized for the Ku Klux Klan in *The Birth of a Nation*. Seeking to capitalize upon the title of his former success, he called his new novel *The Fall of a Nation*. It was turned into a twelve-reel movie by the National Drama Corporation, whose press release said, "The theme of the play is the eternal conflict of autocracy and democracy—and the necessity for the preparedness of democracy against the aggressions of autocratic rule." The plot concerned advocates of peace at any price who weakened a nation's defenses and left it helpless before a foreign foe. The country was invaded and conquered, but then there arose a modern Joan of Arc who organized a secret clan of women who helped the men overthrow the conqueror and restore democracy.

The Fall of a Nation caricatured two real pacifists, William Jennings Bryan and Henry Ford. In the film an actor wearing a skin-hugging cap to make him look bald like Bryan portrays a character called the Honorable Plato Barker and is shown in one scene presiding over a meeting opposing preparedness for war. In another scene the burlesqued Bryan and Ford go out to meet the invaders with flowers in their hands but are captured and forced to peel potatoes under the guns and glares of five soldiers wearing spiked helmets.

Both the novel and the film were unbelievably bad, but nonetheless *The Fall of a Nation* was a landmark movie because it had the first symphonic accompaniment of any full-length motion picture ever made. This score was written by Victor Herbert, the Dublin-born composer and conductor, a man much loved by his fellow Americans who hummed his tunes, but considered by some to be pro-German. *Musical America* said, ". . . the incredibility of many of the scenes is considerably lessened by the effective score that Mr. Herbert has provided. . . . In the Prologue the national airs, *Star-Spangled Banner, Columbia, the Gem of the Ocean,* and *America,* are skilfully interwoven; the bassoon sounds a note of doom as the enemy is plotting; good, honest 'rag-time' is used for the music of the carnival celebrating the end of the European war. . . ."

Press agents for the National Drama Corporation ballyhooed *The Fall of a Nation* as "Thomas Dixon's Stupendous Spectacle . . . the first grand opera cinema . . . a big vital throbbing message to the American people . . . a bugle call to arms for national defense." The movie premiered on the evening of June 6, 1916, in the Liberty theater in New York City, and among those in the audience that night were Mayor John Purroy Mitchel and Mary Pickford. The New York *Times* critic was jubilant about Victor Herbert's score. He said the film itself was "full of thrills" but went on to say there were a "few points that offend against good taste and several points that outrage intelligence." The New York *Clipper*, a sporting journal, gave *The Fall of a Nation* a brutal review, calling the direction bad, the action wearisome, the situations silly, the atmosphere poor, the continuity jagged, the suspense absolutely lacking. In summation, the New York *Clipper* said, "National defense propaganda. Very bad story, poorly constructed, ridiculous in action, and lacking in elementary values."

Among the celebrities at the premiere of *The Fall of a Nation* was Thomas Ince, one of the leading film directors of the nation, who four days previously had premiered his own movie *Civilization*—which promoted pacifism and put down preparedness. Having studied the public reaction to *The Battle Cry of Peace*, he decided there was a market for a film presenting the other side of this national issue. Ince was born into a theatrical family, made his stage debut at the age of seven and in 1916 was vice-president of the Triangle Film Corporation. Working with a $100,000 budget, producing on a grand scale in imitation of D. W. Griffith, he turned out *Civilization*, which the New York *Times* called "an excellently elaborate photo pageant."

The picture was both antiwar and anti-German. It featured a group of women calling themselves the Mothers of Men Society; they hoped to stop the slaughter by refusing to bear any more children to be turned into cannon fodder. Obviously, Ince borrowed this theme from *Lysistrata*, the play by Aristophanes that was first presented in Greece in 411 B.C. Lysistrata convinced the women of Greece that they could end war by refusing their men sexual satisfaction.

Civilization was first shown on Broadway in the Criterion theater on June 2, 1916, with a full orchestra and with offstage singing, both choral and solo. In the film the Mothers of Men Society gave a purple cross to a submarine commander who refused to torpedo a defenseless passenger liner. His crew mutinied, the submarine sank, and all aboard were drowned. The commander's soul went to some spiritual region where Christ appeared and received him with honor. Christ then entered the body of the dead officer and returned to the world, where He took a war-mongering king—perhaps the Kaiser—on a review of battle scenes so horrible as to make the king cry for peace.

Despite the refusal of the sensitive commander to sink a ship, another was torpedoed and her passengers killed in a scene so realistic that the theater audience was touched and Billie Burke fainted. Miss Burke was an actress who had been working in another Triangle picture soon to be released, so Broadway cynics sneered that she was just trying to grab some cheap publicity. However, Miss Burke had been deeply devoted to producer Charles Frohman, who went down with the *Lusitania*, so she may have been genuinely overcome with emotion. While the *Times* critic praised *Civilization* for the lavishness of its production and the beauty of its photography, he added, "Its argument is elementary, a leaf out of the pacifists' primer." After the Presidential election of 1916 William Cochrane declared that the movie helped reelect Wilson, but he was the Democratic national committee's press agent, and press agents tend to call a spade a scepter.

There is a Turkish proverb that says, "A weapon is an enemy, even to its owner." As American manufacturers sold more and more munitions to the Allies, Henry Ford was not the only person who became alarmed. Congressman James Slayden's wife wrote in her diary, "Who was it said, 'Scratch a war scare and you find a capitalist'?"

As early as October 8, 1914, E. I. du Pont de Nemours and Company received its first war contract: Russia ordered 960,000 pounds of TNT for high-explosive shells. Four days later Du Pont got an order from France for 8,000,000 pounds of cannon powder and 1,250,000 pounds of guncotton. Cotton was used to make explosives; every 300 soldiers carried 3 bales of cotton in the shape of cartridges. Before the end of 1914 the Allies had bought a total of 15,600,000 pounds of smokeless powder from Du Pont; by the following March the firm's orders had increased by 350 percent.

In early November, 1914, Charles M. Schwab, head of the Bethlehem Steel Works, was in London climbing stairs in dimly lit office buildings to arrange fat armament contracts; one was a $50,000,000 order for submarines. That same month Jacob H. Schiff, a German-American who headed the New York investment firm of Kuhn, Loeb & Company, asked President Wilson to appeal to American munition makers not to contribute to the carnage in Europe. Wilson replied three weeks later, explaining he had taken so long because he needed time to wrestle with the problem and calling it "one of the most perplexing things I have had to decide." On January 25, 1915, the President publicly declared that "the duty of a neutral to restrict trade in munitions of war has never been imposed by international law or by municipal statute. . . ."

In December, 1914, Democratic Senator Gilbert M. Hitchcock of Nebraska asked the Senate to embargo the sale of arms to the warring nations. On the fifteenth of the month German Ambassador von Bernstorff told our government that Germany acknowledged the right of American firms to export arms and ammunition to either or both of the groups of belligerents; of course, at this very time his secret agents were trying to blow up our munitions plants. By the twenty-second of the month the Allies had ordered 21,621,300 pounds of death-dealing material from the Du Pont Company and the British were suffering from an appalling shortage of ammunition.

As rich manufacturers got richer by selling their products abroad, it was interesting to hear an explanation of the source of rich men's wealth from Daniel Guggenheim, the copper king. On January 21, 1915, at a hearing of the United States Commission on Industrial Relations, Guggenheim said, "These men and women have become wealthy because they have been thrifty." Before long Franklin D. Roosevelt was to write Guggenheim, "The Carnegie Steel Company is making a reduction of seven or eight dollars a ton. . . ." FDR then went on to say, "You know, of course, of the arguments used by many of the opponents of the creation of an adequate defense—especially by people in the central portion of the country—that most of the demand for an increase in the Army and Navy is fostered by those business interests which would derive the greatest financial benefit therefrom. It is needless for me to tell you that I feel sure that nine-tenths of these allegations are entirely false." FDR may have meant what he said, or he may have been hinting that he hoped Guggenheim would keep down copper prices.

Despite widespread unemployment in the winter of 1914–15 there was a boom in the new industry of manufacturing phonographs, and in Thomas Edison's factories his employees began working double shifts. In January, 1915, only half the nation's steel capacity was in use, and the United States Steel Corporation was in financial trouble. But the steel picture soon changed as ever more war orders poured in from abroad. The *Literary Digest* polled editors on the question of an arms embargo; of the 440 editors who responded, 244 opposed such an embargo, 167 favored it, and 29 were noncommittal. On January 16 a ship sailed from New York with two 14-inch guns lashed on her forward deck; they were being sent to Liverpool from the Bethlehem Steel Corporation of Pennsylvania—Schwab's sales mission to Great Britain having paid off.

By February 1 the Allies had ordered 43,398,300 pounds of explosives from the Du Pont Company, and employment began to drop in certain lines of work. England was in the midst of one of its recurrent shell scandals: Lloyd George went to Woolwich arsenal and found workers filling shells with buckets of boiling liquid by hand. In March American subcontractors got their largest single munitions order thus far, while J. P. Morgan and Company was getting its Allied purchasing bureau in running order. More ships sailed from New York with cannon and armored cars for the Allies. Colonel Edward House was in Berlin, where he was told—regardless of what Ambassador Bernstorff had said about our sales of arms—that if the United States really wanted peace, it had better embargo munitions exports.

On May 6, 1915, the Cleveland Automatic Machine Company published a full-page advertisement in a weekly trade journal to promote a machine that produced a new type of shrapnel shell. The copy said:

> The material is high in tensile strength and VERY SPECIAL and has a tendency to fracture into small pieces upon the explosion of the shell. The timing of the fuse for this shell is similar to the shrapnel shell, but it differs in that two explosive acids are used to explode the shell in the large cavity. The combination of these two acids causes terrific explosion, having more power than anything of its kind yet used. Fragments become coated with these acids in exploding and wounds caused by them mean death in terrible agony within four hours. . . .

On June 26, the *Frankfurter Zeitung* published a facsimile of this advertisement on its front page and commented, "It is significant that the American man of feeling glories in its manufacture; the struggle of the wounded is especially terrible. . . ." The German foreign office alerted American Ambassador Gerard to the advertisement, and copies of it were laid on the desk of every member of the Reichstag.

In May the British placed a $100,000,000 order for luddite shell and shrapnel with the Bethlehem Steel Company. By June total American exports reached a record high, and New York hotels swarmed with businessmen competing with one another for orders for lethal devices. The Du Pont Company already had booked more than $100,000,000 in war orders, and its profits were running about 1,000 percent ahead of 1914. Austria-Hungary filed a formal complaint with the American government about the sale of arms to the Allies and asked for an embargo. But on June 14 the German newspaper *Der Montag* published an article by Eugen Zimmerman, a correspondent close to the German foreign office, acknowledging the right of the United States to sell arms and declaring that Germany itself had agreed to this sort of thing by accepting Article 7 of the Hague Convention for Land and Sea Warfare.

War orders poured in so fast that by the summer of 1915 there was a boom in steel and iron, whose workers began getting wage raises, in some instances more than ever before. By November unemployment was down a third from November, 1914, and the value of American exports of explosives had risen to a total of more than $121,000,000. But as prosperity spread across the land, it spawned new problems. Railway terminals began to break down under a volume of traffic greater than at any time in the past. In December, 1915, iron and steel workers in Youngstown, Ohio, struck for higher wages, and the steel industry in general raised wages a second time.

In February, 1916, Walter Lippmann wrote in the *New Republic* that Frederic C. Howe, commissioner of immigration for the port of New York:

> . . . formulates three principles which he believes ought to be worked into any program of preparedness. The first is that the cost of armament should be paid for out of direct taxation graded to throw the chief burden on the well-to-do and the very rich. . . . Commissioner Howe's second postulate is that "there should be no profit from war." This is an impossible ideal, short of complete communism; but if Commissioner Howe means that the chief munitions should be made in government plants, that prices of other munitions should be regulated, and that special war profits should be reached by drastic taxation, then we can heartily agree.
>
> The third point is by far the most interesting because there has been so little discussion of it. It is that the greatest source of diplomatic friction in the modern world centers about finance in backward countries. Commissioner Howe argued against acceptance by the United States of the doctrine that the flag follows the investment of the citizen, that armed force should ever be used to secure concessions, to protect them, or to collect debts. . . .

Howe was so outspoken in his denunciations of munitions makers and other "warmongers" that he was criticized and harassed and even investigated. A Republican, Howe had the tacit support of another Republican leader, William Allen White. In a letter to a friend the Kansas editor sounded like a Socialist when he said, "I am very strongly for government ownership of all plants making arms, armor plates and munitions of every kind. I do not believe that our peace should be at the mercy of a lot of agitators who profit by our warlike activities."

One of the surprises of the war was the enormous volume of artillery shells fired by all combatants. There were times when the artillery fire was so heavy that each side spent 100,000 shells in a single day. This wastage was so stupendous that all of Europe's arsenals and munitions factories were unable to keep up with the demand, and a shortage of ammunition became chronic with both the French and British.

The September, 1915, issue of *La Follette's Weekly Magazine* published this caustic editorial:

> With the first clash of the great European war came President Wilson's solemn appeal. . . . "The United States must be neutral in fact as well as in name." . . . But when you can boom stocks 600 per cent in manufacturing munitions—to the Bottomless Pit with Neutrality! What do Morgan and Schwab care for world peace when there are big profits in world war?. . . The stocks of the Schwab properties which stood at a market value of seven million before they began supplying the Allies . . . are today given an aggregate "value" of forty-nine millions. And now we are about to engage in furnishing the Allies funds. . . . We are underwriting the success of the cause of the Allies. We have ceased to be "neutral in fact as well as in name."

The New York *World* sent Herbert Bayard Swope to Germany as a correspondent. At a press conference in Berlin the chief of the German war press bureau received him and other correspondents at a desk adorned with three shells of American manufacture and said that he himself had been wounded by one of them. Here in America unemployment continued to fall, profits and wages rose, and munitions makers and financiers acquired more and more power. Just before the 1916 Presidential election Alfred du Pont bought a string of newspapers in Delaware. Henry P. Davidson, a leading partner in the House of Morgan, went to London to arrange new loans, and Arnold Bennett, the British novelist, wrote in his diary on October 7, 1916, "Before lunch Mrs. —— took me aside and explained that I had to be polite to Davidson, as if people weren't polite to him he wouldn't let us have any money. She was quite serious."

At the end of 1916 William Allen White wrote in his Emporia (Kansas) *Gazette:*

> As a nation we are rich with blood money. Our prosperity has come from the suffering and tragedy of other nations. We have built up our own wealth on the lives of others. Our Prosperity is cursed and tainted. Some day we shall have our own fiddler to remunerate. "Vengeance is mine, saith the Lord, I will repay!" And he has a little bill against this United States. The year will not be a proud year in our history. . . . It will be known in the future as the sad old, mad old, bad old year of 1916, and the year when our God was our belly as we minded earthly things.

Chapter 18

HENRY FORD'S PEACE SHIP

The second battle of Champagne was fought between the French and Germans on the western front in the autumn of 1915, and in a single day 20,000 soldiers were killed. Twenty thousand young lives snuffed out meaninglessly, for the battle failed to change the relative positions of the two armies. This ghastly news was read by Henry Ford, who stormed out of his Detroit office declaring he would give all his fortune to end the slaughter. Ford was quoted by Theodore Delavigne, a reporter for the Detroit *Free Press*, wire services picked up his story, and soon the world knew that the fifty-two-year-old auto manufacturer and millionaire and pacifist meant business. A deluge of peace proposals swamped Ford, who hired Delavigne away from the newspaper to become his personal press agent for peace.

Ford was intemperate and inconsistent in his denunciations of war, warriors and warmongers. He said the conflict had been started by moneylenders, absentee owners and Wall Street parasites. He also said it was the Jews who began the whole thing. He cried, "New York wants war, but not the United States!" He said, "Do you want to know the cause of war? It is capitalism, greed, the dirty hunger for dollars. Take away the capitalists and you will sweep war from the earth." He made the vague charge that liquor helped trigger war by making Frenchmen and Germans suspicious of one another. He harangued "Wall Street Tories" and "armor-plate patriots." He accused "imperialists and profiteers" of "arming both sides" to exploit "the common people" who would have to "pay the bills." He announced that the Ford Motor Company would absolutely refuse to accept any war orders from any of the belligerents. As for the British and French envoys negotiating loans with the House of Morgan, he snarled that they "ought to be tin-canned out of the country!" He characterized the professional soldier as either "lazy or crazy." He said, "To my mind, the word 'murderer' should be embroidered in red letters across the breast of every soldier!"

Ford's savage pacifism antagonized James Couzens, the vice-president, general manager and treasurer of the Ford Motor Company, the largest and most successful auto-manufacturing firm in the world. From 1905 to 1915 the company was practically, if not legally, a partnership between Ford and Couzens, with Couzens dominant in all business matters. Every time Ford made a pronouncement about war, Couzens flinched. He said, "I was born in Canada, but I am absolutely neutral." At last Couzens became so thoroughly fed up that on October 12, 1915, he resigned all his company titles, telling reporters he was breaking with Ford because of their disagreement about preparedness. In private Couzens snarled, "I decided that I had had enough of his God damn persecution!" This was just one of countless ruptures between friends and relatives over the issue of preparedness versus neutrality or pacifism.

It was on a day early in November, 1915, when Ford said he would give his fortune to end the war. In Detroit at that time was Rosika Schwimmer, a writer and lecturer, a native of Hungary who had come to the United States with documents she claimed proved that belligerents and neutrals alike were receptive to mediation of the war. In the past she had promoted causes such as woman suffrage, birth control and trade unionism; now she was propagandizing for peace. Brilliant and magnetic, she had joined forces with other pacifists such as Jane Addams of Chicago's Hull House. Having gone to Detroit to speak at a peace rally, she read Ford's remarks in a newspaper and decided to try to get to the rich pacifist to win his financial support.

But Ford was so closely guarded by his staff members—especially Ernest Liebold, his secretary—that Madame Schwimmer was unable to approach him. One day when Liebold was away, she got a call from a reporter for the Detroit *News* who alerted her to the secretary's absence, and on November 16 she managed to slip into Ford's office and engage his attention. In her late thirties, she was a heavy woman with a round face and dark complexion, articulate and persuasive, extremely knowledgeable about foreign affairs. Four years later she was to become the Bolshevik ambassador from Hungary to Switzerland. She entered Ford's office carrying a black bag containing "state papers" which she showed him—papers that convinced Ford that one all-out effort could end the war. Psychologically primed, Ford now went off half-cocked. "Well, let's start! What do you want me to do?"

They agreed to meet the next day to work out their program. At their second conference they included Louis P. Lochner, a slender blond young man, a graduate of the University of Wisconsin and a Phi Beta Kappa, a pacifist working for the Carnegie Endowment for International Peace. Lochner had just reached Detroit from Washington, where he had conferred with President Wilson in the company of Dr. David Starr Jordan, president of Stanford University and chairman of the Fifth International Peace Congress. Lochner, like Madame Schwimmer, had come seeking aid from Ford. Ford may or may not have known that she was Jewish, but with his usual lack of tact he again announced that the Jews had started the war and, tapping a pocket, said he had the documents to prove it. Her big-brim hat bobbing as she spoke, Madame Schwimmer explained what she had in mind. Jane Addams had a plan calling for neutral nations to pick delegates to go to The Hague in Holland, where they would organize an unofficial court to consider peace proposals and sit in continuous mediation sessions until all the warring powers could agree to peace terms.

The plan appealed to Ford. "All we know," he said, "is that the fighting nations are sick of war, that they want to stop, and that they are waiting only for some disinterested party to step in and offer mediation." Then he wanted to know what Lochner thought. Decades later Lochner became chief of the Berlin bureau of the Associated Press. Now he urged Ford to see the President and offer to pay the expenses of an unofficial mediation commission until Congress appropriated enough money to sustain it. But if Wilson and the Congress would not agree to create an official commission of this kind, then they could organize an unofficial one and Ford could underwrite its expenses. Ford said he would get the project going with an initial donation of $10,000. The place to start anything big, he added, was New York City. Madame Schwimmer left for the Eastern metropolis while Ford and Lochner agreed to follow her the next day.

When Ford reached Manhattan, he took a suite in the Biltmore hotel and the next day attended a luncheon in the McAlpin. Everyone present was a pacifist. Besides Ford, Madame Schwimmer and Lochner, the others included Jane Addams; Paul Kellogg, editor of a magazine for social workers called *The Survey;* Professor George W. Kirchwey of Columbia University; and Oswald Garrison Villard. All agreed it would be best to send an official commission to Europe, but if they failed to win governmental approval, they would then form their own private group. Half-jestingly, Lochner asked, "Why not a special ship to take the delegates over?" Miss Addams said this would be too flamboyant, but Ford's green eyes sparkled. A mechanic and inventor, a man who felt more comfortable with things than ideas and a businessman with an uncanny feeling for publicity, Ford reasoned that a ship was something solid that could be seen and remembered. "We'll get one!" he cried. He sprang to his feet, picked up the phone and summoned agents of shipping lines. When they arrived, he pretended to be a "Mr. Henry," and when he asked how much it could cost to charter a vessel, they stared at him in amazement, but when he dropped his transparent mask and let them know they were dealing with *the* Henry Ford, they made quick calculations and gave him estimates. Ford let Madame Schwimmer work out the details, and before the end of the day she had chartered a liner owned by the Scandinavian-American line and called *Oscar II.*

Colonel Edward M. House happened to be in Manhattan, and on November 21, 1915, he wrote in his diary:

> Misses Jane Addams, Lilian [*sic*] Wald, and von Schwimmer of Vienna [*sic*] called by appointment this afternoon. It was the same old story of trying to get the President to appoint a peace commission jointly with other neutral nations, to sit at The Hague and to continue making peace proposals until accepted. I explained that the President could not do this officially. They then wanted to know whether he would object to an unofficial commission doing it, and I thought he would not. As usual, I got them into a controversy between themselves, which delights me since it takes the pressure off myself.

House's diary for the following day:

> Henry Ford, the automobile manufacturer, called by appointment. He also came in the role of a pacifist. He brought with him David Starr Jordan's secretary [Louis Lochner], a young man who did most of the talking, despite the fact that I indicated very clearly that I wished to talk to Mr. Ford. Ford's views regarding peace were so crude and unimportant that I endeavored to lead him into a more fruitful field; but just as I got him discussing his great industrial plant at Detroit and the plans for the uplift of his workmen, the young man would break in and turn the tide of conversation into another channel. Ford, I should judge, is a mechanical genius . . . who may become a prey to all sorts of faddists who desire his money.

House nonetheless arranged for Ford to confer with the President in the White House the following day, November 23. By this time Wilson had begun to modify his bias against preparedness. In a speech at the Manhattan Club in New York City on November 4 he had spoken out for the first time for preparedness, although he insisted it should be defensive, not offensive. "We have it in mind," the President had told his listeners, "to be prepared, not for war, but only for defense; and with the thought constantly in our minds that the principles we hold most dear can be achieved by the slow process of history only in the kindly and wholesome atmosphere of peace, and not by the use of hostile force."

Ford went to the White House with Lochner and Dr. Jordan. Jordan was an imposing figure, more than six feet three inches tall, sixty-four years old but looking like an athlete, a man with a rich mellow voice, a scholar with a remarkable knowledge of the classics and also of modern languages. Jordan wore a black Prince Albert coat. Ford wore a plain business suit. Jordan respectfully remained standing until the President asked him to be seated. Ford slumped down into an armchair, threw his left leg over one of its arms and swung his leg back and forth as he chatted.

Henry Ford was a restless man. Unable to stand or sit in the same position very long, he was in constant motion. His long, slim hands were always fluttering across his chest or twitching at his sides. He was of average height—five feet nine—but when he stood up, he looked tall because he held himself erect and had a thin figure and no belly. His forehead was high and broad, his chin narrow and pointed. His hair was gray and neat and lustrous. His ears, which stuck out from his head, were almost as pointed as those of a leprechaun. His father was Irish, his mother Dutch. His glittering green eyes burned within deep sockets. His mouth was so wide and thin and straight it looked like a scar left by the cut of a saber. He had been born on a farm in Michigan, and before he died, there was a year in which he paid $79,000,000 in *taxes*. His mother called him a born mechanic; she told him never to smoke or drink or gamble or go into debt, and he never did. He worshiped Thomas Edison and despised Jews. He could look at a brick wall and tell at a glance how many bricks it contained, coming within 2 percent of the correct total. He played the violin badly and ice-skated well and doted on johnnycakes and collected antiques. In private he spoke easily and swiftly and softly in one-syllable words; in public he suffered such stage fright that the best he could do was to blurt out a few words. Hardheaded, a pragmatist, he nonetheless had a strain of mysticism, believing that "man can do whatever he can imagine." He also said, "I refuse to recognize that there are impossibilities." He hated Wall Street and doubted whether bankers or lawyers knew much about business. He likewise said he detested monopoly and special privilege, although he ran his industrial empire like an absolute monarch. Ford was so rich that in time to come he decided one day to keep on hand $30,000,000 in cash.

Swinging his leg back and forth in the President's study, Ford complimented Wilson on his appearance and asked how he managed to stay so slim. Wilson replied that after office hours he tried to forget business, and besides, he enjoyed a good joke. Lochner asked whether these included Ford jokes. Ford brightened and told a story he had made up: Driving past a cemetery one day, he saw a gravedigger digging such an enormous hole that he asked whether an entire family was to be buried in it. The gravedigger said, no, that just one fellow would be buried there. Then why was it so big? The gravedigger explained that the dead man had been a queer duck who stipulated in his will that he must be buried in his Ford because it had pulled him out of every hole thus far, and he felt sure it could pull him out of this one.

After the laughter faded, Ford explained why he had wanted to see the President. He hoped Wilson would appoint a neutral commission to sit in continuous session until some peace proposal was advanced that could be accepted by all the contending nations. Wilson, who doubtless had been briefed by Colonel House, said he liked the idea of continual mediation, but wished to leave himself free to consider another and perhaps better peace proposal. Ford said he had chartered a ship, which he now offered to the President. "If you feel you can't act," Ford said, "I will." Wilson looked startled, but repeated his position. At the end of this brief discussion, when Ford and Jordan and Lochner reached the lawn of the White House, Ford shook his head in disappointment and said the President had missed a great opportunity. "He's a small man," Ford declared. But at a later date Ford completely revised his opinion of Wilson.

Ford and Lochner went back to New York, and the next day in the Biltmore hotel they held a press conference attended by forty reporters. Uneasy as always when on view, Ford fumblingly told the correspondents, "A man should always try to do the greatest good to the greatest number, shouldn't he?" Then he spoke a line he had tested on Lochner, who had liked it, "We're going to get the boys out of the trenches before Christmas." This meant French and British and Russian and German and Austro-Hungarian boys, since of course the United States was not yet in the war. Much later Fiorello H. LaGuardia jeered, "The only boy Henry Ford ever got out of the trenches was his own son"—who was exempted from the draft. With reporters scribbling notes, Ford explained the plan for continuous mediation and announced he had chartered a ship to take the unofficial delegates abroad. The story was published on the front pages of most New York newspapers and others across the land. The New York *Tribune* published this snide headline:

GREAT WAR ENDS
CHRISTMAS DAY
FORD TO STOP IT

Then came the editorials. Most were faintly critical, savagely negative or fatuously funny. The *Lusitania* had been sunk only six months previously, and Americans still felt hurt or angry. Sly British propaganda fanned feelings against Germany. Theodore Roosevelt and Senator Lodge and General Wood were roaring about the need to arm ourselves against the menace of the Huns. The New York *Times* called Ford "thoroughly well-intentioned" and likely to do "as little harm as good." The New York *World*, usually well disposed toward Ford, characterized his peace ship as an "impossible effort to establish an inopportune peace." Because of his supposedly impossible dream, Ford was being depicted as another Don Quixote. The Baltimore *Sun* suggested that William Jennings Bryan take charge of the vessel, for "if a brutal German submarine should sink her nothing would be lost." Besides being pilloried in editorials, Ford also was vilified in news stories, cartoons, poems and letters to the editor. The New York *Sun* published a cartoon showing Ford standing on a cliff labeled "Peace Ship," shaking his finger at an erupting volcano symbolizing war and crying, "Now you stop it!" Bud Fisher, a cartoonist who had created a popular comic strip called *Mutt and Jeff*, ridiculed Ford in one strip after another. The New York *World* published John O'Keefe's doggerel:

THE FLIVVERSHIP

I saw a little fordship
Go chugging out to sea,
And for a flag
It bore a tag
Marked 70 h.p.
And all the folk aboardship
Cried: "Hail to Hennery!"

Walter Lippmann wrote:

> Mr. Henry Ford's peace trip has aroused violent resentment in America since the day it was announced. Men laugh at it with helpless anger. They regard it as humiliating. They want to break something at the thought of it. Yet there is hardly one of Mr. Ford's opponents who doesn't long for peace, and hope secretly that America may help bring it about. Something in the protests seems a little too loud. May it not be that we are shouting at Mr. Ford because he has done us the inconvenience of revealing some

> of the American character a little too baldly? Is our indignation like that of the man making faces at himself in a mirror?

Decades later two American historians, both former newspapermen, commented on the press treatment of Ford. Mark Sullivan wrote, "One wonders, at this distance, if the newspapers were living up to their functions in the highest way, when they made this attempt at peace an occasion for ridicule." Walter Millis said, "The famous 'Peace Ship' [was] launched, to the undying shame of American journalism, upon one vast wave of ridicule." Ford's ideas about peace may have seemed crude to the sophisticated and devious Colonel House, and Ford may have failed to think the plan through to its logical conclusion, but at a time when blood was being spilled like water he, at least, was trying to do something.

According to Jane Addams, these newspaper attacks kept at home "three leading internationalists who had seriously considered going, and . . . and two others who had but recently accepted." The day Lochner suggested the ship to Ford she had objected that the idea was too flamboyant, but now she changed her mind. Other antiwar movements, said Miss Addams, had been "too grey and negative" and "the heroic aspect of life had been too completely handed over to war." She planned to accompany Ford but got sick and had to stay at home. For a variety of reasons, refusals came from a long list of distinguished Americans. The invitations had been sent out jointly by Ford and Madame Schwimmer, and someone at their headquarters in the Biltmore made the mistake of cabling Rome to ask for the blessings of "His Holiness Pope Pius VII"—who had been dead since 1823; the reigning Pope was Benedict XV. The aggressive Madame Schwimmer regarded the forthcoming trip as her own project and soon reduced Lochner to the post of her general assistant. Ford erred in letting her run everything, for she was an alien—a fact never forgotten by many Americans and other neutrals.

Theodore Roosevelt declared that "Mr. Ford's visit abroad will not be mischievous only because it is ridiculous." Dr. Charles W. Eliot predicted the mission would fail because it was wrong. Ambassador Walter H. Page wrote to Colonel House from London, ". . . Cheer up! It's not at all impossible that Ford and his cargo of cranks, if they get across the ocean, may strike a German mine in the North Sea. Then they'll die happy, as martyrs; and the rest of us will live happy, and it'll be a Merry Christmas for everyone." The London *Spectator* dubbed Ford's vessel Ship of Fools; the name came from a satire called *Ship of Fools* written by Sebastian Brant and published in 1494.

Will Rogers, the cowboy-comedian, ambled onto the stage of the Forty-fourth Street theater in Manhattan, where he was appearing in Flo Ziegfeld's *Midnight Frolic*, and said to the audience, "There seems to be a good deal of talk about gettin' the boys out of the trenches by Christmas. Well, if Henry Ford will take this bunch of girls we've got here tonight, let 'em wear the same clothes as they do here, and march them down between the two lines of trenches, the boys will be out of the trenches before Christmas."

Saturday, December 4, 1915. A raw, cold winter day. Henry Ford emerged from the Biltmore wearing a derby and a dark overcoat with a black fur collar. To waiting reporters, he said, "We've got peace talks going now, and I'll pound it to the end!" He climbed into a Model T touring car with his wife, Clara, his son, Edsel, and a sculptor named Pietro, and they drove through the chill to Hoboken, New Jersey, where the *Oscar II* lay at her berth, scheduled to sail at 2 P.M. She had one smokestack, two masts, and painted on the sides of her hull was the yellow cross of Sweden. Fifteen thousand people were waiting on the pier, and more kept arriving every moment. When Ford stepped out of his car, those closest to him saw that his face was white and he smiled a tight and sickly smile. When he was recognized, according to one reporter, the crowd "went entirely mad." As he took off his derby to wave it in acknowledgment of the cheers, suddenly his silver hair gleamed phosphorescently against his black fur collar. On the dock a band played "I Didn't Raise My Boy to Be a Soldier."

Ford's bodyguard, Ray Dahlinger, cleared a path for him to the gangplank so he could board the ship. Already aboard and standing at a rail was an actor, Lloyd Bingham, wearing a beret and a Windsor tie, a self-appointed master of ceremonies. Through a megaphone Bingham shouted down to the crowd to greet Ford with a "Hip-hip-hurray!" As Ford took up his position at the rail on the promenade deck, someone handed him a big bouquet of American Beauty roses, which he threw, one by one, to the people jammed on the pier below. In the bow of the ship a young Jew leaned down to harangue and jest with the spectators in Yiddish. Near the stern the lieutenant governor of North Carolina was lecturing about the purity and beauty of Southern women. Governor Louis B. Hanna of North Dakota—the only one of the forty-eight governors to accept Ford's invitation—was telling reporters that unlike Ford, he believed in preparedness but was going along for the ride because he wanted to visit relatives in Sweden. The Reverend Jenkin Lloyd Jones of Chicago leaned against a rail, his white beard tumbling halfway down his chest, invoking divine blessings on the expedition.

On the dock the crowd went wild a second time with the appearance of William Jennings Bryan, who wore a wide-brimmed hat. As Bryan pushed his way through the throng, he was kissed by an old woman wearing a white streamer saying PEACE AT ANY PRICE. A prankster handed Bryan a cage containing two squirrels—signifying that Ford also collected nuts—and amid the excitement the former secretary of state accepted the cage and continued to hold it. Reporters who made the trip later christened the squirrels William Jennings Bryan and Henry Ford. Now the correspondents were busy poking their noses into this and that face while batteries of newsreel cameras captured the eccentric embarkation.

Some delegates were late because they had not yet received tickets entitling them to passage on the ship, and when this news reached Captain J. W. Stempel he angrily wagged his Vandyke beard and swore that his ship would cast off at 2 P.M. at the latest, passengers or no passengers. Thomas Edison was seen boarding the vessel, whereupon Lloyd Bingham yelled through his megaphone, "Here's the fellow who makes the light for you to see by! Three cheers for Edison!" The aging inventor was led to the side of his friend Ford. Since so many invited guests had declined to accompany Ford, he was left without any delegate of a truly towering reputation, so he turned to Edison and cried, "You must stay on board! You must stay on board! I'll give you a million dollars if you'll come!" Edison was deaf and did not hear what Ford said. Putting his lips to Edison's ear, Ford screamed, *"I'll give you a million dollars if you'll come!"* Edison smiled and shook his head but told Ford he was heart and soul with him. Tears stained the cheeks of Mrs. Ford, who was persisting until the last moment in her effort to keep her husband from leaving. Judge Ben Lindsey of Denver, one of the Ford delegates, shrank within his coat and mumbled, "Oh, God, why am I here?"

It was long after 3 P.M. when the *Oscar II* cast off and swung her bow into the cold Hudson river, her whistle droning, spectators cheering, pacifists singing hymns, others singing patriotic songs, and when the ship was fifty yards from the pier, a man bulled his way through the crowd to the edge of the dock, dived into the river and frantically began swimming after her. Rescued by a tug, he identified himself as Urban J. Ledoux—known to New Yorkers as an eccentric social worker who liked to call himself "Mr. Zero." And just what did he think he was doing? "Mr. Zero" explained he was warding off torpedoes. Then, after a moment's thought, he decided instead that he was "swimming to reach public opinion."

The whole crazy scene was played up in newspapers and magazines, in speeches and newsreels. Ford was a fool! Sure, his Model T was a good little car, but why didn't Henry stick to making cars instead of trying to run the world? People nodded agreement when Theodore Roosevelt spoke of Ford's "silly mission." Arthur Vandenberg, a Michigan newspaper editor and not yet a United States Senator, called this ark of peace a "loon ship." Democratic Senator Charles S. Thomas of Colorado rose on the floor of the Senate to characterize Ford's peace delegates as "an aggregation of neurotics!" The New York *Times* said that most of Ford's passengers were "rainbow chasers" and "crack-brained dreamers" and "tourists." Still, as Ford told reporters during the voyage, news about his ship was at least driving articles about preparedness off the front pages of newspapers.

Oscar II was heading for Norway, a neutral nation, and would dock at Christiania, now called Oslo. Louis Lochner, who wrote a book about this trip, said there were eighty-three delegates, fifty-four reporters, three photographers, eighteen students and fifty persons on the technical staff. William C. Bullitt, covering the story for the Philadelphia *Ledger*, wrote, "Mr. Lochner never intends to offend any one. He is a gentle soul. He looks like the rabbit in *Alice in Wonderland*, recuperating from a dreadful fright which has scared off all his hair and popped his eyes. But he has the ability . . . to get on people's nerves."

Madame Schwimmer also managed to antagonize people. Imperious, devious-minded, trained in the intricacies of European politics, she enjoyed intrigue for its own sake and was unable to adapt herself to the open personalities of Americans. She spun such an efficient web of espionage that nothing said or done aboard ship escaped her attention. Wherever she went she lugged her now-famous Black Bag with its mysterious "state papers." Reporters had been given the second-class smoking room to use as a press room, and soon they organized themselves into the Friendly Sons of St. Vitus, a drinking society whose motto was "Skoal!" One day when Madame Schwimmer entered their domain, they gave her a friendly round of applause. She glared at them and snapped, "Don't be hypocritical!" Then she accused them of telling Ford she spied on them and added, "I further deny that I am Mr. Ford's mistress!" Nobody had hinted that she was.

About half the delegates were writers. The next largest group consisted of lecturers and special pleaders—diehard pacifists, Socialists, suffragists and single taxers. There also were a few teachers, ministers and minor government officials. However, there were no labor leaders or engineers or scientists or farmers or businessmen or industrialists—except for Ford. With Madame Schwimmer working her black magic backstage and belowdeck, Ford was the center of attention. Mary Alden Hopkins, a magazine writer, rhapsodized, "This silent man with the scholar's brow, the dreamer's wide-set eyes, the executive's mouth, the flickering humor, and the absolute simplicity of thought and action which comes from following high ideals to their logical conclusion—this personality grips the imagination."

A minister asked Ford, "Don't you feel that this is a holy cause?"

"No . . . I don't know what you mean by 'holy.' Instead of a holy cause, I consider this expedition a people's affair."

Another preacher persisted. "Are you not sailing with faith?"

Ford replied, "Yes, but it is faith in the people. I have absolute confidence in the better side of human nature. . . . People never disappoint you if you trust them. Only three out of six hundred convicts in my factory have failed to make good." Ford went on to say he did not expect to be able to bring peace immediately, but rather to hasten it. This comment revealed he was retreating from his promise to get the boys out of the trenches by Christmas. "The chief effect I look for," said Ford, "is psychological."

From the ship he wired Senators and Representatives, urging them "to give the peace mission your support and encouragement so that it may succeed at the earliest possible moment." He also radioed several European rulers to beg for peace. "Enough blood has been shed, enough agony endured, enough destruction wrought."

Next to Ford the best-known man aboard ship was S. S. McClure, the publisher and editor. The day before he left he tossed into his suitcase advance copies of President Wilson's annual message to Congress. The peace ship had sailed on Saturday, December 4, and the President spoke to Congress on Tuesday, December 7. That Tuesday, with the vessel bucking heavy weather, McClure was sitting in the second-class dining salon and happened to mention that he had copies of the President's address. Asked to get a copy and read it aloud, he did.

To an audience of ardent pacifists, Mc Clure read that Wilson was asking Congress for a substantial increase in national defense. Among other things, the President wanted a regular army of 142,000 soldiers and a force of 400,000 "disciplined citizens." Wilson further advocated a five-year program to provide the navy with two battleships and two battle cruisers the first year. He also called for the formation of an advisory council to oversee the mobilization of economic resources to meet our "national necessity."

The moment McClure finished reading, the delegates exploded. Woodrow Wilson, a man they regarded as a pacifist, had betrayed them! Passions rose to such a pitch that some began denouncing McClure, who of course had had nothing to do with the President's shift away from neutrality and pacifism. Maybe McClure himself was a warmonger! Down with McClure! Down with the munitions trust! Amid the uproar, Henry Ford rose to suggest they wait a few days before continuing their discussion of Wilson's message, and the heated delegates dispersed, still grumbling.

Later that afternoon Madame Schwimmer summoned McClure to her stateroom and scolded him for preaching preparedness. Staring at her in amazement, he started to say he was talking facts, but before he could finish, she dismissed him. Then she organized some delegates into a resolutions committee, and they met in a closed session to draft an antipreparedness resolution called the Declaration of Principles of the Ford Peace Ship Party. She said that after all the delegates signed it, the declaration would be wirelessed to Congress.

On December 9 word spread through the ship that the committee was about to hold a meeting in the dining salon. Delegates and reporters gathered there. The Reverend Dr. Charles Aked, a natty British-born minister with a congregation in San Francisco, took the floor and read the declaration. In fuzzy language it declared, first, that the delegates supported Ford's effort to achieve a just and honorable peace and, second, that they disapproved of any increase in armaments by the United States. Madame Schwimmer and other committee members thought they could get everyone's signature without debate, but they reckoned without McClure.

Springing to his feet, he said, "For years I have been working for international disarmament. I have visited the capitals of Europe time and time again in its behalf. But I cannot impugn the course laid out by the President of the United States and supported by my newspaper. I should like to be able to go on working with the party, but I am unable to sign that part of its declaration of principles which would place me in opposition to my government."

Bedlam. Some delegates shouted that they agreed with McClure. Others denounced him at the top of their lungs. Madame Schwimmer accused McClure of corrupting the students in the party by talking to them about preparedness. Lochner cried, "Anyone who accepted the invitation of Mr. Ford and now refuses to sign this resolution came for a free ride!" His remark was resented by a journalist, John D. Barry: "If you push through this resolution and cause a sharp split in the party, we shall be the laughingstock of the whole of Europe!" Madame Schwimmer, Lochner and the Reverend Dr. Aked insisted that everyone approve the declaration or get off the ship at the first port it touched. After listening to this pandemonium, William C. Bullitt of the Philadelphia *Ledger* remarked that "pacifist means a person hard to pacify." Ford said all delegates were welcome to stay aboard.

But the delegation had been split, and it did become the laughingstock of Europe and the rest of the world after correspondents got off stories to their newspapers. The Chicago *Tribune* said, "The dove of peace has taken flight, chased off by the screaming eagle." Arthur Hartzell of the New York *Sun* wrote a dispatch saying, MUTINY ABOARD THE OSCAR II. His phrase, flashed by wireless, was intercepted by the telegraph officer of a passing ship, who radioed the *Oscar II:* ARE YOU IN NEED OF ASSISTANCE? When this inquiry was handed to Captain Stempel, the skipper of the Ford peace ship, he stormed off his bridge demanding the name of the ringleader of the mutiny. Laughing reporters captured McClure and led him forward. The captain grumbled and stalked away, whereupon the correspondents held a mock trial in which McClure was accused, like Socrates, of corrupting the nation's youth. The publisher, who was not amused, was acquitted.

On December 18, 1915, the two-week voyage ended when the *Oscar II* docked at Christiania, Norway, at 4 A.M. in twelve-below-zero weather. Although a few Norwegians boarded her later in the morning, the peace delegates got nothing like the reception promised them by Madame Schwimmer. She and Ford told Norwegian journalists there had been no disagreements among the members of the party. In the afternoon the sea-weary passengers were entertained by the Women's International Peace League, and that evening they gathered in a building at the University of Christiania. But not Ford. During the trip he had been drenched by a wave one morning while taking a brisk walk on deck, and he had caught a cold. After his ship docked, he walked through the cutting cold to a hotel, where he collapsed. Although he received reporters, never did he appear at any public function while in Norway.

Although Norway was officially neutral, most Norwegians favored the Allies and resented the fact that a peace mission had been led to their shores by Madame Schwimmer, a Hungarian and thus a citizen of one of the Central Powers. Ford blunted their resentment by donating $10,000 for a student clubhouse at the university. When he called a press conference, he astonished local reporters by ignoring the subject of peace mediation and talking instead about his new tractor. Saying that his invention was not patented, he declared he would try to convince armament makers that they could make more money by manufacturing tractors than by producing guns. One journalist commented, "He must be a very great man who permits himself to utter such foolishness."

Because of the strife that had developed among the peace delegates, because his cold worsened, because the weather stayed cold, because his hotel suite faced north and was hammered by the wind, Ford lost heart and told Lochner, "Guess I had better go home to mother. . . . You've got this thing started now and can get along without me." Lochner protested that if Ford were to leave his party at the first stop in Europe, his departure would be regarded as an admission of failure. Ford refused to listen. He arranged to give the party $270,000 to see them through the rest of their adventure; the morning of December 23 they were scheduled to leave Norway for Sweden. He had learned that in Bergen he could catch a ship about to sail for America.

At 4 A.M. on December 23 Ford slipped out of the Grand hotel with his bodyguard and a few others. The Hotel stood at twenty-two degrees below zero, and one of the men with Ford did not have time to put on underwear or socks. Gathered in the hotel lobby were some of Ford's peace delegates, who had heard he might desert them. The local branch of the Ford Motor Company had provided him with burly employees, who formed a flying wedge to escort him past the protesters and outside and into a waiting car. Ford was cursed. Fists flew. But he made his getaway. When the rest of the Americans learned their leader had turned tail and run, they felt betrayed and sank into depression. Some resigned and made their way home by various routes.

The others formed themselves into the Neutral Conference for Continuous Mediation and toured the capitals of the neutral nations—Sweden, Denmark and Switzerland—then reached Holland and set up headquarters in The Hague, where they labored for a year trying to end the war. Joined by members of European parliaments, mayors, professors and officers of peace organizations, they held conferences and issued appeals to the governments, parliaments and peoples of the warring nations. Madame Schwimmer remained the controversial head of the group until her resignation in February, 1917.

Ford's peace crusade cost him $465,000. What, if anything, had been accomplished? Opinions differed. Mark Sullivan wrote of the expedition, "After its failure, dying down to an echo of gigantic and exhausted laughter, it deprived every other peace movement in the country of force and conviction." Jane Addams disagreed. She admitted Ford's peace project had been ridiculed, but she argued that in the end it came to be respected even by some of the nations doing battle. Upton Sinclair praised Ford. Others pointed out that the Ford delegates had coordinated the efforts of idealists and pacifists and publicists in neutral countries in their efforts to formulate and popularize terms for a just and lasting peace.

Theodore Roosevelt was delighted with some remarks made by a writer named E. S. Martin:

> Nobody is much good who has not in him some idea, some ideal, that he cares for more than he does for life, even though it is life alleviated by the Ford motor. You help to make life pleasant, but war, Henry, helps to make it noble; and if it is not noble it does not matter a damn, Henry, whether it is pleasant or not. That is the old lesson of Calvary repeated at Mons and Ypres and Liège and Namur. Whether there are more people in the world or less, whether they are fat or lean, whether there are Fords or oxen, makes no vital difference; but whether men shall be willing to die for what they believe in makes all the difference between a pigsty and Paradise. Not by bread alone, Henry, shall men live.

After Ford got home he made a series of strange and even contradictory statements about his peace expedition. Asked what he got out of it, he replied, "I didn't get much peace." Then he added he had learned that Russia was going to be a great market for tractors. He told friends he would rather work at his desk the next quarter century without a vacation than "go through this thing again." He said he was still convinced that the Jews started the war. He declared that the "wrong people" had made the trip and said that if he were to sponsor another peace ship, he would take along "the whole village of Dearborn" rather than the people who "went along before."

But this man—this paradoxical Quixote—made most sense when he said, "I wanted to see peace. I at least tried to bring it about. Most men did not even try."

Chapter 19

THE TOM MOONEY CASE

The threatening letters—more than 200 of them—were all anonymous, all lettered by the same hand and all mailed within the city limits of San Francisco. They were sent to the city fathers and newspaper publishers and the civic leaders planning the city's Preparedness Day parade.

Preparedness Day parades had become a common event all across America by 1916. In city after city anti-administration businessmen and Republicans set aside a day on which citizens would be given flags and placards and set marching behind bands down the streets to demand the nation's immediate arming.

San Francisco scheduled its Preparedness Day celebration for July 22, 1916. California was a one-party state ruled by Republicans. San Francisco was the most industrialized city in the state and the most heavily unionized in the United States. The prime mover behind the forthcoming event was the Pacific Coast Defense League—a front for the San Francisco Chamber of Commerce. Among other things, the league wanted to give military training to kids in grade schools. Another arm of the Chamber of Commerce was its newly organized law and order committee; the name camouflaged the chamber's real purpose, which was to break the power of the unions in the city. On June 22, exactly a month before the Preparedness Day parade, the chamber publicly declared, "The Chamber of Commerce favors the open shop and insists upon the right to employ union or non-union workers, in whole or in part, as the parties involved may elect. . . ." In theory, an open-shop company is one employing either union or nonunion workers, but in practice it means one hiring only nonunion labor.

Many employers ordered their nonunion workers to march in the parade—or be fired. Department stores bought space in newspapers to say things such as "Continued Peace Through Preparedness—Join the March of the Patriots—Join, March and Show Your Colors!" The San Francisco *Chronicle*, the organ of the city's businessmen, published this headline: PATRIOTS' PAGEANT TO CRY: PREPARE! William Randolph Hearst's *Call* and *Examiner* also advocated preparedness. The *News* did not commit itself. The *Bulletin* was against preparedness. Despite the spate of propreparedness propaganda, however, a decision to boycott the parade was made by the city's Irish, Democrats, progressives, Socialists, pacifists, anarchists and labor unions. The San Francisco Labor Council adopted a resolution saying, ". . . we hereby caution all union men and women . . . to be especially careful and make no other protest than their silent non-participation. . . ." R. L. Duffus, a reporter for the antipreparedness San Francisco *Bulletin,* later wrote, "It wasn't considered harmlessly idealistic to be a pacifist any more; it was dangerous, perhaps unpatriotic."

Then the threatening letters began arriving. Fremont Older, editor of the *Bulletin,* got one saying, "Our protests have been in vain in regards to this preparedness propaganda, so we are going to use a little 'direct action' on the 22nd, which will echo around the earth and show that Frisco really knows how, and that militarism cannot be forced on us and our children without a violent protest. Things are going to happen to show that we will go to any extreme, the same as the controlling class will do, to preserve what little democracy we still have left. . . ." The letter said more in this same vein. Older gave the letter to the police and suggested they watch the hall used by the Industrial Workers of the World. The police said they would investigate and also would take special precautions to make sure that no violence occurred during the parade, but Older felt they were not greatly concerned.

Saturday, July 22, 1916. A day brilliant with sunshine. The city's only decorations were flags, but there were tens of thousands of them—small flags held by spectators, larger flags fluttering from tall standards held by the marchers, a big flag hanging from a trolley wire, huge flags draped across the fronts of buildings, a flag so enormous that it was carried horizontally by twenty Civil War veterans.

One flag was waved by the most important man in the parade, Mayor James Rolph, Jr., hardly an able administrator but a friendly man with a dazzling personality, beloved by business and labor alike, known to everyone as Sunny Jim. A showman, Rolph wore gold-heeled cowboy boots, a ten-gallon white stetson, and a frock coat with a camellia in the buttonhole. In 1930 "Sunny Jim" would be elected a Republican governor of California, and three years after that his name would become a household word when he publicly expressed approval of the lynching of two men who had been jailed at San Jose in connection with a kidnapping.

In the reviewing stand on upper Market Street sat a man fated to become far more famous than the mayor. This was George Catlett Marshall, age thirty-five, a captain in the regular army, stationed in San Francisco as the adjutant of the army's western department headquarters; during World War I Marshall became aide-de-camp to General Pershing, and during World War II he became chief of staff.

In an apartment at 569 Dolores Street in the Mission district of the city, a leisurely lunch was being eaten by three anarchists, Emma Goldman, Alexander Berkman and Mary Eleanor Fitzgerald. Miss Goldman, a dumpy middle-aged woman, was Berkman's former mistress, while Miss Fitzgerald was his current love. The previous Thursday Miss Goldman had been scheduled to give a speech entitled "Preparedness—The Road to Universal Slaughter," but she had canceled it when she learned that Fremont Older was to talk that same night at another antipreparedness rally.

The newspapers had said the parade would begin at 1 P.M.; actually, officials planned to get it going at 1:30 P.M. after the police had cleared

Market Street of traffic. A hundred thousand people now thronged Market Street, the city's main artery, a noble thoroughfare 120 feet wide, and they asked one another what was holding things up. The marchers themselves were gathered at the foot of the street along the Embarcadero bordering the waterfront. According to the police, there were 22,400 marchers; according to the *Bulletin*, 22,458; according to the *Chronicle* and *Examiner*, 51,000.

At precisely 1:30 P.M. Police Captain Duncan Matheson looked at his watch, looked up at the clock in the tall Ferry Building and blew a shrill blast on his whistle. The first parade unit started up Market Street. It was led by the parade's grand marshal astride a spirited bay horse, Thornwell Mullally, a director of United Railroads of San Francisco, a man hated by labor because he had helped crush two strikes by streetcar workers, the first in 1907 and the other just two weeks before the parade.

At 1:31 P.M. Mayor Rolph took his first jaunty steps up the street, and now the parade undulated with motion. But—there was something strange. The marchers were quiet, the spectators silent. This mood puzzled reporters on the fire escape outside the fourth-floor city room of the *Chronicle* at 767 Market Street. Their boss, Fremont Older, had not told them about the menacing letter he had received; in fact, the police had asked all local editors to publish nothing about those threats for fear of touching off panic. Edgar T. Gleeson, a *Chronicle* reporter, said, "We felt it, sensed it unmistakably—that crowd was queerly silent."

Although the United States was not at war, the people of San Francisco had begun to feel uneasy for a number of reasons. Munitions ships lay in the harbor, and some that sailed had been crippled by mysterious explosions. Suspicion had fallen on the German consul in San Francisco. Towers holding electrical wires had been bombed. On the Fourth of July some anarchists had held a picnic at Colma, eight miles south of town. And everyone knew that organized labor had boycotted the parade, that the appointment of Mullally as grand marshal was a slap in the face to workers, that the Chamber of Commerce and utility companies were girding for another fight with unions—perhaps a showdown.

Then it happened.

At 2:06 P.M.—at the corner of Market and Steuart streets only a block from the Ferry Building where the parade began and with the leading parade units now far up Market Street and to the left of the other marchers just then passing the Ferry Exchange saloon—a bomb exploded.

Whhhhuuurrrruuuummmmmmmmmppppphhhhh! . . . the blast blew off the top of a man's head . . . it knocked over a row of men at the bar in the saloon . . . it slammed a woman and her daughter to the sidewalk . . . it bowled over marching veterans of the Spanish-American War . . . . it punctured lungs . . . it stripped flesh from the legs of a boy . . . it threw a mounted cop and his horse to the pavement . . . shattered eardrums . . . flung onto the top of a building was a hat with a piece of skull inside it . . . dense white smoke . . . moans . . . "Oh, my God! Oh, my God!" . . . a child's voice: "Mama!" . . . the clink of glass from broken windows . . . bloodstains like red spiders . . . broken legs twisted at crazy angles . . . a cloud of dust . . . eerie silence . . . ten dead . . . forty-four seriously injured. . . .

In the apartment where the anarchists dawdled over lunch, Alexander Berkman was joking about Miss Fitzgerald's cooking when the phone rang. He stepped out of the room to answer it. On the line was a reporter asking whether Berkman would care to comment on the explosion. When Berkman rejoined the two women, his face was grave. "A bomb exploded in the preparedness parade this afternoon," he told them. "There are killed and wounded."

Emma Goldman cried, "I hope they aren't going to hold the anarchists responsible for it!"

"How could they not?" Berkman asked. "They always do."

A *Bulletin* reporter was emerging from a ship chandlery on Steuart Street when the blast occurred, throwing him back inside. He picked himself up, ran outside and stared in horror, then ran to a phone and called in the first spot story of the day. Another *Bulletin* reporter raced to the scene, found a cop and was talking to him when someone showed them a section of steel pipe picked up on the street. The reporter and cop thought it looked like the pipes used by German saboteurs in their shrapnel shells. The reporter telephoned his city editor and said the blast probably was caused by a bomb. The city editor told Fremont Older, whose eyes tightened in anxiety. Older liked to invite all kinds of people to his ranch and had entertained Emma Goldman. The previous Thursday he had spoken at a meeting in Dreamland Rink and denounced this "preparedness nonsense." Now he told his city editor, "They'll probably blame me for this!" In time to come—they did. Fremont Older was accused of being the murderers' adviser and of having foreknowledge of the bomb plot.

To the site of the blast at about 3:30 P.M. came Charles M. Fickert, district attorney of the city and county of San Francisco. With him was a friend, Frederick H. Colburn, a banker and Chamber of Commerce official. Reporters regarded the district attorney as a joke because they knew he liked whores and sometimes patronized two or three a day. They knew that when he ran for office, he had been backed by United Railroads, and the company used him as a tool to quash graft indictments against the firm, and ever since then he had been its cat's-paw. They knew that California Supreme Court Justice Frederick W. Henshaw, the spokesman for the utilities companies, was the Machiavellian influence behind the DA. They knew that one of his closest friends was Frank Drew, attorney for the Chamber of Commerce. They knew that the district attorney was a man who took orders from the businessmen who ran the city.

A bulky man, Fickert liked to recall that he played guard on the Stanford football team that had Herbert Hoover as a water boy. He was less fond of recalling that his teammates called him Boob. Before long Fickert was to declare that Nietzsche was the name of some kind of a bomb, and in a trial connected with the tragedy he was to crib several hundred words from a speech by Daniel Webster. Now, standing amid the rubble on Market Street, he told reporters that his office would supervise the investigation.

A *Bulletin* reporter said, "You know, Mr. D.A., you solve this one and they'll make you governor."

Fickert seldom knew when reporters were teasing him; but his eyes lighted up, and he said, "You know, men—I already think I know who did this."

On Thursday, July 27, five days after the blast, Thomas J. Mooney and his wife were vacationing on the Russian river fifty miles north of San Francisco. Wearing bathing suits, they paddled a rented canoe to Monte Rio, a small resort. Tom took a dip while Rena walked to the railway station to buy beer and a copy of the San Francisco *Examiner.* She kept the paper folded as she walked back to her husband. They shoved off and drifted down the river and then tied up at some willows to munch sandwiches and drink the beer. He unwrapped the sandwiches while she opened the paper.

"Oh, my God, Tom! Look at that!"

He jerked up his head and grabbed the paper from her and saw its banner: BILLINGS, WEINBERG, NOLAN ARRESTED; MOONEYS ESCAPE!

As fast as they could, they paddled back to Monte Rio, where Tom went to the station to send a wire to David A. White, the chief of police of San Francisco. His telegram said: WIFE AND I LEFT SAN FRANCISCO LAST MONDAY 8:45 FOR WEEK'S VACATION AT MONTESANO. SEE BY EXAMINER I AM WANTED BY SAN FRANCISCO POLICE. MY MOVEMENTS ARE AND HAVE BEEN AN OPEN BOOK. WILL RETURN BY NEXT TRAIN TO SAN FRANCISCO. I CONSIDER THIS ATTEMPT TO INCRIMINATE ME IN CONNECTION WITH BOMB OUTRAGE ONE OF THE MOST DASTARDLY PIECES OF WORK EVER ATTEMPTED. . . . TOM MOONEY.

Just to play it safe, he sent a copy of his wire to Fremont Older at the *Bulletin.* Rather than take the time to paddle back upstream, the Mooneys abandoned the canoe and walked three miles to their camp, dressed, packed and caught the 4:15 P.M. train to San Francisco. At Guerneville, several miles down the line, two detectives boarded and arrested the Mooneys and took them off the train at gunpoint.

Such was the beginning of one of the most celebrated cases in history, one compared to the Dreyfus case in France, a case that commanded the attention of President Wilson and the United States Supreme Court and the United States Senate and a succession of California governors, one involving Theodore Roosevelt and Felix Frankfurter and Earl Warren and James J. Walker and Lenin, a case that triggered protests and demonstrations all around the world, a case that made Mooney the most famous prisoner in the nation and kept him behind bars for twenty-two years, five months and twelve days.

Thomas Jeremiah Mooney was born in Chicago on December 8, 1882, which meant that he was thirty-three at the time of his arrest. His mother was an Irish immigrant. His father was a native of Indiana, a coal miner and one of the first organizers of the Knights of Labor.

When Tom was ten, his father died of "miner's pneumonia"—tuberculosis. In parochial school a priest slapped the boy, who walked out and enrolled in public school, but left that, too, at fourteen to go to work in a paper mill in Massachusetts. The family had moved around a lot because the elder Mooney had been blacklisted for his union activities. Tom himself was so quick to protest poor working conditions and low pay that he also was barred from one job after another.

Deciding to become an artist, he scraped up enough money to go to Europe, where he spent much time in museums while also studying conditions of the workingmen of the continent. When he got back to America, he lacked the funds to study art so he became an iron molder, often got into trouble and was often fired. Riding the rails from the East coast to the West, taking jobs here and there as a manual laborer, Tom arrived in California in 1908.

He became a Socialist and made speeches to raise money for Eugene V. Debs, the Socialist candidate for President. Tom also joined the more radical Industrial Workers of the World, but remained a Wobbly only three months. He married a divorced woman named Rena Brink Hermann. In 1910 Tom attended the International Socialist Congress in Copenhagen, Denmark, and met many of the world's greatest Socialist leaders, including Lenin—whom Tom did not find very impressive. After Tom got back to California the San Francisco *Bulletin* described him as "the lusty-voiced, aggressive, belligerent spokesman of the Socialist left-wing." He became active in San Francisco union politics and wanted to run for sheriff but was unable to get enough signatures to place his name on the ballot.

In May, 1913, some linemen who belonged to a local of the Electrical Workers pulled a wildcat strike against the Pacific Gas & Electric Company, a utility that supplied nearly all the electrical power for northern California. Mooney, who by this time was employed in a Berkeley foundry, spent his spare time trying to persuade other workers to walk out. He was arrested on a charge of felonious possession of high explosives, the authorities alleging that he and others planned to blow up one of the two giant steel towers supporting electrical wires spanning the Carquinez Strait in Contra Costa county. His first trial resulted in a hung jury. His second trial—same result. A third jury acquitted Mooney and his codefendants. The jurors did not believe the prosecution because no dynamite had been found. After his acquittal, Tom returned to San Francisco, and he and his wife took a studio in the Eilers Building at 975 Market Street.

Tom Mooney stood five feet ten inches tall and was barrel-chested, strong and restless. He had black eyes and rosy cheeks and bushy black eyebrows and thick black hair and a plump face. A militant union organizer and magnetic orator, his brogue reflecting his Irish ancestry, he nonetheless antagonized many people by always acting as though he alone were in the right. Even those convinced of his innocence in the bombing of the parade found him unbearable, for he was vain and demanding, opinionated and self-righteous.

In 1915 foundry work was scarce in San Francisco, so he got a job as a laborer on the grounds of the Panama-Pacific International Exposition. In July of the following year he began to try to organize the 2,200 nonunion carmen employed by United Railroads; but the company was riddled with spies, and soon private detectives began shadowing him. In his home he kept a file of the names of carmen and their attitudes toward unions—a posssession so precious that one of the Mooneys always stayed at home to guard it.

On July 27, 1916, five days after the bombing of the parade, the *Chronicle* reported that "the police last night raided the rooms of Thomas J. Mooney, agitator and suspected dynamiter, at 975 Market Street, and carried away all the papers, documents and personal effects belonging to Mooney and his wife, Rena Mooney." The *Chronicle*, spokesman for the city's businessmen, called Mooney a "suspected dynamiter" despite his acquittal three years previously.

That same July 27 after detectives took him and his wife off the train at Guerneville, the couple was held in a hotel room until evening and then driven by a roundabout way to San Francisco police headquarters. They were separated, searched, questioned. Both denied having anything to do with the explosion. They were not booked. They were not permitted to see lawyers. They were denied the right to prompt arraignment. They were jailed. During Mooney's trial one of his attorneys was questioning Captain Duncan Matheson, the police officer who had started the parade by blowing his whistle.

"You knew that a man arrested without a warrant, you were at once to take him before the nearest magistrate?"

"Yes, I am familiar with that section of the code."

"Then why didn't you do it?"

"In the interest of justice," said the police captain.

"In the interest of justice?"

"Yes, sir."

When Police Lieutenant Stephen Bunner was being questioned in connection with the violation of the rights of another defendant in the case, he said, "I regard the directions of my superior as sufficient warrant for violating the law."

In all, there were six defendants: along with Mooney and his wife, there was Warren K. Billings, former president of the Boot and Shoe Workers' Union, a man who had served two years in prison for possessing sixty sticks of dynamite; Billings claimed he was not guilty, charging that the explosives had been planted on him by a utility agent. Another defendant was Edward D. Nolan: a few days before the parade was bombed he had returned from Baltimore where he attended a machinists' convention; for a long time he had been on San Francisco employers' blacklists. The fifth defendant was Israel Weinberg, a member of the executive board of the Jitney Bus Operators' Union. The sixth was Belle Lavin, who ran a boardinghouse where Billings lived.

All had been arrested despite the lack of any evidence connecting them with the bombing; this may explain why no warrants were issued, since the issuance of a warrant required at least one complaining witness. James Brennan, an assistant to District Attorney Fickert, later admitted the arrests were made solely on the basis of the defendants' past records and associations.

The April 1, 1916, issue of Berkman's anarchist paper *The Blast* had carried an article by Mooney denouncing preparedness in general but not San Francisco's preparedness parade in particular, since it had not yet been conceived. Mooney was also angry with the Pacific Coast Defense League and said that "they wanted to take kids out of the cradles and make soldiers of them." This was hardly a radical statement—on another occasion, during a Cabinet meeting in Washington Navy Secretary Daniels said, "I hope I shall never live to see the day when the schools of this country are used to give any form of military training. If that happens it will be proof positive that the American form of government is a failure."

Mooney was charged with murder on eight separate indictments. When he was brought to trial, Assistant District Attorney Edward Cuhna made a four-hour opening statement in which he said in part:

> We will offer evidence in this case, gentlemen, to show that some time prior to January first, 1916, this defendant, Thomas J. Mooney, entered into a general enterprise, or undertaking, or conspiracy with a number of other citizens—including Alexander Berkman, M. E. Fitzgerald, E. M. Morton, and Edward D. Nolan, and others—this general proposition—of bringing about an uprising or revolution of those persons in this state of California who were not owners of property, generally speaking those who worked. That this conspiracy had for its object confiscation of private property and the destruction of the government; that in order to bring about the object of this conspiracy, the people in question in this case organized themselves into an organization known as the Blasters. . . .

The assistant DA went on to say that the aim of this alleged revolution included overthrowing the American Federation of Labor, taking over factories, closing the banks, weakening America by fighting preparedness and advocating the assassination of President Wilson.

Mooney's trial and those of the other defendants were complex and protracted, touched off vibrations lasting a quarter century, became the theme of books and plays and motion pictures. His defense attorneys proved by means of photographs and witnesses that when the bomb exploded at 2:06 P.M. on that July 22, Mooney and his wife were watching the parade from the roof of the Eilers Building a mile and a half from the site of the blast. Curt Gentry wrote a big book about the case which he called *Frame-Up*, concluding that he was "inclined toward belief" that the parade had been bombed by German agents.

Nonetheless, Mooney was found guilty and sentenced to death. His sentence later was commuted to life imprisonment, and at last, in 1939, he received an unconditional pardon. An innocent man, he had served twenty-two years, five months and twelve days. Billings, equally innocent, served twenty-three years. All the other defendants were acquitted.

After Herbert Hoover became President, he appointed a National Commission on Law Observance and Enforcement, popularly known as the Wickersham Commission after its senior member, George W.

Wickersham. After careful study of the Mooney case, a commission subcommittee concluded:

> 1—There was never any scientific attempt made by either the police or the prosecution to discover the perpetrators of the crime. The investigation was in reality turned over to a private detective, who used his position to cause the arrest of the defendants. The police investigation was reduced to a hunt for evidence to convict the arrested defendants.
>
> 2—There were flagrant violations of the statutory law of California by both the police and the prosecution in the manner in which the defendants were arrested and held incommunicado, and in the subsequent searches of their homes to procure evidence against them.
>
> 3—After the arrest of the defendants, witnesses were brought to the jail to "identify" them, and their "identifications" were accepted by the police and prosecution, despite the fact that these witnesses were never required to pick the defendants out of a line-up, or to demonstrate their accuracy by any other test.
>
> 4—Immediately after the arrests of the defendants there commenced a deliberate attempt to arouse public prejudice against them, by a series of almost daily interviews given to the press by prosecuting officials.
>
> 5—Witnesses were produced at the trials with information in the hands of the prosecution that seriously challenged the credibility of the witnesses, but this information was deliberately concealed.
>
> 6—Witnesses were permitted to testify at the trials, despite such knowledge in the possession of the prosecution of prior contradictory stories told by these witnesses, as to make their mere production a vouching for perjured testimony.
>
> 7—Witnesses were coached in their testimony to a degree that approximated subornation of perjury. There is strong evidence that some of this coaching was done by prosecuting officials, and other evidence points to knowledge by the prosecuting officials that such coaching was being practiced on other witnesses.
>
> 8—The prejudice against the defendants, stimulated by newspaper publicity, was further appealed to at the trials by unfair and intemperate arguments to the jury in the opening and closing statements of the prosecuting attorneys.
>
> 9—After the trials, the disclosures casting doubt on the justice of the convictions were minimized, and every attempt made to defeat the liberation of the defendants, by a campaign of misrepresentation and propaganda carried on by the officials who had prosecuted them.

Why did elected officials of the city and county of San Francisco do all these things?

One answer came from John B. Densmore, the federal director of general employment, who was told by Labor Secretary W. B. Wilson to investigate the Mooney case. Densmore concluded, "The basic motive underlying all the acts of the prosecution springs from a determination on the part of certain employer interests in the city of San Francisco to conduct their various business enterprises upon the principle of the open shop. There has been no other motive worth talking about."

Bourke Cockran, a lawyer and liberal and orator and Congressman, chief among Mooney's defense attorneys, said, "The motive for the Mooney frame-up was to discredit organized labor by fastening responsibility for a horrible crime on a man known as a 'labor agitator' in the hope that this would discourage workers from joining labor unions."

Emma Goldman wrote, "The bosses who had declared themselves for the 'open shop' had determined to hang Tom Mooney, as a warning to other labour organizers."

Fremont Older said, "Anyone who has a tendency toward pessimism, and in his gloomiest moments declares the human race incapable of any real progress, can find in the Mooney case some justification of his belief."

Soon we were waging war to make the world safe for democracy.

Chapter 20

WILSON'S SECOND MARRIAGE

After the death of Woodrow Wilson's wife his loneliness had been sharpened by the absence of his three daughters. Jessie and Eleanor had married and had homes of their own. Margaret, considered by some flighty and selfish, disliked Washington so much that she was away most of the time. For companionship within the silence of the White House the President turned to his cousin, Miss Helen Woodrow Bones, who had served as a kind of secretary to the late Mrs. Wilson. Miss Bones called him Cousin Woodrow and sat wordlessly beside the distraught widower just to let him know she was there. Sometimes he was so anguished he paced the floor, reminding her of "a splendid Bengal tiger . . . never still, moving, restless, resentful of his bars that shut out the larger life God had made for him."

With few friends in the national capital, Miss Bones began to feel like a prisoner herself, and in the early spring of 1915 she became ill. The isolation and sickness of this shy and gentle woman touched the heart of the White House physician, Dr. Grayson. He was courting Alice Gertrude Gordon, whose friends contracted her first two names into the nickname "Altrude." Her father was James Gordon, a mining engineer who died when she was seventeen. Before his death he asked Mrs. Edith Bolling Galt to look after his daughter, and Mrs. Galt had not only befriended the younger woman, but had made her her ward. Mrs. Galt was the widow of Norman Galt, who had been a Washington jeweler, and she now lived alone with two maids in a small house at 1308 Twentieth Street in Washington.

Miss Gordon introduced Mrs. Galt and Dr. Grayson. One day he told the charming widow that Miss Bones, the President's cousin, was so sick and lonely he would like to bring her to Mrs. Galt's home to cheer her up. Mrs. Galt, a reserved woman with no taste for the social life of the capital, doubted whether she was the proper person to help Miss Bones, but at last she let herself be persuaded. The two liked each other from the start and soon began taking long walks together. They also went for rides in Mrs. Galt's electric car, the first owned by a woman in the city; she drove it recklessly. About the only thing Miss Bones had to talk about was "Cousin Woodrow" and his grief and loneliness. One afternoon when they had finished tramping along muddy paths, Miss Bones told

Mrs. Galt that instead of returning to the widow's house they were going to the White House, where she had ordered tea. Mrs. Galt protested that she could not think of entering the executive mansion with muddy shoes, but Miss Bones said, "Yes, you can—for there is not a soul there! Cousin Woodrow is playing golf with Dr. Grayson and we will go right upstairs in the elevator and you shall see no one. I have had tea with you every time, and Cousin Woodrow asked me the other day why I never brought my friends back there. He really wishes I would have someone in that lonely old house."

So they went to the White House, and just as they stepped out of the elevator on the second floor, they came face to face with the President and Dr. Grayson, who had just returned from their golf game with shoes as muddy as theirs. Miss Bones introduced the widow to the widower. All four laughed at their mutually bedraggled appearance. However, the wealthy Mrs. Galt—whose clothes were designed for her by M. Worth, Paris' reigning couturier—mused that despite her shoes, she was well turned out in a smart black tailored suit and a tricot hat. Miss Bones explained she had brought Mrs. Galt to the White House for a tête-à-tête tea. The President smiled and said, "I think you might ask us."

The men and women went their separate ways to tidy up and then met again in front of crackling logs in the fireplace in the Oval Room on the second floor. Wilson was enchanted by the cheerful Mrs. Galt, who twice made him laugh. Miss Bones later declared, "I can't say that I foresaw in the first minute what was going to happen. It may have taken ten minutes." A short time previously Wilson and Grayson had been taking a drive and passed a woman, to whom the doctor bowed, and after the car passed on, the President asked him, "Who is that beautiful lady?"

That beautiful lady had been born on October 15, 1872, in the small farm community of Wytheville in southwestern Virginia, the seventh of eleven children born to Sallie White Bolling and William Holcombe Bolling. She was the granddaughter, seven times removed, of Pocahontas. Edith's parents had owned plantations which they lost during the Civil War. Her father, who became an attorney and then a judge, would gather his brood around him of an evening to read aloud from the works of Shakespeare and Dickens and Milton. He lacked the money to pay for the formal schooling of the nine children who lived to young adulthood. Edith had only two years of education—one at Martha Washington College in Abingdon, Virginia, the other at Powell's School in Richmond.

When she was eighteen, she paid a long visit to a married sister, Mrs. Alexander Galt, who lived in Washington on a shady cobblestoned street five blocks west of the White House. To the wide-eyed girl from the Virginia backwaters, the capital was a glamorous place. Her sister's husband had a brother, Norman Galt, nine years Edith's senior, and after a four-year courtship they were married. They had no children. A wealthy man, Galt was sole owner of a Washington jewelry shop more than a century old and patronized by the best people in town. The Galts lived comfortably and often vacationed in Europe, where Edith picked up a smattering of culture. In 1908 Galt died, leaving his business to his widow. After supervising it for two years, she sold the store to its employees for a tidy sum, then gave her life to leisure. Lacking creativity, disliking society, devoid of any special interests, she whiled away her days doing nothing in particular. "I appreciated the prosaic quality of my life," she later wrote, "destined to be spent, like millions of others, in a backwater of commonplace."

But she was a rich and handsome widow. Five feet nine inches tall, she had an ample and shapely figure, a full bosom, thick dark hair, big violet eyes whose color she enhanced by wearing orchids, a straight nose set within a round and rosy face, beautiful legs and trim ankles. She combined high spirits with dignity. She listened well and spoke with vivacity. Quick-minded, she was hardly profound, and her opinions tended to be either black or white, for she lacked the ability to make fine distinctions. True to her Southern belle heritage, she was slightly prudish and easily offended by the sight of nude statues. On the subject of suffragettes she was vehement, calling them "disgusting creatures" and "detestable." Much concerned with clothes, she dressed with simple elegance, rarely wearing pins or necklaces. With her sunny personality, radiant smile and dimples, Mrs. Galt was considered one of Washington's most attractive women.

Following that afternoon in March when she first took tea with the President of the United States, she confessed to a sense of glamor about the occasion. On April 7 Miss Bones telephoned to suggest they take a ride instead of going for a walk, and when Mrs. Galt reached the White House, she was surprised to find Wilson in the front seat of a big open touring car beside his chauffeur, a secret service agent sitting on a jump seat. The women took their places in the back.

A week earlier Wilson had written the new police chief of the District of Columbia, ". . . I want you to tell your men that White House cars must obey the traffic regulations. . . . If there is any creature on earth I despise it is the man who by reason of his wealth or his high social position seeks to disregard with impunity minor police regulations." During this late afternoon ride the President spoke not a word. Before leaving his office, he had written to Henry M. Pindell, the owner and editor of two newspapers in Peoria, Illinois, about the issue of whether Americans should be allowed to make transatlantic trips on foreign vessels while German submarines continued to be a threat. "I see no sufficient reason why they should not," Wilson told Pindell, "though the indications are that both sides are feeling just now a little irritated by our consistent and effective neutrality. . . ." Unaware of the problems the President contemplated in silence, Mrs. Galt and Miss Bones "chatted like magpies," as the widow later expressed it.

When the limousine returned to the White House about 5:30 P.M., Wilson came to life. Plaintively he asked Mrs. Galt to stay for dinner, saying that otherwise he and Miss Bones would be left alone. She accepted, but first she wanted to go home to freshen up. That evening the three of them enjoyed a quiet dinner and then sat again before the fireplace to discuss literature. Wilson picked up first one book and then another to read passages aloud, delighting Mrs. Galt with his expressive voice. He told her how close he had felt to his father, an affection that echoed within her because of her warm relationship with her father. They shared another common interest in their Southern heritage and exchanged stories about the people and beauty of that part of the land. "It was the first time I had felt the warm personality of Woodrow Wilson," Mrs. Galt was to write. "A boylike simplicity dwelt in the background of an official life which had to be content with the husks of formal contacts when starving for the bread of human companionship. Thereafter I never thought of him as the President of the United States, but as a real friend. That evening started a companionship which ripened quickly."

On April 28, 1915, a day on which German planes bombed an American tanker in the North Sea, he wrote his first note to her to say he had ordered a book sent to her from the Library of Congress. Two days later he created Naval Oil Reserve Number 3 near Casper, Wyoming, popularly known as Teapot Dome, and that afternoon he sent Mrs. Galt a corsage of golden roses. That evening the charming forty-two-year-old widow appeared in the White House with the corsage pinned to another of Worth's creations, a black charmeuse princess dress with a jet panel in front that created a slender line, and wearing gold slippers to match the golden roses. Once again they dined together.

Then came May 3. With Americans booking passage on the *Lusitania*, Mrs. Galt was driven from her home to the White House to dine once again with the President. This time several guests were present, and when the meal was finished, all strolled out onto the south portico to be served coffee; but soon, to her surprise, Mrs. Galt found herself alone with Wilson.

The tall lean man hitched his chair closer to the buxom widow and stared at her with eyes she considered "splendid, fearless." He said he had asked the others to leave the two of them alone so that he might tell her something he already had told them. Then, speaking quietly but emotionally, he told her he loved her. Mrs. Galt's first reaction was that "the very world seemed tense and waiting." She said the first thing that came to mind, "Oh, you can't love me, for you really don't know me—and it is less than a year since your wife died."

He said, "Yes, I know you feel that—but, little girl, in this place time is not measured by weeks or months or years, but by deep human experience, and since her death I have lived a lifetime of loneliness and heartache. I was afraid, knowing you, I would shock you. But—I would be less than a gentleman if I continued to make opportunities to see you without telling you what I have told my daughters and Helen—that I want you to be my wife. In the circumstances of the spotlight that is always on this house, and particularly on me as the head of the government, whoever comes here is immediately observed and discussed, and—do what I can to protect you from gossip—it will inevitably begin. If you can care for me as I do for you, we will have to be brave about this. But—as I cannot come to your house without increasing the gossip—you, in your graciousness, will have to come here. It is for this reason I have talked to the girls about it, so that they can safeguard you and make it possible for me to see you. They have all been wonderful about it and tell me they love you for your own sake—but would, anyway, for mine!"

She felt mild shock. She told herself she never had expected he would propose to her, although what she sensed unconsciously was something else. There on the south portico of the White House that evening in May, with no other human beings in sight and the city still and the war a blur in their minds, the important man and the woman made important by his love talked in soft voices for more than an hour. At last she told him gently that if she were pressed for a yes or no answer immediately, it would have to be no. Nonetheless, she said she wanted him to know she appreciated the manly way he had expressed his feelings, and she hoped to continue their friendship until she might make a decision.

The next morning Mrs. Galt and Miss Bones went walking in Rock Creek Park. Miss Bones, who knew about her cousin's declaration of love, said nothing about the previous evening until the two sat down on rocks to rest. Then, eyes flashing, she cried, "Cousin Woodrow looks really ill this morning!" And burst into tears. "Just as I thought some happiness was coming into his life—! And now you are breaking his heart!"

Woodrow was depressed? Guilt washed over the widow. Here was a wonderful man, a man who happened to be President of the United States, a gentleman, kind and loving and sensitive, one who had done her the honor to declare his love for her, the nation's chief executive with burdens beyond belief, a suitor who had offered to share his life with her—and what did she do? She hesitated. Why? She was not sure. She felt confused. She knew she was a romantic, and she also knew that if she gave her heart to Woodrow, it would be to the private man and not the public figure. But dare she wait? Had she a right to wait when his need was so great? As she expressed it to herself, she knew she was "playing with fire" because of the intensity of his nature. Perhaps he would not wait too long for her answer.

The day before he proposed Wilson had asked her to accompany him on the Presidential yacht, the *Mayflower*, to New York, where he was to review the Atlantic fleet. She had accepted and now, after more soul-searching, she decided to keep this commitment; after all, she had told Woodrow she wanted to continue their friendship. And so, for the first time other than their automobile rides together, the President and Mrs. Galt appeared together in public. During the trip down the Potomac he suggested they lean awhile on the rail, for he had something he wanted to discuss with her.

By this time the *Lusitania* had been torpedoed and relations were strained between Wilson and Secretary of State Bryan. The President told Mrs. Galt he had received a letter from Bryan announcing that he wanted to resign. Never in her life had she bothered her head about politics or affairs of state, but now—doubtless out of loyalty to Wilson—she snapped, "Good! I hope you can replace him with someone who is able, and who would in himself command respect for the office, both at home and abroad." In this moment the woman with two years of formal education embarked on her career as an adviser to the President of the United States, a career which in the postwar years would find her making decisions affecting the entire nation.

Subsequently, Wilson freely told Mrs. Galt all kinds of state secrets. He acted foolishly—not because there was any danger she might be disloyal, but because he had not known her very long and could not be sure she did not engage in gossip. In those tense times one had to be careful: A young American army officer was about to be appointed as an aide to the White House when it was discovered he was a close friend of a baroness who was under observation by the French secret service. But as time proved, Mrs. Galt did not gossip, and she never did betray a confidence.

She became an almost daily visitor at the White House, whose chief usher considered that "her voice was soft and musical, with a Southern accent." One of the President's secret service guards quickly discovered that Wilson was a jealous man. One day when one of Mrs. Galt's shoelaces came untied, the agent asked whether he might tie it for her, dropped to one knee, and she rested her foot on his other knee, raising the skirt of her handsome tailored suit to reveal a shapely ankle. Wilson pretended not to see this; but his jaw muscles worked angrily and he did not speak to the agent for the next couple of weeks.

And so, that spring and summer of 1915, the President courted the widow, his private happiness plagued by grave public problems: German spies in the United States, German submarine attacks, American loans to the Allies, a hurricane that devastated Galveston, unemployment, neutrality and pacifism and preparedness. His face grew gaunt, and Mrs. Galt thought that his eyes "seemed pools of tragic suffering." On September 3 she went for another ride with him, she and Miss Bones sharing the back seat with the President, the chauffeur and a secret service agent in front. After telling her his problems, he confessed that it was becoming increasingly difficult to keep the United States out of the war.

"And so, little girl," he said, "I have no right to ask you to help me by sharing this load that is almost breaking my back, for I know your nature, and you might do it out of sheer pity."

Despite the presence of the others, Mrs. Galt wound her arms around his neck and said, "Well, if you won't ask me, I will volunteer and be ready to be mustered in as soon as we can."

Theodore Roosevelt told Mark Sullivan that Wilson would not marry again because he wanted to be reelected President and was "too cold-blooded to let his emotions overcome his self-interest." Nonetheless, the day after Mrs. Galt committed herself, a day on which the state department prepared to ask for the formal recall of the ambassador from Austria-Hungary, Wilson told his daughters that he was engaged. Despite her impulsive surrender, Mrs. Galt preferred they delay their marriage until after the election of November, 1916. Though she was a Democrat, she thought the Republicans would win, and by marrying a defeated candidate, she felt she could prove to the world that it was the man himself, not his title, which attracted her.

Reporters had known for months that Wilson was keeping company with the beautiful widow, and they noted in amusement that he was wearing brighter clothes, matching his tie and socks, keeping orchids on his desk—but now news of the engagement leaked out. Ugly rumors began flying. It was whispered that Dr. Grayson had poisoned Wilson's first wife. There was another story to the effect that Ellen had died as the result of a beating Wilson gave her. Word had it that the President was so lovey-dovey with the buxom Mrs. Galt that he neglected his dead wife's grave in Georgia, letting weeds thicken over her remains. People also gossiped that Wilson spent so much time with Mrs. Galt that he now saw less of his adviser, Colonel House, and perhaps there might be a break between the two men. The Colonel himself became concerned and suggested to Wilson that this gossip could be killed if they were seen together more frequently, and on September 24 he let reporters catch him calling at the White House.

When Wilson told House he was engaged, the wily Colonel feigned a delight he did not feel. House had got along well with the first Mrs. Wilson because she never expressed jealousy about the relationship between her husband and his best friend. And after her death the President had leaned ever more heavily on the Colonel, who savored his growing influence. Now here was some rattlebrained widow—handsome, to be sure, but probably scheming—about to interpose herself between Wilson and his alter ego. If Wilson actually married her, where would this leave the Colonel?

Another who began worrying was William Gibbs McAdoo. He had never forgotten that after his own engagement to Eleanor Wilson, the President's youngest daughter, Eleanor had kept the news from her father as long as possible because she was afraid of his wrath. As his three daughters grew into young womanhood, Wilson became a jealous and tyrannical father, trying to discourage them from dating young men and even seeking to prevent them from marrying. Wilson demanded jealously that they love him above all others. Jessie, the middle child, had wrung reluctant approval from her father to marry a college professor, but after the wedding Wilson wrote a friend, "The pang of it is still deep in my heart." McAdoo, who had enjoyed easy access to his father-in-law, now felt concern lest Mrs. Galt come between him and the chief executive.

Joseph Tumulty, the President's secretary, was also vexed and worried. He had adored the late Ellen Wilson. He was opposed to a second marriage because he was a morally conservative man, because he felt it might cost Wilson reelection and because he wondered what the presence of a strange White House mistress would do to his privileged position. There were Democratic politicians other than Tumulty who felt concern about the effect of Wilson's marriage on the November election. Some of the most influential politicians met secretly and finally persuaded Postmaster General Burleson to ask Navy Secretary Daniels to see the President and, in his capacity as a personal friend, beg Wilson to think of the party's success and not jeopardize victory at the polls. Shocked and amused, Daniels flatly refused.

One Saturday evening in September, 1915, Mrs. Galt was alone in her home getting ready to join the President when Dr. Grayson arrived, unannounced and obviously worried. He said the President had sent him to tell her something Wilson could not bring himself to write. "It was this," she later wrote in her memoirs. "Colonel House was at the White House, having just returned from a conference with Secretary McAdoo. They both had been told in confidence of our engagement and, the Colonel said, they had sounded out a few people, particularly newspaper men, who told them the gossip was that should the rumors concerning our engagement be true, Mrs. Peck was going to come out against the

President, saying she had letters from him which would be compromising. . . ."

Years earlier, when Wilson was president of Princeton University, he had left his wife at home to vacation alone in Bermuda, where he met a charming woman. Her maiden name had been Mary Allen, she had married Thomas Peck. After he died, she married a Mr. Hulbert, and after they were divorced, she had resumed the use of her former married name of Peck. Wilson was so taken with the stylish and pretty Mrs. Peck that they fell into a friendship that lasted for many years. He had invited her to Princeton, and then to Washington, to socialize with Ellen and himself. He wrote Mrs. Peck more than 200 letters—warm and friendly letters, to be sure, but hardly love letters. He also lent her $7,500. During the 1912 Presidential campaign there had been rumors about Wilson and Mrs. Peck, and now, apparently, they were to be revived.

Now Dr. Grayson told the horrified Mrs. Galt that the President had sat down in the White House that evening to write her a letter explaining what had happened, but Wilson's hand shook so much that at last he put down the pen, turned to Grayson and said, "I cannot bring myself to write this! You go, Grayson, and tell her everything, and say my only alternative is to release her from any promise." The doctor choked as he repeated this to Mrs. Galt. Then he asked, "What shall I tell him?"

"Tell him," Mrs. Galt said, "I will write."

After Grayson left, she sat down in a big chair by a window where she remained for hours, staring into the blackness of night and a future that looked equally black, thinking, worrying, brooding. Then everything stopped. ". . . as suddenly as the blow had fallen, its weight lifted, and I saw things in their true proportions. It was our *lives* that mattered, not politics, not scandal. If I did not care enough for the man to share his misfortunes, his sorrows, then it was a futile love! I would glory in standing by when the world scoffed and doubted, for in the end he would triumph and vindicate my trust." At dawn, she sat down at her desk, turned on a lamp and wrote a letter to the man she loved.

Early that morning she sent her note to the White House. No reply that day. No reply the next. The woman who once again had pledged her love and allegiance began to feel hurt and humiliated. About noon the third day Dr. Grayson returned, his chiseled features anxious. He was too distraught to shake hands. "I beg that you will come with me to the White House," he said. "The President is very ill and you are the only person who can help. I can do nothing. . . . I know it is a lot to ask after what you have been through, but it is a desperate situation. Neither Miss Margaret nor Miss Bones is here, so I will have to act as chaperone."

"Did the President ask you to come?"

"No . . . I told him I was coming, and he said it would be unfair to you and weak in him to ask it. . . . If you could see him you would not hesitate. He looks as I imagine the martyrs looked when they were broken on the wheel. He does not speak or sleep or eat."

Mrs. Galt asked for time to think and went to her room. Could her letter have fallen into "alien hands," as she expressed it to herself. Did he still care for her? Did he doubt her love? Did he think her incapable of enduring a harsh test? Did he doubt—ah, *yes!* She remembered. She remembered that she had written: "I will stand by."

She and Dr. Grayson hurried to the White House and rode the elevator to the second floor. At the door to Wilson's room the doctor beckoned her to follow him inside. The curtains were drawn, the room dark. "On the pillow I saw a white, drawn face with burning eyes dark with hidden pain. Brooks, the coloured valet, was by the bed. No word was spoken, only an eager hand held out in welcome, which I took to find icy cold, and when I unclasped it we were alone. Strangely in these tense moments things are understood with no need of words. I never asked why he had not answered my letter, only had it reached him. He said, 'Yes.'"

After they were married, he said he wanted to confess something, and from a pocket took her letter, the seal unbroken, the envelope frayed. "I think I am rarely a coward," he told her, "but when this letter came that Sunday morning after a sleepless night, I could not open it, for I felt the world was slipping from under my feet. I was so sure—with your horror of publicity and all the rest of it—that this was the end, and you would never see me again, that I could not bring myself to face the written words. So I put it here, where it has been ever since. Now, with you beside me, I *want* to open it, remembering no matter what the hurt it holds that you came like an angel of light to heal my wound."

Together they read her letter, and then he begged that it never be destroyed.

Some malicious people sneered at Wilson, calling him Peck's Bad Boy, after a book of that title, but there was not a word of truth in the story that Mrs. Peck planned to blackmail or otherwise embarrass Wilson. In fact, at this time Mrs. Peck did not even know that Wilson was engaged to Mrs. Galt. Later the President even wrote her to say that he and Mrs. Galt were about to announce their engagement, adding he knew she would rejoice with him in this "blessing."

Wilson himself wrote the press release about his impending marriage, and Tumulty made copies for White House correspondents. The President slanted the news by making it appear his fiancée was a close friend of his daughters. Tumulty, who was equally eager to soften the impact, persuaded Wilson to couple it with a statement about an issue of the day—votes for women. Despite Mrs. Galt's aversion to woman suffrage, the President had been won over to the cause by his daughters. On October 7, 1915, the New York *Times* published this headline:

PRESIDENT TO WED MRS. NORMAN GALT
INTIMATE FRIEND OF HIS DAUGHTERS;
ALSO COMES OUT FOR WOMAN'S SUFFRAGE

The political part of the President's announcement said, "I intend to vote for woman suffrage in New Jersey because I believe that the time has come to extend that privilege and responsibility to the women of the State, but I shall vote, not as the leader of my party in the nation, but only upon my private conviction as a citizen of New Jersey."

Mrs. Galt wrote in her memoirs:

> Years afterwards when I asked Colonel House to tell me where he got such an unjust impression as he gave the President about Mrs. Peck, he said he had never heard anything about it from anybody; that he and Secretary McAdoo had planned it between them because they thought at the time that a second marriage of the President might prevent his re-election. Colonel House concluded his story: "In that I was mistaken, for I think you have been a great asset." When I asked Mr. McAdoo about it, he said that it was entirely "the Colonel's idea"! This shifting of responsibility between Colonel House and Mr. McAdoo was a matter I never mentioned to my husband because I knew it would make him see red.

Such was her version of this affair. The papers of Colonel House, a man much concerned with his place in history, make it appear that he encouraged Wilson to marry Mrs. Galt, that he had consulted political friends who agreed remarriage would do no political damage to the President. After Wilson married Mrs. Galt and then went on to win reelection, Postmaster General Burleson scoffed, "Poppycock! Didn't cost him five thousand votes in the whole country! Didn't cost him a thousand!" The new Mrs. Wilson never overcame her distaste for Colonel House and in time caused the Colonel to lose influence with the President. (Years later when Wilson introduced her to Mrs. Peck, she remarked that Mrs. Peck was a "faded, rather sweet-looking woman" who talked too much and overstayed her welcome.)

In early October, 1915, the news of the President's engagement crowded the war out of the headlines for a few days. Newspapers made much of Mrs. Galt's connection with Princess Pocahontas, writing not only about her ancestry but also about her looks, personality, and shopping habits and the fact that she opposed giving women the right to vote. She engaged Edith Benham as her social secretary, for now she began receiving a flood of letters. There were requests for everything from money, photographs, automobiles and advice to discarded clothing. One woman wrote to say she was five feet eight inches tall, weighed 140 pounds, had a 38-inch bust and 40-inch hips, was very attractive and only needed fashionable clothes to become a beauty. One day a man Mrs. Galt knew slightly and disliked greatly rushed uninvited into her home, took her in his arms, kissed her, announced that his wife was out of town but would be glad to return for the wedding, cast some flowers at her feet and rushed out again.

Mrs. Galt felt the world had gone mad. Wilson wrote to his daughter Jessie, "Edith is greatly distressed by the foolish (and lying) publicity of which she is being made the object, poor girl, but is fine about it, as about everything else. She is very well indeed, and seems (to me, at least) to grow more radiant and lovely every day." He called on staff members of the Library of Congress to find quotations so that he might include them in his love letters to her. He had a direct telephone line installed between the White House and Edith's home. On days when they were unable to see each other, he sent a messenger with a digest of foreign and domestic news so she would be able to keep in touch with his work.

She was an Episcopalian, he a Presbyterian. They decided to have two clergymen at the wedding ceremony so both faiths would be represented. They planned a small wedding attended only by members of their immediate families. Their marriage license was obtained for them by the head usher. The morning of the wedding Wilson was amused when Hoover said, "Mr. President, I will be on hand tonight as usual to tell you when it is time for the ceremony." Concealing a smile, Wilson asked, "Do you think I will need that, Hoover?"

The evening of December 18, 1915, the day the Ford peace ship docked in Norway, Woodrow Wilson, the twenty-eighth President of the United States, married Edith Bolling Galt in the small drawing room of her home at 1308 Twentieth Street, Washington, D.C. She was forty-three years old. He was fifteen years older. He wore a cutaway coat and gray striped trousers. She wore a plain black velvet gown, a velvet hat trimmed with the feathers of crowned pigeons, and she carried her customary orchids. Her only jewelry was a diamond brooch—a present from the bridegroom. After the ceremony the newlyweds ate a buffet supper and then slipped outside and into a limousine guarded by secret service agents. To avoid crowds, they did not leave Washington from Union Station, but drove to a smaller railway station in Alexandria. There they boarded a private railway car filled with flowers and fruit and sandwiches, departing about midnight for a two-week honeymoon at Hot Springs, Virginia.

> We ran into the siding at Hot Springs about seven o'clock the next morning [wrote Edmund W. Starling of the secret service in his memoirs]. Soon after we stopped I went back to the private car. I entered quietly and walked down the narrow corridor flanking the bedrooms. Suddenly my ear caught the notes of a familar melody. Emerging into the sitting room I saw a figure in a top hat, tailcoat, and gray morning trousers, standing with his back to me, hands in his pockets, happily dancing a jig. As I watched him he clicked his heels in the air, and from whistling the tune he changed to singing the words, "Oh, you beautiful doll! You great big beautiful doll . . . !"

Chapter 21

THE PRESIDENTIAL ELECTION OF 1916

On January 3, 1916, President Wilson and his bride left Hot Springs, Virginia, by special train and returned to Washington, where she became mistress of the White House. The part she liked best was on the southwest corner of the second floor—a suite consisting of a small dressing room and two huge bedrooms, each with its own bath. Every morning a servant brought a tray, set the table for them in front of an open fire and then retired. After that she seldom saw him alone.

At first they breakfasted at eight o'clock sharp. When the President finished eating he would walk into his study and sit down at a desk given to the government by Queen Victoria years before. On the desk stood a student lamp with a green shade that Wilson had used when studying law at the University of Virginia. The desk had a compartment which Mrs. Wilson called the Drawer, and he never entered or left the room without looking into it. She came to resent the Drawer because it held important papers requiring her husband's attention and preventing them from reading or resting. As Wilson's workload increased, he suggested they "steal up on the days in the dark," so after that they ate breakfast at 5 A.M.

The day the Wilsons returned to Washington his name was placed on a Presidential petition in Michigan, and three days later he authorized the filing of his name in Indiana's Presidential primary. By setting in motion the machinery to seek reelection, he acted contrary to his wishes, for he did not care to spend another four years in the White House. He wanted more time alone with his wife, he was tired, he had blinding headaches, he worried about the war, and he seemed unable to strike a balance between neutrality and preparedness.

By relaxing his neutral stance and leaning toward preparedness, Wilson incurred both approval and disapproval. Oswald Garrison Villard declared that Wilson's new preparedness posture was just a bid to win reelection, but the National Security League praised the President's approval of certain defense measures. On January 27 Wilson irritated some Americans and delighted others when he wired congratulations to Kaiser Wilhelm II of Germany, who turned fifty-seven that day. Later that same day Wilson led a preparedness parade in New York City, provoking former Secretary Bryan into snarling that the President had become a jingoist. Theodore Roosevelt publicly accused Wilson of taking forty-one different positions on preparedness.

The Democratic party's 1912 platform had suggested that a President serve only a single term and then be ineligible for reelection. Although Wilson had called this proposal unsatisfactory, he could have used it as an excuse for not running again, if that was what he really wanted. But counterbalancing his aversion to a second term was Wilson's sense of public duty and the reluctance felt by powerful men to relinquish power. He told Colonel House "it would be a delightful relief if I could conscientiously retire" and said a second term might be "an anti-climax." The canniest politician in the Cabinet was Postmaster General Burleson, who said to Wilson's face, "You wanted to be elected in 1912 and you needed a party to nominate you. This time the party and the country need you."

While it remained to be seen whether the country needed Wilson, his party certainly did, for now he was stronger than the party. Although Democratic machine politicians were angry because he ignored their advice and had pushed progressive legislation through Congress, they were realists who recognized Wilson as the party's strongest and therefore most logical candidate.

At about the time Wilson was telling House he wanted to retire, Roosevelt was telling one of his own friends, "Don't imagine that I wouldn't like to be in the White House this minute!" Above everything else Roosevelt wanted to get the United States into the war on the side of the Allies, and since Wilson would not take the lead, Teddy decided to make another run for the Presidency so that he might force the issue. Former President Taft said of Roosevelt, "He is not a real democrat. He has not the spirit that makes him bow to the will of the people."

Roosevelt wrote letters calling Wilson "the worst President by all odds since Buchanan, with the possible exception of Andrew Johnson. . . . I abhor Wilson . . . at heart he is neither a gentleman nor a real man. . . . I am sick at heart over the actions of Wilson . . . he has trailed the honor of the United States in the dust. . . ." He was so passionately *for* war that he actually called Americans cowards. In 1916 he wrote British Ambassador Cecil Spring-Rice, "*Your* country is passing through the flame and will come out cleansed and refined to lofty nobleness. *Mine* is passing through the thick yellow mud-streak of 'safety first' . . . ."

Teddy knew that to take the Presidency from Wilson he would have to avoid a three-cornered race such as that of 1912. This time Teddy hoped to become the nominee of both the Republicans and Progressives. He knew he would have to work hard to win the approval of the Old Guard Republicans, members of a Senate cabal and the leading capitalists of the Eastern Establishment, since they considered him too liberal for their tastes. Since most Progressives adored him, perhaps he could take the Progressive nomination by default. But he was picked by the Progressives, rejected by the Republicans, then rejected the Progressive nomination. Instead of Teddy the GOP named Charles Evans Hughes as its candidate.

Charles Evans Hughes was born in 1862 in Glen Falls, New York, the son of a Welsh-born minister. He attended public schools in Newark, New Jersey, and then in New York City, being graduated from high school when he was thirteen. A year later he entered Colgate University, transferring two years later to Brown University, from which he was graduated third in his class and a member of Phi Beta Kappa. At first he had wanted to be a minister like his father, but he turned to law and taught school for a while to pay his way through law school. He entered Columbia University law school, won his degree and was admitted to the bar in 1884. He took a job with a prestigious Manhattan law firm, married the daughter of the senior partner, worked so hard his health gave way and taught law for two years at Cornell. He was so precise he always took the same number of steps from the classroom door to his desk.

In 1905 Hughes became counsel to the Stevens Committee of the New York state legislature and probed the conduct and rates of gas companies. A master of cross-examination, he did so well that before the end of the year he also became counsel to the Armstrong Committee and investigated insurance companies. His work for these two committees won him a reputation as a brilliant lawyer and investigator.

In 1906 he was nominated for governor by the Republicans—not because the politicians really wanted him but because they wanted to win and he had an impressive record. Winning the election, he developed into one of the most independent state executives in the nation's history. Hughes worked hard, threw party hacks out of his office and "displeased everybody but the voters." Nominated again and winning again, he was so efficient that he gave himself only a half hour for lunch, so austere that when he banned racetrack betting, he was grumblingly called Charles the Baptist. Hughes had organized a Bible class in the Fifth Avenue Baptist Church, the one later taught by John D. Rockefeller, Jr.

In 1910 President Taft appointed Hughes to the United States Supreme Court. No flaming liberal or great dissenter, Hughes was an associate justice whose opinions were solid and analytical—and usually a little left of center. After moving to Washington, he ceased to vote because the trip to New York to cast his ballot took too much time away from his work. In 1915 he began getting letters declaring he was the only man who could reunite the Republican party and urging him to run for the Presidency. At first he reacted with indifference, then with irritation. In a letter to a former governor of New Jersey he said, "It seems to me very clear that, as a member of the Supreme Court, I have no right to be a candidate, either openly or passively."

Roosevelt sent a friend to tell Hughes that Teddy considered the justice "the brainiest man now in public life in the United States" and "the best equipped man" for the Presidency—this, of course, before Roosevelt decided he wanted the GOP nomination himself. In a display of humility rare among public men, Hughes told a newspaper editor, "Your friend Roosevelt can handle the work of the White House and enjoy it. It would take me a whole day to dispose of matters that he could get rid of in an hour." When Roosevelt began seeking the nomination, he regretted his tribute to Hughes, telling a friend, "In international matters and in the present situation, I know I am worth two of Hughes."

Because he stood more than six feet tall and was strong and tenacious, Hughes was called the Long-Legged Bulldog. His figure was slim, erect and lordly, and he walked at a brisk pace with his head held high, his chest out, his Phi Beta Kappa key dancing from the watch chain across his vest. He was an immaculate dresser. More than lordly, Hughes seemed almost godlike in appearance. He had a large and shapely head, a high forehead, a tangle of thick eyebrows, quiet gray eyes, a strong and classical nose, big white teeth. He brushed his reddish brown whiskers from the middle and out toward either side of his face. William Randolph Hearst called him "an animated feather duster," while Roosevelt sneered at him as "the whiskered Wilson." Brilliant and reserved, Hughes spoke coldly and came to be called the Ice Myth.

Perhaps never in the history of American politics had there been two Presidential candidates so similar as Hughes and Wilson, so evenly matched in ability, so astonishingly alike. Both were the sons of ministers, both were fond of sermons; both took law degrees; both were elected to Phi Beta Kappa, both taught school, both were the souls of rectitude; both worked hard; both were highly strung; both had happy marriages.

Hughes was lunching with his family in his Washington home at noon on June 10, 1916, when he learned that the Republicans, at their convention in Chicago, had nominated him as their candidate. Tears filled his gray eyes. He spoke to reporters and then went to his study to write a note resigning from the Supreme Court: "To the President: I hereby resign the office of Associate Justice of the Supreme Court of the United States. I am, sir, respectfully yours, Charles Evans Hughes." This was the first mistake of his campaign. The curt message was an insult to the office of the Presidency; it didn't matter that Hughes had been appointed to the bench by a Republican President. Now that he was about to square off against a President who was a Democrat, he could have been more gracious. A messenger took his note to the White House, and when Wilson read it, his eyes narrowed.

Hughes then wrote the Republicans assembled in Chicago, saying he had not desired the nomination, but now that they had summoned him he accepted their call. This was the first time that any of our major political parties had chosen a Supreme Court justice as their Presidential candidate, and some Americans resented it. They felt there should be no overlapping of the judicial and executive branches of the government.

On June 11 Hughes left Washington for New York to set up campaign headquarters in the Astor hotel on Times Square.

President Wilson's nomination by the Democratic party was certain, but his election was doubtful. Rich men referred to him as that "radical" or "Socialist" in the White House. They resented Wilson's friendliness toward labor, complained that their own interests had not been given a hearing, declared that the men around him were either inept or untrustworthy.

Most Americans judged his foreign policy in terms of their own attitude for or against war. Many admired his domestic program—giving credit to farmers, regulating child labor, lowering the tariff, applying the first income tax, approving the inheritance tax, creating the Federal Reserve System and the Federal Trade Commission and the Clayton Antitrust Act.

Although the Democratic party of 1916 was not a genuinely liberal party, nonetheless, Wilson had, in the words of a prominent Progressive, "hammered the Democratic Congress into a constructive body." Colonel House felt that Wilson's moral strength in the days ahead lay in his willingness to transform his party into a truly liberal one. House told a friend, "I would rather have the President defeated than to have him win by deserting the progressive principles for which we have fought. The Democratic party must change its historic character and become the progressive party in the future."

The Democratic national convention opened in St. Louis on June 14, 1916. From his study in the White House the President controlled almost everything that happened on the bank of the Mississippi river. As the new chairman of the Democratic national committee he had chosen Vance C. McCormick, a retired mayor of Harrisburg, Pennsylvania, and a Pennsylvania newspaper publisher, the very kind of aggressive professional politician Wilson sought. Besides having McCormick in St. Louis, the President was linked with the convention by a direct telephone line, he had written the Democratic party platform and he had sent this platform to St. Louis with his new secretary of war, the diminutive Newton D. Baker. Only fourteen delegate seats were contested.

To the convention came William Jennings Bryan, the former secretary of state, the passionate pacifist and professional politician, a national figure with a large personal following. He did not arrive as a delegate, since he had lost a Nebraska contest for a seat on the floor, but as a working journalist. Bryan had been the Democratic Presidential candidate in 1896, in 1900 and again in 1908. Some Democratic leaders worried lest he try to stampede the delegates into offering him the nomination a fourth time. But when he arrived at his hotel and met reporters in the lobby, he smiled and said, "I have no plan except to report this convention." Then he worked his way through throngs of well-wishers and went to his room. Still, the first time Bryan took his place with other reporters in the press section of the convention hall, all the delegates cheered him.

They had gathered in the Coliseum on the southwest corner of Jefferson and Washington avenues. Erected at a cost of $345,000, opened in 1909 with a revival by evangelist "Gypsy" Smith, the Coliseum could hold more than 10,000 people and was the largest public hall in St. Louis. It stood on the site of a cool damp cave where Joseph Uhrig formerly kept his beer and operated Uhrig's Cave Theatre.

Wilson had chosen Senator Ollie M. James as permanent chairman of the convention; J. W. Wescott, head of the New Jersey delegation to the convention, to place his name in nomination and Martin H. Glynn as the keynote speaker. Glynn had been born in New York state of humble Irish parents, developed into a journalist and economist and a friend of labor, was elected a Congressman and then governor of his native state. Now he was out of office but had a nationwide reputation as an orator. Wilson had told his convention leaders to stress the theme of patriotism, as illustrated by his preparedness program, but when Glynn rose to speak, he launched into a review of historical precedents for Wilson's policy of writing notes instead of making war. Glynn cited a British violation of American neutrality during the Pierce administration; a Canadian attack in the Van Buren administration that killed several American crewmen; another case of a British ship firing on an American vessel—a list of long-gone outrages that had not been met by war but with diplomacy—and he himself considered them so boring that he read fast. But every time he finished a statement about some provocation, the delegates yelled, "What did we do? What did we do?"

"We didn't go to war," he would answer.

Surprised by their emotional response, his face puzzled, he would cite another precedent, and again the crowd would yell, "What did we do? What did we do? What did we do?"

"We didn't go to war!"

Men jumped out of their chairs and danced in the aisles and waved flags and screamed and shouted. This may have been one of the few times in which a history lesson provoked a response like that at a football game. Glynn's keynote address was developing into one of the most effective speeches in the history of American political conventions, oratorical magic so powerful that some delegates actually began weeping. Bryan wept. The spell was broken only when a Texan jumped up to shrill, "And don't forget that that policy also is satisfactory to William Jennings Bryan!" The delegates laughed. Bryan laughed. On and on and on went Glynn about the precedents used by Woodrow Wilson, providing the Democrats with their campaign slogan: "He kept us out of war!"

Later in the convention proceedings Wilson's name was formally presented to the delegates, and he was nominated on the first ballet. A motion was made to declare the nomination unanimous, but an Illinois delegate objected, so officially Wilson was nominated by a count of 1,092 to 1.

The President felt it would be improper to campaign from the White House, so he rented an estate in the resort town of West Long Branch, New Jersey, near the Atlantic and five miles north of Asbury Park. His secretary, Joseph Tumulty, set up an executive office in the Asbury Park Trust Building. During the Gilded Age—the boom period after the Civil War—this seaside area of New Jersey had become the playground of Presidents and millionaires and beautiful if notorious, women such as Lillian Russell and Lily Langtry. Its architecture was flamboyantly Victorian, and Wilson's temporary home was no exception. It was called Shadow Lawn. The grounds included nearly nine acres, while the house was so huge and ornate it almost overwhelmed Mrs. Wilson. "The first impression was awful," she wrote. "We entered a room which looked more like a lounge in a summer hotel—very large, with a staircase, wide enough for an army abreast, opposite the front door." She said the big house had "acres of porches" with "seventeen complete sets of porch furniture, each different, and whenever I passed from one to another I felt as though I were being escorted through a furniture store."

September 2, 1916, was the date on which Wilson would be officially notified that he had been chosen as the Democratic candidate. Special trains brought people and bands to Shadow Lawn, and by ten o'clock that morning men and women sat in chairs and on long rows of seats stretching across the vast lawn. The façade of the house and its tall fluted columns had been garnished with flags and bunting, while carpenters had extended the main porch into a simple platform.

The notification speech was delivered by Senator Ollie James of Kentucky, the largest man in the Senate—so huge that his Senate desk was too small for him—a man with "the face of a prizefighter, the body of an oak and the voice of a pipe organ." When he finished and Wilson rose to stand beside him to prolonged applause, the tall President looked small by comparison. Wilson wore a dark jacket, white shirt, white trousers, white shoes, and his nose glasses glinted in the sunshine. He had labored over his acceptance speech, and now he began by attacking the Republican party, calling it a failure because it served special interests. Later in his talk, he confirmed the fact that he had changed his attitude about neutrality, declaring that "no nation can any longer remain neutral as against any willful disturbance of the peace of the world."

Mrs. Wilson believed her husband would lose the election, so she began to suggest what they might do with their lives afterward. The President gave her a long look and said, "What a delightful pessimist you are! One must never court defeat. If it comes, accept it like a soldier—but don't anticipate it, for that destroys your fighting spirit."

Although Colonel House was not as pessimistic as Mrs. Wilson, he followed his habit of formulating plans to cope with an unpleasant situation. If Hughes actually were elected, there would be a period of sixteen weeks—from November 7, 1916, until March 4, 1917—during which Wilson would have the title of President but no real power. The foreign crisis was too acute to be mastered by a lame-duck President, thought the Colonel. He suggested to Wilson that if he were defeated, he might ask Vice President Thomas R. Marshall and Secretary of State Robert Lansing to resign. Then Wilson could name Hughes secretary of state, tender his own resignation and thus enable Hughes to become President long before the following March. Wilson accepted the Colonel's plan, but without saying so to anyone.

Robert W. Wooley, in charge of publicity for the Democratic national committee, made widespread use of Glynn's convention cry: "He kept us out of the war!" The slogan was used in handbills and plastered on billboards across the land, much to the disgust of some Republicans. One of Wooley's assistants was George Creel, who later became a ghost-writer for Franklin D. Roosevelt. Creel said that one day Wilson stormed into Democratic headquarters, white-faced with anger.

"You are deliberately giving the impression," he observed acidly, "that my policy is one of unchangeable neutrality, no matter what arises! And yet, in speech after speech, I have made it plain that the day may come when we may be *forced* to fight." From a pocket the President pulled some papers, crying, "Here are excerpts that I insist upon having emphasized!"

Creel took one of the papers and read some words Wilson had spoken in the recent past: "We are not going to invade any nation's right, but suppose, my fellow countrymen, some nation should invade our right. What then? I have come here to tell you that the difficulties of our foreign policy . . . daily increase in number and intricacy and danger, and I would be derelict in my duty to you if I did not deal with you in these matters with the utmost candor, and tell you what it may be necessary to use the force of the United States to do."

In his memoirs Creel wrote, "Bob Wooley obeyed the injunction for a while, but when Mr. Wilson's attention seemed safely diverted to other things, 'He kept us out of the war' was resurrected as a slogan. How large a part it played in the election is a question, but Bob always insisted that the ballyhoo swung California."

Wilson said in private, "Any little German lieutenant can put us into the war at any time by a calculated outrage."

Vance McCormick, the Democratic campaign manager, urged Wilson to tour the nation to stump for reelection, but the President refused. "Don't worry, McCormick," Wilson said. "This is exactly what the people want. They want the President at a time like this to stay on the job. Let Hughes run around the country if he wishes to." And Wilson told Bernard Baruch, "I am inclined to follow the course suggested by a friend of mine who says that he has always followed the rule never to murder a man who is committing suicide slowly but surely."

Wilson made political speeches from the porch of his temporary home and then pleased party leaders by visiting Cincinnati, Indianapolis, Chicago, Detroit and Omaha. At the rally in Detroit he emphasized the fact that since 1914 America had "ceased to be a debtor nation and become a creditor nation." But this welcome news was offset by growing inflation. The President also made a quick trip to Pittsburgh, where a man tried to force himself into his limousine in what the secret service considered an assassination attempt. Pope Benedict XV sent Wilson congratulations on his escape from death.

Visitors to Shadow Lawn were screened at the gate by guards and at the front door by Edmund W. Starling of the secret service. One day a self-important political boss from New Jersey arrived, persuaded a guard to let him inside the estate, but was stopped by Starling. The boss demanded the agent take his card to the President. The diplomatic Starling led the boss back to the gate and then sent word to Wilson, who left the luncheon table and came to the front door. Staring at the card through his glasses, never lifting his eyes from it, heavily emphasizing each word, the President said, "I—will—not—see—the—son-of-a-bitch!"

George Creel's first assignment as a press agent for the Democrats was to visit Thomas Edison, for it had been reported the inventor was ready to endorse Wilson. The young man felt nervous about meeting the world-famous sixty-nine-year-old Edison, but went to his New Jersey plant and sat down with him. Although the white-haired scientist was deaf, he refused to wear a hearing aid. Creel put his lips to Edison's ear and asked a question in such a bellow that he startled himself. Edison laughed. "Never mind, son. I've got it all written out." From a pocket Edison pulled crumpled yellow paper with words written in pencil. In this public statement he explained his reasons for quitting the Republican party and ended with the comment "They say Wilson has blundered. Well, I reckon he has, but I notice he always blunders *forward.*"

Wilson donated $2,500 of his own money to the Democratic campaign fund—an amount so small that the campaign managers were worried. In the hope of getting more contributions, Campaign Manager McCormick and Navy Secretary Daniels invited Edison and Henry Ford to McCormick's suite in the Biltmore hotel in Manhattan. Edison and Ford were old friends and very rich. No alcoholic drinks were served. The four men ate at a table in the center of the room under a big chandelier with glass globes dangling from it. When they had finished the first course, Edison pointed and said, "Henry, I'll bet anything you want to bet that I can kick that globe off the chandelier!"

Ford grinned and said he would take the bet. The table was pushed aside. The sixty-nine-year-old Edison began limbering up his legs. Then he froze, fixed his eyes on a globe and suddenly flipped into a kick so high that he shattered it. Next the fifty-three-year-old Ford took up launch position, paused, let fly with his foot—but missed. When the four resumed their luncheon, Edison kept crowing to Ford, "You're a younger man than I am, but I can outkick you!"

Not until the ice cream came were McCormick and Daniels able to bring the two millionaires around to the subject of the needs of the Democratic party. Ford snorted, "All this campaign spending is the bunk! I wouldn't give a dollar to any campaign committee." Edison also refused to donate, pointing out that he had helped with his statement about Wilson blundering forward. Daniels, refusing to give up, argued that the greatest need was newspaper advertisements, which cost money, and ultimately Ford spent $58,800 for pro-Wilson advertisements in 500 newspapers.

When Wilson made his acceptance speech, he declared he wanted no support from any disloyal "hyphenates." And among other things he said, "I neither seek the favor nor fear the displeasure of that small alien element among us which puts loyalty to any foreign power before loyalty to the United States." This infuriated an already enraged Irishman named Jeremiah O'Leary, an Irish-American agitator and president of the American Truth Society. One of the most ardent pro-German propagandists in the East, he always urged Irishmen to stand up whenever "The Watch on the Rhine" was played by a band.

On September 11, 1916, Maine's state elections were carried by such heavy Republican majorities that GOP leaders boasted that "as goes Maine, so goes the nation." O'Leary used this turn of events to send an insulting telegram to the President, predicting his defeat in November and reviling him for "truckling to the British empire."

When Wilson received O'Leary's wire at Shadow Lawn, he called Tumulty in Asbury Park and told him to summon reporters to an afternoon news conference at the estate. When the correspondents arrived, the President gave them his reply to O'Leary: "I would feel deeply mortified to have you or anybody like you vote for me. Since you have access to many disloyal Americans, and I have not, I will ask you to convey this message to them."

This rebuke was masterful propaganda. One of Wilson's biographers said that it "made the front-page of every newspaper and thrilled the country." But it did not thrill William Randolph Hearst, whose New York *American* defended O'Leary as "an American citizen" and attacked Wilson's policies of "submitting to British aggression." This referred to the British search and seizure of American mail, together with other provocative acts plaguing the President.

While Wilson disassociated himself from any support faintly tinged with pro-German sentiment, his Republican rival, Hughes, received the endorsement of the National Council of Teutonic Sons of America. This enraged Theodore Roosevelt. Throughout his entire campaign Hughes was dogged by furious reactions to the approval given him by the "hyphenates"—the German-Americans and Irish-Americans. But Roosevelt's disgust with Hughes' judgment was less acute than his hatred for Wilson, so Teddy swallowed his bile and announced that he strongly endorsed Hughes. Roosevelt also told his Bull Moose followers "not to sulk because our leadership is rejected," and before long what was left of the Progressive party formally endorsed Hughes.

Roosevelt was almost paranoid in his fury at Wilson, screaming at an audience that the President was "kissing the bloodstained hand that slapped his face!" Barnstorming the West in support of Hughes, Teddy kept talking about Wilson, Wilson, Wilson, and what a bad man he was, forgetting to say much about Hughes, the man whose cause he supposedly supported. Wilson, in turn, took some verbal jabs at Roosevelt, with Hughes almost finding himself shunted to the sideline.

At an appearance at Cooper Union in Manhattan, Roosevelt was so overcome by frenzy that toward the end of his talk he threw away his prepared manuscript and shrilled:

> There should be shadows now at Shadow Lawn—the shadows of the men, women and children who have risen from the ooze of the ocean bottom and from graves in foreign lands—the shadows of the helpless whom Mr. Wilson did not dare protect lest he might have to face the danger! The shadows of babies gasping pitifully as they sank under the waves! The shadows of women outraged and slain by bandits! . . Those are the shadows proper for Shadow Lawn—the shadows of deeds that were never done, the shadows of lofty words that were followed by no action, the shadows of the tortured dead!

While Roosevelt antagonized German-Americans and Irish-Americans, Hughes vacillated. Although the Republican candidate had said he too was against "hyphenates," he received further endorsements from the German-American Alliance, the Northeastern Saengerbund and other "hyphenated" groups. Repeated efforts were made to draw Hughes out on the German issue. If he were elected by German votes, would his administration feel beholden to German interests? Hughes responded with generalities about "firmness," "America first," "full guarantee of American rights" and "no divided allegiances." Aware that the election would be close, he did not care to offend the "hyphenates." Their bloc of votes was part of the equation for victory he had worked out. In private Roosevelt complained that the GOP strategists had plans based on "some more or less secret understanding with the German vote."

On October 18 the Hughes campaign erupted in crisis. The Chicago *Journal* said that German Lutheran ministers from all parts of the country had met secretly in Chicago, had received certain pledges from Hughes and then decided to support him. Harold Ickes, a Progressive now supporting Hughes, said in his autobiography, "I have always suspected that this strictly undercover assembly was without the knowledge or consent of the candidate." Ickes added, "The party was playing with dynamite, but the [GOP] high command wanted the German vote for Hughes."

The crisis doubled on October 23, when the New York *Times* published a sensational charge by the Democratic national committee that Hughes had met secretly with German-American and Irish-American groups and made "a campaign deal" with them. According to Democratic leaders, about the middle of September Hughes had conferred with five men representing the American Independence Conference—and one of the five was Jeremiah O'Leary—the same O'Leary who had sent Wilson the insulting telegram. Furthermore, said the Democrats, this alleged meeting occurred *after* O'Leary had libeled the President, *after* Wilson had struck back.

William R. Willcox, the GOP campaign chairman, denied the Republicans had made a secret compact with the Germans, but Hughes admitted that he had met with the five-man committee, and that O'Leary had been present, but declared he had not known who O'Leary was. This probably was true, for Hughes was an honorable man. He went on to state, "I have said nothing in private that I have not said in public."

What Hughes said in public on the campaign trail was hardly exciting, for he had a frosty personality, felt uncomfortable with strangers, had no feel for politics, and was unable to sink his teeth into a meaty issue. Aware of his iceberg reputation, he did his burlesque best to get close to everyone he met. In Reno he attended a barbecue and rodeo and mingled with cowboys. In Detroit he jumped on top of the players' dugout to shake hands with the ballplayers and chat with Ty Cobb. In Butte he struggled into miner's clothing and descended 10,000 feet into a copper mine. At times when his special train pulled into some town, he heard people knocking on the door of his car as early as 5 A.M. and yelling, "Charlie, come out! Come out, or we won't vote for you!"

Since he refused to use a ghost-writer and since he lacked the time to dictate speeches, he hired stenographers to record each speech as he delivered it, had copies given to reporters and received good local press coverage. But the big Eastern newspapers, lacking advance copies, gave scant space to his speeches elsewhere in the country. Whenever he spoke, his wife sat behind him and would pull his coattail when she felt he had talked long enough. A tall woman who dressed in excellent taste, Mrs. Hughes became accustomed to having her husband wave his hand in her direction and exclaim, "Gentlemen—the greatest asset of the Republican party!" On September 22 after giving thirteen speeches in rapid succession, he lost his voice.

Hughes erred in failing to make simple statements about what he intended to do were he to be elected. Walter Lippmann wrote, "The human interest of this campaign is to find out why a man of rare courage and frankness should be wandering around the country trailing nothing but cold and damp platitudes." Another critic commented, "He makes a fine solemn appearance, but the Democratic papers should immediately call on him to unmask physically and intellectually, shave his beard and expose his thoughts and his face."

Hughes fought a clean fight, but the same cannot be said of some other Republicans or anti-Wilson individuals and organizations. The *Irish World* depicted Wilson almost as an antichrist. In Indiana a German Catholic priest slandered the President from the pulpit. There were rumors Wilson had insulted a cardinal, an archbishop and a papal legate. Tumulty, an Irish Catholic, countered by distributing a list of Catholics Wilson had appointed to office. Democrats complained to the Pennsylvania railroad for printing Hughes' campaign speeches on the menus used in its dining cars. In Chicago some people telephoned one another to gossip about Wilson's friend Mrs. Peck, implying he had been her lover. At a dinner party, a reporter who liked the President told a man, "If you can furnish proof of the statement you have just made, sir, surely you are wasting your time to make it here. Mr. William Randolph Hearst and a half dozen other people would gladly pay you twenty-five thousand dollars for proof of the charge you have just preferred."

After it was all over, Wilson lamented to a friend that "the campaign was indeed one of the most virulent and bitter and, I believe, one of the most unfair on the part of the Republican opposition that the country has ever seen, but I think that very circumstance worked to my advantage."

The worst mistake of the campaign was made not by Hughes but by some Republicans in California. The governor of California was Hiram Johnson. Reactionaries called Johnson a liberal, liberals called him a reactionary, and he called himself "a rotten politician." He was wrong in his opinion of himself, for he became one of the greatest vote getters in his state. In the fall of 1916 Johnson was running in the primaries for nomination as the Republican candidate for the United States Senate. When Hughes took his campaign to California, the reactionary Republicans opposing Johnson contrived to keep the governor away from the GOP standard-bearer. This antagonized the powerful Johnson, who won election to the Senate, and helped lose the state to Hughes.

Wilson was scheduled to end his campaign with a rally in Madison Square Garden in Manhattan on November 2, 1916. Although Colonel House was privately conceding New York state and most of the eastern seaboard to the Republicans, he wanted Wilson to make one last great appeal for votes there. New York City was ruled by Tammany boss Charles Murphy, and while Tammany was part of the Democratic party, it disliked Wilson because he gave it no patronage, because he was too progressive to suit Murphy and because it felt Wilson had done nothing to help the Irish rebels in Ireland. Bernard Baruch had offered to donate $50,000 to the state campaign through Murphy, but the boss refused, saying, "I won't take your money because Wilson can't carry the state."

Wilson felt as chilly toward Tammany as Tammany felt toward him. He was in a raw mood when the Presidential yacht docked at Twenty-third Street on the East river in Manhattan. Vance McCormick and Colonel House went aboard for a ninety-minute talk which House later called "the most acrimonious debate I have had with him for a long time." Wilson resented the way his campaign had gone in New York. He was angered by the huge sums of money the Republicans had spent for full-page advertisements in the morning papers that day. He also was furious because the New York papers gave far more news space to the GOP campaign than to his. To the surprise of his advisers he barked that New York was "rotten to the core" and should be wiped off the map. When the Colonel protested that the President had as many friends in the city as elsewhere in the nation, although these friends were not in the money class, Wilson sneered that House and McCormick had "New Yorkitis." He said he was sure he could win the election without any help from the city or state.

Madison Square Garden then occupied a block bounded by Twenty-sixth and Twenty-seventh streets, Madison and Fourth avenues, and early in the evening of November 2 the building was surrounded by a crowd eager to attend the final rally for Wilson. The people were packed so solidly outside that hundreds of cops were necessary to enable the President to push his way to the main entrance. But it was blocked, so Wilson and his wife were led around to the rear and helped up a fire escape and into the hall. A parade to the Garden had been headed by Sheriff Al Smith, who in 1928 was to become the Democratic Presidential candidate. Despite the trouble Wilson had getting inside, the rally went off with perfect timing, the President appearing on the speakers' platform the very second former Governor Glynn finished introducing him. Then the thousands of spectators began cheering and kept on cheering a half hour before the surprised and delighted Wilson could cut a hole in the noise and begin speaking.

On election day, Tuesday, November 7, 1916, the weather was clear across most of the country, and nearly 18,500,000 citizens went to the polls to vote in the thirty-third Presidential election.

That morning Wilson and his wife awakened early at Shadow Lawn, ate a hasty breakfast, then drove to Princeton so he could vote. Mrs. Wilson was unable to cast a ballot because New Jersey had not yet granted suffrage to women. She remained in the Presidential limousine, while he pushed his way through good-natured townspeople and students to enter an old engine house used as a polling place. When he emerged, he was cheered again. By eleven o'clock they were back in their summer home.

A telegraph company had offered to install a special wire to speed election returns to the President, but he had declined with the explanation that he would keep in touch with events through his executive office in nearby Asbury Park.

That afternoon Wilson sat at a desk at Shadow Lawn, talking from time to time on the telephone with Tumulty, and keeping tally on a sheet of paper. As the ladies of his household passed one another, they exchanged admiring whispers about the President's composure. Wishing to break the hushed strain, Mrs. Wilson and some others decided to play Twenty Questions, but Dr. Grayson nervously said he thought he would run into Asbury Park to find out what was happening. Early in the afternoon the first return came from a small fishing village in Massachusetts and showed a slight gain over the size of the vote Wilson got there in 1912. About 4 P.M. returns arrived from Kansas, and these were favorable to the President. In fact, the first trickle of returns seemed to indicate Wilson would win reelection.

But by 7 P.M. he learned he had lost New York, despite the boisterous rally, and in the next two hours he also lost Massachusetts, Connecticut, New Jersey, Illinois, Wisconsin, Indiana and looked as if he were losing Ohio. All were big states with many electoral votes. About 8:30 P.M. Tumulty sat in his office in Asbury Park overlooking the Atlantic when he was told someone was calling from Manhattan with an important message. Tumulty took the call. A man's voice said he did not wish to identify himself, but he was a friend of the Democratic cause. At first Tumulty considered the caller a crank, but he began to listen carefully when the man said, "I shall keep you advised of what is happening in the Republican headquarters. I can only tell you that I will *know* what is happening, and you may rely upon the information I give you."

Republican headquarters was in the Astor hotel on Manhattan's Times Square, and Hughes had taken a suite there for himself and his family. That morning Hughes had awakened early and gone to vote in a small laundry on Eighth Avenue with reporters and photographers following in his wake. Handed ballot number 13, Hughes smiled and said, "This is a lucky omen." At noon he attended a luncheon at the Harvard Club in honor of his campaign manager, William E. Willcox, and although Hughes was genial, some GOP leaders grumbled that Willcox had mishandled the campaign.

In the afternoon Hughes and his wife drove through Central Park, and when they returned to the Astor, he took a nap. His campaign oratory had left him as hoarse as a crow. In early evening, when it was learned Wilson had lost many big states, the Republicans in the hotel began a premature victory celebration, drinking and carousing. Since it looked as though Hughes might become the new President, a secret service agent quietly began guarding the door to his suite.

About 9:30 P.M. in Asbury Park, Tumulty was staring glumly at the ocean when he heard an uproar in the corridor outside his office. The door burst open, and in tumbled White House correspondents. They were led by a reporter for the New York *World* who waved a bulletin announcing that the *World* had conceded Wilson's defeat. This hurt. The *World* was so pro-Wilson that it was regarded as an organ of his administration. The reporters demanded a comment from Tumulty. Masking his panic, the Presidential secretary said, "Wilson will win. The West has not yet been heard from. Sufficient gains will be made in the West and along the Pacific slope to offset the losses in the East."

As the correspondents ran out, the phone rang. Wilson was calling from Shadow Lawn, and he had just heard the news about the *World* from Dr. Grayson. The President laughed. "Well, Tumulty, it begins to look as if we have been badly licked." Tumulty protested, arguing that there were Democratic drifts elsewhere in the country, declaring it was too early to concede anything. Wilson chuckled. "Tumulty, you are an optimist! It begins to look as if the defeat might be overwhelming. The only thing I am sorry for—and that cuts me to the quick!—is that people apparently misunderstood me. But I have no regrets. We have tried to do our duty."

About 10 P.M. the phone rang in Wilson's summer home. His daughter Margaret answered. A tactless friend was calling from New York to console her about "your father's defeat." Margaret sputtered, "Why, he's *not* defeated! What are you talking about?" The caller said, "The flashlight from the New York *Times* building—white for Wilson, red for Hughes—has already flashed red, conceding the election to the Republicans." Margaret snapped, "Impossible! They can't know yet! In the West they're still at the polls!"

When Margaret reported the conversation to Mrs. Wilson, the President's wife felt, as she wrote in her memoirs, "All along I had felt in my bones that the Opposition was too rich and too strong for us." She may have absorbed this attitude from Colonel House, who had said, "It is true that we have organized wealth against us, and in such aggregate as never before."

The Republicans spent $2,445,421 on the campaign, the Democrats $1,808,348.

Dr. Grayson tried to console Wilson by predicting he could make a comeback such as Grover Cleveland had done. By way of reply, Wilson told one of his favorite stories: After Appomattox a Confederate veteran limped home, his arm in a sling, to find his house and barn had been burned, his fences ruined, his stock driven away, his family scattered. Staring glassy-eyed, the soldier said, "I'm glad I fought, but I'm damned if I'll ever love another country!"

Wilson was glad he had arranged to turn the government over to Hughes as soon as possible after a Hughes victory. He had spelled out his plan in a letter, sealed the envelope with wax and on the envelope he had written "Most Confidential," underlining the words. He had given the letter to Colonel House, who gave it to Frank Polk, one of House's cronies and the counselor of the state department. Polk had this vital letter in his pocket when he went to Democratic headquarters in the Biltmore hotel in Manhattan, and there he gave it to Secretary of State Robert Lansing. Shortly after 10 P.M. Wilson went to bed believing he had been defeated. He slept soundly.

Long before election day the Democrats had planned a victory celebration in the Biltmore. The host was Henry Morgenthau, Sr., a financier and real estate promoter who had almost adored Wilson since a day, years before, when one of Wilson's speeches had made him weep. Colonel House had declined to attend the banquet, and now he had something important to do.

At about the time Wilson fell asleep in New Jersey the Colonel left his apartment at 115 East Fifty-third Street in Manhattan in the company of Thomas W. Gregory, the U.S. attorney general. From reporters and other sources the Colonel had heard that Wilson seemed to be losing the election. He and Gregory walked to a bar association library to look up points of law about the resignation of the President, the plan that House had suggested to Wilson. They discovered it would be necessary for Wilson to convene the Senate to confirm Hughes as secretary of state, and only after that would Hughes become eligible to assume the Presidency prior to the regular inauguration day of March 4.

In the Biltmore the Democrats were holding more a wake than a banquet. Almost every new return showed Hughes leading Wilson. Vance McCormick, the Democratic campaign leader, seemed to have aged in hours; one observer said he had turned a greenish yellow. The politicians slouched around with their jackets off and their shirts rumpled, drinking to erase the pain of defeat. Among the dejected men was Franklin D. Roosevelt, and when he left to take a sleeper back to Washington, he was convinced Wilson had lost. Morgenthau later told House "there never was such a morgue-like entertainment in the annals of time."

Starling, the secret service agent, visited the GOP headquarters in the Astor and found "the place was a bedlam—everyone was celebrating victory." Another Republican celebration was under way in the Metropolitan club, known as the Millionaires' Club, at the northeast corner of Sixtieth Street and Fifth Avenue. Rich men were whooping it up at having defeated Wilson, pausing long enough to issue this statement: "It is a great constructive victory . . . a national triumph. . . . America may again hold her head up among the nations of the world. . . ." Out on Long Island Theodore Roosevelt expressed "my profound gratitude as an American proud of his country that the American people have repudiated the man who coined the phrase about this country that it is 'Too proud to fight.' "

When Charles Evans Hughes awakened from his nap in the Astor, he found darkness had fallen. He walked to a window and gazed down on Times Square. Hundreds of thousands of people swarmed over sidewalks and streets, chanting, "Hughes! Hughes! Hughes!" His wife led their three daughters to the window so they might bask in the greatest moment in the history of the family. Two brass bands disturbed the night air. Searchlights made passes at an enormous flag roped across the façade of the hotel, while on the roof a big electric sign spelled out HUGHES. Skyrockets rainbowed into the sky. In Times Square Hughes saw a permanent commercial electric sign saying U.S. TIRES, and he joked, "Perhaps they will complete that tomorrow by adding—'of Wilson.'"

The Hughes family sat down to a late supper in their suite. In New York the betting was running 10 to 7 in his favor. Further election returns suggested the Republicans would carry every state outside the solidly Democratic South. Now New York papers other than the *World* were declaring that Hughes had won. Told that reporters were begging for a statement, Hughes said, "Wait till the Democrats concede my election. The newspapers might take it back." Influential Republicans swept into the suite to urge him to step out onto the balcony to accept the acclaim of the thousands below, but he said, "If I have been elected President, it is because the people of this country think that I'll keep my shirt on in an emergency. I'll start right now by not yielding to this demand, when I am not positive that I have been elected." At 1:30 A.M. Hughes went to sleep again.

About 3 A.M. Wednesday, November 8, Herbert Bayard Swope arrived at the damp Democratic party in the Biltmore. The first journalist to win a Pulitzer Prize, the redheaded, electric and articulate Swope was city editor of the *World*, and with so much happening he had been unable to stay at his desk. He bounded into a sanctum occupied by five of the party's biggest names—McCormick, chairman of the national committee; Thomas L. Chadbourne, a corporation lawyer; Treasury Secretary McAdoo; Henry Morgenthau; and Bernard Baruch. They were tired and glum, and the floor was strewn with papers.

Swope shouted, "You fellows are a lot of damn quitters!" Then, chattering like a machine gun, he said California was the key to the election, and if they let California Democrats believe Wilson had lost, the professional politicians on the Pacific coast would begin trading off what votes they had to the Republicans. There also was the danger that the Republicans might try to steal the election in California. Baruch agreed. His brother had told him a telegraph operator at GOP headquarters had said returns from some Western states were being held up by Republicans because they were favorable to Wilson.

There also was a rumor of a Wall Street plot to pull off a coup that would give the election to Hughes. Swope snarled at the politicians to get off their asses and on the phone to California to tell the leaders out there to hold the line. Swope revived McCormick, who began placing long-distance calls with never-say-die orders. *Watch out*, McCormick warned, *for skulduggery*. One Californian replied that if anyone came near his headquarters with any fancy ideas, he had better bring his coffin with him.

Meredith Snyder, the reform Democratic mayor of Los Angeles, later told Josephus Daniels:

> I did not close my eyes all night until the result of the election was declared. Shortly after the polls closed I ordered that every ballot box be sealed, and I stationed policemen in every booth with orders to shoot any man who should lay the weight of his

> hands on the ballot box. We kept vigilant watch, and a staunch Democrat was assigned as watcher in every booth. Nothing was left undone to see that there was no tampering. I knew that the fate of the Presidency in the next four years would be settled in those boxes, and I staked my life that the votes would be counted as cast.

At 5 A.M. Wednesday Colonel House awakened in his Manhattan apartment and reached for the phone by his bed. Reporters told him the far West was going Democratic. House then called Democratic headquarters in the Biltmore to urge that telegrams be sent to county chairmen in every doubtful state, warning them to remain alert and pay no attention to reports that Hughes had been elected.

Swope had left the Biltmore and returned to the *World*, where he persuaded other editors to hedge the banner in the paper's next edition by ending it with a question mark. So the *World*'s next edition asked: HUGHES ELECTED IN CLOSE CONTEST?

At 4 A.M. Wilson's daughter knocked at her stepmother's bedroom door and awakened her. Margaret had just talked with McCormick at headquarters in Manhattan, and he told her better news was coming in and he had not given up hope. Margaret asked, "Shall we wake Father and tell him?" Mrs. Wilson said, "Oh, no! Do let him sleep."

An hour later Wilson awakened believing he had lost the election. He walked into his bathroom and began shaving. Margaret knocked on the door and shouted that the New York *Times* had come out with an extra saying that now the election was in doubt. Thinking his daughter was joking, Wilson laughed. "Tell that to the marines!"

By daybreak Tumulty was awake in his Asbury Park office. From Democratic headquarters he heard much the same news McCormick had reported to Margaret. With more and more returns coming in from the Midwest and West, there now was a trend for Wilson. Ohio had not been captured by Hughes but actually had gone for Wilson by a majority of 60,000 votes. Wilson also took Kansas, Utah was leaning toward him, while North and South Dakota were switching to the Democrats. From this time forward, state after Western state fell into the Democratic column.

About 8 A.M. Hughes awakened in the Astor and saw newspapers published before the trend had begun to shift. In one editorial after another he was hailed as the new President. Soon, though, Hughes was shown bulletins telling a different story.

This was one of the most confused Presidential races ever held in the United States. Franklin D. Roosevelt, back home in Washington, told his wife that this Wednesday, November 8, was "the most extraordinary day of my life." Not since 1888 when Republican Benjamin Harrison and Democratic Grover Cleveland battled it out at the polls had there been any American election so close and uncertain. Former President Taft wrote a friend, "The fate of the nation is trembling in the balance."

About 1 P.M. the mysterious stranger called Tumulty again, and said,

"George Perkins is now at Republican headquarters and is telephoning Roosevelt and will soon leave to inform Roosevelt that, to use his own words, 'the jig is up,' and that Wilson is elected." Moments later the puzzled Tumulty read a statement issued to the press at GOP headquarters: "George Perkins is on his way to confer with Mr. Roosevelt." Months later the anonymous caller visited Tumulty at the White House, and although he would not identify himself, he explained that he had wiretapped Republican headquarters in the Astor.

A few days after the election Franklin D. Roosevelt twitted Theodore Roosevelt, telling an audience that "a certain distinguished cousin of mine is now engaged in revising an edition of his most noted historical work, *The Winning of the West.*"

Wednesday afternoon Mr. and Mrs. Wilson and Dr. Grayson drove from Shadow Lawn to Spring Lake to play golf. Someone asked, "How is your game today, Mr. President?" Wilson smiled, waved and replied that Grayson had him three down, but he didn't mind since he was four states up over yesterday's returns. At the eighth hole he was told that California seemed to be going for him and he was likely to be reelected.

Wilson's middle daughter, Jessie, married to Francis B. Sayre, had just given birth to a daughter in Williamstown, Massachusetts, and wanted the President to attend the christening as the child's godfather, so late in the afternoon he and the ladies in his family motored to Sandy Hook to board the Presidential yacht. Margaret retired to her cabin about 9:30 P.M., but the others strolled the deck until the lights of Manhattan came into view. The vessel touched land to put ashore a Chinese cook who was ill and also to get the latest election returns from a waiting messenger. Wilson went into the smoking salon to read under a lamp. While it was true the Democrats were gaining in the West, the outcome of the election remained in doubt.

On Thursday, November 9, Republican leaders met in the Astor in a conference from which they excluded Willcox, their campaign manager, because of his inept handling of the Hughes campaign. The New York *Herald* said Hughes had been "handicapped by bungling campaign management from the start." In the national capital Franklin Roosevelt wrote his wife, "If Wilson is elected, I shall wire as follows: 'The Republican party has proved to its own satisfaction, I hope, that the American people cannot always be bought.' I hope to God I don't grow reactionary with advancing age."

Thursday evening Justice and Mrs. Hughes saw a Broadway show called *Nothing But the Truth;* it starred William Collier. At one point in the plot the star's stage sweetheart gave him some money to invest, asking, "Is it absolutely safe?" Collier paused, glanced at Hughes in the orchestra, then ad-libbed, "I can't tell until I hear from California." Hughes joined in the laughter.

About 5:30 A.M. Friday, November 10, secret service agent Starling awakened aboard the Presidential yacht and walked to the galley for coffee. There he met Arthur Brooks, the President's black valet. Brooks grinned and waved a telegram and cried, "Safe at last! The boss has won for certain!"

"Does he know?"

Brooks shook his head no.

Starling said uneasily, "You know what would happen if I woke him up to tell him? I'd be fired! Nothing is so important that it can't wait until breakfast, he thinks."

The valet and the agent almost worshiped Wilson. There in the galley of the yacht in the dimness before dawn that November 10, Starling nursed his mug of coffee in his hands and mused that Wilson "stood for something bigger than me, bigger than himself, bigger than America. He stood for the hope of the world." Then, raising his eyes to the valet, the agent murmured, "It was a funny election. The Republicans celebrated and the Democrats won."

The British ambassador wrote his foreign office that "the elections have clearly shown that the great mass of the Americans desire nothing so much as to keep out of the war."

PART III

The Edge of the Storm

Chapter 22

THE ZIMMERMANN TELEGRAM

London had a mysterious room known only to the elect and guardedly called Room 40. It was hidden headquarters of the cryptographic section of British naval intelligence, and it was here that men worked at breaking German codes. This undercover work was directed by Sir Reginald Hall, perhaps the most astute intelligence officer produced by World War I. Since the British do not scorn amateurs so much as is the habit of Americans, among the professionals in Room 40 were two gifted amateur cryptographers, one a publisher, the other a Presbyterian pastor. They were asked to decipher a coded message which British agents had intercepted, and in one of the most spectacular coups of its kind they broke the German diplomatic code. When they handed their translation to Admiral Hall, he may have felt his heart beat faster, for he realized that the message could change the course of the war.

The telegram was from German Foreign Secretary Arthur Zimmermann in Berlin to Von Eckhardt, the German minister to Mexico and stationed in Mexico City:

BERLIN, JANUARY 19, 1917

ON THE FIRST OF FEBRUARY WE INTEND TO BEGIN SUBMARINE WARFARE UNRESTRICTED. IN SPITE OF THIS IT IS OUR INTENTION TO KEEP NEUTRAL THE UNITED STATES OF AMERICA. IF THIS ATTEMPT IS NOT SUCCESSFUL WE PROPOSE AN ALLIANCE ON THE FOLLOWING TERMS WITH MEXICO: THAT WE SHALL MAKE WAR TOGETHER AND TOGETHER MAKE PEACE. WE SHALL GIVE GENEROUS FINANCIAL SUPPORT, AND IT IS UNDERSTOOD THAT MEXICO IS TO RECONQUER THE LOST TERRITORY IN NEW MEXICO, TEXAS, AND ARIZONA. THE DETAILS ARE LEFT FOR YOUR SETTLEMENT. YOU ARE INSTRUCTED TO INFORM THE PRESIDENT OF MEXICO OF THE ABOVE IN THE GREATEST CONFIDENCE AS SOON AS IT IS CERTAIN THERE WILL BE AN OUTBREAK OF WAR WITH THE UNITED STATES, AND WE SUGGEST THAT THE PRESIDENT OF MEXICO ON HIS OWN INITIATIVE SHOULD COMMUNICATE WITH JAPAN SUGGESTING ADHERENCE AT ONCE TO THIS PLAN; AT THE SAME TIME OFFER TO MEDIATE BETWEEN GERMANY AND JAPAN. PLEASE CALL TO THE ATTENTION OF THE

PRESIDENT OF MEXICO THAT THE EMPLOYMENT OF RUTHLESS SUBMARINE WARFARE NOW PROMISES TO COMPEL ENGLAND TO MAKE PEACE IN A FEW MONTHS.

ZIMMERMANN

The Zimmermann wire left Admiral Hall conflicted. He thought it should be publicized because it might provoke the Americans and perhaps bring them into the war on the British side, but at the same time he did not want to let the Germans know his men had broken their diplomatic code. Furthermore, the flamboyant admiral considered British Foreign Secretary Arthur J. Balfour too timid for his taste. But duty is duty, so Hall gave the Zimmermann telegram to Balfour and for nearly a month, as Hall had feared, Balfour did nothing.

Taking matters into his own hands, Hall leaked the news to Edward Bell of the American embassy in London. Bell was horrified. Germany was about to resume unrestricted submarine warfare? Coax Mexico into attacking the United States? Turn Japan against America? These possibilities were so disturbing that Bell wondered whether the intercepted telegram was genuine or merely a German hoax. Hall convinced Bell it was genuine. Hall urged Bell to tell Walter Hines Page, the American ambassador to Great Britain, but not to let the British foreign office know he had tipped off the Americans.

On February 24, 1917, after a long and suspenseful wait, Balfour finally and formally gave Page a copy of the Zimmermann telegram. Balfour lied to Page, saying it had just been received. At eight thirty that evening the state department in Washington received a cable from Page reporting the contents of the telegram, and Secretary of State Robert Lansing hurried to the White House to show it to Wilson. When the President heard the news, he exclaimed, "Good Lord!" and his face went gray. Then he wondered whether the telegram was a forgery, but when he was convinced that it was real, he looked up and said, "This means war."

Frank Polk, counselor to the state department, telephoned Colonel House to break the news and to ask him to use his influence with Wilson to make the telegram public. Polk knew that if Americans learned of Germany's scheme they would react angrily and thus strengthen any action Wilson might take against Germany in defense of American rights on the sea. Agreeing with Polk, House wrote Wilson urging him to have the dispatch publicized. The President agonized over this decision, but at last he acquiesced with the sad realization that the telegram might incite national resentment beyond the danger point.

The Zimmermann telegram had been flashed from Berlin to Washington, where German Ambassador Von Bernstorff had relayed it to his colleague in Mexico City. In doing this, Bernstorff had used American diplomatic cable facilities, for Wilson had previously granted the ambassador the use of cable facilities to promote peace. Bernstorff's perfidy angered the President.

Since the British did not want the Germans to learn they had broken their code, Balfour had asked Page to ask Wilson to declare it was the Americans who had intercepted and deciphered the telegram. At the state department a search was made for a copy of the coded telegram, and when it was found, it was wired to the American embassy in London. Admiral Hall sent a cryptographer to the embassy to decipher the telegram in the presence of a representative of the U.S. embassy staff, thus verifying its true contents. Then the American was shown how to break the code and deciphered it himself. This farce enabled the Americans to say with a pale semblance of truth that they had broken the code.

Wilson had decided to publicize the wire—but how could he do so without making it seem like an Anglo-American ploy to get the United States into the war? Secretary Lansing was opposed to issuing an official news release lest it appear the Wilson administration was using the German telegram to pressure stubborn Congressmen fighting an administration bill to arm American merchant ships against U-boat attacks.

At 6 P.M. on February 28 Lansing telephoned Edwin M. Hood of the Washington bureau of the Associated Press. Hood was a veteran correspondent of such renown that in the early days of the McKinley administration he had been offered the post of assistant secretary of the navy; now he covered the state department on a daily basis. Lansing asked Hood to come to his home that evening.

The moment the AP man arrived, and even before the two exchanged greetings, Lansing pledged him to secrecy. Then they sat down, and Lansing told Hood he was about to get one of the most amazing stories of his career—but only under certain conditions: He could not disclose the story's source. No administration official could be quoted. It might even be necessary for the state department to deny knowledge of the story after its publication. Would Hood agree to these conditions? Yes. Lansing then told him about the Zimmermann telegram.

Hood was so startled that he hesitated. This explosive story was sure to touch off repercussions, and it was contrary to the Associated Press practice to put on its wires any story that did not identify its source. But after long thought, Hood said, "I think we can use it."

Hood left Lansing's home and telephoned the house of the AP's bureau chief, Jackson S. Elliott. After Elliott heard the story, he pondered the responsibilities the AP would assume and then told Hood, "Go ahead! I'll be right down." Hood next called Lional C. Probert, the AP news editor, told him what was happening and said Lansing had promised to have the text of the telegram ready in a sealed envelope to be picked up by a messenger. Hood warned Probert that if anyone learned of his connection, it then would be correctly assumed it had been leaked to him by the state department; therefore, to live up to his agreement with Lansing, Hood asked that the story be handled by someone else in the office.

The bureau was busy that evening of February 28 because Senators and Representatives were ramming bills through their respective houses before the expiration of the second session of the sixty-fourth Congress on March 3, the day before Wilson's second inauguration. All the veteran AP men were tied up with this legislation. Looking around his office,

Probert saw twenty-eight-year-old Stephen T. Early. In 1913 Early had joined the AP, now his regular beat was the war and navy departments, and he had come to know Franklin Roosevelt, who in time to come would make Early his press secretary. Probert called Early to his desk and said, "You're to go to Secretary Lansing's home on Eighteenth Street and bring back whatever Lansing gives you. Then you're to forget you ever saw the secretary tonight. That's all! No questions."

The puzzled young reporter ran to Lansing's red brick house. A servant ushered him into a reception room, and Lansing walked down the stairs clad in a long dressing gown. Reaching into a pocket, the secretary brought out a big envelope and handed it to Early. The envelope was unmarked. Taking it from Lansing, Early ran back to the office.

Probert grabbed the envelope. As Early returned to his desk to watch and wonder, Probert disappeared within an inner office with David Lawrence and Bryan Price and the night editor, Horace Eppes. They decided to keep the story off the wires until very late so other correspondents would be unable to check its origin with government officials. This delay also gave the shirt-sleeved cigar-puffing Probert time to think through the style of the story he had decided to write himself. Typing with one finger, he wrote more than two columns of copy.

The AP teletype machines had alerted member newspapers to be ready to receive a very important story. At about midnight Probert walked back into the news room and gave his copy to a man at a machine. The story began this way: "By the Associated Press . . . Washington, D.C., Feb. 28—The Associated Press is enabled to reveal that Germany, in planning unrestricted submarine warfare and counting its consequences, proposed an alliance with Mexico and Japan to make war on the United States, if this country should not remain neutral. . . ." The story included the full text of the Zimmermann telegram.

This was the first time in the history of the Associated Press that its member newspapers had been asked to accept an explosive story on no authority but that of the AP itself. From newspapers all over the nation came inquiries on the story's origin, but the AP refused to disclose its source. Rival correspondents called the story a fraud.

The next morning Lansing held a news conference in his office in the state department building. Huge and handsome and impressive, the secretary of state was renowned for his courtesy and tact. After Stephen Early had received the envelope from him the previous evening, Lansing received a call from Elliott, the AP bureau chief, who had told him the AP would transmit the story if Lansing later answered three questions to be put to him by an AP man. Lansing had hesitated until he heard Elliott's three questions and proposed answers.

Now, with the press conference under way, a hundred reporters shouted questions at the secretary of state, who parried all of them. The frustrated and furious correspondents agreed among themselves that the Associated Press had made a colossal mistake. Then the AP reporter stepped forward, and he and Lansing went through the ritual agreed on.

"Mr. Secretary, did you know that the Associated Press had this story last night?"

"Yes."

"Did you deny its authenticity?"

"No."

"Did you object to the Associated Press carrying the story?"

"No."

Lansing disappeared behind the draperies covering the door to his private office. End of press conference

When Americans heard the news, at first they were dumbfounded and then they were infuriated. Germany scheming to help Mexico and Japan make war on the United States? Outrageous! When reporters reached Theodore Roosevelt at his home on Long Island and told him about the Zimmermann telegram, Teddy reacted with a stream of profanity directed against Wilson. Then, recovering his poise, he flashed his famous grin and said, "Boys, I'm sorry, but you have now heard some of the more or less—mostly less—justly famed Roosevelt profanity. . . . I don't want to apologize for it. This man is enough to make the saints and the angels—yes, and the apostles—swear, and I would not blame them. My God! Why doesn't he do something? It's beyond me!"

The Zimmermann note radicalized the West and Southwest, where most Americans were pacifists because they thought war would never touch them. Now the people in that part of the country read with apprehension that an estimated 100,000 Germans were in Mexico, that they had bought wireless stations on the West coast, that more than 700 Germans had obtained passports from the Mexican consulate in New York City for emigration to Mexico.

The New York *Times* and other papers published reports that there was a 6,000-man army in Mexico ready to attack the United States. The rumors spread in widening circles; newspaper readers read that Germany was intriguing with many nations in Central and South America, that a German submarine had reached Peru in the hold of a ship, buried under coal.

Americans shuddered at visions of a German army suddenly falling on the Southwest, of trained German reservists springing into action in the heart of the country, of bombs hidden under every bridge, of every tennis court concealing a gun emplacement for German artillery.

On March 10, 1917, Navy Secretary Daniels was out of town, so Franklin Roosevelt was acting secretary. He went to the White House and said, "President Wilson, may I request your permission to bring the fleet back from Guantanamo, to send it to the navy yards to have it cleaned and fitted out for war and be ready to take part in the war if we get in?"

Wilson said, "I am very sorry, Mr. Roosevelt. I cannot allow it."

Roosevelt pleaded, but the President refused, saying of the fleet, "No, I do not wish it brought north."

The disappointed Roosevelt said a bit curtly, "Aye, aye, sir!" And started to leave.

Wilson said, "Come back!"

When Roosevelt returned to Wilson's desk, the President said, "I am going to tell you something I cannot tell the public. I owe you an explanation. I don't want to do anything. I do not want the United States to do anything in a military way, by way of war preparations, that would allow the definitive historian in later days to say that the United States had committed an unfriendly act against the Central Powers."

"The definitive historian of the future?" Roosevelt asked.

"Yes," Wilson replied. "Probably he won't write until about the year 1990 and when he writes the history of this World War, he may be a German, he may be a Russian, he may be a Bulgarian—we cannot tell—but I do not want to do anything that would lead him to misjudge our American attitude sixty or seventy years from now."

Chapter 23

THE UNITED STATES GOES TO WAR

Woodrow Wilson sat in his study in the White House awaiting the arrival of Frank Cobb. The President had made a great decision, a lonely decision, and now he wanted to discuss it with his friend, the editor of the New York *World*. He had sent word to Manhattan asking Cobb to join him, but his request was slow in reaching Cobb, who got a tardy start for the national capital.

Much had happened since the two were last together. Germany had resumed unrestricted submarine warfare, neutral shipping was terrorized, the United States had broken diplomatic relations with Germany, and Wilson had asked Congress for the authority to arm American merchant ships. The House quickly passed his armed ship bill, but the Senate was prevented from acting because of a filibuster by seven Republicans and five Democrats led by Senator Robert La Follette—a "little group of willful men," Wilson angrily called them. Secretary of State Lansing then told Wilson that under existing law he had the right to arm vessels without Congressional approval, so this was done.

The President had asked Congress to convene in extraordinary session on April 2, 1917, and what he had in mind was to ask for a declaration of a state of war between the United States and Germany. At long and painful last Wilson had become convinced of the inevitability of war. Aware his address to Congress would be critical and historic, Wilson took great pains in preparing it, writing the first draft in longhand, editing it by hand and on the typewriter, then writing the final draft on his Hammond. This work went on for days. On the night of March 31 he was unable to sleep, so he got out of bed and put on a bathrobe and slippers and took his small typewriter out onto the south portico of the White House. His wife rose, went to the kitchen and got a bowl of milk and some crackers, which she silently placed at his side. In the silence of the night he completed his war message.

In the sixteenth century the French essayist Montaigne wrote about a leader of antiquity, saying, "I should rather know the truth of the talk he had in his tent with one of his close friends on the eve of the battle than the speech he made the next day to his army, and what he did in his study or in his own room than what he did in public and in the Senate."

We know what Woodrow Wilson did on the eve of battle because of

Frank Cobb. The editor did not reach the White House until one o'clock the morning of April 2, the very day Wilson was scheduled to go before the Senate and House to ask for war. The President was waiting in his study. Cobb had never seen him looking so worn. When he told the President he looked as though he had not rested, Wilson admitted he had not been sleeping well. He said he was probably going before Congress to ask for a declaration of war, and he'd never been so uncertain about anything in his life. For nights he had been lying awake going over the whole situation, over the provocation given the United States by Germany, over the probable feeling in the nation, over the consequences to the settlement and to the world at large if America entered the conflict.

Tapping some sheets on the typewriter table beside him, the President said he had written a message and expected to go before Congress with it as it stood. He said he couldn't see any alternative, that he had tried every way he knew to avoid war. "I think I know what war means," Wilson said. But he asked Cobb whether there was any possibility of avoiding war, anything he might have done and failed to do.

Cobb replied that his hand had been forced by Germany and that so far as he could see, America *couldn't* keep out of war. Wilson looked at Cobb bleakly and said, "Yes, but do you know what that means?" He said war would overturn the world we had known, that so long as we remained out of it, there was a preponderance of neutrality, but that if we joined with the Allies, the world would go off the peace basis and onto a war basis.

In a choked voice Wilson said, "It would mean that we should lose our heads along with the rest and stop weighing right and wrong. It would mean that a majority of people in this hemisphere would go war-mad, quit thinking and devote their energies to destruction." A declaration of war, the President continued, would mean that Germany would be beaten and so badly beaten that there would be a dictated peace, a victorious peace.

"It means an attempt to reconstruct a peace-time civilization with war standards, and at the end of the war there will be no bystanders with sufficient power to influence the terms. There won't be any peace standards left to work with. There will be only war standards."

This, said the President, was what the Allies thought they wanted, and they would expect to have their own way in the very thing America had hoped against and struggled against. Cobb later wrote: "W. W. was uncanny that night. He had the whole panorama in his mind." He went on to say that so far as he knew he had considered every loophole of escape, and as fast as they were discovered, Germany deliberately blocked them with some new outrage.

Wilson then began to talk about the consequences to the United States. He had no illusions about the fashion in which America was likely to fight the war. He said when a war got going, it was just war and there weren't two kinds. War required illiberalism at home to reinforce the men at the front. We couldn't fight Germany and maintain the ideals of government that all thinking men shared. He said we would try it, but it would be too much for us.

"Once lead this people into war and they'll forget there ever was such a thing as tolerance. To fight you must be brutal and ruthless, and the spirit of the ruthless brutality will enter into the very fibre of our national life, infecting Congress, the courts, the policeman on the beat, the man in the street. Conformity would be the only virtue, and every man who refused to conform would have to pay the penalty."

Wilson confessed his fear that the Constitution would not survive war, that free speech and the right of assembly would vanish. He said a nation couldn't put its strength into a war and keep a level head—it had never been done.

In anguish, the President begged the editor, "If there is any alternative, for God's sake, let's take it!" Cobb said he saw no alternative. Resignedly, Wilson said that if he had it to do all over again he would take the same course, but—it was just a choice of evils.

It was late when Cobb left the White House deep in thought and the President went to bed. That night over Washington the sky paled and gave birth to Monday, April 2, 1917, a day on which the American people passed through the looking glass of fate and emerged into a new kind of reality. Wilson woke up early and from a window watched the rain. It was Monday of Holy Week. Reporters saw a messenger emerge from the White House with a sealed envelope, the President's typescript of his war message on its way to the public printer. Colonel House arrived from New York by night train and reached the executive mansion for breakfast, or so he had hoped, but had time for only a word with Wilson before the President left with his wife to play golf in the spring rain. Wilson muttered he had a headache.

Some Cabinet members and government officials got in touch with the Colonel to ask what the President planned to say to Congress, but since House had not seen the message, he sidestepped their inquiries with the generalization that "it will meet every expectation." In early afternoon Wilson read his speech to the Colonel, who said he considered it the greatest of Wilson's career. House did suggest he delete a phrase which seemed to urge the German people to revolt against their own government, and Wilson took this advice.

"I asked him," House later wrote, "why he had not shown the Cabinet his address. He replied that, if he had every man in it would have had some suggestion to make and it would have been picked to pieces if he had heeded their criticism. He said he preferred to keep it to himself and take the responsibility. I feel that he does his Cabinet an injustice. . . . I have noticed recently that he holds a tighter rein over his Cabinet and that he is impatient of any initiative on their part."

Up on Capitol Hill the legislators were organizing the sixty-fifth Congress, and there were the usual procedural delays, so until they were ready to hear him, there was nothing Wilson could do but wait. He waited. Nervously. To kill time, and also to enhance the prestige of the three Cabinet members soon to be engaged in waging war, he left the White House at 4:40 P.M. and strolled across West Executive Avenue to the old and imposing state-war-navy building just west of the executive mansion.

With a secret service agent at his side, he slipped into a big room where Navy Secretary Daniels was ending a press conference, taking a seat in the rear so that he might not be noticed by the reporters. They bombarded Daniels with questions. After they left, Wilson asked him, "Do you have to go through this ordeal every day?" Daniels smiled and replied, "Twice every day—but, being a newspaperman, I am only taking some of my own medicine." Wilson left Daniels and dropped in to see State Secretary Lansing and War Secretary Baker. Lansing warned Wilson that he should be accompanied by a strong military force when he drove to the Capitol later in the day, but Wilson scoffed at his fears.

The city was tense. Newspapers had said we were about to go to war with Germany and had further reported the nation's militant mood. This was not wholly true. Colonel House had heard from a friend back from a two-week tour of the Midwest that the people out there did not want war but were willing to follow the President. On the flag-draped streets men and women walked through the rain wearing white armbands and badges saying KEEP OUT OF WAR, but into Union Station pulled trains filled with flag-waving Pilgrims of Patriotism. Other trains brought thousands of pacifists determined to make one last stand against war. Each was armed with a white tulip.

The pacifists were led by the same Dr. David Starr Jordan who had conferred with Wilson in the company of Henry Ford about the Ford peace ship. Senator La Follette had failed in an attempt to persuade the metropolitan police to grant the pacifists a parade permit. During the morning the demonstrators had swarmed to the White House to try to see the President, only to be repulsed. Then they attempted to storm the state-war-navy building but once again were turned back. Now they drifted up the wet pavement and sidewalks of Pennsylvania Avenue to the Capitol, where some perched on the steps while others invaded the Senate and House buildings.

A knot of Massachusetts pacifists reached the office of Senator Henry Cabot Lodge and demanded he see them. They were told the Senator was busy. They shrilled that they were his constituents and had a right to speak with him. At last the white-haired and bearded Lodge stepped outside his door to listen. The delegation's spokesman was Alexander Bannwart, who had played baseball in New England under the name of Al Winn. He asked what Lodge intended to do when the President requested that we go to war. Lodge replied that he planned to support the President. Bannwart became abusive.

Lodge reacted angrily, snapping, "National degeneracy and cowardice are worse than war! I regret that I cannot agree with your position, but I must do my duty as I see it."

"Anyone who wants to go to war," Bannwart snarled, "is a coward! You're a damned coward!"

The former ballplayer was thirty-six, while the Senator was sixty-seven. Lodge had begun to back away from the irate pacifists, but when Bannwart called him a coward, he shouted back, "You're a damned liar!" Lodge struck Bannwart. Bannwart struck back, knocking Lodge against the closed half of the double door. The other pacifists rushed the Senator. A Western Union messenger, seeing an old man under attack, sprang forward to help Lodge, and secretaries poured from his office to rescue him. Bannwart was badly beaten and hauled off to jail. During this melee, the other pacifists escaped. Although Lodge had struck the first blow and yelled, "I'm glad I hit him first," Bannwart was charged with assault. After he apologized, he was released from jail. Through the Senate office building ran the news that Lodge had punched a pacifist, had struck our first blow for freedom.

Other truculent pacifists marched from office to office seeking Senators and Representatives, invading the office of Vice President Marshall, tumbling into the office of Speaker of the House Champ Clark; but Capitol guards were called, and the legislators hastily closed their doors, while out on the Capitol steps the police broke up an incipient demonstration. The members of the peace army then adjourned to a hall next door to an armory used by the national guard and were jeered by the young citizen soldiers.

That afternoon in New York City a crowd tried to attack a pacifist speaking on the street, but it was held off by policemen. Some pacifists had been inspired by a sermon given the previous day—Sunday—in Manhattan by Dr. John Haynes Holmes, pastor of the Community Church of New York, who said, "If war is right, then Christianity is wrong—false—a lie. If Christianity is right, the war is wrong—false—a lie."

Congress convened at noon. The House of Representatives had a curiosity—the first woman ever elected to that branch of government. She was Jeannette Rankin, born in 1880 on a ranch in Montana, a social worker and suffragette who had helped the women of her state win the right to vote—six years before passage of the Nineteenth Amendment. She was a Republican and a pacifist. This meant that even as she took her seat, she was in a minority, for a poll had proved the vast majority of Congressmen were in favor of war. Miss Rankin entered the chamber wearing a dark blue silk and chiffon suit with an open neck and wide white crepe collar and cuffs, and she carried a bouquet of yellow and purple flowers given to her at a suffrage breakfast.

Wilson was scheduled to speak to the joint session in the House chamber, and people were so eager to hear him tip the scales of history that fabulous prices were paid for tickets of admission. By early afternoon men and women thronged the doorkeepers. Every elevator bore a sign saying NO ADMITTANCE TO GALLERIES EXCEPT BY CARDS. Amid all this tension and bustle a general's wife told a Congressman's wife in a trembling voice that all these preparations meant war, "and we are utterly unprepared, and we will be just annihilated!" Asked how this would happen, the general's wife explained the Germans would "just come over in their ships and submarines and *do* it!"

Wilson remained in the White House, and as the day stretched out like a rubber band, he fidgeted more and more. At last word came that Congress had completed its organization and would receive him at 8:30 P.M. The President sat down to an early dinner with Colonel House and members of his family, and they talked about everything and anything but his forthcoming speech and the advent of war. As daylight faded, the rain fell harder and the wind increased and lightning flicked the sky. As

Bernard Baruch left his hotel to drive to the Capitol, he stopped before entering his car so that he might stare; for the first time ever the white dome of the Capitol was lit by floodlights on the ground, rays of light made porous by the rain and mist.

At 8:20 P.M. the President left the White House for the brief ride up the avenue to the Capitol, and on the glistening streets were thousands of people eager to get a glimpse of him this historic evening. In addition to his usual secret service detail, and despite his protest that he needed no extra protection, he was guarded by marines and foot soldiers and two troops of cavalry from Fort Myer, ordered to duty by War Secretary Baker.

The Capitol was guarded by soldiers, policemen, secret service agents and even post office inspectors; some stood vigil on the roof. Their instructions were to be on the alert for any pacifist who might try to harm the President. The House chamber was jammed, with every seat taken and with people standing on the floor and in the galleries. Navy Secretary Daniels looked around and decided with a sense of awe that never in the history of Washington had there been gathered such an assemblage of powerful and colorful men. For the first time in memory the Supreme Court justices, clad in business suits rather than their black robes, sat in a body on the floor of the House directly in front of the Speaker's desk. "Like Saul among the prophets," in Daniels' phrase, sat Chief Justice Edward D. White, who was seventy-two years old and a former Confederate soldier. Recently the old jurist had told a Cabinet member, "I wish I were thirty years younger. I would go to Canada and volunteer."

Behind the justices sat Cabinet officers, their wives wearing evening dresses, and behind them the foreign diplomats in full regalia, the British and French ambassadors smiling expectantly. Along the front row of one gallery sat Mrs. Wilson and her mother and Margaret Wilson. The room was warm and brilliantly lit. The House was called to order, double doors opened in the rear and in marched Vice President Marshall followed by the Senators, most of them wearing or carrying tiny American flags. It was noted that Senator La Follette was flagless. A murmur arose when people saw Senator Lodge, for his face was slightly puffed as a result of his fight earlier in the day. Everyone settled down. Then, from outside the chamber, a clatter of horse hooves on pavement.

A stir at the door. The President appeared. The time was 8:32 P.M. Everyone rose and greeted him with a sustained ovation. As Wilson strode down the center aisle, his black suit and thin figure made him seem taller than he really was, and those closest to him saw his muscles knotted like marbles under the skin. His face was pale and tight. Mounting the rostrum, he took his place behind a wooden lectern set on a marble surface and opened a printer's copy of his message. House Speaker Clark banged his gavel and announced, "The President of the United States!" Wilson gave a slight bow; his gray eyes peered down at the justices and Cabinet members and then lifted to a gallery to search for his wife. His attention turned to his manuscript, and he began speaking clear and solemn tones in his tenor voice:

> Gentlemen of the Congress, I have called the Congress into extraordinary session because there are serious, very serious, choices of policy to be made, and made immediately, which it was neither right nor constitutionally permissible that I should assume the responsibility of making. . . .

This was an era before American Presidents sent soldiers to foreign countries to fight without obtaining Congressional approval.

Wilson declared Germany was warring on all mankind by unleashing unrestricted submarine warfare, by sinking hospital ships and relief ships, by shooting down American vessels and taking American lives, by denying the use of arms to neutrals to defend themselves. His audience listened in absolute silence until he said, "There is one choice we cannot make, we are incapable of making: we will not choose the path of submission—"

Starling of the secret service, who sat to the President's right, saw a sudden motion from the corners of his eyes. He tensed for action. Then he relaxed, realizing that the man who had moved was Chief Justice White. The old warrior had dropped his hat on the floor, and now he raised his arms above his white head and cracked the palms of his hands together in a sharp slap. White jumped to his feet—looking ten feet tall, Daniels thought—and from his throat there ripped the rebel yell that had sounded at Shiloh and Gettysburg, the Confederate war cry, a sound that drove icicles up the spines of Daniels and Wilson and Baruch and others of Southern blood, while from the floor and galleries there rolled an avalanche of applause. White's face trembled, and tears ran like pearls down his furrowed cheeks.

The President paused, and when he resumed speaking, he said, "—and suffer the most sacred rights of our nation and our people to be ignored or violated." From that moment until the end of the speech the chief justice, like the leader of a Greek chorus, applauded everything Wilson said. The President's voice trembled when it hit the core of his message:

> . . . With a profound sense of the solemn and even tragical character of the step I am taking and of the grave responsibilities which it involves, but in unhesitating obedience to what I deem my constitutional duty, I advise that the Congress declare the recent course of the Imperial German government to be in fact nothing less than war against the government and people of the United States; that it formally accept the status of belligerent which has thus been thrust upon it; and that it take immediate steps not only to put the country in a more thorough state of defense, but also to exert all its power and employ all its resources to bring the government of the German empire to terms and end the war. . . .

Wilson continued speaking when—*crash!* The sound seemed to come from the overhead skylight. The President lifted his white face in instant anxiety. People stirred nervously. Wilson was talking about going to war, and everyone knew there were German agents in this country and bombings and dynamitings. What was this? Soon it was learned that a soldier on the roof had dropped his rifle.

Except for Wilson's first inaugural address, this speech was the best thus far in his career, a tapestry of colorful rhetoric and balanced phrases. After unfurling image after golden image, he came to the place where he said, "The world must be made safe for democracy," and Secretary Daniels thought that as Wilson spoke this phrase, "the spirit of the Covenanter flashed from his eyes." Senator John Sharp Williams of Mississippi reacted with a slow and deliberate clapping that touched off other applause whirring across the floor like a threshing machine.

The President finished his thirty-six-minute oration with a masterful rhetorical flourish: "To such a task we can dedicate our lives and our fortunes, everything that we are and everything that we have, with the pride of those who know that the day will come when America is privileged to spend her blood and her might for the principles that gave her birth and happiness and the peace which she has treasured. God helping her, she can do no other."

His eloquence was stunning. When he had finished, there was a long moment in which no one moved or spoke or hardly breathed. Then the people jumped to their feet, waving flags, applauding, shouting, screaming, roaring, all eyes locked on the tall man with the sad face on the rostrum, some eyes suddenly wet and seeing him as through a mist, hearts bursting with a sense of glory. Now had a halt been called to the evil that stalked the earth; now began the frenzy that was to change the tone of American life for generations to come. Ahead lay sacrifices, of course, the pain that purges, indelible deeds, passions parading as patriotism. This was the most dramatic moment in American history since the Civil War, the wildest acclaim Wilson had ever received, but the adulation was not unanimous, for there stood Senator La Follette, with lips of steel, arms folded high on his chest for all to see his defiance, and there stood two or three other Senators in mute and helpless protest against the war.

The President nodded once or twice, his spectacles trembling on his nose, and then he turned and left the rostrum and began walking out of the chamber. Men pressed forward to congratulate him, and his hand was taken by Senator Lodge, often his enemy, who said, "Mr. President, you have expressed in the loftiest manner possible the sentiments of the American people!" Starling walked with his right shoulder touching Wilson's left shoulder, and the agent felt the President sag into him for support in his exhaustion. They waited for Mrs. Wilson to extricate herself from the crowd in the gallery and join them, and then the President put on his tall silk hat, stepped outside and heard a roar from the waiting crowd, got into his limousine and drove back to the White House past thousands of cheering flag-waving spectators. Wilson sat still. Secretary Daniels said, "If I should live a thousand years, there would abide with me the reverberation of the fateful ominous sounds of the hoofs of the cavalry horses as they escorted Mr. and Mrs. Wilson back to the White House."

Five minutes after Wilson left the Capitol the House was called on to adopt a rule making possible swift passage of a war appropriations bill while the Senators, back in their own chamber, heard a summons to the members of the foreign relations committee to meet at ten o'clock the next morning to draft a declaration of war.

Wilson, relieved the tension was over and the die cast, sat down in the Oval Room with his family and Colonel House to discuss the evening's events. From beyond the gates to the grounds, now guarded by soldiers, came cheers and the tramp of marching feet. Before going to bed, he had a few minutes alone with his secretary at the long table in the Cabinet room. "Tumulty," he quavered, "think what it meant—the applause of the people at the Capitol and the people lining the avenue as we returned! My message tonight was a message of death to our young men. How strange to applaud that! . . . Our life till this thing is over . . . will be full of tragedy and heartaches." From a pocket he pulled a handkerchief to wipe away tears and then let his head sink down onto the table. And wept.

Theodore Roosevelt was fishing for devilfish in the Gulf of Mexico. He was a guest aboard a houseboat owned by a Virginia tobacco trader named Russell Coles, whose hobby was killing sharks and giant manta rays. Before leaving the houseboat to board a launch to take him to the fishing grounds, Teddy had delivered a tirade against pacifists. Out in open water he slammed a harpoon two feet inside a devilfish, the barbed iron held, and the wounded creature towed the launch a half mile before Cole's crew could haul it onto the deck, where they hacked it to death. When the fishermen returned, they found the dead giant ray measured 16 feet 8 inches from fin to fin. Roosevelt grinned and told reporters, "Good sport—but not the sort of thing to recommend to a weakling."

Riding north on the train taking him home, he learned that Wilson had asked Congress for a declaration of war. He stopped in Washington and went to the White House with the intention of congratulating the President, but Wilson was attending a Cabinet meeting and Roosevelt would not wait. But he took time to find Senator Lodge and praise him for punching a pacifist.

Roosevelt said publicly, "The President's message is a great state paper which will rank in history with the great state papers of which Americans in future years will be proud. It now rests with the people of the country to see that we put in practice the policy that the President has outlined and that we strike hard, as soon and as efficiently as possible, in an aggressive war against the government of Germany." Privately, though, Roosevelt wrote James Bryce that Wilson's message was "a terrible indictment of everything he has done and said, and everything he has left undone and unsaid, during the past two years and eight months. I will forgive him everything if he will see that America fights not only with swords but with hatchets also."

Winston Churchill, first lord of the British admiralty, later wrote:

> Step by step the President had been pursued and brought to bay. By slow merciless degrees, against his dearest hopes, against his gravest doubts, against his deepest inclinations, in stultification of all he had said and done and left undone in thirty months of carnage, he was forced to give the signal he dreaded and abhorred. Throughout he had been beneath the true dominant note of American sentiment. He had behind his policy a reasoned explanation and massive argument, and all must respect the motives of a statesman who seeks to spare his country the waste and horrors of war. But nothing can reconcile what he said after March, 1917, with the guidance he had given before. What he did in April, 1917, could have been done in May, 1915.

Franklin and Eleanor Roosevelt had sat in the House to listen to Wilson's war message, and when the President finished, Eleanor felt half-dazed by a sense of impending change. Now FDR told the press that "no statement about American national honor and high purpose more clear or more definite . . . could be made. It will be an inspiration to every true citizen no matter what his political faith, no matter what his creed, no matter what the country of his origin."

Colonel House, aware of Wilson's need for praise, not only tendered his personal congratulations, but also passed along comments from others. The Colonel said the speech had stirred the world even more than he had anticipated. Ignace Paderewski, the Polish pianist and statesman, declared the world had never seen Wilson's equal. Sir William Wiseman, head of British intelligence work in the United States, thought Wilson's address could not have been more perfect had it been written by Shakespeare. When Wilson's name was mentioned in the British House of Commons, he was cheered. After Wilson spoke, the stock market rose. Across the country excited people staged demonstrations and scores of organizations pledged support of the impending war. State legislators and governors passed resolutions praising the President. His war message was read aloud in French to all French schoolchildren; British aviators dropped German translations of it behind the German lines; Italian pilots scattered other copies over Austria.

But—

William Jennings Bryan, who had been in Miami as Wilson spoke, was sick with despair. Democratic Senator James Vardaman of Mississippi said, "Things look gloomy. God alone can save this republic, it seems to me, from the horrors of the European slaughter." Senator La Follette said Europe was "cursed with a contagion . . . a deadly plague, whose spread threatens to devastate the civilized world." La Follette thought that regardless of "material loss, or commercial inconvenience," we should "keep our people at home" and "quarantine against it" as if it were "the Black Death."

The Danish Socialist press accused Wilson of catering to capitalists. The American Socialist party passed a resolution saying, "Our entrance into the European conflict at this time . . . will give the powers of reaction in this country the pretext for an attempt to throttle our rights and to crush our democratic institutions." This foreboding matched Wilson's own gloomy vision of brutalities to come.

The American Constitution gives Congress sole power to declare war. On Tuesday, April 3, 1917, the Senate and House began to act on a war declaration prepared by Secretary of State Lansing with the approval of President Wilson. As finally adopted, this historic document says:

> Resolved by the Senate and House of Representatives of the United States of America in Congress assembled, That the state of war between the United States and the Imperial German Government which has thus been thrust upon the United States is hereby formally declared; and that the President be, and he is hereby, authorized and directed to take immediate steps not only to put the country in a thorough state of defense, but also to exert all of its power and employ all of its resources to carry on war against the Imperial German Government and to bring the conflict to a successful determination.

Tuesday morning the Senate foreign relations committee met and adopted this resolution, although the committee chairman, Senator William J. Stone, cast a lone vote against it. When the Senate itself met Tuesday noon, various Senators read into the record thousands of letters, telegrams, petitions and memorials they had received from all over the country; these filled twenty-four pages of the *Congressional Record*. Then Senator Gilbert M. Hitchcock of Nebraska took the floor, read the war resolution and asked unanimous consent for its immediate consideration.

Senator La Follette rose and said, "Mr. President, I ask that the joint resolution go over for the day under the rule. I object to the request for unanimous consent." He was invoking a Senate rule saying a single Senator could compel a bill to be delayed a day to give Senators time to study it. Hitchcock, believing La Follette was objecting because the resolution had not yet been printed in sufficient numbers by the government printing office, assured him that within five minutes every Senator would have a printed copy on his desk. With an exasperating smile, La Follette said, "I ask for the regular order." The presiding officer, Vice President Marshall, started to sustain La Follette's objection, but the Democratic floor leader, Senator Thomas S. Martin, broke in, saying, "The joint resolution goes over, of course, but I have a right to make some comments upon—"

"I have asked," La Follette interrupted, "for the regular order, and I ask for a ruling upon that request."

Martin began to talk about "the momentous consequences involved in this joint resolution—"

La Follette interrupted again. "It is quite unnecessary for the Senator to call my attention to the momentous consequences of this joint resolution. I think I realize them quite as fully as he does." Again he demanded the regular order—a parliamentary ploy to end debate.

The Vice President ruled the resolution must go over one day. Martin angrily moved adjournment. When another Senator sought recognition, Martin "cut him short with a roar like a wounded bull," objecting to the introduction of business of any sort until disposition of the war resolution. In violation of Senate rules, Martin was applauded by spectators in the galleries. Agreeing to meet at ten the following morning, the Senate adjourned, and Senate leaders went into conference to form a plan to thwart the filibuster they expected from La Follette and other Senators opposed to the war.

A New York *Times* correspondent wrote a snide article saying, "And while [the leaders] were conferring on the street floor of the Capitol on the way to save the nation from the undeserved imputation of being laggardly to meet the President's call to arms, Senator La Follette far underground below their feet, in a little cubbyhole of a room in the sub-basement reached by a labyrinth, was busily whispering cheek by jowl with a dozen pacifists."

That day the stock market slumped, and the Washington *Herald* said, "Wall Street was angered at the attitude taken by Senator La Follette." He clipped this story, mounted it on a sheet of Senate stationery and wrote in the margin: "Wall Street's anger is a matter of utter indifference to me. It may not be so with others. Be that as it may, I have never experimented with the dubious business of trying to serve two masters—the people of the country and the interests of Wall Street." Years later La Follette wrote, "I should have been a traitor to the people, in my opinion, had I not voiced and voted my opposition to a declaration of war. Despite . . . the vast war propaganda with which the country has been flooded . . . the American people were in their hearts at that time opposed to war, and I believe the instinct of the people was sound."

Tuesday evening Franklin H. Giddings, a professor of sociology at Columbia University, said in Manhattan, "We read tonight that a declaration of war that might have been made today was delayed by one Robert La Follette. Men have often made up lists of 'immortals.' Among the 'immortals' whose 'immortality' is sure are Robert La Follette, William Jennings Bryan, James Buchanan, Benedict Arnold and Judas Iscariot." That same night in Cambridge, Massachusetts, students from the Massachusetts Institute of Technology made an effigy of La Follette, set it afire on the banks of the Charles and danced an Indian war dance around it, singing and hooting and jeering.

On Wednesday, April 4, 1917, the Senate convened at 10 A.M. and continued to sit until 11:15 P.M. Its members were debating the war resolution, and as they debated, the House waited and Wilson waited. In the afternoon the President and his wife rode through Rock Creek park, and that evening they went to Belasco's theater to see *Very Good Eddie*, which Wilson did not find very good.

During the Senate's long debate only five Senators spoke against the war resolution. Three were progressive Republicans—La Follette of Wisconsin, George Norris of Nebraska and Asle Jorgenson Gronna of North Dakota. Two were Democrats—James K. Vardaman of Mississippi and William J. Stone of Missouri.

La Follette had introduced a bill calling for a referendum on war before

Congress acted on this grave question, but it had been defeated. Senator Gronna referred to the referendum when he said, "We criticize European monarchies for forcing their subjects into war against their will, but we refuse to ascertain by a referendum vote of the American people whether they desire peace or war. . . . I shall vote against war because I believe it would have been possible to maintain an honorable peace."

Senator Norris rose and said, "I am most emphatically and sincerely opposed to taking any steps that will force our country into the useless and senseless war now being waged in Europe. . . ." He declared that although both Great Britain and Germany had violated American neutrality, the administration had submitted in the case of Britain and protested only against Germany. Since the start of war Americans had lent $2.2 billion to the Allies. Norris argued that "the enormous amount of money loaned to the Allies in this country has been instrumental in bringing about a public sentiment in favor of our country taking a course that would make every bond worth a hundred cents on the dollar and making the payment of every debt certain." He added that "the enormous profits of munition manufacturers, stockbrokers and bond dealers must be still further increased by our entrance into the war." Then he uttered a line that haunted him for the rest of his life: "We are going into war upon the command of gold!"

Here and there on the Senate floor Norris saw gleams of hostility from his colleagues and sensed, as he later wrote, that "the friendships of years were dissolving into misunderstanding." But his heart felt calm because he was convinced he was right. Norris said, "I know that I am powerless to stop it. I know that this war madness has taken possession of the financial and political powers of our country. . . . I feel that we are committing a sin against humanity and against our countrymen. I would like to say to this war god: You shall not coin into gold the lifeblood of my brethren. . . . I feel that we are about to put the dollar sign upon the American flag."

Senator James Reed of Missouri leaped up and cried, "If that be not giving aid and comfort to the enemy on the very eve of the opening of hostilities, then I do not know what would bring comfort to the heart of a Hapsburg or a Hohenzollern!" As for the remark that "we are about to put the dollar sign upon the American flag," Reed characterized it as "near to treason!"

Moments before 4 P.M. that Wednesday, April 4, 1917, just as the President was leaving the White House for a ride through a park, Senator La Follette rose from his Senate seat. Other Senators who had been idling in the smoking room hurried in, while in the crowded galleries men and women leaned forward expectantly. Robert La Follette was known as "Fighting Bob" and "The Little Giant." For a while in 1912 he had been the Progressive candidate for President; he had whipped the Wisconsin bosses and given that state honest government. As governor, Congressman and then Senator he had won a national reputation as an honest man concerned with the welfare of the people; he had been praised by President Wilson and Louis Brandeis and William Allen White and others. He was known to be incorruptible and stubborn—and a pacifist.

Now he opened a manuscript on his desk and began reading in a firm voice. All eyes locked on this short solid man with the brushed-back hair and expressive hands, and for almost three hours he spoke, and only three times was he interrupted. He was existing at the tip of his soul, sacrificing himself to his faith in reason, annihilating his reputation in an attempt to avert a national catastrophe.

La Follette rejected the doctrine of supporting the President without asking whether the President was right or wrong. Point by point he dissected Wilson's war message, and step by step he traced what he called diplomatic blunders made by the President and the state department. He said that from forty-four states he had received 15,000 letters and telegrams that opposed the war in a ratio of 9 to 1. He challenged the administration and the Congress to submit the issue of war to the people. He declared the United States had "submitted to Great Britain's dictation."

"The poor, sir, who are the ones called upon to rot in the trenches, have no organized power, have no press to voice their will upon this question of peace or war, but, oh, Mr. President, at some time they will be heard!"

He predicted inflation and criticized "the non-taxable bonds held by Morgan and his combinations, which have been issued to meet this war." It was silly to believe that Germany's submarine warfare was "a warfare against mankind," since many neutral nations did not subscribe to this concept. Make the world safe for democracy? Why, of all those nations with which we were about to ally ourselves, only France and now the czarless Russia were true democracies.

La Follette said that "we should not seek to hide our blunder behind the smoke of battle, to inflame the mind of our people by half-truths into the frenzy of war in order that they may never appreciate the real cause of it until it is too late."

He continued to speak as darkness fell and lights were lit in the Senate chamber and men and women wearing evening clothes came to the galleries, and the British ambassador came to listen and so did Cabinet members. Very quietly La Follette finished speaking at 6:45 P.M., took his manuscript and walked to the rear of the floor to speak to his secretary.

Mississippi Senator Williams sprang to his feet. His voice quivering with emotion, he said, "Mr. President, if immortality could be attained by a verbal eternity, the Senator from Wisconsin would have approximated immortality. We have waited and have heard a speech from him which would have better become Herr Bethmann-Hollweg of the German parliament than an American Senator! In fact, he has gone much further than Herr Bethmann-Hollweg ever dared to go—"

La Follette stood in the rear of the room with his back to the speaker. Glaring at La Follette, Williams raised his voice and shouted, "I fully expected before he took his seat to hear him defend the invasion of Belgium—the most absolutely barbarous act that ever took place in the history of any nation anywhere! I heard from him a speech which was pro-German, pretty near pro-Goth and pro-Vandal, which was anti-American President and anti-American Congress and anti-American people!"

Without so much as glancing at Williams, La Follette vanished inside the cloakroom. When the Mississippi Senator finished speaking, six other Senators took the floor to urge passage of the war message.

At 11:11 P.M. the vote began. People were packed in the aisles on the floor and crouched on the steps of the galleries. Almost half the membership of the House thronged the rear of the Senate to hear the results. The Senators were tense and quiet, and the silence tightened as the clerk called the roll. Many answered in tremulous voices. La Follette was now back at his desk, and when his name was called, he responded with a clear "No!" At last the clerk announced the Senate had adopted the war resolution by a vote of 82 to 6. There were 8 absentees; each sent word he would have voted for war—except for Senator Thomas P. Gore of Oklahoma. The Senate's fateful decision was greeted with silence.

As La Follette left the Senate floor, he was avoided by his colleagues, and as he walked toward his office a man stepped forward and handed him a rope.

Thursday, April 5, 1917, was another stormy day, so the President did not leave the White House. At 10 A.M. the House of Representatives began to debate the war resolution, and for nearly the next seventeen hours the oratory flowed. Now the House chamber was filled to overflowing with spectators who sat in wet clothes after coming through the rain, and all that morning, all afternoon, and on into the night a northeastern storm dashed rain against the Capitol as more than 100 Congressmen voiced their opinions about the great issue.

Midnight came and went, turning Thursday into Good Friday, a day devoted to fasting and penance, and at last the House began voting. When the clerk called the name of Miss Rankin, everyone turned to stare at the woman from Montana, and after a moment of silence she got to her feet, her troubled eyes staring straight ahead. "I want—" Her voice broke. "I—want to stand by my country," she said, "but I cannot vote for war." Her voice broke into a sob: "I vote No." She sank back into her chair and shielded her face with her hands and wept.

On droned the impersonal voice of the clerk, and at 3:12 A.M. the House of Representatives voted 373 to 50 to go to war with Germany.

Shortly before dawn the metropolitan police got a call from the center of the business district at 14th and H streets, and a cop investigated and found the effigy of a man dangling from a shop. The effigy was five feet tall, made of white cloth stuffed with newspapers, and it had eyes and a nose and a mouth crudely sketched in black paint. Running down its back was a broad yellow streak. One side of this figure bore the name STONE, for Senator Stone of Missouri who had voted against war, while painted on the other side was the name LA FOLLETTE. From its feet fluttered a streamer saying TRAITORS.

On Friday, April 6, 1917, President Wilson was lunching in the state dining room with his wife and Helen Bones when he received word the joint Congressional declaration of war had been delivered to the executive office. He ordered the document brought to the office of Ike Hoover. Quickly finishing his meal, Wilson left the dining room and walked to the head usher's office, followed by the two women and Starling of the secret service.

When an important document is to be signed by the President, it is customary for him to be attended by Congressional leaders who guided the measure through both houses, by Cabinet members, by reporters and photographers. On this day of transcendent importance, however, Wilson acted informally. Into Hoover's office walked Rudolph Forster, executive clerk of the White House.

"How are you, Rudolph?" Wilson asked. "You have the proclamation?"

"Yes, sir. Shall I take it to your study?"

"No. I'll sign it here."

Wilson sat down at Ike Hoover's desk.

"Give me a pen," he said.

His wife said, "Use this one." She handed him a gold fountain pen he had presented to her.

"Stand by me, Edith."

She moved to a position just behind him on his right. Miss Bones stood beside her. Forster stood behind the President's chair. Starling stood at Wilson's left elbow. Beside Starling stood Hoover, with a blotter in his hand. The President bent over the parchment, his jaw muscles hardening, swiftly read the document, saw that it already had been signed by Vice President Marshall and House Speaker Clark, and then in a firm hand he wrote: "Woodrow Wilson."

The time was 1:20 P.M.

Ike Hoover pressed a button that buzzed in the executive office, alerting Byron McCandless, aide to Navy Secretary Daniels. McCandless ran out onto the lawn of the White House and raised both hands over his head. He was seen, as it had been intended he should be seen, by a navy officer at a window in the nearby state-war-navy building. Within moments there flashed to every navy ship and shore installation the news that the United States was officially at war with Germany.

Chapter 24

THE DRAFT ACT

Three days after Congress declared war Theodore Roosevelt bustled into Washington bursting with ambition. He went to the home of his daughter Alice and her husband Nicholas Longworth, a Congressman, and the first person he called was his relative, Franklin Roosevelt. The former President asked the assistant secretary of the navy to arrange an interview for him with War Secretary Baker. FDR met with Baker and said Theodore wanted permission to raise a division of soldiers, become their commanding officer and lead them into battle in France.

This was hardly news to Baker. At the outbreak of war in August, 1914, Theodore had begun to dream of a "Roosevelt Division," and as the war went on, his idea became so obsessive that family members began teasing him about it. When it seemed the United States would never take up arms, Roosevelt said lightly that he might recruit his division in Canada and go anyway. As Alice remembered it, someone in his home pointed out that if he did this, he would be unable to fight under the American flag. Roosevelt chuckled that he could put a bull moose in a corner of the British flag, or else a bison. Teasingly, a relative said a more appropriate emblem would be a dodo.

On February 3, 1917, the day Wilson told Congress the United States was severing diplomatic relations with Germany, but two months before it declared war, Roosevelt had written Baker to say he was canceling a planned Jamaica vacation so that he might hold himself in readiness to receive authorization to raise a division. Between Roosevelt and Baker there then developed one of the most curious correspondences in American history. Teddy sent a deluge of letters and telegrams to the secretary of war.

Roosevelt's immaturity, romanticism and violence came to full flower in his determination to lead men into battle—even if it meant his death. Nineteen years had passed since he'd charged up San Juan Hill in Cuba during the Spanish-American War, an exploit that had proved his courage but little else, and now he was fifty-eight and nearly a shell—blind in one eye and slightly deaf. He still carried a would-be assassin's bullet in his chest, and his health had been sapped by fevers and injuries three years before during a trip up a wild river in Brazil. In fact, Roosevelt did not have much longer to live. Privately he called himself an old man, but he wrote William Allen White, "I think I could do this country most good by dying in a reasonably honorable fashion, at the head of my division in the European War."

At the time the preparedness debate was dragging out, Roosevelt had opened a private recruiting station in New York, written his old Rough Rider friends and prepared lists of the men he wanted to take to France with him. There still was such magic in the old man that he got an overwhelming response. He announced he was receiving more than 2,000 applications a day and declared he soon would be able to offer the government the services of a quarter million men.

Among those who wanted to fight under Roosevelt were some sons or grandsons of great Civil War officers—Philip Sheridan, Stonewall Jackson, Fitzhugh Lee, Simon Bolivar Buckner and Nathan Bedford Forrest. Teddy's volunteer division would be officered at the upper echelon by regulars and in the lower ranks by business and professional men. "The broncho-buster type," he was careful to say, "will be very much lacking." The moment he got permission to form his division he would assemble his men at Fort Sill, Oklahoma, for six weeks' training, take them to France for combat training, then lead them to the front "in the shortest possible time."

Roosevelt pointedly reminded Baker that he was "a retired Commander-in-Chief of the United States Army, and eligible to any position of command over American troops to which I may be appointed." Baker showed all of Teddy's messages to Wilson, and after reading one of them, the President cried, "This is one of the most extraordinary documents I have ever read! Thank you for letting me undergo the discipline of temper involved in reading it in silence!"

Although Wilson disliked Roosevelt, he seemed sentimentally inclined to grant Teddy his wish. However, there was an abundance of negative factors. It had been an American tradition at the onset of war for patriots and politicians to issue personal calls for volunteers whose commander they would become. Wilson's desk was piled with petitions from Senators, Indian fighters, Texas rangers and Southern colonels eager to raise a company, regiment or division for service in France. Since Wilson was about to ask Congress to pass a draft law, his appeal would be weakened were he to deny these petitions while making an exception for Roosevelt.

This was a young man's war—and Roosevelt was old. This was a mechanized war best fought by professionals—and Roosevelt was a dilettante. Marshal Joseph Joffre of France had told Baker it cost from 10,000 to 15,000 lives to train a major general—and Wilson was not about to sacrifice young Americans to Roosevelt's thirst for glory. Chief of Staff Hugh Scott had told Baker that to name Roosevelt to command would be to repeat the mistake Lincoln made in the early part of the Civil War by appointing political generals. Wilson had selected General John J. Pershing as commander of the American Expeditionary Force, and Pershing was likely to be embarrassed to have in France a former President of the United States, a man legendary for his acts of insubordination when he held lesser positions. When Louisiana Governor John M. Parker interceded for Roosevelt, Wilson protested he was not playing politics with this issue, but it was a fact that Teddy was the most glamorous leader of the war party and might become the Republican candidate for President in 1920. Wilson told Tumulty, "I really think the best way to treat Mr. Roosevelt is to take no notice of him."

To take no notice of Theodore Roosevelt, however, was like trying to ignore a hurricane.

Baker told Franklin Roosevelt he would be pleased to see Theodore Roosevelt, and as a courtesy to the former President, he would call on him at the Longworth mansion. When Baker arrived, he found the first floor filled with Senators, reporters and close friends of Roosevelt. The thick-waisted Roosevelt greeted Baker jovially, put his arm through Baker's and led him to an upstairs bedroom so they could talk privately.

Lowering the aim of his ambition, Roosevelt told Baker, "I am aware that I have not had enough experience to lead a division myself, but I have selected the most experienced officers from the regular army for my staff." This was hardly a diplomatic remark for a civilian to make to the secretary of war. Furthermore, a Roosevelt division would have drawn heavily from the cadre of officers so badly needed to create an army in a land where none existed. But the patient Baker took no offense.

After Baker left, Roosevelt told a friend, "I had a good time with Baker. I could twist him around my finger if I could have had him about for awhile. . . . He will do exactly what Wilson tells him to do, he will think exactly as Wilson wants him to think. . . . He has the blindest faith in the general staff and the graduates of West Point. He doesn't realize that a muttonhead, after an education at West Point or Harvard, is a muttonhead still."

The next day Alice Roosevelt drove her father to the White House, for Baker had told Teddy the President wished to see him. It was twelve noon when Roosevelt appeared at the front door. Tumulty greeted him and led him into the Red Room, where he was received by Wilson. The two sat down, Tumulty took a chair nearby, and Roosevelt was surprised to see that a door to the room had been left open. Teddy was of course familiar with the Red Room and its walls of cerise silk, a sofa said to have belonged to Dolley Madison standing in a corner on the east side, another sofa in the northwest corner once owned by Martha Washington's granddaughter. When Roosevelt was President, he had felt so offended by the ornate Tiffany mantel and cornices of the fireplace that he had them removed.

Roosevelt and Wilson had met before. Wilson had once lunched in Teddy's home on Sagamore Hill on Long Island. When Roosevelt was President, he had gone to Princeton, New Jersey, to attend an army-navy football game and was entertained by Wilson, then president of the university. But that was long ago. The two had not seen one another since 1912, when they had become political opponents, and since then they had developed into archrivals. Wilson was well aware of all the nasty names Roosevelt had called him. Now Teddy grinned and begged Wilson to think of their old hostilities as nothing but "dust on a windy street." He jested that if the President would let him take his division to France, he would promise not to come home alive.

Wilson said the war on the western front was no Charge of the Light Brigade, no romantic escapade. He told Roosevelt he was preparing legislation to draft men into the army. Roosevelt promised to support this measure but argued that selective service did not obviate the need for a volunteer division, swiftly formed and sent abroad as a token of our intentions.

"I could arouse the belief that America is coming," Roosevelt said. "I could show the Allies what was on the way."

Wilson said the general staff opposed the volunteer system, and he added that his desk was piled high with requests from other individuals asking to create their own units. Far from being animated by any ill will toward Roosevelt, Wilson went on, he felt inclined to overrule the general staff and urge that the colonel be granted his wish, but under the circumstances he was not sure this could be done. After about an hour the two shook hands and parted with mutual compliments.

As the Presidential secretary escorted Roosevelt out of the Red Room into the main hall and toward the front entrance of the White House, Teddy clapped him on the back and cried, "By Jove, Tumulty, you are a man after my own heart! Six children, eh? Well, now, you get me across and I will put you on my staff, and you may tell Mrs. Tumulty that I will not allow them to place you at any point of danger."

When Roosevelt walked out onto the north portico, he was met by thirty reporters and a crowd of watching people. He waved, grinned and puffed out his chest as photographers snapped pictures. Then the correspondents closed in on him to get his statement. Roosevelt declared he had had a bully interview with the President. Mr. Wilson had received him with the utmost courtesy and consideration, patiently listening as he outlined his plan to raise a division to go to France.

"I am heart and soul for the proposal of the administration for universal obligatory military training and service. I would favor it for three million men. You can call it conscription if you wish, and I would say yes. The division that I ask permission to raise would be raised exclusively among men who would not be taken under the conscription system. They would either be over twenty-five or of the exempted class, and they would eagerly enlist to go to the front."

Roosevelt stopped and turned to the bareheaded Tumulty, who was listening to his every word. Waving his arms, Roosevelt laughed. "If I say anything I shouldn't, be sure and censor it." Turning back to the reporters, Roosevelt added, "I'm already under orders."

At a later date Roosevelt growled, "If Tumulty came along it might be as a sort of watchdog to keep Wilson informed. I'll have a place for him, but it won't be the place he thinks!"

When Tumulty walked back into the White House, the President asked, "Well, and how did the colonel impress you?"

Tumulty said he had been taken with Roosevelt's buoyancy and charm.

"Yes," Wilson mused, "he is a great big boy. I was, as formerly, charmed by his personality. There is a sweetness about him that is very compelling. You can't resist the man. I can easily understand why his followers are so fond of him."

At the end of his performance, and as he drove back to his daughter's home, Roosevelt sank into dejection. He understood the language of diplomacy; he understood that Wilson was denying his request.

In the following days he went to work on members of Congress, now debating selective service, asking them to insert in their draft bill a provision authorizing him to raise not one but *four* volunteer divisions. This touched off such a legislative furor that for two weeks the nation's war effort was paralyzed over the solitary issue of whether Teddy Roosevelt was to have his way. At last the Senate and House agreed to a compromise letting Wilson alone decide whether to accept or reject Teddy's volunteers. The day the President signed the draft act he issued a statement saying:

> It would be very agreeable to me to pay Mr. Roosevelt this compliment and the Allies the compliment of sending to their aid one of our most distinguished public men, an ex-President who has rendered many conspicuous public services, and proved his gallantry in many striking ways. Politically, too, it would no doubt have a very fine effect and make a profound impression. But this is not the time or the occasion for compliment or for any action not calculated to contribute to the immediate success of the war. The business now in hand is undramatic, practical, and of scientific definiteness and precision.

Eleanor Roosevelt felt that Wilson's decision was a bitter blow from which Theodore never recovered. On May 25, 1917, he began the gloomy work of disbanding his paper division, sneering not too privately at the man who had, in effect, regarded him as Don Quixote.

"Wilson—that skunk in the White House!"

Between the outbreak of the war in August, 1914, and the American declaration of war in April, 1917, a few preparedness measures had been adopted by the Wilson administration and private groups and individuals, but now it became apparent that not enough had been done to meet the tests that lay ahead.

Long before we went to war, many American youths had enlisted in the British, Canadian and French armies. There was no law against enlisting in a foreign army, provided the enlistment took place outside the United States, and neither Wilson nor Congress sought to pass such a law. Some Americans living in Paris in August, 1914, organized a volunteer regiment to fight with the French. William Faulkner of Mississippi, who later won the Nobel Prize for literature, joined the Canadian air force and was sent to France. Samuel Insull of Chicago, the British-born utilities king, did all he could to help Americans enlist under the British colors. T. S. Eliot of St. Louis, who also won the Nobel Prize for literature, was living in London when war began, and after the United States entered it, he tried to enlist in the American navy but was rejected because of poor health. Sculptor Jacob Epstein of Manhattan's lower east side had also taken up residence in London and become a British citizen, but he was not eager to fight. His Scottish-born wife asked George Bernard Shaw for help in getting Epstein deferred, but the artist was drafted into the British army, refused a commission, fell ill and was discharged. In July, 1917, after

America went to war, the British held a "British Recruiting Week" in the United States.

In the summer of 1915, acting alone but with the approval of Teddy Roosevelt, General Leonard Wood had established a system of voluntary military training. At Plattsburgh, New York, he had opened an officers' training camp for business and professional men, expanded it the following summer, trained more than 12,000 officers.

As German armies won one military success after another in France, and as the British navy violated the rights of American ships on the Atlantic, President Wilson began to hedge his position on neutrality. On May 27, 1916, in a speech before the League to Enforce Peace, Wilson said, "We are participants, whether we like it or not, in the life of the world. The interests of all nations are our own also. We are partners with the rest. What affects mankind is inevitably our affair as well as the affair of the nations of Europe and Asia."

On August 29, 1916, Congress set up a Council of National Defense consisting of six Cabinet members and an unpaid civilian advisory board; its purpose was to plan for the industrial mobilization of the nation in case of war. That same day Wilson asked Congress to give him the power to take over the nation's railways in an emergency and "to operate them for military purposes." On September 2, 1916, accepting the Presidential nomination a second time, Wilson said, "We have provided for national defense upon a scale never before seriously proposed. . . ." On September 7, 1916, Congress passed a shipping act authorizing the creation of the United States Shipping Board; this five-man board had the power to build, buy, lease or requisition merchant vessels for commercial use and as naval auxiliaries.

But despite these things, when the United States declared war on Germany, it barely had an army—only a little more than 200,000 soldiers, not enough to plug a gap on the western front, where more than 6,000,000 men were locked in combat.

As late as six weeks before the United States went to war, the army was so unprepared it had no plan to organize and equip a large military force, no plan for sending masses of men to France, none for building bases and lines of communications for an American front. General Pershing called the war department inert and wrote, "When the Acting Chief of Staff went to look at the secret files where the plans to meet the situation that confronted us should have been found, the pigeon-hole was empty."

Wilson, wavering between neutrality and preparedness, had considered war planning "a very dangerous situation." He also had thrown a fit of anger when he learned the general staff had plans for fighting Germany, telling War Secretary Baker, "I think you had better stop it." The lack of preparation was due to Wilson's indecision, to Baker's reluctance to act, to the nation's divided soul, to the historic inadequacy of its military establishment, to the fact that Congress had placed limitations on military personnel and funds.

The European combatants were organized into armies of three to five corps, with each corps consisting of two divisions, while the American army had no organized unit larger than a regiment. A divisional structure existed—on paper—but not since the Civil War had American soldiers taken to the field as a division. General Hunter Liggett, head of the War College, said that one well-trained, well-equipped foreign soldier could whip ten brave but untrained Americans

When fighting began in Europe in 1914, the authorized strength of the American army was 100,000 men. From that time, and up until the declaration of war, the administration, Congress and the people debated the issue of the size of the army and how to get it. Wilson's secretary of war, Lindley M. Garrison, said the military establishment was far too small; he stressed the need for a larger standing army, trained reserves and more militiamen. Wilson objected, saying, "We must depend in every time of national peril, in the future as in the past, not upon a standing army, but upon a citizenry trained and accustomed to arms."

But as the United States neared war, Wilson asked Garrison to recommend ways to strengthen the military establishment. Garrison gave him a plan calling for a large regular army and militia, together with a so-called continental army of 400,000 men who would enlist for six-year tours of duty and receive short training periods every year. Garrison urged Wilson to make this plan public, but Wilson refused.

News of the plan nonetheless leaked out, and preparedness advocates, including members of the National Security League, began touting Garrison's continental army—a phrase used during the Revolutionary War for the regular troops of the Colonial army. Some Southern Senators and Congressmen disliked the idea of a continental army and the eclipse of the national guard because they felt that states' rights would be weakened. They rallied around Representative James Hay, chairman of the House military affairs committee, who offered a substitute plan that would expand the state militia. The Garrison plan would put the continental army under federal control. The Hay plan would keep the national guard under state control. Wilson, fearful of losing Congressional support, opted for Hay and the national guard. Garrison became so angry he resigned, and Franklin Roosevelt wrote, "My one regret is that the Cabinet has not more Garrisons."

On March 7, 1916, Wilson named Newton D. Baker of Ohio as Garrison's successor, and on June 3 Congress passed the National Defense Act. This provided for expansion of the regular army from 100,000 to 175,000 enlisted men, 42,750 noncombatant troops and their officers, and the federalization of the national guard—in all, about 235,000 soldiers. The act also authorized the establishment of an officers' reserve training corps at universities, colleges and military camps. Theodore Roosevelt angrily called the act "as foolish and unpatriotic a bit of flintlock legislation as was ever put on the statute books. It is folly, and worse than folly, to pretend that the National Guard is an efficient second line of defense."

His reasoning took on greater weight with the passage of time and the Allied loss of men, munitions and money. If America were to save Britain, France and Russia from defeat, obviously it would have to raise a huge fighting force as quickly as possible. The National Defense Act provided for 235,000 men to be raised in five annual increments ending in July, 1921—but now time was running out. Could the country depend on volunteers to flesh out a gigantic fighting machine, or would it have to resort to conscription—the draft? The two living former Presidents, Roosevelt and Taft, favored the draft, but Wilson was against it.

Wilson knew that conscription was a dirty word to most Americans, for it smacked of autocracy; after all, Germany and Austria-Hungary traditionally drafted men into their armies. Besides, American history teemed with tawdry tales about the draft.

However much Americans loved freedom, they had resisted impressment into the military in the Revolutionary War, the War of 1812 and the Mexican War of 1846. Washington, Jefferson and Madison had failed in their attempts to persuade Congress to pass selective service legislation. When a draft was proposed in 1812, Daniel Webster denounced what he called this foul attack on the Constitution and the rights of states. During the Mexican War 40,000 soldiers finished their one-year enlistments just as General Winfield Scott was marching on Mexico City, so gleefully they about-faced and wandered home.

During the Civil War Lincoln ordered Northern governors to draft men if they could not fill their quotas with volunteers, whereupon riots erupted in Wisconsin and Indiana while there were threats of riots in Pennsylvania. Worst of all, in New York City in July, 1863, there occurred a draft riot that was the most brutal and shameful episode in that city's history; the police estimated 1,155 persons were killed.

With all this in mind, Senator James Reed of Missouri now warned War Secretary Baker that blood would run through the streets if men were drafted for military service. Millions of native-born Americans still opposed participation in the war, while 10,000,000 others—13 percent of the population—had been born in Germany. Wilson had these German-Americans in mind in his speech calling for war: "They are, most of them, as true and loyal Americans as if they had never known any other fealty or allegiance. They will be prompt to stand with us in rebuking and restraining the few who may be of a different mind and purpose."

By the time Wilson made this speech he had changed his mind and decided it would be necessary, after all, to draft men. He ordered the war department to write a Selective Service Act, and a small group of officers went to work. Much of this bill was composed by Hugh S. Johnson, deputy provost marshal general, who later became a prominent New Dealer in the administration of Franklin Roosevelt.

On April 5, 1917, Baker gave Congress the suggested bill and then went before the House military affairs committee to explain its features. It provided that the regular army be brought to full war strength, that the national guard be federalized, that 500,000 men should be drafted with a second 500,000 to be called when the President deemed necessary. All together, this would raise more than 1,727,000 soldiers. All males between the ages of twenty-one and thirty inclusive were to be subject to the draft, and they would be drafted in proportion to the populations of the various states.

Many members of Congress resisted this bill, urging that the volunteer system be given a fair test before the draft was introduced as a last resort. Democratic Congressman Stanley H. Dent of Alabama, who had replaced Hay as chairman of the House military affairs committee, flatly refused to offer the measure to the House. Democratic Claude Kitchin of North Carolina, the House floor leader, also washed his hands of the bill. House Speaker Champ Clark of Missouri, also a Democrat, took the floor to make a speech in which he said that "conscript" and "convict" meant the same thing. Earlier in the war George Bernard Shaw had equated conscription with slavery.

It was a Republican born in Germany, Congressman Julius Kahn of California, the ranking GOP member of the House committee on military affairs, who led the fight in the House for passage of the draft act. Long an advocate of preparedness, he had helped organize the National Defense League.

In both houses of Congress the draft debate was long and bitter. Tumulty kept in close touch with the situation on the Hill and informed the President there was "almost panic in our ranks" over the conscription plan. The *Congressional Record* was filled with pages of comment by worried legislators: ". . . The news of rioting all over the United States will add more joy to the German heart than any other news which could be conveyed. . . . Conscription is another name for slavery. . . . We shall Prussianize America. . . . It will produce a sulky, unwilling, indifferent army. . . ."

John F. "Honey Fitz" Fitzgerald, a former mayor of Boston and a grandfather of John Fitzgerald Kennedy, wanted to tax all aliens $100 apiece and draft them into service. As Congressional bickering continued, former President Taft wrote Baker, 'Why are a lot of them such fools that they want to commit the blunders of previous wars in regard to the volunteer system and insist on going down through the slough of mistakes that England has just been through?"

The Selective Service Act was passed by the House 397 to 24, by the Senate 81 to 8, and was signed into law by the President on May 18, 1917.

What members of Congress did not know as they debated the draft was that the machinery to put it into effect already had been prepared. Baker and his generals felt they were racing against time, since Germany seemed to be defeating the Allies, so they wanted to be ready to set the wheels turning the moment Congress voted for the bill. Forty million forms would be needed to register the 10,000,000 men of draft age. The printing of the forms began in strict secrecy lest the news leak to draft opponents and enrage them.

The man charged with the administration of the draft was Enoch H. Crowder, provost marshal general. Physically weak but strong-minded, he exemplified the intellectual military man; his thoughts flashed so fast he kept two secretaries busy. Just as he began planning the draft organization, an accident put him on crutches, but energetically he would tap-tap-tap down the hall to Baker's office in the state-war-navy building. Crowder often spoke up to his superior, although most of the time the two worked harmoniously.

Baker had told Crowder to get the 40,000,000 forms printed despite the fact that Congress had not yet approved the draft act, and lacking an appropriation, the secretary of war secretly diverted $250,000 of war department funds to pay for the printing and the salaries of the postal clerks who would distribute them. Hugh Johnson, who carried out many of Crowder's orders, later wrote, "Printing in advance of the statute was absolutely illegal, but we figured . . . that the worst we could lose was our jobs and maybe spend some weeks in jail."

Crowder and Johnson met with the public printer, Cornelius Ford, who wasn't sure he could print so many forms without discovery but said he would try. He bought paper in trainload lots and set the federal presses turning. As the millions upon millions of forms flipped off the presses, the conspirators found themselves faced with the problem of storage. Drawn into the secret was Washington's postmaster; after all, he had charge of a depot where the nation's surplus mail sacks were stored. Soon postal workers were stuffing draft forms into the sacks, then hiding them here and there in the huge post office building. But when the printing job was only half-finished, every bag was full and every square foot of space in the post office was filled, with sacks stacked to the ceiling. And of course there was the danger that some disgruntled postal worker might tip off an antidraft legislator or some newspaper to this huge and illegal operation.

Crowder and Baker decided to write every governor and mayor and sheriff in the country to explain their predicament—a calculated risk. The sacks of draft forms would be sent to these public officials, the forms would be taken out and stored in any available vaults, the empty sacks would be returned to Washington. The public men all around the country were asked to say nothing about this to anyone, and in a remarkable example of mass patriotism, not a single official betrayed this trust, although a Philadelphia newspaper got word of what was happening.

Baker had asked Wilson to make registration day "a festival and patriotic occasion" to take the edge off the resentment many Americans felt at the thought of conscription. Specifically, Baker wanted a lofty Presidential draft proclamation. Although Wilson wrote his own state papers, it was left to Hugh Johnson to compose a proclamation which would then be signed by Wilson. Crowder warned Johnson his work probably would be love's labor lost, since Wilson was likely to reject Johnson's text and then prepare his own. Johnson spent two days soaking himself in Wilson's style, finally imitating it so well that the President changed only a few words before signing it. Government printers set part of the Presidential proclamation in Gothic type associated with legal and religious documents, to make it appear impressive, and many newspapers published it under the heading "Call to Arms."

Since the administration did not want the people to feel the heavy hand of bureaucracy, an attempt was made to give the draft organization the appearance of decentralization. Authority began with the President and then descended through General Crowder to the state governors. The governors nominated members of 4,650 local draft boards—all civilians, all friends and neighbors of the boys about to be drafted. In the beginning the board members served without pay; before the end of war they were offered fees about equal to jury duty pay, although few applied for this remuneration. Also created were 1,319 medical boards and 160 district boards. The district boards, also staffed by civilians, handled appeals from local draft boards.

The first registration day was Tuesday, June 5, 1917. Governors, mayors, chambers of commerce and other individuals and groups did all they could to invest with patriotism this first nationwide conscription in the history of the United States. From the docks of Boston to the quays of San Diego, from the forests of Oregon to the swamps of Florida, young men appeared at schools and churches and city halls, some willingly, some resentfully, to offer themselves to the service of a faraway war few understood.

Each registrant filled out a form asking his name, address, age, physical features and reason for claiming exemption—if any. Then he was handed a green card certifying he had registered for the draft. A Philadelphia youth tore up a questionnaire and was sent to jail for a year. In Springfield, Illinois, a man and his wife were jailed for ninety days for advising their son not to register.

In Butte, Montana, 600 miners paraded to protest registration. When Navajo Indians drove away an Indian agent sent to take their names, the New York *Times* solemnly said there was danger they might go on the warpath. The Ute also refused to register, and the young braves of draft age put on their bear-dance costumes, got drunk and fled to the hills. Raymond Moore of Kansas City refused to sign the registration form and was jailed and then visited by his sister, who wept and said he was causing his mother much anguish. Some Texans opposed to the draft organized the Farmers' and Laborers' Protective Association, drifted into Dallas to buy weapons and muttered about making a stand in the woods against anyone thinking he could put them into uniform. General Crowder said that in the course of the war some fifteen to twenty persons were killed in what he called "pitched battles between resisters and county and state forces."

One of the worst clashes occurred near Heber Springs, Arkansas. A clutch of mountain boys holed up in the home of old Tom Adkisson and swore they danged well warn't goin' down into the valley to register. Tom belonged to an offshoot of the Baptist sect and agreed with his preacher that killing was wrong, dead wrong. Well, Sheriff Duke of Cleburne county knew the law, knew the boys had to come out and register, so he took four men and advanced on Tom's place at dawn and yelled for the draft dodgers to surrender. Instead of prisoners, he got a spatter of lead from maybe twenty hidden riflemen and finished up with one dead posse man, name of Porter Hazlewood. That misty morning the sheriff and his remaining deputies beat a retreat to beef up their forces, then returned about noon twenty-five strong.

That's when the battle began. Bullets whanged back and forth between the lawmen and the outlaws, while in defiance of all danger a small, redheaded mountaineer woman, Mrs. Ida Simmons, stood in the open, waving her arms, singing hymns and cursing the officers. Old Tom got winged as he ducked past a gap in his fence; but he managed to slip away, and so did all the young men he was trying to protect. The sheriff allowed as how he wouldn't let it go at that, so he asked the governor for help. The governor turned out something called the Home Guard, along with a machine-gun company, and for a week they trailed old Tom and the boys through the backwoods.

At last the weary young men gave up, and the last to turn himself in was old Tom himself—wounded, but grim and game and bellowing that he took responsibility for the whole ruckus. Old Mother Blakeley summed up the feelings of the mountain folk when she said, "Men, hit's wrong to kill! I know they tell terrible things on them German soldiers, but they hain't got over here yit an' hit'll be plenty o' time fer to fight when they jump on us in our own kentry!"

On registration day a total of 9,660,000 young men appeared as ordered to sign up for the draft. The government wanted 687,000 of them immediately, so the next step was to determine which of the registrants should be called to duty. Crowder decided the fairest way to do this would be to hold a national lottery.

The drawing began the morning of July 20, 1917, in the public hearing room of the Senate office building. President Wilson was present, and so were Secretary Baker, General Crowder, ranking members of Congress and other dignitaries. A big glass bowl was filled with 10,500 black capsules containing slips bearing numbers from 1 to 10,500. In each of the 4,650 local draft offices across the country the men had been registered on numerical lists; the local board with the largest list had 10,500 names. A general took a large wooden spoon bedecked with red, white and blue bunting and stirred the capsules in the bowl.

Photographers edged in as Baker was blindfolded and led to the table. At 9:49 A.M. the secretary of war plunged in his hand and brought out a single capsule as cameras clicked. Baker had drawn number 258. It was verified by three tellers, recorded by six tallymen and chalked on a blackboard behind Baker. Reporters ran out of the room to telephone or wire their offices everywhere in the nation. From coast to coast young men stood anxiously in front of newspaper buildings which soon displayed hastily scrawled bulletins announcing that 258 was the magic number, the first of many, for the drawing continued until two o'clock the following morning.

In Greenville, Mississippi, a man named G. M. Bradshaw saw the first number and ran to the local telegraph office to wire Baker: THANKS FOR DRAWING 258—THAT'S ME! Alfred A. Primeau told Chicago reporters, "It is more honor than I have ever had before." Early that day in the Flushing area of New York City a bartender had tossed a coin with his brother to determine which would enlist and which would stay home to support their widowed mother; the brother had called the toss which meant he had to enlist, but now the bartender, Andrew Yaros, learned Baker had drawn his number—258. In small towns where the registration list did not reach 258, the man holding the closest number was selected.

Now local draft boards swung into action, bringing out of hiding the millions of stored forms. White postcards summoned men to report for physical examinations, and doctors thumped chests and examined tongues and noted deformities and listened to requests for exemption. Each man was given seven days to file a claim to stay home.

James Thurber, who later became a cartoonist and satirist for the *New*

Yorker magazine, was at this time a twenty-two-year-old student at Ohio State University in Columbus, and years later he wrote an amusing piece called "Draft Board Nights." A childhood accident had robbed him of the sight in one eye, and his other eye was so weak that eventually he went totally blind. Thurber wrote:

> . . . I was called almost every week, even though I had been exempted from service the first time I went before the medical examiners. Either they were never convinced that it was me or else there was some clerical error in the records which was never cleared up. Anyway, there was usually a letter for me on Monday ordering me to report for examination on the second floor of Memorial Hall the following Wednesday at 9 P.M. The second time I went up, I tried to explain to one of the doctors that I had been exempted. "You're just a blur to me," I said, taking off my glasses. "You're absolutely nothing to me," he snapped, sharply.
>
> I had to take off my clothes each time and jog around the hall with a lot of porters and bank president's sons and clerks and poets. Our hearts and lungs would be examined, and then our feet; and finally our eyes. That always came last. When the eye specialist got around to me, he would always say, "Why, you couldn't get into the service with sight like that!" "I know," I would say. Then a week or two later I would be summoned again and go through the same rigmarole. The ninth or tenth time I was called, I happened to pick up one of several stethoscopes that were lying on a table and suddenly, instead of finding myself in the line of draft men, I found myself in the line of examiners. "Hello, doctor," said one of them, nodding. "Hello," I said. . . .

Thurber said some men were so desperate to escape the draft that they drank ink, swallowed nails and hairpins, and one even gulped down a small watch. There is further evidence that some men called to service mutilated themselves, while a few even committed suicide.

Draft dodging now became a way of life for thousands upon thousands. The administration had decreed that no marriage contracted after April 6, 1917, was grounds for escaping the draft, but despite this ruling, many young men quickly took brides. Those who mobbed marriage license bureaus were sneeringly called "cupid recruits." On July 31 a total of 164 marriages had been performed by early afternoon in the New York City municipal marriage chapel, where the daily average was only 15 or 16. City Clerk Patrick Scully fumed that "any man who thus seeks to hide behind a woman's skirt is a moral and physical coward!" The Reverend Percy Stickney Grant took a softer line: "Marriage has assumed an air of joyous adventure, in place of the rather sad solemnity that might be expected at times like these. American youth has declared that death shall not conquer." Interestingly, the draft exposed more bigamists than the courts could punish.

The left-wing magazine *The Masses* published a cartoon showing an army doctor examining a draftee lacking a head and exclaiming, "At last—a perfect soldier!" In another issue the magazine offered this slogan: "Knit a straitjacket for your soldier boy!" Robed members of the Ku Klux Klan hunted down draft dodgers, dewy-eyed maidens contemptuously handed yellow feathers to young men in civilian clothing, and Franklin Roosevelt spoke out publicly against "slackers." When Theodore Roosevelt's son Quentin volunteered as a pilot, he was joined by Hall Roosevelt, a brother of Eleanor Roosevelt, who cheated on the eye examination to qualify. Eleanor's Grandmother Hall, out of touch with the times, asked why Hall had not bought a substitute, as was done by gentlemen during the Civil War. Eleanor snapped at her grandmother that "gentlemen" owed the same duty to their country as other citizens and considered it unthinkable to pay someone to risk his life for them. Robert H. Jackson, then a lawyer and later a justice of the United States Supreme Court, believed we should have remained out of the war and said, "My grandfather bought his way out of the draft in the Civil War and I was never ashamed of it."

Alfred I. du Pont of the enormously wealthy du Pont family later confessed, "My war record consisted in staying home and trembling in my shoes for fear I would be eaten alive by a Boche." Huey Long, then a young man of twenty-four, asked exemption on the grounds he was a notary public. Many years later, after he was elected Senator for Louisiana, after a revulsion against the war set in, Huey said on the floor of the Senate, "I did not go into that war. I was within the draft age. I could have gone, except for my dependents. I did not go because I did not want to go, aside from that fact. . . . I did not go because I was not mad at anybody over there, for another reason. I did not go because it was not the first time in history that the sons of America had volunteered themselves as cannon fodder under the misguided apprehension that it was going to be a fight for humanity," when in reality they had been used to centralize "the wealth of the United States and of the world in the hands of a few."

Jack Dempsey was twenty-two in 1917 and two years away from winning the world's heavyweight boxing championship, but he escaped the draft. In an autobiography as told to Bob Considine and Bill Slocum, Dempsey said:

> I followed the law. My draft board never called me. It never called me because it felt I was entitled to deferment. I was never charged with failing to register for the draft, which is draft dodging in its basic meaning. I was charged with defrauding the government in connection with the papers I filled out. The public had a quicker way of saying it. I was charged with being a slacker. God only knows how many people called me that—yelled it, loud and clear, in front of thousands of people in fight crowds or theaters. People would yell it from passing automobiles, or call it out a window as I passed. But a funny thing: Nobody ever called me a slacker to my face. Those thousands of people who elected themselves my judges handed down their decisions from a safe distance. Nobody ever made the charge in print. But they hinted

> at it in a way that said as much but was libelproof. I got so damned fed up that I decided to join the Navy.

In 1915 Henry Ford had declared he would refuse to accept war orders from any of the belligerents, but by early 1917 he had changed his mind and begun to aid the Allies. After the American declaration of war he told a Detroit reporter, "Everything I've got is for the government, and not a cent of profit." His only son, Edsel, was twenty-three in 1917 and secretary of his father's corporation. Edsel wanted to enlist, but his father refused him permission, darkly telling a friend that if Edsel were put into uniform, "certain interests" who disliked "the Ford system" of doing business would "have seen to it" that Edsel never returned.

When Edsel's draft number came up, attorneys for the Ford Motor Company appealed his case to his local draft board, arguing that the son was indispensable to the Ford interests since he was helping fill war orders. When the board could find no reason to exempt Edsel, some family representatives appealed to the White House. The President never ruled on this matter, but in the end Edsel was exempted under an army regulation concerning men in war industries. Theodore Roosevelt lamented that "young Mr. Ford, in ease and safety, is in the employ of his wealthy father." Teddy's son-in-law, Congressman Nicholas Longworth, said that of the seven men in the world who were sure to get through the war unscathed, six were sons of the Kaiser while the seventh was Edsel Ford.

Perhaps the strangest exemption was granted to Conrad Aiken, the poet. In 1917 he was eighteen, but he refused to serve in the army on the grounds that as a poet he was engaged in an "essential industry"—not to be classified with billiard marking, setting up candlepins, or speculation in theater tickets. He won his case and went on to win a Pulitzer Prize for literature.

Despite the many men who tried to escape the draft, there were more who were eager to fight.

Actor John Barrymore was thirty-five and not subject to the draft law, but he tried to enlist, only to be rejected—for varicose veins. A beautiful man with a classical profile, Barrymore was so disappointed that he and another man went on a colossal drunk and threw plates around the dining room of the Astor hotel on Times Square.

Franklin D. Roosevelt was the same age as Barrymore, and he also wanted to volunteer, partly because he believed that a good war record was necessary to get him into the White House; as a young man he had decided that someday he would become President. He asked Navy Secretary Daniels to ask Wilson to let him resign his navy post and don a uniform. Daniels spoke to the President, who said, "Neither you nor I nor Franklin Roosevelt has the right to select the place of service" because that place had already been "assigned" by the country. Roosevelt then made a personal plea to Wilson, who persisted in his refusal.

F. Scott Fitzgerald, who became a great American novelist, scorned patriotism but was attracted by the romantic notion of the gallant man staring into the eyes of death. He wrote a cousin, "Updike from Oxford or Harvard says 'I die for England' or 'I die for America'—not me I'm too Irish for that—I may get killed for America—but I'm going to die for myself." Dean Rusk, a small boy in Georgia, dug trenches, read about battles and cut soldiers' pictures from newspapers.

The day Congress declared war William Jennings Bryan abandoned his lifelong pacifism, erupted in patriotism and wired Wilson to ask to be enrolled in the army as a private. The former secretary of state was fifty-seven. He told Secretary Daniels that although he had been a colonel during the Spanish-American War, he did not now seek a command because he was "too old to learn the art of war." Wilson responded, "I am sure that the whole country will believe that you are ready to serve in any way that may set its interests forward." Nonetheless, Bryan's offer was not accepted.

War Secretary Baker, forty-six, became so fed up with his desk job that he asked Chief of Staff Scott to send him to France as a second lieutenant. According to Baker, who could laugh at himself, the general replied, "You don't know enough to be a second lieutenant!"

Many American and British parents were quick to offer their sons to the god of war, causing Bertrand Russell to muse, "I had supposed until [now] that it was quite common for parents to love their children, but the War persuaded me that it is a rare exception." Theodore Roosevelt gave a rousing war speech in Detroit, and a woman rose in the balcony with an American flag in her hand and cried, "I have two sons! I offer them!" When the applause ended, Teddy replied, "Madame, if every mother in the country would make the same offer, there would be no need for any mother to send her sons to war."

Former President Taft had a nineteen-year-old son named Charles P. Taft II who left Yale to enlist. Weeks later he married Eleanor Chase, and just before he sailed for France, he got a letter from his father saying, "Demoralization exists as never before in France and you will be almost raped unless you brace yourself. It is such a comfort to know that you have your sweet, loving wife, Eleanor, to whom you have plighted your faith and whose appealing fond glances will always rise before you when you are confronted by sinful love."

John Nance Garner, a Texas Congressman who became Vice President under Franklin Roosevelt, had a son named Tully. The day after the House passed Wilson's war declaration Tully visited his father's office, and Garner asked, "Son, how do you feel about going to war?" Tully replied, "I aim to go, Dad." Garner exploded, "Hell, it's not a matter of *aiming* to go! You *are* going! I couldn't have cast my vote to send other boys to war if I hadn't known I was sending my own."

After we entered the war many members of Harvard's class of 1912 enlisted, but not so one of their classmates, Joseph P. Kennedy. One of them remembered: "They took pride in not being drafted, and they didn't appreciate a man not going into the war, as, for instance, in the case of Joe."

Joyce Kilmer was graduated from Columbia in 1908, six years later wrote his famous poem "Trees," was thirty-one in 1917. He had four children, and his wife was pregnant with their fifth; but he enlisted and went to France and took a bullet in his brain. The death of this American poet was remembered during World War II when an embarkation station in New Jersey was named Camp Kilmer.

Conscientious objectors were a problem.

There is a long history to the subject of conscientious objectors. More than 500 years before the birth of Christ the Chinese philosopher Lao-tse condemned war and defended conscientious objectors. Mark Anthony exempted Jews from military service because they would not bear arms on their Sabbath. In the first century and a half of the Christian era few Christians served in the Roman army, but as the Catholic church grew in power and wealth, it began to denounce men refusing to fight. Napoleon allowed the pacifist Mennonites to serve as hospital workers. During the Revolutionary War in this country conscientious objectors sometimes were exempted from militia service by paying a fine or by paying double or triple taxes. During the Civil War conscientious objectors in the North could escape service by payment of $300.

The draft law of 1917 was considerate of sects whose creeds opposed fighting—Mennonites, Quakers, Dunkers, Russian Dukhobors, Seventh-day Adventists, Jehovah's Witnesses, Molokans and Plymouth Brethren. Although their members were not exempted from the draft, they were allowed to serve as noncombatants.

A distinction was drawn between *sincere* and *insincere* CO's, although this distinction was hard to maintain. In general, a *sincere* objector meant someone objecting to all wars, while an *insincere* objector meant someone opposing this particular war. Most of the so-called *insincere* CO's, of course, were of German birth or descent. War Secretary Baker stretched the law to let anyone with "personal scruples against war" be considered a conscientious objector.

There were 1,400 men who refused to serve in any capacity; a majority were native-born Americans. For the first time ever the government used intelligence tests on men being considered for the service, and these showed that the balky 1,400 were above average in intelligence. Most intelligent of all were those opposing the war on political grounds, many of them Socialists who absolutely refused to take part in a war they believed was due to capitalism. One CO was Carl Naessler, a former Rhodes scholar and a professor of philosophy.

President Wilson created a board of inquiry "to discover and weigh and measure the secret motives which actuated the objector to resist authority." One board member was Harlan Fiske Stone, dean of Columbia University's school of law and later a justice of the United States Supreme Court. He personally interrogated a nonreligious objector named Ernest L. Meyer, who later wrote about this experience in his diary.

Stone asked, "You are a member of no church?"

"No, sir."

"Socialist?"

"I share many of their beliefs, but I am not a member of the party."

"What would you do if you were attacked, or a burglar entered your house and tried to rape your wife or mother?"

"Resist him. . . . Try to save my wife."

"Then," Stone asked, "how can you maintain your position in opposition to war? You sanction the use of force."

Meyer answered, "I see no analogy whatever in your comparison. I can't concede that this is a defensive war. . . . You imply . . . one side is an innocent wife or mother and the other side a fiend. I can't admit this. . . . I am dealing with one individual. But in war we are dealing with nations. . . . America, as the outstanding neutral, could have exerted enough pressure to bring about peace without resorting to arms."

"Other means have been tried. They failed."

"They were not tried," Meyer insisted, "with the same vigor, the same sacrifice, that we have mobilized in the war."

"Your country made the choice," Stone declared. "It is up to you to abide by it."

Stone detested these "glib talkers," as he called them, and dealt with them harshly.

Wilson and Baker took a softer line toward the CO's than did Stone, some generals and newspapers and educators and churchmen and others. The President said, "I have little enough sympathy with the conscientious objector, but I am sure we all want to avoid unnecessary harshness and injustice of any sort."

Theodore Roosevelt snarled that most CO's were "slackers, pure and simple, or else traitorous pro-Germans" who should "permanently be sent out of the country as soon as possible." Some extremists wanted all CO's shot out of hand. The canon of the Episcopal Cathedral of St. John the Divine in Manhattan characterized CO's as "wolves in sheep's clothing." The New York *Times* published a ferocious editorial about CO's, declaring that "if he puts his belief into practice, we should either put him to death or shut him up in an asylum as a madman." Nicholas Murray Butler, the president of Columbia University, declared "no one has less sympathy with these morally half-witted people than I have."

General Leonard Wood, in charge of Fort Riley and Camp Funston in Kansas, raged at an order by Secretary Baker to segregate the CO's and treat them with "kindly consideration." All objectors sent into Wood's jurisdiction knew they were in for a bad time. One of the CO's at Fort Riley was Evan Thomas, a brother of Socialist leader Norman Thomas, and soon Evan was going through hell. To protest the brutal treatment of the CO's he went on a hunger strike, was put in solitary confinement, became so weak he was removed to a base hospital, was cursed by a doctor, was told he would wind up in a straitjacket, was tortured by being scrubbed with a stiff brush, was forcibly fed.

At last Evan Thomas was court-martialed and found guilty of disobeying the order of an officer to eat. He was sentenced to life imprisonment. Subsequently, as Norman Thomas sarcastically phrased it, General Wood "in his mercy" reduced his sentence to twenty-five years.

Evan was sent to Fort Leavenworth, where he found a group of

Molokans, a Russian pacifist sect which had migrated to this country during President Grant's administration on the assurance that the United States never conscripted its citizens. The jailed Molokans refused to work under military orders, so they were placed in solitary, abused by guards, compelled to sleep on cement floors, manacled nine hours a day in a standing position to the bars of their cells. They were also forbidden to read or write or even talk. Evan smuggled a letter out of Leavenworth to his brother Norman, and their mother went to see Secretary Baker to protest this treatment. Baker told her the stories simply were not true. Since he was a sensitive and compassionate man, one must assume he really did not know what was happening in Leavenworth.

Torture was inflicted on CO's in other parts of the country as well. Philip Grosser was sent to Alcatraz island in the San Francisco bay; most of the time he was kept in solitary confinement; the rest of the time he was chained to the door of his cell. In camps and in penitentiaries here and there across the land the CO's were beaten and jabbed with bayonets, and some were hung upside down with their faces in human excrement.

Horrors of this kind were not inflicted on all objectors. One young man who refused to serve was Roger Baldwin, who later became director of the American Civil Liberties Union. He was found guilty and sentenced to a year in jail, and ironically he began serving his term the day the war ended, November 11, 1918, trudging through the confetti-strewn streets of Manhattan to board a ferry to enter a prison in Newark, New Jersey. There he was treated well by an Irish warden who said he wanted no part of "England's war."

One youth began the war as a CO and ended it as a mass killer. His name was Alvin York. He was a mountaineer from Pall Mall, Tennessee, six feet tall with hair the color of fire, fond of bootleg booze and gambling and rough-and-tumble fighting—until he got religion. In 1915 he joined the Church of Christ in Christian Union, became an elder, and when the draft came along, he tried to explain to his draft board that he agreed with the Lord: "Thou shalt not kill." The local board members knew Alvin was a crack rifleman who could "drive the cross" of a half-inch penciled X on a piece of paper pinned to a tree 200 feet away. Just what this country needed.

York declared himself a conscientious objector, made three appeals against the draft, was thrice denied, and finally was sent to a camp in Georgia. There he asked for a job as a noncombatant, but a Captain Danforth, aware of his reputation as a marksman and a Bible believer, went to work on him with Biblical quotations: "I bring you not peace but a sword. . . . He that hath no sword, let him sell his garment and buy one." York argued a little; but mostly he listened, and when he went home on leave, he knelt on a hill and had a talk with the Lord, who said it was all right for him to fight in a just cause.

So Alvin York was sent to France with the American Expeditionary Force, was promoted to corporal, and during the Argonne battle on October 8, 1918, he became an American folk hero. A German officer and five men leaped from a trench and advanced toward York in single file like wild turkeys, who are methodical in their habits, and the Tennessee mountaineer shot them as he had shot turkeys—the last first, then the next to last, and so on until he killed the officer, out in front, who had not known what was happening behind him.

Nor was that all. Armed only with a rifle and revolver, York then killed a total of twenty Germans, took a fortified hill and forced the surrender of 132 Germans and thirty-five machine guns. General Pershing called York the outstanding soldier of the AEF, while Marshal Ferdinand Foch of France went further, describing York's feat as "the greatest thing accomplished by any private soldier of all the armies of Europe." York was decorated with the Croix de Guerre and the Congressional Medal of Honor, and in 1941 Gary Cooper portrayed him in a film called *Sergeant York*.

On July 9, 1917, President Wilson announced that the following August 5 all state militiamen would be brought under federal control. This angered many of the country folks in Oklahoma. In 1916 they had voted for Wilson because they thought he would keep America out of war, but after the declaration of war and passage of the draft act, they felt he had betrayed them. Men would lift their eyes from the sticks they were idly whittling, spit tobacco juice and sneer at the President, calling him Big Slick. Why should they or their sons or nephews or cousins leave the valleys and flatlands to go to France to fight some German farmers wearing a different uniform? What the hell was the war all about, anyway? As it was, they had enough trouble just keeping alive.

In the cotton-growing region southeast of Oklahoma City the tenant farmers endured poverty as miserable as that in Asia. The sandy soil was nearly barren, the sharecroppers were in bondage to landlords, the few farmers lucky enough to own their own property were indebted to banks that charged them 20 to 40 percent interest on loans, while the general stores demanded even higher interest rates. Poverty and malnutrition sickened bodies and dulled minds; only a few people in the region could read or write.

In the South Canadian valley of Oklahoma, in Seminole and Hughes and Pontotoc counties, the Socialist party had polled more than a third of the votes in the Congressional election of 1914. These regional Socialists were not sophisticates or intellectuals, like the national leaders of the party, but crude and unlettered radicals with a tendency to violence because of years of suffering. And their own murky radicalism was exceeded by men belonging to other minority groups that came into existence in that part of the country.

One was the Working Class Union, founded in 1914 in Van Buren, Arkansas, by Dr. Wells Le Fevre. Then it affiliated with the Industrial Workers of the World, and locals were established up and down Oklahoma's valley. To join the union, one had to swear a secret oath on a Bible and a six-shooter. Although the union's official posture was one of mild radicalism, its leaders did nothing to cool the extremists who flocked into the locals. Another radical organization in this part of Oklahoma was a smaller homegrown group called the Jones Family. Some members of the union and the family also belonged to the Socialist party but were too poor to pay even the meager party dues. There was no formal link between these two groups and the Socialist party; the overlapping membership was a matter of preference.

The night of August 3, 1917—two days before the national guard in every state was to be drafted en masse into the regular army—more than 100 tenant farmers and sharecroppers gathered on Spears Hill a couple of miles from Sasakwa, Oklahoma. As the hours ticked by, they were joined by 400 other men, all angry, all muttering about revolution. At this encampment they lit fires which shone on the hard, pinched faces of poor whites, some blacks and some Indians. They ate barbecued beef and an Indian green corn dish call tomfuller. This, together with the fact that this was the season of the annual green corn dance of the nearby Shawnee, gave this event the name of the Green Corn Rebellion.

All wore ragged clothes, were poorly armed and thoroughly confused. Their plan was nothing less than to march to Washington, take over the government, and end America's participation in the war. But many of the young rebels were so ignorant they were not even sure of the location of the capital. They believed a rumor that when they got to Chicago, they would be joined by 190,000 Wobblies—members of the Industrial Workers of the World—and march with them to the East coast. Sons of the soil, they expected to feed off the land as they moved to their goal. Later it was said that Germany had given them money to buy arms and ammunition, but this simply was untrue; many carried nothing but ancient rifles.

Local Socialist leaders, hearing about their encampment and their impossible dream, rushed to the scene to warn they did not stand a chance of getting to Washington, let alone overthrowing the government. But the tattered stubborn men, more in touch with their bellies than their minds, argued that while the Socialist party only *talked* about ending the war, they intended to do something about it. For openers they turned livestock loose in fields and cut a few telegraph wires, but things went wrong from the start. Some rebels tried to blow up a bridge; their dynamite would not explode.

This pathetic rebellion was put down in a couple of days. Sheriffs deputized posses, who captured the hazy-minded radicals without firing a shot. The authorities did not find it necessary to declare martial law, to call out the militia or to ask for help from army units in the state. About 450 bewildered men were arrested.

Some were tried in federal court and found guilty. Most got suspended sentences when they promised to go back to their patches of earth and behave themselves. Others were jailed for sixty days to two years, while the leaders of the Green Corn Rebellion were sent to the federal penitentiary at Leavenworth, Kansas, to serve sentences of three to ten years.

In July, 1918, a madcap reporter named Gene Fowler left Denver for New York to take a job on a Hearst newspaper in Manhattan. One hot day that month Fowler decided to visit a pool to see an exhibition by

Duke Kahanamoku, the Hawaiian swimmer. When he got there, he saw a cluster of police wagons and men in civilian clothes stopping young men to see their draft cards. A deputy U.S. marshal approached Fowler and ordered him to produce his. The young reporter had left it at home. The deputy then asked to see his other credentials, whereupon the irrepressible Fowler demanded to see his. With a snarl the deputy asked his destination, and Fowler replied he was on his way to fire on Fort Sumter. "Oh!" the deputy barked. "A wise guy, eh? You're going downtown to the clinkeroo!" Fowler was put in a police van, driven to the Harrison Street jail and thrown into the bullpen. Other reporters managed to convince the cops that he was not a draft dodger, so at last a sergeant gave him a voucher certifying he was properly registered.

Four registration days were held during the course of the war and a total of 23,456,021 men between the ages of eighteen and forty-five were registered—half the adult male population of the United States. Of this number, more than 4,800,000 actually donned uniforms. They included the 2,810,296 men selected for service, together with 2,000,000 others who anticipated the draft by enlisting in the army or navy. Eighteen percent of all draftees were foreign-born. Thirteen percent were black.

The government granted exemption from service to 56,830 members of religious sects opposed to war. A total of 337,649 men tried to dodge the draft, and the government brought legal action against 220,747 of them, and of these 163,738 were found and arrested and tried. Some were acquitted while others were convicted and jailed, some for as long as ten years.

A total of 3,989 men sought exemption as conscientious objectors. Of this number more than 1,300 accepted noncombatant duty, 1,299 were furloughed for alternate duty on farms and the like, while 504 were court-martialed and sent to prison. One man was tried and convicted in only eighteen minutes. Seventeen CO's were sentenced to death—but their sentences were not carried out.

Chapter 25

CONSTRUCTION OF THE CAMPS

In the spring of 1917 Congress was so busy debating a draft bill that it was slow to act on an emergency war appropriations bill that included an item calling for $60,000,000 to erect barracks for the men about to be drafted. While the army wanted to turn civilians into soldiers as fast as possible, it had not a cent for construction of the camps.

Quartermaster General Henry G. Sharpe asked Frederick Snare to visit his office in the state-war-navy building in Washington. Snare arrived on May 12, 1917. He was a partner in the New York construction firm of Snare & Triest, and in the previous weeks he had been negotiating a contract to build a subway station in the Flatbush section of Brooklyn.

The general asked the businessman to sign a $3,000,000 contract to build an army camp at Chickamauga, Georgia. But—as Sharpe was quick to tell Snare—there was a catch: At the moment the army lacked the money to pay him. Was Snare willing to risk his fortune to start work without federal funds, to face bankruptcy should the war suddenly end, to wait to be reimbursed only after Congress appropriated the money? The general said he knew this was much to ask of anyone, but every day's delay in housing soldiers meant a day's delay in their training and thus a day's delay in getting them to France.

The contractor walked over to a window to stare abstractedly out at the national capital, deep in thought. Then he turned to the general and said, "I'll do it." Sharpe beamed and summoned a secretary and dictated the government's first emergency camp contract, which Snare then signed.

Existing army posts were inadequate to billet all the men about to be drafted, so entire soldier-cities had to be created—within ninety days. No construction project of such proportions had been undertaken since the building of the Panama Canal. It was one of the most impressive construction feats in the history of the world. In terms of the numbers of men to be housed, it was like building Philadelphia from scratch. In terms of space, it was like roofing all Manhattan, all Atlantic City and one square mile more.

War Secretary Baker made all the big decisions, such as how many camps were needed and where they should be located. The city fathers of hundreds of communities wanted the camps built near their hometowns because that would be good for local business. They appealed to their representatives in Washington, but to favor one city over another was to make political enemies, so Senators and Congressmen were happy to be able to say that only the secretary of war could pick the sites. Municipal rivalry was intense. In Kentucky the cities of Louisville and Lexington began feuding, spokesmen for each community alleging the other place was no fit site to quarter soldiers.

Southerners flinched at the thought of black soldiers from the North being stationed in Dixie and perhaps upsetting the status quo—meaning segregation of the races. The governor of South Carolina went to Washington to argue against quartering black enlisted men in the South. Universities and colleges offered their campuses as centers for the training of officers.

Baker decided on the construction of sixteen cantonments to house the national army and sixteen camps for the federalized national guard. The word "cantonment" comes from the French, was used by the British and means the quartering of troops in temporary structures. Each one was to be made of wood and was to cost from $7,000,000 to $14,000,000. Since militiamen were accustomed to living in tents, each camp would be made mainly of canvas and cost from $2,000,000 to $4,000,000. Most canvas cities would go up in the warm Southland while the wooden cantonments would arise farther north and stretch across the land from Massachusetts to the state of Washington.

On May 19, 1917—a day before a massive mutiny by soldiers in the French army—there was created within the office of the quartermaster general a cantonment division, later renamed the construction division. It was charged with housing the new American army. Before America entered the war, an officer had made a model of a Napoleonic barracks one story high, but it was decided instead to construct two-story barracks since one roof could cover two floors and thus double the number of men to be sheltered. For advice about the design of the soldier-cities the army turned to the nation's foremost town planners.

Each camp would house one division. Each barracks would house 150 men—one company, although infantry companies later were increased to 250 men. The standard design was a street 3 miles long lined on both sides by an average of 1,200 two-story barracks 43 feet wide and 140 feet long, backed by other rows of buildings—mess halls, lavatories, warehouses, offices, hospitals and stables. It would be necessary to build water and sewage systems, bring in railway lines and construct terminals, provide lighting and heating facilities and link each camp with one another and Washington by telephone and telegraph systems.

All this colossal construction work was to be done by private contractors at a profit of 3 percent—although some got as much as 4½ percent. Baker and Samuel Gompers, the president of the American Federation of Labor, agreed that the men who built the camps should be paid the union scale prevailing in each separate community. While there were plenty of skilled workers, the nation suffered from a lack of unskilled labor. Chinese businessmen living in this country offered to import Chinese laborers to meet the need, but Baker declined because, among other things, Gompers would be sure to explode at such an arrangement. The British used gangs of Chinese laborers behind their lines in France. One American contractor aroused the wrath of Jews by advertising for "Christian" carpenters.

Construction of the camps and cantonments began in June, 1917. At thirty-two sites scattered from Massachusetts to Georgia to California to Washington, lumber began arriving in a total of 80,000 freight cars—enough to make a boardwalk 12 inches wide and 1 inch thick that would stretch to the moon and halfway back again. As the lumber was unloaded, it was sawed into duplicate parts of precisely the same length and shape, which were then fitted together to construct a total of 43,254 buildings. The parts were so standardized and the work so routine that a building could be put together in two days. In a couple of camps some barracks went up in only an hour and a half.

Work was proceeding nearly on schedule when a crisis erupted on July 16, 1917. Contractors told the government they were running out of lumber. This was one day after 50,000 lumbermen, most of them members of the Industrial Workers of the World, struck the logging camps of the Northwest. Since lumber was the only big industry on the coast in which the eight-hour day did not prevail, Baker asked the lumber barons to grant the shorter working hours the strikers wanted, but the *American Lumberman* editorialized: "It is really pitiable to see the government . . . truckling to a lot of treasonable, anarchistic agitators . . . playing into the hands of our enemy." The Lumbermen's Protective Association refused to raise wages but did collect a $500,000 "fighting fund" to try to break the strike. President Wilson ordered a mediation commission to investigate, and the commission condemned the resistance of the lumber kings to an eight-hour day. The war department ordered a colonel to recruit a "Loyal Legion of Loggers and Lumbermen." The discontented workers of the Northwest got their eight-hour day in December, but by this time the camp construction had been thrown off schedule.

There were other problems, as well. In parts of the country where metal was scarce the contractors installed wooden pipes. Swarms of mosquitoes interrupted work on Camp Upton at Yaphank, Long Island. At this site the army had rented land for 88 cents an acre but then found the remains of an oak forest and had to spend $200 an acre to pull out stumps.

By October 15, 1917, the thirty-two camps and cantonments were declared finished, although draftees were to find that this announcement was only relatively true. In only a little more than ninety days there had been created quarters for 1,372,718 men at a cost of more than $218,000,000—a feat which the President's secretary said would "stand for all time as a building miracle." Baker agreed, saying, "In spite of the stupendous difficulties involved, the entire housing enterprise was completed practically on schedule, constituting one of the most remarkable accomplishments of the war."

Meantime, local draft boards had been processing almost 1,000,000 men to select the 687,000 the President sought in his first draft call. General Pershing, the commander of the American Expeditionary Force and already in France to boost Allied morale, cabled a request for at least 1,000,000 soldiers by May, 1918. Now that the camps were said to be ready, from all points of the compass in the United States the draftees began leaving their hometowns and heading for the new soldier-cities to begin six weeks of basic training. Since the railroads were unable to move such masses simultaneously, they went in batches.

A wave of emotion swept the land as they took this first step in a journey that could end in a grave in France. Mothers and grandmothers, aunts and sisters, nieces and girlfriends touched for the last time the warm hands and cheeks of their beloved men, kissed them, wished them well, wept and fainted. Fathers and grandfathers, uncles and brothers shook hands a little too vigorously and grinned too widely and then turned away to touch eyes suddenly moist. Little girls tugged at the jackets of their big brothers, while small boys puffed out their chests and bragged about what their brothers would do to those dirty Huns.

Journalist Mark Sullivan described a scene at Peru, Indiana:

> Among those who came to see the draftees off was the local post of the Grand Army of the Republic, a tottering handful of very old men come to give a blessing to their grandsons, grandsons destined to substitute, in the newer generation's experiences, Belleau Wood for Gettysburg, St. Mihiel for Bloody Angle. The Civil War veterans wore their army uniforms, and evidently had been at great pains to get together what was left of the fife and drum corps that had played them off to war some fifty years before. Now once more it played *Rally 'Round the Flag, Boys* to old men who could no longer rally. As one watched them saying good-bye to the younger men, one wondered how much the furtive tears in their eyes were for their own long-gone youth, how much for the fate that might await their grandsons.

Youths who had cut no great figure in their hometowns suddenly found themselves local celebrities. They were partied and petted and praised by chambers of commerce, Rotary clubs, local branches of state councils of defense, welfare societies, churches and the like. With the departure of the first draftees from the District of Columbia, the Senate recessed early so the Senators could march with them along Pennsylvania Avenue. In Dallas a reporter couldn't quite understand when a father seeing his son off to war said, "I'd rather have my son go to heaven in France than to hell in America."

Some dressed up in their Sunday best to go to war, but John L. Barkley of Holden, Missouri, later said he felt like a fool because he wore overalls as he boarded a train that would take him to Funston, Kansas. In Southern railway stations bands serenaded the departing draftees with "Dixie," while in the North it was "Marching Through Georgia." In all parts of the country, though, the most popular song for the occasion was "Auld Lang Syne."

Whenever a troop train stopped at a station along the route, the local women appeared with baskets of food to stuff the young men. For many the trip to camp was the first journey they had ever made any distance outside their tiny towns, and a Virginia mountaineer exclaimed in amazement, "Bud, if this old world is as big the other way as she is this side, she's a hell-buster for sartain!"

Some men, having had liquor pressed on them by patriotic bartenders or having brought along their own bottles, were drunk when they boarded the trains. In Arizona one trainload of cowboys and Indians and miners "were drunk, and not just drunk, but extravagantly and supremely drunk." During the next twenty-four hours they threw a porter off the moving train, and when it stopped in Trinidad, Colorado, they looted a bar, lassoed civilians and provoked a fight among the pets they had brought along—a bulldog, a goat and a wildcat.

At long and spine-jolting last, hung-over and homesick, weary and dazed, the men arrived at their camps to find carpenters driving the last nails and electricians stringing the last wires. Gone was their brief glory, and now they struggled to adjust to a new and strange and drab environment. One man described his cantonment as "a desolate wilderness of sand and scrub oak and famous for nothing but our great national bird—the mosquito."

They were bellowed out of the troop trains by sergeants and corporals who displayed the traditional contempt of regular army noncoms for draftees, yelled into ragged formations and looked up and down. The uneasy young men in civilian clothes averaged five feet seven and a half inches in height and weighed an average of 141½ pounds. For some reason or other, the recruits from Kansas and Missouri were larger than most. But when they reached France, the shorter Frenchmen were impressed with their size and vigor; Napoleon had reduced the stature of the French people by killing off the tallest and sturdiest men in his wars.

Then, stretching cramped muscles, trying to smooth their crumpled suits, the draftees were marched into the camps and along unfinished roads, shuffling through dust and over debris left by workmen, hearing carpenters' hammers clattering like—well, was that the way a machine gun sounded? Then they reached their barracks, many still unfinished, and dumped their suitcases and cardboard cartons on the wooden floor and had their cots assigned to them. The lucky ones, that is.

Cots had not been delivered to some camps. There were shortages of every kind. Blankets were so scarce that worried officers ordered noncoms to ride into the nearest town to buy all they could—and the hell with red tape or money! The officers had cause to worry, for some men fell ill as a result of the absence of blankets and uniforms. Even when uniforms arrived, they sometimes were too small. And their civilian clothes, which they stripped off for the last time, were collected and sent to the people of Belgium.

The trainees began their life in the army by cleaning up the mess left in camp by construction workers, and only after a week or so did they settle down to military routine. There were not enough rifles. There were not enough machine guns. There were not enough tanks. There were not enough artillery guns. Lacking fieldpieces, they ran through artillery drill using logs. Lacking hand grenades, they practiced lobbing rocks. They whittled sticks to look like carbines and presented arms with broomsticks, and when Theodore Roosevelt heard about this he went into a spasm of rage. One man made a ninety-minute trolley trip into Indianapolis to buy oil and rags to clean his rifle when he got it. Some men studied horseshoeing without horses. At Camp Colt near Gettysburg, Pennsylvania, a young officer named Dwight D. Eisenhower was supposed to train thousands of men in tank warfare, but he was without a single tank.

After the nation's industries tooled up and began mass-producing the necessary weapons and gear, some city boys who never had fired a gun found it difficult to learn marksmanship. Alvin York, the sharpshooting mountaineer, thought that the boys from the streets were just plain dumb. In his words, they missed everything but the sky. "Of course," he drawled, "it warn't no trouble nohow for me to hit them big army targets—they was so much bigger than turkeys' heads."

Besides the lack of equipment, there was a shortage of qualified instructors. At one camp a young reserve second lieutenant sat up all night with a manual to learn how to strip and then reassemble the .45 automatic pistol so that the next morning he might teach the trick to his men. "It was," said Charles L. Bolté, "a case of the blind leading the blind."

At Fort Leavenworth, Kansas, a handsome second lieutenant with green eyes and sandy hair refused to let his military duties prevent him from rewriting a novel he had begun before leaving Princeton University. His name was F. Scott Fitzgerald. At first he hid his writing pad inside a book called *Small Problems for Infantry*, and after he was caught he worked in the officers' club amid smoke and talk and rattling newspapers. He began writing every Saturday at 1 P.M. and kept at it until midnight. At 6 A.M. Sunday he would resume his labor of love and scribble until 6 P.M. By holding to this schedule, Fitzgerald completed the rewrite of his book, which he called *The Romantic Egotist*. While it never was published, he used passages from it in his postwar novel *This Side of Paradise.*

Edward Streeter was another who wrote in camp. Pretending naïvete, he described the raw life of the rookie in a series of spurious letters later published in a book called *Dere Mable* that became the big best seller of the year 1918. In *Dere Mable* he caught the tone of the confused citizen-soldier in passages such as this:

> . . . Were doin baynut drill now. I cant say nothin about it. Its not for wimens ears. We have one place where we hit the Hun in the nose an rip all the decorashuns offen his uniform all in one stroke. Then theres another where you give him a shave an a round haircut an end by knocking his hat over his eyes. Then the wiperzup come over with a lot of bums and do the dirty work. I an the rest of the fellos go ahead an take another trench. I havent been able to find out yet where we take it.

In 1917 songwriter Irving Berlin was so rich and famous that when he was drafted as a private one paper published this headline: U.S. TAKES BERLIN. He trained at Camp Upton at Yaphank, Long Island, where he wrote the music for and starred in a soldier show called *Yip-Yip-*

Yaphank, which had a cast of 277, played to packed houses and earned thousands of dollars for the camp fund. Among the songs he wrote for the show was "Oh, How I Hate to Get Up in the Morning," and it so exactly expressed the feelings of his fellow soldiers that it became one of the hit tunes of the war.

While farm boys did not mind being awakened at 5:30 A.M. reveille, to rise at that hour was torture to men born and bred in cities. Then began the day's schedule: mess, physical drill, close-order drill, manual of arms, bayonet practice, extended order, lectures by officers including combat-wise French and British officers, rest, grenade drill, aiming and sighting, athletic instruction, close-order drill, inspection of men and living quarters and streets, mess, extended order drill, gas mask drill, more lectures, close-order drill, platoon movements, rifle instruction, advance guard and reconnaissance, rest, mess, and then the blowing of taps at 10 P.M.

Six weeks of this rigorous training changed the recruits: Their faces became bronzed, their muscles hardened, their backs straightened, their shoulders squared off. They were marched and marched and marched until a 25-mile hike that had taken them three days when they arrived in camp now took a single day. Exercise and outdoor life made them so ravenous that many a buck private could eat as much as three civilians.

Now strong of body and proud of their uniforms, they were irresistible to little boys. Journalist Ida M. Tarbell wrote, "It was startling to see a baby of three years slip away from his mother, walk down the aisle to where a soldier boy was sitting, watch him silently with wide-open eyes, get a little bolder, stretch out his hand and stroke his clothes, get a little bolder still and ask if he might put on his cap."

Many soldiers were better clothed, better fed and better housed than they had been at home, and their health was much better. The army's daily ration was 4,761 calories, and the men were fed on an allowance of 39.07 cents per man per day. The quality of the food and its preparation varied from camp to camp. Some rookies exulted that they feasted like lords while others complained, calling canned beef "monkey-meat" and canned salmon "goldfish." Now that the men were in camp they consumed 75 percent more tobacco than they had at home—two pounds of chewing and smoking tobacco and one pound of cigars and cigarettes a month. They were told not to waste anything, and when a major saw a private throw away a half-smoked cigarette he ordered him to bury the butt in a hole ten feet deep to learn to appreciate conservation.

Now that a national army was being formed the question of what to call our soldiers arose. They referred to one another as Buddy, a variant of "brother." German soldiers addressed one another as Kamerad, the British were called Tommy Atkins or Tommy, the French fighting men were known as Poilus. New Zealanders were Kiwis and the Australians were Aussies.

The Cleveland *Press* suggested that our soldiers be called Sammies, after Uncle Sam, and Roy Howard of the United Press ordered Westbrook Pegler to use this term when he went to France as a correspondent. The French called our boys Teddies, after Teddy Roosevelt whom they admired, but French newspapers dropped the nickname when General Pershing said it lacked national significance. Frenchmen then switched to Sammies, but our men disliked it so much that it too soon faded from the language.

The name Yanks won wide currency, partly because in his song called "Over There" George M. Cohan had written that "the Yanks are coming." The word derived, of course, from "Yankee," which had been in the English language since 1789. However, Southern-born soldiers disliked being called Yanks or Yankees because their grandfathers had fought the "damned Yankees" in the Civil War. During a reunion of Confederate veterans in Washington the President reviewed their parade from a low stand in front of the White House, and one old fellow hobbled over and Wilson leaned down to shake his hand. The veteran later shook his head in bewilderment and said, "I'd never thought I'd live to see the day when I'd shake hands with a son-of-a-bitch of a Yankee President!" He did not know Wilson had been born in Virginia.

As early as 1856 American infantrymen had been called doughboys. While the origin of this word is shrouded in mystery, there are a couple of legends concerning its genesis. According to one version, foot soldiers trudging through the Southwest kicked up the white dust of adobe clay and became powdered with it, so Spaniards in that part of the country called them dobies, which evolved into do-boys and then doughboys. There is another story claiming that an officer—doubtless an infantryman—wrote that foot soldiers were called doughboys because they were the flower of the army. In any event, Americans and then foreigners finally called our soldiers doughboys.

Never in the history of this nation had so many Americans from such widely separated parts of the country come together in such intimate association, one resulting in cultural cross-fertilization. Loggers from Oregon chowed with clam diggers from Connecticut, corn huskers from Kansas, grocery clerks from New Jersey, fruit pickers from Florida, hillbillies from Arkansas, miners from Colorado, mailmen from Michigan, cowboys from Wyoming, reporters from Missouri.

Eighteen percent were foreign-born, and some spoke no English. Extremists had tried to exclude from the army all men with German names, but some enlisted and others were drafted, and when they reached the front, they astonished enemy soldiers by shouting at them in German. American soldiers spoke fifty-one different languages, including Gaelic, Tagalog, and several American Indian tongues. When the AEF got to France a few Indian soldiers manned wireless sets and spoke their tribal languages, thoroughly confusing the Germans listening in on their conversations. Since bravery is not a virtue peculiar to the people of any particular race, Congressional Medals of Honor were bestowed on men with such diverse names as Bailey, Bertoldo, Gerstung, Kraus, Krotiak, McCarthy, Moskala, Ozbourn, Perez, Truemper.

Most of the men in the camps were unmarried, all were young and lusty, so their sex life became a matter of concern to government officials and army officers. On leave many rookies stationed in Kansas and Missouri would head directly for Kansas City's Twelfth Avenue, which had so many prostitutes that it was nicknamed "Woodrow Wilson Avenue—a piece at any price."

French Premier Georges Clemenceau wrote Secretary Baker to offer to build houses of prostitution for American soldiers in France. Baker read this letter in the presence of Raymond B. Fosdick, chairman of the Commission on Training Camp Activities, then smiled a wry smile and exclaimed, "For God's sake, Raymond, don't show this to the President or he'll stop the war!"

In an official report, Fosdick wrote:

> The position taken by the American Expeditionary Forces in regard to the problem of prostitution is unique among the armies of Europe on both sides of the battle-line. In the French and British armies and with the German and Austrian troops, licensed houses of prostitution have been generally permitted under the supervision of army medical staffs. General Pershing has from the start refused to tolerate this approach to the problem, and has insisted upon a policy of repression as opposed to the system of reglementation [*sic*] in vogue in the other armies.

At a Washington meeting of the advisory commission of the Council of National Defense, Dr. Franklin Martin, director general of the American College of Surgeons, read aloud a recommendation by a military medical committee that sexual continence be advocated as the best preventative of veneral disease. In other words, all our soldiers, sailors, marines and coast guardsmen were expected to abstain from intercourse as long as the war lasted. The absurdity of this recommendation enraged one commission member, Samuel Gompers. Springing to his feet, he shook his finger at Martin and shouted, "What have you been doing? Sold out to the so-called social hygienists? Real men will be men!"

Baker took a pragmatic attitude toward sexuality and VD, saying that "venereal disease had robbed commanders of battalions which might have turned the tide of history." He noted that VD had incapacitated one-third of an American regiment during our war in the Philippines. Navy Secretary Daniels mixed pragmatism with morality, declaring the government had "the duty of leaving nothing undone to protect these young men from that contagion of their bodies which will not only impair their military efficiency, but blast their lives for the future and return them to their homes a source of danger to their families and to the community at large."

General Leonard Wood said in a memo:

> With reference to the vice question, I am in favor of its absolute eradication. It is one of the greatest menaces to military efficiency, and I shall insist to the best of my ability on this being done in all towns and areas adjacent to or near cantonments and training-camps, and to this end will extend the fullest military cooperation. Where local authorities are unable or unwilling to

> take the necessary measures to eradicate this evil, they should at least restrict it to the smallest possible area in order that soldiers may be kept out of it and thereby protected against moral and physical contamination.

The general wrote this memo on July 25, 1917.

Five days later, on a warm afternoon in New York City, Senator Warren G. Harding of Ohio and a girl entered the Imperial hotel on the east side of Broadway between Thirty-first and Thirty-second streets. Friends had told him that this second-rate hotel was a safe place for a clandestine affair. The Republican Senator's companion was Nan Britton, who worked as a secretary for the United States Steel Corporation. She was twenty years old; he was fifty-one. Married to a woman five years older than himself, Harding had just begun an affair with Miss Britton which was to be consummated in bed this very day.

Miss Britton looked younger than her age and wore a short pink linen dress that enhanced her girlish appearance. She remained in the waiting room while the future President of the United States registered under the name of Hardwick or Warwick—she never was quite sure. Because of the obvious difference in their ages and the guilty knowledge that they were about to engage in an illicit liaison, neither spoke as they rode an elevator to an upper floor. The bellboy ushered them into a big room and raised the windows, but they were so high above Broadway they could not hear the street noises below. At last Warren and Nan were alone, and at last she became his bride, as he expressed it.

The phone rang. Harding picked up the receiver and growled, "You've got the wrong party!" The next moment they heard a rap on the door, and seconds later the door was opened from the outside with a key and in marched two hotel detectives. One of them pulled out a notebook and asked Nan her name. She whispered to Harding, "What shall I tell them?" The Senator slumped on the edge of the bed with his naked feet dangling and replied in a stricken voice, "Tell them the truth. They've got us." Nan told the detective with the pad what her real name was and where she worked. Harding interrupted to lie that she was twenty-two years old. Nan was so naïve that she corrected him and gave her true age.

Trying to reason with the detectives, Harding argued that he and the girl had disturbed none of the hotel guests and therefore should be allowed to depart peacefully. "Let this poor girl go!" he begged. But every time Harding opened his mouth the man with the notebook snarled, "You'll have to tell that to the judge!" He said a police car was en route to the hotel to take them to the station house.

The second detective picked up the Senator's hat and examined it. Stamped in gilt on the sweatband inside was the name W. G. Harding. The detective showed this to his partner, they conferred in whispers, and then both men stopped blustering and became respectful. They let the couple dress and led them downstairs and out of the hotel by a side entrance. As Harding stepped into a cab, he slipped a $20 bill to one of the men and then leaned back against the seat and sighed. "Gee, Nan! I thought we wouldn't get out of that under a thousand dollars!"

The following month—August, 1917—the war and navy secretaries declared that no red-light district would be permitted within five miles of any army or navy base. There were 116 such districts scattered about in the country, and this ban vexed many people in the communities it would affect. They tolerated prostitution because they considered it inevitable, but they did not wish to defy the government because they also wanted the money sure to be spent in their cities by servicemen stationed nearby.

The nation's most famous whorehouse district was Storyville, an area of twenty-eight city blocks in and near the quaint French Quarter of New Orleans. Storyville was so renowned that some visitors to the Crescent City on the bank of the Mississippi took conducted tours of it. Sidney Story, a New Orleans broker and city alderman, had studied the regulation of prostitution in Europe, and in 1897 he submitted to the city council an ordinance to permit prostitution to flourish in a certain area. The council passed the measure, which took effect on October 1 of that year, and the newly created district soon took the name of Storyville—much to the disgust of Alderman Story.

Now the madams and whores and pimps were safe from interference from the police, provided they remained within this reserve, but just to make doubly certain, they left dollars and quarters on the doorsteps of brothels for the cops to find and pocket. Tours of the area usually began with a drink in a saloon called the Arlington Annex at the corner of Basin and Iberville streets. Regarded as the unofficial city hall of Storyville, the Annex was owned by Thomas C. Anderson, better known as Tom, a former state legislator and now the political boss of the fourth ward. Tom also owned at least two prosperous bawdyhouses and had a financial interest in several others. The Annex was two stories high, had a balcony around the second floor and never closed. Tom advertised that it had private rooms for "the fair sex," and he boasted that it was noted "the states over for being the best-conducted café in America."

Advertising played an important part in Storyville's success. A half dozen publications chronicled the beauty and talents of the madams and girls alike, and of these periodicals perhaps the most interesting was the *Blue Book*. Reputedly financed by Tom Anderson, the first issue of the *Blue Book* appeared in 1902 and every year or so afterward. It was six inches by four and a half inches, had forty to fifty pages, cost a quarter and was sold in saloons, hotels, railway stations and at steamboat landings. It was printed on blue paper, its cover was decorated with a floral design, and its name was printed in red ink. Each edition opened with the warning that it must not be mailed.

"To know the right from the wrong," the *Blue Book* said, "to be sure of yourself, go through this little book and read it carefully, and then when you visit Storyville you will know the best places to spend your time and money, as all the BEST houses are advertised."

One of the best places, as such matters go, was Miss Lulu White's bagnio at Basin and Bienville streets, a few doors from the Annex. Three stories high, it was called the Mahogany Hall because one of its rooms was furnished in mahogany and decorated in the comfortable Victorian style. A New Orleans songwriter named Spencer Williams, author of the famous "Basin Street Blues," celebrated Miss Lulu's establishment in a number called "Mahogany Hall Stomp."

Lulu's advertisement in the *Blue Book* said:

> Nowhere in this country will you find a more popular personage than Madame White, who is noted as being the handsomest octoroon in America, and aside from her beauty, she has the distinction of possessing the largest collection of diamonds, pearls, and other rare gems in this part of the country. To see her at night is like witnessing the electrical display on the Cascade, at the late St. Louis Exhibition. Aside from her handsome women, her mansion possesses some of the most costly oil paintings in the Southern country. Her mirror-parlor is also a dream. There's always something new at Lulu White's that will interest you. "Good time" is her motto.

Storyville had three categories of brothels: posh parlor houses where the minimum was $5, houses charging from $2 to $3 and flimsy cribs where naked girls waited for customers unable to afford the higher rates. Some *Blue Book* advertisements were nothing but lists of names, addresses and the color of the prostitutes—black and white and every shade in between. The city fathers would not let white and black women work in the same house but permitted them to occupy adjoining premises.

Many of the best brothels were North Basin Street mansions three and four stories high, expensively furnished, some with mirrored ceilings and walls, elegantly decorated and decorous in mood, where rich men were courteously received. A few even had ballrooms in which orchestras began playing about 7 P.M. and continued until closing time at dawn.

Most of the musicians were black and talented and soon to become famous, for it was in Storyville that ragtime turned into jazz. More than 100 jazz musicians developed this uniquely American art form in Storyville's brothels, cabarets, saloons and dives. Their favorite off-hour hangout was a one-story wooden shack known at first as Lete Lala's and later as the Big 25.

Among these black instrumentalists, composers and band leaders was Ferdinand Joseph La Menthe, better known as Jelly Roll Morton; he was a pianist and composer and singer who began his musical career in the brothels of Storyville in 1902. Another was drummer Warren "Baby" Dodds, later praised as "one of the greatest figures in New Orleans jazz." Then there was Joseph "King" Oliver, who played the cornet and led his own band and became the idol of Louis Armstrong.

"Satchmo" Armstrong, destined to develop into the greatest of all the New Orleans jazz artists, was a teen-ager in 1917, too young and inexperienced to play in a bawdy house or saloon, but romping through Storyville and acquiring skill on the trumpet. Years later he said, "I spent all my young days around those whores and pimps and gambling fellers and some of the baddest people what was ever born. . . . The kids from the third ward were so bad they carried pistols on them in holsters just like those real cowboys. An' you think they wouldn't shoot to kill? . . . Huh!"

Late in August, 1917, Bascom Johnson, a representative of the army and navy departments, left Washington for New Orleans to confer with the mayor, Martin Behrman, telling Behrman his city had to comply with the ban on red-light districts. The mayor protested. He was told that Baker and Daniels would make no exceptions. Storyville simply had to be closed. Behrman made two trips to Washington in the hope that he, a Democrat, could persuade the Democratic administration to rescind its order. He argued that men will be men and that New Orleans was an old-world kind of city with a relaxed attitude toward sex. Secretary Daniels gave him short shrift, declaring that the navy would abolish its bases in and near New Orleans unless Storyville was cleaned up.

The defeated mayor went home and presented the city council with an ordinance dooming the red-light district. In his remarks to council members, Behrman said, "Pretermitting [overlooking] the pros and cons of legislative recognition of prostitution as a necessary evil in a seaport the size of New Orleans, our city government has believed that the situation could be administered more easily and satisfactorily by confining it within a prescribed area. Our experience has taught us that the reasons for this are unanswerable, but the navy department of the federal government has decided otherwise."

On October 9 the council adopted this decree, which ruled that after midnight of November 12, 1917, it would be unlawful to operate a brothel or house of assignation anywhere in New Orleans. Days later the New Orleans *Times-Picayune* quoted William Railly as charging that the elegant bawdy houses had been promised protection by city officials and would be allowed to reopen after the deadline. Railly was president of the Citizens' League of Louisiana, which for years had waged unsuccessful war against Storyville. The mayor asked the district attorney to convene a grand jury to investigate the charge, but the league was unable to prove its allegation. Fire insurance firms canceled policies on property in Storyville, and then the state fire marshal probed an alleged plot to burn down the district.

The residents of Storyville thought their unofficial mayor, Tom Anderson, was so influential that he could prevent the district from being closed. With the approach of the deadline Tom called the city's power brokers, calm as ever, but soon it became apparent to all that not even he could hold off the reckoning. Tom had a mistress who later became his wife, Gertrude Dix, the madam of a "palatial home" in the district, and on November 11 she asked a civil court judge for an injunction restraining the city from enforcing the ordinance. Her attorney argued that the area was operated under the law "for the protection of public morals and public health, good order and the peace of the community." Gertrude's house was burdened with a $6,000 mortgage she would have to pay off over the next two years.

"Having confidence in the good faith of the city," she had invested $15,000 in furnishings, and the threat to the district and thus her property was confiscatory, according to her lawyer, and therefore unconstitutional. But the judge denied her request, holding that "the subject matter of the ordinance is clearly within the police power of the city." Later that same day the state supreme court refused to issue a writ of mandamus to compel the judge to grant the requested injunction. With the collapse of this last-minute legal maneuver to save Storyville, all hope fled.

Furniture men and secondhand dealers swarmed through the streets to buy furniture and bric-a-brac, and since this was a buyers' market, the girls were cheated and knew it. Tempers flared. Toward midnight of November 12 two police captains and fifteen extra cops entered the area to take up precautionary posts.

Rich madams hired wagons to haul away their furniture and paintings and other valuables, while the crib girls shouldered mattresses and staggered away, carrying birdcages and calling out to pet dogs frolicking at their feet. Tom Anderson slumped over drinks in his café. And the midnight air was stained with lamentation gushing from one open doorway after another, the sound of music, of jazz pumping like blood, a syncopated dirge dark with despair, saxophones and trumpets and drums, a sad psalm celebrating an art born of black men now dispossessed and about to begin an exodus leading to—what? Like their daddies and granddaddies before them, the musicians had been robbed of pride and work, so about all they had left was soul, their soul music, the blues.

Before the deadline a girl from Storyville had left the district to take a job in a shrimp-packing factory, but when the other women learned about Edna Wallace's past, they refused to work with her, so Edna walked her bitterness back to the district and shot herself. There was hushed talk about Edna as midnight neared, some tears, and for the last time a madam reached into her stocking for money to tip her house pianist, always called the professor, and then he closed the keyboard and the other instrumentalists wiped saliva from the mouthpieces of their clarinets, gulped a final shot of booze, said good-bye and walked into the night.

A few jazz musicians had already left New Orleans, but after that midnight of November 12, 1917, others headed north to Chicago, a swinging city with cabarets that could use a hot band, while some pushed on to New York. And so, because of concern about the sex habits of soldiers, jazz left its birthplace on the Mississippi delta and began to spread out over the United States and finally all the world, an orphan of a distant storm called war.

Before passage of the draft act many blacks had been eager to enlist in the army, hoping that by serving their country they could rid themselves of their status as second-class citizens, but recruiting stations generally refused to accept them. Black men were barred altogether from the marine corps and permitted to serve in the navy only in menial capacities.

With enactment of the selective service law and the drafting of men regardless of race, blacks proudly donning uniforms were shocked and angered to be called "niggers" and "coons" and "darkies" by some white officers. Soon after work began on the training camps a group of men led by Dr. Joel E. Spingarn of the NAACP petitioned the army to give blacks an opportunity to earn commissions as officers. As a result, a black officers' camp was established at Fort Des Moines in Iowa, and four months after its creation 639 black men were commissioned as infantry lieutenants and captains.

The army also decided to form an all-black division, the 92d division, but instead of being trained together, the men were drilled at seven different camps scattered all the way from Camp Grant in Illinois to Camp Upton on Long Island. The 92d was the only division never brought together as a single unit until it reached the front in France. A second all-black division, the 93d division, never reached full strength, and after being trained at different sites, its members were sent abroad piecemeal and then incorporated within the French army.

Southerners were so afraid the army would send black men from the North to train in the South that it was necessary for federal officials to call a conference in Washington to discuss the issue. Out of this meeting came an agreement that Northern blacks would be drilled above the Mason and Dixon line, but this arbitrary scheme worked such hardship on the army's training program that at last black servicemen were sent wherever there were facilities for handling them.

And trouble came. Black draftees complained that white officers assigned them to labor battalions although some were qualified for other duties requiring higher skills and intelligence. At Camp Lee near Petersburg, Virginia, white guards patrolled the grounds outside a prayer meeting to keep blacks from entering and participating. At Camp Greene near Charlotte, North Carolina, there were five YMCA buildings for white soldiers, but none for the 10,000 blacks there; one had a sign saying: THIS BUILDING IS FOR WHITE MEN ONLY.

Resentment against discrimination reached fever pitch among the black soldiers of the 24th infantry regiment at Camp Logan near Houston, Texas. Local cops rousted them, called them names and tried to keep them off the public streetcars. Violence erupted on August 23, 1917, after a white policeman used force in arresting a black woman and then beat up a black soldier who tried to help her. Near the scene was a black military policeman who asked the cop about the condition of the bleeding black soldier and, instead of getting an answer, got a pistol whipping.

When news of these outrages reached camp, the black soldiers exploded in such wrath that their worried white officers quickly disarmed them lest they start rioting. But about 100 black soldiers broke into an army ammunition storage room, armed themselves and marched on the city's police station. This touched off a race riot in which black soldiers and white civilians exchanged gunfire that killed seventeen whites and two blacks. The governor of Texas placed Houston under martial law, influential Texans protested to Secretary Baker about billeting blacks in the South, the army pulled the black troops out of the city, and the raw situation was discussed by President Wilson at a Cabinet meeting. The embittered whites of Texas did their legal best to bring the black soldiers to trial in one of the state's civil courts, but the army said it intended to maintain control of its soldiers and would institute courts-martial. Although no indictments were returned against a single white cop or army officer, 156 black soldiers were arrested and thrown into a stockade.

Many were charged with murder, and as defense counsel the NAACP retained a white lawyer with special credentials, A. J. Houston, a son of Sam Houston, the Texas hero for whom the city had been named. Sixty-three blacks were tried in a military court. Five were condemned to death. Forty-one were sentenced to prison for life. Four others got long jail terms. Then a second court-martial was held, and eleven more black soldiers were condemned to be hanged.

James Weldon Johnson, a black writer and former diplomat, now secretary of the NAACP, tried to save the sixteen condemned men by appealing to Emmet J. Scott, a black man serving as special assistant to Secretary Baker. Johnson also gave the President a 12,000-name petition asking for executive clemency. Wilson agreed to have the records reviewed, and as a result, some sentences were commuted. But on December 11, 1917, thirteen black soldiers were hanged for their part in the Houston riot.

Chapter 26

MAKING THE TOOLS OF WAR

One evening in the spring of 1917 Bernard M. Baruch went to a White House reception and was approached by Wilson's military aide, who saluted and said the President wanted to see him. Baruch wondered whether he had made some mistake for which he was about to be rebuked. He was chairman of the committee on raw materials, minerals and metals of the advisory commission of the Council of National Defense. He was led to the President by the officer, who saluted again and backed away, leaving Baruch face to face with Wilson. Curious guests watched from a respectful distance.

Wilson told Baruch an American syndicate had bought several Austrian ships in anticipation of the American declaration of war, and what with the shortage of American shipping this combine wanted to sell the vessels to the government at a handsome profit. Although the President had ordered a federal official to try to prevent this profiteering, nothing much had been done. Now he was turning this assignment over to Baruch. Wilson concluded, "You use all the influence you think the President has—but get those ships!"

Baruch, who knew that the man he was replacing was also at the reception, asked Wilson to tell him his chore was being given to Baruch. At first Wilson said he saw no reason to do this, but he finally agreed and summoned the man to inform him that Baruch would handle the matter of the Austrian ships. The man sputtered, "But, Mr. President—"

Wilson snapped, "There are no more *buts!*"

Baruch immediately left the White House, glancing at his watch and noting that the time was 9:58 P.M. Hurrying to his suite in the Shoreham hotel, he began calling one syndicate member after another. One lived in Washington, while the others were in New York. Armed with Presidential authority and the force of his own personality, Baruch persuaded the businessmen seeking a windfall that it would be unwise for them to profit at the expense of the government.

The next morning Baruch called Wilson. He held his watch in his hand as the phone rang in the White House and saw that the time was 8:58 A.M.—eleven hours to the minute since he had taken on the assignment. Baruch reported to an astonished President that he had obtained all the Austrian ships for the government at no profit whatsoever. When Wilson hung up, he began to wonder whether in Baruch he had found the superman he sought, one capable of administering the entire economy of the United States.

Before the United States got into the war, it told our Allies to help themselves, so money was mustered and machines were made and the weapons of war flowed to our friends—the British, French, Russians and Italians. Between 1914 and 1917 American exports to Europe rose from $1.5 billion to $4.3 billion. As a result, by the time we declared war on Germany, many factories were committed by contract to the production of arms for the Allies, we were short of most war matériel, our natural resources had not been mobilized, and our industry faced the task of doing in two years what Germany had been doing the previous forty years. Except for a few commodities such as rubber and nitrate, the United States was so rich in everything that it was more self-contained than any other country in the world. Potentially. But ore in the earth killed no enemy; ore had to be mined to make a gun to kill a Hun.

One of Baruch's colleagues on the advisory commission was a Detroit industrialist named Howard E. Coffin, who said, "Twentieth century warfare demands that the blood of the soldier must be mingled with from three to five parts of the sweat of the man in the factories, mills, mines and fields of the nation in arms."

Consider all that was needed to make a shell for a gun: scores of raw materials of many kinds; numerous technological processes; many manufactured units; a variety of machines; a range of skills. Grosvenor B. Clarkson, the director of the United States Council of National Defense, expressed it this way: "The ore-miner in Minnesota, the coal-miner in Pennsylvania, the coke-maker in West Virginia, the brass-worker in Connecticut, the copper-miner in Arizona, the maker of chemicals in New York, of explosives in Delaware, of milling machinery, of steel, of iron, the transport-workers—all these and many more must synchronously converge their efforts or there will be no shell."

On August 29, 1916, an act of Congress created a Council of National Defense charged with doing anything and everything necessary to beef up industry to help defend the nation. The council consisted of six Cabinet members—the secretaries of war, navy, interior, agriculture, commerce and labor—augmented by an advisory commission, a kind of executive committee for the council, comprised of seven businessmen, industrialists and Gompers of the AFL.

Soon it became apparent that the six federal officials and seven private citizens were not functioning as well as had been hoped. Too many men made too many individual decisions. Operations were loose; there was an overlapping of authority and a clash of egos. Slowly it was seen that what was needed was one man with supreme authority, an industrial czar. Wilson, who had known Baruch for several years, had named him to the commission, but in a moment of frustration Baruch had scribbled a note to himself: "What is everybody's job is nobody's job." But even as the defense program became more snarled and impotent, there was resistance to the thought of making one man the economic dictator of America. Besides, where could such a superman be found?

Back in October, 1915, Baruch had drafted a plan for unifying all economic efforts in behalf of defense, and in the end his plan became the basis for the War Industries Board, a board created by the President by executive order, as an extension of the Council of National Defense. To head the new board, Wilson chose a Cleveland industrialist named Frank A. Scott; but Scott's health broke down, and he resigned. The second chairman of the War Industries Board was Daniel Willard, president of the Baltimore & Ohio Railway, and he did his best; but his health also snapped, so he too resigned, leaving a clutch of unsolved problems.

Grosvenor B. Clarkson wrote a book called *Industrial America in the World War*, in which he cited some of these mind-boggling problems:

> Should locomotives go to Pershing to help him get ammunition to the front or should they go to Chile to haul the nitrate without which there could be no ammunition? Should steel go to destroyers whose mission was to sink submarines or to the merchant ships the submarines had thinned to the point of breaking down of the food supplies of the Allies? Should brass go to binoculars without which cargo ships could not leave port or to the shells without which they need not go at all? Should nitrate go to munitions without which guns were useless or should they go to fertilizers without which artillerymen would be foodless?
>
> Should acetone, indispensable for British explosives, go to the powder mills or to airplanes which needed it for their wings? Should chrome steel go to indispensable army trucks or indispensable army munitions? Should women be condemned to steelless corsets or tinless preserved vegetables? Should cranes go to American wharves for loading ships for France or to French wharves for unloading the same ships? Should ships from Brazil bring coffee to bolster civilian morale or manganese for fighting steel? Should coal go to Italy to power munitions plants there or to coke here for steel for those plants? Should long-staple cotton go to tires for army trucks or to fabric for airplanes?

To level such mountainous problems seemed to call for the wisdom of Solomon. Wilson knew that to replace Willard he had to find a man with vision, character, experience, stamina and the ability to weld the business-industrial complex into a monolithic instrument capable of waging war and guaranteeing peace. It was also important that the man he chose be without any particular vested interests. So the President began to think about Bernard Baruch. Baruch was a pragmatist and also something of a visionary. Although he moved in the upper echelons of business, he was essentially a loner. He talked the language of business, although he never had to meet a payroll. A Wall Street speculator who had made millions playing the market, he had closely studied the structure of the economy. He was not a specialist but a generalist. He had no links to this bank or that corporation.

Men who had watched Baruch rise to riches never quite understood him. When in the company of others, he would sit very still with his blue-gray eyes boring straight as a laser beam into the eyes of the speaker of the moment, soaking in every word, and then suddenly he would lean forward and speak a simple profound truth. What others failed to comprehend was that Baruch made all his big decisions in his unconscious, rather than in his conscious mind. His reasoning was not so much logical as intuitive. Men who prided themselves on their logic failed to note that Baruch thought the way artists and philosophers think, absorbing masses of data, relaxing their minds, then receiving flashes of insights from their unconscious.

Herbert Hoover said he liked to deal with Baruch because of the swiftness with which he went to the heart of a problem, although Baruch was the most inarticulate smart man he knew.

Bernard M. Baruch was born in South Carolina on August 19, 1870. His father was Dr. Simon B. Baruch, a Jew who had left Poland in protest against the repression of liberty, and when Bernard was a grown man, he would kiss his father and proudly introduce him to his friends. Dr. Baruch came to America and married Belle Wolfe, a descendant of a Portuguese Jew who had settled here before the Revolutionary War. When their son was young, the family moved to New York, where Bernard attended the College of the City of New York and won renown as both a scholar and an athlete.

He began his career as a broker's boy on Wall Street at $3 a week, and by the time he was thirty he had made and lost $1,000,000. Then he went on to pile up a fortune estimated at $10,000,000—maybe more. Unlike most self-made men, he did not become conservative when he became wealthy; by the time he was forty he was a political liberal. Taking neither his politics nor his economics from Wall Street, he had a warm interest in human beings and a cool fascination with the structure of the economy.

He was forty-eight years old when he became the second most powerful man in the United States. He was tall and handsome and pink-cheeked, with prematurely gray hair. A reserved man with sharp, patrician features, dignified in all his dealings, autocratic or democratic as the occasion warranted, forever courteous, a smile on his lips, boyish in his enthusiasm, he was mature enough to accept blame for whatever went wrong. He had a photographic memory, disliked paper work, carried a few notes in his vest pocket and felt pleased when Wilson called him Dr. Facts.

As chairman of the War Industries Board he occupied a one-room office in a ramshackle building in Washington and always left his door open. He liked chocolate sodas, and one was brought to him every afternoon at three o'clock by a brash eighteen-year-old named Billy Rose.

In the future Rose was to become a showman second only in American history to Phineas Barnum. Born in New York, short of stature but tall of ego, Rose first won national attention at the age of eighteen when he became the shorthand king of the world. His skill and renown won him a job with the War Industries Board, where he managed to get into

Baruch's office to offer to recruit a battery of shorthand experts. Rose had learned that the board's stenographic staff averaged only 80 to 90 words a minute, while he could easily write 200. He also urged Baruch to replace the board's sluggish typewriters with faster ones. This double-pronged offer was enough to interest Baruch, but the clincher came when Rose asked, "Mr. Baruch, how would you like to have by dinner-time every night a complete text of everything you said to anybody and what anybody said to you?"

Baruch replied, "That would be wonderful, young man, but it isn't possible."

"I'll show you!" Rose cried. "I'll capture everything you say, whether on the phone or in conference."

Baruch agreed. He then fell into the habit of telephoning Billy Rose in the middle of the night to dictate whatever he had on his mind.

The young New Yorker became indispensable to the chairman of the War Industries Board. One day Baruch handed him a letter and told him to deliver it to the President in the White House. When Rose got there, he found the executive mansion teeming with Cabinet members, Senators and dignitaries who looked like diplomats. Rose handed the letter to a Presidential secretary and was asked to wait in case there was a reply. Moments later the male secretary returned with a puzzled look on his face and said, "The President would like to see you."

The kid from the sidewalks of New York was trembling with excitement as he entered the President's study. Wilson smiled and said, "I understand you're quite a shorthand writer." Baruch, of course, had mentioned Rose to Wilson. This was in the days when a battle was being waged between those who wrote Gregg shorthand and those who used the Pitman method. Rose, who specialized in Gregg, knew that Wilson's shorthand was of the Pitman variety.

"I hear you're pretty good yourself, Mr. President."

Wilson said, "I don't get much chance to practice these days. Mr. Baruch tells me you can write two hundred words a minute. I wonder if you'd give me a little demonstration?"

Handing a pad and pencil to Rose, the President picked up a New York newspaper and in his precise speech read aloud an editorial at the rate of about 150 words a minute. When he finished, he said, "Now let's hear you read it back."

The way Rose told it later, "Well, as every stenographer knows, it's the reading back that counts. I shot the editorial back at him a good deal faster than he had dictated it. And then I started at the bottom of the page and read the editorial backwards."

It is not necessary to believe the last part of Rose's comment, since he tended to exaggerate everything. But Wilson was impressed. Then the boy took the newspaper from the President and gave him the pad and pencil, saying, "I wonder if you'd mind writing for me, Mr. President."

Wilson took off his glasses, rubbed them on his sleeve, pinched them back onto the bridge of his nose and said, "Don't go too fast."

Rose read the editorial at about 100 words a minute and then asked Wilson to read it back. When the President finished, Rose said he had not made a single mistake, and Wilson sighed with satisfaction. Rose reached over and took the President's shorthand notes, saying, "If you don't mind, sir, I'd like to keep them."

With a smile, Wilson remarked, "We'll exchange."

The youth left the White House and floated back to the WIB building. When he reached his desk, a phone rang, and Baruch's secretary said the chief wanted to see him. Smugly musing that this was pretty good for a kid from Delancey Street, Billy Rose walked into Baruch's office, and the secretary said, "The boss wants you to get him a chocolate soda."

Before Baruch and the War Industries Board took control of the nation's economy, bureaucratic rivalry had created incredible confusion in the war program. The government had no central purchasing agency; each federal bureau entered the war with its own independent purchasing system. In the army alone there were eight different purchasing bureaus. The various branches of government and a host of bureaucrats vied with one another in buying and stockpiling goods, grabbing everything in sight.

The quartermaster general and army medical department took all available canvas duck, leaving none for haversacks. The commanding officer of the government arsenal at Rock Island, Illinois, cornered the nation's leather market without regard for the needs of other branches of government, and although he later admitted he had done wrong, he added, "I went on the proposition that it was up to me to look after my particular job."

General Pershing was dismayed when he learned that some factories were signing contracts they could not fill and that different arms of the government were bidding against one another. For example, the corps of engineers and the quartermaster corps engaged in a lively contest for lumber, causing its price to rise.

Secretary of War Baker went to the basement of the navy-war-state building in Washington and found crates piled from floor to ceiling. Each was earmarked for the adjutant general's office. All were sealed. What did they contain? Baker returned to his office and telephoned the adjutant general to ask what was in the crates. Typewriters. The general said he knew he would have to have a lot of typewriters, so he had bought all he could because if he had not bought them the army or navy would have cornered them.

Down through the ages crafty men have known that the royal road to riches is to create a monopoly. Aristotle told the story of how an ancient Greek philosopher named Thales had proved that even a man devoted to pure thought could make a fortune if he put his mind to it. Familiar with astronomy and weather forecasting, Thales decided one winter that the following year there would be an abundance of olives, so for next to nothing he bought all the oil presses he could at a time when no one else cared to bid for them. The next year the olive harvest was plentiful, as he had predicted, so men who wanted to make olive oil had to rent Thales' presses at the exorbitant prices he charged, thus making him rich.

During World War I a young American used the same kind of scheme to make a financial killing. Closely studying the needs of the Allies, he discovered one item that had not been cornered—parts for machine guns. He furthermore found that these parts were made in small machine shops scattered up and down the Atlantic seaboard and could be bought at shamefully low prices. Borrowing some money, he traveled from shop to shop, organizing them into a combine, a monopoly that could demand and get very high prices, and soon he was a millionaire.

The Northeastern section of the United States had the greatest concentration of factories, and about 50 percent of the first war orders were given to manufacturing plants in New York, Pennsylvania, Massachusetts and Ohio. The scores of bureaucratic purchasing agencies turned as by a reflex to this part of the country, failing to check with one another. As a result, transportation, power, factories, fuel, labor and finance became strained to the point of collapse.

To help untangle this snarl Franklin Roosevelt, the assistant secretary of the navy, boasted that he broke enough laws to go to jail for 900 years, while Baruch's WIB counsel warned Baruch that he himself could be sued personally for a loss involving anyone carrying out his orders. "At first," Baruch wrote, "this seemed a paralyzing opinion, but since I had already issued enough orders to have my fortune swallowed up many times over, there was nothing to do but go ahead as I had been doing."

Interagency rivalries and wrangles resulted in perhaps the worst tangle of disordered effort the world had known. There were tanks without engines, airplanes without wings, too much freight and too few freight cars, cargoes without docks to receive them, ships unable to sail for want of anchor chains, shiploading cranes jammed on docks too flimsy for their weight. When army officers were told they would get 21,000,000 pairs of shoes, they insisted upon 10,000,000 more. The officers also demanded ten times more bridles and saddles than they could use. One young officer said, "My instructions are to go and get . . . regardless of . . . whom it hurts."

Baruch scolded his own uncle, a Chicago merchant named Henry Lytton, for an advertisement urging the public to buy extra suits and overcoats while they still were available. He also spurned influence peddlers who swarmed around the WIB building seeking contracts for clients. One of these middlemen had a habit of waiting for Baruch outside his hotel every morning, his clients in tow, to approach the WIB chairman and engage him in what must have seemed to onlookers like a confidential conversation. Baruch was polite, but since he and this man said nothing of importance, he was puzzled until his secretary explained that he was being used. The next time the man approached, Baruch told him off in a voice loud enough to be heard by the man's clients, and that was the end of that.

Baruch also resisted pressure from the husband of a relative of President Wilson, who pestered Baruch's first assistant, Alexander Legge, with overtures in behalf of a war contractor. Legge became so exasperated that one day he said to Baruch, "I'm going to throw him out by the nape of the neck unless you say I can't."

"Chuck him out, Alec!"

The next time the man entered the WIB office Legge blistered him verbally, making plain that he was not wanted on the premises. Subsequently the man complained to Wilson's son-in-law, William G. McAdoo, about the board's attitude toward him, and McAdoo reported this to Baruch.

"Mac," said Baruch, "I'm doing just what you would do and I can't do otherwise."

A little later Baruch attended a meeting in the White House, and when it ended, the President said, "Baruch, I'd like to see you. Will you please remain?" As the other men filed out of the President's study, Wilson and Baruch stood near each other gazing out a window and across the lawn toward the Potomac. When all the others had left, the President broke the silence, mentioned the husband of one of his relatives and then said, "Baruch, I understand you've ordered him to keep away from the War Industries Board and denied him the right of coming there to find a contract."

"Yes, sir, Mr. President, but—"

"You don't have to give me any *buts!* You did exactly the right thing."

Americans were fortunate to have a President and economic czar who were totally incorruptible. The more one studies history, the more it becomes apparent that one constant in human nature is greed. For example, as our soldiers got to France and some were killed, the mothers of the casualties became known as Gold Star Mothers. While they were being organized, a committee began to design an official armband which would display as many stars as the numbers of sons a woman had lost. Ida M. Tarbell later wrote:

"The idea had not been noised about before a gentleman high in the counsels of the nation came to us with the request that we make the badge not of black as decided but purple—purple velvet. His reason was that a friend of his, a manufacturer of velvet, had on hand some thousands of yards of purple velvet which he would like to dispose of."

In the summer of 1917, when Baruch was chairman of the raw materials committee but before he became chairman of the WIB, he was summoned to the White House to see the President. Wilson said he had heard from Navy Secretary Daniels that the steel industry was charging exorbitant prices for its products, especially ship plates. Baruch offered to meet with steel executives, and Wilson agreed, telling him to act as his personal representative.

The steel barons agreed to a conference in the Manhattan office of the United States Steel Corporation, whose board chairman was Elbert Gary. After the outbreak of war the first orders to U.S. Steel called for barbed wire—mile after mile of barbed wire for the trenches of the Allies. Then came a deluge of other demands—steel for shells, shrapnel bars, guns, trucks, locomotives, railway cars. By the middle of 1915 U.S. Steel was operating at 90 percent of capacity and exporting a third of its products. In 1916 the corporation earned $333,000,000. In 1917 its earnings rose to $530,000,000. Between 1915 and 1919 its profits equaled the combined pay of all the 2,000,000 American soldiers while they were in France.

Baruch, who moved in the nation's highest financial circles, had met

Elbert Gary socially and said of him, "I never knew a man more devoted to anything than Gary was to the United States Steel Corporation." Gary was short, vain, humorless, foppish. He was asking 4¼ cents per pound per ship plate, a price Baruch considered far too high for the government to pay. At the conference in his office Gary replied that he thought this a fair price; in any event, that was what the steel industry would continue to charge. Baruch argued that big business was missing a chance to show the public that in time of war it put the welfare of the government and the people ahead of its own interests, but Gary would not budge. Baruch urged Gary to call the White House and talk to the President, but Gary refused—and declared the conference at an end.

The next morning the angry and chagrined Baruch headed for uptown Manhattan and the mansion owned by Henry C. Frick, which later became the Frick Museum. Chairman of the finance committee of U.S. Steel, Frick was a quiet man with a well-trimmed gray beard which he stroked while speaking. Baruch argued the government's case for lower steel prices, finally asking, "What do you think is the right price for ship plates?"

"Baruch, that's not a fair question. After all, I'm chairman of the finance committee and a director in the company."

"I know that—but I'm not here to see you in that capacity. This country is at war and I have come here by the President's direction to obtain from you, as a patriotic citizen, certain information for his guidance in the performance of his duties."

"What precisely does the President wish to know?"

"I have already told you that the manufacturers are charging the Allies four and one-quarter cents per pound for ship plates."

Frick nodded.

"The President would like to learn from you—if you can tell—what the production cost of ship plates is."

Frick said tersely, "Two and a half cents is enough."

"Including a profit?"

"Only sufficient to safeguard the manufacturer against loss—which is only fair and proper. Mind you—that is the cost to the United States Steel Corporation. I have no information respecting costs to other companies."

Baruch thanked Frick and left.

Armed with this information, Baruch once again sought out Gary and learned that he was dining at the Metropolitan club at Fifth Avenue and Sixtieth Street. Popularly called the Millionaires' Club, it was restricted and white. Baruch felt that any man excluded from any club for any reason should never enter it, but now he swallowed his pride, walked into the club and asked that his name be taken to Mr. Gary.

Word came back that Mr. Gary was in conference and could not see him. Baruch said, very well, he would wait—because the matter was important. He waited. He waited a half hour and then he sent up a card on which he had written: "My message is from the President and I must return tonight." He meant to Washington, of course. No reply. An hour passed. At last Gary appeared and gave Baruch a minute and said he thought the government would accept his judgment that the steel price was fair. And walked out.

Later there were other negotiations and at last the steelmen agreed on a price of 3¼ cents per pound per ship plate. But this agreement covered only the steel they sold to the United States government; they would continue to charge the Allies and the public whatever the traffic would bear. Wilson flushed with anger. He wanted the same price for the same product regardless of the customer.

Ship plates were merely one product among many made by the steel industry, and prices on these other commodities continued to soar. Connellsville coke had sold at $1.67 a ton in September, 1915; it reached $12.25 by July, 1917. Basic pig iron that sold at $12.59 in June, 1915, brought $52.50 a ton in June, 1917. The following September the War Industries Board drew up a price schedule for coke, iron and steel.

Then came a stormy meeting in which WIB representatives faced sixty-five tough steel executives. Baruch was there, but the government's case was presented by Robert Lovett, vice-chairman of the board, a man so dignified and with such a leathery face that Baruch thought he might be part Indian. Gary, who had begun his career as a corporation lawyer, opened for the steelmen by questioning the government's authority to fix prices. Lovett said, "A gentleman of your eminent qualifications in law requires no information from me on that point."

Baruch sat with a face like a mask as the steelmen trotted out experts to talk about what it cost to run the steel industry. At last Baruch addressed Gary. "I've listened with a great deal of interest to your witnesses. May I ask if you concur in their testimony?"

Gary's eyes were like ice as he replied, "I can't see that that matters!"

"That," Baruch said quickly, "is a sufficient answer for the record!"

Baruch then showed Gary a letter from the President declaring that he would commandeer the United States Steel Corporation or any other business upon the recommendation of the War Industries Board. Gary read it with a blank face and handed it back, saying, "You haven't got anybody to run the steel company."

"Oh—yes—I—have, Judge!"

"Who?"

"Oh, we'll get a second lieutenant or somebody to run it."

Gary looked pained.

"But that won't trouble you very much," Baruch added, his voice an iceberg. "If those mill towns find out why we've taken over, they'll present you with your mills—brick by brick."

Gary rose and walked some distance away, and Baruch saw all his fingers rubbing against one another, and then suddenly Gary turned around and walked back and asked, "Can't we fix this up?"

Baruch let his voice melt. "Sure we can."

Gary said he wanted to confer privately with his people, and when they returned to the conference table, a steelman who had been friendly with Baruch for years thrust his face near Baruch's face and waggled his finger and shouted, "Bernie, the steel people thought you were friendly to them, but they've found out you're their arch-enemy! They'll never forgive you as long as you live!"

Once again Baruch's voice froze. "Is that the steel people's message to me?"

"It is!"

Baruch roared, "All right! If that's their message to me, let me give you my answer—!" And in sentences that flowed like lava he told the steelmen exactly what he thought of them until they crumpled and compromised and agreed to the lower prices the government wanted.

Years later Baruch wrote:

> The steel industry accepted these new prices in good faith and they remained almost unchanged till the end of the war. It has been estimated that this regulation of steel prices saved the government more than a billion dollars. The steel industry also did a superb job of production; but there is no question that profits, especially of the great integrated companies, were still excessive.
>
> The government's interference with the affairs of the U.S. Steel Company always rankled Judge Gary, and he never forgave the threat I had made. After the war he publicly charged that subversive influences in the government, meaning WIB, had sought to nationalize the steel industry as the first step in undoing America's free enterprise system. I had to set the record straight and publicly reveal the uncooperative attitude of the steel industry in the midst of war that had compelled the government to resort to a show of force.

Navy Secretary Josephus Daniels had the problem of trying to find oil and gasoline to power ships and run machines because British and French demands had drained the resources of American oil companies. He was therefore in a receptive mood when an aide said an inventor had come to Washington with the claim that he could provide fuel at a very low cost.

Ushered into Daniels' office, John Andrews introduced himself and came quickly to the point. "I can furnish a substitute for gasoline at a cost of two cents a gallon, which would put every oil company in the world out of business, and I have come to offer it exclusively to the navy."

Daniels was astonished, for this claim seemed too good to be true. Trying not to show too much excitement, he began to question the inventor about his substitute, saying that of course he would need proof. Andrews replied, "You need not take my word. All I ask is an opportunity to demonstrate what I claim."

Into the office just then came Franklin Roosevelt, assistant secretary of the navy, and Senator Benjamin R. Tillman, chairman of the Senate naval affairs committee. Daniels asked Andrews to repeat what he had said and Andrews did.

Tillman said, "Josephus, snap him up! Don't let him get away!"

Roosevelt said, "Chief, it is worth trying. I say he should be given the opportunity to prove he can do what he says."

Daniels told Andrews that he would get in touch with officials at the Brooklyn navy yard in New York and order them to provide facilities for testing the gasoline substitute.

A couple of days later a Packard drove into the navy yard with

Andrews and a man who introduced himself as a banker from McKeesport, Pennsylvania. They were met by Captain E. P. Jessup, a senior engineering officer, two other officers and a civilian serving as secretary of the naval consulting board. Jessup asked the visitors to drive to a laboratory where Andrews could put on his demonstration. Outside the laboratory, mounted on a test block, was a three-cylinder motorboat engine. The only equipment the inventor had was a one-gallon metal can and a small black bag.

Jessup examined the can to make sure it was empty. It was. The inventor was handed a bucket of fresh water. He got into the rear of the Packard with the bucket of water, his can and his black bag. Although it was an open touring car, the navy men were unable to see what Andrews did. Moments later Andrews handed the can to Jessup, who could tell by its weight that it was full. Jessup then peered into the bucket, which now seemed to contain one gallon less of water than before. Searching the car, Jessup saw no evidence of any fluid having been spilled anywhere.

Jessup carried the inventor's metal can inside the laboratory, followed by Andrews and the others, then handed it to Andrews. The inventor poured the liquid from the can into the open feed tank of the engine, and to prove it was not gasoline, he held a lighted match near the flowing fluid.

Admiral George E. Burd, manager of the naval yard, said, "Mr. Andrews, while it is true the water is gone from the bucket, and we did not see what you did with it if you did not use it in your can, yet we did not actually see you mix the liquid, and even if it runs the engine we cannot certify that you used the water in the can."

"Give me the bucket," said Andrews, and from the bucket he poured a half gallon of water directly into the engine's feed tank. This assured the officers that at least a third of the mixture was water.

Andrews said, "Start the engine."

The engine was started, a slight carburetor adjustment was made, the engine developed 75 percent of its rated horsepower and used up all the water and the other liquid in the tank.

Impressed but still cautious, the officers asked the inventor to return the next day.

This time they did not let him get into his car to mix his stuff but put him in a small concrete room without a drain and so bare there was no place to hide anything. Andrews made no protest. He entered the room with his little can and bag and bucket of water, and soon emerged with the can full of fluid. Same result. The engine worked as though it were burning gasoline. Every time he poured in more water he took from a pocket a tiny vial and squeezed six or seven drops of a green fluid into the feed tank.

Now the officers were convinced the inventor had something worthwhile, although they did not know what chemicals he was using. A lieutenant commander was told to take Andrews back to Washington to see Secretary Daniels again.

By the time the inventor entered the secretary's office Daniels had read an approving report prepared by the navy's bureau of engineering. Andrews asked Daniels whether he was satisfied with this report.

Replying that he was, Daniels said he now wanted to talk about how much Andrews wanted for the sale of his formula to the navy.

"Two million dollars."

Daniels said this seemed like a fair price. But before he could ask the President to allocate such a sum, Daniels must insist that Andrews prove he had a large supply of his secret chemicals and that their cost would not be prohibitive.

"You told me," Andrews said, "that if the test was satisfactory, the navy would buy it. Your officers who saw the demonstration inform me that I did all I claimed. Therefore, I will sell it to the navy for two million dollars and guarantee the exclusive possession, but I will not give the secret preparation that propels the engine until I get the money!"

Daniels protested that the government could not pay until he met these two conditions—quantity and price.

"Give me the money," Andrews insisted, "and I assure you there will be no difficulty about quantity and price."

Daniels said he would not spend public money to buy "a pig in a poke."

Heatedly accusing Daniels of not living up to their agreement, the inventor stomped out of the office, angrily declaring he knew another country that would not haggle over price. Daniels was so surprised by this hasty departure that he forgot to ask Andrews where he lived.

Daniels ordered a naval officer to locate Andrews' residence, but this officer could find no trace of the inventor. Word of this affair leaked to the naval editor of a New York newspaper, a man named Meriwether who had been graduated from Annapolis, and he set out on his own to try to find Andrews. He traced him to a house in a suburb of Pittsburgh, and Andrews told Meriwether, "Come to see me tomorrow morning at nine o'clock and I will give you the information you want."

Early the next day the editor returned to the house but found it empty. The neighbors knew nothing. The man who said he had found a substitute for gasoline was never heard of again.

The war on the western front consumed explosives at an incredible rate. In a single artillery barrage 80,000 shells fell in an area only 500 yards by 1,000 yards, killing every soldier in that area and maddening and deafening others nearby. Towns and fields were blown off the face of the earth. George Bernard Shaw lamented "the utter divorce of the warrior from the effects of his soulless labor. He has no sight or knowledge of what he is doing: he only hands on shells or pulls a string. And a Beethoven or a baby dies six miles off."

By the autumn of 1917 American munitions plants were producing more than 1,000,000 pounds of smokeless powder a day, but General Pershing cabled from Europe that even this was not enough. He said, "Under pain of incurring disaster, and to avoid calamity," the United States must "furnish all powders and explosives needed for present contracts with the French government" and also "furnish by December three hundred tons per day of explosives and two hundred tons per day of powder for French consumption."

General William Crozier, chief of ordnance, decided that only the Du

Pont Company had the experience necessary to assume the job of increasing the supply of smokeless powder, and so he drafted an agreement with the Du Ponts to erect and operate a government-owned plant capable of making 1,000,000 pounds per day. Objection came, however, from the War Industries Board, which had not been consulted. WIB officials said that such a contract would enable the Du Ponts to make a profit of $60,000,000 to $70,000,000 at the expense of the government. At the WIB it was felt that there were civilian experts other than the Du Ponts who could construct such a plant. Secretary of War Baker agreed, and the Du Pont contract was canceled.

Bernard Baruch summoned to Washington a mining engineer named D. C. Jackling and told him to build the powder plant. Within nine months civilian technicians created a new town named Nitro near Charleston, West Virginia, and a factory that could produce 625,000 pounds of powder a day. But even its output failed to meet the needs Pershing had outlined.

Jackling had been given the title of director of the United States government explosive plants units. He asked the Du Ponts to build and operate another smokeless powder factory, one larger than that at Nitro, one that would become the largest factory of its kind in the world.

That autumn of 1917 the government and the Du Ponts began negotiating, the Du Ponts demanding a 10 percent commission on construction and 15 percent for operations. The WIB told Baker that under these terms the Du Ponts would earn $13,500,000 net on construction and $10,000,000 more for one year's operations. Agreeing that this was profiteering, Baker blocked the contract; there was such a pressing need for powder, however, that negotiations were resumed.

The War Industries Board proposed that the Du Ponts be guaranteed the flat sum of $1,000,000 over and above the cost of construction and operation. Later, when the plant was completed, if the government and the Du Ponts were unable to agree on additional compensation, the matter would be submitted to arbitration. The Du Ponts rejected this proposal. Years later Pierre du Pont complained to a Senate committee that Baker had strongly implied that he regarded the Du Ponts as "a species of outlaws." Pierre said he especially resented Baker's remark that "the time has come for the American people to demonstrate that they can do things for themselves."

After three months of wrangling the government and the Du Ponts signed a contract that guaranteed the company gross profits of about $2,000,000. To build Old Hickory, as the new plant was to be called, the Du Ponts formed a new corporation, the Du Pont Engineering Corporation. Old Hickory was to cost twice as much as the Panama Canal. A seven-mile railroad was built between Nashville and the site of the complex, ground was broken on March 8, 1918, and in addition to the plant itself, a whole new city was built to house the workers.

This was one of the most gigantic construction feats in the history of the nation. To run the plant at capacity each day, there was needed 1,500,000 pounds of nitrate of soda; 675,000 pounds of sulfur; 4,500 tons of coal equivalent to 100 carloads; 100,000,000 gallons of water, or as much as was used by a city of 1,000,000 inhabitants.

On June 1, 1918, two months ahead of schedule, production began on the first unit, one that made sulfuric acid. The first batch of smokeless powder was produced on July 2. Old Hickory's 30,000 workers now lived in the new city with its own light and water and sewage system and incinerator; it had hospitals and churches and schools and hotels and restaurants and amusement halls and YMCA and YWCA buildings. The entire complex was completed ninety-six days earlier than the contract specified, and Du Pont made not only all the powder it said it would, but 13,000,000 pounds more.

Pershing's request had been more than met. By the end of the war all the powder plants in the country were daily producing six times as much smokeless powder as had been made in all of 1914. Old Hickory itself cost the government more than $85,000,000, but when peace came and the plant was closed, the government was able to salvage less than $4,000,000 on its expenditure. And years later a Senate munitions committee said that since the Du Pont Engineering Corporation had been capitalized for only $5,000, with each share of the original stock selling for $1, the Du Ponts grossed nearly $2,000,000, or a profit of 39,231 percent.

During the Civil War the Lincoln administration had to pay excessive prices to contractors furnishing food and clothing to the Union soldiers; Lincoln contemptuously called these profiteers "harpies." The Spanish-American War was disgraced by scandals in furnishing supplies for the army. Since President Wilson had written a history of the United States, he was aware of the sharp practices of some contractors in time of war, and warned that "no true patriot will permit himself to take toll of [our soldiers'] heroism in money or seek to grow rich by the shedding of their blood." Navy Secretary Daniels had said that after war was declared, the first order should be to "mobilize against profiteers." Daniels went further: He suggested that anyone profiteering in blood money should be forced to wear the letter *P* on his chest.

Irvin S. Cobb, the journalist and war correspondent, wrote that "at the back of my brain always has been the conception of a bloated abortion with dollar marks on its flanks to denote its sponsors and a dripping steel snout and knuckles of brass; a ravaging monster which is never emptied yet never is filled up; and it dragging its gross belly across the face of the land, rending and spoiling what all it does not devour."

In Britain George Bernard Shaw wanted to finance the war by confiscating income not engaged in maintaining a reasonable standard of living. In the United States Republican Senator William S. Kenyon of Iowa demanded the conscription of wealth as well as manpower, while Senator La Follette of Wisconsin said in a letter, "Well, my friend, it is a part of the topsy turvy times that we are 'traitors,' 'disloyal,' and 'partners of the Kaiser,' while the men who have been undermining our government and robbing the people, are the only 'patriots' and friends of the dear old flag."

Bernard Baruch agreed with a report of the President's mediation commission that "with the exception of the sacrifices of the men in the armed service the greatest sacrifices have come from those at the lower rung of the industrial ladder." Price McKinney of McKinney Steel confessed, "We are all making more money out of this war than the average human being ought to."

United States Steel Corporation's profits on its common stock rose from 11 percent in 1913 to 39.15 per cent in 1917; in this same period its profits on preferred stock shot up from 22.54 to 75.37 percent. Between 1915 and 1918 E. I. du Pont de Nemours & Company grossed more than $1.2 billion and paid dividends of 458 percent on the par value of its stock.

Journalist Richard Harding Davis angrily wrote from the French capital, "In Paris, we hear that on Wall Street there are some very fine bargains. We hear that in gambling in war brides [slang for fat war contracts] and ammunition everybody is making money. Very little of that money finds its way to France. Some day I may print a list of the names of those men in American who are making enormous fortunes out of this war, and who have not contributed to any charity or fund for the relief of the wounded or of their families."

Dr. Alvin Johnson, an educator and a founder of the New School for Social Research, wrote in his memoirs:

> War has always been attended by an orgy of profiteering. How could it be otherwise? The demand for war matériel is insatiable and instant. There is no time for bargaining with the suppliers of arms and munitions. The army purchasing agent asks not, How much but, How soon? If a billion dollars' worth of smokeless powder and high explosives is to be shot away, what does it matter that the army paid two billion for it? Anyway, it was assumed that the victorious Allies would collect the whole cost of the war from the defeated enemy countries. Why try to bargain down our own purveyors, profiteering, in the last analysis, at the expense of the enemy?

Most war contracts were let on a cost-plus basis. A cost-plus contract is one in which it is agreed to pay the manufacturer the total costs of producing an article, plus an additional fixed percentage of the cost. But, as historian Charles A. Beard noted, "Under the cost-plus system no one was interested in economy; if the producer of raw materials raised his prices, the war contractor would smile and pass on the extra charge with an increase in his commission. If a trade union struck for higher wages, the manufacturer could grant the demand with a friendly shrug, for the additional expense meant a larger commission garnered from the beneficent government."

According to tax returns from 7,000 corporations, their net earnings in the prewar years 1911–13 averaged 11 percent on invested capital. In the early part of the war many industries saw their profits rise more than 100 percent.

In 1914 there were 6,000 Americans with taxable incomes of between $30,000 and $40,000; by 1918 there were 15,400 people in this bracket. Although no one knows for sure, economist George Soule has said that the war produced 42,000 millionaires.

However, not every businessman or industrialist was avaricious. Many executives left richly rewarding positions in private business to work for some war agency in Washington at a dollar a year. One was Baruch; not only did he refuse to accept a federal salary, but he paid from his own pockets some expenses that ran into thousands of dollars. Another notable exception was George Eastman, the "Kodak King." He was one rich man who welcomed a rise in taxes. He made his manufacturing facilities and some of his staff available to the government and then refused to accept any profits for his war work.

Another wealthy man, Senator Henry Cabot Lodge of Massachusetts, was not so generous. Although he accused the government of "spending money like drunken sailors," when the Wilson administration responded to agitation for putting down profiteering, Lodge attacked the President for trying "to carry on a war against American business and a war against Germany at the same time."

To siphon off excessive war profits and produce greater revenues for defense, Congress passed the nation's first excess profits tax on March 3, 1917. This was a graduated tax on all profits exceeding a fixed percentage of capital investment, or of average profits, over a given period. On October 3 of the following year the excess profits tax was replaced by the War Revenue Act, which made the income tax the chief source of revenue. Nonetheless, this second measure imposed a graduated excess profits tax of from 20 to 60 percent on corporations and individuals.

Before the war it was the practice of manufacturers to design and make and market many kinds or styles of a given commodity; by giving customers a wide range of choices, the manufacturers hoped to beat their competition and win preeminence in a given field. But after we got into the war and the military began demanding almost everything that was produced, no longer could manufacturers satisfy the whims of fashion or the allure of variety. Diversification became a luxury no longer tolerable if we were to win the war.

The government, headed by Baruch, called for standardization of products and processes, the production of interchangeable parts, the reduction of styles and sizes. Civilians had to sacrifice novelty, content themselves with fewer choices and reduce their desires. They were forced to adopt that attitude of which Emerson spoke when he said that Thoreau made himself rich by making his wants few. Some consumers reacted at first with irritation and outrage, but others were surprised to learn that a paucity of *things* can heighten spirituality.

So many Frenchmen had been killed in battle and so many Frenchwomen wore black to mourn them that Parisian dressmakers decreed that their 1918 fashions would alleviate this gloom by emphasizing colors and an abundance of fabrics. The couturiers furthermore reasoned that the opulence of their new styles would loosen the purse strings of the prosperous and less mournful Americans. But when the War Industries Board learned that the latest Paris designs called for more cloth, an executive of the board's conservation division visited Jean J. Jusserand, the French ambassador to the United States, and asked him to intercede. As requested, the ambassador passed the word to the couturiers, who reluctantly agreed to pare down their styles; thus the material that would have gone into women's gowns was made available to manufacture uniforms and tents and airplane wings and the like.

Women wore corsets, corsets had steel braces, and steel was needed to make guns and shells and tanks, so steel was left out of corsets at a savings of 300 tons of the precious metal. There was such a demand for leather for harnesses for horses and the Sam Browne belts worn by officers and so forth that a savings was effected by reducing the height of women's shoes and ruling that no new lasts could be produced.

Mrs. James L. Slayden, the wife of a Democratic Congressman from Texas, wrote in her diary:

> Another one of those preposterous appeals has come in, this time from the "Patriotic Economy League" . . . recommending "economy and simplicity in dress and a curtailment of purely social activities." They also ask me to sign three pledges to that effect "for the duration of the war." The names of some of those sponsoring and signing this appeal are of women who, I have no doubt, spend more in a month than [her husband's] entire salary—Mrs. Medill McCormick, Mrs. William Corcoran Eustin, Mrs. Peter Goelet Genny, etc., etc.

Treasury Secretary McAdoo tried to set a good example by ostentatiously wearing patches on his pants, igniting witticisms in the press. Germany led the world in the sophistication and magnitude of its chemical industry, and when we could no longer import German-made synthetic dyes, the color went out of American clothes. Baruch said that if the war had lasted much longer, our civilian population "would have been clothed in serviceable, if drab, apparel."

In the ardor to conserve everything nothing was too small to be ignored. A spool of thread contained 150 yards of thread. By increasing this to 200 yards per spool, fewer spools were needed, and thus more wood was saved for more vital purposes. This change also freed 600 railway cars that would have been required to transport the greater number of spools of thread. By reducing typewriter ribbon colors from 150 to a mere 5, by furthermore cutting back on the tinfoil and tin boxes in which the ribbons came, the United States saved 395 tons of steel and seven tons of pig iron. A hardware wholesaler reduced by more than half the 90,000 items he was accustomed to advertising in his catalogue.

No longer could a farmer choose a plow from among the 326 styles and sizes available; plows were reduced to only 76 kinds. Instead of 784 drills and other planting machines, only 29 were offered for sale. Buggies had come in 232 varieties, but it was found that 4 were enough. Boys had had their pick of 6,000 kinds of pocketknives, but to save metal, only 100 varieties became available. Baby carriages were standardized. The government forbade the manufacture of coffins made of brass, bronze or copper, and it also curtailed the styles and sizes of steel caskets. Even the varieties of wooden coffins were reduced by 85 percent.

Wool was needed to make uniforms, so manufacturers of men's clothing had to alter their styles to save on fabric. Sack suits could be made in only ten models, while models of boys' suits were reduced to three. The consumption of cloth by the manufacturers of men's clothing was reduced 12 to 15 percent by eliminating outside pockets, shortening coats, narrowing the width of facings, etc.

The United States saved 2,265 tons of steel by paring down the numbers of bicycle designs and stripping the vehicles of extras. By applying this principle to the manufacture of motorcycles, the nation saved 600 tons of steel, 9 tons of aluminum, 13½ tons of brass, 12½ tons of copper, and 12 tons of rubber. Taking the tin out of children's toys and the like conserved 75,000 pounds of pig iron. Changes in the packaging of various products freed 2,325 freight cars to haul the tools of war.

Hardly any consumer goods were unaffected by the government's demands that civilians do with less to give the soldiers more, but all in all, there were surprisingly few complaints.

In time of war a government can bend a balky industry to its will by using the ultimate power of commandeering—seizing a plant or facility and forcing it to aid the military effort.

The first few months after we went to war with Germany there was no unified program of commandeering. Instead, this and that arm of government grabbed what it wanted regardless of the needs of other agencies. The army insisted on preferential treatment. So did the navy. So did the shipping board and every other wartime agency. The result was confusion and error.

For example, the army took over the Southern Pacific coastline ships plying between New York and New Orleans and Galveston; but Treasury Secretary McAdoo had just become director of the railroads, and he declared the ships were under his jurisdiction and therefore the army's commandeering order was to be ignored.

Baruch sympathized with an aide who ordered cement from a plant 500 miles away only to find plenty of cement available only 10 miles away. A Buffalo manufacturer shipped steel bars to a Cincinnati plant that converted the bars into projectile forgings, which then were shipped back to Buffalo to be machined. Crosshauling. An intricate problem. Freight piled up at ports until trains were unable to reach them and had to unload in fields 30 miles away. As the transportation system broke down some railway yards became so chaotic that cranes had to lift freight cars off tracks and trundle them to a main line to get them on their way again.

In a single year the army got 21,700,000 blankets, or more than the normal consumption of blankets by 100,000,000 American civilians in two and a quarter years. In 1918 the army bought far more woolen socks than the entire normal annual production in the nation. The army called for twenty suits of underwear for each soldier in France on the theory that because of vermin, the underwear could be worn only one week and then would have to be thrown away. Had this surrealistic order been met it would have strained and perhaps broken the nation's knitting industry. But fewer union suits were made; instead, delousing equipment was made to free the soldiers of lice.

To end interagency bickering, the President finally wrote the heads of all executive agencies to declare that the "commandeering power should not hereafter be exercised over any of the agencies of the country without first consulting the chairman of the War Industries Board." That, of course, meant Baruch.

In the spring of 1918 the WIB told the auto industry to reduce its production of passenger cars. In the last six months of the year it could make only a fourth as many cars as it had delivered in 1917, and by 1919 the industry would have to shift entirely to war work. However, in defiance of this order many auto manufacturers did not taper off their production or reduce their inventories; they furthermore continued to stockpile fuel and raw materials.

One manufacturer flatly refused to limit production, arguing that the board was acting arbitrarily, rather than in the public interest. Since he had enough coal and other supplies on hand, he would do as he wished. When word of this rebellion reached Baruch, he summoned a naval officer assigned to the WIB and ordered him to commandeer the manufacturer's supply of coal. The officer got in touch with the businessman and relayed the chairman's order.

The manufacturer asked in amazement, "You wouldn't do that—would you?"

Baruch's man said grimly, "So far as I'm concerned, it's already done! So far as you are concerned, it will be accomplished tomorrow morning."

The manufacturer gave in.

On another occasion a lumber manufacturer dared Baruch to commandeer his mills, saying that Baruch knew damned well the government could not run them efficiently.

"Quite true," Baruch said quietly, "but by the time we commandeer those mills you will be such an object of contempt and scorn in your home town that you will not dare show your face there. If you should, your fellow citizens would call you a slacker, the boys would hoot at you, and the draft men would likely run you out of town."

The lumberman also fell into line.

There was such a scarcity of lumber and other building materials that the War Industries Board had to restrict private construction. No private citizen was allowed to erect any structure worth more than $2,500. This was almost a deathblow to the building trades and their subindustries; it hurt carpenters, bricklayers, plumbers, cement makers, steamfitters and the like. It also hurt businessmen in need of new offices, farmers planning to build a new barn, homeowners who wished to enlarge their houses.

The reaction to this ban was instantaneous and furious. William M. Calder, a Republican Senator from New York and a former contractor, gave the Senate a resolution demanding that the WIB explain why a $4 billion industry, "than which it seems to me there can be few more essential," should be put out of business.

Baruch wrote the Senate a letter explaining the situation. He began by saying that representatives of the construction industry had been consulted and all had agreed on the necessity of curtailing private production if the United States were to win the war. Although the country needed 21,000,000 tons of steel and iron, it was producing only 17,000,000 tons. In the face of a shortage of fuel essential to the war program, the production of private building materials was consuming 30,000,000 tons of coal. A quarter of the railway capacity was being used to haul items intended for private construction. At a time when not enough men were available to work in war plants, thousands of laborers were engaged in private construction.

The ban on nonwar construction fell especially hard on schools and churches, so many individuals and delegations went to Washington to plead that exceptions be made in behalf of projects in their hometowns.

Chicago wanted to erect a big building to memoralize American soldiers but was turned down. Evangelist Billy Sunday was refused permission to construct another wooden tabernacle. An influential Democratic Congressman from New York had a growing family and wanted to add a wing to his home, but he withdrew his application after learning that many houses, schools and hospitals in his district had been denied exemptions, realizing a bad impression would be created if he got special attention.

John F. Hylan, the mayor of New York City, asked permission to spend $8,000,000 to build some new public schools, and while it was politically ticklish for the Wilson administration to antagonize the mayor of the largest Democratic city in the country, he too had to bow to the board's system of priorities. Herbert Bayard Swope, formerly of the New York *World* and now Baruch's press agent, wrote Hylan a reply which Baruch signed and Wilson characterized as a great letter. It said in part, "He serves best who saves most."

The winter of 1917–18 was the coldest in human memory—some said the coldest in recorded history. In camps here and there across the country some draftees still wore their civilian clothing for lack of uniforms; they shivered in tents and barracks lacking fuel; they drilled with wooden guns. There was a scarcity of all kinds of fuel and the railroads had broken down. Brigadier General William Crozier vowed at a Senate committee hearing that all camps would be supplied with rifles within ten days—and then he did the unthinkable. He criticized his superior, Secretary of War Baker, calling Baker responsible for all sins of commission and omission in the production of the weapons of war.

This cry was taken up by George Harvey, the vituperative editor of *Harvey's Weekly*, who called Newton Baker "Newtie Cootie" and said that the army secretary "sat on top of a pyramid of confusion which he has jumbled together and called a war machine." Harvey ended his article with the words "We need a butcher, not a Baker; a he-man to run a he-war." This was a slap at Baker's diminutive size and his interest in reading the classics.

Others then opened up on Baker, who felt so hurt he offered his resignation to the President, who refused it. So Baker stayed at his post but thereafter wore such a stoical mask that an assistant wondered how "in the face of all this maddening business" the secretary could look so serene. Baker softly told a friend, "If you took my heart out, you'd see the heel-prints on it."

The worst attack came from Democratic Senator George E. Chamberlain of Oregon, chairman of the Senate's powerful military affairs committee. On January 19, 1918, he spoke in New York at a luncheon of the National Security League. By this time there was a movement afoot to create a bipartisan Cabinet, and the man most often mentioned as Baker's replacement was Theodore Roosevelt. Teddy was present at the luncheon, one among many influential Republicans eagerly lapping up the words of the discontented Senator.

Chamberlain declared, "The military establishment of America has fallen down. There is no use to be optimistic about a thing that does not exist; it almost stopped functioning. Why? Because of the inefficiency in every department of the government of the United States. I speak not as a Democrat but as an American citizen!"

Roosevelt sprang to his feet and led the cheering.

When Navy Secretary Daniels read Chamberlain's remarks, he wondered whether the Senator had suddenly gone mad and said as much to the numbed Baker. A biographer and historian named Ray Stannard Baker (no relation to the secretary of war) wrote in his diary that day: "The attack is largely traceable to the great business interests of the country, which resent government control of the railroads and the mines, chafe under taxation, fear the growing power of labor. . . . Several New York papers which supported Wilson's re-election, now in a rampaging mood of hostile criticism."

The President flared in anger. He resented this assault on Secretary Baker, who had his affection as well as his confidence, but Wilson knew he could not ignore the attacker, since he was chairman of a powerful committee. Wilson wrote Chamberlain to ask whether his luncheon remarks had been quoted correctly. Yes, Chamberlain replied, correctly. The President then issued a statement branding Chamberlain's comments as "an astonishing and absolutely unjustifiable distortion of the truth."

Chamberlain planned to call Baker to testify before his committee in private, but Baker, his dander up, insisted upon testifying in public. So the little secretary of war marched up the hill to the Capitol, sat down before a row of hostile Senators and began with a brisk announcement to the chairman that he proposed to review the whole course of the war and the part the war department had played in it.

Speaking without notes, Baker held forth a total of five astonishing hours, admitting there had been delays in providing our troops with uniforms and guns and ammunition, but nonetheless weaving facts and figures into a persuasive argument to the effect that never in history had any army the size of the American army been raised and equipped so swiftly. Navy Secretary Daniels sat and listened and later said, "No such speech, restrained and fortified with logic and evidence, had been heard in the Capitol in a generation. I was as happy at Baker's victory as I was enraptured by his unstudied eloquence."

When the committee took a luncheon break, Senator Ollie James, the elephant-sized Democrat from Kentucky, rushed to the White House, ran into Wilson's office and panted, "Jesus, Mr. President! You ought to see that little Baker! He's eating 'em up!"

After lunch Baker resumed testifying, and by the time he finished he had demolished Chamberlain. Chamberlain did follow Baker with a three-hour speech and introduced a bill calling for a war Cabinet of "three distinguished citizens of demonstrated executive ability" with "full control of the war under the direction and supervision only of the President," but Baker had done such a good job of countering Chamberlain's arguments that the bill failed to pass.

The President, as proud of Baker as though Baker had been his son, nevertheless was unwilling to let matters go at that. He did not want a coalition Cabinet. He felt, instead, that despite all his authority as President and commander in chief of the army and navy, he lacked the total clout he needed to do an effective job of administering the war program.

Wilson struck back by drafting a bill that would give him limitless powers. He gave his bill to Senator Thomas S. Martin, a Democrat from Virginia, and asked him to introduce it into the Senate. Martin, who felt that Presidential authority already had been stretched too far, was so startled when he read the measure and saw that it would give Wilson total power, that he refused to shepherd it through the upper chamber. Wilson then turned to Democratic Senator Lee S. Overman of North Carolina, who agreed to sponsor the bill that came to be known as the Overman Act. Appealing to other Senators, Overman said, "Everybody has been making criticism about the red tape in the departments. The President wishes to cut it. Let us give him the scissors with which to do so."

But some Senators trembled lest they hand the President not a pair of scissors but a scepter. One of them cried, "We might as well abdicate!" The bill would grant Wilson greater war powers than those exercised in Great Britain by Prime Minister Lloyd George or in France by Premier Clemenceau.

The Overman Act authorized the President to coordinate or consolidate executive bureaus, agencies and federal offices in the interest of economy and the more efficient concentration of governmental operations in matters relating to the conduct of the war. It would remain in force as long as the war lasted and for six months afterward. And to make sure there were no limitations whatsoever on Presidential power, the sixth and last section of the bill said that "all laws or parts of laws conflicting with the provisions of this Act are to the extent of such conflict suspended while this Act is in force."

Wilson ordered Tumulty to manipulate the press and stir citizens into pressuring their legislators to pass the measure, there ensued a long and bitter struggle between the President and the Congress, some Senators and Representatives stood fast, but since there had been such a clamor for greater efficiency, a majority of them finally passed the Overman Act, and Wilson signed it on May 20, 1918.

Now, in law and in fact, Woodrow Wilson was the political dictator of the United States of America.

Alexis de Tocqueville, that astute French witness to American democracy, wrote in the nineteenth century: "War does not always give democratic societies over to military government, but it must invariably and immeasurably increase the powers of civil government; it must almost automatically concentrate the direction of all men and the control of all things in the hands of the government. If that does not lead to despotism by sudden violence, it leads men gently in that direction by their habits."

Woodrow Wilson did not become a benign despot overnight or even consciously. He had worried about the presence of German spies and saboteurs in the United States, the victories of German armies in Europe, the menace of German submarines in the Atlantic, the diminution of food and ammunition and other necessities among the Allies. He had been angered by Theodore Roosevelt's attacks on him during the preparedness debate, by savage Republican assaults on his character during the 1916 Presidential campaign and now by Congressional criticism of his conduct of the war effort. He continued to believe that God had chosen him as President of the United States. He was quick to credit himself with noble motives and equally quick to discredit others for allegedly ignoble ones. He was not always the idealist he thought he was. He was far from being an evil man, but evil is not necessarily arbitrary or even conscious; there is truth in the platitude that the road to hell is paved with good intentions. Wilson, now the political dictator of America, firmly believed in democracy and capitalism, and so did Baruch, the nation's economic dictator. However, the pressures of war led both of them, gently but inexorably, to adopt attitudes resulting in the advent of something new and dangerous—the military-industrial complex.

Baruch had faith in the economic law of supply and demand, but unlike most of his contemporaries, he also believed that time was necessary to let this law unfold to the benefit of all. With the war raging, with Germany seemingly about to defeat the Allies, time was of the essence; there simply was not enough time in which to let the economic water find its own level. Victory had to be forced, democracy had to be rationed, capitalism had to bend—or so it appeared.

Capitalists abandoned their cherished ideal of free competition, industrialists threatened with nationalization surrendered to the needs of the government, and the Wilson administration rewarded them in part by relaxing antitrust laws—with the people paying the price. Borrowing concepts from the business world, the government also created its own corporations.

Bureaucrats and businessmen learned how to work together—not without friction, not without recriminations, but at least to the mutually satisfying end of winning the war. Generals and admirals exchanged views with board chairmen and came to understand one another. Scientists and professors offered their brains to government and industry, and soon they too began talking much the same language. Since it was easier for the government to deal with the heads of a few huge labor unions, rather than many smaller ones, the trade union movement fell into line.

In their *History of the American People* Harry J. Carman and Harold C. Syrett said:

> World War I accelerated earlier trends toward the concentration of control over American industry and finance. During the last months of the war, economic competition within the United

States virtually ceased as the government assumed responsibility for the regulation of the quantity, quality, prices, and distribution of many goods. Although some businessmen objected to the extent of government control, they did not object to the profits that were provided by the wartime planned economy. . . . Before World War I, businessmen fought each other; after the war they combined to present a united front against consumers.

Chapter 27

THE LIGHTER SIDE OF LIFE

In August, 1914, the first month of the war, American newspapers and magazines began publishing stories saying that a huge Russian army had landed in Great Britain.

This was no invasion, since Russia and Britain were Allies. According to the articles, the czar's soldiers were passing through the British Isles en route to France to fight the Germans on the western front. Other Russian armies already were battling the Germans on the eastern front.

The way American newspaper readers heard the news, Russian soldiers had boarded troop transports at Archangel, sailed to Norway, transferred to ordinary steamers, continued to Aberdeen, Scotland, where they disembarked, then filed into troop trains that sped them to ports on the English Channel for transshipment to France.

In Great Britain and on the continent only a few papers published this story, for as soon as the war began, the Allied governments had imposed press censorship, so over there the rumor was spread mainly by word of mouth. It was brought to the United States by Americans who sailed back from England and on their arrival in New York were interviewed by shipboard reporters; by a Scottish nobleman who wrote his American brother-in-law that Cossacks had marched across his estate in Perthshire; by Americans from Massachusetts to Oregon who had a friend who had an acquaintance who knew a man who claimed to have seen trainloads of bearded Russians disembarking from vessels in Scotland. Everyone seemed to believe that all Russian soldiers wore long black beards. In one version or another, the alleged facts were published in the New York *Times*, the New York *Evening Sun*, New York *Evening Post*, the New York *World*, the *Journal of Commerce* and the *Literary Digest*, among others.

The presence of any Russian soldiers on British soil was fascinating enough, but equally piquant were their supposed numbers: At first it was said there were 500,000 of them. Later the figure was revised downward to 250,000, then 125,000 and at last it held at an estimated 70,000 to 80,000 men.

Overlooking certain flaws in the story, many people were quick to believe it because of colorful details: A Scottish army officer said he had seen the Russian warriors in "long gaily-colored coats and big fur caps," armed not with rifles but bows and arrows, tending their own horses that looked "just like Scottish ponies, only bonier." An Oxford professor said a colleague had been summoned to interpret for them. In the Edinburgh railway station a porter saw them stamp snow off their boots. The townspeople of Yarmouth were kept awake all night by the tramp of soldiers wearing astrakhan tunics. The residents of Redhill saw a train laden with cannon of a kind unknown in the British army.

A farmer was awakened by the sound of an unscheduled train and looked out his window and saw bearded faces peeping between the slats of drawn blinds on the train windows. A British officer confided to friends that Russians had traveled through Britain in the "utmost secrecy." Ten thousand foreign soldiers were seen after midnight in London, marching along an embankment toward Victoria Station. Some Britons who spoke Russian swore they had talked with the Russians in their native language. One man said the Russians were mounted and armed with bayonets; another said they were foot soldiers equipped with swords.

Over the next few weeks Britons were split into those who believed these stories and those who scoffed at them, the debate raging in homes and clubs and newspaper offices. Snow on boots in August? Bows and arrows? Cavalrymen carrying bayonets? Ridiculous! But what about that dispatch from Amsterdam saying a large force of Russians was being sped to the western front! And what about the people of Paris hanging around railway stations in hope of seeing the arrival of Cossacks?

Some said the rumor began in an English railway station where a porter spoke to Scottish soldiers whose troop train was making a brief stop; he asked where they came from and they replied "Ross-shire"; they spoke in thick Scottish accents and the English porter thought they said "Russia." But two London newspapers declared their belief that the Russians had come and soon would be fighting in France. In another London newspaper office, though, an editor offered to bet 25 to 1 that there was not, and never had been, any Russian force in Britain.

On September 15, 1914, the British government officially denied all versions of the rumor.

Not until the end of the war did the true story emerge. There had been no Russians in Great Britain. The rumor was a hoax intended for propaganda purposes. The story had been deliberately planted by agents of the British secret service, partly in the hope of misleading and frightening the Germans, partly to bolster morale at home. Horatio H. Kitchener, the British secretary of state for war, furthered the ruse by sending transports laden with sundry goods from Scottish ports to Archangel, to create confusion, and he had the ships insured in Holland, where the Germans were sure to hear of them. Kitchener also ordered British troop trains to travel with blinds drawn down on the windows so as to arouse curiosity and generate rumors. The government's official denial was also a part of the scheme, for had there really been Russians in Britain it would have been natural for authorities to deny it. It is possible that alleged eyewitnesses, or at least some of them, were acting under orders from the secret service. The rest was done by the imaginations of hoodwinked people.

The hoax was effective to some extent, for German staff officers in Belgium and northern France became afraid they soon would find themselves fighting the Russians on two fronts, and deployed their own troops to meet this expected emergency.

In 1915 a rich American made a proposal so controversial that it touched off a storm of criticism.

The man was John Wanamaker, who had established the country's largest retail men's clothing store in Philadelphia, and who had served as postmaster general of the United States between 1889 and 1893. Civil service reformers had criticized the circumstances of his appointment to the Cabinet, as well as his use of the spoils system while in office. In 1914, after the Germans conquered and occupied Belgium and Belgian citizens began to die of starvation, Wanamaker donated enough money to stock two ships with food, clothing and medical supplies and then send the vessels to Belgium.

On July 22, 1917, the seventy-seven-year-old merchant attended a ceremony to accept the chairmanship of the Philadelphia branch of the National Security League. When he got up to speak, he startled his audience by suggesting the United States buy Belgium from Germany.

"Raise billions!" he cried. "Buy Belgium! Instead of putting money into ships, this country should borrow a great sum—a hundred billion dollars if necessary—and buy Belgium and give it its freedom when it is able to take care of itself."

While imperialistic nations had purchased tropical colonies from other great powers, there seemed no precedent for the purchase of a European nation of ancient lineage and unique culture. Not only was there no precedent, but Wanamaker's proposal raised questions of legality and morality, of the feelings of the Belgians themselves, of paying blackmail to Germany, of buying something from someone who did not own it, of raising the enormous sum of which he spoke. Wanamaker was criticized so severely that six days after he spoke he resigned his new chairmanship with the complaint his remarks had been misinterpreted.

The Belgians were being helped by Herbert Hoover. After finishing his job of overseeing the rescue of Americans trapped in Europe at the start of war, Hoover had formed the Committee for Relief of Belgium and Northern France. In a monumental operation he directed the relief of 10,000,000 people in this area who had been victimized by the German occupation and the Allied blockade. From all belligerents he obtained agreements for the protection of the food, clothing and medical supplies sent to the stricken people. He was probably the only American allowed to move freely between London, Paris, Brussels and Berlin.

Hoover, who was to become the thirty-first President of the United States, nonetheless once found himself staring into a German gun. In one volume of his memoirs he told the story:

. . . At the end of September 1916, on one of my perpetual North Sea crossings, I came to the Hook of Holland from Brussels to take the Dutch boat for Harwich. The requirement was as usual to be on board in the evening as the boat left at daylight. One slept comfortably at least until then.

Late next morning I was awakened by a gruff voice telling me in German to keep still. The man wore the uniform of a German marine. As he pointed a revolver with the seeming calibre of a beer glass I had no inclination to raise a disturbance. He seemed wholly disinclined to carry on a conversation, but every little while repeated his words of little comfort. Combining feeble German with gestures, I suggested that I might ring the bell over the bunk. To this he made no ultra-violent objection.

When the Dutch steward arrived he informed me that we had been captured at daylight by the Germans and taken into Zeebrugge. So far as I was concerned it had been a most peaceable battle. With the steward as a messenger to the German officer in command I obtained the privilege of getting up and going on deck in search of breakfast. There I found that we were in Zeebrugge harbor, surrounded by four or five German destroyers. All the passengers except myself and an elderly Dutch gentleman had been crowded onto the stern deck and were being examined by one or two German officers seated behind tables.

One of the officers asked if I were Mr. Hoover. On my reply he courteously told me that we would be delayed some hours, but that when they had done with their search of the mail and passengers we would be allowed to proceed to England. . . .

When the search was over and we were waiting for a signal to depart I was standing with the Dutch gentleman observing proceedings from the upper deck. Suddenly an explosion broke in our faces and my companion fell in a heap. It flashed through my mind that we were being fired upon from the shore. Then a Dutch sailor yelled "Aeroplane!" I looked up to see a French plane circling over us, kindly dropping a bomb each time it came around. It came around five times. The first bomb had struck the bow of a barge fifty feet away, and the Dutch passenger had been slightly hurt with splinters. My neck had a crick in it for a week from the earnestness of my interest in the next four rounds from that plane. The bombs did not strike either us or the German destroyers, but the expectation that the aim would be better next time was absorbing. . . .

Hoover was still in Europe on April 6, 1917, when the United States declared war on Germany, and that day he got word that President Wilson wanted to talk to him in person. The morning of May 4 Hoover reached the White House, where he was asked by the President to supervise food production and distribution in the nation for the duration of the war. Hoover agreed, although he stipulated that he receive no salary for this new position and wanted to continue as head of Belgian relief. On May 19 Wilson appointed him the head of a new Food Administration.

An able administrator, Hoover did a masterful job in the face of grave difficulties and despite the jokes made about him by Americans forced to endure wheatless days and meatless days and other kinds of privations. He was wise in his selection of subordinates, some of whom became famous for their resourcefulnesss. One in particular.

People spread a story that may have been untrue and certainly was more grisly than funny. According to this anecdote, a Norwegian immigrant died at his home in North Dakota. His family wanted to ship his body back to Norway for burial but was told that under wartime regulations nothing but necessities could be sent abroad. The problem was brought to the attention of one of Hoover's assistants, who sympathized with the grieving family. Carefully checking regulations, he decided the corpse could be shipped overseas if it were crated within a box marked "Animal fats, not edible."

On July 17, 1917, the New York *Times* reported that Mrs. Franklin D. Roosevelt, the wife of the assistant secretary of the navy, had been selected by the conservation division of the Food Administration as a model for large households in the matter of conserving food. The article told how she managed for a family of seven with ten servants. She was careful when she herself did the grocery shopping, she made sure her cooks wasted no food, and she ordered the laundress to use soap sparingly. By closely following helpful hints from the Food Administration, she was able to keep down the family food budget despite the rise in the cost of food.

FDR was away from their Washington home when this new story broke, but he read it in the *Times* and burned with anger. Writing Eleanor a letter lacking any kind of salutation, Roosevelt said, "All I can say is that your latest newspaper campaign is a corker and I am proud to be the husband of the Originator, Discoverer and Inventor of the New Household Economy for Millionaires! Please have a photo taken showing the family, the ten cooperating servants, the scraps saved from the table and the handbook. I will have it published in the *Sunday Times*."

Charles Lathrop Pack, a forest conservationist, organized the National War Garden Commission as an affiliate of the American Forestry Association, and it stimulated the development of domestic "war gardens" to augment the national food supply during the emergency. These gardens came to be called Victory Gardens, and among the hundreds of thousands of Americans who planted them were the Marx Brothers.

During the war the comedians lived temporarily in the Chicago suburb of La Grange; from there they left to play one-night stands in the Middle West. They were much under the influence of their redoubtable mother, Minna Schoenberg Marx, whom they called "Minnie," and at first they agreed when she suggested they turn to farming to do their patriotic bit and also make extra money.

As Kyle Crichton tells the story in his biography of the brothers, they bought a five-acre farm with a dilapidated chicken house built by a former owner. All right. They would raise chickens. Setting alarm clocks for five in the morning, they would leap out of bed to take care of their flock, but this early hour soon took its toll of actors accustomed to sleep until noon. Groucho would sit down under a tree with a book and refuse to move. Chico wandered into town to play pool. Harpo blasted away at rats with a secondhand .22 rifle. Zeppo, who hated the taste of chicken, would turn his hand to nothing until it was time to slaughter them, and then he would chop off the heads of chickens "with the zest of Attila."

Unwilling to admit their flocks were dying of neglect and disease, the brothers made a halfhearted attempt to sustain their reputation as chicken farmers by resorting to fraud. When a friend from Chicago was expected to spend a country weekend with them, they went to a local grocery store, bought fresh eggs and hid them in nests in the hen house. The next morning Gummo tried to impress their visitor by "finding" the eggs. "How's this for nice fresh eggs!" Their friend took one look and laughed. "Very efficient! Lay them with the label already stamped!"

The chicken farm failed. Next the Marx Brothers decided to raise guinea pigs to sell to laboratory technicians in hospitals, but so many other people had the same idea that this plan failed as well. Okay, so they would plant a truck garden. The patriotic word from Washington was that every tomato was a bullet aimed at the Kaiser's heart. Woodchucks and weasels ravaged everything but the tomatoes and cucumbers, so they pinned their dwindling hopes on the two acres they had planted in potatoes. At the end of the growing season, however, all they could harvest was a single bucket of spuds, and these were too small and gnarled to be worth much. Their experiment with agriculture left the brothers with little but food for thought.

Not only was a Victory Garden planted on the White House lawn but sheep were brought in to graze as well. In the spring of 1917 as the nation geared for war and a manpower shortage began to develop, President Wilson decided he could release some White House gardeners for essential work if he got sheep to crop the grass. Before the gardeners left to find other work, however, they carefully protected every tree, bush and flower bed from the animated lawn mowers.

On April 30, 1917, eight sheep were turned loose on the lawn, much to the surprise, then amusement of passersby. Tended by a man wearing a cap, overalls and sweater and carrying a long stick, the sheep added a pastoral touch to a city feverish with excitement. Mrs. Wilson felt annoyed at those critics who deplored what they considered to be a lack of dignity at the nation's executive mansion.

Besides cropping the grass, as they were expected to do, the sheep also multiplied until there were eighteen in the flock. When they were sheared they produced 98 pounds of wool, which Mrs. Wilson divided equally among the forty-eight states for auction by the American Red Cross, bringing in almost $100,000 for its war work.

Many of the supplies for the American Expeditionary Force left for France from the port of Hoboken, New Jersey. Some quartermaster officer at Hoboken either overestimated the number of Jewish boys serving in France or the number of holidays in the Jewish calendar, for almost a shipload of matzoth was sent abroad.

The unleavened bread was made in ten-inch squares and packaged in glazed paper stamped in Hebrew. Laurence Stallings wrote that when one battalion was given two days' field rations the doughboys were surprised to find the matzoth. Some Jewish soldiers in the outfit apologized to their buddies, but after the Gentile soldiers tried the bread they waved aside all embarrassed comments. They liked the crisp unsalted freshness of the bread, and they were bored with the dreary diet of corned beef they called monkey meat. Happily they made themselves a matzo-monkey-meat hash. A Catholic chaplain chuckled that Rome had missed a good thing in the culinary department.

Most black soldiers sent to France worked so hard and fought so bravely that they were acclaimed back home. For example, on July 26, 1918, a well-meaning editorial writer for the Milwaukee *Sentinel* singled out two units for praise, saying, "Those two American colored regiments fought well and it calls for special recognition. Is there no way of getting a cargo of watermelons over there?"

One day in March 1917 Lewis J. Selznick was lolling in his posh Park Avenue apartment when he learned Czar Nicholas II had abdicated the throne of Russia under pressure from revolutionaries. Selznick was the son of Russian immigrants, and when young, he had been so poor he had to leave school; but he worked hard, became a jewelry merchant and then developed into one of the most powerful producers in the history of the motion-picture industry. A flamboyant man, Selznick decided the czar's abdication gave him a chance to grab even more publicity for himself. Summoning his secretary, he dictated a cablegram in the Russian language. In English, it said:

> NICHOLAS ROMANOFF
> PETROGRAD, RUSSIA
> WHEN I WAS A POOR BOY IN KEIV [*sic*] SOME OF YOUR POLICEMEN WERE NOT KIND TO ME AND MY PEOPLE STOP I CAME TO AMERICA AND PROSPERED STOP NOW HEAR WITH REGRET YOU ARE OUT OF A JOB OVER THERE STOP FEEL NO ILLWILL [*sic*] WHAT YOUR POLICEMEN DID SO IF YOU WILL COME NEW YORK CAN GIVE YOU FINE POSITION ACTING IN PICTURES STOP SALARY NO OBJECT STOP REPLY MY EXPENSE STOP REGARDS YOU AND FAMILY
>
> SELZNICK
> NEW YORK

The former czar did not reply.

Late in April 1917 British and French war commissions arrived in the United States seeking money, men and arms. The French commission was led by Marshal Joseph J. Joffre, supreme commander of all the French forces, so kind a man that his adoring soldiers called him Papa Joffre but so old-fashioned that he refused to speak on the telephone. Navy Secretary Daniels took the ranking officers of the missions aboard the Presidential yacht to sail fifteen miles down the Potomac to Mount Vernon, Virginia, where they placed wreaths on the grave of George Washington.

Daniels asked Joffre whether he was frightened when he went into battle. Instead of giving a direct answer, the marshal told the secretary this story:

> Early in the war a French officer, who had long been retired, returned to active service. He had grown fat and soft in retirement, but nothing could dissuade him from donning the uniform and going to the front. When the first call to battle came, he found he was frightened and was trembling like an aspen leaf. It distressed him greatly because his body was shaking as he prepared to go where the fighting was fiercest. He struck himself on his breast and said: "What do you mean, you miserable carcass, to tremble so and disgrace me in the presence of my troops!" And then, caressing his body, he said in tender tones: "But forgive me for my harshness. If you knew where I was going to take you today, you would tremble more than you do!"

Early in the summer of 1917 Irvin S. Cobb decided to try to enlist in the army. He knew he had almost no chance of being accepted because he was forty-one years old, thirty pounds overweight, with fallen arches and one abnormally large lung. Furthermore, while in France in 1914 as a correspondent for the *Saturday Evening Post*, he had acquired a hernia carrying wounded soldiers out of hospital trains at Maubeuge after litter-bearers had dropped from exhaustion. Nevertheless, he thought that if he were taken into the service, he might be of some help in military intelligence. In his autobiography, *Exit Laughing*, he said his motives may have been vanity or patriotism—he wasn't sure.

As fat and funny as Falstaff, a seasoned newspaperman who knew his way around, Cobb took direct action by seeking an audience with President Wilson. His first step was to place a long-distance call to Tumulty, whom Cobb fondly characterized as a man as wily as Cardinal Richelieu. Tumulty told Cobb to appear at the White House a couple of days later toward the end of the afternoon. As Cobb approached the executive mansion, he saw a crowd standing on the sidewalk, peering through the guarded gates.

Tumulty always referred to Wilson as the Governor. He said to Cobb, "The Governor is going to see you as soon as he gets rid of a lot of boll weevils, mostly long-winded babies from up on Capitol Hill. Their idea of a conference is a weekend party. So sit down and rest your face and hands. . . . No, be gee, I've got an idea! An excursion outfit of nice people from out in the Wheat Belt—Nebraska, Kansas, somewhere out there—have been hanging around for hours hoping to get a glimpse of the Governor. They want to go back and tell the folks they saw him, anyhow. Until this minute it looked as though they were going home disappointed. But now—well, you come along with me."

Tumulty led Cobb into the President's office and told him to sit down at the desk with his back the door and the top of his head showing above the President's chair.

"Now," said the secretary with a grin, "start fiddling with papers or something. Pretend you're signing state documents—that would be a nice touch. But whatever you do, don't turn that face of yours sideways. That'll kill the show and what's worse, maybe get me killed, to boot."

Cobb struck a pose and Tumulty walked out, leaving the door ajar. In a minute or so Cobb heard the shuffle of feet in the corridor, heard excited murmurs and the voices of ushers urging the throng to keep moving. The impish Cobb grinned to himself, aware that the people from the Midwest thought they were seeing their President hard at work at his desk. When all was silent again, he quickly got out of the chair, and moments later Wilson entered, unaware of what had happened.

The President smiled at Cobb, whom he knew by reputation, asked him to be seated and then ordered a hovering attendant to leave them alone. Cobb later wrote of Wilson, "He looked fit and fine-drawn, trained down like a racing whippet. His eyes were not dulled even after a long and arduous day, but were swift and keen behind his glasses. His scholarly face showed no heavy lines of fatigue and hardly any suggestion of strain."

Ashamed of bothering the President over something so trivial, Cobb mumbled that he wanted to join the army.

"See here," Wilson responded, "as commander in chief of the armed forces of the United States I could issue you one of those phony commissions. . . ." When Cobb heard the word "phony," he laughed to himself because he knew Wilson's reputation as a lord of language. Cobb told Wilson that if he failed to get a commission, the *Saturday Evening Post* planned to send him back to the front, and when the President heard this, he said, "That's where I am ordering you, as a loyal citizen, to go."

As Cobb left the office, the President did something astonishing—he brushed the correspondent's shoulder with his bent arm. Cobb, well aware that Wilson was no backslapper, wrote in delight, "I don't believe many men were hugged that summer, even fleetingly, by Woodrow Wilson."

A husky fifteen-year-old boy was so eager to get into the army that when he appeared at a recruiting station and was asked his age, he said he was "over eighteen." But despite his heft, he looked so young that he was closely questioned, and at last he had to confess his true age. Rebuked for making a false statement, the boy insisted he had not lied. He explained that before presenting himself he had taken off both shoes and in the sole of each of them he had inserted slips of paper on which he had written EIGHTEEN.

In naval training camps throughout the country the trainees were fond of reciting:

> I never thought I'd be a gob—
> You see, dad owns a bank;
> I thought at least I'd get a job
> Above a captain's rank.
> But woe to me, alack! alas!
> They've put me in white duds;
> They don't quite comprehend my class—
> They've got me peeling spuds.

In the fall of 1918 Captain Harry S. Truman was commanding Battery D of the 129th field artillery in the battle of Meuse-Argonne. One night German artillery fire zeroed in on his outfit, pouring in such a barrage that it began to appear the entire unit would be blown off the map. The terrified doughboys abandoned their equipment and began to scatter. The captain from Missouri, his spectacles reflecting bursting shells, was riding a horse. It stumbled and threw him into a shell hole. Truman scrambled to his feet and cut loose with a barrage of his own—a verbal barrage.

"It was beautiful!" a gunner later cried. "He called us every name west of the Mississippi. We stopped like whistled-after rabbits and in two minutes were back lammin' it at the Germans."

Truman's unit silenced the enemy batteries, losing only one of their own men. After that night a good way to get a busted nose was to say anything nasty about Captain Truman, who later became a major, then the President of the United States.

President Wilson's swearing was pretty much confined to mild words, such às "rats!," but when angered he sometimes let himself cry "damn!" One day he told Secretary Daniels a man had accused him of profanity because he had said "damn!"

"My critic," Wilson said, "was unaware of the fact that when some Democrats, wishing to impeach a Federalist judge, charged him among other things with profanity on the bench, specifying that he used the word 'damn,' the court held that 'damn' was not profanity but just a way of being emphatic. Perhaps I should not have let my temper get the best of me when I used that emphatic word, but at least that decision acquits me of being guilty of profanity."

And Wilson's eyes twinkled.

In July, 1918, Franklin D. Roosevelt went to France to inspect naval bases. At St.-Nazaire some huge 14-inch American naval guns were being mounted on railways cars so that they might blast away at the German lines from various spots on land. Already scheming to quit his sub-Cabinet post, Roosevelt decided that what he most wanted to do was to don a uniform and be assigned to this naval railway battery. He spoke of this to the admiral in charge. The admiral asked, "Can you swear well enough in French to swear a French train on a siding and let our big guns through?"

Fairly fluent in French, Roosevelt grinned and cried, "Listen!—" With that he launched into a long and colorful string of French oaths, some real, some imaginary. The admiral was so impressed he promised to accept Roosevelt in his outfit with the rank of lieutenant commander if he could persuade the secretary of the navy to give him a commission.

On March 23, 1918, the Germans had begun bombarding Paris from a distance of eighty miles with a 150-ton cannon called Big Bertha. According to William Manchester, this monster was serviced by sixty seamen commanded by a full admiral, although it was fired from the land rather than the sea. Its shells weighed 200 pounds or more, and before every firing the admiral and his staff studied atmospheric pressure, humidity, temperature, the curvature of the earth and extensive mathematical data. Each shot cost 35,000 marks. Big Bertha was more an instrument of terror than an effective weapon of war; although it killed more than 1,000 Parisians in twenty weeks, there were days when it did nothing more than damage a few roofs in the French capital. On August 8 the bombardment stopped.

That spring everyone in the United States became aware of Big Bertha, and it even figured in Flo Ziegfeld's *Follies* in New York City. Among Ziegfeld's comedians were Eddie Cantor, W. C. Fields and Will Rogers. Cantor decided to play a practical joke on Rogers. He told the Oklahoma cowboy, "Will, I've thought of a gag you can use, and, if you can, it's yours. Tell'em that no matter what the Germans invent, we can always go 'em one better. Tell 'em you have inside information that we have just invented a long-range gun that will shoot from Staten Island to Berlin, and if it doesn't kill a man—it will take him prisoner."

Rogers laughed, said he liked the gag and would work it into his monologue that evening. Cantor then went to W. C. Fields and told him the same story, cautioning him not to mention it until he got onstage. Cantor knew Fields was scheduled to appear at a time when Rogers would be in his backstage dressing room. So Fields incorporated the joke in his act, and the audience laughed. Later that evening Will Rogers strolled onstage, twirling his lariat, and repeated the story, unaware that the audience had just heard it. Naturally, there was no reaction.

As the puzzled Rogers walked off into the wings, he met Cantor, who asked, "How did the story go, Will?"

"It was a failure," Rogers muttered. "I never had a gag fall so flat."

Before the end of the evening someone in the cast told Rogers how he had been taken by Cantor, and the cowboy-comedian became so angry he refused to speak to Cantor. The next day, though, Rogers forgave him.

The joke heard twice in the same evening by a *Follies* audience spread to Europe, where it underwent a slight change. After the war President

Wilson went to Paris, and after he got back he talked to his Cabinet members about the huge 14-inch American guns fired from land by our sailors; it was after they went into action that the Germans stopped bombarding the French capital with Big Bertha. In a jovial mood, Wilson said, "I heard a good story about the big fourteen-inch naval guns in France. They created a great sensation as they were carried about the country to the battle front. One man said: 'They kills everybody within one hundred miles and hunts up the next of kin and kills all of them.' "

In the spring of 1918 the third Liberty Bond campaign was launched, and federal officials sought the help of celebrities to make it a success. Among them were movie stars—Douglas Fairbanks, Mary Pickford, Marie Dressler and Charles Chaplin. They went to Washington, were paraded through the streets and then driven to a football field to speak to a huge crowd. As Chaplin awaited his turn, he stood on the ground beneath a platform made of crude boards and decorated with flags and bunting. Beside him stood a tall handsome young man whom he learned was Franklin D. Roosevelt. The British-born comedian told FDR that never in his life had he made a serious public speech, and he felt nervous.

"There's nothing to be scared about," Roosevelt told Chaplin. "Just give it to them from the shoulder. Tell them to buy Liberty Bonds. Don't try to be funny."

When Chaplin was introduced, he leaped onto the speakers' platform and began a rapid-fire speech: "The Germans are at your door! We've got to stop them! And we *will* stop them if you buy Liberty Bonds! Remember, each bond you buy will save a soldier's life—a mother's son!—will bring this war to an early victory!"

Chaplin was so voluble and excited that he twisted his body and lost his balance, grabbed at Marie Dressler, who stood beside him, and the two of them fell off the platform and onto FDR.

After the end of the rally the Hollywood stars were driven to the White House and ushered into a room to wait to see the President. A door opened, an attendant appeared, and they were ordered to form a line and then take one step forward. In walked President Wilson.

Mary Pickford was the first to speak. "The public's interest was most gratifying, Mr. President, and I am sure the bond drive will go over the top."

Chaplin, as he later confessed in his autobiography, was so nervous and confused that he butted in, "It certainly was and will—"

Wilson stared at Chaplin as though he wondered who he was, made no response, but launched into an anecdote about a politician who liked his liquor. Chaplin later wrote, "We all laughed politely, then left."

At another bond rally that spring the main attraction was Douglas Fairbanks, the swashbuckling athlete with the sunny grin. He wore a tailored military uniform and greatcoat, and his hands were encased in enormous boxing gloves. Lettered in white on one glove was the word "Victory" while the other spelled out "Liberty Bonds."

To the delight of the spectators Fairbanks staged a fake boxing match with another actor impersonating the Kaiser and wearing boxing gloves saying "*Kultur*" and "*Kamerad.*" On the western front the Germans who wanted to surrender would yell "*Kamerad!*," meaning "Comrade." The man playing the part of the German emperor was a German-American named Gustav von Seyffertitz; after the war began, he changed his name to C. Butler Clonebaugh. The symbolic fight was watched by still another actor made up like Uncle Sam, a fourth disguised as the devil, and a pretty girl with a crown spelling out "Justice."

Naturally, Fairbanks decked the "Kaiser."

At a Cabinet meeting in the White House there was talk of appointing a comptroller general of railroads, and someone raised the question whether it should be spelled "comptroller" or "controller." President Wilson laughed and said:

"Once upon a time a man built a small lumber railroad. He was a practical man, not well educated, but knew enough to keep his books. The railroad prospered and the owner employed an elderly man to keep books, and he signed himself 'Controller.' When he died the business had grown and the owner employed a young efficiency expert. When he brought in his first report he spelled his title comptroller, not controller, as had his predecessor. The old man didn't like the change and said so very emphatically. 'Since when was there a "P" in controller?' The young man got even by quietly saying, 'I think it was the last time you watered the stock.'"

Chapter 28

THE EAST ST. LOUIS MASSACRE

One of the most significant changes to occur in this country because of the war was the mass migration of black people from the South to the North.

Back in about 1880 a stream of blacks had begun to flow across the Mason and Dixon line, but not until 1916 did this stream swell into a tidal wave. It is impossible to exaggerate the historic importance of this movement, for not only was it one of the largest migrations on any continent in any century, but it set in motion a series of sociological, economic, political, racial and humanistic developments felt throughout our society to this very day.

When the European war began in 1914, the South was deep in depression, and the blacks suffered most because they lived at the bottom of the economic scale. In the years just previous to the war Southern harvests had been poor, the boll weevil was killing the cotton, and 1915 and 1916 floods left thousands of blacks homeless and destitute.

Black fieldhands lucky enough to work on plantations were paid only 50 to 75 cents a day, while black factory workers felt fortunate to get $1.25 to $2 a day. On plantations their housing was miserable, crop settlements were unfair, and they were charged exorbitant interest rates. And in a variety of ways white people discriminated against the blacks.

When the industrial North began getting orders from the Allies, when immigration declined, when white workers entered the military, Northern plant owners and managers began searching for a new supply of labor. They placed help-wanted advertisements in Southern newspapers and sent glib labor agents south to try to recruit black workingmen. Southern blacks read black newspapers such as the militant Chicago *Defender* and learned of job opportunities in the North. Northern blacks wrote their Southern relatives about the openings in the industrial cities. Referring to lynchings in the South, the Chicago *Defender* said, "To die from the bite of frost is far more glorious than at the hands of a mob." The *Christian Recorder* prophesied, "If a million Negroes move north and west in the next twelve-month it will be one of the greatest things for the Negro since the Emanicipation Proclamation."

Southern blacks were so quick to respond that Southern white newspapers urged them to stay at home, rhapsodizing about the

Southland, where " . . . the cotton is blooming in the old patch, roasting ears are hanging green from the stalks, red-hearted watermelons are ripe under the shady vines, blackberries are winking through the leaves."

Northern cities braced themselves for an invasion. Texas-born Attorney General Gregory muttered darkly about a "colonization conspiracy." Georgia-born Treasury Secretary McAdoo ruled that no one might pay in advance the cost of transporting any Southern black to the North. In Jacksonville, Florida, city officials passed a law requiring Northern migration agents to pay $1,000 for a license fee, and in several Southern towns whites threated blacks with violence should they try to leave.

Railroads, eager to profit from this migration, added extra coaches to north-bound trains, and by the summer of 1916 tens of thousands of blacks were heading north to "the land of promise." Down in Dixie whites worried about the disappearance of fieldhands essential to plantation life, the flight of their black house servants, the loss of factory workers. In Georgia the Macon *Telegraph* nervously wrote about the white farmers who awakened morning after morning to find their black help had left for Cleveland, Pittsburgh, Chicago and Indianapolis. In Washington the labor department expressed concern about this "great migration."

Even today no one can be sure of the size of this movement. While estimates ranged from 150,000 to 750,000, it would seem that between 1916 and 1920 more than 500,000 blacks moved North. Far more made the change in the 1920's. Most migrants settled in the big cities of the North because that was where the big factories were located. Chicago's black population grew fourfold in two years.

Few migrants were paid the $4 a day they had been promised by some of the smooth-talking labor agents, and most blacks soon found working conditions and housing far less attractive than they had been led to expect. But they settled down and helped make cars and trucks and electrical products, ammunition and iron and steel; they labored in meat-packing plants and coal mines and shipyards. At a steel mill in Maryland a black man broke the world's record for driving rivets into steel ships. At Hog Island near Philadelphia a black pile-driving crew set another world's record for driving piles.

One of the Northern cities attracting the blacks was East St. Louis, the chief railway and manufacturing center of southern Illinois. Located on the east bank of the Mississippi river opposite the larger city of St. Louis, Missouri, and with twenty-seven railroad lines radiating out in all directions, East St. Louis was a gateway to the North and West. Smoky, brawny, bustling, the city was thick with mills, factories, warehouses, stockyards and packing plants.

Its industries were controlled by corporations such as the Aluminum Ore Company, the Republic Iron and Steel Company, the American Steel Foundries Company controlled, for the most part, by Republican capitalists living in New York, Chicago and elsewhere. In short, the city's wealth was controlled by nonresidents. Sherwood Anderson said that East St. Louis was "nobody's home . . . the most perfect example, at least in America, of what happens under absentee ownership." Elliott Rudwick, who wrote a well-documented book about the East St. Louis, riot, made this point: "Civic responsibility often began and ended with a membership card in the East St. Louis Chamber of Commerce."

These huge corporations enjoyed doing business in the city because the corrupt city and county governments favored them with ridiculously low property tax assessments. The capitalists did not much care what went on in town so long as they piled up profits under this tax dodge. The meat-packing industry, which employed the greatest number of workers in the city, found another way of saving money. From the state of Illinois the companies obtained a charter to incorporate on the north side of town a village named National City. This tiny municipality of only a few hundred residents had its own mayor, aldermen and, most important, a tax assessor who just happened to work for one of the meat-packers. But when a fire broke out, the owners of National City instantly forgot their independence and turned for help to the fire department of East St. Louis.

With the corporations paying less than their fair share of taxes, small householders were forced to pay disproportionately large real estate taxes, while the city's largest single source of revenue came from fees charged to operate saloons—of which there were many. The absentee capitalists got along very well indeed with the graft-ridden Democratic machine that ran both the city and county governments. Mayor Fred Mollman was a stooge beholden to the boss of bosses, Locke Tarlton, who held the juicy chairmanship of the East St. Louis Levee Board. A Congressional committee later reported that "one of the picturesque sights . . . was to see Locke Tarlton with a stack of $5 bills in his hands publicly paying the negroes who helped him win an election."

East St. Louis was a wide-open town, as raw as a frontier settlement, a city where laws had been ignored for so long that to many people they had almost ceased to exist. Because the politicians were corrupt and careless and inefficient, the municipality was bankrupt. City councilmen took bribes. Police jobs were political appointments, and any man who wished to go on the force had to contribute to the mayor's campaign fund. Since the starting salary for a new cop was only $70 a month, many policemen supplemented their incomes by renting houses to whores. Realtors profited by charging prostitutes $30 to $100 for a house that would have brought in only $15 a month as a home for decent citizens.

When St. Louis and Chicago and other towns in the area temporarily closed their red-light districts in 1915, the prostitutes had flocked into East St. Louis. There they paid law officers for protection and were afraid to go to court because they knew that juries were bought. The city's lawlessness also made it a favorite retreat for criminals, who opened cocaine dives and gambling joints and held cockfights. The nearby hamlet of Brooklyn offered "wine rooms," one owned by Brooklyn's chief of police, Tony Speed. The specialty of the house was "twelve-block whiskey" because "you take a drink, walk twelve blocks, and fall flat on your face."

East St. Louis was a gamblers' mecca. There were slot machines, craps, faro, roulette and chuck-a-luck, and the town was a clearinghouse for the St. Louis racing interests. Constables and deputy sheriffs moonlighted as procurers and bouncers in some of the city's haunts—The Bucket of Blood, The Monkey Cage, The Yellow Dog, Uncle John's Pleasure Palace, Aunt Kate's Honkytonk. In a community of 70,000 people there were only 52 cops; a Chicago grand jury estimated that at least 1,000 officers were needed. Ten thousand residents were black, but there were only 6 black cops on the police force.

Vice, graft, corruption, prostitution, gambling, murder, community apathy and race prejudice were so widespread that late in 1917 a Congressman gasped, "I had never dreamed that such a condition existed in this country—or on the face of the earth!"

Prior to 1913 the city's entire labor force had been white. Early in 1917, though, with war orders rolling in and business booming, local plant managers discovered that the migration to the North had given them more black laborers than they could use. This labor surplus delighted them, since they could use it as a weapon to resist attempts to unionize white workers, to keep down wages. In 1916 common laborers earned 17 to 20 cents an hour. By 1917 they were getting from 17 to 27 cents an hour; but the cost of living had risen more than this, and their wage scale was lower than in nearby cities.

The black men from the South, glumly aware they could get nothing like the $4 a day promised them by labor agents, willingly accepted any job, however dirty and unpleasant, that was offered them. Some worked in a plant owned by the East St. Louis Cotton Seed Oil Company as long as twelve hours a day for only 16 2/3 cents an hour. Mayor Mollman said in alarm that unless these conditions were corrected, there was sure to be a holocaust.

The tension in this blue-collar town was between unorganized and unskilled whites, on the one hand, and unorganized and unskilled blacks, on the other hand. Whenever a black was hired, his new boss warned him against joining any union—an unnecessary admonition, since black workers were suspicious of organized labor. Over the previous years they had been excluded from the white men's unions. The American Federation of Labor occasionally expressed friendship, but its national officers were really uninterested in organizing blacks, while AFL President Gompers was notoriously unsympathetic toward them. Michael Whalen, president of the Central Trades and Labor Councils of East St. Louis, was quoted in a newspaper as saying, "The chief objection to the negroes is that they would not unionize and would not strike." And this labor organization sent the mayor a letter demanding "drastic action . . . to get rid of" the migrants.

By now the black workers from the South were disenchanted with "the land of Lincoln." White workers resented them. White employers used them as pawns in a power struggle with unions. White foremen charged them 25 cents a day for the privilege of working. Since there was absolutely no job security, blacks were laid off at the whim of the bosses. Blacks had to take the dirtiest and most dangerous jobs. Some factories did not install washrooms, lockers or safety devices until compelled to do so by the state.

Blacks were excluded from parks, playgrounds, theaters. Confined in ghettos, they had to pay high rentals for hovels lacking running water or sanitary facilities. Black children were often locked at home alone during the day because their mothers worked as maids and were unable to pay anyone to look after them. When rain fell, the water backed up and overflowed into muddy streets, so workmen walking to plants and children going to school had to wade through the muck; some children who sat in school with wet feet caught colds and even came down with pneumonia.

Despite an 1874 state law banning segregated school systems, black girls and boys had to attend segregated schools. In defiance of another state law of 1885, blacks were excluded from restaurants and hotels. Blacks who broke any law whatsoever were locked inside segregated sections of the city and county jails. But the white realtors who owned the blacks' shacks could break the law by renting substandard housing and never be punished, because the realtors and corporations controlled the corrupt local government.

Burton K. Wheeler, who later became a United States Senator from Montana, says in his memoirs that Bruce Bielaski, head of the investigative division of the justice department, told him that "most of the labor troubles in the big cities was [*sic*] caused by the miserable working conditions maintained by large corporations." A Congressional committee later declared that "the employers of labor paid too little heed to the comfort or welfare of their [black workers]."

Elliott Rudwick, a sociologist who wrote a book about East St. Louis, said that "corporation managers were most heavily responsible for the social climate which culminated in the race riot." Thomas Canavan, one of the town's overlords, in a self-serving remark intended to exonerate himself from complicity in these horrible conditions, declared, "The prime cause of the trouble was the avarice of the manufacturers." But C. B. Fox, general manager of the Aluminum Ore Company and a former president of the local Chamber of Commerce, remarked, "You can do too much . . . welfare work."

On May 28, 1917, rumors flicked through the city: A black had shot a white man during a holdup . . . accidentally . . . no, the shooting was done in cold blood . . . a white woman had been insulted . . . two white girls had been shot . . . another white woman had been wounded.

Inflamed by these stories, 3,000 whites erupted into the streets shouting about ropes and lynchings, yelling that pawnshops were selling guns to blacks. Mobs raced through the downtown section, beating every black in sight. A restaurant, a barbershop and saloons patronized by blacks were invaded by white toughs who whipped every black they could find and then demolished some of these establishments. Unarmed and terrified blacks were beaten and kicked and left bleeding in the gutters. Two or three blacks were shot, but none died. That night hundreds of blacks carrying cheap suitcases fled across the two bridges leading to St. Louis.

This was the city's first mass attack of whites against blacks, but soon it was followed by other incidents. The mayor appealed to Illinois Governor Frank O. Lowden, who sent national guardsmen into the city but withdrew most of them by June 20. Tension increased: The whites feared the blacks would retaliate by massacring them on the Fourth of July, while the blacks babbled that the whites intended to slaughter them on that same holiday.

Early Sunday evening, July 1, there were reports of several more assaults by whites on blacks. Later that night a Ford driven by a white man and filled with other whites cruised along a street in a black section, and guns were fired into black homes. When the car returned, the black homeowners shot back and hit the vehicle, which speeded up and vanished into the night. The report reaching the police was that blacks were armed and rampaging.

A police car—also a Ford—was sent to investigate. The driver and his companion on the front seat were detectives in civilian clothes. Uniformed cops sat in the back while Roy Albertson, a reporter for the St. Louis *Republic,* stood on the running board. He said that when the squad car turned off Tenth Avenue and into Bond Avenue, it met "more than 200 rioting negroes . . . [who] without a word of warning opened fire."

One detective was killed almost instantly, while the other died the next day. In later testimony before a Congressional committee the reporter admitted the killings might have been the result of mistaken identity. The detectives rode in a Ford—and the attacking car had been a Ford. The squad car's headlights were weak and the nearest streetlight was around the corner and fifty feet away. But in the morning edition of the *Republic* the day after the shooting Albertson's story had depicted the black gunmen as so calloused that they opened fire on the white officers who had come to help them.

On the morning of July 2 the bullet-riddled police car was displayed in front of the downtown police station, its blood-stained upholstery looking "like a flour sieve, all punctured full of holes." White men walking to work stopped and gaped and growled and muttered about revenge. A white lawyer announced he would gladly serve as counsel for "any man that would avenge the murders." Thousands of whites regarded the murders and the squad car as proof that the blacks really planned to rise and massacre all of them.

By 9:30 A.M. on Monday, July 2, 1917, downtown streets teemed with angry whites. The mayor, who had solicited the political support of poor whites and blacks, was afraid to leave his office lest he be attacked by white workers. The previous night he had telegraphed national guard headquarters in the state capital of Springfield, and now he mistakenly believed six militia companies were racing toward the city. Some prominent citizens urged him to deputize a civilian army to prevent mobs from burning down the town, but his will was so paralyzed that he was unable to decide anything.

While he trembled in his office, a mob met in the nearby Labor Temple and listened to speakers roar at them to get guns and then come back to the business district. Some already were armed. When the men left the hall, they meandered in ragged military formation along a main thoroughfare peopled with far more whites than blacks because the nearest Negro ghetto was about two miles away, and just as they reached Broadway, the first black was shot.

Observers said the militant whites were "in good humor . . . like waiting for a circus parade." At a street intersection hundreds of people watched as thirty bullies stopped a streetcar by pulling its trolley arm off the overhead wire. Among the passengers were Mr. and Mrs. Edward Cook of St. Louis and their teen-age son. They were blacks who had spent the morning fishing in nearby Alton, and now they were on their way home. A white man reached through an open window and grabbed Mrs. Cook's dress, partly tearing it off and yelling, "Come on out, you black bitch! We're going to kill you!" Another white man boarded the stalled streetcar and bellowed, "All you white people get out! We're going to kill these niggers!"

Mrs. Cook shrieked that her family did not live in East St. Louis and that they had not hurt anyone. The man who tore her dress then grabbed her husband by the collar, dragged him to the rear platform, knocked him down and shot him. The second white man seized her son and began dragging him away. Mrs. Cook screamed, "You've killed my husband! Don't kill my boy!" But the man jerked her boy away and beat him over the head with a revolver.

The man who had killed her husband ran back to her and pulled her off the streetcar, and several men then beat and kicked her and tore out her hair. One white man jumped into the melee screaming, "Don't kill the women folks!" As the brutes turned on him, Mrs. Cook crawled away on her hands and knees toward a store and collapsed in the doorway. Now another white man, a tall man, ran up to protect her, shielding her body with his and begging her pursuers, "Don't beat her any more!" Then he glanced down at her and said, "I'm not going to let them kill you. Stay back there!" Turning back toward her attackers, the tall white man screamed, "In the name of the Lord, don't kill the woman!"

She survived. She survived to tell her story to a jury, and she ended with these words: "And then some way or other they got me into the ambulance and there was another fellow lying there, a colored fellow on the side of the ambulance, and I saw he had a big handkerchief and I took it and wiped the blood out of my eyes and when I looked down I saw my husband lying there and my boy right under me. They had their eyes open and they were dead."

The violence spread. At first it occurred in the business district, where whites outnumbered blacks. Several blacks were knocked down and beaten and white men strolled up to them as they lay bleeding and shot them. When the corpses were put in an ambulance, some white spectators clapped their hands and cheered.

White whores attacked frightened black women. Carlos F. Hurd of the St. Louis *Post-Dispatch* wrote about the fury of these white prostitutes "dressed in silk stockings and kimonos, with last night's paint still unwashed on their cheeks." Hurd went on to say: "I saw negro women begging for mercy and pleading that they had harmed no one, set upon by white women of the baser sort, who laughed and answered the coarse sallies of men as they beat the negresses' faces and breasts with fists, stones and sticks. I saw one of these furies fling herself at a militiaman who was trying to protect a negress, and wrestle with him for his bayonetted gun, while the other women attacked the refugee."

At 8:40 A.M. twenty-seven national guardsmen and three officers had arrived in the city, but instead of the six full companies the mayor expected, only small units trickled in during the next several hours. Many militiamen were farmhands, most had been in the guard less than two months, some wore overalls instead of uniforms, many were ignorant and prejudiced against blacks, and they were led by an officer who knew nothing about riot control measures. One guardsman told the crowds, "The black skunks are no friends of ours!"

Near the place where the whore had attacked the militiaman some white men surrounded two black men who held trembling hands over their heads in surrender, but they were clubbed to the street with the butts of guns. White girls ran up and kicked the blacks, spattering their stockings with blood, while white men watched and grinned. Some black women were actually scalped. Four black children were slaughtered. Mobs chanted, "Get a nigger! Get a nigger! Get another!"

Late that afternoon at a distance from the business district some black shacks were set on fire. White men lay in wait with weapons to pick off fleeing blacks as one might shoot running rabbits. A reporter for the St. Louis *Republic* wrote:

> A crazed negro would dash from his burning home, sometimes with a revolver in his hand. Immediately revolvers by the score would be fired. He would zig-zag through the spaces between the buildings. Then a well-directed shot would strike him. He would leap into the air. There were deep shouts, intermingled with shrill feminine ones. The flames would creep to the body. The negro would writhe, attempt to get up, more shots would be fired. The flames would eat their way to him. . . .

With the help of fire-fighting equipment rushed across the river from St. Louis, local firemen tried to douse the blazes, only to be threatened by mobs. At least one fire hose was slashed by a white man. As firemen tried to put out one fire, others would be started by rioters elsewhere. Attempts were made to burn black schools. Whites broke the windows of one Negro home, crawled inside, banged on the piano, then looted the place. Two militiamen threw the corpses of several blacks into a creek.

And all this cruelty was performed coolly, according to several reporters. One journalist said that "this was not the hectic and raving demonstration of men suddenly gone mad." Paul Y. Anderson of the St. Louis *Post-Dispatch* felt his belly hurt as he watched whites attacking six black men. One cried, "My God! Don't kill me, white man!"

Elsewhere three armed whites saw a wounded black sprawled in a gutter. One gunman cried, "Look at that bastard! Not dead yet!" The whites fired at the prone figure, then ran away. Standing near a burning hovel was a white soldier who was jeered by whites: "Whatcha doin' with a gun? You couldn't even shoot it!" The young militiaman retorted, "The hell I can't!" And raised his rifle and shot at several blacks.

White men tried to hang a black from a telephone pole with a clothesline which broke, so someone got a stronger rope. A reporter ran to some soldiers and begged them to stop the lynching, but the guardsmen just stood there and did nothing. Carlos Hurd of the *Post-Dispatch* wrote:

> I saw the most sickening incident of the evening when they got a stronger rope. To put the rope around the negro's neck, one of the lynchers stuck his fingers inside the gaping scalp and lifted the negro's head by it, literally bathing his hand in the man's blood. "Get hold and pull for East St. Louis," called the man as he seized the other end of the rope. The negro was lifted to a height of about seven feet and the body left hanging there for hours.

Cops smashed cameras and arrested photographers and one reporter in an attempt to suppress telltale evidence. Laughing policemen let themselves be held "captive" by cynically winking mobs, while other whites beat and shot blacks. Hurd was so outraged by what he saw that he wrote,

> For an hour and a half last evening I saw the massacre of helpless Negroes at Broadway and Fourth Street in downtown East St. Louis where a black skin was a death warrant.
>
> I have read of St. Bartholomew's night, I have heard of the latter-day crimes of the Turks in Armenia, and I have learned to loathe the German army for its barbarity in Belgium. But I do not believe that Moslem fanatics or Prussian frightfulness could perpetrate murders of more deliberate brutality than those which I saw committed in daylight by citizens of the state of Abraham Lincoln. . . .

In terms of the numbers of killed and injured, the East St. Louis massacre of July 2, 1917, was the worst race riot thus far in the twentieth century. We will never know exactly how many died. The NAACP and the Chicago *Defender* estimated that from 100 to 200 blacks were slaughtered. A Congressional committee, aware that there was no way to make sure, decided that 39 blacks had been killed. The county coroner said 9 white people lost their lives; some were accidentally slain by wild-shooting whites.

Hundreds may have been wounded, but the precise figure could not be determined because injured blacks were afraid to go to hospitals controlled by whites. The Congressional committee said 312 buildings were destroyed; a state deputy fire marshal estimated property damage at $373,605; other estimates were higher.

And, in a shocking indictment of the American dream, it was learned that 6,000 to 7,000 terrified black men, women and children fled from the horrors of the massacre by swarming across the two bridges to St. Louis, Missouri, where many were sheltered in the municipal lodging house.

The day after the riot the President's secretary told Washington reporters the details were so sickening he had difficulty reading them. Tumulty urged Wilson to express his "deep disapproval" of the "terrible things" that had happened in East St. Louis, and the President issued a strong public statement denouncing mob violence. However, when a delegation of Baltimore blacks asked for an appointment with Wilson, Tumulty advised him to decline the request with the excuse that he was busy with pressing international affairs. Tumulty felt that if the administration gave little attention to the matter, the tension would subside.

He was wrong. The Boston *Journal* declared that the status of the blacks had declined since the Southern Democrats had taken control in Washington in 1913. The St. Louis *Post-Dispatch* and St. Louis *Globe-Democrat* claimed that Illinois must not rest until the guilty were brought to justice. Thomas Swann of the Freedman's Foundation asked Wilson for federal action. H. H. Harrison of the Liberty League of Negro Americans urged blacks to get weapons to defend themselves. In a Chicago jail black prisoners went on a rampage when they heard the news of East St. Louis. The city's Chamber of Commerce passed a resolution urging black workers to return from St. Louis, promising them protection. An AFL spokesman denied that labor unions were responsible for the riot.

The evening of July 6, 1917, a reception was held in Carnegie Hall in Manhattan to celebrate the Russian revolution and honor the new republic's first ambassador to the United States. Mayor Mitchel introduced the principal speaker, Theodore Roosevelt, who was greeted with cheers. Seated on the platform was Samuel Gompers, president of the AFL, and many in the audience were Russian Socialists. Roosevelt departed from his prepared text and began to condemn the riot, saying, "Before we speak of justice for others it behooves us to do justice within our own household. Within the week there has been an appalling outbreak of savagery in a race riot in East St. Louis, a race riot for which, as far as we can see, there was no real provocation, and which, whether there was provocation or not, was waged with such an excess of brutality as to leave a stain on the American name. . . ."

Gompers rose. When Roosevelt was President, Gompers had gone to the White House to express displeasure at something Teddy had said in public, and he spoke so vigorously that Roosevelt banged his desk with his fist and cried, "Mr. Gompers, I want you to understand, sir, that I am the President of the United States!" Gompers' eyes had blazed as he too banged the desk and shouted back, "Mr. President, I want you to understand that I am the president of the American Federation of Labor!"

Now, standing in Carnegie Hall, Gompers opened with the remark that he approved the "general sentiments" expressed by Roosevelt, then added, "But I want to explain a feature of the East St. Louis riots with which the general public is unacquainted. . . . I wish I had brought with me a copy of a telegram received today from Victor Hollander, secretary of the Illinois Federation of Labor. I can tell you that not only labor men but a member of the Chamber of Commerce of East St. Louis warned the men engaged in luring Negroes from the South that they were to be used in undermining the conditions of the laborer in East St. Louis. The luring of these colored men to East St. Louis is on a par with the behavior of the brutal, reactionary and tyrannous forces that existed in old Rome!"

Gompers was applauded. Roosevelt, his face red with fury, asked the chairman for permission to say a word in response, then moved to the center of the stage and resumed speaking. Unaware that the riot had been caused more by economic rivalry than race prejudice, Roosevelt said:

"I am not willing that a meeting called to commemorate the birth of democracy and justice in Russia shall seem to have given any approval of or apology for the infamous brutalities that have been committed on Negroes at East St. Louis. Justice with me is not a mere phrase or form of words. How can we praise the people of Russia for doing justice to men within their boundaries if we in any way apologize for murder committed on the helpless? In the past I have listened to the same form of excuse advanced on behalf of the Russian autocracy for pogroms of Jews. Not for a moment shall I acquiesce in any apology for the murder of women and children in our own country! I am a democrat of democrats! I will do anything for the laboring man except what is wrong!"

Roosevelt strode over to Gompers, shook his fist in his face and shrilled, "I don't care a snap of my finger for any telegram from the head of the strongest labor union in Illinois! This took place in a Northern state, where the whites outrank the Negroes twenty to one. And if in that state the white men cannot protect their rights by their votes against an insignificant minority, and have to protect them by the murder of women and children, then the people of the state which sent Abraham Lincoln to the Presidency must bow their heads!"

Gompers leaped out of his chair and barked, "Investigate afterward, not before—"

Roosevelt hammered his fist closer to Gomper's nose and shouted, "I'd put down the murders first and investigate afterwards!"

Socialist leader Eugene V. Debs called the riot "a foul blot upon the American labor movement. . . . Had the labor unions freely opened their door to the Negro instead of barring him . . . and, in alliance with the capitalist class, conspiring to make a pariah of him, and forcing him in spite of himself to become a scab . . . the atrocious crime at East St. Louis would never have blackened the pages of American history."

No one in his right mind suggested that *all* the white people of East St. Louis had taken part in the horrors. Many blacks fleeing from mobs found refuge in the homes of compassionate whites. Mrs. Cook, the black woman whose husband and son were killed, never forgot the two anonymous white men who protected her from the fury of the crowd. Interestingly, though, after a paper printed a story about a white grocer who hid some blacks in his cellar, the grocer demanded a retraction.

But to the dismay of good people in the days following the riot it became clear that many whites, perhaps most, felt no remorse for what had happened. The city had a Mardi Gras mood. A postman said, "The only trouble with the mob was that it didn't get niggers enough. You wait and see what we do to the rest when the soldiers go. We'll get every last one of them!" Ominous black hands were painted on black property. White insurance men canceled fire policies on homes owned by blacks. New attempts were made to burn down black shacks. Landlords brutally evicted black tenants. Furniture dealers demanded the return of merchandise being purchased on the installment plan.

A New York reporter interviewed some leading citizens and then wrote a composite of their opinions: "Well, you see, too many niggers have been coming in here. When niggers come up North they get insolent. You see they vote here, and one doesn't like that. And one doesn't like their riding in the street cars next to white women—and, well, what are you going to do when a buck nigger pushes you off the sidewalk?"

The blacks who had fled to St. Louis were afraid to return to their homes and jobs. Vigilante committees were organized in nearby towns. Hundreds of white men and women cheered when charred corpses were removed from the smoking shells of what had been black homes. The morgue became a tourist attraction. People strolled around showing off souvenirs—bits of hats and shirts and jackets stripped from the dead. And on a street a militiaman stood over a cinder that had been a torso and told grinning spectators, "There's one nigger who'll never do no more harm!"

Two years before the riot Dr. Sigmund Freud had written an article called "Thoughts for the Times on War and Death." He said, "Our conscience is not the inflexible judge that ethical teachers are wont to declare it, but in its origin is 'dread of the community,' and nothing else. When the community has no rebuke to make, there is an end of all suppression of the baser passions, and men perpetrate deeds of cruelty, fraud, treachery and barbarity so incompatible with their civilization that one would have held them to be impossible."

The NAACP and other black groups wrote letters and held parades to try to pressure the President and the Congress into sponsoring federal legislation to guarantee real freedom and justice for all Americans regardless of race. On July 28, 1917, 10,000 black men, women and children marched along Manhattan's Fifth Avenue behind muffled drums and carrying banners saying:

WE ARE MALIGNED AS LAZY AND MURDERED WHEN WE WORK
WE HAVE FOUGHT FOR THE LIBERTY OF WHITE AMERICANS IN 6 WARS, OUR REWARD IS EAST ST. LOUIS
PRAY FOR THE LADY MACBETHS OF EAST ST. LOUIS

New York police prevented the marchers from displaying a reproduction of a cartoon from the New York *Evening Mail*. It showed the President holding a paper saying, "The world must be made safe for democracy," while at his feet there knelt a black woman with two children, her arms outspread; in the background could be seen smoke from the burning homes of East St. Louis. The caption read: "Mr. President, why not make America safe for democracy?"

When the parade was over, a group of black leaders entrained for Washington and called at the White House. Tumulty told them that while it would be impossible for them to see the President, they could rest assured he understood their feelings. After listening to "general and platitudinous phrases," the black men left, disappointed and angry.

A young man wrote a letter saying he refused to serve in the army unless the President and justice department made some realistic move to protect black people from mobs. His letter was published in a Virginia newspaper, the Norfolk *Journal and Guide,* which then was banned from the mail by the Richmond postmaster. The editor of the paper hired a lawyer who managed to get this ban lifted. A black minister about to become an army chaplain asked how his nation, "with so much filth in her own back-yard," could take part in a "world-cleaning expedition."

But neither the President nor his attorney general cared to institute a federal inquiry into the massacre. They held that the federal government had no legal right to intervene, since there was no evidence proving the rioters had violated any federal statutes.

However, four investigations and several trials were held. The investigations were held by: (1) the labor committee of the Illinois State Council of Defense; (2) a board of inquiry, which reported to the adjutant general of the Illinois national guard; (3) a grand jury of St. Clair county, in which East St. Louis was located; and (4) a House Select Committee to Investigate Conditions in Illinois and Missouri Interfering with Interstate Commerce between these States.

It was the inactivity of the Wilson administration that prompted Congress to investigate. The House took the lead because a move to launch an inquiry did not get far in the Senate. Two racist Senators—Tillman of South Carolina and Vardaman of Mississippi—declared that the riot had its roots in biology, not region, and proved that East St. Louis illustrated the "dauntless spirit of the white man" who would never yield to a "congenitally inferior race."

Republican Congressman Leonidas C. Dyer of Missouri became the prime mover in the House. He said the riot had interfered with interstate commerce and therefore Congress was entitled to look into the matter. St. Louis shipping firms were having trouble hiring black men because they were afraid to make deliveries in East St. Louis. Managers of packing plants in East St. Louis reported the riot had delayed the fulfillment of government war contracts. So the House established the select committee.

Its five members went to East St. Louis and held hearings there from the middle of October to the middle of November in 1917. After taking 5,000 pages of testimony, they returned to Washington and spent months analyzing their data. The full testimony of these hearings was never printed—supposedly for reasons of economy—although the committee issued a twenty-four-page report read into the *Congressional Record.* This report was a stinging indictment of white rule in East St. Louis, spelling out the ways in which politicians, employers and labor leaders had created an emotional and economic climate that resulted in the massacre.

C. W. Middlekauf, an assistant attorney general of Illinois, called the riot "the greatest crime in the history of the state." One of his colleagues, James Farmer, told a jury that the white mobs of East St. Louis had been more savage than the Indians formerly roaming the area.

After several court trials nine white men were sent to the penitentiary; only four were charged with homicide. Twelve blacks were imprisoned; eleven had been convicted of killing the two detectives riding in the Ford squad car the night before the riot.

A black writer, Jessie Fauset, wrote an article called "A Negro on East St. Louis" that was published in *Survey* magazine on August 18, 1917. He said: ". . . We, the American Negroes, are the acid test for occidental civilization. If we perish, we perish. But when we fall, we shall fall like Samson, dragging inevitably with us the pillars of a nation's democracy."

Chapter 29

THE REIGN OF TERROR

On April 2, 1917, when President Wilson asked Congress to declare war he said "we act without animus, not in enmity," and the next morning the New York *Tribune* published this banner:

THE PRESIDENT CALLS FOR WAR WITHOUT HATE

Wilson told a friend, "Charles Lamb, the English writer, made a very delightful remark that I have long treasured in my memory. He stuttered a little bit, and he said of someone who was not present, 'I h-h-hate that m-man.' And someone said, 'Why, Charles, I didn't know you knew him.' 'Oh,' he said, 'I-I-I don't. I-I can't hate a m-man I know.' That," Wilson concluded, "is a profound human remark. You cannot hate a man you know."

This is not necessarily true; furthermore, this Wilsonian comment leaves a certain sad latitude to human behavior. If you cannot hate a man you know, have you the moral right to hate a man you do not know? Apparently so, in the opinion of Billy Sunday. At a revival meeting the evangelist taught children in the audience to hiss the German flag. And as he delivered the opening prayer at a session of the House of Representatives, he called the Germans "one of the most infamous, vile, greedy, avaricious, bloodthirsty, sensual and vicious nations" in history, then went on to describe them as "that great pack of wolfish Huns whose fangs drip with blood and gore!"

Like Billy Sunday, most American ministers were red-hot partisans of the war, although a few thought it possible for our soldiers to whip the Germans without hating them. Disagreement came from our leading army officers, who equated hatred and patriotism. General Pershing complained the doughboys did not feel enough hatred for the enemy—a condition he blamed on the press. By means of posters and pep talks and snarling sergeants, the draftees were indoctrinated with the belief that the Germans had committed unspeakable atrocities in Belgium; this, as we have seen, was not the whole truth.

During bayonet practice men charged dummies labeled "Hun" or "Fritz" and savagely disemboweled their straw guts. A YMCA instructor wrote a manual called *Hand-to-Hand Fighting* in which he preached: "Eyes. Never miss an opportunity to destroy the eyes of the enemy. In all head-holds, use the fingers on the eyes. They are the most delicate points in the body and easy to reach. The eye can be easily removed with the finger."

The American Peace Society said it was permissible to bayonet even a decent German soldier, for this freed him of a tyranny he had chosen as his form of government. Freedom through death. Navy Secretary Daniels, a decent but perhaps naïve man, wrote in his diary that "one American soldier did shoot a German in the back, but they found out he was crazy." In New York City an Episcopal priest asked, "Was Jesus a pacifist?" and then answered, "Christ was the greatest fighter the world has ever seen!" A Yale divinity professor urged our soldiers to "see Jesus Christ Himself sighting down a gun barrel and running a bayonet through an enemy's body."

In the spring of 1917 Franklin Roosevelt was afraid of a German submarine attack on New York or some other port along the Atlantic. He even worried about a U-boat assault on his favorite vacation spot, the island of Campobello in the Bay of Fundy off the coast of Maine. He wrote his wife, "I meant to tell you that if by any perfectly wild chance a German submarine should come into the bay and start to shell Eastport or the Pool, I want you to grab the children and beat it into the woods. Don't stay to see what is going on. I am not joking about this, for though it is 500 to 1 against the possibility, still there is just that one chance."

As a matter of fact, German shells did land on the soil of continental United States during World War I.

On Sunday, July 21, 1918, the U-156 surfaced off Massachusetts near the resort town of Orleans on Cape Cod. Without warning, and within sight of hundreds of people relaxing on the beach, the sub opened fire on a tug called the *Perth Amboy*. The tug was heading from Gloucester to New York and towing three barges—two empty and one laden with stones. Aboard were forty-one persons, including three women and five children.

For ninety minutes the U-boat raked the craft, wounding three men and sinking the tug. A call for help was sent to a naval air station at Chatham south of Orleans. The fliers, who were playing baseball, dropped their gear and ran to their planes. Four took off and sped to the scene, dropping bombs that forced the enemy sub to submerge. One pilot was so excited he bombed the U-boat with a monkey wrench. During its attack the sub fired 147 shots, and 4 hit the mainland. Since it ignored the military base at Chatham and chose instead to attack an innocent tug and barges, the people regarded the attack as an example of the German strategy of terror.

Alarmists appealed to the ladies of the Boston auxiliary of the National Security League to register their cars to carry virgins to safety in the event of an invasion. Kansas residents thought they saw German aircraft overhead. Through Michigan ran a rumor that a strange species of pigeon was flying messages to Canada from German agents in the United States. San Francisco citizens worried about an attack by German zeppelins. There were reports of German planes operating out of mountain hideaways in Montana.

A Congressman suggested that if the Germans made a simultaneous attack on our eastern and western shores, the seaboard people should retreat to safety behind the Allegheny and Rocky mountains. Robert R. McCormick, publisher of the Chicago *Tribune* and a self-proclaimed military expert, preached fortress warfare. For the safety of the nation, he argued, bastions should be constructed at Albany, Buffalo, Pittsburgh, Atlanta, Vicksburg, Houston and "the passes of the Sierra Nevadas and the Rocky Mountains." From these strongholds, McCormick insisted, we would be able to defend ourselves against invaders.

Spy fever swept the land. Democratic Senator George E. Chamberlain of Oregon introduced a bill to make the entire United States "a part of the zone of operations conducted by an enemy"; anyone publishing anything endangering our military successes should be considered a spy and therefore subject to the death penalty by courts-martial. This bill, which fortunately did not pass, would have castrated civil courts and created a military dictatorship.

Millions of Americans gave quick credence to the conspiratorial theory of history. Even George Washington had been victimized by such savage wrongheadedness, writing to Thomas Jefferson, "I am accused of being the enemy of America and subject to the influence of a foreign country." During the Civil War President Lincoln's wife had been accused of being a Confederate sympathizer. Now, in 1917, some people whispered that President Wilson's wife secretly sympathized with the Germans. Mayor Mitchel of New York accused New York Senator Robert F. Wagner of "working in the interest of the German government." George B. McClellan, Jr., a former mayor of New York, was accused of being a German agent.

Colonel House put a spy on the trail of Bernard M. Baruch, chairman of the War Industries Board, but the federal agent became such an admirer of the loyal and hard-working Baruch that he disclosed his identity to Baruch and begged forgiveness. Publisher William Randolph Hearst was placed under surveillance and the government smuggled an agent into his home in the guise of a butler. Hearst lived in a posh apartment on Riverside Drive in Manhattan and people whispered that the colored lights winking from his windows were signals to German subs lurking in the Hudson river below; actually, the lights were refractions from his stained-glass windows. In a restaurant a woman hissed at Hearst, "*Boche!*" He bowed and replied, "You're right, madame. It is all bosh."

St. Louis beer baron Adolphus Busch had a married daughter, Mrs. Hugo Heisinger, who was accused of spying because she had a wireless set in her home; it belonged to a servant studying wireless at the local YMCA. Federal agents heard that a German spymaster had been put ashore by a U-boat and had then toured army camps trying to persuade our soldiers to mutiny; when they caught him, he turned out to be a harmless Baltimore plumber. It was rumored that a German spy stood in the dome of the capitol at Hartford, Connecticut, peering through a telescope at a nearby munitions plant. Superpatriots alerted people to watch out for "gloaters"—anyone who seemed to smile or otherwise show satisfaction at news of German victories.

Long after the war Eugene O'Neill revealed, "I was a victim of war hysteria." In his twenties and already writing plays, O'Neill summered at Provincetown, Massachusetts, and sometimes took his typewriter to the beach to work, occasionally accompanied by another writer named Harold De Polo. Across the dunes some distance away was a government radio station, whose chief saw sun glint from O'Neill's typewriter and concluded he was a German agent flashing signals to an enemy ship. One evening while O'Neill and De Polo were dining in a hotel, some federal agents "pounced on us at the point of a revolver and carried us to the lockup in the basement of the Town Hall. We were held incommunicado for several hours. They wouldn't even let us see a lawyer."

Senator Harding of Ohio was romancing not only Nan Britton, but also the wife of the owner of a department store, and his married mistress was so pro-German in her remarks that Harding anxiously warned her she was being trailed by government agents. Zona Gale, a Wisconsin writer who later won a Pulitzer Prize, was a pacifist carefully watched by her neighbors in Portage. A phantom ship allegedly was transporting ammunition from one of our harbors to Germany. The mayor of New Orleans banned masks during Mardi Gras lest such disguises let spies slip through the city.

Back in 1908, during President Roosevelt's second term, Congress had created a bureau of investigation within the justice department, the genesis of the noted Federal Bureau of Investigation. J. Edgar Hoover joined the bureau on July 26, 1917. At that time the bureau chief was A. Bruce Bielaski, a native of Maryland who took his college degree from Columbia University.

In March, 1917, before we entered the war, Bielaski got a letter from a Chicago advertising man, A. M. Briggs, who said he wanted to organize a nationwide group of loyal Americans to help the bureau protect the nation; its members would pay their own expenses. Bielaski was interested because he had only 400 agents; before the end of the war his force grew fivefold. He showed Briggs' letter to Attorney General Thomas W. Gregory, the third man to hold this Cabinet post in the Wilson administration. Born in Mississippi, the son of a doctor who enlisted in the Confederate army and was killed during the Civil War, Gregory had helped Colonel House promote Wilson's nomination for the Presidency, and in 1916 he was appointed attorney general largely with the Colonel's aid. Gregory told Bielaski to encourage Briggs. Days later Briggs formed the American Protective League, with headquarters in Chicago.

Anyone could join. No applicant had to take any test to determine his sanity, efficiency or experience in investigative work. All that was required was the zeal of a true-blue American to hunt down the enemies of the state. There was such a rush of men and women to become spies and informers that within three months the league had almost 100,000 members, and at its peak it consisted of 250,000 members. Branches were established in every major city in the country. So great was the scramble to join that enlistments had to be suspended awhile to enable the national office to catch its breath and obtain another supply of badges.

These badges cost 75 cents and said "American Protective League, Secret Service Division." They were to be worn concealed and shown only in an emergency. Badge holders were clearly told they were not official representatives of the federal government and had no right to make arrests, but in their ardor they nonetheless engaged in illegal searches and made illegal arrests, often giving the impression they really were federal agents. Labor leaders complained that some employers used league members to intimidate strikers.

At first the bona fide agents of the bureau of investigation sneered at these "greenhorns" and "voluntary detectives," but they shut up when their superiors warned that they could lose their jobs if they continued to carp at members of the league. Henry G. Clabaugh of the bureau's Chicago office dutifully reported, "Without exaggeration, I think the Chicago division of the A.P.L. did 75 percent of the governmental investigation work of the Chicago district throughout the war."

Attorney General Gregory boasted that "several hundred thousand private citizens, most of them members of patriotic bodies," worked for him for nothing, "keeping an eye on disloyal individuals and making reports of disloyal utterances, and seeing that the people of the country are not deceived." In addition to this corps of snoopers, secret or semisecret intelligence agencies were created within the state, war, navy and post office departments.

Telephone wiretapping, first used in New York in 1895, was resumed on a large scale in 1917. The federal government set up a huge switchboard in the Custom House near the Battery, tapped the lines of hundreds of aliens and kept relays of stenographers taking notes on private telephone conversations.

President Wilson did not much care for the American Protective League, but he knew little about the work of the justice department and accepted Gregory's assurances that the league consisted of a fine body of men and women. Treasury Secretary McAdoo was neither so gullible nor so trusting. Three months after its formation he protested to Gregory about its use of the words "Secret Service" on its badges and literature; after all, the real secret service was an arm of his own treasury department.

"You will recall," McAdoo wrote, "that during the American Revolution a voluntary organization . . . was formed under the title *Sons of Liberty*. It committed grave abuses and injustices. This *Secret Service* division of the American Protective League contains the same evil potentialities."

But the superduper snoopers of the APL kept their ears open in offices and factories and mines and mills and churches and schools and restaurants and trains and ships and ferries and stores, alert to any overtone or undertone of disloyalty, remembering all they overheard, writing notes and then sending reports to Washington where huge dossiers were compiled on the behavior of innocent citizens.

In the previous century George Canning, the British statesman, had written about three tailors who worked on Tooley Street in London and presented the House of Commons with a petition beginning with the words: "We, the people of England—"

And so it was now in the United States in 1917 and 1918. Everyone and his friends believed they were the voice of the people. They, and they alone, knew who were the enemies of the state, who were the spies and radicals and revolutionaries. To themselves they arrogated the powers of policemen and judges and juries. In their zealous patriotism they subscribed to the either/or proposition of patriotism or anarchy.

They were not just members of the American Protective League, but belonged to other groups such as the American Anti-Anarchy Association, the Knights of Liberty, the Liberty League, the American Rights League, the Ku Klux Klan, the Anti-Yellow Dog League, the Sedition Slammers and the Terrible Threateners. F. Scott Fitzgerald called them "wine-bibbers of patriotism—which, of course, I think is the biggest rot in the world."

The star-spangled sadists went to work.

Anything mindful of German culture became suspect. Vigilantes inspected public libraries and invaded private homes and burned books by Goethe and Heine and Kant, broke Victrola records that preserved the music of Beethoven and Bach and Wagner. School after school forbade the teaching of the German language, while in clubs and churches and halls there was a ban against speaking German.

With trembling fingers frightened people plucked their gardens free of bachelor buttons, which was Germany's national flower. Sauerkraut was renamed Liberty cabbage, hamburger became Salisbury steak, German measles were called Liberty measles, German dishes disappeared from restaurants, seed catalogues referred to German clover as Liberty clover, and bartenders removed pretzels from their free lunch counters.

On the streets people so often kicked dachshunds, a favorite dog among Germans, that their owners began referring to them as Liberty pups. Men owning German shepherd dogs risked arrest as German spies. Baltimore changed the name of German Street to Redwood Street. Statues of German heroes such as Goethe, Frederick the Great and Steuben were disfigured or toppled from their pedestals. In Manhattan the Bank of Germany changed its name to the Bank of Europe. John Burroughs, the gentle naturalist, shot woodchucks nibbling his corn and whooped, "Another dead Hun!"

Palm readers, soothsayers and spiritualists made fortunes by telling disturbed people what to believe, while mediums comforted parents with messages allegedly received from their sons killed in battle. A London scientist claimed to have found a treatment that could make a soldier invulnerable to the bullets flying all around him and killing his comrades. Franklin Roosevelt's mother solemnly assured him that a building across the Hudson river from Hyde Park was filled with German ammunition. People believed there was a plot to destroy crops in South Dakota. There was talk of the Germans putting ground glass in food, poisoning water, even poisoning Red Cross bandages.

Teachers were forced to take oaths promising to support the Constitution. For emphasizing the Sermon on the Mount, ministers were unfrocked, driven from their pulpits, and at least fifty-five were arrested.

Dr. Karl Muck, the elderly and prestigious conductor of the Boston Symphony Orchestra, was arrested. In New Jersey the mayor of East Orange refused to let violinist Fritz Kreisler play a concert there because Kreisler once had been a lieutenant in the Austrian army. A man was tied to the end of a cannon. A ninety-year-old man was forced to kiss the American flag. A woman was ridden on a rail, a man was led around by a dog chain attached to his neck, houses were painted yellow, and some unfortunates had German iron crosses painted on their bodies with black paint.

A tabernacle was burned down, and bombs exploded in the Carnegie mansion in Manhattan, the Bronx county courthouse, St. Patrick's cathedral and the governor's mansion in California. States passed censorship laws, certain people were forbidden to speak in public, a man was prosecuted for talking too loud, another was jailed for laughing at draftees, and cops closed meetings where Russian was spoken.

In Eureka, California, something happened that had the sour taste of the future, of Nazi Germany when Hitler youths spied on their parents: A man was sentenced to five years at hard labor for criticizing President Wilson—on the testimony of his own daughter.

As Goethe once said, nothing is so frightening as ignorance in action.

It was not just faceless fanatics or masked mobs that indulged in an orgy of intolerance, for noted individuals and institutions also ran amok.

Elihu Root, who had served as secretary of war and then secretary of state, said there were certain men walking the streets of New York who should be shot for treason. The *Wall Street Journal* editorialized, "We are now at war, and militant pacifists are earnestly reminded that there is no shortage of hemp or lamp-posts." Theodore Roosevelt declared, "He who is not with us, absolutely and without reserve of any kind, is against us and should be treated as an enemy alien." In Texas a federal judge told a jury, "If any man deserves death it is a traitor, and I wish I could pay for the ammunition."

George Herbert Kinsolving, the Protestant Episcopal bishop of Texas, declared that the mayor of Chicago, "Big Bill" Thompson," was "guilty of treason and ought to be shot. There is only one way of punishing treason; that is by death to the man that is guilty. I am in favor of the firing squad and a stone wall as the proper means of combating treachery to the United States. What this country needs is a few first-class hangings."

A federal judge said that Senator La Follette should be executed by a firing squad. Nicholas Murray Butler said of La Follette, "You might just as well put poison in the food of every American boy that goes to his transport as permit this man to talk as he does." J. G. Phelps Stokes, who resigned from the Socialist party because it opposed the war, wrote to Vice President Marshall and House Speaker Clark to propose a Congressional investigation of La Follette, two other Senators and three Congressmen. Stokes said, "If any are guilty, let the guilty be shot at once without an hour's delay." Hanged and burned in effigy were several well-known men, among them Mayor Thompson, Senator La Follette,

William Randolph Hearst and former Congressman Charles A. Lindbergh.

George Bernard Shaw said that one had to accept madness as sanity when all the world had gone mad because sanity, after all, was only that madness upon which the world agreed.

Charles A. Lindbergh, Jr., is remembered as the first aviator to fly the Atlantic alone, while his once-famous father is all but forgotten.

The elder Lindbergh was elected to Congress in 1906, then reelected for five successive terms. He introduced and at first fought almost alone for the resolution resulting in the Pujo Committee of 1912, the one that bared the money trust. Senator Norris of Nebraska said, "When the true history of Congressional action on the so-called Money Trust is written, it will be found that the gentleman from Minnesota is entitled to more credit than any other member." Congressman Lindbergh lived in Little Falls, Minnesota. In 1916 he ran for the Senate, instead of the House, but was defeated and left the Capitol for the last time on March 3, 1917.

He lost his Senate race largely because during his campaign he said he agreed with the antiwar stance of the Socialists and because of his remarks about "war propaganda—dollar plutocracy versus patriotic America" and a "nation muzzled by false national honor." Three days before he left his desk on the floor of the House he prophesied, "The man who reasons and exercises good sense today may be hung in effigy tomorrow by the jingoes."

In July, 1917, he used his own money to publish a book charging that the war had been caused by an "inner circle" of industrialists and financiers who made whopping profits from the agony of millions of Americans. Critics savagely attacked his book as a "Red" document whose author was a "Gopher Bolshevik." Federal agents entered the plant where his book had been printed and forced its owners to destroy the bookplates, as well as every copy of the book in stock.

In 1918 Lindbergh ran for governor of Minnesota as a progressive Republican with the endorsement of the Farmers Non-Partisan League. This league had been organized three years earlier in North Dakota by a former Socialist, Arthur C. Townley, as an agrarian reaction against the abuses of the grain trade in that state and in Minnesota. Its program included a demand for hail insurance, state rural credits, tax reform, and state-owned grain elevators, mills and packinghouses. By the end of 1917 the league had elected a governor and a majority of members of the lower house of the North Dakota legislature, and early in 1918 its influence swept into Minnesota. By July, 1918, about 50,000 Minnesota farmers, miners and factory workers belonged to the league.

It was furiously opposed by Minnesota's new Public Safety Committee, a superpatriotic group formed to hunt down "traitors" and "subversives." The committee chairman was a bigot named John F. McGee who, in the words of Kenneth S. Davis, "promptly set out to destroy in the name of God and patriotism all whose social and economic views differed from his own." McGee said that in Minnesota the "disloyal element" consisted largely of Germans and Swedes—and

Lindbergh's father had been born in Sweden. McGee also declared that the justice department had been a dismal failure in ferreting out subversives. He went to Washington to testify in behalf of Senator Chamberlain's ill-fated bill to place the entire country under military control, and in one emotional outburst he shouted, "Where we made a mistake was in not establishing a firing squad in the first days of the war! We should get busy now and have that firing squad working overtime!"

Lindbergh fumed when McGee denounced every member of the Farmers Non-Partisan League as "traitors." His gubernatorial campaign became a duel between himself and the Minnesota Public Safety Committee, but he fought fair while the committee stooped to terror and violence. Town after town denied him the use of halls, bullies broke up his meetings, shots were fired at his car, he was hanged and burned in effigy, and almost every newspaper in the state branded him a "traitor."

One day he was about to address 10,000 people in a grove in southern Minnesota when the local sheriff and dozens of deputies planted themselves in front of the speakers' platform, pulled out guns and implied they were ready to kill rather than let the rally proceed. The farmers who had come to hear Lindbergh muttered and surged toward the officers, who raised their weapons. Lindbergh raised his arms to command attention. In the hush that followed he said the sheriff was wrong to "suppress a discussion of the serious economic issues facing us," but he thought it would "do our cause more harm than good to have a bloody riot." He urged the people to "adjourn a few miles south into the state of Iowa, which still seems to be a part of these United States." The farmers followed him to an Iowa farm whose owner had offered his property as a meeting ground, and there Lindbergh argued for state ownership of public utilities and every other natural monopoly, as well as of grain elevators and mills. He insisted that the real issue in America was "the control of finance by a few."

He lost the primary, and the national press hailed his defeat as a triumph for "loyalty." Sixteen-year-old Charles A. Lindbergh, Jr., admired his father's courage and drove him from place to place in Minnesota during the campaign, but he had no interest in politics and instead of listening to the speeches, he remained at a distance from the speakers' platform tinkering with the family Ford.

In August, 1916, President Wilson had established the Council of National Defense, and after the United States went to war, he asked all state governors to create similar state councils to work with, and under the direction of, the national council. Each of the forty-eight state councils organized branches in every county and city. They were supposed to supervise such things as the conservation of food and the sale of Liberty Bonds and to help with draft registration, but many degenerated into repressive pressure groups insisting on total conformity, "100 percent Americanism," and the quashing of almost all the rights of minorities and individuals.

A case in point was the Council of Defense of Henry county, Missouri. It was headed by a self-crowned patriot, the Reverend A . N. Lindsay, and it had a special method of dealing with anyone suspected of "speaking or acting in a disloyal way." One householder after another began to receive a white card saying, "You have been reported to the Committee of Patriots and Patriotism as in your attitude and utterances dangerous and disloyal. We recommend CAUTION and a complete change of attitude. [Signed] Committee of Patriots."

Should the suspect fail to mend his ways to the satisfaction of the bigots, a week later he got a blue card saying, "The White Card meant CAUTION; the Blue WARNING. Every flag in our Country waves to protect you—your life and property. Your duty is to defend your Country's Flag with your life. [Signed] Committee of Patriots."

If the suspect continued to speak his mind, he was sent a red card with this imperious command: "If unjustly reported, or if you desire to avoid Summary Action, report at once your change of front to the Postmaster. No harm will come to you if you continue in your devotion to your Country in its hour of need. FINAL. [Signed] Committee of Patriots."

The Reverend M. Lindsay urged the justice department to adopt his early warning system, but the department declined to do so.

Governor Lowden of Illinois asked Samuel Insull of Chicago to organize an Illinois State Council of Defense. Insull was born in London in 1859, became an American citizen in 1896, and in 1917 he lived in opulence as he administered a cluster of utility firms worth more than $175,000,000. In the plenitude of his idealism, before his spectacular fall from power in the Thirties, he robbed tens of thousands of families of their life savings. Insull never smiled at an employee and poet Edgar Lee Masters thought he had a "barracuda curl to his lip."

In August, 1917, Insull put together an organization that became a model for other state councils. At the top was an executive committee heavily weighted with businessmen. Then the members of the executive committee were organized into three-man subcommittees. They recruited volunteer workers, speakers and publicists and enlisted the state's newspaper editors as propagandists. Local committees soon were holding daily, sometimes hourly meetings in public buildings and churches and homes the length and breadth of Illinois. An army of 2,000 orators addressed more than 700,000 people a week, pounding into their heads themes such as "the proper war spirit" and "appreciation of the ideals of true patriotism and love of country." English-born profit-greedy Insull was telling Americans how to be good Americans.

Whatever he said was Gospel. In *The Big Money* John Dos Passos wrote, "War shut up the progressives (no more nonsense about trustbusting, controlling monopoly, the public good) and raised Samuel Insull to the peak. He was head of the Illinois State Council of Defense. *Now,* he said delightedly, *I can do anything I like.* With it came the perpetual spotlight, the purple taste of empire. If anybody didn't like what Samuel Insull did he was a traitor. Chicago damn well kept its mouth shut."

Self-important patriots descended on homes occupied by foreign-born people and bawled out demands that they cancel subscriptions to foreign-language papers, learn English overnight and instantly begin teaching their children the Declaration of Independence and the

Constitution. In one case some women knocked on the door of a tenement in the Bohemian section of Chicago and their leader began grandiloquently: "We are here in the interests of Americanization!"

The Bohemian-born woman of the house faltered. "I'm sorry, but you'll have to come back next week."

"*What!* You mean you have no time for our message? That you want to put off your entrance into American life?"

The frightened woman cried, "No! No! We're perfectly willing to be Americanized. Why, we never turn any of them away! But there's nobody home but me. The boys volunteered, my man's working on munitions, and all the rest are out selling Liberty Bonds. I don't want you to get mad, but can't you come back next week?"

In downstate Illinois just north of East St. Louis there was a town called Collinsville, and in it lived a young miner, Robert Paul Prager. He was registered as an enemy alien, had taken out his first citizenship papers, and although he professed Socialist leanings, he had no record of any overt act of disloyalty. One day he made a speech to fellow miners about Socialism, and when this news got around, followed by the rumor that he was hoarding dynamite to blow up the mine in which he worked, a drunken mob marched to his house, pulled him out and dragged him down a street. The town's four cops rescued him and hid him in the cellar of city hall, but the mob found him there, hauled him out again and forced him to walk barefoot through the streets carrying an American flag. He begged in broken English for a German-speaking interpreter so that he might explain himself more clearly, but when this request was refused, when he knew he had to die, he prayed aloud in German for three minutes and then was hanged.

This lynching took place on April 4, 1918.

Across the country newspapers printed headlines such as GERMAN HANGED BY MOB IN ILLINOIS. In a hushed Senate chamber in Washington tight-faced legislators listened to Senator Borah read an article about the lynching. Governor Lowden ordered state officials to investigate. It was proved that Prager had said nothing disloyal and was not hoarding dynamite. His murder was discussed in the German Reichstag and by members of Wilson's Cabinet. As had happened after the riot in East St. Louis, the Wilson administration decided there were no legal grounds for federal intervention in Illinois. The President issued a public statement denouncing the mob spirit, and so did Theodore Roosevelt. Eleven men were indicted and then acquitted by a local jury in only twenty-five minutes. During the trial a defense attorney said that all the defendants had done was to engage in "patriotic murder."

"Every war," wrote George Bernard Shaw, "produces a Reign of Terror."

On April 7, 1917, the day after the United States declared war on Germany, the Socialists met in emergency session in St. Louis. During the election the previous year their Presidential candidate, Allen J.

Benson, had polled 585,113 popular votes, but not a single electoral vote. The 200 delegates now gathered in St. Louis represented the 80,126 dues-paying members of the Socialist party. Most were middle-class and native-born; fewer than a dozen had been born in Germany, Austria or Ireland. They had gathered to discuss the war and to define the attitude the party should take toward it.

One hundred and forty of the delegates voted to adopt a resolution that came to be known as the "St. Louis Proclamation," a sharp indictment of American participation in the war. It declared that "in all modern history there has been no war more unjustifiable than this war." It said that "no greater dishonor has ever been forced upon a people than that which the capitalist class is forcing upon this nation against its will." Then, in a prescient sentence, it said that "our entrance into the European conflict at this time . . . will give the powers of reaction in this country the pretext for an attempt to throttle our rights and to crush our democratic institutions."

The "St. Louis Proclamation" weakened the Socialist party because many delegates who voted against it became so bitter that they quit the party, some went to work for the government, and they savagely criticized their former friends. Among these dropouts was Charles Edward Russell, who publicly spoke of his former associates as "dirty traitors" who should be "driven out of the country." W. J. Ghent left the party with a dramatic flourish, writing a letter to his old friend Morris Hillquit that ended with these words:

> You are my enemy and I am,
>
> Yours,
> W. J. Ghent

Hillquit ran for mayor of New York in the fall of 1917 on the Socialist ticket, won more votes than any Socialist candidate for that office before or since, but placed third in a four-cornered race. Theodore Roosevelt slandered Hillquit as a "Hun . . . inside our gates" while Charles Evans Hughes called him "unpatriotic" and "treasonable."

Of all the war measures passed by Congress and approved by Wilson, none was more controversial than the Espionage Act of 1917 and its amended and tightened version known as the Sedition Act of 1918.

Wilson felt censorship was necessary to deal with people who could not be relied on to observe "a patriotic silence about everything whose publication could be of injury." His secretary disagreed. Tumulty considered a few publishers vicious and irresponsible but believed the average publisher was reasonable. At the request of the President the attorney general drafted an Espionage Act which Gregory said was meant to punish willful attempts to hamper the conduct of the war and to prevent the publication of vital information or its transmission to the enemy.

After this administration measure was introduced into Congress, House Speaker Clark declared that "the press censorship in the bill is in flat contradiction with the Constitution." Another who worried was Arthur Brisbane, the Hearst editor and columnist; he wrote to ask the President whether the act would be used to shield him from criticism. In a letter of reply Wilson said he approved of the pending legislation but had no intention of letting any part of it apply to him or his official acts. "I can imagine no greater disservice to the country," Wilson said, "than to establish a system of censorship that would deny to the people of a free republic like our own their indisputable right to criticize their own public officials." This sentence was significant because Wilson failed to practice what he preached. As we have seen, a California man was sentenced to five years at hard labor simply for criticizing the President.

Tumulty warned Wilson that many people believed the Espionage Act was "really a gigantic machine, erected for the despotic control of the press . . . by a host of small bureaucrats." During legislative jockeying over the bill the President gave in on a few minor points, but by writing to the chairman of the House judiciary committee and by conferring with Senators in the White House, he rammed it through both houses and signed it on June 15, 1917.

And he did this despite the First Amendment to the Constitution, which says, "Congress shall make no law . . . abridging the freedom of speech, or of the press."

The new Espionage Act called for twenty years in prison and/or a fine of up to $10,000 for anyone found guilty of aiding the enemy, obstructing recruiting, or causing insubordination, disloyalty, or refusal of duties in the armed services. It gave the postmaster general the power to deny mailing privileges to any newspaper or magazine alleged to be treasonable or seditious.

Treasonable? What was treason? Who defined it? Our founding fathers had been so sensitive to the dangers of wild and irresponsible accusations of treason that they had defined the word in the Constitution rather than leave the definition to Congress. Article III, Section 3, of the Constitution says: "Treason against the United States shall consist only in levying war against them, or in adhering to their Enemies, giving them Aid and Comfort. No Person shall be convicted of Treason unless on the Testimony of two Witnesses to the same overt Act, or on Confession in open court . . ." However, Section 3 goes on to say that "the Congress shall have Power to declare the Punishment of Treason."

Wilson urged his attorney general to prosecute as traitors the editors of an obscure sheet called *The Peoples' Counsellor*, declaring that "one conviction would probably scotch a great many snakes." Gregory declined to act, arguing that such action would be unconstitutional. Wilson considered the Socialist party "almost treasonable." His opinion was not shared by Bielanski, the head of the bureau of investigation. Bielanski wrote to Gregory, "The meetings engineered by the Socialists are now covered throughout the United States without any specific instructions and I think there is a need rather for more caution than more vigorous efforts in the matter of handling Socialistic gatherings." He meant that federal agents were watching the Socialists, but he saw no immediate need to prosecute them.

What was it Wilson had told Cobb of the *World* in the White House the night of April 1, 1917? "Once lead this people into war and they'll forget there ever was such a thing as tolerance. . . ." Now Wilson himself forgot.

Although individuals and mobs were taking the law into their own hands, although zealous United States district attorneys were crowding courts with spurious cases, although federal judges were making impassioned speeches in the guise of instructions to juries, although juries were convicting innocent people, although the states passed their own espionage acts and syndicalism laws, although the land churned in an orgy of intolerance, Wilson poured oil on the bonfire by asking Congress to tighten the Espionage Act.

In 1798 Congress had passed a Sedition Act to silence criticism of the administration and to strengthen its hand in an impending war with France. Thomas Jefferson had denounced that first Sedition Act as contrary to the First Amendment, and after he became President in 1801 he pardoned everyone convicted under the act, while Congress eventually repaid all fines.

According to historian Richard B. Morris, the new Sedition Act of 1918 was aimed chiefly at Socialists and pacifists. Another target was the Industrial Workers of the World. Some IWW leaders were proclaiming that the war crisis should be used to destroy capitalism and the President told his attorney general that IWW members "certainly are worthy of being suppressed." When Wilson had delivered his war message, he expressed confidence that Americans of German birth would prove loyal to their adopted land, but added "should there be disloyalty, it will be dealt with with a firm hand of stern repression." Subsequently he had become convinced that there existed a genuinely subversive movement which was determined to destroy American liberty.

At Wilson's request Democratic Senator Thomas J. Walsh of Montana presented the Senate with a bill modeled after Montana's criminal syndicalism act, the most repressive law of its kind among all the states and one that opened a new chapter in the legal history of America. Walsh's proposed measure was even more severe than the 1798 Sedition Act and as extreme as any similar law in effect in any nation of Europe during World War I.

Senator Johnson of California denounced the bill as unnecessary and unconstitutional. Senator Borah of Idaho protested that "it is not necessary to Prussianize ourselves in order to destroy Prussianism in Europe." Tumulty warned Wilson that the law would get the administration "into very deep water." The bill prohibited "contemptuous or slurring language about the President," but that phrase was deleted after Theodore Roosevelt snarled, "If it is passed I shall certainly give the government the opportunity to test its constitutionality."

But Congress failed to resist pressure from the White House, and despite squabbles and dire warnings, both houses passed the Sedition Act, which was signed into law by the President on May 16, 1918. Now anyone could be jailed for twenty years and/or fined $10,000 for obstructing the sale of Liberty Bonds, inciting insubordination, discouraging recruiting, or uttering, writing or publishing "any disloyal, profane, scurrilous, or abusive language" about the flag, the armed forces, their uniforms, the Constitution or the form of government of the United States.

The intent of the law was bad enough, but the looseness of its language made it worse. Exactly what was "disloyal, profane, scurrilous, or abusive language"? Nowhere in the law were these adjectives clearly defined. And in the absence of precise definitions, the law was interpreted and misinterpreted by men who tended to believe that because they were patriotic, they were omniscient. So people were punished for advocating heavier taxation instead of bond issues, for calling conscription unconstitutional, for saying that war is contrary to the teachings of Christ, for arguing that the people themselves should have been entitled to decide on war by means of a referendum, for criticizing the Red Cross, for doubting the utility of knitting socks for soldiers.

The law's vague language troubled Attorney General Gregory, who was otherwise hardly noted for his sensitivity to civil liberties. To the eighty-eight United States attorneys he sent a circular asking them to administer the new law "with discretion" and not use it to suppress legitimate criticism of the government. Gregory's special assistant, John Lord O'Brian, felt even more apprehensive. O'Brian said the law "covered all degrees of conduct and speech, serious and trifling alike, and in the popular mind gave the dignity of treason to what were often neighborhood quarrels or barroom brawls."

The Sedition Act, a model of totalitarianism, perhaps the most dangerous law ever passed by Congress, gave almost unlimited powers to a bigot who happened to be the postmaster general of the United States, Albert S. Burleson.

Burleson was born in Texas in 1863, the son of a major in the Confederate army. He obtained a fine education, read widely, passed the bar, practiced law, was elected to Congress in 1899 and served fourteen years before accepting Wilson's nomination as postermaster general. A political conservative and professional politician, who seldom let principles interfere with his pragmatism, Burleson became the chief dispenser of patronage in the Wilson administration and the most hated man in the Cabinet.

Bald, blunt and cocky, eccentric in his appearance and behavior, Burleson wore a black coat and wing collar and looked like a country preacher. He was so pompous that behind his back the President called him "the Cardinal." Agriculture Secretary David F. Houston said of Burleson, "He does everything just as if he were killing snakes, and there is really only one way to deal with him, as I told him, and that is to give him what he wants or to kill him."

Wilson's bodyguard, Starling, wrote in his memoirs that Burleson:

> . . . looked and acted like an extremely sly gentleman. He was so astute and secretive that his left hand never knew what his right was doing. He used to come over from the Postoffice Department through the east entrance of the White House, along the lower corridor past the laundry, following in part the same passageway that the President used in going between the White House and executive offices. Rain or shine, he carried an

> umbrella and briefcase, and if the weather was bad he wore overshoes, tiptoeing as he walked. We finally began to call that passageway "Pussyfoot Alley."

Burleson was contemptuous of freedom of the press. Navy Secretary Daniels wrote in his diary:

> . . . In the afternoon the Burlesons and the Cranes came on board the *Sylph* and we had a delightful sail. Burleson talked about his course in denying the use of the mails to disloyal newspapers. He had in mind shutting up some big newspapers. He said he was going to advise W. W. to give a garden party and invite members of Congress who had stood by him and leave out men like Weeks, La Follette, and others, so the country could see they were not trusted. He was full of the idea, and that it would pillory those not invited before they could go out to the country and speak against the plan before the second draft was called.

Daniels, a former newspaper editor as well as a Cabinet member, protested to Burleson that it was contrary to American ideals to deny the mails to newspapers unless it had been established that they were convicted of treasonable utterances. Daniels might have saved his breath. In a later diary entry he wrote:

> Gag Tom Watson: Burleson wanted something done to Tom Watson, editor of a paper in Georgia, who was writing bitterly about the policy of the Government, particularly against the draft. "It is a Socialist paper and should be suppressed." Wilson listened to B's blast, and answered: "We can not go after all the Damn Fools. Everybody knows Watson is a fool. We have better and more important things to do."

Thomas E. Watson was worse than a fool; he was a bigot who used his periodical to make savage assaults on Catholics and blacks and Jews. But—a point Burleson failed to grasp—Watson attacked Socialism along with almost everything else, so he hardly could be said to be publishing "a Socialist paper." It would seem that anyone opposing the draft must be a Socialist who deserved to be gagged. And although Wilson had suggested restraint, the postmaster general barred Watson's publication from the mail.

Freedom of press vanished as Burleson revoked the second-class mailing privileges of one periodical after another and denied others even first-class delivery. By the end of war he had killed almost every Socialist paper and magazine, muting the few that remained alive. Republican Senator Lawrence Y. Sherman of Illinois, who had opposed the Sedition Act, charged in the Senate that Burleson was making a fortune by using convicts on his Texas property. This accusation was further aired by "Red Tom" Hickey, editor of *Rebel*, the organ of the Tenant Farmers Union. In what may have been a case of personal spite, Burleson put *Rebel* out of business too.

Herbert Croly, editor of *The New Republic,* wrote Wilson to protest Burleson's repressive acts. Wilson assured Croly he was concerned about censorship but said he had discussed the matter with Burleson and believed his postmaster general was "inclined to be most conservative in the exercise of these great and dangerous powers." On another occasion Wilson wrote Burleson, "I am willing to trust your judgment after I have called your attention to a suggestion."

Norman Thomas went to see Burleson to make a personal protest. Thomas was editor of a periodical called *The World Tomorrow,* and the author of an article entitled "The Acid Test of Our Democracy," in which he criticized American intervention in Russia. The politician roared at the intellectual, "You're worse than Gene Debs! If I had my way, I'd not only kill your magazine but send you to prison for life!"

Washington correspondents also complained about Burleson's arbitrary exclusion from the mail of mildly leftist publications, but Wilson refused to discuss the issue with them. Cobb of the New York *World* became anxious when his newspaper was denied the use of the telegraph to distribute criticism of Burleson, and since the editor had access to the President, he warned Wilson that relations between the newspapers and the administration were "intolerably tangled."

Norman Thomas was a member of a committee that met with Colonel House to say that Wilson was making trouble for himself by jailing liberals and pacifists while allowing reactionary Republicans to flourish. The colonel tut-tutted them. "Trust the President. He'll win."

Federal agents tapped Thomas' telephone. With Burleson's approval, local postmasters opened private letters and read them. Whenever they found any remark they considered disloyal, they asked the government to prosecute. For example, Conrad Kornmann of Sioux Falls, South Dakota, wrote a friend that he was opposed to the Liberty Loan; he was fined $1,000 and stuffed in jail for ten years. L. N. Legendre of Los Angeles was jailed for two years for saying, "This is a war fostered by Morgan and the rich." He said no more than Senator Norris, who declared, "We are going into war upon the command of gold." He said no more than Henry Ford, who asked, "Do you want to know the cause of war? It is capitalism, greed, the dirty hunger for dollars."

Robert Goldstein of Los Angeles produced a film called *The Spirit of '76* which showed Patrick Henry defying England and Thomas Jefferson signing the Declaration of Independence. One scene depicted British redcoats bayoneting Americans in the Wyoming Valley massacre near Wilkes Barre, Pennsylvania, in 1778. Not only had this really happened, but, according to the British commanding officer, the British had Indian allies who scalped 227 Americans. But the Wilson administration considered the film an insult to the British, now an ally. Goldstein was fined $500 and put behind bars for ten years. This stiff sentence was so pleasing to Attorney General Gregory that he had a record of the case published as a pamphlet.

Kate Richards O'Hare was the wife of Frank O'Hare, who edited a Socialist paper in St. Louis, and she was an active Socialist agitator on her own. In North Dakota she made a speech criticizing the draft and was arrested and charged with violation of the Espionage Act. Tried in a federal court in Fargo, she was found guilty of discouraging enlistments and sentenced to five years in jail. The temper of the times showed in a remark by the trial judge: "This is a nation of free speech; but this is a time of sacrifice, when mothers are sacrificing their sons, when all men and women who are not at heart traitors are sacrificing their time and their hard-earned money in defense of the flag. Is it too much to ask that for the time being men shall suppress any desire which they may have to utter words which may tend to weaken the spirit, or destroy the faith or confidence of the people?"

When Socialist leader Eugene V. Debs heard of the conviction of Mrs. O'Hare he wrote her, "I cannot yet believe that they will ever dare to send you to prison for exercising your constitutional rights of free speech, but if they do . . . I shall feel guilty to be at large." His turn came later.

Rose Pastor was an immigrant cigarmaker who had won attention when she married a rich New Yorker, J. G. Phelps Stokes, the president of the Nevada Central Railroad. Despite his wealth and social standing, he became a Socialist. Mrs. Stokes supported the Wilson administration during the early part of the war but soon changed her mind. In Kansas City she made a mildly antiwar speech before the Woman's Dining Club and a Kansas City *Star* reporter wrote an article garbling her statements and declaring that she favored American participation in the war. More interested in truth than fearful of punishment, she wrote Ralph Stout, managing editor of the *Star*, to complain that her remarks had been twisted, since she did not support the war. She said, "No government which is *for* the profiteers can also be *for* the people, and I am for the people while the government is for the profiteers."

This was no inflammatory remark by a wild radical. The government was trying to cope with profiteering by means of price-fixing, taxation and other measures, but had no success except for price-fixing. Early in the war many industries increased their profits by more than 100 percent. The United States Steel Corporation, which had made a 5 percent profit before the war, earned a 25 percent profit in 1917. During a Congressional hearing Bernard Baruch testified the copper kings were making such whopping profits that the War Industries Board had considered taking over the mines. Republican Senator William S. Kenyon of Iowa demanded the conscription of wealth as well as manpower. President Wilson spoke of the sacrifices being made by our soldiers and then said, "No true patriot will permit himself to take toll of their heroism in money or seek to grow rich by the shedding of their blood." But more and more businessmen became millionaires.

Rose Pastor Stokes was charged with violation of the Espionage Act. In Kansas City she went on trial before a federal grand jury and pleaded not guilty. The judge in his charge to the jury said that in her speech to the members of the women's club she was trying to incite them to mutiny because of their influence over men of military age. She was found guilty and sentenced to ten years in the penitentiary. Her conviction was later set aside on appeal.

George Creel of the Committee on Public Information sent Wilson a clipping from the Kansas City *Post* that demanded the indictment of the managing editor of the *Star* for publishing Mrs. Stokes' letter. Wilson wrote his attorney general, "Don't you think there is some way we could bring this editor to book?" Gregory replied that the government had no case against Ralph Stout.

On June 8, 1917, fire broke out 2,400 feet belowground in a copper mine in Butte, Montana, and 164 workers died of suffocation. A strike was called by electricians in all the copper mines of that area, and when mine managers brought in other men to do their work, they were joined in their walkout by the metal trades workers. Then the strikers organized a joint strike committee dominated by former members of the defunct Western Federation of Miners and members of the Industrial Workers of the World.

The committee demanded dismissal of state mine inspectors and observance of all mining laws and called for an end to the blacklisting of union members or organizers. The strikers also wanted an increase in wages from $4.75 to $6 a day. Although copper prices more than doubled between 1914 and 1917, and although House Speaker Clark charged that copper companies had "held a gun to Uncle Sam," the Montana mineowners refused to increase wages or meet any other demands. William A. Clark, a former United States Senator now living in a mansion in Butte, swore he would rather flood his mines than recognize any union.

Butte, called the world's greatest mining town, was like a clock wound too tightly. In hobbled Frank H. Little, a member of the general executive board of the IWW. He had a leg in a cast owing to an accident suffered in Oklahoma while on his way back from Bisbee, Arizona, which he had visited to investigate the kidnapping of more than 1,000 striking Arizona copper miners.

Although Frank Little was blind in one eye, he saw much evil. He boasted of being half-Indian, was tough and brave and impulsive and brash—very brash. During the Ludlow massacre in Colorado he had denounced militiamen as "uniformed scabs." Now the *Anaconda Standard*, published in Butte by the powerful Anaconda Copper Mining Company, quoted him as saying that "the I.W.W. do not object to war, but the way they want to fight it is to put the capitalists in the front trenches, and if the Germans don't get them the I.W.W. will. Then the I.W.W. will clean out the Germans."

Burton K. Wheeler, then United States attorney for Montana, was besieged with demands that he prosecute Frank Little under the Espionage Act. He showed a copy of the act to L. O. Evans, Anaconda's chief counsel, and asked him to cite any section he could use to take legal action against Little. "Evans' only reply," according to Wheeler, "was that district attorneys everywhere else in the country seemed to be able to find ample grounds for prosecution—but he could not point to any provision of the law under which Little could be prosecuted."

On the evening of July 31, 1917, Little made a speech in a ball park in

Butte and then returned to his hotel, put on pajamas and went to bed. After midnight six masked armed men broke in, worked him over, dragged him outdoors, tied him to the rear of a car and dragged him miles along a dirt road. When they came to a trestle of the Milwaukee railroad, they stopped the car, cut him loose, prodded him around in front and in the glare of headlights pinned a sign on him. Then they hanged him from the trestle.

The sign said FIRST AND LAST WARNING! 3–7–77. D-D-C-S-S-W. These numbers had been used by Western vigilantes to refer to the dimensions of a grave—three feet wide, seven feet long, seventy-seven inches deep. As for the letters, Wheeler's friends believed that the *W* symbolized him, while the others may have signified the names of other strike leaders.

The murder of Frank Little shocked the miners and heightened the anxiety of some mineowners. More than 3,000 strikers walked behind the hearse the three miles to the cemetery while 10,000 other people watched in silence. A coroner's jury declared that Frank Little had been killed by unknown persons. Wheeler believed, but was unable to prove, that he had been lynched by agents of some copper company. He issued this statement:

> The lynching of Frank Little, said to be an international officer of the IWW, is a damnable outrage, a blot on the state and county. There is no excuse for this murder. The murderers should be apprehended and given the severest penalty of the law. My office and every special agent in my jurisdiction will assist the state and county authorities to catch the men who committed the awful deed. Every good citizen should condemn this mob spirit as unpatriotic, lawless, and inhuman. . . . My department made a thorough investigation of the case and we could not by any stretch of the imagination have indicted Little.

The killers were never found. Vice President Marshall said, "The governor of Montana had been too busy to issue the announcement of a statutory reward for the apprehension of the men who did the hanging." Wilson warned of "the great danger of citizens taking the law into their own hands." Senator Walsh of Montana condemned the lynching and called for legislation "to curb the violence of agitators who oppose the constituted government of the country." Walsh also wanted laws to "suppress agitators who in the name of labor are treasonably trying to tie up industries of the country."

In Helena, Montana, the *Independent* editorialized, "There was but one comment in Helena, 'Good work: Let them continue to hang every IWW in the state.'" Another Western newspaper said Butte had "disgraced itself like a gentleman." And on the floor of the House of Representatives in Washington a Congressman asked rhetorically whether those who professed no allegiance to the United States "have any right to squeal when citizens of this country hang one of them occasionally?"

Humorist Kin Hubbard once wrote, "It seems like the less a statesman amounts to, the more he loves the flag."

The Wilson administration set out to destroy the Industrial Workers of the World.

The IWW had been organized in Chicago in 1905 by 203 men representing more than forty groups of workers. Among its sponsors were leaders of the Western Federation of Miners, the remnants of the American Labor Union and the Socialistic Trade and Labor Alliance—the economic arm of the Socialist Labor party, which should not be confused with the Socialist party.

While the American Federation of Labor was willing to work within the capitalistic system, the IWW wanted workers to capture and control all production. Such, in brief, is the theory of syndicalism. The AFL was organized by crafts—the carpenters in one union, the plumbers in another, etc. The IWW wanted to pull all workers, regardless of their skills, into a single army, one big union.

The IWW constitution said "the working class and employing class have nothing in common; there can be no peace so long as hunger and want are found among millions of working people and the few who make up the employing class have all the good things of life." The wage system must be abolished. Capitalism had to perish. Only by direct action, and finally a general strike, could every ship and train and mill and mine be immobilized; then the toilers would take and hold everything produced by their labor. "There is but one bargain that the IWW will make with the employing class—the complete surrender of industry to the organized workers."

This was radicalism, to be sure, a threat not only to the capitalistic system, but also to the very form of government, and rich men shuddered whenever they thought about the Wobblies. Men of means found neither logic nor solace in the words of an earlier radical named Thomas Jefferson, who had said in his first inaugural address: "If there be any among us who wish to dissolve this union, or to change its republican form, let them stand undisturbed, as monuments of the safety with which error of opinion may be tolerated where reason is free to combat it."

Between 1914 and 1917 the IWW grew in strength—perhaps in rough proportion to the growth of profits by industries producing arms for the Allies. Between 1917 and 1920 a total of twenty-one states and two territories passed criminal syndicalism laws aimed at the IWW. Most state laws reproduced the wording of the Idaho law, which defined criminal syndicalism as "the doctrine which advocates crime, sabotage, violence, or other unlawful methods of terrorism as a means of accomplishing industrial or political reform." For violation of these laws most states could impose sentences of ten years in prison and/or a fine of $5,000. In South Dakota the penalty was twenty-five years and/or $10,000. One state supreme court after another upheld the constitutionality of these criminal syndicalism laws.

During the first two years of the European war the Wobblies concentrated more on the domestic class struggle than the international conflict, but in 1916 they adopted this resolution: "We condemn all wars and for the prevention of such, we proclaim the anti-militaristic propaganda in time of peace, thus promoting class solidarity among the workers of the entire world, and, in time of war, the General Strike in all industries."

But when the United States entered the war, the IWW failed to call a general strike, although its members engaged in scattered strikes. Frank Little had been the only member of the IWW's general executive board who had favored direct action against the war—and he had been murdered.

As profits rose, as prices soared, as wages lagged behind, even rank-and-file members of the AFL became angry. In 1917 there were 4,450 strikes involving more than 2,300,000 workers. The Wobblies were so articulate and inflammatory that they were blamed for most of these strikes, but a Presidential commission on industrial relations determined that only a small minority of the strikes had been called by the IWW, while most had been staged by disgruntled members of the AFL.

Nonetheless, it was rumored that the IWW was financed by the Germans. Senator Henry F. Ashurst of Arizona sneered that IWW stood for "Imperial Wilhelm's Warriors," others said the initials meant "I Won't Work," and Theodore Roosevelt declared that "the I.W.W. is a criminal organization." Evangelist Billy Sunday screamed about "that God-forsaken crew of I.W.W.'s" who "would have a firing squad at sunrise if I was running things!" IWW organizers were beaten, and vigilantes began making illegal raids on Wobbly offices.

On September 5, 1917, federal agents aided by local patriots raided forty-eight IWW halls across the country. This was done despite the Fourth Amendment to the Constitution, which says: "The right of the people to be secure in their persons, houses, papers, and effects, against unreasonable searches and seizures, shall not be violated." In the IWW halls the agents of the justice department took possession of five tons of letters, newspapers, propaganda pamphlets and other documents.

This data was analyzed, part of it was presented to a grand jury in Chicago, and on September 28, 1917, the jury handed up indictments against 166 Wobbly leaders. The next day, in a nationwide sweep, federal officers arrested more than 1,000 Wobblies, including most of those named in the indictments. They were accused of interference with the nation's war program. Obviously, an entire organization was being threatened with extinction.

This was admitted by the leading prosecutor, a Utah corporation lawyer named Frank K. Nebeker, who said in his opening statement that "it is the I.W.W. which is on trial here." The mass trial began on April 1, 1918, in a federal courtroom in Chicago, with 101 defendants at the bar of justice. Lasting five months, it was the longest criminal trial in American legal history up to that time.

The presiding judge was Kenesaw Mountain Landis, an eccentric and cantankerous man who had been appointed to the bench by President Roosevelt. In 1907 Landis had won national attention when he fined the Standard Oil Company more than $29,000,000 for accepting rebates from the Chicago and Alton Railroad on oil shipments—although the fine was never collected.

After the United States entered the war, the judge attracted further attention by his bizarre courtroom behavior. Author Henry F. Pringle said "few men have been as zealous in the suppression of minorities, and his charges to juries were dangerously close to patriotic addresses." Even if the judge had been less extreme in his patriotism, according to Pringle, "it is doubtful if he could have been impartial in trying men charged with sedition and conspiracy against the government," for his only son was a flier in France and Landis lived in constant dread of a telegram announcing the boy's death. As the Wobbly trial dragged on through the hot summer of 1918, the judge often left his bench to stroll around the courtroom.

He ruled out of order a defense attempt to read into the record the conclusion of the Commission on Industrial Relations that "the overwhelming mass of the laboring population is in no sense disloyal. . . . With the exception of the sacrifices of the men in the armed services, the greatest sacrifices have come from those at the lower rung of the industrial ladder." But the judge listened when Wobblies testified that they had sons fighting in France, that they bought Liberty Bonds, that they had worked in munitions plants and loaded arms aboard ship.

The trial hit a peak when William D. Haywood took the stand. The one-eyed, rugged and moody Wobbly leader testified for three days. He created a sensation with his unsupported charge that in Southern lumber camps the bosses gave heroin and cocaine to black workers. "They knew," Haywood declared, "that when they became addicted to the drugs, that they were sure to return to their jobs. It was the strongest method of holding them—stronger even than the chains of chattel slavery or the whips of the turpentine bosses."

After a five-month trial in which they heard a million words of testimony, the jurors took less than an hour to reach their verdict: *Guilty*. All 101 defendants were found guilty of trying to destroy the capitalistic class, "not by political action," but by force and violence with the ultimate aim of "the forcible revolutionary overthrow of all existing governmental authority in the United States." Haywood was sentenced to twenty years in jail and fined $30,000; released on bail, he fled to Russia. Fourteen other defendants received the same sentence. Thirty-three others got ten years. Another thirty-five got five years. The remaining eighteen were given shorter sentences. Their fines totaled more than $2,500,000.

The only black defendant was Ben Fletcher, the leader of Philadelphia's dockworkers, and he cracked a wry joke about the court's decision: "Judge Landis has been using bad English today. His sentences are too long."

In the spring of 1918 Eugene V. Debs was sixty-two years old and ill and angry. A veteran labor leader and America's prime apostle of Socialism, he had been the Socialists' Presidential candidate in 1900, 1904, 1908 and 1912. In thorough agreement with the party's "St. Louis Proclamation," he said, "I abhor war. I would oppose war if I stood alone. When I think of a cold, glittering steel bayonet being plunged into the white, quivering flesh of a human being, I recoil with horror."

Now federal agents were raiding Socialist headquarters across the country, Socialist periodicals were being banned from the mails, uniformed soldiers were attacking civilians on streets and disrupting meetings they considered unpatriotic. In Tulsa, Oklahoma, hooded men snatched seventeen Wobblies from the police, then whipped and tarred and feathered them. In Newport, Kentucky, a peace-loving minister, the Reverend Herbert S. Bigelow, was seized by a mob, thrown into a car, driven to a forest, stripped and lashed with a blacksnake whip. His hair was doused with gasoline, and his attackers were about to set it on fire when they were frightened away. They had snarled they were acting "in the name of the women and children of Belgium."

Debs, in a memorable phrase, said that civilization needed to be civilized. He had heart trouble and drank too much, but his frail body and anguished heart were still capable of expressing outrage. In speeches and articles he protested against these atrocities and seethed with resentment at what he felt were Wilson's pretensions of democracy. He lived in Terre Haute, Indiana, and early in June, 1918, he was visited by his former campaign manager, Noble C. Wilson. Debs said he thought the time had come for him to make an all-out remonstrance against the war and its ugly echoes in America.

"Of course," he said with a chuckle, "I'll take about two jumps and they'll nail me—but that's all right!"

On June 16 Debs arrived in Canton, Ohio, an industrial center and the home of former President William McKinley. He was scheduled to speak at the Ohio convention of the Socialist party. The rally was to be held in Nimisilla park, but while being driven there, Debs insisted upon stopping at the Stark county workhouse, across the street from the park, to visit three Socialists imprisoned for opposing the war. The warden had strung them up by their wrists for two days.

It was a hot day, but Debs wore a tweed jacket and vest. He looked a little like Lincoln, for he was tall and slender and gawky, had a high forehead, big ears and a long neck. Despite the sweetness of his smile, his blue eyes were veiled with sadness. James Whitcomb Riley, the Hoosier poet, wrote that "God was feeling mighty good the day He created Gene Debs." Self-educated and well read, Debs had developed an oratorical style that was masterful in its simplicity. Whenever he became intoxicated with the passion of his theme, the melancholy faded from his eyes, which then seemed to burst into flame, and he would lean over the edge of the platform, his right arm extended and his long forefinger jabbing here and there as he denounced capitalism.

Twelve hundred people stood in front of a plain wooden bandstand devoid of any American flag. A local Socialist opened the rally by reading the Declaration of Independence and then introduced Debs. Smiling, he moved to the front of the platform while the prisoners in the nearby jail pressed against their bars to try to hear him. Debs began by saying, "I have just returned from a visit over yonder, where three of our most loyal comrades are paying the penalty for their devotion to the cause of the working class. . . ."

As he spoke, federal agents and members of the American Protective League moved through the crowd checking draft cards. The United

States attorney for the northern district of Ohio had hired a young man to record Debs' speech in shorthand, but the youth was so inept and Debs spoke so fast that he got only patches of the remarks. The local Socialists, aware of the significance of this meeting, had employed a local attorney as their own stenographic reporter.

Sweat laced Debs' face as he paced the platform, every now and then wheeling around and ramming his finger toward someone in the audience. "It felt," a man said later, "exactly as if that forefinger was hitting you in the nose." Debs said, "I realize that in speaking to you this afternoon there are certain limitations placed upon the right of free speech. I must be exceedingly careful, prudent, as to what I say, and even more careful and prudent as to how I say it—"

Laughter.

"I may not be able to say all I think—"

More laughter, followed by applause.

"But I am not going to say anything that I do not think. I would rather a thousand times be a free soul in jail than to be a sycophant and coward in the streets! They may put those boys in jail—and some of the rest of us in jail—but they cannot put the Socialist movement in jail. . . ."

Debs spoke for two hours, the stenographers scribbling. He denounced "Wall Street Junkers" and "the gentry who are today wrapped up in the American flag." He said that "in every age it has been the tyrant, the oppressor and the exploiter, who had wrapped himself in the cloak of patriotism or religion or both, to deceive and over-awe the people." He said that each of the 121 federal judges in the land held "his position, his tenure, through the influence and power of corporate capital." He declared that "the purpose of the Allies is exactly the purpose of the Central Powers."

A transcript of Debs' speech was sent to the federal office in Cleveland, and thirteen days later a grand jury indicted him for alleged violations of the Espionage Act. He was arrested on June 30, 1918, as he was about to enter the Bohemian Gardens in Cleveland to speak at a Socialist picnic. This was a Sunday, most offices were closed, and the authorities refused to let him arrange bail, so that night he slept in a cell. The next day a Cleveland Socialist put up the $10,000 bail and when he was released, he told friends, "I had a hunch that speech was likely to settle the matter."

He remained free until his trial began September 9 in federal district court in Cleveland. He retained four Socialist lawyers but hardly used them because he admitted he had made that Canton speech, while denying there was anything criminal about it. His attorneys made the sole argument that the Espionage Act violated the guarantee of freedom of speech as set forth in the First Amendment of the Constitution. The case was heard by David C. Westenhaver, judge of the United States court of the northern district of Ohio and once a law partner of Secretary of War Baker. The twelve jurors were all retired, averaged seventy-two years of age, and each was worth from $50,000 to $60,000.

Sure he would lose the case, Debs began to do some heavy drinking. His lawyers decided that one of them would have to devote all his time to keeping Gene sober. For two days the prosecution proved what Debs had already conceded—that he indeed had made that speech in Canton. When the government rested, the defense rested, for it had no witnesses to present. Then the judge agreed to let Debs speak in his own behalf.

At 2 P.M. on September 11, 1918, the courtroom darkened by a passing thundershower, Debs, dressed in a worn gray suit, rose and began speaking quietly. He went on talking for almost two hours, and when he finished, some jurors were weeping. A federal agent leaned across a table and whispered to a reporter, "You've got to hand it to the old man—he came through clean." When court adjourned, Debs walked into a corridor where a girl handed him roses and fainted at his feet.

The next day the judge told the jurors to find the defendant not guilty on those counts dealing with ridicule of the federal government. He instructed them to deliberate on other counts charging that Debs willfully and knowingly tried to obstruct the draft act. The jury was out six hours, and Debs spent this time regaling friends with anecdotes about Abraham Lincoln. About 5 P.M. the jurymen filed back inside, and one read the verdict: guilty as charged on two counts of the indictment. The judge said he would impose sentence on September 14.

When court reconvened on that date, the clerk asked whether the defendant cared to make a final statement. He did. Rising from his chair and beginning to speak as he approached the bench, talking without notes, Eugene Debs delivered a speech that was to become an American classic and be printed and reprinted in anthologies; Heywood Broun called it "one of the most beautiful and moving passages in the English language."

> Your honor, [Debs began] years ago I recognized my kinship with all living things, and I made up my mind that I was not one whit better than the meanest on earth. I said then, and I say now, that while there is a lower class, I am in it, while there is a criminal element I am of it, and while there is a soul in prison, I am not free. . . . I look upon the Espionage law as a despotic enactment in flagrant conflict with democratic principles and with the spirit of free institutions. . . . I am opposed to the social system in which we live. . . . I believe in fundamental change, but if possible by peaceful and orderly means. . . .
>
> I am thinking this morning of the men in the mills and factories, of the men in the mines and on the railroads. I am thinking of the women who for a paltry wage are compelled to work out their barren lives; of the little children who in this system are robbed of their childhood and in their tender years are seized in the remorseless grasp of Mammon and forced into industrial dungeons, there to feed the monster machines while they themselves are being starved and stunted, body and soul. I see them dwarfed and diseased and their little lives broken and blasted because in this high noon of our twentieth century Christian civilization, money is still so much more important than the flesh and blood of childhood. In very truth, gold is god. . . .

When Debs finished, the judge said he considered himself second to none in his sympathy for the poor and suffering, but he was amazed by "the remarkable self-delusion and self-deception of Mr. Debs, who assumes that he is serving humanity and the downtrodden." Calling himself "a conservator of the peace and a defender of the Constitution of the United States," the judge then imposed sentence: ten years' imprisonment.

Debs' attorneys said they would appeal to the United States Supreme Court and challenge the constitutionality of the Espionage Act. During the appeal Debs could live at home in Terre Haute, but he was forbidden to leave the northern federal district of Ohio. He was at once amused and irritated when federal agents raided the home of his former campaign manager, Nobel C. Wilson, confiscated Socialist literature and letters and never returned any of these documents. The agents also found a box they thought might contain dynamite and began opening it gingerly. Debs' friend laughingly warned them to be careful lest they get their noses blown off. The box was full of charcoal tablets.

Not until March 10, 1919, when the war had been over for four months did the Supreme Court pass on the Debs case. All nine justices sustained the verdict of the lower court. Their unanimous opinion was written by Justice Oliver Wendell Holmes. In another opinion only a week earlier Holmes had said free speech could be abridged only in case of "a clear and present danger" to public safety, but he did not cite his own doctrine in this decision. Regarded as a champion of free speech, Holmes told a friend he guessed Chief Justice White had asked him to write the opinion in the Debs case as a strategic move. "I hated to have to write the Debs case," Holmes confessed. Still, this New England aristocrat had little in common with the Midwestern proletariat. He felt contemptuous of the "poor fools whom I should have been inclined to pass over. The greatest bores in the world are the come-outers who are cock-sure of a dozen nostrums."

Holmes thought Debs, a noted agitator, was rightly convicted of obstructing the recruiting service," held that the jury had acted properly and declared the Espionage Act constitutional. But when Holmes began to receive "stupid letters of protest," he wrote a friend, "Now I hope the President will pardon him and some other poor devils with whom I have more sympathy."

As for Debs, he told the press, "Great issues are not decided by courts, but by the people. I have no concern in what the coterie of begowned corporation lawyers in Washington may decide in my case. The court of final resort is the people, and that court will be heard from in due time."

According to Claude Bowers—journalist, historian, diplomat—when the President heard Debs had been arrested, he said, "I never meant my law to be used like that." *My* law. Wilson's words. But when outraged telegrams and letters poured into the White House, he vowed never to pardon him.

Many disagreed with Wilson. Bowers said of Debs, "He was not a traitor. He was not a revolutionist. He was, rather, an evolutionist." The New York *Times* editorialized, "Mr. Debs was convicted for making a socialist speech. No sane person considers him a criminal." Harold J. Laski, an English political scientist who corresponded with Holmes, said of Wilson, "I must get off my chest my sense of passionate indignation at his refusal to pardon Debs."

In April, 1919, sick and old, at a time when federal prisons still overflowed with people convicted under the Espionage and Sedition acts, Debs entered the penitentiary at Moundsville, West Virginia. Two months later he was transferred to the federal penitentiary in Atlanta, Georgia. In 1920 he ran a fifth time as the Socialist candidate for President, the first man to seek this highest office while behind bars. Although he was defeated by the Republican candidate, Warren G. Harding, he polled 919,779 popular votes.

On January 31, 1921, only about a month before the end of his second term, Wilson received from his attorney general a recommendation that he commute Debs' sentence. On this sheet of paper Wilson scrawled one word, "Denied." Then he turned to his secretary and said explosively:

"I will never consent to the pardon of this man! While the flower of American youth was pouring out its blood to vindicate the cause of civilization, this man, Debs, stood behind the lines, sniping, attacking, and denouncing them. Before the war he had a perfect right to exercise his freedom of speech and to express his own opinion, but once the Congress of the United States declared war, silence on his part would have been the proper course to pursue. I know there will be a great deal of denunciation of me for refusing this pardon. They will say I am cold-blooded and indifferent, but it will make no impression on me. This man was a traitor to his country and he will never be pardoned during my administration!"

On December 25, 1921, President Harding commuted Debs' sentence, but did not restore his citizenship.

About eight o'clock the morning of August 23, 1918, workmen were idling at the corner of Houston and Crosby streets in Manhattan when leaflets fluttered down on their heads. Looking up, they saw someone throwing the circulars from a window on the fourth floor of a hat factory. Some men snatched the brochures from the air while others stooped down to pick them up from the street. There were two kinds of leaflets—one printed in English, the other in Yiddish. The one in English denounced the dispatch of American troops to Russia and was signed "Revolutionists," while the one in Yiddish called for a general strike in America in support of Soviet workers, and it was signed "The Rebels."

Someone called military intelligence, and soon two army sergeants arrived on the scene. Having walked up to the fourth floor of the hat factory, they arrested Hyman Rosansky. When he was questioned, he said that a couple of weeks earlier he had attended an anarchist meeting where he'd met three men; the previous night they had given him a package of leaflets and asked him to throw them out a window to the people below. The evening of the day of his arrest he was supposed to meet with the other men, so the military police set a trap and captured six other persons—five men and a girl.

They said they lived in a six-room apartment on East 104th Street. All had been born in Russia, all had lived in the United States a few years, though none had become an American citizen, and all were anarchists except one, who was a Socialist. Their leader was Jacob Abrams.

Twenty-nine years old and the eldest of the prisoners, he later testified he had been denied permission by the federal government to return to Russia to fight the Germans. The girl was Molly Steimer, and she was twenty-one years old.

They were interrogated in the presence of several army sergeants by Thomas J. Tunney, a New York police inspector who had written a book about bombers called *Throttled*. Emma Goldman, the anarchist leader, said "every one of those youths was subjected to the severest third degree." Zechariah Chafee, Jr., a Harvard law professor who studied the case, said "the charges of brutality seem disquietingly specific and sincere." However, policemen and soldiers alike denied they had threatened or struck the prisoners. Nonetheless, one of them, Jacob Schwartz, died the day before all were to come to trial; Emma Goldman said he died of injuries suffered at the hands of cops wielding blackjacks in the Manhattan prison called the Tombs. The federal judge who heard the case wisecracked, "There is no evidence who killed Schwartz any more than there was evidence as to who killed Cock Robin."

The surviving prisoners refused to tell where the pamphlets had been printed, but among Abrams' papers the investigators found a bill for a printing press and paper, and these led them to a basement at 1582 Madison Avenue. Entering with a search warrant, they found a motor-driven press, a hand-operated press, stacks of blank paper the size of the leaflets and English and Hebrew type like that used in printing the circulars. The janitor was a woman who said she had seen Abrams and Hyman Lachowsky, another prisoner, working in the basement room she had rented to Abrams for $8 a month.

The five men and the girl were indicted on a charge of conspiring to violate the Espionage Act. They were *not* to stand trial for making pacifist remarks or uttering pro-German sentiments; rather, they were to be prosecuted for agitating against the government's Russian policy.

This 1918 policy—still a controversial subject—was the result of a long chain of complex events. Under Czar Nicholas II Russia had entered the war on the side of Britain and France and suffered many defeats at the hands of the Germans. Russian revolutionaries had forced the czar to abdicate and then murdered him, a provisional government took power, it was overthrown by the Bolsheviks, Lenin rose to power, Russia made peace with Germany, and civil war broke out between Soviet and anti-Soviet forces.

Then the Allies intervened in northern Russia. Book after book has been written about the events that led to the landing of 9,000 American soldiers on Russian soil, but the subject remains so complex, confusing and controversial that no definitive statement can be made about it.

Here is an outline of what happened: Dissident Russians challenged the authority of the new Soviet regime, set up their own provisional governments and fought the Bolsheviks on many fronts. The Soviets were known as the Reds while the anti-Soviet forces were called the Whites. The civil war between these groups was complicated by the so-called Czechoslovak Legion. It consisted of Czech and Slovak soldiers who had been captured by the Russians, together with deserters from the Austro-Hungarian army who were eager to fight against Germany and

Austria-Hungary for the independence of their countries. After the Soviets made peace with the Central Powers, the Czech Legion turned on the Reds, fought them, captured all the principal cities along the Trans-Siberian railway from the Urals to the Pacific.

The British and French begged Wilson to intervene in Russia to steady the Soviet government, to protect Allied supplies stored in Russia, and to reopen the eastern front. The President hesitated. American military intervention was opposed by state department officials, Chief of Staff Peyton C. March, Herbert Hoover and others. But at long and foolish last the President gave in to Allied appeals and sent American troops to Russia to join the British, French and Japanese forces there. Ultimately thirty-six bewildered doughboys were killed in clashes with armed partisans on Russian soil, and the last of the American forces did not withdraw until the early part of 1920.

It was this American expedition to Russia that had angered the six persons now charged with violating the Espionage Act. Before their arrest they had distributed 9,000 copies of their two leaflets.

The English brochure said: " . . . You people of America were deceived by the wonderful speeches of the masked President Wilson. His shameful, cowardly silence about the intervention in Russia reveals the hypocrisy of the plutocratic gang in Washington. . . . Will you allow the Russian revolution to be crushed? . . . There is only one enemy of the workers of the world and that is CAPITALISM. . . ."

The Yiddish leaflet sneered at the President as "his Majesty, Mr. Wilson." It warned Russian immigrants that the American government was making bullets "not only for the Germans but also for the Workers Soviets of Russia. Workers in the ammunition factories, you are producing bullets, bayonets, cannon, to murder not only the Germans, but also your dearest, best, who are in Russia and are fighting for freedom. . . . Workers, our reply to the barbaric intervention has to be a general strike!"

The trial began on October 10, 1918, in the United States courthouse in New York before Judge Henry De Lamar Clayton. For eighteen years Clayton had served in the House of Representatives as a Democratic Congressman from Alabama, and as chairman of the House judiciary committee he had given his name to the Clayton Antitrust Act of 1914. *Abrams v. United States* was his first important Espionage Act case and was assigned to him only because the city dockets were crowded. Although the New York *Times* praised Judge Clayton for his "half-humorous" remarks, defense counsel and some spectators were appalled by his fumbling and prejudiced comments: "After listening carefully to all [the defendants] had to say, I came to the conclusion that a capitalist is a man with a decent suit of clothes, a minimum of $1.25 in his pockets, and a good character."

The prosecution proved that after American intervention in Russia the defendants decided to protest what they regarded as an attack on the Russian revolution. (The revolution had been praised by Wilson and Roosevelt, among others.) Professor Chafee has pointed out, "Since we had not declared war upon Russia, protests against our action there could not be criminal unless they were also in opposition to the war with

Germany." But the English-language leaflet had ended with this postscript: "It is absurd to call us pro-German. We hate and despise German militarism more than do your hypocritical tyrants. We have more reasons for denouncing German militarism than has the coward of the White House."

During the trial Abrams was asked, "You are opposed to German militarism in every form?"

"Absolutely."

"You would overthrow it and help overthrow it, if you could?"

"First chance."

Agreement came from all the other defendants except Molly Steimer, who testified, "The war between the United States and Germany does not concern me because I wish to see militarism throughout the entire world crushed by the workers . . . the workers of the United States who are working in munition factories ought to stop producing munitions which are used for the killing of Russians. I care nothing about interfering with the war with Germany because it does not matter to me."

Defense counsel Harry Weinberger offered to prove through the testimony of certain federal officials that American intervention in Russia was not part of our war with Germany, but the judge refused. His ruling was technically correct, since such testimony had nothing to do with the overt acts of the defendants, but it gave a great advantage to the prosecution, since the trial was being held at a time when many Americans believed that Bolsheviks were nothing but German spies.

Weinberger argued that Wilson had broken the law by sending troops to Russia without the consent of Congress or the knowledge of the American people. Therefore, the defense attorney said, the defendants had acted in a just and laudable manner in calling public attention to our penetration of a country with which we were at peace. He was fined for contempt of court.

One defendant was acquitted, but the other five were found guilty of violating the Espionage Act. Although the prosecution agreed that Hyman Rosansky had been duped into throwing the leaflets from the building, he nonetheless was sentenced to three years in prison. Molly Steimer was put away for fifteen years and fined $500. Jacob Abrams, Samuel Lipman and Hyman Lachowsky were fined $1,000 each and sent to jail for twenty years.

The punishment could not have been more severe, Professor Chafee commented, had the defendants conspired to tie up every munition plant in the country and actually succeeded in doing so. It also is interesting to note that in 1918 a man from South Dakota was convicted of threatening the life of the President and received a sentence of two years and six months.

Sentences in the Abrams case were imposed on October 25, 1918, during a Congressional election campaign. The defense attorney argued for bail pending appeal to the United States Supreme Court declaring that in the course of the campaign some Republicans had uttered statements as extreme as anything said by the defendants. Bail was granted, whereupon two defendants went to New Orleans and tried to stow away on a ship bound for Mexico. Molly Steimer used her temporary freedom to hand out anarchist literature on the sidewalks of New York and then was returned to prison.

November 10, 1919, a year after the end of war, the Supreme Court voted seven to two to sustain the verdict of the lower court. The majority opinion was written by Justice John H. Clarke, who was considered a mild liberal. He said that while the defendants had urged only that workers make no arms that could be used in Russia, and although America was not at war with Russia, the necessary consequences of their propaganda would have hampered the war with Germany. He furthermore held that they were willing to cripple the American effort to beat Germany if they thereby also crippled American intervention in Russia.

Dissenting opinions were submitted by Justices Louis D. Brandeis and Holmes, with Holmes writing their minority opinion. *Abrams v. United States* had been the sixth Espionage Act case considered by the Supreme Court, and in the five previous cases Holmes and Brandeis had upheld the convictions. But now Holmes could not go along with the majority. Some students of jurisprudence consider his dissenting opinion in the Abrams case the best opinion he ever wrote. Max Lerner calls it "the greatest utterance on intellectual freedom by an American, ranking in the English tongue with Milton and Mill." Holmes said:

> [The leaflets] in no way attack the form of government of the United States. . . . Congress certainly cannot forbid all effort to change the mind of the country . . . sentences of twenty years' imprisonment have been imposed for the publishing of two leaflets that I believe the defendants had as much right to publish as the Government has to publish the Constitution of the United States now vainly invoked by them. . . .
>
> Even if I am technically wrong . . . the most nominal punishment seems to me all that possibly could be inflicted . . . when men have realized that time has upset many fighting faiths, they may come to believe even more than they believe the very foundations of their own conduct that the ultimate good desired is better reached by free trade in ideas—that the best test of truth is the power of the thought to get itself accepted in the competition of the market, and that truth is the only ground upon which their wishes safely can be carried out. That, at any rate, is the theory of our Constitution. It is an experiment, as all life is an experiment.

On the night of July 11, 1917, in the mining town of Bisbee, Arizona, a group of leading citizens, including a friend of Theodore Roosevelt's, met secretly and decided to kidnap more than 1,000 men the next day.

Bisbee was booming because the Allies needed copper to make wire and manufacture alloys such as brass. Their call for copper benefited the United States more than any other country, for it was the world's greatest producer of this reddish metal. In 1914 525,529 metric tons were mined; by 1917 production had risen to 872,065 tons. Before the war copper had cost about 15 cents a pound; by March, 1917, the price had risen to 37 cents. Since it cost only 8 to 12 cents to mine 1 pound of copper, the copper companies made huge profits. In fact, a Congressional committee heard that profits ranged from 33 to 300 percent.

Bisbee sat in the center of the Warren mining district, one of the richest copper districts in America. The seat of Cochise county, located on the Southern Pacific Railroad 100 miles southeast of Tucson and less than 10 miles from the Mexican border, Bisbee perched on the steep slopes of a canyon called Mule Pass Gulch, a part of the Mule Mountains, 5,300 feet above sea level. Most of its mines were owned by the Phelps-Dodge Corporation—which also owned the largest hotel, department store, hospital, library and other enterprises and institutions.

The miners were angrily aware of the windfall profits of the copper companies. On June 15, 1917, a convention of Bisbee miners had asked the operators for a minimum wage of $6 a day for underground work and $5.50 for surface work. They also wanted changes in working conditions. The operators refused even to meet with the miners, let alone consider their demands, and so on June 27 the workers had struck.

Phelps-Dodge officials claimed the strike was called by the Industrial Workers of the World. Actually, it came on a signal from the International Union of Mine, Mill and Smelter Workers, which was an affiliate of the American Federation of Labor. The IWW and AFL had been vying for members in the copper country of Arizona. A federal commission later declared that "here, as elsewhere, there was . . . no machinery for the adjustment of difficulties between the companies and the men which provided for the determination of alleged grievances by some authoritative and disinterested tribunal."

A subsequent army survey found that 381 of the strikers belonged to the AFL, 426 were IWW members, and 360 were affiliated with no union. The copper barons and their controlled press denounced the strikers as "pro-German." However, the army survey showed that 199 of the men were native Americans, 468 were naturalized citizens, and of the foreign-born 141 were British, 82 Serbs and 179 Slavs. Other than the Slavs, there were few Austro-Hungarians and few Germans.

The mine managers, hiding their hunger for profits behind patriotism, banded together with other businessmen in a so-called Loyalty League. They rumbled that the strikers and their sympathizers should be run out of town, while the copper firms began stockpiling arms and ammunition, hiring more guards and gunmen. In a 1915 strike for higher wages the miners had been beset by criminals imported from the underworlds of various cities.

Sheriff Harry Wheeler asked Arizona Governor Thomas F. Campbell to ask for federal troops. The sheriff based his request on the fact that the state militia had been drafted into federal service. Actually, there was no need to appeal for outside help, since the strikers were behaving themselves. They engaged in no violence. In fact, some townspeople said there was less petty crime than usual because the IWW told bootleggers to sell no more booze during the strike. In normal times Bisbee was a tough town with a reputation for an occasional Johnson Day Picnic—local slang for a barroom brawl. After the strike began, an army officer twice surveyed conditions and found everything peaceful, so the federal government rejected the governor's request for soldiers.

When the town worthies met on the night of July 11, they included the managers and other officials of the Copper Queen Consolidated Mining Company, which was a division of the Phelps-Dodge Corporation, and officers of the Calumet and Arizona Mining Company. Without consulting their own attorneys, the United States attorney in Arizona or the law officers of the state or county or town, they decided to deport all strikers and strike sympathizers. There was one exception: At the last minute the conspirators managed to persuade the sheriff to help them rid the town of all undesirables. To do so without attracting the attention of the outside world, they also decided to seize control of the local telephone and telegraph offices.

Then the vigilantes struck.

As dawn seeped over the bleak landscape of Bisbee, 2,000 men fanned through the streets and broke into private homes. They wore white handkerchiefs on their sleeves so they could recognize one another. All had been deputized by the sheriff. They stopped every man on the street to ask him his business, and if they disliked his reply, they arrested him and led him to a baseball park converted into a temporary concentration camp. They frightened wives and children when they smashed into houses to grab sleepy men in bed and then drag them away.

They arrested not only strikers, but lawyers and tradesmen and property owners as well. Although the vigilantes pretended they were acting for patriotic reasons, it later was learned that among those nabbed were 472 who had registered for military service, 205 who had bought Liberty Bonds and 520 who had donated money to the Red Cross.

Now, for the first time, violence flared. A deputy was killed as he tried to arrest a Wobbly and then the IWW man was slain by another deputy. Within an hour or so 1,186 astonished men found themselves detained in an improvised concentration camp in the open under a broiling sun. Then a kangaroo court convened, and each prisoner was given the choice—at the point of a gun—of returning to work, going to jail or being deported from the state. Infuriated by this violation of their civil liberties, the men refused to call off their strike.

So they were marched out of the ball park through a gauntlet of gunmen to the railway tracks, where they were prodded into a twenty-seven-car cattle train provided for the occasion by the Southern Pacific Railroad. The train pulled out toward the east, passed armed men stationed here and there along the right-of-way, crossed the Arizona state line and entered New Mexico and bumped to a stop at the town of Columbus. The city fathers of Columbus refused to let the out-of-state vigilantes unload their prisoners, so the train took them back to a tiny desert town called Hermanas. There the men were dumped out amid sagebrush and onto sand stretching to the horizon, and for the next thirty-six hours they had nothing to eat.

For two days no one outside the Southwest knew about this illegal and brutal deportation. In a subsequent lawsuit the Associated Press accused Phelps-Dodge officials of throwing such a scare into a telegrapher that he did not flash the news to the AP, but a court ruled there was no statute covering this offense. The corporation later said it regretted this censorship of the news by what it called "subordinate officials." The plight of the stranded men was brought to the attention of the war department in Washington, and on the morning of July 14 a company of soldiers reached Hermanas, put the men aboard a train and took them to Columbus. There they were given food and shelter by the federal government until September 12.

Having been snatched away from homes and families, most miners wanted to return to Bisbee to join their families and claim their possessions. But again they ran into trouble. The vigilantes had taken over the functions of law officers and the courts and continued to reign illegally until late in August. A vigilante committee decided whether a man would be allowed to get his clothes and other belongings. The sheriff, a puppet of the vigilantes, said he had heard from a chambermaid that there was "a plan on foot when they go down in the mines to get their clothing . . . that they were to block those tunnels. . . ."

When news of the deportation reached "Big Bill" Haywood, the founder of the Industrial Workers of the World, he called it an outrage. Previously he had denied that the IWW had called the strike, while other IWW leaders had denounced the rumor that the Germans were behind it. The affair also was discussed in the House of Representatives by Congresswoman Jeannette Rankin of Montana, another copper-producing state, who explained to her colleagues the blacklisting system used by copper companies against workers they considered unruly. However, in defiance of mounting public criticism, the Bisbee vigilantes arrested all unemployed men in town and charged them with vagrancy.

An angry President Wilson sent the Arizona governor a telegram deploring the persecution of citizens of the state. He also appointed a federal commission to investigate, and for its chairman he selected Secretary of Labor William B. Wilson. On November 6, 1917, this commission issued a scathing report. It declared that the strike was neither pro-German nor seditious but "appeared to be nothing more than the normal results of the increased cost of living, the speeding up processes to which the mine management had been tempted by the abnormally high market price of copper."

In the report Chairman Wilson addressed himself to Sheriff Wheeler, saying, ". . . on the strength of rumors . . . you directed the picking up of twelve hundred people here, some only for a brief period and some, as we are informed, here for a long time, and under the authority to use whatever power is necessary, you undertook to use that power not only within your bailiwick, but outside your own bailiwick . . . where you had no authority and where you were not authorized or directed to use power."

The report, signed by all four members of the commission, was written mainly by Felix Frankfurter, the commission counsel, who later became a justice of the United States Supreme Court. Years later, in a letter summarizing the commission's report, Frankfurter said, "It did not put anybody in jail—partly because of the existing state of law, and partly because of the incompetence of those who administered what law there was. It did not take any vengeance on the perpetrators of the deed."

A subsequent Arizona governor, George P. Hunt, sent the state legislature a message denouncing the "mob of nearly two thousand men directed by county authorities . . . [who] under cover of darkness, calmly, premeditatedly, deliberately, swooped down at dawn upon the homes of unsuspecting, unoffending miners, who committed no violence, nay more, who had threatened no violence, but who had every lawful reason to feel secure as citizens under the guarantees vouchsafed by the Constitution of the United States."

Theodore Roosevelt sided with the vigilantes. He said in a letter that "one of the prominent leaders in that deportation was my old friend, Jack Greenway." Disregarding the fact that the Bisbee strike had not been called by the IWW, ignoring the further fact that the strikers had neither threatened nor engaged in violence, Roosevelt went on to say that "the I.W.W. is a criminal organization. . . . No human being in his senses doubts that the men deported from Bisbee were bent on destruction and murder."

A federal grand jury indicted the sheriff and twenty-one leading citizens of Bisbee for violating the rights of the men they deported. However, the indictment was invalidated by a United States circuit court, whose decision was upheld in *United States v. Wheeler.* Then the state of Arizona obtained an indictment accusing 224 businessmen, the sheriff, many of his deputies and some policemen of illegal kidnapping. One case came to trial; but after several weeks the defendant was acquitted, and after that the charges against all the other defendants were dismissed.

So, as Frankfurter said, no one was punished for capturing 1,186 men, throwing them into a temporary concentration camp, shoving them into cattle cars, transporting them to another state, marooning them in a desert without food or water.

Theodore Roosevelt, who had once written that "there is a Doctor Jekyll and Mr. Hyde in nations as in individuals," took no consistent stand about this reign of terror. While he castigated Wilson for letting Burleson censor the mails, he endorsed loyalty oaths for teachers, wanted to prohibit the teaching of German in schools, urged that German-language papers be forced to switch to English, approved of the prosecution of two Columbia University students for advising other students not to register for the draft, endorsed the indictment of the periodical called the Milwaukee *Socialist*.

Neither did Franklin D. Roosevelt speak out against this massive suppression of civil liberties. Instead, he approved of the Espionage and Sedition acts and sometimes denounced "slackers." To a U.S. attorney who prosecuted four persons for distributing Socialist antiwar literature, FDR wrote, "Pamphlets of this kind are undoubtedly attacks not on the individuals who make up the government but on duly constituted government itself, and I cannot help feeling that in certain parts of the country especially every effort should be made to stamp them out."

War Secretary Baker became worried, however, and on April 10, 1918, he wrote:

> The spirit of the country seems unusually good, but there is a growing frenzy of suspicion and hostility toward disloyalty. I am afraid we are going to have a good many instances of people roughly treated on very slight evidence of disloyalty. Already a number of men and some women have been tarred and feathered, and a portion of the press is urging with great vehemence more strenuous efforts at detection and punishment. This usually takes the form of advocating "drum-head courts-martial" and "being stood up against a wall and shot," which are perhaps none too bad for real traitors, but are very suggestive of summary discipline to arouse mob spirit, which unhappily does not take time to weigh evidence.

Herbert Hoover wrote in his memoirs that "emotion had replaced all reason."

"We may well wonder in view of the precedents now established," Charles Evans Hughes mused, "whether constitutional government, as hitherto maintained in the Republic, could survive another great war, even victoriously waged."

Years later Montana Senator Burton K. Wheeler recalled, "I went through the First World War hysteria and I wouldn't have believed the American people could so completely lose their sense of balance."

According to journalist and historian Mark Sullivan, "The prohibition of individual liberty in the interest of the state could hardly be more complete."

Alvin Johnson, an economist and editor and a founder of the New School for Social Research, said in his autobiography, "A screaming hurricane of hate swept America."

"Democracy in America," in the opinion of Wisconsin Senator Robert F. La Follette, "has been trampled under foot, submerged, forgotten."

In his book *The Challenge to American Freedom*, Donald Johnson wrote, "Few people have ever been so intolerant of their fellow-men as Americans in the First World War."

Kansas editor William Allen White lamented that an orgy of intolerance swept the land and added, "The war has a throttle grip on our thinking."

And Ernest Sutherland Bates wrote a book called *The Story of Congress* in which he said that "the first result of the war 'to make the world safe for democracy' was to eliminate democracy from the United States."

What went wrong? While there is no single answer or simple answer, perhaps the reign of terror was due to a combination of the following factors:

Fear—Until the United States entered the war, there really *were* German spies and saboteurs in this country. After the war declaration almost all of them fled, but Americans could not be sure they were gone.

Change—All change produces stress on the human mind and body, and the faster and more radical the change, the greater the stress. Americans were caught off guard by the outbreak of war, were unable to understand its complex causes, and after they got into the conflict, their lives were so intimately affected by it that they lost their emotional balance.

Identity—The importance of the individual diminished with the growth of population, decline of religious faith, explosion of science and technology, rapid rise of war production, shift of attention from the village to the world, increasing complexity of life. A powerless nobody could feel like an important somebody by wrapping himself in the flag, by identifying himself with something bigger than himself, with some glorious cause.

Elitism—This glorious cause was the Americanization of the entire world. Consciously or unconsciously, many Americans regarded themselves as the chosen people. Herman Melville, an otherwise brilliant man, wrote in a wrongheaded moment, "We Americans are the peculiar, chosen people—the Israel of our time; we bear the ark of the liberties of the world. . . . God has predestined, mankind expects, great things from our race; and great things we feel in our souls. The rest of the nations must soon be in our rear." Republican Senator Albert J. Beveridge of Indiana once said, "We will not renounce our part in the mission of our race, trustee under God of the civilization of the world." Some of those who believed that the United States had a divine mission were willing to wink at tawdry means to this end.

Religion—Some might argue that this nation went berserk for want of religious scruples; after all, during the war fewer than a third of all Americans were church members. But this reasoning shatters on the fact that an overwhelming majority of ministers and priests and rabbis were passionately for war, and some made savage remarks. The predominant attitude of the nation's religious Establishment was an eye for an eye, a tooth for a tooth.

Nationalism—As religion declined, nationalism rose. Worship of God began to give way to worship of the state. Many people felt that the proper thing to worship was the United States of America. Those who gave all their faith to the state could speak, as one lawyer did in court, of "patriotic murder." The individual human being is a reality; the state is an abstraction. Still, in the servive of this abstraction, some people were willing to kill that greatest of all realities—life.

Absorption—There is a yoga maxim that says, "We become what we hate." Because of stories about German atrocities, prowar propaganda, an outburst of patriotism and the misguided belief that everyone should conform in a time of peril, many Americans absorbed the very hatred they professed to hate. The Irish writer and mystic, George William Russell, known as AE, clearly explained this concept: "By intensity of hatred nations create in themselves the characters they imagine in their enemies. Hence it is that all passionate conflicts result in the interchange of characteristics."

Madness—A portion of mankind, perhaps a majority, has been mad in every land in every century. The proof of this proposition is to be found in the Crusades, the Inquisition, the dancing mania of Italy, the witch-hunt in Massachusetts. Since madness is contagious, it can infect nations as well as individuals—an idea expressed by Theodore Roosevelt when he spoke of the coexistence of a Dr. Jekyll and Mr. Hyde in nations. Sometimes the dogma of institutions can plunge a people into madness. To retain his sanity, a man needs his private vision, and so does a nation. The Bible says, "Where there is no vision the people perish."

Chapter 30

THE INFLUENZA PANDEMIC

Albert Gitchell felt sick. He was a company cook at Camp Funston in Kansas and before breakfast on Monday morning, March 11, 1918, he reported at hospital building Number 91. When army doctors found he had a fever of 103 degrees, a sore throat, headache and muscular pains, he was placed in a contagious ward.

To this same building moments later came Corporal Lee W. Drake, who also had a fever of 103 and all of Gitchell's other symptoms. No sooner had the corporal been put to bed when Sergeant Adolph Hurby arrived, coughing, and then two other sick soldiers wobbled in. By noon 107 feverish men had been admitted to the army hospital, all with low pulse, a drowsy feeling and inflammation of the nose, throat and bronchi. Then, day after day, and with appalling swiftness, the number of cases jumped—100, 300, 1,000.

General Leonard Wood wrote the governor of Kansas, saying, "There are 1,440 minutes in a day. When I tell you there were 1,440 admissions in a day, or practically one a minute, you will realize the strain put upon our nursing and medical force. The nurses and medical personnel did admirably. The influx of patients for two or three days was like the wounded coming back from the battlefield."

Influenza had struck this army post of 26,000 men in the geographic center of the country. Overcrowded, like most other military posts, it already had endured eruptions of pneumonia, measles, mumps, and even 200 cases of spinal meningitis. As one kind of quarantine flag was hauled down, a new one was broken out. The camp was dismal and dirty, its thousands of horses and mules produced 9,000 tons of manure a month, and dust storms clotted the nostrils and mouths of the suffering soldiers. But this new epidemic was worse than the previous ones—far worse. In fact, this was one of the beginnings of not just an epidemic but a pandemic—a worldwide plague that was to kill 21,000,000 people around the earth before it ended.

Influenza pandemics had ravaged the world before—in 1781, 1832, 1847 and 1889. With the exception of a few remote islands, the plague of 1918 exploded in every area on earth, although scientists were unable to pinpoint the site of its origin. Camp Funston appeared to have been the first place in the United States to be afflicted. Many people thought that the country of origin had been Spain, and so the plague took the name of Spanish influenza. "Influenza" is an Italian word dating back to 1504, when astrologers coined it to describe the influence of the stars and planets on human beings. Since nations are like people in their tendency to ascribe evil to neighbors or foreigners, in 1918 the French blamed the Spaniards, the Spaniards blamed the French, and the Americans blamed eastern Europe.

The flu pandemic erupted all around the earth within weeks. This was due to the facts that the disease is highly contagious, it is communicated by one person to another, and that the war had transported more people from continent to continent than ever before in history. It raced around the world in three waves: The first wave began in March, 1918; the second toward the end of September, 1918; the third early in March, 1919.

On June 1, 1918, the New York *Times* reported that a disease resembling influenza was spreading through northern China—"like a tidal wave," according to an American doctor in Shanghai. The Chinese called it Chunking fever. Before the end of June the flu was felling German soldiers and miners and spreading through German cities. A few cases were seen among the doughboys fighting in France, although at first General Pershing denied there was any infection in the American Expeditionary Force.

By July health officials at New York, Boston and other Atlantic ports were fumigating ships arriving from Spain. British soldiers in Flanders called the malady the Flanders grip. The French called it *la grippe*. The Japanese called it wrestlers' fever.

On August 12 the Norwegian liner *Bergensfjord* docked at the army base in Brooklyn after a dreadful voyage. During the trip 100 passengers had been stricken with an illness "resembling influenza"; 4 died and were buried at sea. Eleven semiconscious passengers were taken off ship on stretchers and rushed to the Norwegian Hospital in Brooklyn; within hours 1 of the 11 died. New Yorkers became alarmed, but city health officials declared there was no danger of an epidemic occurring in the city. Seldom was any prediction so wrong. Soon another ship docked with 11 more passengers burning with fever. Then a third vessel with 2 dead and 25 sick.

Boston was hit hard. Patients overflowed the 1,236-bed Chelsea naval hospital overlooking the city's harbor. The commanding officer of the hospital wrote to his superiors in Washington that "the congestion of the ships as well as the repeated intercourse with the civilian population is believed to be a menace to the health of the personnel and may have its influence upon the present prevalence of influenza."

Then the plague rampaged up and down the East coast, began showing up in army camps and naval stations, leaped to the West coast and touched off nationwide panic. While the New York *Times* devoted columns of space to news of the flu, other newspapers seem to have played it down lest the people become so terrified they lose their heads.

Having read about the dirty work done in this country by German spies and saboteurs, some officials and many ordinary people believed a growing rash of rumors. A lieutenant colonel said he thought flu germs had been brought here in enemy submarines. A toxicologist claimed to have found a relationship between the flu germs and the poison gas released on the western front in France. His statement was followed by horror stories alleging that these gases permeated all space, dipping and rising and dipping again, and some people believed that by the time the gas clouds had traveled around the world every human being would be stricken. In a small town in Illinois a seven-year-old girl looked up at the sky and saw clouds and thought they were smoke from Europe and began screaming.

In the coal-mining community of Clearwater, Pennsylvania, a sheriff arrested "a dangerous enemy alien" found near a mine with stolen dynamite caps, and since seven cases of flu had been reported in town, it was felt the man might also be carrying flu germs. In New Mexico a woman swore that a German sympathizer had put something in the drinking water at an Arizona mining camp, some substance that felled sixty miners with an ailment like the flu. In Providence, Rhode Island, evangelist Billy Sunday said in a sermon, "We can meet here tonight and pray down an epidemic, just as well as we can pray down a German victory. The whole thing is a part of their propaganda. It started over there in Spain, where they scattered germs around. . . . There's nothing short of hell they haven't stooped to do since the war began. Darn their hides!"

In 1918 much less was known about influenza than is known today. Only after the war was it discovered that the disease is caused by a filtrable virus. An acute ailment, it is characterized by fever, prostration, aches and pains, and inflammation of the respiratory mucous membranes. The onset is swift and often marked by chilly sensations. The patient feels anxious and depressed, and some victims hallucinate because of their high fever. In mild cases the temperature rises to 101 or 102 degrees and lasts two to three days. In severe cases the fever may shoot up to 103 or 104 degrees and continue four or five days.

Owing to the lack of enough oxygen in the blood, the lips and ears turn blue. Breathing is rapid and shallow. The pulse may run fast and feebly, indicating that the heart is strained by the poison in the system. The flu is so exhausting that some patients may die from the mere effort of leaning forward or turning over to enable a doctor to put a stethoscope against the back to check the condition of the lungs.

Acute symptoms usually subside quickly after the fever breaks, although weakness, sweating and fatigue may persist for days or even weeks. If there are no complications, most victims recover—but the most dangerous complication is secondary bacterial pneumonia. In 1918 there was no specific medication for the flu, no miracle drug, no effective vaccine, so the only treatment was bed rest, good nursing care, a light diet, the ingestion of lots of fluids and the use of laxatives if necessary. Not until the year 1943 was the first pracitcal vaccine against the flu developed.

During the American flu epidemic of 1890 the death rate was highest among the middle-aged and elderly, but in 1918 the chief victims were young adults—those between the ages of twenty and forty. Dr. Warren T. Vaughan, acting surgeon general of the army, said, "The husky male either made a speedy and rather rapid recovery or was likely to die.

Nature overdoes the resistance, kills the invading organisms too rapidly and sets free such an amount of poison that death occurs. . . . Infection, like war, kills the young, vigorous, robust adults."

Thomas Wolfe, who later became a major American novelist, was eighteen and a student at the University of North Carolina at Chapel Hill in the fall of 1918 when his mother wired: COME HOME AT ONCE. BEN HAS PNEUMONIA. Ben was Wolfe's elder brother and hero. Wolfe hurried back to his home town of Asheville, and when he reached the boardinghouse his mother ran, he found that Ben was dying. Pneumonia had developed in both lungs. Ben had not received the proper kind of care, for which the other children blamed their mother During postmortems it was a commonplace for doctors to talk about "wet lungs" or "dripping lungs," and now Wolfe heard the family physician say of Ben, "Not all the doctors and nurses in the world can help him now. . . . He's drowning! Drowning!"

In time to come Thomas Wolfe referred to Ben's death as the most tragic experience of his life, and in his novel *Look Homeward, Angel* he recorded his horror in one of the most moving passages he ever wrote:

> . . . Then, over the ugly clamor of their dissention, over the rasp and snarl of their nerves, they heard the low mutter of Ben's expiring breath. The light had been re-shaded; he lay, like his own shadow, in all his fierce gray lonely beauty. And as they looked and saw his bright eyes already blurred with death, and saw the feeble beating flutter of his poor thin breast, the strange wonder, the dark rich miracle of his life surged over them in its enormous loveliness. They grew quiet and calm, they plunged below all the splintered wreckage of their lives, they drew together in a superb communion of love and valiance, beyond horror and confusion, beyond death. And Eugene's eyes grew blind with love and wonder; an enormous organ-music sounded in his heart, he possessed them for a moment, he was a part of their loveliness, his life soared magnificently out of the slough of pain and ugliness. He thought: "That was not all! That really was not all!" . . . The rattling in the wasted body, which seemed for hours to have given over to death all of life that is worth saving, had now ceased. The body appeared to grow rigid before them. . . . But suddenly, marvellously, as if his resurrection and rebirth had come upon him, Ben drew upon the air in a long and powerful respiration; his gray eyes opened. Filled with a terrible vision of all life in the one moment, he seemed to rise forward bodilessly from his pillows without support—a flame, a light, a glory—joined at length in death to the dark spirit who had brooded upon each footstep of his lonely adventure on earth; and, casting the fierce sword of his glance with utter and final comprehension upon the room haunted with its gray pageantry of cheap loves and dull consciences and on all those uncertain mummers of waste and confusion fading now from the bright windows of his eyes, he passed instantly, scornful and unafraid, as he had lived, into the shades of death.

The worst plague ever to afflict mankind was the Black Death of 1347–51 that killed 75,000,000 people. The second worst was the influenza pandemic of 1918–19, which took 21,640,000 human lives. In Spain 80 percent of the population fell sick. In the United States almost 1 out of every 4 persons was stricken, and a total of 500,000 Americans died. Forty-six of the forty-eight states were affected, thirty-six being especially hard hit. Across the country the death rate became fifty times greater than usual. In Philadelphia the death rate soared 700 percent above normal. In New York City more than 19,000 died of the flu. In Baltimore, day after day, the *Sun* published five and six columns of death notices.

The daily routine of life flickered and faded and finally seemed like a slow-motion sequence in a film. The frightful disease affected commerce, industry, show business, education, cultural events, elections, the war program—everything. It killed half as many soldiers as fell in battle in France. Because it was so very contagious, people were afraid to leave their homes and mingle with others. Whole families were wiped out within a few days. Weddings were postponed. Conventions were canceled. Out-of-town buyers stayed away from Manhattan. So many workers were stricken, or afraid to go to their jobs, that there was a decrease in the production of coal and ships and trucks and many other commodities.

German propagandists published a story saying that flu victims lay in heaps on the sidewalks of New York, and although this was an exaggeration, the reality was terrifying. In Queens, one of the five boroughs of the city, so many gravediggers came down with the flu that in some cemeteries the dead lay unburied so long that at last the mayor ordered city engineers to use heavy equipment to scoop out graves. Baltimore ran out of coffins. Chicago ran out of hearses. The Cook county coroner asked Chicago transit officials to drape trolley cars in black and use them as makeshift hearses.

In the national capital the Senate and House closed their galleries to everyone except reporters; parades and Liberty Loan rallies were outlawed, all schools closed, and the United States Supreme Court adjourned to avoid bringing lawyers to what Justice Holmes called "this crowded and infected place." The flu felled half the workers of Herbert Hoover's food administration. The entire District of Columbia was declared a "sanitary zone." With a patient in every bed in every hospital in Washington, and with new admissions being placed on cots and mattresses on the floors of hospital corridors, the only way to make room for still more patients was to station undertakers at hospital doors ready to remove bodies as fast as the victims died. Congress appropriated $1,000,000 to fight the pandemic, while the Red Cross allocated $575,000.

When the district's health officer learned that sorrowing families were being overcharged for funerals, he lashed out at what he called "the coffin trust." A young woman who had left Oklahoma to work in the war capital died. Two girlfriends had her body prepared for shipment back home, then learned to their anguish that the bill came to $350—or more than their combined salaries for an entire month.

The district health officer got a tip from a railway dispatcher that the Washington railroad terminal had two carloads of coffins consigned to Pittsburgh; breaking several laws, he commandeered the entire shipment for the District of Columbia. Philadelphia had a shortage of coffins until a firm that manufactured streetcars turned to the production of coffins in its woodworking shop. The acting health commissioner of Buffalo, New York, announced that the city would make its own coffins. Angrily he added, "They will not be $1000 caskets or even $100 caskets. They will be plain, with plain handles, and respectable . . . the casket business is a worse trust than oil. The health department will make them and will sell them at cost to the families needing them and will give them to the families of the poor."

Some Philadelphia cemeteries collected $15 burial fees from the families of flu victims and then said they would have to dig the graves themselves. A few Philadelphia druggists charged $52.40 a gallon for prescription whiskey—it being a widely held belief that booze helped or cured the flu. The mayor of New York City heard so many complaints about overcharging by druggists and doctors that he issued a public warning declaring that with the help of newspapers he would "pin upon them a badge of shame that will last longer than their ill-gotten gains." In Atlanta, Georgia, landlords evicted tenants simply because they had been taken ill; an army officer was turned out of his Peachtree Street apartment with a fever of 103 degrees. H. L. Mencken, the so-called Sage of Baltimore, listened in horror to the crunch of undertakers' wagons trundling past his home.

The federal government quarantined the Mexican border. The Boston Stock Exchange closed. The New York Public Library stopped circulating books. In California the famous Santa Barbara mission shut its doors for the first time in its history. East St. Louis authorities locked every public building, including churches. George Cardinal Mundelein of Chicago prohibited long masses and long sermons in his diocese. James Cardinal Gibbons of Baltimore banned public funerals for all Catholic victims. In some cities everyone who went out in public had to wear a gauze mask over his mouth and nose. Some streetcar conductors refused to pick up any passengers without masks. In San Francisco a cabdriver picked up three men wearing gauze masks who robbed him.

The New York *Times* urged its readers to make no unnecessary phone calls because of the illness of 2,000 of the city's telephone operators. Service on the New York Central Railroad worsened because so many crew members were laid up with the flu. Omaha's packing plants had to try to get along with nearly a third of their workers missing. A boxing promoter canceled a fight that would have starred Jack Dempsey. Hollywood suspended all movie production for three weeks, and as klieg lights flickered off in one studio after another, some pessimists croaked that this was the end of the film industry.

A lot of people said they knew how to cure the flu

An Englishman recommended snuff. In Walter Reed hospital in Washington word got around that chewing tobacco was the thing, so many soldiers bit and chewed and choked and spat. In Georgia an elderly doctor suggested sprinkling sulfur in one's shoes. In Oklahoma another physician urged removal of the tonsils and pulling all the teeth. In Chicago a snake charmer attracted a large crowd, and then a con man extolled the virtues of "Spanish Influenza Remedy." Other alleged remedies were Borden's malted milk, Gude's Pepto-Mangan and Phez—Pure Juice of the Loganberry."

A Cleveland woman wrote to War Secretary Baker, "Cut up two large onions and add to them rye flour until there is formed a thick paste; make it into a cake, wrap it in a thin white cloth and apply it to the chest." From a man in Leavenworth, Kansas, the war department received a telegram advising, "Rinse the mouth with lime water, inhale hot water and turpentine fumes." Some Minnesota and Michigan physicians believed the only cure was plenty of fresh air, so chilled and aching flu patients were wheeled onto porches overlooking snowscapes.

In a letter to the New York *Herald* a Boston doctor recommended nudity. A Pasadena woman announced, "The formula is this—saturate a piece of cotton or small clean white rag if cotton is not available, with alcohol, adding three drops of chloroform and place between the patient's teeth, letting him inhale the fumes of the alcohol and chloroform."

At last Rupert Blue, the surgeon general of the United States, felt it necessary to issue this warning: "The Health Service urges the public to remember that there is as yet no specific cure for influenza and that many of the alleged cures and remedies now being recommended by neighbors, nostrum vendors and others do more harm than good."

An Omaha printer, Anton Schneckenberger, nursed his sick wife and nine children and then said, "My wife had made careful charts for each child, listing on them the medicine for each, the time of taking and a place for all kinds of records. Five took one kind of cough medicine and . . . three took another kind. The charts enabled me to keep from getting the medicines mixed up. I used ice water and cloths and three ice bags at their heads, and hot water bottles at their feet. From Saturday night until Tuesday noon I had only two hours rest. By the time I would reach the last, the first would want something." In Philadelphia a social worker found a man dead in bed, and nearby lay his flu-ravaged wife, who had delivered herself of twins with no assistance and then managed to survive on a single apple.

One of the most pitiful results of the plague were the children orphaned when both parents succumbed to the disease. In New York City alone more than 400 children survived their fathers and mothers and had to be cared for by city officials. Mary McCarthy, who lived to become a major American writer, was six years old and living in Seattle. Both her parents died of the flu. Later she wrote:

> We, my three younger brothers and I, spent five years together in Minneapolis, in the custody of a severe great-aunt and her sadistic husband. Two blocks away, my McCarthy grandparents, dwelling in sumptuous middleclass style, instilled in us the contrast between wealth and penury by occasional treats and vacations; it was thought beneficial that we should know we were orphans and fitted for a different destiny than our well-tended

cousins. Today, some of my relations allege my literary successes and my brother Kevin's career as an actor as proof that the harsh formula followed in our upbringing produced results; nevertheless, I cannot feel grateful. Nor do I believe that artistic talent flowers necessarily from a wounding of the stem on which it grows, as in some gardening-operation where a plant is slashed to make it branch.

In an article for the *Encyclopaedia Britannica* a professor wrote that "of insanities traceable to influenza, melancholia is twice as frequent as all other forms put together." He noted that in the flu epidemic in Paris in 1890 the suicide rate rose by 25 percent. William James once speculated about the relationship between sanity and body temperature. In 1918 everyone who came down with the flu became feverish, and when the fever reached 104 or 105 degrees, the patients became deranged.

This time there was a tripling of the suicide rate in France. In Winthrop, Massachusetts, a man, his wife and their three children were stricken, and his fever turned him into a madman. Someone called the police, who had to fight to lace him into a straitjacket so they could take him to a hospital. In Washington, D.C., a telephone worker was alone for three days with a burning fever, tried unsuccessfully to kill himself by slashing his throat, then managed to take his life by jumping out a window.

Something like this happened to Edgar Ansel Mowrer, a foreign correspondent for the Chicago *Daily News*. He and his wife caught the flu in Padua, Italy, and his infection turned into pneumonia. In his memoirs Mowrer described what happened:

> Then began our purgatory. . . . [An American Red Cross nurse, acting on a doctor's orders] continued to excite me with more caffein . . . my brain grew more wildly active . . . great resolutions began to form in me. Was I afraid to die? Or only afraid of suffering, of the pain in my chest, of the fiery applications? My death was certain. But let it come all at once, not slowly, with padded lungs and a sleepless racing heart! At this point something occurred to decide me.
>
> Suddenly a great coughing shook me, causing me unspeakable pain. Out of my lips shot a clot of greenish mucus. I stared at it there on the pillow. God, anything was better than slow corporeal deliquescence, anything . . . even death.
>
> That was it: suicide was what I had been thinking of. It was so easy; you just pierced your throat beside the glottis and out on the red stream from the gaping jugular you hurried forth into oblivion. Or you blew out your brains with a revolver (but I no longer had a revolver). Or you drown—that was it! A mere washbasin would do, just enough water to cover the nose and mouth, a little will-power.
>
> Giddy but determined, I arose from the soiled pillow and tottered into the dressing-room. (How good the marble floor felt to feverish feet!) You turned a faucet, and when the basin was full you plunged in your face and breathed the waters of release! I

> tried hard. Twice I drew the liquid in through my nostrils; but then my nerve failed me; I raised my head and choking, crying with disappointment, I returned to the bed. I lacked the courage of suicide. And by my mad act, I had doubtless spoiled what little chance I might previously have had of recovering. What humiliation! I had loaned my revolver, but there were my paper clipping scissors, and I could reach my jugular.
>
> Just then Lilian came in and, like a maniac, I told her I had decided to take my life; whereupon I again got out of bed. She wrestled with me a minute and threw me back, telling me, I do not know in what words, of her two dreams and how God could not betray me . . . would save me.

Some of the most important people in the world came down with the flu. King George V of Great Britain and his prime minister, David Lloyd George, were stricken but survived. Kaiser Wilhelm II of Germany fell ill at his headquarters in France. King Alfonso XIII of Spain was put to bed with a fever of 102.2 degrees. Georges Clemenceau lost a son to the disease. General Pershing was kept in bed several days, but he continued to work hard over a formula demanding the unconditional surrender of the Germans. Death took Ezra bin Abbas, heir apparent to the khedive of Egypt. Dr. Sigmund Freud suffered in his home in Vienna. Elsie Janis, an actress who entertained American troops in France, went to bed with infected lungs. Mrs. Wellington Koo, the wife of the Chinese ambassador to the United States, died in Washington. Samuel Gompers, president of the American Federation of Labor, lost the apple of his eye—his twenty-three-year-old daughter Sadie.

Another victim was Jacob Edwin Meeker, a Republican Congressman from Missouri. In October, 1918, he left the national capital and returned to his home state to look into the need for more gauze masks for sick soldiers at Jefferson Barracks. There he was stricken with the flu. For several months the forty-year-old Representative had been engaged to his secretary, Mrs. Alice V. Redmon, a widow with four children, but their wedding had been postponed again and again because of war work and politics. Meeker now lay critically ill in Jewish hospital in St. Louis. A doctor took Mrs. Redmon aside to say that her betrothed was not likely to live another day. Bursting into tears, she sobbed that she wanted to marry him anyway. So the wedding was held at his bedside with the bride and judge and doctors and nurses wearing hospital gowns. A mask covered the mouth of the dying Congressman, who panted so hard he was hardly able to make the proper responses. The couple were pronounced man and wife, and seven hours later he died.

Franklin Roosevelt had gone to Europe on an inspection tour. On September 8, 1918, he reached Brest, France, to sail back to the United States. Flu was raging through Brest when he arrived, and he stood in a chilling rain at a funeral before boarding ship. Roosevelt, who had driven himself hard while abroad and not got enough sleep, walked into his cabin and collapsed.

Besides the flu, he was suffering from double pneumonia and

threatened by suffocation from the congestion in his lungs and bronchial tubes. So many other passengers had also been taken ill that the ship was like a floating hospital. Several died during the voyage home and were buried at sea. And FDR almost died in the middle of the Atlantic.

A message was wired to his family in New York City, and his wife and mother arranged to have an ambulance waiting at the dock to speed him to his mother's house at 47 East Sixty-fifth Street, his own adjoining house having been rented. There he stayed in bed a long time, his wife taking care of his correspondence, and it was because of this that Eleanor Roosevelt found letters proving that her husband was having an affair with a woman named Lucy Mercer.

Another kind of sorrow came to George W. Perkins, the millionaire and politician who had played such an important role at both the Progressive and Republican conventions in Chicago in 1916. His son, also named George, had married Katherine Trowbridge, a daughter of the head of the physics department at Princeton University. The banker became extremely fond of his daughter-in-law. Young Perkins entered the army and was sent overseas, while his wife remained with her mother in the family home in Princeton, New Jersey; her father was also in the service and away from home. By this time Katherine was pregnant.

In September, 1918, as her confinement neared, Perkins telephoned her almost every day from his home in Riverdale, New York. Because his wife was in Oregon visiting a married daugher, and he was all alone in his Riverdale mansion, Perkins had asked Katherine to come visit him and she said she would do so on Monday, September 30. But that day her mother called Perkins to say that Katherine had a bad cold and planned to stay in bed. On Tuesday she became feverish. Wednesday her temperature became normal again, but by Thursday it was obvious that she was a very sick girl.

Mrs. Trowbridge was unable to find a nurse in Princeton because many nurses had entered the military and because the others were busy taking care of flu victims. The worried mother telephoned Perkins to ask for his help. In New York he found not only a nurse, but a doctor as well, and drove them to Princeton. By this time Katherine had a fever of 103 and had developed pneumonia. Perkins, a man usually obsessed with profits and power, now forgot everything in his passion to save the life of his beloved daughter-in-law and his unborn grandchild. Remaining at the Trowbridge home, he sent to New York for a second nurse and another specialist. He also obtained oxygen tanks and other medical supplies. Nothing helped. Seven months pregnant, Katherine died on October 7.

The banker was torn apart by grief. He had never been a particularly introspective or emotional man, but now that he had lost this lovely daughter-in-law he saw life in a different light. To his son he wrote letters that may have been clumsy, since Perkins knew nothing of felicitous phrasing, but letters nonetheless powerful because of their raw honesty and leaden sorrow. "I feel as though a great line or deep mark has been made in my life. . . . It cannot be that women with Spirits like my mother and your dear wife can die. . . . Each hour I say to myself more & more often, that there *must* be a plan in it all. . . ."

The flu caused havoc not only in the civilian population but also created a crisis in the military, spreading from one training camp to another, attacking sailors aboard ship, felling soldiers being transported to France, infecting thousands in the American Expeditionary Force. From his French headquarters General Pershing kept calling for more and more fighting men, but so many fell ill in the United States that it was impossible to give him all he wanted.

The horrors of the plague were described by Dr. Rufus Cole at Camp Devens near Boston:

> . . . It was cold and drizzling rain, and there was a continuous line of men coming [into the hospital] from the various barracks, carrying their blankets, many of the men looking extremely ill, most of them [blue] and coughing. There were not enough nurses, and the poor boys were putting themselves to bed on cots, which overflowed out of the wards on the porches. We made some inquiries about the cases, went to the laboratory, and then down to the autopsy room. Owing to the rush and the great numbers of bodies coming into the morgue, they were placed on the floor without any order or system, and we had to step amongst them to get into the room where an autopsy was going on.
>
> When the chest was opened and the blue, swollen lungs were removed and opened and Dr. Welch saw the wet, foamy surfaces with little real consolidation, he turned and said, "This must be some new kind of infection or plague," and he was quite excited and obviously very nervous. . . . It was not surprising that the rest of us were disturbed, but it shocked me to find that the situation, momentarily at least, was too much even for Dr. Welch.

At Camp Dodge, Iowa, medical officers wrestled with the problem of trying to fit 8,000 patients into a 2,000-bed hospital. At Camp Meade, Maryland, more than 11,000 soldiers—a fourth of the complement—became totally disabled, and every twenty-four hours 1,500 new flu cases were reported. At Camp Grant, Illinois, 10,713 soldiers—a third of all the men stationed there—tossed feverishly in the base hospital, infirmaries and barracks; German prisoners held at the camp were not infected.

At Camp Fremont, California, a gritty silence prevailed; no one could leave camp, use the telephone or even write letters home. An absolute quarantine was imposed upon the 4,000 men stationed at the naval training station on Goat Island in San Francisco Bay; they marched at a distance from one another, slept twenty feet apart, telephones were swabbed with alcohol, and once an hour drinking fountains were sterilized with blowtorches.

Relatives and friends worried about their young men in camps and bases scattered throughout the country. Senator La Follette wrote an anxious letter to his son Philip, a second lieutenant stationed at Norman,

Oklahoma: "You are in my mind these days when I am here all by myself. You seem a long way off—alone among strangers. Won't you arrange with someone there upon whom I can depend to *wire me* if you should happen to get sick—and *to do it promptly*. You will poo poo this—but do it just for my comfort."

Chief of Staff Peyton March wired General Pershing: EPIDEMIC HAS NOT ONLY QUARANTINED NEARLY ALL CAMPS BUT HAS FORCED US TO CANCEL OR SUSPEND NEARLY ALL DRAFT CALLS. In the camps in this country the number of deaths began to match the numbers of men falling in battle overseas. The flu halted almost all activity at two coast guard stations and made invalids of 60 percent of the members of a machine-gun battalion at Camp Funston, Kansas. At most military posts in the United States the epidemic lasted an average of five weeks. A field artillery regiment that departed from Fort Sill, Oklahoma, to head to New York City to embark for France left its dead and dying at almost every railway station through which it passed.

An infantry regiment left a staging area near Yonkers, New York, marched through the town to the Hudson river to board ferries that would take the men to Hoboken, New Jersey, where they were scheduled to board the *Leviathan* for the voyage to France, and what happened to them has been described by Colonel E. W. Gibson:

> We had proceeded but a short distance when it was discovered that the men were falling out of ranks, unable to keep up. The attention of the commanding officer was called to the situation. The column was halted and the camp surgeon was summoned. The examination showed that the dreaded influenza had hit us. Although many men had fallen out, we were ordered to resume the march. We went forward up and up over the winding moonlit road leading to Alpine Landing on the Hudson where ferry boats were waiting to take us to Hoboken. The victims of the epidemic fell on either side of the road, unable to carry their heavy packs. Some threw their equipment away and with determination tried to keep up with their comrades. Army trucks and ambulances, following, picked up those who had fallen and took them back to the camp hospital.

The rest of the men of the 57th pioneer infantry regiment were herded onto the *Leviathan*, which then sailed for Brest.

> The ship was packed [the colonel wrote] and conditions were such that the influenza bacillus could breed and multiply with extraordinary swfitness. We went much of the way without convoy. The U-boat menace made it necessary to keep every port hole closed at night, and the air below decks where the men slept was hot and heavy. The number of sick increased rapidly.
>
> Washington was apprised of the situation, but the call for men for the Allied armies was so great that we must go at any cost. The sick bay became overcrowded and it became necessary to evacuate the greater portion of Deck E and turn that into sick

> quarters. Doctors and nurses were stricken. Every available doctor and nurse was utilized to the limit of endurance. The conditions during the night cannot be visualized by anyone who had not actually seen them . . . groans and cries of the terrified added to the confusion of the applicants clamoring for treatment, and altogether a true inferno reigned supreme.

The same sad scene was reenacted on other troopships bound for Europe. When the *Olympic* docked in Southampton, England, of the soldiers aboard her 2,300 had the flu and 119 had died during the voyage. General Pershing finally admitted:

> Influenza in the Army had assumed very serious proportions, over 16,000 cases additional having been reported during the week ending October 5th. Large numbers of cases were brought in by our troop ships. The total number of cases of influenza treated in hospitals was nearly 70,000, of whom many developed a grave form of pneumonia. The death rate from influenza rose now to 32 per cent of cases for the A.E.F. and was as high as 80 per cent in some groups.

American Expeditionary Force hospitals overflowed with more flu patients than battle casualties. The plague killed 25,000 American soldiers. This was almost half as many as the 52,429 soldiers who died in battle. The flu did not change the course of the war itself since it crippled Allied and enemy armies in about equal proportions. But the navy suffered more than the army. The navy, with only about a tenth of the men in the army, lost 5,000 sailors to the disease. At the peak of the plague more than 120,000 officers and sailors were stricken—nearly a fourth of the navy's personnel.

On October 6, 1917, the United States government had offered life insurance to every soldier, sailor, marine, coast guardsman, aviator and nurse. By law, none had to sign up for a policy but pressure to do so was exerted by officers. The insurance could be obtained in multiples of $500 for any amount from $1,000 to $10,000 at a premium ranging from 63 cents a month per $1,000 to $3.35. An officer of the Metropolitan Life Insurance Company said, "When Uncle Sam put a value of $10,000 on the life of a buck private, it woke a lot of people up."

Nearly twelve times more servicemen took out life insurance than had been predicted by the government. When Pershing learned from Treasury Secretary McAdoo that they had bought $19 billion worth of policies, he cabled the secretary: ALL RANKS OF THE A.E.F. APPRECIATE DEEPLY THE GENEROUS MEASURES THE GOVERNMENT HAS TAKEN TO PROVIDE INSURANCE FOR THEIR FAMILIES, IN PROOF OF WHICH MORE THAN 90 PER CENT OF THE MEN HAVE TAKEN OUT INSURANCE.

At the peak of the flu pandemic the Metropolitan Life Insurance Company received 5,000 to 6,000 claims a day—far more than usually arrived in a single week. Every few hours a wicker truck the size of a desk was trundled out of the mail department, laden with claims. So many company claim approvers were in the military that the claims department was shorthanded; once it was six weeks behind in its work. Not since the San Francisco earthquake and fire of 1906 had such a wave of claims swept over the insurance companies of the world. And in the end they paid more money to the beneficiaries of flu victims than to the survivors of our men killed in battle.

The influenza pandemic of 1918–19 killed more than 21,000,000 people around the world, or more than 1 percent of the world's population, and 10,000,000 more than lost their lives in the war itself.

Epilogue

Suddenly it was all over.

An armistice took effect at 11 A.M. on November 11, 1918, and on the wasted fields of a dozen widely scattered fronts the last soldier died, the last gun belched, the thunder of war boomed for the last time. Where all had been noise there now was a voice. For a moment mankind held its breath. The people of the earth went numb in this prayed-for hour and then opened smothered throats and screamed in relief.

When news of the armistice reached a Prussian hospital, a wounded soldier named Adolf Hitler threw himself onto his bed to weep and swear revenge. In military terms the Allied Powers had defeated the Central Powers and saved the world from the awful evil of Prussian militarism. In human terms, however, no one won and everyone lost. The butchered flesh and blasted property and wasted dollars and withered hopes were a price almost too high to pay. In a very real sense it had been a world war, since it was fought not only by armies in the field, but by entire populations who devoted their lives and muscles and minds and goods to the destruction of the enemy on the land, in the air, on the sea and beneath it.

World War I was the bloodiest in the history of mankind. The death toll was twice the total of all casualties in all wars between 1790 and 1913. In the worst single battle, the first battle of the Somme in 1916, more than 1,030,000 soldiers became casualties. The battle of Meuse-Argonne in 1918 was the equivalent of seven Gettysburgs.

The statistics were staggering: 65,000,000 men under arms; 30,000,000 engaged in combat; 12,000,000 killed or missing; 20,000,000 wounded; 21,000,000 dead of the flu; 4,000,000 civilians massacred.

Although the American forces took fewer casualties than the Allied nations of Russia, France, Great Britain and Italy, 50,000 doughboys died in combat, 230,000 were wounded, 63,000 died of disease, 4,500 were taken prisoner. Mere figures—except to mothers who lost sons, wives who lost husbands, children who lost fathers. Only an abstraction—except to American veterans who had lost both arms and both legs and cynically called themselves the Oysters.

The 1,563 days of the war cost all the belligerents $331 billion. During the first two years alone they spent more than twice as much as the total cost of all the other wars waged in the nineteenth and twentieth centuries. During the one year, seven months and five days the United States was at war it spent $35 billion—ten times more than the Civil War and as much every two days as the entire cost of the Revolutionary War.

The editor of a journal named *The Scholastic* figured that the total cost of the war could have furnished:

1. Every family in Britain, France, Belgium, Germany, Russia, Canada, Australia and the United States with a $500 one-acre lot holding a $2,500 house filled with $1,000 worth of furniture;
2. A $5,000,000 library for every city of 200,000 inhabitants in each of these countries;
3. A $10,000,000 library for every such community;
4. A fund that at 5 percent interest would yield indefinitely enough money to pay $1,000 a year to 125,000 teachers and 125,000 nurses;
5. Still enough money left to buy all property and all wealth in France and Belgium.

In one of the great pendulum swings of history the war shifted the balance of power from Europe to the United States. It changed the political map of Europe. It toppled three empires—the German, the Rusian, the Austro-Hungarian. It deposed two kings—the king of Bulgaria and the king of Greece. It created seven new republics—Austria, Hungary, Czechoslovakia, Poland, Finland, Lithuania and Estonia. It spawned Communism in Russia, Fascism in Italy, Nazism in Germany. It revolutionized the nature of warfare. It elevated businessmen and scientists to the priesthood of a materialistic society. It launched a tidal wave of political, social and economic changes that finally crashed over the earth in World War II.

Because of the war Americans burst beyond the horizon to make their presence felt abroad as never before. Of the 4,000,000 Americans mustered into service, 2,000,000 were sent overseas and 1,000,000 engaged in combat. Those posted to distant lands saw places and people so strange that they suffered culture shock, for they learned that their way of doing things was not the only way. As a result, they lost their parochial viewpoint, and although they matured a little, they hardly became overnight sophisticates—despite a popular song that asked how you gonna keep 'em down on the farm after they've seen Paree?

Apart from the damage done by German saboteurs and the German submarine attack on the coast of Massachusetts, the United States suffered none of the physical ravages of war, while much of Belgium and France was left as pitted and barren as the moon.

But ordinary Americans were taxed more heavily than ever before, and some had their savings sunk by inflation, while thousands of profiteers became millionaires and corporations emerged stronger than in the past. The United States revolutionized its banking system, changed from a debtor nation to a creditor nation, became the financial center of the world, lent more than $8 billion to the Allies. Domestic finance became ever more entwined with international finance. In Europe all credit was exhausted, national debts multiplied, currencies were devalued, and the vanquished peoples were saddled with heavy indemnities—but between 1914 and 1920 American wealth increased two and a half times.

Americans had fought and worked and sacrificed and saved to win a war to end all war and make the world safe for democracy—so they thought. On armistice day they were told by President Wilson, "Everything for which America fought has been accomplished." This was far from the truth. Actually, the war weakened democracy. It turned Wilson into a dictator—benign, for the most part, but nonetheless a dictator. It centralized government. It strengthened authoritarianism. It created the military-industrial complex. It paralyzed the progressive movement. It undermined religion. It ironed the interesting wrinkles of individuality into flat conformity. It brutalized minds. It seared souls.

Soon after the war Wilson wanted the United States to join the League of Nations, then in the process of being organized, since he regarded it as a guarantor of peace. When the Senate divided on the issue of joining, the President took his case to the people, traveling across the country to make a series of speeches. On September 5, 1919, addressing an audience in St. Louis, he said:

> . . . Why, my fellow citizens, is there any man here or any woman, let me say is there any child here who does not know that the seed of war in the modern world is industrial and commercial rivalry? The real reason that the war that we have just finished took place was that Germany was afraid her commercial rivals were going to get the better of her, and the reason why some nations went into the war against Germany was that they thought Germany would get the commercial advantage of them. The seed of the jealousy, the seed of the deep-seated hatred was hot, successful commercial and industrial rivalry.

The peoples of blood-soaked Europe sank back exhausted, but in the United States, which had entered combat so late in the day, the passion of patriotism and poison of propaganda had done their work all too well. The Europeans were overwhelmed, Americans unsatisfied. Emotionally, the war had ended too soon for Americans. They had focused their hatred on the unspeakable Huns—but now this target had been snatched away from them. They continued to quiver with hatred, with the tension of surplus energy seeking some outlet, and became like a keg of dynamite left near a hot stove. Energy can burst outwardly in an explosion or inwardly in an implosion. When they exploded, they exploded both ways. In need of new targets for their undischarged fury, Americans found an external enemy in the Bolsheviks and an internal enemy in domestic radicals and nonconformists.

The war altered the consciousness of all mankind. Most people had assumed that the world was rational, but an entire world at war was obviously a world gone mad. Most had considered man reasonable, but the war demonstrated that passions are stronger than reason. Whatever their religion, most people had believed God to be a just deity, but the slaughter was so senseless that God Himself became a casualty of war. Progress was not inevitable, after all. Peace was not permanent. The perfectability of man was brought into question.

It is the common condition of mankind to prefer illusions to reality because raw reality is too painful to bear, but the war stripped away one illusion after another, exposing the very soul of man, and then it became obvious that man's image of himself and his essence are nothing alike. People were disappointed with the world, their leaders, themselves. They suffered psychic shock—almost fatal shock. Trying to protect what was left of their sanity, they reacted in terms of their individual personalities, retreating into sadness, apathy, sensuality, cynicism. A few even embraced madness as a way of life. In Zurich in 1916 some artists and writers launched a movement called Dadaism, a cultural counterpart of political anarchy, a nihilistic philosophy that ridiculed civilization and glorified irrationality.

No, reality was not at all what most people had thought it was before the war. Now they were forced to look at life through a new prism. Now some realized that the future itself had been changed. It was argued by historians such as Brooks Adams of the United States, Arnold Toynbee of England and Oswald Spengler of Germany, that World War I marked the beginning of the decline of Western civilization. Perhaps civilization is like an organism in that it is born, blooms, decays, then dies. Perhaps the future was to be a long slide into revolutions ending in wars and wars ending in revolutions, the clamping of iron controls upon the masses by the classes, the rich getting richer and the poor getting restless, a rising tide of color, a titanic clash between East and West, an almost endless era of tyranny and imperialism and domestic conflicts.

Selected Bibliography

ADAMS, BROOKS, *The Law of Civilization and Decay*. New York, Alfred A. Knopf, 1951.
ADAMS, FRANKLIN P., *The Diary of Our Own Samuel Pepys*. New York, Simon and Schuster, 1935. 2 vols.
ADAMS, JAMES TRUSLOW, *The March of Democracy*. New York, Charles Scribner's Sons, 1932. 2 vols.
———, *The Epic of America*. Boston, Little, Brown, 1933.
———, ed., *Dictionary of American History*. New York, Charles Scribner's Sons, 1940. 7 vols.
ALLEN, FREDERICK LEWIS, *The Big Change: America Transforms Itself, 1900–1950*. New York, Bantam Books, 1961.
ALPERT, HOLLIS, *The Barrymores*. New York, Dial, 1964.
Americana Annual, 1923. New York, Encyclopedia Americana Corp., 1923.
American Year Book, 1913–1920. New York, Independent Corp.
ANGLE, PAUL M., *The American Reader*. New York, Rand McNally, 1958.
Annals of America. Chicago, Encyclopaedia Britannica, Inc., 1968. 18 vols.
Army Almanac (no editor named). Harrisburg, Pa., Stackpole Co., 1959.
ASBURY, HERBERT, *The French Quarter*. New York, Alfred A. Knopf, 1936.

BAKER, LIVA, *Felix Frankfurter*. New York, Coward-McCann, 1969.
BARNHART, CLARENCE L., *The New Century Cyclopedia of Names*. New York, Appleton-Century-Crofts, 1954. 3 vols.
BARUCH, BERNARD M., *Baruch: The Public Years*. New York, Rinehart and Winston, 1960.
BATES, ERNEST SUTHERLAND, *The Story of Congress, 1789–1935*. New York, Harper & Brothers, 1936.
BEARD, CHARLES A, and BEARD, MARY R., *The Rise of American Civilization*. New York, Macmillan, 1930.
———, *A Basic History of the United States*. Philadelphia, Blakiston Co., 1944.
BELL, H. C. F., *Woodrow Wilson and the People*. Garden City, Doubleday, Doran, 1945.

BERGMAN, PETER M., *The Chronological History of the Negro in America*. New York, Harper & Row, 1969.

BERKY, ANDREW S., and SHENTON, JAMES P., eds., *The Historians' History of the United States*. New York, G. P. Putnam's Sons, 1966. 2 vols.

BERNSTEIN, JOSEPH M., *Writings and Speeches of Eugene V. Debs*. New York, Hermitage Press, 1948.

BINING, ARTHUR CECIL, *A History of the United States*. New York, Charles Scribner's Sons, 1950. 2 vols.

BINKLEY, WILFRED E., and MOOS, MALCOLM C., *A Grammar of American Politics*. New York, Alfred A. Knopf, 1949.

Biographical Directory of the American Congress, 1774–1949. Washington, United States Government Printing Office, 1950.

BISHOP, JOSEPH BUCKLIN, *Theodore Roosevelt and His Time*. New York, Charles Scribner's Sons, 1920. 2 vols.

BLUM, JOHN M., *Joe Tumulty and the Wilson Era*. Boston, Houghton Mifflin, 1951.

BOWERS, CLAUDE G., *Beveridge and the Progressive Era*. New York, Literary Guild, 1932.

BOYER, RICHARD O., and MORAIS, HERBERT M., *Labor's Untold Story*. New York, Cameron Associates, 1955.

BRIDGWATER, WILLIAM, and SHERWOOD, ELIZABETH J., eds., *The Columbia Encyclopedia*. New York, Columbia University Press, 1952.

BRITTON, NAN, *The President's Daughter*. New York, Elizabeth Ann Guild, 1927.

BROOK-SHEPHERD, GORDON, *The Last Hapsburg*. New York, Weybright and Talley, 1968.

Brooklyn Daily Eagle Almanac, 1913–1920. New York, Brooklyn Daily Eagle.

BURKE, W.J., and HOWE, WILL D., *American Authors and Books*. New York, Gramercy Publishing Co., 1943.

BURNS, JAMES MACGREGOR, *Roosevelt: The Lion and the Fox*. New York, Harcourt Brace, 1956.

BUTLER, NICHOLAS MURRAY, *Across the Busy Years*. New York, Charles Scribner's Sons, 1940.

BUTTERFIELD, ROGER, *The American Past*. New York, Simon and Schuster, 1957.

CAMPBELL, JOSEPH, ed., *The Portable Jung*. New York, Viking, 1971.

CARLSON, OLIVER, *Brisbane: A Candid Biography*. New York, Stackpole Sons, 1937.

CARMAN, HARRY J., and SYRETT, HAROLD C., *A History of the American People*. New York, Alfred A. Knopf, 1952. 2 vols.

CARR, WILLIAM H. A., *The Du Ponts of Delaware*. New York, Dodd, Mead, 1964.

CARRUTH, GORTON, *The Encyclopedia of American Facts and Dates*. New York, Thomas Y. Crowell, 1959.

CHALMERS, DAVID M., *Hooded Americanism*. Garden City, Doubleday, 1965.

CHURCHILL, ALLEN, *The Improper Bohemians*. New York, E. P. Dutton, 1959.
———, *Over Here!* New York, Dodd, Mead, 1968.
CHURCHILL, WINSTON S., *The World Crisis*. Charles Scribner's Sons, 1949.
CLARKSON, GROSVENOR B., *Industrial America in the World War*. New York, Houghton Mifflin, 1923.
COBB, IRVIN S., *Exit Laughing*. Indianapolis, Bobbs-Merrill, 1941.
COFFMAN, EDWARD M., *The War to End All Wars*. New York, Oxford University Press, 1968.
COIT, MARGARET L., *Mr. Baruch*. Boston, Houghton Mifflin, 1957.
Collier's Encyclopedia. New York, Crowell Collier and Macmillan, 1966. 24 vols.
COMMAGER, HENRY STEELE, ed., *Documents of American History*. New York, Appleton-Century-Crofts, 196[illegible].
CONGDON, DON, ed., *Combat: World War I*. New York, Delacorte, 1964.
CONKLIN, GROFF, ed., *The New Republic Anthology, 1915–1935*. New York, Dodge, 1936.
COOPER, PAGE, *The Bellevue Story*. New York, Thomas Y. Crowell, 1948.
COWLES, VIRGINIA, *1913: An End and a Beginning*. New York, Harper & Row, 1967.
———, *The Russian Dagger*. New York, Harper & Row, 1969.
CRANSTON, RUTH, *The Story of Woodrow Wilson*. New York, Simon and Schuster, 1945.
CREEL, GEORGE, *Rebel at Large*. New York, G. P. Putnam's, 1947.
Current Biography, 1940–1973. New York, H. W. Wilson Co., 35. vols.

DANIELS, JOSEPHUS, *The Wilson Era*. Chapel Hill, University of North Carolina Press, 1946.
DARROW, CLARENCE, *The Story of My Life*. New York, Charles Scribner's Sons, 1934.
DAVIS, KENNETH S., *Soldier of Democracy: A Biography of Dwight Eisenhower*. Garden City, Doubleday, Doran, 1945.
———, *The Hero: Charles A. Lindbergh and the American Dream*. Garden City, Doubleday, 1959.
———, *FDR: the Beckoning of Destiny*. New York, G.P. Putnam's Sons, 1972.
DAWES, CHARLES G., *A Journal of the Great War*. Boston, Houghton Mifflin, 1921. 2 vols.
DAY, DONALD, ed., *Franklin D. Roosevelt's Own Story*. Boston, Little, Brown, 1951.
———, ed., *Woodrow Wilson's Own Story*. Boston, Little, Brown, 1952.
DENNIS, R. ETHEL, *The Black People of America*, New Haven, Readers Press, 1970.
DEWEERD, HARVEY A., President Wilson Fights His War. New York, Macmillan, 1968.
Dictionary of American Biography. New York, Charles Scribner's Sons, 1964. 12 vols.

DOS PASSOS, JOHN, *U.S.A.* New York, Houghton Mifflin, 1946. 3 vols.

———, *Mr. Wilson's War.* Garden City, Doubleday, 1962.

DULLES, FOSTER RHEA, *The United States Since 1865.* Ann Arbor, University of Michigan Press, 1959.

DUNNER, JOSEPH, ed., *Handbook of World History.* New York, Philosophical Library, 1967.

EASTMAN, MAX, *Enjoyment of Living.* New York, Harper & Brothers, 1948.

EATON, HERBERT, *Presidential Timber: A History of Nominating Conventions, 1868–1960.* New York, Free Press of Glencoe, 1964.

EDWARDS, PAUL, ed., *The Encyclopedia of Philosophy.* New York, Macmillan and the Free Press, 1967. 8 vols.

ELLIS, EDWARD ROBB, *The Epic of New York City.* New York, Coward-McCann, 1966.

Encyclopedia Americana. New York, Americana Corp., 1952. 30 vols.

Encyclopaedia Britannica. Chicago, Encyclopaedia Britannica, Inc., 1945. 24 vols.

Encyclopaedia Britannica, The New Volumes. New York, Encyclopaedia Britannica, Inc., 1922. 3 vols.

FADIMAN, CLIFTON, ed., *The American Treasury.* New York, Harper & Brothers, 1955.

FALLS, CYRIL, *The Great War.* New York, G.P. Putnam's Sons, 1959.

FAY, SIDNEY BRADSHAW, *The Origins of the World War.* New York, Macmillan, 1948.

Federal Writers' Project of the Works Progress Administration. Various states, various publishers, various years. 36 vols.

FIELD, CARTER, *Bernard Baruch: Park Bench Statesman.* NewYork, McGraw-Hill, 1944.

FLEISCHMAN, HARRY, *Norman Thomas.* New York, W. W. Norton, 1964.

Flexner, Abraham, An Autobiography. New York, Simon and Schuster, 1960.

FOSDICK, RAYMOND B., *John D. Rockefeller, Jr.: A Portrait.* New York, Harper & Brothers, 1956.

———, *Chronicle of a Generation.* New York, Harper & Brothers, 1958.

FOWLER, GENE, *Skyline.* New York, Harper & Brothers, 1962.

FRANKLIN, JOHN HOPE, *From Slavery to Freedom.* New York, Alfred A. Knopf, 1956.

FREDERICKS, PIERCE G., *The Great Adventure: America in the First World War.* New York, E.P. Dutton, 1960.

FREUD, ERNST L., *Letters of Sigmund Freud.* New York, Basic Books, 1960.

FREUD, SIGMUND, and BULLITT, WILLIAM C., *Thomas Woodrow Wilson, A Psychological Study.* Boston, Houghton Mifflin, 1966.

FRIED, ALBERT, ed., *A Day of Dedication: The Essential Writings & Speeches of Woodrow Wilson.* New York, Macmillan, 1965.

FURMAN, BESS, *White House Profile*. Indianapolis, Bobbs-Merrill, 1951.

FURNAS, J. C., *The Americans: A Social History of the United States, 1587–1914*. New York, G.P. Putnam's Sons, 1969.

GARRATY, John A., *Henry Cabot Lodge*. New York, Alfred A. Knopf, 1953.

———, *Right-Hand Man: The Life of George W. Perkins*. New York, Harper & Brothers, 1960.

GENTRY, CURT, *Frame-up: The Incredible Case of Tom Mooney and Warren Billings*. New York, W. W. Norton, 1967.

GEORGE, ALEXANDER L., and GEORGE, JULIETTE L., *Woodrow Wilson and Colonel House: A Personality Study*. New York, John Day, 1956.

GERHART, EUGENE C., *America's Advocate: Robert H. Jackson*. Indianapolis, Bobbs-Merrill, 1958.

GINGER, RAY, *The Bending Cross: A Biography of Eugene Victor Debs*. New Brunswick, Rutgers University Press, 1949.

GOLDMAN, EMMA, *Living My Life*. New York, Alfred A. Knopf, 1934.

GRAHAM, HUGH DAVIS, and GURR, TED ROBERT, eds., *The History of Violence in America*. New York, Frederick A. Praeger, 1969.

GRAMLING, OLIVER, *AP: The Story of News*. New York, Farrar and Rinehart, 1940.

GRAYSON, REAR ADMIRAL CARY T., *Woodrow Wilson: An Intimate Memoir*. New York, Rinehart and Winston, 1960.

GREEN, ABEL, and LAURIE, JOE, Jr., *Show Biz from Vaude to Video*. New York, Henry Holt, 1951.

GREW, JOSEPH C., *Turbulent Era*. Boston, Houghton Mifflin, 1952. 2 vols.

GRAYSON, REAR ADMIRAL CARY T., *Woodrow Wilson: An Intimate Memoir*. New York, Holt, Rinehart and Winston, 1960.

GUNTHER, JOHN, *Inside U.S.A.* New York, Harper & Brothers, 1946.

HACKER, LOUIS M., and KENDRICK, BENJAMIN B., *The United States Since 1865*. New York, F. S. Crofts, 1932.

HAGEDORN, HERMANN, *Leonard Wood*. New York, Harper & Brothers, 1931. 2 vols.

———, *The Roosevelt Family of Sagamore Hill*. New York, Macmillan, 1954.

HALSEY, FRANCIS WHITING, ed., *The Literary Digest History of the World War*. New York, Funk & Wagnalls, 1920. 10 vols.

HAMPTON, BENJAMIN B., *History of the American Film Industry*. New York, Dover Publications, 1970.

HARBAUGH, WILLIAM HENRY, *Power and Responsibility*. New York, Farrar, Straus and Cudahy, 1961.

HARNSBERGER, CAROLINE THOMAS, *Treasury of Presidential Quotations*. Chicago, Follett Publishing Co., 1964.

HART, JAMES D., ed., *The Oxford Companion to American Literature*. New York, Oxford University Press, 1948.

HARVEY, GEORGE, *Henry Clay Frick*. New York, Charles Scribner's Sons, 1928.

HELM, EDITH BENHAM, *The Captains and the Kings*. New York, G. P. Putnam's Sons, 1954. HENDERSON, ROBERT M., *D.W. Griffith: His Life and Work*. New York, Oxford University Press, 1972.

HENDERSON, ROBERT M., *D. W. Griffith: His Life and Work*. New York, Oxford University Press, 1972.

HENDRICK, BURTON J., *The Life & Letters of Walter H. Page*. Garden City, Garden City Publishing Co., 1927. 2 vols.

HERZBERG, MAX J., *The Reader's Encyclopedia of American Literature*. New York, Thomas Y. Crowell, 1962.

HICKS, GRANVILLE, *John Reed*. New York, Macmillan, 1936.

HINSHAW, DAVID, *A Man from Kansas: The Story of William Allen White*. New York, G. P. Putnam's Sons, 1945.

HOEHLING, A.A., *The Great Epidemic*. Boston, Little Brown, 1961.

HOEHLING, A. A., and HOEHLING, MARY, *The Last Voyage of the Lusitania*. New York, Henry Holt, 1956.

HOLBROOK, STEWART H., *The Age of the Moguls*. Garden City, Doubleday, 1954.

———, *Dreamers of the American Dream*. Garden City, Doubleday, 1957.

HOOVER, HERBERT, *Years of Adventure, 1874–1920*. New York, Macmillan, 1951.

HOOVER, IRWIN HOOD (IKE), *Forty-Two Years in the White House*. Boston, Houghton Mifflin, 1934.

HORNE, CHARLES E., ed., *Source Records of the Great War*. (No city named), National Alumni, 1923. 6 vols.

HOWE, MARK DEWOLFE, ed., *Holmes-Laski Letters*. Cambridge, Harvard University Press, 1953.

HOYT, EDWIN P., JR., *The House of Morgan*. London, Frederick Muller, 1968.

HUGHES, H. STUART, *Oswald Spengler*. New York, Charles Scribner's Sons, 1952.

HURD, CHARLES, *Washington Cavalcade*. New York, E. P. Dutton, 1948.

———, *The Compact History of the American Red Cross*. New York, Hawthorn Books, 1959.

HURWITZ, HOWARD L., *An Encyclopedic Dictionary of American History*. New York, Washington Square Press, 1968.

HUTCHINS, ROBERT MAYNARD, ed., *Great Books of the Western World*. Chicago, Encyclopaedia Britannica, Inc., 1952. 54 vols.

HUTHMACHER, J. JOSEPH, *Senator Robert F. Wagner*. New York, Atheneum, 1968.

JAMES, MARQUIS, *Alfred I. Du Pont: The Family Rebel*. Indianapolis, Bobbs-Merrill, 1941.

———, *The Metropolitan Life*. New York, Viking, 1947.

JENSEN, AMY LA FOLLETTE, *The White House*. New York, McGraw-Hill, 1965.

JESSUP, PHILIP C., *Elihu Root*. New York, Dodd, Mead, 1938. 2 vols.

JOHNSON, ALLEN, ed., *Dictionary of American Biography*. New York, Charles Scribner's Sons, 1964. 12 vols.

JOHNSON, ALVIN, *Pioneer's Progress*. New York, Viking, 1952.
JOHNSON, CLAUDIUS O., *Borah of Idaho*. New York, Longmans, Green, 1936.
JOHNSON, HUGH S., *The Blue Eagle from Egg to Earth*. Garden City, Doubleday, Doran, 1935.
JOHNSON, THOMAS H., ed., *The Oxford Companion to American History*. New York, Oxford University Press, 1966.
JONES, MAX, and CHILTON, JOHN, *Louis: The Louis Armstrong Story*. Boston, Little, Brown, 1971.
JOSEPHSON, MATTHEW, *The President Makers*. New York, Frederick Ungar, 1964.
JUNG, CARL G., *Jung's Psychology and Its Social Meaning*. New York, Grove Press, 1953.
———, *Two Essays on Analytical Psychology*. New York, Meridian Books, 1956.
———, *The Undiscovered Self*. Boston, Little, Brown, 1958.

KANE, HARNETT T., *Queen New Orleans*. New York, William Morrow, 1949.
KANE, JOSEPH NATHAN, *Facts About the Presidents*. New York, H. W. Wilson, 1959.
———, *Famous First Facts*. New York, H. W. Wilson, 1964.
KELLER, HELEN REX, *The Dictionary of Dates*. New York, Macmillan, 1934. 2 vols.
KELLOGG, CHARLES FLINT, *NAACP: A History of the National Association for the Advancement of Colored People*. Baltimore, Johns Hopkins Press, 1967.
KEMLER, EDGAR, *The Irreverent Mr. Mencken*. Boston, Little, Brown, 1950.
KENNAN, GEORGE F., *The Decision to Intervene*. Princeton, Princeton University Press, 1958.
KIPLINGER, W. M., *Washington Is Like That*. New York, Harper & Brothers, 1942.
KIRSCHTEN, ERNEST, *Catfish and Crystal*. Garden City, Doubleday, 1960.
KOENIG, LOUIS W., *The Invisible Presidency*. New York, Rinehart, 1960.
———, *Bryan: A Political Biography*, New York, G. P. Putnam's Sons, 1971.
KORNBLUH, JOYCE L., *Rebel Voices: An I.W.W. Anthology*. Ann Arbor, University of Michigan Press, 1964.
KULL, IRVING S., and KULL, NELL M., *A Short Chronology of American History, 1492–1950*. New Brunswick, Rutgers University Press, 1952.
KUNITZ, STANLEY J., and HAYCRAFT, HOWARD, eds., *Twentieth Century Authors*. New York, H. W. Wilson, 1942.

LA FOLLETTE, BELLE CASE, and LA FOLLETTE, FOLA, *Robert M. La Follette*. New York, Macmillan, 1953. 2 vols.
LANDAU, CAPTAIN HENRY, *The Enemy Within: The Inside Story of German Sabotage in America*. New York, G.P. Putnam's Sons, 1937.

LANGER, WILLIAM L., *An Encyclopedia of World History.* Boston, Houghton Mifflin, 1968.

LANGFORD, GERALD, *The Richard Harding Davis Years.* New York, Holt, Rinehart, 1961.

LASH, JOSEPH P., *Eleanor and Franklin.* New York, W. W. Norton, 1971.

LAVER, JAMES, *The Age of Optimism: 1848–1914.* New York, Harper & Row, 1966.

LE BON, GUSTAVE, *The Crowd: A Study of the Popular Mind.* New York, Macmillan, 1896.

LECKIE, ROBERT, *The Wars of America.* New York, Harper & Row, 1968. 2 vols.

LEISH, KENNETH W., ed., *The American Heritage Pictorial History of the Presidents of the United States.* New York, American Heritage Publishing Co., 1968. 2 vols.

LERNER, MAX, ed., *The Mind and Faith of Justice Holmes.* New York, Modern Library, 1943.

L'ETANG, HUGH, *The Pathology of Leadership.* New York, Hawthorn Books, 1970.

LEVIN, N. GORDON, JR., *Woodrow Wilson and World Politics.* New York, Oxford University Press, 1968.

LIEF, ALFRED, *Brandeis: The Personal History of an American Ideal.* New York, Stackpole Sons, 1936.

The Lincoln Library of Essential Information. Buffalo, Frontier Press, 1955.

LINK, ARTHUR S., *Wilson: The Road to the White House.* Princeton, Princeton University Press, 1947.

———, *Wilson: The New Freedom.* Princeton, Princeton University Press, 1956.

———, *Wilson: The Struggle for Neutrality.* Princeton, Princeton University Press, 1960.

———, *Wilson: Confusions and Crises.* Princeton, Princeton University Press, 1964.

———, *American Epoch: A History of the United States Since the 1890's.* New York, Knopf, 1963.

LIPPMANN, WALTER, *Early Writings.* New York, Liveright, 1970.

LONGWORTH, ALICE ROOSEVELT, *Crowded Hours.* New York, Charles Scribner's Sons, 1933.

LORANT, STEFAN, *The Glorious Burden: The American Presidency.* New York, Harper & Row, 1968.

LORD, WALTER, *The Good Years: From 1900 to the First World War.* New York, Harper & Brothers, 1960.

LUHAN, MABEL DODGE, *Movers and Shakers.* New York, Harcourt Brace, 1936.

LUNDBERG, FERDINAND, *America's 60 Families.* New York, Vanguard, 1937.

LYON, PETER, *Success Story: The Life and Times of S. S. McClure.* New York, Charles Scribner's Sons, 1963.

MADISON, CHARLES A., *Critics & Crusaders.* New York, Henry Holt, 1947.

———, *Leaders and Liberals in 20th Century America*. New York, Frederick Ungar, 1961.

MALONE, DUMAS, and RAUCH, BASIL, *Empire for Liberty*. New York, Appleton-Century-Crofts, 1960. 2 vols.

MANCHESTER, WILLIAM, *Disturber of the Peace: The Life of H. L. Mencken*. New York, Harper & Brothers, 1951.

MARKMANN, CHARLES LAM, *The Noblest Cry: A History of the American Civil Liberties Union*. New York, St. Martin's Press, 1965.

MARTIN, MICHAEL, and GELBER, LEONARD, *The New Dictionary of American History*. New York, Philosophical Library, 1952.

MASON, ALPHEUS THOMAS, *Harlan Fiske Stone*. New York, Viking, 1956.

———, *Brandeis: A Free Man's Life*. New York, Viking, 1956.

MATHEWS, MITFORD M., ed., *A Dictionary of Americanisms*. Chicago, University of Chicago Press, 1956.

MCADOO, ELEANOR WILSON, *The Woodrow Wilsons*. New York, Macmillan, 1937.

MCCLELLAN, GEORGE B., *The Gentleman and the Tiger: An Autobiography*. Philadelphia, J.B. Lippincott, 1956.

MCDONALD, FORREST, *Insull*. Chicago, University of Chicago Press, 1962.

MCGOVERN, GEORGE S., and GUTTRIDGE, LEONARD F., *The Great Coalfield War*. Boston, Houghton Mifflin, 1972.

MCLEAN, EVALYN WALSH, *Father Struck It Rich*. Boston, Little, Brown, 1936.

MCLOUGHLIN, WILLIAM G., JR., *Billy Sunday Was His Real Name*. Chicago, University of Chicago Press, 1955.

MILLER, HOPE RIDINGS, *Embassy Row: The Life and Times of Diplomatic Washington*. New York, Holt, Rinehart and Winston, 1969.

MILLIS, WALTER, *Road to War: America 1914–1917*. Boston, Houghton Mifflin, 1935.

MINOR, HENRY, *The Story of the Democratic Party*. New York, Macmillan, 1928.

MIZENER, ARTHUR, *The Far Side of Paradise*. Boston, Houghton Mifflin, 1949.

MORISON, SAMUEL ELIOT, *The Oxford History of the American People*. New York, Oxford University Press, 1965.

MORRIS, LLOYD, *Postscript to Yesterday: America, the Last Fifty Years*. New York, Random House, 1947.

MORRIS, RICHARD B., ed., *Encyclopedia of American History*. New York, Harper & Row, 1961.

MORRIS, RICHARD B., and IRWIN, GRAHAM W., eds., *Harper Encyclopedia of the Modern World*. New York, Harper & Row, 1970.

NEARING, SCOTT, *The Making of a Radical*. New York, Harper & Row, 1972.

NEVINS, ALLAN, and HILL, FRANK ERNEST, *Ford: Expansion and Challenge, 1915–1933*. New York, Charles Scribner's Sons, 1957.

New York Times.

New York Times Film Reviews, 1913–1970. New York, Arno Press, 1971.

New York Times Index, 1913–1920. New York, The New York Times.

NORRIS, GEORGE W., *Fighting Liberal, an Autobiography*. New York, Macmillan, 1945.

NOWELL, ELIZABETH, *Thomas Wolfe: A Biography*. Garden City, Doubleday, 1960.

PALMER, FREDERICK, *Newton D. Baker*. New York, Dodd, Mead, 1931. 2 vols.

PARKS, E. TAYLOR, and PARKS, LOIS F., *Memorable Quotations of Franklin D. Roosevelt*. New York, Thomas Y. Crowell, 1965.

PERSHING, JOHN J., *My Experiences in the World War*. New York, Frederick A. Stokes Co., 1931. 2 vols.

PHELPS, WILLIAM LYON, *Autobiography with Letters*. New York, Oxford University Press, 1939.

POGUE, FORREST C., *George C. Marshall: Education of a General*. New York, Viking, 1963.

PORTER, KIRK H., and JOHNSON, DONALD BRUCE, *National Party Platforms, 1840–1964*. Urbana, University of Illinois Press, 1966.

PRINGLE, HENRY F., *The Life and Times of William Howard Taft*. New York, Farrar & Rinehart, 1939. 2 vols.

———, *Theodore Roosevelt*. New York, Harcourt, Brace, 1956.

PUSEY, MERLO J., *Charles Evans Hughes*. New York, Macmillan, 1951. 2 vols.

RAMSAYE, TERRY, *A Million and One Nights: A History of the Motion Picture*. New York, Simon and Schuster, 1926.

RENSHAW, PATRICK, *The Wobblies: The Story of Syndicalism in the United States*. London, Eyre & Spottiswoode, 1967.

RICHARDS, WILLIAM C., *The Last Billionaire: Henry Ford*. New York, Charles Scribner's Sons, 1948.

RIDER, FREMONT, *Rider's New York City: A Guide-Book*. New York, Henry Holt, 1923.

Roosevelt, Theodore, The Works of, National Edition. New York, Charles Scribner's Sons, 1926. 20 vols.

ROSEBLOOM, EUGENE H., *A History of Presidential Elections*. New York, Macmillan, 1964.

ROWAN, RICHARD WILMER, *The Story of Secret Service*. Garden City, Doubleday, Doran, 1937.

RUDWICK, ELLIOTT, *Race Riot at East St. Louis*. New York, Atheneum, 1972.

RUSSELL, FRANCIS, *The Shadow of Blooming Grove*. New York, McGraw-Hill, 1968.

SAYERS, MICHAEL, and KAHN, ALBERT E., *Sabotage! The Secret War Against America*. New York, Harper & Brothers, 1942.

SELTZER, LEON E., ed., *The Columbia Lippincott Gazetteer of the World*. New York, Columbia University Press, 1952.

SEYMOUR, CHARLES, *The Intimate Papers of Colonel House*. Boston, Houghton Mifflin, 1926. 2 vols.

SHANNON, DAVID A., *The Socialist Party of America*. New York, Macmillan, 1955.
SILLS, DAVID L., ed., *International Encyclopedia of the Social Sciences*. New York, Macmillan and the Free Press, 1968. 17 vols.
SINCLAIR, ANDREW, *The Available Man: The Life Behind the Masks of Warren Gamaliel Harding*. New York, Macmillan, 1965.
SLAYDEN, ELLEN MAURY, *Washington Wife*. New York, Harper & Row, 1963.
SMITH, ARTHUR D. HOWDEN, *Mr. House of Texas*. New York, Funk & Wagnalls, 1940.
SMITH, GENE, *When the Cheering Stopped: The Last Years of Woodrow Wilson*. New York, William Morrow 1964.
SORENSEN, CHARLES E., with WILLIAMSON, SAMUEL T., *My Forty Years with Ford*. New York, Collier Books, 1962.
SOULE, GEORGE, *Prosperity Decade*. New York, Rinehart, 1947.
SPENGLER, OSWALD, *The Decline of the West*. New York, Alfred A. Knopf, 1926. 2 vols.
SPIVAK, JOHN L., *A Man in His Time*. New York, Horizon Press, 1967.
STALLINGS, LAURENCE, *The Doughboys*. New York, Harper & Row, 1963.
STARLING, COLONEL EDMUND, with SUGRUE, THOMAS, *Starling of the White House*. New York, Simon and Schuster, 1946.
STARR, JOHN, *Hospital City*. New York, Crown, 1957.
STEARN, GERALD EMANUEL, ed., *Gompers*. Englewood Cliffs, Prentice-Hall, 1971.
STIMSON, HENRY L., and BUNDY, MCGEORGE, *On Active Service in Peace and War*. New York, Harper & Brothers, 1948.
STONE, IRVING, *Clarence Darrow for the Defense*. Garden City, Garden City Publishing Co., 1943.
———, *They Also Ran: The Story of the Men Who Were Defeated for the Presidency*. Garden City, Doubleday, Doran, 1945.
STUART, GRAHAM H., *The Department of State*. New York, Macmillan, 1949.
STUDENSKI, PAUL, and KROOS, HERMAN E., *Financial History of the United States*. New York, McGraw-Hill, 1952.
SULLIVAN, MARK, *Our Times*. New York, Charles Scribner's Sons, 1916. 6 vols.
SWANBERG, W. A., *Citizen Hearst*. New York, Charles Scribner's Sons, 1961.
SWARD, KEITH, *The Legend of Henry Ford*. New York, Rinehart, 1948.
SWEET, WILLIAM WARREN, *The Story of Religion in America*. New York, Harper & Brothers, 1950.

TARBELL, IDA M., *All in the Day's Work: An Autobiography*. New York, Macmillan, 1939.
TAYLOR, EDMOND, *The Fall of the Dynasties*. Garden City, Doubleday, 1963.
TAYLOR, TIM, *The Book of Presidents*. New York, Arno Press, 1972.
TEBBEL, JOHN, *The Life and Good Times of William Randolph Hearst*. New York, E. P. Dutton, 1952.

These Eventful Years: The Twentieth Century in the Making. New York, Encyclopaedia Britannica, Inc., 1924. 2 vols.
TIMMONS, BASCOM N., *Garner of Texas*. New York, Harper & Brothers, 1948.
TOYNBEE, ARNOLD J., *A Study of History*. New York, Oxford University Press, 1957. 2 vols.
TUCHMAN, BARBARA W., *The Guns of August*. New York, Macmillan, 1962.
———, *The Proud Tower*. New York, Macmillan, 1966.
———, *The Zimmermann Telegram*. New York, Macmillian, 1971.
TUMULTY, JOSEPH P., *Woodrow Wilson as I Knew Him*. Garden City, Doubleday, Page, 1921.

UNTERMEYER, LOUIS, *Makers of the Modern World*. New York, Simon and Schuster, 1955.

VAN ALSTYNE, RICHARD W., *American Diplomacy in Action*. Stanford, Stanford University Press, 1947.
VOSS, CARL HERMANN, *Rabbi and Minister: The Friendship of Stephen S. Wise and John Haynes Holmes*. Cleveland, World Publishing Co., 1964.

WALDROP, FRANK C., *McCormick of Chicago*. Englewood Cliffs, Prentice-Hall, 1966.
WALL, JOSEPH FRAZIER, *Andrew Carnegie*. New York, Oxford University Press, 1970.
Webster's Biographical Dictionary. Springfield, G. & C. Merriam Co., 1943.
WEIGLEY, RUSSELL F., *History of the United States Army*. London, B. T. Batsford, 1967.
WEINTRAUB, STANLEY, *Journey into Heartbreak*. New York, Weybright and Talley, 1971.
WENDT, LLOYD, and KOGAN, HERMAN, *Big Bill of Chicago*. Indianapolis, Bobbs-Merrill, 1953.
WERNER, M. R., *Bryan*. New York, Harcourt, Brace, 1929.
WEYL, NATHANIEL, *The Battle Against Disloyalty*. New York, Thomas Y. Crowell, 1951.
WHEELER, BURTON K., with HEALY, PAUL F., *Yankee From the West*. Garden City, Doubleday, 1962.
WHIPPLE, LEON, *The Story of Civil Liberty in the United States*. New York, Vanguard, 1927.
White, William Allen, The Autobiography of. New York, Macmillan, 1946.
———, *Selected Letters*. New York, Henry Holt, 1947.
WHITEHEAD, DON, *The FBI Story*. New York, Random House, 1956.
Who's Who in America, various years. Chicago, A. N. Marquis Co.
Who Was Who in America, 1897–1942. Chicago, A. N. Marquis Co., 1943.

WILLIAMS, NEVILLE, *Chronology of the Modern World: 1763 to the Present*. New York, David McKay, 1967.

WILSON, EDITH BOLLING, *My Memoir*. Indianapolis, Bobbs-Merrill, 1939.

WINKLER, JOHN K., *The Du Pont Dynasty*. New York, Reynal & Hitchcock, 1935.

World Almanac, 1913–1920. New York, Press Publishing Co.

The World's Greatest Books. New York, Wm. H. Wise, 1941.

WRIGHT, CHESTER WHITNEY, *Economic History of the United States*. New York, McGraw-Hill, 1949.

YELLEN, SAMUEL, *American Labor Struggles*. New York, S. A. Russell, 1936.

Index

MICHAEL IAN

Edward Robb Ellis was born in Kewanee, Illinois, in 1911. At fourteen he knew he wanted to become a journalist and an author. At sixteen he began keeping the diary that the *Chicago Tribune* has called "a jewel of Americana."

In his long newspaper career he worked at the *New Orleans Item*, covering Huey Long, Louis Armstrong, as well as the city's hungry workers and the colorful French Quarter. In the 1930s he joined the *Oklahoma City Times*, writing about the Great Depression, dust storms, and Eleanor Roosevelt. The beginning of World War II found him at the *Peoria Journal-Transcript*, from where he moved to Chicago, where he became a feature writer for the United Press. During the war Ellis edited a navy newspaper on Okinawa. In 1946 the Chicago Newspaper Guild named him the best feature writer in the city.

In 1947 Ellis joined the *New York World-Telegram*, where he remained for the next fifteen years, winning wide attention for his feature stories about world leaders, Nobel laureates, and Hollywood stars. After retiring from reporting in 1962, Ellis embarked on a career as a full-time author, publishing *The Epic of New York City*, which the *New York Times* called "a magnificent modern chronicle." *A Nation in Torment*, Ellis's narrative history of the Great Depression, received the Friends of American Writers Literary Award in 1970. In 1975 he published *Echoes of Distant Thunder*. In 1995 *A Diary of the Century*, Ellis's own selections from his prodigious journal, was published. He is also an associate editor of *The Encyclopedia of New York City*.

Mr. Ellis lives in New York City, tending his 15,000-volume library and faithfully recording his life and times in the pages of his epic diary.